Migration, Globalization, and Ethnic Relations

An Interdisciplinary Approach

Edited by

Mohsen M. Mobasher
University of Houston-Downtown

Mahmoud Sadri
Texas Woman's University

Upper Saddle River, New Jersey

Library of Congress Cataloging-in-Publication Data

Migration, globalization, and ethnic relations : an interdisciplinary approach/[edited] by
Mohsen Mobasher and Mahmoud Sadri.
p. cm.
Includes bibliographical references.
ISBN 0-13-048389-3
1. Emigration and immigration—Social aspects—United States. 2. Immigrants—United
States—Social conditions. 3. Immigrants—United States. 4. United States—Ethnic relations.
I. Mobasher, Mohsen, II. Sadri, Mahmoud.
JV6475.M53 2004
304.8'73—dc21

2003051712

Publisher: Nancy Roberts
Editorial Assistant: Lee Patterson
Production Liaison: Joanne Hakim
Director of Marketing: Beth Gillette Mejia
Marketing Assistant: Adam Laitman
Manufacturing Buyer: Mary Ann Gloriande
Cover Art Director: Jayne Conte
Cover Design: Bruce Kenselaar
Cover Illustration/Photo: Jeff Greenberg/Photo Edit; The New York Public Library; James Willis/Getty Images
Cover Image Specialist: Karen Sanatar
Composition/Full-Service Project Management: Brenda Averkamp/Carlisle Communications
Printer/Binder: Hamilton Printing Company

Credits and acknowledgments borrowed from other sources and reproduced, with permission, in this textbook appear on appropriate page within text.

Pearson Education LTD, London
Pearson Education Singapore Pte. Ltd
Pearson Education Canada, Ltd
Pearson Education—Japan
Pearson Education Australia PTY, Limited
Pearson Education North Asia Ltd
Pearson Educación de Mexico, S. A. de C.V.
Pearson Education Malaysia Pte. Ltd
Pearson Education, Upper Saddle River, New Jersey

10 9 8 7 6 5 4 3 2 1
ISBN: 0-13-048389-3

To The Memory of Our Fathers
Morteza Mostafavi Mobasher
and
Fathollah Sadri

Contents

Preface

During the last few years, a number of anthologies have attempted to familiarize their readers with the history, causes, and consequences of immigration. In our view, these anthologies, their salient accomplishments notwithstanding, have had limited success in two significant areas: First, they have seldom portrayed the rapidly changing nature of immigration in the context of globalization and its far-reaching consequences for the lives of immigrants and the restructuring of the U.S. economy and society. Second, most of the existing readers have been confined either to particular regions such as New York and Los Angeles or to particular topics in immigration such as immigration policy, immigrant women, and immigrants' labor-force participation. We have endeavored to surmount both of these limitations in this book.

Our goal has been to put together an anthology that blends some of the classic essays on immigration with some of the most rigorous current scholarship examining various dimensions of immigration. Far from attempting to present an exhaustive array of topics in the ever-expanding immigration literature—which would have required the inclusion of issues such as refugees, second-generation immigrants, political participation, and the effect of immigration on sending societies—we have tried to include works that illustrate, with the help of appropriate case studies, the foremost theoretical and substantive foci of migration research. The twenty-seven essays in this book examine the integration of new immigrants into U.S. society and the influence of this integration on ethnic relations, social inequality, and social mobility of immigrants. They also examine the effect of immigration on immigrants' gender roles and family relations.

The title of this book reveals another of its unique features, that is, the interdisciplinary nature of the collection. Some of the articles are written by anthropologists and are based on ethnographic accounts. Others are written by sociologists, urban analysts, and political scientists who have combined a variety of research methods and presentation styles to address multifarious dimensions of migration in their respective fields. Finally, we have done our utmost to be meticulous in our effort. No readings in this book have been abridged, which we consider essential for the preservation of the integrity of original sources.

We would like to thank Prentice Hall's publisher Nancy Roberts for a most cooperative and collegial relationship throughout this project. Lee Peterson and Brenda Averkamp's continuous administrative and procedural guidance helped us stay on the publisher's "straight and narrow." We would be in remiss if we neglected to acknowledge the conscientious and meticulous labors of Brenda Averkamp of Carlisle Publishers Services and freelancer Key Metts. As the project editor and the copy editor of this project, respectively, they have left no stone unturned in order to ascertain that the final product is as accurate as humanly possible. Special thanks are due to Walter F. Carroll (Bridgewater State University), Douglas V. Davidson (Western Michigan University), and James L. Litwin (Owens Community College), the three reviewers who read our original prospectus and provided us with many helpful comments and suggestions. Finally, we would like to acknowledge Maryam Mobasher's tireless efforts in assembling a comprehensive bibliography for this book.

EDITORS' INTRODUCTION

The Industrial and democratic revolutions of the eighteenth century ensured the global triumph of modern capitalism. The attendant colonization of vast territories in every continent and the revolutionary advances in the technologies of transportation and communication—from steamships to the telegraph—in the nineteenth century transformed immigration from sporadic and usually catastrophic events in the traditional world to sustained patterns of movement and resettlement of population around the world in the modern era.

The population history of the United States as the largest recipient of immigrants in modern times records a marked surge of immigration in the last two centuries. Between the 1820s and 1920s, during which two great waves of immigrants reached U.S. shores, almost 40 million people entered the United States (Healey, 1995). The largest groups of immigrants in the first wave were primarily of northern and western European origins, that is, from Ireland, England, Germany, Canada, France, and the Scandinavian countries. Later, during the 1880s, the second wave of immigration originated in eastern and southern Europe, that is, Austria-Hungary, Poland, Russia, and Italy. The former were known as "Old Immigrants" and the latter as "New Immigrants." In this period the scale and impact of European immigration dwarfed the arrivals from non-European countries. These consisted of Asians arriving chiefly from China and, later, from Japan to the West Coast of the United States in response to the labor demands of the mining and railroad industries. The flow of immigration from far eastern Asia as well as eastern Mediterranean regions was sharply curtailed by the passage of restrictive laws such as the Chinese Exclusion Act of 1882, and the National Origin Act of 1924. The exclusionary effects of the National Origin Act and its "quota system" were eventually obliterated by the Immigration Act of 1965, which quickened the pace of what has come to be known as the third wave of immigration. Now, almost four decades later, the volume of immigration to the United States is again approaching the levels of European immigration of the early twentieth century and the United States has become the desired destination of millions of immigrants from Mexico, the Caribbean, Central America, South America, Asia, and Africa.

The centrality of immigration to the understanding of the history, culture, economy, and politics in the United States has generated a concomitant social scientific interest in the processes of acculturation and incorporation of immigrants and their descendants in American society. Members of the Department of Sociology at the University of Chicago led the first systematic study of the immigrant communities and careers. The five-volume seminal work of W. I. Thomas and Florian Znaniecki titled "Polish Peasant in Europe and America" (1927) was one of the first fruits of this labor. Robert E. Park, a central figure in the department, trained a generation of scholars with interests in the lives of immigrants and their descedents. Even the titles of the books written by Park's younger colleagues and students: "The Gang" (Thrasher, 1927), "The Hobo" (Anderson, 1923), "The Ghetto" (Wirth, 1928), "The Gold Coast and the Slum" (Zorbaugh, 1927), and "Taxi Dance Hall" (Cressey, 1932) suggest their interest in the social problems directly or indirectly related to the lives of immigrants. Chicago, as a hub of the meatpacking, steel, and wheat exchange industries, had attracted numerous immigrants. Park and his colleagues studied the immigrants' struggle to adjust to life in the metropolis. Park's famous race relations cycle theory (1950a) predicted that the majority of the immigrants, having gone through stages of "contact," "competition," and "accommodation," will arrive at the final stage of "assimilation" into mainstream U.S. society. For those who couldn't complete this transition, Jane Addams, an associate of the Chicago sociologists, founded the famous "Hull House" that attended to some of their needs (Vidich and Lyman, 1985, Hannerz, 1991).

The ebbing of the immigration flow pursuant to the Exclusion Act of 1924 was accompanied by a waning of social scientific interest in the lives of immigrants and the impact of immigration on U.S. society. However, Congress's Hart-Celler Act of 1965 reinvigorated not only the flow of immigration into the United States from across the world but a renewed interest in the study of immigration in the United States. As the essays in this book testify, this interest shows no signs of abating; rather, it has gathered steam in the intervening decades as it has followed the complex developments of the third wave of immigration. Since 1965, more than 22 million legal immigrants have been admitted to the United States (U.S. Department of Justice, 1998).

The new immigration to the United States, however, has several distinctive features that separate it from earlier waves of immigration. First, unlike the European immigration, which was followed by a long hiatus, the entry of Asians and Latin Americans is continuously affected by an ongoing flow of fresh arrivals from abroad. Second, whereas European immigrants were scattered across more national-origin groups and languages, new immigrants are linguistically more concentrated and geographically more clustered. Finally, in contrast to the European immigrants who entered the United States during its economic boom with opportunities for upward mobility, new immigrants are entering a highly stratified society characterized by high income inequality and growing labor-market segmentation that will provide fewer opportunities for economic advancement (Massey, 1995). The economic and technological restructuring of U.S. society has changed the distribution and organization of jobs, creating structural unemployment and low-income employment throughout society. The effects of economic and industrial changes are most palpable in the economic activities of immigrants and racial minority groups. The new ethnic populations are heavily over-represented in exactly those industries that are most affected by ongoing economic and technological changes (Waldinger, 1986; Waldinger et al., 1990). Furthermore, the shift from labor-intensive to highly automated production has caused a dramatic decline in the demand for unskilled and semiskilled migrant workers. Thus, with the concentration of growth in the high-technology and service sectors that demand technical proficiency and strong interpersonal communication, immigrants with inadequate skills are either prodded into marginal economic positions or forced to look for more viable routes to upward economic mobility; hence, the expansion of small business ownership in ethnic zones (Auster and Aldrich, 1984; Boissevain, 1984; Waldinger et al., 1990). In the meantime, a smaller, skilled prospective immigrant population has gained unprecedented access to legal and employment opportunities in the United States.

New research has followed the contours of the patterns, populations, and problems of recent immigration. As a result, contemporary scholarship has engaged in a critique and reevaluation of the classical literature on immigration and has engendered new theories. Not only have classical paradigms such as "assimilation" been, for the most part, replaced with new concepts such as "incorporation," but novel terminology has also emerged that captures new realities of immigration in notions such as "segmented assimilation," "transmigration," "chain migration," "return migration," "transnationality," "middleman minorities," "ethnic economies," and "ethnic enclaves."

Organization and Focus of This Book

Given the unique demographic characteristics of new immigrants and the distinctive structural features of contemporary U.S. society, the immigrants in the new wave have different economic, cultural, and political problems of adaptation than their counterparts in the past. The twenty-seven essays in this book examine the integration of new immigrants into American society and the influence of this integration on ethnic relations, social inequality, and social mobility of immigrants. They also examine the impact of immigration on immigrants' gender roles and family relations.

The readings are organized in five parts. Part I maps out major theoretical discussions of international migration and areas of needed immigration research. The readings in Part II examine changes in the economy and immigration, and their effect on the new structures of ethnicity in the United States. The essays in Part III explore the impact of globalization on the process of incorporation of immigrants into U.S. society. Part IV examines various modes of incorporation of immigrants into their new society. Part V addresses the increasingly significant issues of gender and migration.

Together, the essays in this book underline the fact that the new patterns of immigration exhibit intriguing continuities, as well as discontinuities, with the past. The twenty-first century, thus, promises to be no less a century of immigrants than the twentieth century was. It is our firm belief that as long as immigration continues to be an issue of pivotal significance for U.S. economy, politics, culture, and, indeed, identity, systematic and interdisciplinary studies of this phenomenon will remain a fundamental requirement for comprehending the past, present, and future of American society. We hope that this book will make a contribution to this scientifically significant and morally noble effort.

PART I

IMMIGRATION: THEORIES AND RESEARCH

Part I maps out major theoretical discussions of international migration and areas of needed immigration research. This part is essential to the reader's understanding of the causes and consequences of migration.

In the first selection, "Theories of International Migration: A Review and Appraisal," Douglas S. Massey and his collaborators launch a systematic review of five competing economic and sociological theories of immigration. They examine the various means through which immigration is sustained and perpetuated.

The second reading is Alejandro Portes's judicious essay titled "Immigration Theory for a New Century: Some Problems and Opportunities." In this sweeping account, Portes enumerates current problems and promising trends in immigration research. According to Portes, the themes of transnational communities, the new second generation, households and gender, state and state-systems, and cross-national comparisons have great potential for research in this area.

In the third article in this section, "The New Diaspora: African Immigration to the United States," April Gordon uses a combination of "push–pull" factors to examine current patterns, future trends, and consequences of African immigration to the United States.

"Return Migration," by George Gmelch, concentrates on this relatively neglected but important phenomenon and its effect on the host and sending communities. After summarizing various studies on the topic, Gmelch develops a typology for return migration and discusses the motives for migration and readjustment of migrants upon returning home.

In the fifth piece, "Filling in Some Holes: Six Areas of Needed Immigration Research," Herbert J. Gans pinpoints six specific areas that need further immigration research. To fill these "holes," Gans proposes that researchers ask new questions about this topic, especially after the Immigration Act of 1965.

Part I concludes with Silvia Pedraza-Bailey's ground-breaking "Immigration Research: A Conceptual Map," in which she provides a "historiography of immigration research." Pedraza-Bailey compares the paradigm shifts in immigration research in history and sociology and identifies several major questions that immigration scholars need to investigate.

Theories of International Migration: A Review and Appraisal

✦ Douglas S. Massey ✦ Joaquín Arango ✦ Graeme Hugo ✦ Ali Kouaouci ✦ Adela Pellegrino ✦ J. Edward Taylor

Over the past 30 years, immigration has emerged as a major force throughout the world. In traditional immigrant-receiving societies such as Australia, Canada, and the United States, the volume of immigration has grown and its composition has shifted decisively away from Europe, the historically dominant source, toward Asia, Africa, and Latin America. In Europe, meanwhile, countries that for centuries had been sending out migrants were suddenly transformed into immigrant-receiving societies. After 1945, virtually all countries in Western Europe began to attract significant numbers of workers from abroad. Although the migrants were initially drawn mainly from southern Europe, by the late 1960s they mostly came from developing countries in Africa, Asia, the Caribbean, and the Middle East.

By the 1980s even countries in southern Europe—Italy, Spain, and Portugal—which only a decade before had been sending migrants to wealthier countries in the north, began to import workers from Africa, Asia, and the Middle East. At the same time, Japan—with its low and still declining birth rate, its aging population, and its high standard of living—found itself turning increasingly to migrants from poorer countries in Asia and even South America to satisfy its labor needs.

Most of the world's developed countries have become diverse, multiethnic societies, and those that have not reached this state are moving decisively in that direction. The emergence of international migration as a basic structural feature of nearly all industrialized countries testifies to the strength and coherence of the underlying forces. Yet the theoretical base for understanding these forces remains weak. The recent boom in immigration has therefore taken citizens, officials, and demographers by surprise, and when it comes

Massey, Douglas et al. 1993. "Theories of international migration: A review and appraisal." *Population and Development Review*. Volume 19, No. 3 (September 1993):431–466. Reprinted with permission of the Population Council.

to international migration, popular thinking remains mired in nineteenth-century concepts, models, and assumptions.

At present, there is no single, coherent theory of international migration, only a fragmented set of theories that have developed largely in isolation from one another, sometimes but not always segmented by disciplinary boundaries. Current patterns and trends in immigration, however, suggest that a full understanding of contemporary migratory processes will not be achieved by relying on the tools of one discipline alone or by focusing on a single level of analysis. Rather, their complex, multifaceted nature requires a sophisticated theory that incorporates a variety of perspectives, levels, and assumptions.

The purpose of this article is to explicate and integrate the leading contemporary theories of international migration. We begin by examining models that describe the initiation of international movement and then consider theories that account for why transnational population flows persist across space and time. Rather than favoring one theory over another *a priori,* we seek to understand each model on its own terms in order to illuminate key assumptions and hypotheses. Only after each theory has been considered separately do we compare and contrast the different conceptual frameworks to reveal areas of logical inconsistency and substantive disagreement. In undertaking this exercise, we seek to provide a sound basis for evaluating the models empirically, and to lay the groundwork for constructing an accurate and comprehensive theory of international migration for the twenty-first century.

The Initiation of International Migration

A variety of theoretical models has been proposed to explain why international migration begins, and although each ultimately seeks to explain the same thing, they employ radically different concepts, assumptions, and frames of reference. Neoclassical economics focuses on differentials in wages and employment conditions between countries and on migration costs; it generally conceives of movement as an individual decision for income maximization. The "new economics of migration," in contrast, considers conditions in a variety of markets, not just labor markets. It views migration as a household decision taken to minimize risks to family income or to overcome capital constraints on family production activities. Dual labor market theory and world systems theory generally ignore such micro-level decision processes, focusing instead on forces operating at much higher levels of aggregation. The former links immigration to the structural requirements of modern industrial economies, while the latter sees immigration as a natural consequence of economic globalization and market penetration across national boundaries.

Given the fact that theories conceptualize causal processes at such different levels of analysis—the individual, the household, the national, and the international—they cannot be assumed, *a priori,* to be inherently incompatible. It is quite possible, for example, that individuals act to maximize income while families minimize risk, and that the context within which both decisions are made is shaped by structural forces operating at the national and international levels. Nonetheless, the various models reflect different research objectives, focuses, interests, and ways of decomposing an enormously complex subject into analytically manageable parts; and a firm basis for judging their consistency requires that the inner logic, propositions, assumptions, and hypotheses of each theory be clearly specified and well-understood.

Neoclassical Economics: Macro Theory

Probably the oldest and best-known theory of international migration was developed originally to explain labor migration in the process of economic development (Lewis, 1954; Ranis and Fei, 1961; Harris and Todaro, 1970; Todaro, 1976). According to this theory and its extensions, international migration, like its internal counterpart, is caused by geographic differences in the supply of and demand for labor. Countries with a large endowment of labor relative to capital have a low equilibrium market wage, while countries with a limited endowment of labor relative to capital are characterized by a high market wage, as depicted graphically by the familiar interaction of labor supply and demand curves. The resulting differential in wages causes workers from the low-wage country to move to the high-wage country. As a result of this movement, the supply of labor decreases and wages rise in the capital-poor country, while the supply of labor increases and wages fall in the capital-rich country, leading, at equilibrium, to an international wage differential that reflects only the costs of international movement, pecuniary and psychic.

Mirroring the flow of workers from labor-abundant to labor-scarce countries is a flow of investment capital from capital-rich to capital-poor countries. The relative scarcity of capital in poor countries yields a rate of return that is high by international standards, thereby attracting investment. The movement of capital also includes human capital, with highly skilled workers moving from capital-rich to capital-poor countries in order to reap high returns on their skills in a human capital-scarce environment, leading to a parallel movement of managers, technicians, and other skilled workers. The international flow of labor, therefore, must be kept conceptually distinct from the associated international flow of human capital. Even in the most aggregated macro-level models, the heterogeneity of immigrants along skill lines must be clearly recognized.

The simple and compelling explanation of international migration offered by neoclassical macroeconomics has strongly shaped public thinking and has provided the intellectual basis for much immigration policy. The perspective contains several implicit propositions and assumptions:

1. The international migration of workers is caused by differences in wage rates between countries.

2. The elimination of wage differentials will end the movement of labor, and migration will not occur in the absence of such differentials.

3. International flows of human capital—that is, highly skilled workers—respond to differences in the rate of return to human capital, which may be different from the overall wage rate, yielding a distinct pattern of migration that may be opposite that of unskilled workers.

4. Labor markets are the primary mechanisms by which international flows of labor are induced; other kinds of markets do not have important effects on international migration.

5. The way for governments to control migration flows is to regulate or influence labor markets in sending and/or receiving countries.

Neoclassical Economics: Micro Theory

Corresponding to the macroeconomic model is a microeconomic model of individual choice (Sjaastad, 1962; Todaro, 1969, 1976, 1989; Todaro and Maruszko, 1987). In this scheme, individual rational actors decide to migrate because a cost-benefit calculation leads them to expect a positive net return, usually monetary, from movement. International migration is conceptualized as a form of investment in human capital. People choose to move to where they can be most productive, given their skills; but before they can capture the higher wages associated with greater labor productivity they must undertake certain investments, which include the material costs of traveling, the costs of maintenance while moving and looking for work, the effort involved in learning a new language and culture, the difficulty experienced in adapting to a new labor market, and the psychological costs of cutting old ties and forging new ones.

Potential migrants estimate the costs and benefits of moving to alternative international locations and migrate to where the expected discounted net returns are greatest over some time horizon (Borjas, 1990). Net returns in each future period are estimated by taking the observed earnings corresponding to the individual's skills in the destination country and multiplying these by the probability of obtaining a job there (and for illegal migrants the likelihood of being able to avoid deportation) to obtain "expected destination earnings." These expected earnings are then subtracted from those expected in the community of origin (observed earnings there multiplied by the probability of employment) and the difference is summed over a time horizon from 0 to n, discounted by a factor that reflects the greater utility of money earned in the present than in the future. From this integrated difference the estimated costs are subtracted to yield the expected net return to migration.

This decision-making process is summarized analytically by the following equation:

$$ER(0) = \int_0^n [P_1(t)P_2(t)Y_d(t) - P_3(t)Y_o(t)]e^{-rt}dt - C(0)$$

where $ER(0)$ is the expected net return to migration calculated just before departure at time 0; t is time; $P_1(t)$ is the probability of avoiding deportation from the area of destination (1.0 for legal migrants and <1.0 for undocumented migrants); $P_2(t)$ is the probability of employment at the destination; $Y_d(t)$ is earnings if employed at the place of destination; $P_3(t)$ is the probability of employment in the community of origin; $Y_o(t)$ is earnings if employed in the community of origin; r is the discount factor; and $C(0)$ is the sum total of the costs of movement (including psychological costs).

If the quantity $ER(0)$ is positive for some potential destination, the rational actor migrates; if it is negative, the actor stays; and if it is zero, the actor is indifferent between moving and staying. In theory, a potential migrant goes to where the expected net returns to migration are greatest, leading to several important conclusions that differ slightly from the earlier macroeconomic formulations:

1. International movement stems from international differentials in both earnings and employment rates, whose product determines expected earnings (the prior model, in contrast, assumed full employment).
2. Individual human capital characteristics that increase the likely rate of remuneration or the probability of employment in the destination relative to the sending country (e.g., education, experience, training, language skills) will increase the likelihood of international movement, other things being equal.
3. Individual characteristics, social conditions, or technologies that lower migration costs increase the net returns to migration and, hence, raise the probability of international movement.
4. Because of 2 and 3, individuals within the same country can display very different proclivities to migrate.
5. Aggregate migration flows between countries are simple sums of individual moves undertaken on the basis of individual cost-benefit calculations.
6. International movement does not occur in the absence of differences in earnings and/or employment rates between countries. Migration occurs until expected earnings (the product of earnings and employment rates) have been equalized internationally (net of the costs of movement), and movement does not stop until this product has been equalized.
7. The size of the differential in expected returns determines the size of the international flow of migrants between countries.
8. Migration decisions stem from disequilibria or discontinuities between labor

markets; other markets do not directly influence the decision to migrate.

9. If conditions in receiving countries are psychologically attractive to prospective migrants, migration costs may be negative. In this case, a negative earnings differential may be necessary to halt migration between countries.

10. Governments control immigration primarily through policies that affect expected earnings in sending and/or receiving countries—for example, those that attempt to lower the likelihood of employment or raise the risk of underemployment in the destination area (through employer sanctions), those that seek to raise incomes at the origin (through long-term development programs), or those that aim to increase the costs (both psychological and material) of migration.

The New Economics of Migration

In recent years, a "new economics of migration" has arisen to challenge many of the assumptions and conclusions of neoclassical theory (Stark and Bloom, 1985). A key insight of this new approach is that migration decisions are not made by isolated individual actors, but by larger units of related people—typically families or households—in which people act collectively not only to maximize expected income, but also to minimize risks and to loosen constraints associated with a variety of market failures, apart from those in the labor market (Stark and Levhari, 1982; Stark, 1984; Katz and Stark, 1986; Lauby and Stark, 1988; Taylor, 1986; Stark, 1991).

Unlike individuals, households are in a position to control risks to their economic well-being by diversifying the allocation of household resources, such as family labor. While some family members can be assigned economic activities in the local economy, others may be sent to work in foreign labor markets where wages and employment conditions are negatively correlated or weakly correlated with those in the local area. In the event that local economic conditions deteriorate and activities there fail to bring in sufficient income, the household can rely on migrant remittances for support.

In developed countries, risks to household income are generally minimized through private insurance markets or governmental programs, but in developing countries these institutional mechanisms for managing risk are imperfect, absent, or inaccessible to poor families, giving them incentives to diversify risks through migration. In developed countries, moreover, credit markets are relatively well-developed to enable families to finance new projects, such as the adoption of new production technology. In most developing areas, in contrast, credit is usually not available or is procurable only at high cost. In the absence of accessible public or affordable private insurance and credit programs, market failures create strong pressures for international movement, as the following examples show.

Crop insurance markets. Whenever farm households put time and money into sowing a crop, they are betting that the investment will pay off at a future date in the form of a product that can be sold for cash to purchase desired goods and services, or which can be consumed directly for subsistence. Between the time a crop is planted and harvested, however, human or natural events may reduce or eliminate the harvest, leaving the family with insufficient income or food for subsistence. Likewise, the introduction of new agricultural technology (such as high-yielding seeds or new methods of cultivation) may alter the objective and/or subjective risks confronting farm households. Using a new seed variety may increase a farmer's yield if the development expert is right; but if he or she is wrong, the household faces the prospect of having insufficient food or income.

In developed countries, these sorts of objective and subjective risks are managed through formal insurance arrangements, whereby agricultural producers pay a fee to a company or a government agency to insure the crop against future loss. The insuring institution assumes the risk to the future crop, and should a drought or flood destroy the harvest or a new technology backfire, it pays the producer for the insured market value of the crop, thereby guaranteeing the economic well-being of the family. If crop insurance is not available, families have an incentive to self-insure by sending one or more workers abroad to remit earnings home, thereby guaranteeing family income even if the harvest fails.

Futures markets. Whenever a household sows a cash crop, it assumes that the crop, when harvested, can be sold for a price sufficient to sustain the family or improve its well-being. In making this bet, however, there is a risk that the price for the crop may drop below expected levels, leaving the family with insufficient income. In developed countries, price risk is managed through futures markets that allow farmers to sell all or part of their crop for future delivery at a guaranteed price. Investors assume the risk of loss should prices fall below the guaranteed price, and they reap the gain should prices rise above this level. Most developing countries lack futures markets, and when they exist, poor farm households generally lack access to them. Migration offers a mechanism by which farm families can self-insure against income risks arising from crop price fluctuations.

Unemployment insurance. Nonfarm families, as well as many farm households, depend on wages earned by family workers. If local economic conditions deteriorate and employment levels fall, or if a family member is injured and cannot work, the household's livelihood may be threatened by a reduction or loss of income. In wealthy countries, governments maintain insurance programs that protect workers and their families from this risk, but in poor countries such unemployment and disability programs are absent or incomplete in their coverage, again giving families incentives to self-insure by sending workers abroad.

If employment conditions in foreign and local labor markets are negatively correlated or are uncorrelated, then international migration provides a way of reducing the risk to family wages and guarantees a reliable stream of income, in the form of remittances, to support the family. Moreover, migration fulfills this insurance function whether or not remittances are actually observed. Migrants, like formal insurance contracts, only have to pay out if losses are realized. The existence of an implicit or explicit insurance arrangement, however, can have an important effect on a household's economic behavior, and the desire to acquire this insurance may be primary motivation for families to participate in international migration.

Capital markets. Households may desire to increase the productivity of their assets, but to do so they need to acquire capital to make additional investments. Farm families, for example, may seek to irrigate their fields, apply fertilizers, buy scientifically improved seeds, or acquire machinery, but they may lack the money to purchase these inputs. Nonfarm families may seek to invest in the education or training of household members, or to acquire capital goods that can be used to produce goods for sale on consumer markets, but again they may lack money to cover these costs. In developed countries, investments are funded either through private savings or borrowing, both of which are greatly assisted by access to a sound and efficient banking system. Borrowing can also provide protection against consumption risk if income is variable. In many developing countries, however, savings institutions are unreliable or underdeveloped, and people are reluctant to entrust their savings to them.

In poor countries, the needed funds may also be difficult to borrow because the family lacks collateral to qualify for a loan, because there is a scarcity of lending capital, or because the banking system provides incomplete coverage, serving mainly the needs of the affluent. For poor families, the only real access to borrowing is often from local moneylenders who charge high interest rates, making transaction costs prohibitive. Under these circumstances, migration again becomes attractive as an alternative source of capital to finance improvements in productivity and ensure stability in consumption, and the family has a strong incentive to send one or more workers abroad to accumulate savings or to transfer capital back in the form of remittance.

A key proposition in the foregoing discussion is that income is not a homogeneous good, as assumed by neoclassical economics. The source of the income really matters, and households have significant incentives to invest scarce family resources in activities and projects that provide access to new income sources, even if these activities do not necessarily increase total income.

The new economics of migration also questions the assumption that income has a constant effect on utility for an actor across socioeconomic settings—that a $100 real increase in income means the same thing to a person regardless of local community conditions and irrespective of his or her position in the income distribution. The new economic theorists argue, in contrast, that households send workers abroad not only to improve income in absolute terms, but also to increase income *relative* to other households, and, hence, to reduce their *relative* deprivation compared with some reference group (see Stark, Taylor, and Yitzhaki, 1986, 1988; Stark and Yitzhaki, 1988; Stark and Taylor, 1989, 1991; Stark, 1991).

A household's sense of relative deprivation depends on the incomes of which it is deprived in the reference-group income distribution. If $F(y)$ is the cumulative income distribution and $h[1-F(y)]$ represents the dissatisfaction felt by a household with income y from not having an income that is slightly higher than y (i.e., $y + \Delta$), then the relative deprivation of a household with income y can be expressed conceptually as:

$$RD\,(y) = \int_{y}^{ymax} h[1 - F(z)]dz$$

where *ymax* is the highest income found in the community. In the simple case where $h[1 - F(y)] = 1 - F(y)$, this expression is equivalent to the product of two terms: the share of households with income greater than y, and the average difference between these higher household incomes and y (Stark and Taylor, 1989).

To illustrate this concept of relative income, consider an increase in the income of affluent households. If poor households' incomes are unchanged, then their relative deprivation increases. If household utility is negatively affected by relative deprivation, then even though a poor household's absolute income and expected gains from migration remain unchanged, its incentive to participate in international migration increases if, by sending a family member abroad, it can hope to reap a relative income gain in the community. The likelihood of migration thus grows because of the change in *other* households' incomes. Market failures that constrain local income opportunities for poor households may also increase the attractiveness of migration as an avenue for effecting gains in relative income.

The theoretical models growing out of the "new economics" of migration yield a set of propositions and hypotheses that are quite different from those emanating from neoclassical theory, and they lead to a very different set of policy prescriptions:

1. Families, households, or other culturally defined units of production and con-

sumption are the appropriate units of analysis for migration research, not the autonomous individual.

2. A wage differential is not a necessary condition for international migration to occur; households may have strong incentives to diversify risks through transnational movement even in the absence of wage differentials.

3. International migration and local employment or local production are not mutually exclusive possibilities. Indeed, there are strong incentives for households to engage in both migration and local activities. In fact, an increase in the returns to local economic activities may heighten the attractiveness of migration as a means of overcoming capital and risk constraints on investing in those activities. Thus, economic development within sending regions need not reduce the pressures for international migration.

4. International movement does not necessarily stop when wage differentials have been eliminated across national boundaries. Incentives for migration may continue to exist if other markets within sending countries are absent, imperfect, or in disequilibria.

5. The same expected gain in income will not have the same effect on the probability of migration of households located at different points in the income distribution, or among those located in communities with different income distributions.

6. Governments can influence migration rates not only through policies that influence labor markets, but also through those that shape insurance markets, capital markets, and futures markets. Government insurance programs, particularly unemployment insurance, can significantly affect the incentives for international movement.

7. Government policies and economic changes that shape income distributions will change the relative deprivation of some households and thus alter their incentives to migrate.

8. Government policies and economic changes that affect the distribution of income will influence international migration independent of their effects on mean income. In fact, government policies that produce a higher mean income in migrant-sending areas may *increase* migration if relatively poor households do not share in the income gain. Conversely, policies may reduce migration if relatively rich households do not share in the income gain.

Dual Labor Market Theory

Although neoclassical human capital theory and the new economics of migration lead to divergent conclusions about the origins and nature of international migration, both are essentially micro-level decision models. What differ are the units assumed to make the decision (the individual or the household), the entity being maximized or minimized (income or risk), assumptions about the economic context of decision-making (complete and well-functioning markets versus missing or imperfect markets), and the extent to which the migration decision is socially contextualized (whether income is evaluated in absolute terms or relative to some reference group). Standing distinctly apart from these models of rational choice, however, is dual labor market theory, which sets its sights away from decisions made by individuals and argues that international migration stems from the intrinsic labor demands of modern industrial societies.

Piore (1979) has been the most forceful and elegant proponent of this theoretical viewpoint, arguing that international migration is caused by a permanent demand for immigrant labor that is inherent to the economic structure of developed nations. According to Piore, immigration is not caused by push factors in sending countries (low wages or high unemployment), but by pull factors in receiving countries (a chronic and unavoidable need for foreign workers). This built-in demand for immigrant labor stems from four fundamental characteristics of advanced industrial societies and their economies.

Structural inflation. Wages not only reflect conditions of supply and demand, they also confer status and prestige, social qualities that inhere to the jobs to which the wages are attached. In general, people believe that wages should reflect social status, and they have rather rigid notions about the correlation between occupational status and pay. As a result, wages offered by employers are not entirely free to respond to changes in the supply of workers. A variety of informal social expectations and formal institutional mechanisms (such as union contracts, civil service rules, bureaucratic regulations, company job classifications) ensures that wages correspond to the hierarchies of prestige and status that people perceive and expect.

If employers seek to attract workers for unskilled jobs at the bottom of an occupational hierarchy, they cannot simply raise wages. Raising wages at the bottom of the hierarchy would upset socially defined relationships between status and remuneration. If wages are increased at the bottom, there will be strong pressure to raise wages by corresponding amounts at other levels of the hierarchy. If the wages of busboys are raised in response to a shortage of entry-level workers, for example, they may overlap with those of waitresses, thereby threatening their status and undermining the accepted social hierarchy. Waitresses, in turn, demand a corresponding wage increase, which threatens the position of cooks, who also pressure employers for a raise. Workers may be aided in their efforts by union representatives or contracts.

Thus the cost to employers of raising wages to attract low-level workers is typically more than the cost of these workers' wages alone; wages must be increased proportionately throughout the job hierarchy in order to keep them in line with social expectations, a problem known as structural inflation. Attracting native workers by raising entry wages during times of labor scarcity is thus expensive and disruptive, providing employers with a strong incentive to seek easier and cheaper solutions, such as the importation of migrant workers who will accept low wages.

Motivational problems. Occupational hierarchies are also for the motivation of workers, since people work not only for income, but also for the accumulation and maintenance of social status. Acute motivational problems arise at the bottom of the job hierarchy because there is no status to be maintained and there are few avenues for upward mobility. The problem is inescapable and structural because the bottom cannot be eliminated from the labor market. Mechanization to eliminate the lowest and least desirable class of jobs will simply create a new bottom tier composed of jobs that used to be just above the bottom rung. Since there always has to be a bottom of any hierarchy, motivational problems are inescapable. What employers need are workers who view bottom-level jobs simply as a means to the end of earning money, and for whom employment is reduced solely to income, with no implications for status or prestige.

For a variety of reasons, immigrants satisfy this need, at least at the beginning of their migratory careers. Most migrants begin as target earners, seeking to earn money for a specific goal that will improve their status or well-being at home—building a house, paying for school, buying land, acquiring consumer goods. Moreover, the disjuncture in living standards between developed and developing societies means that even low wages abroad appear to be generous by the standards of the home community; and even though a migrant may realize that a foreign job is of low status abroad, he does not view himself as being a part of the receiving society. Rather he sees himself as a member of his home community, within which foreign labor and hard-currency remittances carry considerable honor and prestige.

Economic dualism. Bifurcated labor markets come to characterize advanced industrial economies because of the inherent duality between labor and capital. Capital is a fixed factor of production that can be idled by lower demand but not laid off; owners of capital must bear the costs of its unemployment. Labor is a variable factor of production that can be released when demand falls, so that workers are forced to bear the costs of their own unemployment. Whenever possible, therefore, capitalists seek out the stable, permanent portion of demand and reserve it for the employment of equipment, whereas the variable portion of demand is met by adding labor. Thus, capital-intensive methods are used to meet basic demand, and labor-intensive methods are reserved for the seasonal, fluctuating component. This dualism creates distinctions among workers, leading to a bifurcation of the labor force.

Workers in the capital-intensive primary sector get stable, skilled jobs working with the best equipment and tools. Employers are forced to invest in these workers by providing specialized training and education. Their jobs are complicated and require considerable knowledge and experience to perform well, leading to the accumulation of firm-specific human capital. Primary-sector workers tend to be unionized or highly professionalized, with contracts that require employers to bear a substantial share of the costs of their idlement (in the form of severance pay and unemployment benefits). Because of these costs and continuing obligations, workers in the primary sector become expensive to let go; they become more like capital.

In the labor-intensive secondary sector, however, workers hold unstable, unskilled jobs; they may be laid off at any time with little or no cost to the employer. Indeed, the employer will generally lose money by retaining workers during slack periods. During down cycles the first thing secondary-sector employers do is cut their payroll. As a result, employers force workers in this sector to bear the costs of their unemployment. They remain a variable factor of production and are, hence, expendable.

Thus, the inherent dualism between labor and capital extends to the labor force in the form of a segmented labor market structure. Low wages, unstable conditions, and the lack of reasonable prospects for mobility in the secondary sector make it difficult to attract native workers, who are instead drawn into the primary, capital-intensive sector, where wages are higher, jobs are more secure, and there is a possibility of occupational improvement. To fill the shortfall in demand within the secondary sector, employers turn to immigrants.

The demography of labor supply. The problems of motivation and structural inflation inherent to modern occupational hierarchies, together with the dualism intrinsic to market economies, create a permanent demand for workers who are willing to labor under unpleasant conditions, at low wages, with great instability, and facing little chance for advancement. In the past, this demand was met partially by two sets of people with social statuses and characteristics conducive to these sorts of jobs: women and teenagers.

Historically women have tended to participate in the labor force up to the time of their first birth, and to a lesser extent after children had grown. They sought to earn supplemental income for themselves or their families. They were not primary breadwinners and their principal social identity was that of a sister, wife, or mother. They were willing to put up with low wages and instability because they viewed the work as transient and the earnings as supplemental; the positions they held were unthreatening to their main social statuses, which were grounded in the family.

Likewise, teenagers historically have moved into and out of the labor force with great frequency in order to earn extra money, to gain experience, and to try out different occupational roles. They do not view dead-end jobs as problematic because they expert to get better jobs in the future, after completing school, gaining experience, or settling down. Moreover, teenagers derive their social identities from their parents and families of orientation, not their jobs. They view work instrumentally as a means of earning spending money. The money and the things that it buys enhance their status among their peers; the job is just a means to an end.

In advanced industrial societies, however, these two sources of entry-level workers have shrunk over time because of three fundamental socio-demographic trends: the rise in female labor force participation, which has transformed women's work into a career pursued for social status as well as income; the rise in divorce rates, which has transformed women's jobs into a source of primary income support; and the decline in birth rates and the extension of formal education, which have produced very small cohorts of teenagers entering the labor force. The imbalance between the structural demand for entry-level workers and the limited domestic supply of such workers has increased the underlying, long-run demand for immigrants.

Dual labor market theory neither posits nor denies that actors make rational, self-interested decisions, as predicted by microeconomic models. The negative qualities that people in industrialized countries attach to low-wage jobs, for example, may open up employment opportunities to foreign workers, thereby raising their expected earnings, increasing their ability to overcome risk and credit constraints, and enabling households to achieve relative income gains by sending family members abroad. Recruitment by employers helps to overcome informational and other constraints on international movement, enhancing migration's value as a strategy for family income generation or risk diversification.

Although not in inherent conflict with neoclassical economics, dual labor market theory does carry implications and corollaries that are quite different from those emanating from micro-level decision models:

1. International labor migration is largely demand-based and is initiated by recruitment on the part of employers in developed societies or by governments acting on their behalf.

2. Since the demand for immigrant workers grows out of the structural needs of the economy and is expressed through recruitment practices rather than wage offers, international wage differentials are neither a necessary nor a sufficient condition for labor migration to occur. Indeed, employers have incentives to recruit workers while holding wages constant.

3. Low-level wages in immigrant-receiving societies do not rise in response to a decrease in the supply of immigrant workers; they are held down by social and institutional mechanisms and are not free to respond to shifts in supply and demand.

4. Low-level wages may fall, however, as a result of an increase in the supply of immigrant workers, since the social and institutional checks that keep low-level wages from rising do not prevent them from falling.

5. Governments are unlikely to influence international migration through policies that produce small changes in wages or employment rates; immigrants fill a demand for labor that is structurally built into modern, post-industrial economies, and influencing this demand requires major changes in economic organization.

World Systems Theory

Building on the work of Wallerstein (1974), a variety of sociological theorists has linked the origins of international migration not to the bifurcation of the labor market within particular national economies, but to the structure of the world market that has developed and expanded since the sixteenth century (Petras, 1981; Portes and Walton, 1981; Sassen, 1988, 1991; Castells, 1989; Morawska, 1990). In this scheme, the penetration of capitalist economic relations into peripheral, noncapitalist societies creates a mobile population that is prone to migrate abroad.

Driven by a desire for higher profits and greater wealth, owners and managers of capitalist firms enter poor countries on the periphery of the world economy in search of land, raw materials, labor, and new consumer markets. In the past, this market penetration was assisted by colonial regimes that administered poor regions for the benefit of economic interests in colonizing societies. Today it is made possible by neocolonial governments and multinational firms that perpetuate the power of national elites who either participate in the world economy as capitalists themselves, or offer their nation's resources to global firms on acceptable terms.

According to world systems theory, migration is a natural outgrowth of disruptions and dislocations that inevitably occur in the process of capitalist development. As capitalism has expanded outward from its core in Western Europe, North America, Oceania, and Japan, ever-larger portions of the globe and growing shares of the human population have been incorporated into the world market economy. As land, raw materials, and labor within peripheral regions come under the influence and control of markets, migration flows are inevitably generated, some of which have always moved abroad (Massey, 1989).

Land. In order to achieve the greatest profit from existing agrarian resources and to compete within global commodity markets, capitalist farmers in peripheral areas seek to consolidate landholding, mechanize production, introduce cash crops, and apply industrially produced inputs such as fertilizer, insecticides, and high-yield seeds. Land consolidation destroys traditional systems of land tenure based on inheritance and common rights of usufruct. Mechanization decreases the need for manual labor and makes many agrarian workers redundant to production. The substitution of cash crops for staples undermines traditional social and economic relations based on subsistence (Chayanov, 1966); and the use of modern inputs produces high crop yields at low unit prices, which drives small, noncapitalist farmers out of local markets. All of these forces contribute to the creation of a mobile labor force displaced from the land with a weakened attachment to local agrarian communities.

Raw materials. The extraction of raw materials for sale on global markets requires industrial methods that rely on paid labor. The offer of wages to former peasants undermines traditional forms of social and economic organization based on systems of reciprocity and fixed role relations and creates incipient labor markets based on new conceptions of individualism, private gain, and social change. These trends likewise promote the geographic mobility of labor in developing regions, often with international spillovers.

Labor. Firms from core capitalist countries enter developing countries to establish assembly plants that take advantage of low wage rates, often within special export-processing zones created by sympathetic governments. The demand for factory workers strengthens local labor markets and weakens traditional productive relations. Much of the labor demanded is female, however, and the resulting feminization of the workforce limits opportunities for men; but since the new factory work is demanding and poorly paid, women tend only to work a few years, after which time they leave to look for new opportunities. The insertion of foreign-owned factories into peripheral regions thus undermines the peasant economy by producing goods that compete with those made locally; by feminizing the workforce without providing factory-based employment opportunities for men; and by socializing women for industrial work and modern consumption, albeit without providing a lifetime income capable of meeting these needs. The result is the creation of a population that is socially and economically uprooted and prone to migration.

The same capitalist economic processes that create migrants in peripheral regions simultaneously attract them to developed countries. Although some people displaced by the process of market penetration move to cities, leading to the urbanization of developing societies, inevitably many are drawn abroad because globalization creates material and ideological links to the places where capital originates. The foreign investment that drives economic globalization is managed from a small number of global cities, whose structural characteristics create a strong demand for immigrant labor.

Material links. In order to ship goods, deliver machinery, extract and export raw materials, coordinate business operations, and manage expatriate assembly plants, capitalists in core nations build and expand transportation and communication links to the peripheral countries where they have invested. These links not only facilitate the movement of goods, products, information, and capital, they also promote the movement of people by reducing the costs of movement along certain international pathways. Because investment and globalization are inevitably accompanied by the buildup of transportation and communication infrastructure, the international movement of labor generally follows the international movement of goods and capital in the opposite direction.

Ideological links. The process of economic globalization creates cultural links between core capitalist countries and their hinterlands within the developing world. In many cases, these cultural links are longstanding, reflecting a colonial past in which core countries established administrative and educational systems that mirrored their own in order to govern and exploit a peripheral region. Citizens of Senegal, for example, learn French, study at lycées, and use a currency directly tied to the French franc in economic transactions. Likewise, Indians and Pakistanis learn English, take British-style degrees, and join with others in a transnational union known as the British Commonwealth. Even in the absence of a colonial past, the influence of economic penetration can be profound: Mexicans increasingly study at U.S. universities, speak English, and follow American consumer styles closely.

These ideological and cultural connections are reinforced by mass communications and advertising campaigns directed from the core countries. Television programming from the United States, France, Britain, and Germany transmits information about lifestyles and living standards in the developed world, and commercials prepared by foreign advertising agencies inculcate modern consumer tastes within peripheral peoples. The diffusion of core country languages and cultural patterns and the spread of modern consumption patterns interact with the emergence of a transportation/communication infrastructure to channel international migration to particular core countries.

Global cities. The world economy is managed from a relatively small number of urban centers in which banking, finance, administration, professional services, and high-tech production tend to be concentrated (Castells, 1989; Sassen, 1991). In the United States, global cities include New York, Chicago, Los Angeles, and Miami; in Europe, they include London, Paris, Frankfurt, and Milan; and in the Pacific, Tokyo, Osaka, and Sydney qualify. Within these global cities, a great deal of wealth and a highly educated workforce are concentrated, creating a strong demand for services from unskilled workers (busboys, gardeners, waiters, hotel workers, domestic servants). At the same time, the shifting of heavy industrial production overseas; the growth of high-tech manufacturing in electronics, computers, and telecommunications; and the expansion of service sectors such as health and education create a bifurcated labor market structure with strong demand for workers at both the upper and lower ends, but with relatively weak demand in the middle.

Poorly educated natives resist taking low-paying jobs at the bottom of the occupational hierarchy, creating a strong demand for immigrants. Meanwhile, well-educated natives and skilled foreigners dominate the lucrative jobs at the upper tier of the occupational distribution, and the concentration of wealth among them helps to fuel the demand for the type of services immigrants are most willing to meet. Native workers with modest educations cling to jobs in the declining middle, migrate out of global cities, or rely on social insurance programs for support.

World systems theory thus argues that international migration follows the political and economic organization of an expanding global market, a view that yields six distinct hypotheses:

1. International migration is a natural consequence of capitalist market formation in the developing world; the penetration of the global economy into peripheral regions is the catalyst for international movement.

2. The international flow of labor follows the international flow of goods and capital, but in the opposite direction. Capitalist investment foments changes that create an uprooted, mobile population in peripheral countries while simultaneously forging strong material and cultural links with core countries, leading to transnational movement.

3. International migration is especially likely between past colonial powers and their former colonies, because cultural, linguistic, administrative, investment, transportation, and communication links were established early and were allowed to develop free from outside competition during the colonial era, leading to the formation of specific transnational markets and cultural systems.

4. Since international migration stems from the globalization of the market economy, the way for governments to influence immigration rates is by regulating the overseas investment activities of corporations and controlling international flows of capital and goods. Such policies, however, are unlikely to be implemented because they are difficult to enforce, tend to incite international trade disputes, risk world economic recession, and antagonize multinational firms with substantial political resources that can be mobilized to block them.

5. Political and military interventions by governments of capitalist countries to protect investments abroad and to support foreign governments sympathetic to the expansion of the global market, when they fail, produce refugee movements directed to particular core countries, constituting another form of international migration.

6. International migration ultimately has little to do with wage rates or employment differentials between countries; it follows from the dynamics of market creation and the structure of the global economy.

The Perpetuation of International Movement

Immigration may begin for a variety of reasons—a desire for individual income gain, an attempt to diversify risks to household income, a program of recruitment to satisfy employer demands for low-wage workers, an international displacement of peasants by market penetration within peripheral regions, or some combination thereof. But the conditions that initiate international movement may be quite different from those that perpetuate it across time and space. Although wage differentials, relative risks, recruitment efforts, and market penetration may continue to cause people to move, new conditions that arise in the course of migration come to function as independent causes themselves: migrant networks spread, institutions supporting transnational movement develop, and the social meaning of work changes in receiving societies. The general thrust of these transformations is to make additional movement more likely, a process known as cumulative causation.

Network Theory

Migrant networks are sets of interpersonal ties that connect migrants, former migrants, and nonmigrants in origin and destination areas through ties of kinship, friendship, and shared community origin. They increase the likelihood of international movement because they lower the costs and risks of movement and increase the expected net returns to migration. Network connections constitute a form of social capital that people can draw upon to gain access to foreign employment. Once the number of migrants reaches a critical threshold, the expansion of networks reduces the costs and risks of movement, which causes the probability of migration to rise, which causes additional movement, which further expands the networks, and so on. Over time migratory behavior spreads outward to encompass broader segments of the sending society (Hugo, 1981; Taylor, 1986; Massey and García España, 1987; Massey, 1990a, 1990b; Gurak and Caces, 1992).

Declining costs. The first migrants who leave for a new destination have no social ties to draw upon, and for them migration is costly, particularly if it involves entering another country without documents. After the first migrants have left, however, the potential costs of migration are substantially lowered for friends and relatives left behind. Because of the nature of kinship and friendship structures, each new migrant creates a set of people with social ties to the destination area. Migrants are inevitably linked to nonmigrants, and the latter draw upon obligations implicit in relationships such as kinship and friendship to gain access to employment and assistance at the point of destination.

Once the number of network connections in an origin area reaches a critical threshold, migration becomes self-perpetuating because each act of migration itself creates the social structure needed to sustain it. Every new migrant reduces the costs of subsequent migration for a set of friends and relatives, and some of these people are thereby induced to migrate, which further expands the set of people with ties abroad, which, in turn, reduces costs for a new set of people, causing some of them to migrate, and so on.

Declining risks. Networks also make international migration extremely attractive as a strategy for risk diversification. When migrant networks are well-developed, they put a destination job within easy reach of most community members and make emigration a reliable and secure source of income. Thus, the self-sustaining growth of networks that occurs through the progressive reduction of costs may also be explained theoretically by the progressive reduction of risks. Every new migrant expands the network and reduces the risks of movement for all those to whom he or she is related, eventually making it virtually risk-free and costless to diversify household labor allocations through emigration.

This dynamic theory accepts the view of international migration as an individual or household decision process, but argues that acts of migration at one point in time systematically alter the context within which future migration decisions are made, greatly increasing the likelihood that later decisionmakers will choose to migrate. The conceptualization of migration as a self-sustaining diffusion process has implications and corollaries that are quite different from those derived from the general equilibrium analyses typically employed to study migration:

1. Once begun, international migration tends to expand over time until network connections have diffused so widely in a sending region that all people who wish to migrate can do so without difficulty; then migration begins to decelerate.

2. The size of the migratory flow between two countries is not strongly correlated to wage differentials or employment rates, because whatever effects these variables have in promoting or inhibiting migration are progressively overshadowed by the falling costs and risks of movement stemming from the growth of migrant networks over time.

3. As international migration becomes institutionalized through the formation and elaboration of networks, it becomes progressively independent of the factors that originally caused it, be they structural or individual.

4. As networks expand and the costs and risks of migration fall, the flow becomes less selective in socioeconomic terms and more representative of the sending community or society.

5. Governments can expect to have great difficulty controlling flows once they have begun, because the process of network formation lies largely outside their control and occurs no matter what policy regime is pursued.

6. Certain immigration policies, however, such as those intended to promote reunification between immigrants and their families abroad, work at cross-purposes with the control of immigration flows, since they reinforce migrant networks by giving members of kin networks special rights of entry.

Institutional Theory

Once international migration has begun, private institutions and voluntary organizations arise to satisfy the demand created by an imbalance between the large number of people who seek entry into capital-rich countries and the limited number of immigrant visas these countries typically offer. This imbalance, and the barriers that core countries erect to keep people out, create a lucrative economic niche for entrepreneurs and institutions dedicated to promoting international movement for profit, yielding a black market in migration. As this underground market creates conditions conducive to exploitation and victimization, voluntary humanitarian organizations also arise in developed countries to enforce the rights and improve the treatment of legal and undocumented migrants.

For-profit organizations and private entrepreneurs provide a range of services to migrants in exchange for fees set on the underground market: surreptitious smuggling across borders; clandestine transport to internal destinations; labor contracting between employers and migrants; counterfeit documents and visas; arranged marriages between migrants and legal residents or citizens of the destination country; and lodging, credit, and other assistance in countries of destination. Humanitarian groups help migrants by providing counseling, social services, shelter, legal advice about how to obtain legitimate papers, and even insulation from immigration law enforcement authorities. Over time, individuals, firms, and organizations become well-known to immigrants and institutionally stable, constituting another form of social capital that migrants can draw upon to gain access to foreign labor markets.

The recognition of a gradual build-up of institutions, organizations, and entrepreneurs dedicated to arranging immigrant entry, legal or illegal, again yields hypotheses that are also quite distinct from those emanating from micro-level decision models:

1. As organizations develop to support, sustain, and promote international movement, the international flow of migrants becomes more and more institutionalized and independent of the factors that originally caused it.

2. Governments have difficulty controlling migration flows once they have begun because the process of institutionalization is difficult to regulate. Given the profits to be made by meeting the demand for immigrant entry, police efforts only serve to create a black market in international movement, and stricter immigration policies are met with resistance from humanitarian groups.

Cumulative Causation

In addition to the growth of networks and the development of migrant-supporting institutions, international migration sustains itself in other ways that make additional movement progressively more likely over time, a process Myrdal (1957) called cumulative causation (Massey, 1990b). Causation is cumulative in that each act of migration alters the social context within which subsequent migration decisions are made, typically in ways that make additional movement more likely. So far, social scientists have discussed six socioeconomic factors that are potentially affected by migration in this cumulative fashion: the distribution of income, the distribution of land, the organization of agriculture, culture, the regional distribution of human capital, and the social meaning of work. Feedbacks through other variables are also possible, but have not been systematically treated (Stark, Taylor, and Yitzhaki, 1986; Taylor, 1992).

The distribution of income. As we have already noted, people may be motivated to migrate not only to increase their absolute income or to diversify their risks, but also to improve their income relative to other households in their reference group. As a household's sense of relative deprivation increases, so does the motivation to migrate. Before anyone has migrated from a community, income inequality within most poor, rural settings is not great because nearly all families live close to the subsistence level with minimal outside incomes. After one or two households have begun participating in foreign wage labor, however, remittances increase their incomes greatly. Given the costs and risks associated with international movement, moreover, the first households to migrate are usually located in the middle or upper ranges of the local income hierarchy.

Seeing some families vastly improve their income through migration makes families lower in the income distribution feel relatively deprived, including some of them to migrate, which further exacerbates income inequality and increases the sense of relative deprivation among nonmigrants, inducing still more families to migrate, and so on. Income inequality and relative deprivation go through a series of phases, being low at first, then high as the rate of outmigration accelerates, then low again as a majority of households participate in the migrant workforce, reaching a minimum when practically all families are involved in foreign wage labor (Stark, Taylor, and Yitzhaki, 1986; Stark and Taylor, 1989; Stark, 1991; Taylor, 1992).

The distribution of land. An important spending target for migrants from rural communities is the purchase of land. But land is purchased by migrants abroad typically for its prestige value or as a source of retirement income rather than as a productive investment. International migrants are likely to use their higher earnings to purchase farmland, but they are more likely than nonmigrants to let the land lie fallow since foreign wage labor is more lucrative than local agrarian production. This pattern of land use lowers the demand for local farm labor, thereby increasing the pressures for outmigration. The more outmigration, the more people have access to the funds necessary to buy land, leading to additional purchases by migrants and more land withdrawn from production, creating still more pressure for out migration (Rhoades, 1978; Reichert, 1981; Mines, 1984; Wiest, 1984).

The organization of agrarian production. When migrant households do farm the land they own, moreover, they are more likely than nonmigrant families to use capital-intensive methods (machinery, herbicides, irrigation, fertilizers, and improved seeds) since they have access to capital to finance these inputs. Thus migrant households need less labor per unit of output than nonmigrant households, thereby displacing local workers from traditional tasks and again increasing the pressures for outmovement (Massey et al., 1987). The more migration, the greater the capitalization of agriculture and the greater the displacement of agrarian labor, leading to still greater migration.

The culture of migration. As migration grows in prevalence within a community, it changes values and cultural perceptions in ways that increase the probability of future migration. Among the migrants themselves, experience in an advanced industrial economy changes tastes and motivations (Piore, 1979). Although migrants may begin as target earners seeking to make one trip and earn money for a narrow purpose, after migrating they acquire a stronger concept of social mobility and a taste for consumer goods and styles of life that are difficult to attain through local labor. Once someone has migrated, therefore, he or she is very likely to migrate again, and the odds of taking an additional trip rise with the number of trips already taken (Massey, 1986).

At the community level, migration becomes deeply ingrained into the repertoire of people's behaviors, and values associated with migration become part of the community's values. For young men, and in many settings young women as well, migration becomes a rite of passage, and those who do not attempt to elevate their status through international movement are considered lazy, unenterprising, and undesirable (Reichert, 1982). Eventually, knowledge about foreign locations and jobs becomes widely diffused, and values, sentiments, and behaviors characteristic of the core society spread widely within the sending region (Massey et al., 1987; Alarcón, 1992).

The regional distribution of human capital. Migration is a selective process that tends, initially at least, to draw relatively well-educated, skilled, productive, and highly motivated people away from sending communities. (As pointed out earlier, however, migration tends to become less selective over time as the costs and risks fall because of network formation). Sustained outmigration thus leads to the depletion of human capital in sending regions and its accumulation in receiving areas, enhancing the productivity of the latter while lowering that of the former. Over time, therefore, the accumulation of human capital reinforces economic growth in receiving areas while its simultaneous depletion in sending areas exacerbates their stagnation, thereby further enhancing the conditions for migration (Myrdal, 1957; Greenwood, 1981, 1985; Greenwood, Hunt, and McDowell, 1987). Programs of school construction and educational expansion in sending areas reinforce this cumulative migration process because raising educational levels in peripheral rural areas increases the potential returns to migration and gives people a greater incentive to leave for urban destinations at home or abroad.

Social labeling. Within receiving societies, once immigrants have been recruited into particular occupations in significant numbers, those jobs become culturally labeled as "immigrant jobs" and native workers are reluctant to fill them, reinforcing the structural demand for immigrants. Immigration changes the social definition of work, causing a certain class of jobs to be defined as stigmatizing and viewed as culturally inappropriate for native workers (Böhning, 1972; Piore, 1979). The stigma comes from the presence of immigrants, not from the characteristics of the job. In most European countries, for example, jobs in automobile manufacturing came to be considered "immigrant jobs," whereas in the United States they are considered "native jobs."

Viewing international migration in dynamic terms as a cumulative social process yields a set of propositions broadly consistent with those derived from network theory:

1. Social, economic, and cultural changes brought about in sending and receiving countries by international migration give the movement of people a powerful internal momentum resistant to easy control or regulation, since the feedback mechanisms of cumulative causation largely lie outside the reach of government.

2. During times of domestic unemployment and joblessness, governments find it difficult to curtail labor migration and to recruit natives back into jobs formerly held by immigrants. A value shift has occurred among native workers, who refuse the "immigrant" jobs, making it necessary to retain or recruit more immigrants.

3. The social labeling of a job as "immigrant" follows from the concentration of immigrants within it; once immigrants have entered a job in significant numbers, whatever its characteristics, it will be difficult to recruit native workers back into that occupational category.

Migration Systems Theory

The various propositions of world systems theory, network theory, institutional theory, and the theory of cumulative causation all suggest that migration flows acquire a measure of stability and structure over space and time, allowing for the identification of stable international migration systems. These systems are characterized by relatively intense exchanges of goods, capital, and people between certain countries and less intense exchanges between others. An international migration system generally includes a core receiving region, which may be a country or group of countries, and a set of specific sending countries linked to it by unusually large flows of immigrants (Fawcett, 1989; Zlotnik, 1992).

Although not a separate theory so much as a generalization following from the foregoing theories, a migration systems perspective yields several interesting hypotheses and propositions:

1. Countries within a system need not be geographically close since flows reflect political and economic relationships rather than physical ones. Although proximity obviously facilitates the formation of exchange relationships, it does not guarantee them, nor does distance preclude them.

2. Multipolar systems are possible, whereby a set of dispersed core countries receive immigrants from a set of overlapping sending nations.

3. Nations may belong to more than one migration system, but multiple membership is more common among sending than receiving nations.

4. As political and economic conditions change, systems evolve, so that stability does not imply a fixed structure. Countries may join or drop out of a system in response to social change, economic fluctuations, or political upheaval.

Evaluation of Theories

Because theories proposed to explain the origins and persistence of international migration posit causal mechanisms at many levels of aggregation, the various explanations are not necessarily contradictory unless one adopts the rigid position that causes must operate at one level and one level only. We find no *a priori* grounds for such an assertion. As stated earlier, it is entirely possible that individuals engage in cost-benefit calculations; that households act to diversify labor allocations; and that the socioeconomic context within which these decisions are made is determined by structural forces operating at the national and international levels (Papademetriou and Martin, 1991). Thus, we are skeptical both of atomistic theories that deny the importance of structural constraints on individual decisions, and of structural theories that deny agency to individuals and families.

Rather than adopting the narrow argument of theoretical exclusivity, we adopt the broader position that causal processes relevant to international migration might operate on multiple levels simultaneously, and that sorting out which of the explanations are useful is an empirical and not only a logical task. Each model must be considered on its own terms and its leading tenets examined carefully to derive testable propositions. Only then can we clearly specify the data and methods required to evaluate them empirically.

The neoclassical economic model yields a clear empirical prediction that, in principle, should be readily verifiable: that the volume of international migration is directly and significantly related, over time and across countries, to the size of the international gap in wage rates. Regression analyses testing the theories of Lewis (1954) and Ranis and Fei (1961) should therefore contain transnational wage differentials as the leading predictor, with geographic distance between countries perhaps entered as a proxy for the costs of movement.

Later refinements of the neoclassical model, however, suggest that the pertinent factor in migration decisionmaking is the *expected* earnings gap, not the absolute real-wage differential (Todaro, 1969, 1976; Todaro and Maruszko, 1987). At any point in time, expected earnings are defined as real earnings in the country under consideration multiplied by the probability of employment there. Although typically estimated as one minus the unemployment rate, the likelihood of employment is probably more appropriately measured as one minus the underemployment rate, given the pervasiveness of sporadic, part-time employment in low-skill jobs within developing regions. They key predictor of international migratory flows is thus an interaction term that cross-multiplies wages and employment probabilities. A statistical test for the significance of this interaction term, compared to a regression model where real wages alone appear, constitutes a critical test comparison between the Ranis–Fei and the Todaro versions of neoclassical theory. (See Todaro, 1980, and Greenwood, 1985, for reviews of the substantial empirical research literature testing the Todaro model.)

A logical corollary of both models, however, is that international movement should not occur in the absence of an international gap in either observed or expected wages, and that movement between countries should cease when wage differentials have been erased (net of the costs of movement, monetary and psychological). International flows that occur in the absence of a wage gap, or that end before a gap has been eliminated, represent anomalous conditions that constitute prima facie evidence challenging the assumptions of neoclassical economic theory.

At the individual level, the Todaro model and its successors predict that individual and household characteristics that are positively related to the rate of remuneration or the probability of employment in destination areas will increase the probability of migration by raising the expected returns to international movement. Hence, the likelihood of emigration is predicted to be reliably related to such standard human capital variables as age, experience, schooling, marital status, and skill. The propensity for international migration is also expected to vary with a household's access to income-generating resources at home (such as owning land or supporting a business enterprise), since these will affect the *net* return to movement.

Since human capital variables that affect rates of employment and remuneration in destination areas also tend to affect wage and employment rates in place of origin, a key empirical issue is where the effect of human capital is greater, at home or abroad. Given the fact that international migration involves a change of language, culture, and economic system, human capital acquired at home generally transfers abroad imperfectly (see Chiswick, 1979). In this case, international migrants may be *negatively* selected with respect to variables such as education and job experience.

Among rural Mexicans, for example, the economic returns to schooling have historically been greater in urban areas of Mexico that in the United States. Whereas an undocumented migrant with a secondary education gets the same minimum-wage job in Los Angeles as one with no schooling at all, that education would qualify the same person for a clerical or white collar job in Mexico City, thereby raising the likelihood of rural-urban migration and lowering the probability of international movement (Taylor, 1987).

This pattern of negative selectivity cannot be hypothesized universally, however, since selection on human capital variables depends on the transferability of the skill or ability under consideration, which itself is determined by social, economic, and historical conditions specific to the countries involved. In general, any social change that affects the market value of human capital in either society has the potential of shifting the size and direction of the relationship between specific predictor variables and the likelihood of international movement.

Thus it is nearly impossible, *a priori,* to predict the direction of the relationship between an individual background variable and the probability of migration, and it is consequently difficult to derive a convincing test of neoclassical economic theory at the micro level in a reduced-form regression—that is, one in which the probability of migration is modeled directly as a function of individual and household variables. In general, the only universal prediction that can be offered is that human capital should somehow be reliably related to the likelihood of international movement, but the strength and direction of the relationship is impossible to know in the absence of historical information about the countries involved. Only after the historical circumstances have been clearly specified and their influence on the returns to specific forms of human capital clarified, can a critical test of the neoclassical microeconomic model be formulated.

A more formal alternative is to model the probability of migration structurally as a function of the expected income differential, and simultaneously model the expected-income differential as a function of individual and household variables. In this way, the effects of individual background variables on migration through their influence on the expected-earnings differential can be tested explicitly. In addition, the possible effects of these variables on migration independent of their influence on expected earnings can be explored (Taylor, 1986). In the absence of structural tests, it is difficult to falsify microeconomic theory by examining individual regressions. The only evidence that could conceivably cast serious doubt on the validity of the human capital theory of migration would be the complete absence of a relationship between human capital and migration.

In contrast to neoclassical economic theory, the new economics of migration focuses on the household or family, rather than the individual, as the relevant decision-making unit; and it posits that migration is a response to income risk and to failures in a variety of markets (insurance, credit, labor), which together constrain local income opportunities and inhibit risk-spreading. The most direct test of this theory would be to relate the presence or absence of such market imperfections to households' propensities to participate in international migration. If the new economics of migration is correct, households confronted by the greatest local market imperfections should be most likely to adopt an international migration strategy, other things being equal.

Unfortunately, other things generally are not equal. Typically there is a high correlation between market imperfections and other variables (namely low wages and incomes) that are the focus of the neoclassical (human capital) migration model. The greatest challenge of this direct test, then, is to isolate the influence of market imperfections and risk on international migration from the role of other income and employment variables.

One of the most distinguishing contributions of the new economics of migration is its integration of migration decisionmaking with migrants' remittance behavior and households' remittance use—aspects of migration that hitherto have been treated separately in the literature. If risks to income and a desire to overcome local constraints on production are the driving forces behind migration, then the outcomes of migration (e.g., the patterns and uses of remittances) should reflect this fact. A number of indirect tests of the new economics model are available.

If risk diversification is the underlying motivation, then migrant remittances should be greatest in households most exposed to local income risks and in periods when this risk is most acute (e.g., during a severe drought, as demonstrated by Lucas and Stark, 1985). If a primary motivation of migration is to overcome risk and credit constraints on local production stemming from market failures, then migration and remittances should positively influence local income-generating activities (Lucas, 1987; Taylor, 1992). Such findings would provide evidence in favor of the new economics of migration, because positive effects of migration on local production activities are ruled out by neoclassical economic theory, as are risk effects. Neoclassical theory focuses on an individual's maximization of expected income and assumes that markets are complete and well-functioning.

The new economics of migration also places migration within a broader community context, specifically linking a household's migration decision to its position in the local income distribution. The theory of relative deprivation predicts that a household's odds of sending migrants abroad are greater the larger the amount of income earned by households above it in the reference income distribution, and more generally, the greater the income inequality in the reference community. A systematic test of this proposition requires a multilevel statistical model that not only contains the usual individual and household-level predictor variables, but also incorporates the community characteristic of income inequality, or an operational measure of relative income. Stark and Taylor (1989) found that relative income was more significant than absolute income in explaining international labor migration within a sample of rural Mexican households, except at the two extremes of the income distribution.

The new economic model can also be tested at the aggregate level. Unlike the neoclassical model, risk diversification allows for movement in the absence of international differences in wages or employment rates, because it links migration not just to conditions in the labor market but to failures in the capital and insurance markets as well. In order to test this conceptualization, regressions predicting international population movements should contain, as independent variables, indicators of the presence or absence of insurance programs (e.g., crop insurance and unemployment insurance), the presence or absence of key markets (e.g., futures and capital markets), levels of market coverage (per capita measures of market participation), and transaction costs (e.g., insurance and interest rates). In general, deficiencies in these ancillary markets are predicted to increase the size of international flows and to raise the likelihood that particular households send migrants abroad, holding constant conditions in the labor market.

Although dual labor market theory posits a bifurcated occupational structure and a dual pattern of economic organization for advanced industrial societies, in practice it has proved difficult to verify this segmented market structure empirically (Cain, 1976; Hodson and Kaufman, 1982). Usually the distinction between "primary" and "secondary" sectors is arbitrary, leading to great instability in empirical estimates and a high degree of dependency of results on the decision rule chosen to allocate jobs to sectors (Tolbert, Horan, and Beck, 1980; Hodson and Kaufman, 1981; Horan, Tolbert, and Beck, 1981, but see Dickens and Lang, 1985, for an exception to this criticism).

Rather than attempting to verify the empirical structure of the labor market, therefore, a more efficacious strategy might be to focus on the theory's predictions regarding patterns of international movement, which are quite specific and objectively testable. Piore and others argue that immigration is driven by conditions of labor demand rather than supply. In statistical models that regress secular trends in international migration on changing market conditions in sending and receiving countries, one should therefore observe a higher degree of explanatory power among receiving-country indicators compared with those for sending countries. If real wages and employment conditions are entered into an equation predicting movement between Turkey and Germany, for example, German indicators should dominate in terms of predictive power.

Being demand-based, the dual labor market approach also predicts that international flows of labor begin through formal recruitment mechanisms rather than individual efforts. In principle, it should be easy to verify this proposition simply by listing the major international migration flows that have emerged since 1950 and documenting which ones were initiated by formal recruitment procedures, either public or private. If most or all of the flows are traceable to some sort of recruitment program, then a key prediction of dual labor market theory will have been sustained. In his book, Piore does not undertake this exercise; he refers only to several cases that happen to be consistent with his theory (for an example of such an exercise, however, see Massey and Liang, 1989).

One last prediction of dual labor market theory is that secondary-sector wages are flexible downward, but not upward. Over time, therefore, fluctuations in wage rates in jobs filled by immigrants should not be strongly related to fluctuations in labor supply and demand. During periods of low labor immigration and high labor demand, wages in receiving countries should not rise to attract native workers because of institutional rigidities, but during periods of high immigration and low demand there is nothing to prevent wages from falling in response to competitive pressure. We thus expect an interaction between changes in wages rates and whether or not immigration was contracting or expanding during the period: the effect is expected to be zero in the former case and negative in the latter. We also expect a widening wage gap between these jobs and those hold by native workers over time.

Although world systems theory constitutes a complex and at times diffuse conceptual structure, it yields several relatively straightforward and testable propositions, the first of which is that international flows of labor follow international flows of capital, only in the opposite direction. According to Sassen and others, emigrants are created by direct foreign investment in developing countries and the disruptions that such investment brings. Thus, we should observe that streams of foreign capital going into peripheral regions are accompanied by corresponding outflows of emigrants.

This basic migratory process should be augmented by the existence of ideological and material ties created by prior colonization as well as ongoing processes of market penetration. If one were to specify a model of international migration flows to test world systems theory, therefore, one would want to include indicators of prior colonial relationships, the prevalence of common languages, the intensity of trade relations, the existence of transportation and communication links, and the relative frequency of communications and travel between the countries.

Finally, world systems theory specifies not only that international migration should flow from periphery to core along paths of capital investment, but also that it is directed to certain "global cities" that channel and control foreign investment. Although the theory does not provide specific criteria for defining a "global city," a set of operational criteria might be developed from information about capital assets and corporate headquarters. One could then examine the relative frequency of movement to global cities, as opposed to other places within the developed or developing world.

Network theory leads to a series of eminently testable propositions. According to Piore, Massey, and others, once someone has migrated internationally, he or she is very likely to do so again, leading to repeated movements over time. Thus the likelihood of an additional trip should increase with each trip taken; the probability of transnational migration should be greater among those with prior international experience than among those without it; and the likelihood of additional migration should increase as the amount of foreign experience rises.

A second proposition is that controlling for a person's individual migrant experience, the probability of international migration should be greater for individuals who are related to someone who has prior international experience, or for individuals connected to someone who is actually living abroad. Moreover, the likelihood of movement should increase with the closeness of the relationship (i.e., having a brother in Germany is more likely to induce a Turk to migrate there than having a cousin, a neighbor, or a friend); and it should also rise with the quality of the social capital embodied in the relationship (having a brother who has lived in Germany for ten years is more valuable to a potential emigrant than having one who has just arrived, and having one who is a legal resident is better than having one who lacks residence documents).

Another hypothesis stems from the recognition that international movement requires migrants to overcome more barriers than does internal movement. In addition to the normal costs of travel and searching for work are the costs of learning and adapting to a new culture, the costs of acquiring appropriate documentation, and, if acquiring legal papers is impossible, of evading arrest and deportation. In general, the greater the barriers to movement, the more important should network ties become in promoting migration, since they reduce the costs and risks of movement. We should thus observe that network connections are systematically more powerful in predicting international migration than internal migration. Taylor (1986) finds this differentiated effect of migration networks for a sample of Mexican households.

Within households, we should also be able to detect the effect of social capital on individual migration behavior. In general, members of households in which someone has already migrated abroad should display higher probabilities of movement than those from households that lack migratory experience. If network theory is correct, for example, a common vector by which migratory behavior is transmitted is from fathers to sons (Massey et al., 1987). Dependent sons whose fathers are active or former international migrants should be more likely to emigrate than those whose fathers lack foreign experience.

Finally, at the community level, one should be able to observe the effect of the prevalence of network ties. People should be more likely to migrate abroad if they come from a community where many people have migrated and where a large stock of foreign experience has accumulated than if they come from a place where international migration is relatively uncommon (Massey and García España, 1987). Moreover, as the stock of social ties and international migrant experience grows over time, migration should become progressively less selective and spread from the middle to the lower segments of the socioeconomic hierarchy. In general, then, individual or household migration decisions need to be placed within a local setting, suggesting the need for multi-level analytic models incorporating indexes of network connections within the community.

Institutional theory argues that disparities between the supply of and demand for entry visas into core receiving societies create a lucrative niche for entrepreneurs to provide licit and illicit entry services, and that the exploitation that results from this disparity will also prompt humanitarian organizations to intervene on immigrants' behalf. The establishment and growth of institutions dedicated to facilitating immigration constitutes another form of social infrastructure that persists over time and increases the volume of international population movements.

Although it may be feasible through case studies to document such institutional development and its effect on immigration, it is more difficult to link institutions to aggregate population flows or micro-level migration decisions in an analytically rigorous fashion. On special surveys, migrants and nonmigrants might be asked whether they are aware of institutions providing support to immigrants, and responses to this question may be used to predict the likelihood of movement. Or the presence of such organizations might be documented across communities and used to predict the rate of outmigration at the community level, or, in a multi-level model, the probability of emigration at the individual or household level.

Lastly, the theory of cumulative causation states the general hypothesis that migration sustains itself in such a way that migration tends to create more migration. This hypothesis follows from the proposition that individual or household decisions are affected by the socioeconomic context within which they are made, and that acts of migration at one point in time affect the context within which subsequent decisions are made. Migration decisions made by families and individuals influence social and economic structures within the community, which influence later decisions by other individuals and households. On balance, the changes at the community level increase the odds of subsequent movement, leading to migration's cumulative causation over time (Massey et al., 1987; Massey, 1990b).

The systematic testing of this theory poses substantial data demands. In order to test for cumulative causation at the aggregate level using cross-sectional data, complicated recursive systems of structural equations must be specified, and these typically require instrumental variables that are difficult to define and identify, especially in international data sets. Ideally the theory should be tested using multi-level longitudinal data, which contain variables defined at the individual, household, community, and perhaps even national levels, all measured at different points in time. Only with such a data set can the reciprocal feedback effects of individual or household decisions on social structure be discerned and measured.

The theory of cumulative causation, while in many ways still rudimentary in its development, does point to several factors as particularly important in channeling the feedback between individual behavior and community structure. The first factor is migrant networks, suggesting the need to gather detailed information about kin and friendship ties between migrants and nonmigrants. A second factor is income equality, which requires the accurate measurement of household income. A third is land distribution, which requires detailed data on land tenure and ownership. A fourth, pertaining only to rural areas, is the nature of agrarian production, which requires information on the use of irrigation, machinery, hired labor, herbicides, pesticides, and improved seeds by both migrant and nonmigrant families. The last and perhaps most difficult factor to measure in testing for cumulative causation is culture, which requires information about beliefs, values, and normative practices.

Ideally all of these factors should be measured longitudinally, although in some cases—culture, for example—this would be next impossible. Given the difficulty of securing longitudinal information on changes in the prevalence of migrant networks, the degree of income inequality, the skewness of land distribution, and the capital intensiveness of agricultural production, an alternative strategy might be to rely on geographic diversity in these factors across communities, specifying recursive structural equation systems to model the feedbacks, but this approach raises serious technical issues with respect to identification and instrumentation.

The final conceptual scheme we discussed was the systems perspective, which argues that causal forces operating at a variety of levels lend a degree of permanence to international flows and over time lead to the emergence of stable migration systems. These systems are characterized by relatively large flows of migrants between member countries compared with flows from outside the system. Verifying the existence of such systems is a straightforward empirical matter of establishing some threshold of intensity for inclusion of a flow within a systemic structure, and then applying it to identify those prevailing in the world today. Some efforts along these lines have already been attempted (Zlotnik, 1992).

Conclusion

Theories developed to understand contemporary processes of international migration posit causal mechanisms that operate at widely divergent levels of analysis. Although the propositions, assumptions, and hypotheses derived from each perspective are not inherently contradictory, they nonetheless carry very different implications for policy formulation. Depending on which model is supported and under what circumstances, a social scientist might recommend that policymakers attempt to regulate international migration by changing wages and employment conditions in destination countries; by promoting economic development in origin countries; by establishing programs of social insurance in sending societies; by reducing income inequality in places of origin; by improving futures or capital markets in developing regions; or by some combination of these actions. Or one might advise that all of these programs are fruitless given the structural imperatives for international movement growing out of market economic relations.

Whatever the case, given the size and scale of contemporary migration flows, and given the potential for misunderstanding and conflict inherent in the emergence of diverse, multiethnic societies around the world, political decisions about international migration will be among the most important made over the next two decades. Likewise, sorting out the relative empirical support for each of the theoretical schemes and integrating them in light of that evaluation will be among the most important tasks carried out by social scientists in ensuing years. We hope that by explicating the leading theories of international migration and by clarifying their underlying assumptions and key propositions, we have laid the groundwork for that necessary empirical work.

Note

The authors are members of the IUSSP Committee on South-North Migration, which is currently undertaking a systematic examination of theories of international migration and the evidence supporting them. The committee is chaired by Douglas S. Massey, who took primary responsibility for writing the text of this presentation, but the ideas, concepts, and conclusions expressed in the article are the collective work of all committee members. The committee welcomes comments and criticisms from interested readers.

Immigration Theory for a New Century: Some Problems and Opportunities[1]

✦ Alejandro Portes, *Princeton University*

ABSTRACT

This essay examines some of the pitfalls in contemporary immigration theory and reviews some of the most promising developments in research in this field. As a data-driven field of study, immigration has not had to contend with grand generalizations for highly abstract theorizing. On the contrary, the bias has run in the opposite direction, that is toward ground-level studies of particular migrant groups or analysis of official migration policies. As the distillate of past research in the field and a source of guidance for future work, theory represents one of the most valuable products of our collective intellectual endeavor. Ways to foster it and problems presented by certain common misunderstandings about the meaning and scope of scientific theorizing are discussed.

At the turn of the century, many immigrants launched their American careers not only in new cities and new jobs, but with new names. How this happened symbolized the confident and careless way in which the country treated its newcomers then. At Ellis Island, busy immigration inspectors did not have much time to scrutinize papers or to struggle with difficult spellings. When needed, they just rebaptized the immigrant on the spot. Thus, the German Jew who, flustered by the impatient questioning of the inspector, blurted out in Yiddish, "Schoyn Vergessen" (I forget), upon which the inspector promptly welcomed "Sean Ferguson"

Portes, Alejandro. 1997. "Immigration theory for a new century: Some problems and opportunities." *The International Migration Review*. Volume 31, Issue 4:799–825. Reprinted with permission.

to America. Poor penmanship plus the similar sound of their native "G" and the English "H," left half an Ukrainian family named Heskes, and the other half Gesker (Kraut, 1982).

That sort of symbolic violence reflected well the position of immigrants in the American pecking order and simultaneously gave them a powerful first shove toward assimilation. The country was young then, in the midst of its major period of industrial expansion, and poised for world hegemony. The role that newcomers were expected to play in the American labor market was transparent, and the Immigration Office was confidently in control. Out of these foreign masses received so unceremoniously in their American ports of entry grew new urban forms, new institutions, new social problems, and a changed concept of what the nation was about. By World War II, the off spring of those Eastern Europeans pro-cessed and often rebaptized at Ellis Island were in the trenches. In Norman Mailer's (1948) classic war novel, most of the platoon led by the Anglo-Saxon lieutenant Hearn were children of immigrants—the Italian Minetta, the Jew Goldstein, the Mexican Martinez.

In the army, as in society, ethnicity was securely established at the core of a man's identity. Women at the time followed a similar, but subordinate, course. It is not necessary for my purposes to inflict upon the reader yet another rendition of assimilation theory, the melting pot, and the other concepts that emerged at the time to explain the American immigrant experience. It suffices to make two general points. First, these theories and concepts, arising out of the momentous historical experience of turn-of-the-century immigration, represent our intellectual legacy as we set out to make sense of similar events taking place today. Research on present-day immigration started with the attempt to use assimilation, amalgamation, melting pot, cultural pluralism, and other concepts stemming from that earlier era as interpretive guides for contemporary events.

Second, a good part of that legacy was flawed, in part by stereotypical characterizations of immigrant groups but, more important, by a persistent focus on relatively superficial aspects of the process of adaptation. Issues of language, cultural habits, and spatial patterns commonly took precedence over the structural forces driving immigration. Debates took place on whether the widespread adoption of English and Anglicization of immigrant names meant that "Anglo hegemony" was paramount or whether the incorporation of items of Italian, Mexican, and Chinese cuisine into the American menu indicated that a "melting pot" was underway. Those debates ended indecisively because they never addressed the fundamentals of immigration and remained at the level of public perceptions of the process. Those fundamentals were grounded in political economy and, with few exceptions, exemplified by the works of Enrique Santibáñez (1930), Gerald Rosenblum (1973), and Brinley Thomas (1973), among others, the research literature on immigration did not address them systematically.

As we prepare to confront the challenge of advancing immigration theory in the contemporary world, we will do well to reflect on the course traveled so far. It has involved describing the novelty and complexity of contemporary immigration, culling concepts and insights from the classic literature on the subject and, simultaneously, getting rid of the dead weight of irrelevant debates. Overall, we are well poised to confront the present challenge because the contributions of social scientists from different disciplines have grounded the study of today's immigration firmly on its fundamental realities: the sustained demand for an elastic supply of labor, the pressures and constraints of sending Third World economies, the dislocations wrought by struggles for the creation and control of national states in less developed regions, and the microstructures of support created by migrants themselves across political borders.

Contemporary immigration theory has not only sought to understand the fundamental forces driving the process, but has even gone beyond them to explore how social networks, community normative expectations, and household strategies modify and, at times, subvert those structural determinants. This rapid advance suggests that the task of an introductory essay should be to summarize the main theoretical perspectives and research findings and comment on how they relate to one another. This will not do, however, because several quality reviews already exist and because many of the articles in this issue are also devoted to covering the same terrain. Instead, I will use this opportunity to invite reflection into what may be some of the major pitfalls as we move toward more encompassing and more powerful theoretical models and what are the lines of investigation that offer greatest potential to further this movement.

Immigration Theory for a New Century: Four Common Pitfalls

It seems to me that there are four important misconceptions about the ways that we go about developing theory. Some are misconceptions about what this type of activity entails; others refer to the weight of evidence as it is brought to bear on the products of that activity. Each such problem may be introduced by a somewhat rash statement whose meaning I will then seek to clarify.

Theories Do Not Grow Additively

A first misconception is that the accumulation of evidence leads to theoretical innovation. Generally, this is not the case. Data, whether quantitative or qualitative, may accumulate endlessly without producing any significant conceptual breakthrough. Indeed, much of what we do as part of our everyday work is simply to produce information on one aspect or another of social reality within the intellectual frameworks already in place, without altering them to any significant extent. Ideas, especially those of a broader reach, are few and far between and certainly do not emerge out of masses of data. There is one sense, however, in which the presence of information does lead to conceptual innovation. This happens when puzzles emerge from the accumulated evidence requiring new explanations.

Contradictions may not be self-evident, and indeed it is a theoretical gift to be able to identify them and single them out for analysis. People had seen Chinese and Japanese immigrants engage in small business on the West Coast for decades. Similarly, everyone knew that Jewish and Italian pawnshops, liquor stores, and clothing stores proliferated in urban ghetto areas in the East. Books and articles were even written on the subject but, until Edna Bonacich came along, nobody had asked the obvious questions: Why is small entrepreneurship so widespread among some first-generation immigrants, but not others? And why do they locate their businesses in low-income areas, precisely where the market for most goods and services is poorer? Out of the analysis of this puzzle came the theory of middleman minorities, a keystone to understand the economic adaptation path followed by a number of immigrant groups and the predecessor of later concepts such as ethnic niches and ethnic enclaves (Bonacich, 1973; Bonacich and Modell, 1980). When Korean stores were systematically looted during the 1992 riots in Los Angeles, those familiar with the theory had an indispensable tool to understand what was happening and why.

The contemporary literature provides other good examples. We know that immigrants have been coming by the tens of thousands during the last decades and that the destinations of many are the core of large cities. These are the very areas that have been undergoing a rapid process of de-industrializaation, shedding thousands of jobs. Why should job-seeking immigrants want to go there? Why indeed should the flow continue at all in the absence of such opportunities? Saskia Sassen focused on that particular puzzle, and her analysis yielded the concepts of a "degraded manufacturing sector" and increasing service sector demand in "global cities" which have proven useful for the analysis of immigrant employment and adaptation in recent years (Sassen, 1989, 1991).

After the concept of ethnic enclave came along, a question that emerged was how could these small ethnic firms retain their labor force. Several authors observed that while entrepreneurs fared well economically, the same was not the case with their employees. Family members and new arrivals provided part of the requisite labor supply, but they did not satisfactorily answer the question of how the more long-term and skilled positions required for the survival of these firms could be staffed. Thomas Bailey and Roger Waldinger (1991) tackled this particular puzzle, developing the concept of "informal training system," a mechanism that not only replenishes the supply of entrepreneurs in immigrant communities, but can offer attractive mobility opportunities for the more experienced and skilled workers. The metaphor of the enclave as a "business engine" rather than as a den of relentless exploitation contributed to our understanding of these structures and of the reasons why apparently exploited workers remain there.

Theoretical breakthroughs do not arise out of additional data, but out of the ability to reconstitute a perceptual field identifying connections not previously seen. Such insights require that we gain some distance from reality in order to identify patterns lost at close range. For purposes of theory, more is not necessarily better, since an avalanche of empirical content can make the task of working out solutions at some level of generalizability more difficult.

Theories Do Not Necessarily Correspond to People's Perceptions

The study of immigration has been, for the most part, data-driven. This is a healthy feature, but it has a significant drawback, namely the tendency to put to test theoretical propositions by comparing them with individual self-reports. All theory worthy of the name requires simplification and abstraction. Hence, actors involved in a given process may not be aware of the broader issues at play or may have a different opinion of them. The various stages of the process of acculturation and assimilation, described in Richard Alba and Victor Nee's essay, may be at variance with how immigrants themselves view their situations. Thus, a group can be in rapid process of assimilation according to some external standard, while their members may still consider themselves quite foreign to the receiving society (Alba and Nee, 1997).

People's subjective orientations are certainly important and represent a legitimate field of study but, unless a theory specifically refers to them (such as theories of ethnic identity), it is improper to make them a standard of evaluation. In my hometown of many years, Baltimore, Korean immigrants have developed a vigorous middleman economy in the midst of the African-American inner city. Yet when confronted with the concept and its implications, many Korean entrepreneurs would balk and vigorously deny that they are doing this. The usefulness of the theory does not hinge on these reactions, but on how well it can explain and predict these immigrants' patterns of economic adaptation, residential settlement, and relationships with the native minority population.

Once made, the point is obvious, but I believe that it is worth emphasizing since claims to the "higher authority" of the actual participants are a common occurrence. The theory of social capital as it applies to immigrant and ethnic communities provides a case in point. In an article published in 1993, Julia

Sensenbrenner and I discussed "bounded solidarity" and "enforceable trust" as sources of social capital in these communities, allowing members to gain access to economic resources otherwise unavailable to them and to conduct business transactions flexibly (Portes and Sensenbrenner, 1993). The problem comes when investigators try to fit these concepts into everyday perceptions. For some, the theory of social capital suggests that immigrants go about spouting love messages about the solidarity they feel to one another and how trustworthy their fellow ethnics are. Nothing can be further from the truth.

In the heart of Cuban Miami, shopkeepers bicker nonstop with each other, denounce others' unethical business practices, and would be hard put to say a kind word about many of their business associates. Similar tendencies of everyday disagreements and competition are evident in Min Zhou's (1992) description of New York's Chinatown and in the Nee's account of its San Francisco counterpart (Nee and Nee, 1992). These are not cozy environments and, at close range, they appear quite "unsolidaristic." Sources of social capital and their effects are not observable at this level; they manifest themselves instead over time and in aggregates of multiple individual transactions. Bounded solidarity emerges as an aggregate "elective affinity" on the choice of business partners, employees, and customers, and in patterns of associational participation. Enforceable trust is reflected in the routine behavior of participants in business transactions, relative to how similar operations are conducted on the outside.

The town of Otavalo in the Ecuadorean Andes has become justly famous for the economic success of its indigenous population. Based on a dense web of ethnically bounded networks, Otavalans have been able to fan all over the world selling their woolens, native crafts, and even their folk music. In street fairs of large North American and European cities, one can readily spot Otavalans wearing their characteristic pigtails and felt hats. They peddle ponchos, CDs of Andean music, and the crafts of other indigenous tribes, sold as their own. However, when David Kyle (1995) visited the town to inquire on the origins of Otavalan entrepreneurship, he found a community riven with factions and, on the surface at least, in conflict with itself. It was only after several layers of public discourse had been peeled off that the patterns of cooperative entrepreneurship and ethnic-bounded business support began to emerge.

There is a second related practice that also does harm to theoretical progress. This may be called the "pseudo-test" and consists of dressing up modest empirical findings as if they were suitable for examining a general hypothesis. The purpose is to exalt the significance of a particular study by linking it up with broader theoretical concerns but, in the process, invalid inferences are made. There are two variants of the problem. The first occurs when individual instances of marginal importance are held up as contradicting general propositions. Obviously, it is valid to call attention to individual negative findings, but one must have a sense of proportion. A case study of a small group of immigrants cannot, for example, invalidate a general theory supported by large-scale trends. I suspect that this is what Alba and Nee (1997) have in mind when they complain about how many past critiques of assimilation theory have been grounded on partial evidence. Alba and Nee recognize problems and exceptions to what they call the "canonical statement" by Milton Gordon (1964), but they argue that these difficulties do not entirely eliminate the value of his perspective.

A more serious variant occurs when measurement and sample selection fit the theory awkwardly, but the researcher goes on anyway to draw conclusions about its validity. In the short and eventful life of the concept of ethnic enclave (Wilson and Martin, 1982; Portes and Bach, 1985), there have been several such instances. In some cases, theoretical predictions derived from the concept have been supported for the wrong reasons; in others, they are rejected with data that bear little resemblance to the original formulation. In a recent article, the enclave is defined as Hispanic businesses in New York City and the negative evidence consists of the lower wages and poor working conditions of immigrant women employed by these firms, relative to those in nonethnic employment (Gilbertson, 1995). To my knowledge, there is no such thing as a "Hispanic" enclave in New York since there is no immigrant nationality that goes by that name. Nor is there anything in the finding of worse employment conditions for a cross-section of immigrant workers in ethnic employment that contradicts the original predictions. The real questions, from the standpoint of that theory, are the viability of these firms, their capacity to spawn new enterprises, and the extent to which workers can become entrepreneurs themselves.

Theoretical insights in the social sciences have the character of a public good. They are not covered by any special form of protection and, once formulated, enter the public domain to be freely used by anyone. This is necessary in order to submit new ideas to logical scrutiny and to the test of empirical evidence, but it has its downside. This consists of theories being invoked rather than seriously examined, either to add luster to modest finding or to serve as a foil for contrary arguments. In recent years, social scientists have become increasingly respectful of empirical evidence and leery of doing violence to it. As a result, a methodological literature on issues of measurement, sampling design, and data analysis has grown rapidly. The same respect has not yet been accorded to the basic elements of theory—concepts and propositions—which, as free public goods, have been handled with considerably less concern. As abstracted knowledge, theory is the end product of the scientific enterprise and the necessary guide for its future development. The study of immigration has not had to contend with extremely abstract notions and operates instead at a data-sensitive middle range. For that very reason, concepts that capture and synthesize insights from past research should not be simply invoked, but examined with careful attention to their scope and original definitions.

Typologies Are Not Theories

In her analysis of self-identification among second-generation Caribbean youth, Mary Waters (1994) distinguishes between the immigrant-identified, ethnic-identified and American-identified members of her sample. Studies of the undocumented population commonly distinguish between "visa-over-stayers" and "entries-without-inspection" (EWIs). Similarly, research on legal arrivals usually separate refugees and asylees from quota and nonquota immigrants and, more recently, from the amnestied population (INS, 1996). Along the same lines, Rubén Rumbaut and I developed a typology of manual labor immigrants, professional immigrants, immigrant entrepreneurs, and political refugees as the framework for our description of contemporary U.S.-bound immigration (Portes and Rumbaut, 1996).

Typologies such as these are valid intellectual exercises, but they are not theories. This is self-evident in administrative categories, such as those employed by the Immigration and Naturalization Service. The distinction, for example, between refugees and asylees or between visa-overstayers and EWIs does not say anything about the causal origins of each flow or its particular patterns of adaptation. All that these terms reflect is primarily an accident of bureaucratic processing. Typologies such as those of Waters (1994) or Rumbaut and Portes (1996) may become building blocks for theories, but, by themselves, they do not amount to a theoretical statement because they simply assert differences without specifying their origins or anticipating their consequences.

The point is again evident once made, but it is worth emphasizing because the field of immigration encourages and depends on such categorical distinctions both for research and for administrative purposes. Typologies enter the construction of theory in one of two ways: as interaction effects or as categorical endogenous values. As interaction effects, typologies specify the scope that certain propositions can take or the way that their predictions vary between different categories of people. To take a familiar example from a related field, the typology of labor market segmentation predicts differential effects of human capital variables in the primary and secondary sectors of the labor market. Years of education are expected to have a significant effect on wages in primary sector employment, but not in the secondary (Edwards, Reich, and Gordon, 1975; Gordon, 1972). This is an interaction effect. To take a second example, the effects of acculturation are expected to be benign among children of professional immigrants and entrepreneurs, but problematic among the offspring of labor immigrants, especially those living in close proximity to impoverished inner-city areas. This interaction is the core of the concept of segmented assimilation (Fernández-Kelly and Schauffler, 1994; Portes and Zhou, 1993).

Waters' (1994) typology provides an example of a categorical endogenous variable. The three types of self-identification that she describes can be interpreted as the range of a variable to be explained through various characteristics of immigrant families and the social context that receives them. In turn, these types of identification may be expected to have differential effects on other aspects of immigrant children's social and educational adaptation. An earlier example is Irvin Child's well-known typology of "conformists," "escapists," and "rebels" to describe the stance taken by Italian-American youth to the conflict between their parents' efforts at cultural preservation and the pull of the American mainstream (Child, 1943). This is also a categorical endogenous variable in need of explanation and which is expected, in turn, to have some significant consequences on individuals so classified.

To rank as a full-fledged theory, a statement should have four elements: first, a delimitation and description of some patch of reality; second, an identification and definition of a process or characteristic to be explained (the dependent variable); third, one or more explanatory factors and their types of effects, additive or interactive; fourth, a logical link to at least one other similar proposition. By coding as 1 the presence of each of these four elements, it is possible to build a hierarchy of statements used in the course of theory construction as listed below:

Historical accounts of the origins of certain immigrant communities and their present characteristics provide examples of the first type of endeavor. They are descriptive case studies, limited in scope to a certain space and time and focused on a specific sequence of events. Oscar Handlin's (1972) classic study of

Description of Specific Instances	Identification of an Issue or Problem in Need of Explanation	Identification of Explanatory Factors	Links With Other Predictive Statements	
1	0	0	0	= Case Study
1	1	0	0	= Empirical Generalization
1	0	0	0	= Theoretical Statement
1	1	1	1	= Theory

the Boston Irish; Thomas and Znaniecki's (1984) *The Polish Peasant in Europe and America*; and William Foote Whyte's (1955) *Street Corner Society* are classic examples. Illsoo Kim's (1981) study of Koreans in New York City; Alex Stepick's (1992) account of the Haitian community in South Florida; and Terry Repak's (1995) monograph on Central Americans in Washington, D.C., provide contemporary ones. These studies, which not incidentally are at the core of the immigration literature, are not theory. They provide, instead, the basic materials for the development of theoretical statements and, subsequently, the empirical ground and means to test them.

Along with monographs on particular immigrant groups, we often encounter in the literature statements like: "Mexicans have low levels of entrepreneurship"; "Chinese settle in spatially clustered areas"; Fillipinos have the greatest propensity to acquire U.S. citizenship." These statements, which are sometimes confused with theory, are empirical generalizations. They contain two elements: a referential statement to a certain period, place, or category of people and a statement of fact about the value or values taken by a certain variable. In each case, there is an assertion that people or events possess specific values or fit into particular profiles, but there is no explanation of how this state of affairs comes about. In contrast to broad descriptive statements, the specific contribution of empirical generalizations is to focus on a limited aspect of reality worthy of attention. As such, they provide a more proximate building block for theory.

A theoretical proposition contains both a universal quantifier specifying its scope of predication and a statement of a relationship between something to be explained and possible factors leading to it. In the best formulations, there is a specification of the character of that relationship (whether additive or interactive) and some clarification of those social contexts in which the prediction is or is not expected to hold. Typologies that specify interaction effects fit here. Because immigration theorizing has generally proceeded at a low level of abstraction, it is perhaps important to note that theoretical statements possess two other characteristics, often missing from those discussed in the literature: first, they are not constrained to a single time and place; second, they can support subjunctive conditionals.

A statement like "among Cuban refugees who arrived between 1960 and 1970 in Miami, social connections in their country of origin led to ready access to business loans" is not a theoretical proposition. Nor is the following, that could be drawn from Robert Smith's excellent monograph on long-distance Mexican migration: "In the village of Ticuaní, Puebla, during the 1980s, the greater the number of migrant families going to New York, the faster the rate of completion of local public works" (Smith, 1992). Such statements are accidental universals that specify causal relationships in a particular locality or migrant group, but that lack the requisite level of generality to qualify as theoretical propositions. The latter can "travel"—that is, they are applicable in times and places other than those that gave rise to them in the first place. Thus a theory of long-distance migration and remittances limited to Mexicans in New York or a theory of entrepreneurship limited to Cubans in Miami would be suspect.

Second, theoretical propositions possess an element of logical necessity that is absent from other statements. This is best seen if one attempts to transform an empirical generalization into a causal proposition. "All immigrants in Salt Lake City are undocumented." This may be true, but it would not support the subjunctive conditional: "For every immigrant, if he or she were in Salt Lake City, he or she would be undocumented." There is nothing about being in Salt Lake that necessarily brings about the condition "undocumented." Compare this with Massey's theory of cumulative social networks, which predicts that the greater the number of present or former migrants a person in a sending area knows, the greater the probability that he or she will also migrate (Massey and García Españia, 1987; Massey and Espinosa, 1996). This can be transformed into the conditional: "For every person in a sending area, if he or she were to maintain contacts with present or former migrants, he or she would also be more likely to migrate than others with identical characteristics." Migrant networks are not an accident, but contain the necessary causal element to produce the predicted outcome.

Philosophers of science such as Ernest Nagel (1961) are content to label isolated theoretical propositions "theories." I would prefer to reserve the label for those interrelated sets of propositions that not only "travel" in the sense of being applicable to different spatial and temporal contexts, but that also tell a coherent story about certain finite aspects of reality. For all its empirical shortcomings, the "canonical" statement of assimilation developed by Gordon (1964) and summarized by Alba and Nee (1997) exemplifies such a theory. With the help of a few auxiliary assumptions, we can formalize it into a series of logically interrelated causal propositions about the trajectory or trajectories that immigrants are expected to follow after their initial settlement.

Zolberg's theory of the role of the state system in the origins and control of international migration flows provides a second example. His insight that enforced borders represent the crucial dividing line between the developed world or "core" and the increasingly subordinate economic periphery can be transformed into a series of propositions about between-country economic inequalities, the role of migration flows in ameliorating them, and that of political borders in reproducing the global hierarchy (Zolberg, Suhrke, and Aguayo, 1986; Zolberg, 1989). One of the significant merits of this theory is that it links anew the study of immigration with broader issues of political economy, thus avoiding an exclusive focus on the characteristics and adaptation process of individual migrants.

I have dwelt in such laborious detail over typologies and levels of theory because, in my view, this is the area in the field of immigration that stands in need of greatest attention. While we may rightfully complain about the lack of a parental nationality question in the decennial census or the surprising lack of a national longitudinal survey of immigrants, the fact is that empirical knowledge about contemporary immigration has grown by leaps and bounds in recent years and can be expected to continue doing so. On the other hand, the cumulative character of the enterprise depends on the insertion of the case monographs and typologies developed in the field into some sort of coherent framework that only theory can provide. While abstract speculation may have bedeviled other fields of inquiry, the problem with one so close to the ground as immigration is precisely the opposite. There is some danger that qualitative studies of immigrant communities and quantitative analyses of their economic and political adaptation may pile up without any systematic guide as to what all this information means and how can it be brought to bear, in a focused way, on major policy concerns.

There Is No Overall Encompassing Theory of Immigration

The pitch for theory has its limits too. The final issue is, in a sense, the opposite of that just discussed. There does not seem to be much danger that someone might be attempting a grand theory of immigration any time soon but, just in case, I would like to argue that this kind of endeavor would be futile. The reason is that the different areas that compose this field are so disparate that they can only be unified at a highly abstract and probably vacuous level. For starters, consider the division between macrostructural issues, such as the role of global capitalist expansion on the onset of migrant flows or the power of the state system to regulate such movements, and microstructural issues, such as the effect of community networks on individual decisions to migrate. Contrary to much conventional wisdom about the need to integrate microstructural and macrostructural theories, I would argue that, in the case of immigration, the two levels are not fungible.

The theory that colonial capitalist penetration played a significant role in the initiation of large-scale labor migration from less developed countries says nothing about who among the population of those countries was more likely to migrate, nor can it be tested at the level of individual decision-making. It requires comparative historical data to establish the existence of such a relationship between overt or covert capitalist penetration and the timing and volume of labor outflows. (For variants of this theory, see Portes and Walton, 1981; Sassen, 1988.) Similarly, individual-level processes of acculturation and labor market incorporation cannot simply be aggregated into structural effects. A hundred thousand Mexican immigrants trying to learn English and find jobs in Houston, Texas, will have a very different impact there than the same number doing this in Boston, Massachusetts, or Charlotte, North Carolina. Mexican immigrants in Houston are a familiar and expected presence, and their paths of cultural adaptation and labor market participation have been charted by past immigrant generations. Such is not the case in the industrial cities of the Northeast, much less in the emerging metropolitan areas of the South.

Over a decade ago, Robert Bach and I proposed a four-fold categorization of topics around which existing theories of immigration could be organized. Although subject to modification, the classification seems still serviceable. These topics were: the origins of immigration, the directionality and continuity of migrant flows, the utilization of immigrant labor, and the sociocultural adaptation of immigrants (Protes and Bach, 1985).

Each of these topics may be approached theoretically at a close-range level or from a broad structural perspective. For example, the issues of what particular places migrants go to and how long a particular movement lasts may be examined at the level of aggregate labor demand and the past history of labor recruitment in sending areas, as Michael Piore (1979) has done, or at the level of cross-national networks pointing individual immigrants in a particular direction and sustaining the flow over time, as Douglas Massey (Massey et al. 1987) or Sherri Grasmuck and Partricia Pessar (1991) have. Although obviously interrelated, each of these areas requires separate attention and, hence, mid-range theories targeted on one or two of them are preferable to an all-encompassing statement. A general theory of immigration must climb to such a level of abstraction as to render its predictions vacuously true. To say, for example, that international labor migration and immigrant sociocultural assimilation are both "equilibrium restoring processes" may be readily accepted without this assertion advancing in any way our understanding of either.

In a related vein, the method of analytic induction deserves a final comment. Analytic induction is the attempt to progressively refine explanation of a particular phenomenon until all exceptions have been taken into account. The method was popular in sociology and anthropology during the fifties and early sixties because it offered the promise of a gradual progression toward explaining the full range of a given phenomenon (Robinson, 1951; Turner, 1953). That popularity quickly faded when it was discovered that applications of the method ended up redefining the problem until it was co-terminous with its explanation. The attempt to account for a social phenomenon in its entirety leads to circular reasoning because it inexorably reduces the conceptual space between the thing to be explained and its alleged causes.

Though no one uses the term *analytic induction* anymore, the logic of the method creeps in all the time in the analysis of social phenomena. To take an example from a related field, political scientist Robert Putnam redefined the concept of "social capital" from the original statements by James Coleman (1988), who had defined it as an individual or family resource stemming from participation in certain social structures. In Putnam's analysis, social capital became instead a collective feature of communities and even countries, measured by such variables as high levels of voting, high associational participation, and a civic culture. The concept was redefined in this fashion in order to serve as an explanatory factor of differences between cities or countries in democratic governance. Gradually, cause and effect come together until the reasoning becomes circular. Differences between the well-governed cities of northern Italy and the poorly governed ones of the Italian South are thus explained as follows: " . . . 'civic' communities value solidarity, civic participation, and integrity and here democracy works. At the other pole are 'uncivic' regions like Calabria and Sicily, aptly characterized by the French term *incivisme*. The very concept of citizenship is stunted here" (Putnam, 1993:36). In other words, if your town is "civic," it does civic things; if it is "uncivic," it does not.

Theory-building is a delicate enterprise where novel and useful ideas occur rarely and where they are constantly exposed to the risks of misuse and misinterpretation or, alternatively, to the threat of conceptual overreach. We cannot explain everything, but we can explain some things with a reasonable margin of certainty. A set of midrange theories designed to do this by drawing on the wealth of historical and contemporary research on immigration seems the strategy most worth pursuing.

A Sampler of Themes for Immigration Research and Theory

Despite the set of pitfalls just seen, there is reason to be optimistic about theoretical progress in the field of immigration. Part of this optimism is based on what has been accomplished in exploring the structural determinants of contemporary migrant flows and the microstructures that sustain them over time. A second factor underlying this optimism is the research programs started in recent years that hold the promise not only of adding to our stock of information, but also of expanding immigration theory in new directions. To my knowledge, none of these programs began with a clearly delineated theoretical agenda, but their own subject matter dictated the development of new typologies, concepts, and propositions. The list is nonexhaustive and certainly biased towards my own interests and preferences. While other topics of equal merit may be identified, the following ones provide a sampler of research issues with significant theoretical potential.

Transnational Communities

Transnational communities are dense networks across political borders created by immigrants in their quest for economic advancement and social recognition. Through these networks, an increasing number of people are able to lead dual lives. Participants are often bilingual, move easily between different cultures, frequently maintain homes in two countries, and pursue economic, political and cultural interests that require their presence in both. In a pioneering statement on the topic, Linda Basch and her collaborators describe their initial attitude toward this emergent phenomenon:

> We define "transnationalism" as the process by which immigrants forge and sustain multi-stranded relations that link together their societies of origin and settlement. We call these processes transnationalism to emphasize that many immigrants today build social fields that cross geographic, cultural, and political borders. . . .An essential element. . .is the multiplicity of involvements that transmigrants sustain in both home and host societies. We are still groping for a language to describe these social locations. (Basch, Glick-Schiller and Blanc-Szanton, 1994:6)

That puzzled attitude toward a novel phenomenon is what makes the study of this topic promising from a theoretical standpoint. In a recent essay, Glick-Schiller (1996) argues that similar processes of back-and-forth movement and intensive investments and contracts with sending countries also took place among European immigrants at the turn of the century. I agree, but I would add that the present transnational communities possess a distinct character that justifies coining a new concept to refer to them. This character is defined by three features: the number of people involved, the nearly instantaneous character of communications across space, and the fact that the cumulative character of the process makes participation "normative" within certain immigrant groups.

As studies by Basch and associates (1994), Glick-Schiller and associates (1992), Guarnizo (1994), Goldring (1992), and others show, the numbers involved in transnational activities of different sorts—economic, political and social—can represent a significant proportion of the population of both sending areas and immigrant communities. In this sense, they become a novel path of adaptation quite different from those found among immigrants at the turn of the century. This path is reinforced by technologies that facilitate rapid displacement across long distances and instant communication. The "astronauts"—Chinese entrepreneurs who live in Monterrey Park and other California cities, but make their living by commuting by air across the Pacific—could not have existed in an earlier era (Fong, 1994). Nor could have the immigrant civic committee, described by Robert Smith (1992) who traveled, over the weekend, to the interior of Mexico to inspect public works in their village in order to be back at work in New York City by Monday.

These communication facilities, added to the economic, social, and psychological benefits that transnational enterprise can bring, may turn these activities into the normative adaptation path for certain immigrant groups. Just as in the Mexican towns described by Massey and Goldring (1994), migration north is the "thing to do" during adverse economic times, so involvement in transnational activities may become the thing to do for immigrants otherwise confined to dead-end jobs and an inferior, discriminated status. That path is, of course, at variance with those envisioned by the "canonical" assimilation perspective, with direct implications for immigration theory.

Elsewhere, I have argued that the construction of transnational communities by immigrants is a process driven by the very forces promoting economic globalization, as common people are caught in their web and learn to use new technologies (Portes, 1996). Involvement in these emerging activities may represent an effective response of popular groups to the new forces unleashed by globalization and the strategies of large corporate actors. The aphorism, "capital is global, labor is local," may still hold on the aggregate, but it is being increasingly subverted by the these grassroots initiatives based on long-distance networks and a newly acquired command of communication technologies.

The New Second Generation

A second line of research has to do with the adaptation process of the second generation. The case for the second generation as a "strategic research site" is based on two features.[2] First, the long-term effects of immigration for the host society depend less on the fate of first generation immigrants than on their descendants. Patterns of adaptation of the first generation set the stage for what is to come, but issues such as the continuing dominance of English, the growth of a welfare-dependent population, the resilience or disappearance of culturally distinct ethnic enclaves, and the decline or growth of ethnic intermarriages will be decided among its children and grandchildren. For example, the much debated issue of the loss of English hegemony in certain American cities heavily affected by immigration will not be settled by immigrants, but by their offspring. Loyalty to the home language among the foreign born is a time-honored pattern; in the past, the key linguistic shift has taken place in the second generation (Lieberson, 1981; Lieberson and Hansen, 1974; Veltman, 1983). Whether this is occurring today represents a major issue for the cities and communities where today's immigrants concentrate.

Second, the experiences of the present second generation cannot be inferred from those of children of earlier European immigrants. The "canonical" statement of assimilation theory may be reread as an abstracted version of the typical course of adaptation among these earlier children of immigrants. With exception, that course featured an orderly progression from the poverty and discrimination endured by the first generation to the rapid acculturation of the second generation and its gradual economic advancement. By the third generation, the loss of "ethnic" linguistic and cultural traits, as well as the disappearance of earlier labor market disadvantages, could be virtually complete.

There are reasons to doubt that a similarly benign and straightforward course will be followed by members of today's second generation. First, the proliferation of transnational activities among first generation immigrants complicates the course of adaptation to be followed by their offspring and renders its outcome uncertain. Second, discrimination against nonwhites and changing requirements of the American labor marker create obstacles for economic progress and the fulfillment of rising aspirations among many second generation youth. Third, and perhaps more insidiously, these difficulties can be readily interpreted within the adversarial framework developed in the innercity among descendants of earlier labor migrants. The blocked mobility experienced by these groups became translated over time into an oppositional stance toward mainstream society. Socialization into the outlooks and role models provided by this segment of the American population creates yet another hazard in the process of social and economic progress of today's children of immigrants.

The concept of segmented assimilation was coined to call attention to these alternative and not always benign paths and to signal differences with the normative course described by earlier theory. A telling example is the alternative interpretations given to the speed of acculturation across generations yesterday and today. The fact that children of immigrants often become their "parents' parents" as their knowledge of the new language and culture races ahead has been repeatedly noted, both at the turn of the century and today.

But there is a difference. Whereas the phenomenon of generational role reversal was expected and even celebrated as it took place among children of Europeans, today it compares unfavorably with other acculturation paths and is even regarded as a danger signal. At the time of Irving Child's (1943) study, Italian-American youth who refused to take the step of joining the American cultural mainstream were dubbed "escapists." Today, Zhou and Bankston (1994) describe how Vietnamese-American children who take the same step become prime candidates for downward assimilation. The reason is that rapid acculturation and generational role reversal undercuts parental authority to control youth as they enter an increasingly complex society, marked by the ready availability of counter-cultural models.

The pattern where the first and second generations learn the ways of American society at different paces may be labeled "dissonant acculturation." The opposite—consonant acculturation—occurs either because parents acculturate at the same speed as their children or because the process is slowed among youth by the influence of the co-ethnic community (Portes and Rumbaut, 1996). This last path, dubbed "selective acculturation," has been associated in studies by Waters (1994), Gibson (1989), Suarez-Orozco (1987), Fernández-Kelly and Schauffler (1994), and others with consistently more favorable adaptation outcomes among second generation children than those brought about by role reversal. In any case, the typology of dissonant, consonant, and selective acculturation across generations and the different evaluations placed on each type in the research literatures of the 1940s and of the 1990s offer a promising point of departure for theory and for a more sophisticated understanding of the social sequel to large-scale migration.

Households and Gender

For a number of years, the field of immigration studies tended to neglect the role of gender. At present, a new wave of studies is redressing this imbalance. The significance of research on women goes beyond covering a previously neglected segment of the migrant population. Instead, like class and race, gender represents a master dimension of social structure and focus on this dimension can yield novel insights into many phenomena. For this to become reality, the analytic focus cannot be exclusively women (or men for that matter), but the socially patterned relationships between the sexes as they influence and, in turn, are influenced by the process of immigration. As Patricia Pessar notes (1996), "the challenge still remains to branch out from a concentration on female immigrants in order to apply appropriately gender-inflected research questions and methods to both men and women."

There is indeed a variable geometry of relationships between the sexes that is not adequately captured by a single-sex focus or by an unnuanced repetition of the realities of sexual exploitation and subordination. The latter do exist, but they do not exhaust the story. As in the case of class and race, the multiple configurations found in different social contexts is what makes the study of gender relations both interesting and capable of yielding new theoretical insights. A cautionary note must be introduced here about analyses that concentrate exclusively on the individual motivations of household members and the conflict of interests between them. This has often become the center of gender-focused studies.

Undoubtedly, men, women, and children within a household may differ and even struggle for conflicting goals. But an exclusive focus on these internal disagreements makes us lose sight of two other important considerations. First, households can still act as units despite internal differences. Hence, it is possible to theorize at the level of household strategies. An exclusive concentration on individual motivations would do away with the possibility of understanding how these small social units pull resources to organize a process as complex as international migration.

Second, there can be differences between people's perceptions and their actual behavior. On this point, the earlier warning against making respondents' definitions of the situation the ultimate test for theoretical propositions comes in handy. Such definitions are important, but they do not exhaust all there is about a particular social process and may even be at variance with the actual conduct of households when examined in the aggregate. Put differently, theory can exist at different levels of abstraction. Reducing everything to the individual plane would unduly constrain the enterprise by preventing the utilization of more complex units of analysis—families, households, and communities, as the basis for explanation and prediction.

States and State-Systems

The analysis of the role of state and state-building on the onset of refugee flows, pioneered by Zolberg and his associates, offers an example of a fourth line of investigation with significant theoretical promise (Zolberg, Suhrke, and Aguayo, 1986; Zolberg, 1989). Detailed accounts of the process leading to major legislation, such as the Immigration Reform and Control Act of 1986, do exist, but they have not been transformed into a systematic theoretical analysis of both the external pressures impinging on the state and the internal dynamics of the legislative and administrative bodies dealing with immigration.

Recent work by Hollifield (1992) and Freeman (1995) has begun to move in the direction of a general model of the political forces promoting immigration in the advanced Western democracies. Freeman even provides a typology of countries according to how their particular histories and political systems affect the play of these forces. But, as his critic Rogers Brubaker (1995) points out, the model still has to be fleshed out to specify the conditions under which restrictionist and antirestrictionist discourses come into vogue and the adaptation of state agencies to conflicting pressures and demands. There is a need for greater information about the inner workings of state legislative and administrative bureaucracies in order to advance this area of immigration theory beyond the plane of broad generalities.

The research questions that lie at the core of this line of inquiry and that hold the potential for theoretical innovation are twofold:

1. How is it that, in the face of widespread public opposition to the continuation of large-scale immigration, governments in the receiving countries have proven unable or unwilling to prevent it?

2. Why is it that recent laws and administrative measures designed to control immigration often end up having consequences that are almost the opposite of those originally intended?

The economic concepts of "path dependence" and its sociological equivalent, "cumulative causation," offer suitable points of departure for the analysis of the first question, insofar as they can guide the explanation of recalcitrant immigration flows in the face of widespread public opposition. (For a more detailed discussion of the concepts and related ones in economic sociology, *see* Portes, 1995.) Yet an inside analysis of how the legislative and administrative branches of the modern state operate to neutralize the manifest public will against mass immigration is only in its early stages. The outside forces and agents that promote continuation of an open door policy are easy enough to identify, but the internal dynamics of state agencies, the ways they absorb information and react to conflicting pressures, are not. The recent review of determinants and constraints of governmental immigration policies in Western Europe by Hollifield (1996) offers a promising point of departure for addressing this question.

Similarly, the Mertonian concept of "unintended consequences" may be used with profit in the analysis of the second question (Merton, 1936, 1968). It fits well what happened to certain pieces of recent legislation, most notably the Immigration Reform and Control Act of 1986. The process by which this set of measures, manifestly designed to control immigration, ended up promoting it has been analyzed by a number of authors. Missing still is a broader set of propositions explaining how such a paradoxical outcome could come about and to what extent the same set of forces can explain or predict similar results elsewhere. For instance, French, German, and Scandinavian policies designed to reverse labor migration have generally ended up promoting further immigration and the emergence of permanent ethnic settlements. (For a recent review of the German case, see Kurthen, 1995; for the French experience, see Body-Gentrot, 1995, and Hollifield, 1994; for the Danish case see Enough, 1994.) The extent to which a common theoretical model is applicable to those experiences and recent American ones remains on open question.

As several political analysts have emphasized, migration control and the perpetuation of social and economic inequalities between advanced countries and the Third World are closely intertwined. The extent to which states succeed in maintaining such controls or are derailed in their enforcement efforts represents a central policy concern as well as a topic of considerable theoretical import.

Cross-National Comparisons

The vigorous resurgence of the sociology of immigration in recent years has been, by and large, a single-country phenomenon. I am less clear about development in the other social sciences, but what seems certain is that the wave of novel research and theory on immigration in the United States has not been accompanied by a comparative thrust of similar vigor. To be sure, numerous conferences on the topics have been convened that bring together North American, European, and, sometimes, Asian scholars. Comparative reports also have been published that examine how specific policies, such as amnesty programs for illegal aliens, have fared in different advanced countries. Applied research agencies like the Urban Institute and the Rand Corporation have been notably active in these policy comparisons.

These efforts are valuable, but they are not theory. Conferences seldom yield more than a collection of papers that describe how things have evolved in different countries. Applied policy reports do not usually contain general concepts or propositions that help explain present events or anticipate future ones. In the absence of theory, predictions generated by these reports commonly assume an immutable social reality. For example, projections about the ethnic composition of the population of countries receiving mass immigration assume that the race/ethnic classifications currently in vogue will not be affected by the presence of immigrants and their subsequent patterns of adaptation. Under similar assumptions, projections made in the early twentieth century would have predicted that the American population would become mostly nonwhite fifty years later since the bulk of Eastern and Southern European immigrants arriving at that time were not considered "white" in the popular and academic racial taxonomy of the time.

Along the same lines, projections made today about the size of the non-white population by mid twenty-first century do not take into account the effects of the process of segmented assimilation. As it unfolds, it is likely that descendants of immigrants classified today as Asian, as well as some groups coming from Latin America and classified initially as Hispanic, will enter the mainstream, intermarry, and become sociologically "white," redefining the meaning and scope of the term. By the same token, other groups who are phenotypically white or mestizo, may become sociologically "black," as this racial term is used today because of a failed process of second generation adaptation (see Fernández-Kelly, and Schauffler, 1994; Waters, 1994).

In the absence of theory, what we have today is mostly an amorphous mass of data on immigration to different countries and a series of concepts whose scope seldom exceeds those of a particular nation-state. Needed are explicitly comparative projects that focus on research topics at a higher level of abstraction than those guiding policy concerns and that employ a common cross-national methodology. Each of the four topics outlined—the rise of transnational communities, the adaptation process of the second generation, gender cleavages and household strategies, and the enactment and enforcement of state immigration laws—is amenable to such comparative analysis.

Other subjects that have been dealt with at length in the North American immigration literature lack a comparative dimension. To cite but three examples: the role of social networks and social capital in initiating and sustaining migration flows in different national contexts; the types of immigrant enterprise that exist in different advanced societies and their role in the economic and social adaptation of immigrants; the patterns of race/ethnic self-identification of first and second generation immigrants in countries that promote rapid legal integration while tolerating ethnic differences (the United States), those that promote legal integration but resist the rise of ethnic subcultures (France), and those that delay indefinitely legal integration (Germany) (Hollifield, 1994; Munz and Ulrich, 1995).

Systematic cross-national research is useful for three purposes: first, to examine the extent to which theoretical propositions "travel," that is, are applicable in national contexts different from that which produced them; second, to generate typologies of interaction effects specifying the variable influence of causal factors across different national contexts; third, to themselves produce concepts and propositions of broader scope. In some cases, large-*N* quantitative designs with nation-states as units of analysis are appropriate. In most cases, however, what Przeworski and Teune (1970) call the "small-*N* maximum differences" design or Kohn (1987) the "nation-as-context" design would be most appropriate. The reason is that these designs are most appropriate to understand how the specific characteristics of national societies condition the validity of the set of mid-range theories that structure the field of immigration.

Conclusion

The inventory of theoretical pitfalls and potentially strategic research sites outlined in this essay is meant to be neither exhaustive nor representative of a consensus in our field. They represent a personal vision and hence are subject to well-justified critiques of incompleteness and topical bias. In my defense, I will only adduce that the inventory is based on long experience attempting to tease regularities out of empirical data and that, even if not consensually agreed upon, it may still provide the basis for useful discussion.

Because of rising public interest in immigration, greater priority has been given to the field by the media, foundations, and government agencies. This is both a blessing and a curse, as the new availability of resources has also given rise to a babel of voices seeking access to them. Applied research has its functions, but it can also lead the field astray by focusing on superficial issues and bureaucratically defined problems. The pressure for "policy relevant" results should not distract us from the painstaking development of concepts and propositions that alone can advance social science knowledge and provide a sound basis for both public understanding of immigration and policies that do not backfire on their original goals.

Notes

1. Revised version of the keynote address to the conference "Becoming American/America Becoming: International Migration to the United States," sponsored by the Social Science Research Council, Sanibel Island, Florida, January 18–21, 1996. I thank Robert K. Merton, Aristide Zolberg, and the editors for their comments on the original version. Responsibility for the content is exclusively mine.
2. The concept of "strategic research site" was coined by Merton (1987:10–11) to refer to an area of research where processes of more general import are manifested with unusual clarity. In his words, "the empirical material exhibits the phenomenon to be explained or interpreted to such advantage and in such accessible form that it enables the fruitful investigation and the discovery of new problems for further inquiry."

The New Diaspora: African Immigration to the United States

✦ APRIL GORDON*

INTRODUCTION

Africans are on the move: rural-urban migration, labor migration to neighboring countries, and refugee flows are widespread phenomena in Africa that touch most people's lives from the largest cities down to more remote villages. In addition to these movements, growing numbers of Africans are entering the stream of international migration away from the continent, not just from the country, of their birth. This exodus is what I refer to as the "new diaspora."

This paper looks at a particular aspect of the new diaspora—immigration to the United States. In the current spotlight focused on immigration to the U.S., little attention has been paid to the growing numbers of African immigrants, an omission I seek to address. My focus is on the causes of the new diaspora, its history and current trends, the origins of migrants, the consequences for Africa and the U.S., and the prospects for future immigration. Based on an analysis of the data, it is my contention that there are five major factors that account for the patterns in African migration currently observable. They are as follows:

1. globalization and integration of the world economy
2. economic and political development failures in Africa
3. immigration and refugee policies in Europe and the United States
4. anglophone background
5. historic ties of sending countries to the United States

**Associate professor of sociology, Winthrop University, Rock Hill, SC 29733. Professor Gordon is the author of* Transforming Capitalism and Patriarchy: Gender and Development in Africa, *co-editor of* Understanding Contemporary Africa, *and author of numerous articles and papers on Africa and development issues.*

Gordon, April. 1998. "The new diaspora: African immigration to the United States." *Journal of Third World Studies.* Volume 15, Issue 1:79–100. Reprinted with permission of *Journal of Third World Studies.*

International Migration: An Overview

Since the end of World War II, a dramatic expansion of the global capitalist economy is linking countries of the world together into a complex network of trade, finance, and technology flows. This global economy includes a global division of labor among countries, with Western industrial nations playing the leading role in providing manufactured goods, capital, technology, and markets. Previously colonized Third World countries largely provide primary goods and cheap labor, although a growing number of NICs (newly industrializing countries) and NIC "wannabes" have been industrializing as a result of foreign investments by multinationals and their own development efforts.

One result of expanding global trade and economic integration is that global gross national product (GNP) has grown to unprecedented heights. But most of the benefits so far have gone to already-wealthy countries. After more than three decades of so-called development in the Third World, the gap between the richest and poorest countries has widened greatly. In 1960, the poorest 20% of the world's people received 2.3% of global income; in 1991 their share was only 1.4%. By contrast, the richest 20% increased their share of world income from 70% to 85%. This amounts to 60 times more income than that received by the poor. The distribution of economic activity is equally skewed: most jobs, trade, and production are located in rich countries. Unfortunately, most job seekers are in the world's poor countries, as will be most of the one billion new workers in the next twenty years.[1] Many of these people will find meager or no job opportunities in their own countries.

The disparity in opportunity and living standards between the have and have-not countries is widely known to the world's struggling masses. One response is international migration. Although leaving one's country of birth is often a last resort for more and more of the world's people in poor countries, the costs of migration are low compared with the likely gains.[2] This is especially true where the gap between growing aspirations, education, and skills in a population and the ability of the country to adequately employ people and compensate them with decent living conditions is great. Stated more simply, the decision to migrate to another country often reflects the failure of development at home.[3]

Political turmoil is closely linked to this failure of economic development. As pressures of poverty, rapid population growth, disease and illiteracy, and environmental degradation mount, they produce a "volatile cocktail of insecurity."[4] Resulting war, civil strife, state-sponsored terrorism, riots, and other forms of political violence can lead to the displacement of large numbers of people as migrants, refugees, or asylees. In the late twentieth century, compared with previous centuries, more wars are taking place, and they are lasting longer and causing more devastation. Since 1945 there have been 130 wars, most of them civil wars. Between 1989 and 1992 alone, of the eighty-two armed conflicts counted by the UN, only three were between countries; the rest were internal conflicts. In other words, most of today's wars are caused by the "failure of societies to hold themselves together."[5] According to Papademetriou, both internal and regional conflicts, often based on religion and ethnicity, are precipitating unprecedented high levels of international migration.[6]

The economic and political factors associated with international migration that I have discussed thus far focus on the lack of economic development and political stability in many Third World countries. These are the major push factors in migration; i.e., pressures that compel people to leave their own countries. Pull factors, i.e., those that draw people to particular destinations, are equally important. The post–World War II expansion of the industrial economies of Western Europe and

North America (especially the United States) has led to immigration policies in these countries designed to meet a burgeoning demand for cheap labor. Globalization has made possible a massive transfer of resources like technology and capital; labor has become another form of large-scale resource transfer. Although more than half of recent international migration flows are between developing countries, the flow from the Third World to industrial nations has grown to unprecedented levels. That developed countries are a magnet for the world's migrants is evident from statistics. In 1990, half of the world's migrants (excluding those naturalized, which would increase even more the number in developed countries) were in industrial countries: 15–20 million were in Western Europe, 15–20 million were in North America, and 2–3 million were in the industrial nations of Asia (e.g., Japan, Taiwan).[7] Virtually all of this migration was deliberately initiated by industrial nations.[8]

In Western Europe large-scale labor recruitment, often from previous colonies, began in the 1960s and ended after 1973, when energy crises and recessions led to restrictive immigration policies. After dropping in the early 1980s, the number of migrants and foreign-born population in Western Europe has risen to about 180,00 per year—many of these foreigners are from the Third World.[9] It would seem reasonable that as Europe's policies have become more restrictive, some migrants might be selecting more welcoming countries as their destination, if they have a choice to do so. Professionals and other skilled migrants would be especially likely to have a greater range of choices about where to migrate. Europe also might lose some of its luster as a destination due to discriminatory limits placed on migrants' rights (including rights to citizenship) and social mobility. Buechler writes that in Europe, migrants work mostly in poorly paid manual, unskilled, or semiskilled jobs natives won't do—regardless of their prior skills or background.[10]

Since 1965 the United States has offered an attractive alternative for many such migrants. Before 1965 restrictive policies made it difficult for any one not from Western Europe or Canada to migrate to the United States. In 1965 the law abolished previous country quotas and made it easier for Third World migrants to come to the U.S. This and subsequent policy changes have set new priorities for admitting migrants: reuniting families of American citizens and legal permanent residents and recruiting needed workers. Between 1965 and 1990 about 270,000 people were admitted each year based on a preference system, each with a numerical ceiling. The ceilings were raised in 1990, especially for workers and professionals. The number of immigrant visas rose to 406,000 between 1991 and 1994 and to 421,000 after that. As a result of the 1965 law, a decline in European immigration, the 1980 Refugee Act (that enabled large numbers of Cubans, Vietnamese, and other Southeast Asians to enter the United States), and illegal immigration (mostly from Mexico and a few other Latin American countries), most migrants coming to the United States are now from the Third World.[11] According to Appleyard, from 1985 to 1989, over 85% of immigrants were from less developed countries.[12] Although many Third World migrants confront discrimination and low wage jobs when they arrive, over time immigrants experience a surprisingly high level of social mobility, as evidenced by per capita income. For instance, economist Barry Chiswick reports that immigrants who came to the U.S. in the 1950s and 1960s earned more than their native-born counterparts 15 to 20 years later.[13]

Massey et al. explain the current Third World-to-industrial world migration flow in terms of world systems theory and dual labor market theory. Modern industrial societies have a built-in demand for workers at the bottom of the labor hierarchy, which encourages migration from less developed to more developed economies. The economic niches available to immigrants reflect the globalization of the world's economies. Once migrant paths are established, the movement of other migrants becomes easier because there are networks of kin and friends in the host country. Services for migrants also become established. All of these factors combine to encourage an acceleration of migration.[14]

While part of the picture, this ignores a central element of Third World migration to the United States. Almost a fourth of legal migrants are well-educated, professional, technical, and skilled workers (due in part to the U.S.'s selective immigration policies). They are at the top not the bottom of the labor hierarchy. Champion contends that this reflects a new "post-industrial migration" pattern that has succeeded earlier labor and family reunification migration. These post-industrial migrants, composed of highly skilled workers, clandestine migrants, and asylum seekers, are often temporary workers at both the upper and lower ends of the labor hierarchy.[15]

Professionals and other skilled workers are typically the best their countries have to offer. It is not usually the absolute wage gap between the U.S. and their own countries that motivates them to migrate but the relative gap between their salaries and working conditions and those considered acceptable at home for people of their education and skills. Professionals who earn enough at home to sustain a middle-class standard of living and who are reasonably satisfied about their chances for advancement seldom migrate, according to Portes and Rumbaut.[16]

Globalization of economies, lack of development and political stability in Third World countries, and immigration policies that reflect the need for labor in the receiving industrial countries have thus far been proposed as the major factors explaining international migration from the Third World to the United States. But these alone do not explain why certain countries or individuals, not others, dominate migration flows nor do they explain the particular destination choice of migrants. As Portes and Rumbaut observe,

> Migration flows do not arise spontaneously out of poverty. Equally undeveloped countries and regions may have very different migration histories and sizable outflows may originate in more rather than less developed areas. The beginnings of these movements are rooted in the history of prior economic and political relationships between sending and receiving nations. Through such processes were molded social contexts that rendered subsequent calculations of "rewards" and "costs" of migration intelligible.[17]

Thus an important element in understanding the migration flow to a receiving nation is the existence of linguistic and historical economic or political ties.

The Origins and Causes of African Emigration

In the first diaspora to the U.S. during the slave period, an estimated 10 to 20 million Africans were transported to the Americans. After the importation of slaves ended in the 1800s, few Africans arrived. For example, from 1891 to 1900 immigration data show only 350 Africans coming to the U.S. Between 1900 and 1950, during the colonial period in Africa, over 31,000 Africans immigrated to the United States, an average of well over 6,000 per decade, still a trickle in the overall number of immigrants.

Most of the immigrants listed as "African" were from Egypt and South Africa and, presumably, few were black Africans. However, in the 1950s, the beginning of Africa's independence period, the number of immigrants doubled from the previous decade; it doubled again in the 1960s. It is here, beginning in the 1950s and after independence, that the origins of the new diaspora of black Africans to the U.S. originates. Although most came for an education and returned to Africa, a few remained and provided a nucleus for those who began arriving and staying in greater numbers in the 1970s.[18]

During the 1950s and 1960s, Egyptians and South Africans continued to be the largest nationalities in the African immigrant flow. However, several black African countries were represented in more significant numbers; eg., Ethiopians, Ghanaians, Kenyans, Liberians, Nigerians, Cape Verdeans, Tanzanians, and Ugandans. Immigration data do not indicate what proportion of these migrants were whites fleeing black liberation struggles and newly independent, black-ruled states, and how many were black Africans. But, as will be discussed in the next section of this paper, it is unequivocal that the number of black African immigrants to the U.S. began to grow dramatically in the 1970s. Examining the major factors behind this increase is my focus in this section.

As I discussed in the previous section, economic globalization, lack of development, political instability, industrial nations' immigration policies, and linguistic and historical ties are the major factors that account for Third World immigration to developed countries in general. The same factors enable us to understand African immigration to the U.S.

Sub-Saharan Africa, like most other developing regions, has been integrated into the global economy primarily as a source of cheap primary goods and cheap labor. Initially, African labor was exploited within colonial boundaries, but after World War II African labor was often actively recruited by ex-colonial European powers as competition increased for more expensive European labor. For example, France gave its former African colonies favored nation status and formed agreements with such African states as Senegal, Mauritania, and Mali to promote labor migration. By 1960, about 20,000 Sub-Saharan Africans were in France; 120,000 in the late 1980s.[19]

The British were less hospitable to immigrants from their former African colonies. Beginning in 1962, Africans in England were denied full social and political rights. They were subject to four immigrant control and three race relations acts that gradually withdrew their citizenship rights. Pass laws and voucher systems were introduced in order to "terminate black settler immigration and to induce repatriation."[20] In 1971, the British passed an immigration act to expressly limit immigration from its former colonies.[21]

By 1974, anti-immigrant sentiment was at a high level in all European countries with large Third World immigrant populations. In France, the largest importer of African immigrants, legal immigration was stopped in 1974, although illegal immigration continued there and elsewhere in Europe. In the late 1980s more liberal policies designed to legalize undocumented aliens, control immigrant flows, and promote family reunification were introduced. However, anti-immigrant sentiment, especially toward those deemed "unassimilable" (mostly Third World people), grew as the French economy went into recession and unemployment grew along with increasing numbers of highly visible, culturally distinct foreign immigrant workers.[22]

Notably, at the same time as European economies were experiencing a declining need for African labor and were seeking to limit immigration, African economies began confronting severe development failures and economic crises. When population growth rates of 3% or more per year are factored in, between 1969 and 1979, most of Africa's economies grew at an average of less than 1% a year. The crisis deepened in the 1980s as mounting debt, stagnant or declining output, falling investment, and rising unemployment worsened. By the end of the decade, most countries were compelled to undertake World Bank-International Monetary Fund structural adjustment programs (SAPs) to try to stabilize if not reverse their economic slide. By some estimates, two-thirds of Africa's population is now living in absolute poverty.[23] In a recent World Bank report, Africa is said to be the one continent that has been, for the most part, "left behind" by the benefits of the global economy.[24]

Political instability is linked with and exacerbates the economic crisis of the continent. Two-thirds of all the victims of war during the 1980s were Africans. In 1991 alone, military conflict affected one-third of Africa's fifty-four countries.[25] As of 1994, Africa has surpassed Asia as the world region with the most refugees. Of the ten countries in 1995 with the most people living as refugees, eight were in Sub-Saharan Africa.[26] The economic and human toll of these conflicts are devastating to a continent that is already the world's poorest.

Both economic and political failure are major push factors for international migration in Africa. Most of the international migrants, including refugees, in Africa have gone to other more developed African countries.[27] Just three countries—Cote d'Ivoire, Nigeria, and South Africa—receive half of Africa's migrants.[28] But the flow to Europe and the United States grows as well.

As several researchers point out, most African immigrants are responding to push factors at home, namely economic and political development failures.[29] In Europe especially, many of these migrants are doing lower-skilled jobs despite the fact that they are among the more skilled and educated citizens of their own countries.[30] From 1960 to 1989, an estimated 70,000–100,000 highly skilled African workers and professionals left their countries to go to Europe or, secondarily, the United States. This amounts to 30% of Sub-Saharan Africa's highly skilled labor stock.[31] Kane adds that a third of all college graduates have left the continent.[32] As an anecdotal illustration of this, Skinner writes that there are more Togolese doctors in France than in Togo.[33]

It may seem odd that it is not the more impoverished and desperate who migrate to countries like the U.S. (i.e., the "huddled masses") but the educated and skilled. Understanding the dynamics of economic globalization can explain this seeming conundrum. Both the deterioration of Africa's economies (due to oil price shocks, declining terms of trade, and so on) and the dualism of labor immigrant selection in industrial nations (either at the bottom or at the top of the labor hierarchy)—reflect current competitive pressures and other economic dynamics resulting from global economic integration. As Logan suggests, in less-developed countries with stagnating or deteriorating economies, such as most of those in Sub-Saharan Africa, it becomes impossible to absorb trained manpower. Emigration to developed countries becomes the only or most desirable alternative for many such workers.[34] On the other hand, the unskilled, perhaps due to a combination of financial, educational, and language constraints, migrate primarily to neighboring African countries in search of work.[35]

SAPs designed to combat Africa's economic problems create, at least in the short run, conditions that actually increase the pressures on the educated and skilled to emigrate. By forcing governments to lay off public sector workers, open their economies to foreign competition, and lower wages, SAPs have compounded the plight of Africa's middle classes, whose living standards have declined drastically. A couple of examples can suggest the magnitude of the problem. By 1984 in Ghana, real wages were only 13% of what they were a decade earlier; agricultural wages also collapsed. Between 1960 and 1990, GNP per capita fell 1.5% per year. If household incomes had declined as much as real wages, most families would have starved.[36] Similarly, in Uganda between 1972 and 1984, the index of real wages fell from 100 to 9. As a result, Chazan et al. report that all over Africa professionals, government workers, and university personnel are leaving their countries.[37]

Environmental problems in many African countries have made it even harder for countries to combat their problems or create enough jobs in urban areas. At the 1994 UN Conference on Desertification in Paris, Burkina Faso's Hama Arba Diallo pointed out that countries with major drought and desertification problems produce the most emigrants to Western Europe and North America.

People are left with no alternative but to emigrate.[38] Cape Verde is a striking example of this. As Foy reports, Cape Verde has been subject to periodic drought, landlessness, a stagnant economy, and a rapidly growing population. There are far more Cape Verdeans and those of Cape Verdean descent living outside the country than in it,[39] and according to Davidson, in the 1970s an estimated majority of young Cape Verdeans intended to emigrate.[40] There are two ways to escape the islands' problems, according to many Cape Verdeans: "death and emigration."[41]

African Immigration to the U.S.

With the British becoming increasingly unreceptive to the arrival of their previous colonial subjects in the 1960s and the French and other European countries following suit in the 1970s, the influx of Africans to Europe became more difficult, although the influx of both legal and illegal immigrants was by no means halted. Collinson reports that since the 1970s there has been a nearly universal stop to legal labor migration in Western Europe.[42] Fortuitously, during this same period, changes in U.S. policy were making it easier for Third World people, including Africans, to come to the U.S.[43]

In 1965 the quota system that previously favored Europeans was replaced with a preference system that favored the entry of immediate relatives of U.S. citizens and permanent residents or of those with skills needed by the economy. A new emphasis was also placed on humanitarian concern in the acceptance of refugees. These changes have produced a dramatic shift away from Europe to Asia and Latin America as the main geographic source for immigrants to the U.S. Until the early 1970s these changes had relatively little impact on the number or proportion of immigrants from Sub-Saharan Africa, largely because newly independent African economies were growing, and Europe and Africa were the logical and preferred hosts for most Africans who did migrate. But as Africa's economies and political systems began to fail (culminating in the crises of the 1980s) and more developed African and European economies became unreceptive to foreign immigrants, the entré to the U.S. provided by U.S. immigration policy began to attract more Africans.

U.S. immigration and refugee policies underwent further alteration in the 1980s and 1990s that have had and will have a major positive influence on African immigration. In 1980, a new Refugee Act, more in conformity with the 1967 United Nations Protocol on Refugees, was passed. This allowed the president in consultation with Congress to review the worldwide refugee situation. On the basis of the number of refugees needing resettlement and which refugees were of "special humanitarian concern" to the U.S., refugee admission ceilings were set among the areas of the world. Under the new law, refugees are eligible to adjust to permanent resident status after one year in the United States. In 1986, in response to growing public alarm over illegal immigration, the Immigration Reform and Control Act (IRCA) was passed. Among its provisions was the offer of the legal permanent resident status to undocumented aliens with roots in the U.S. Between 1986 and 1992 (after which almost all eligible aliens had attained permanent resident status), there was a huge increase in the number of immigrants, most of them from Third World countries. Another contributing factor in the upsurge of immigrants in the early 1990s was the passage of the Immigration Act of 1990. This act was designed to increase the number of skilled and employed immigrants compared to those admitted for reasons of family reunification. A cap of 675,000 immigrants was set to take effect in 1995. About 71% of immigrant visas were to be issued for family members and about 21% for employment-based immigrants. This is a significant change. For instance, between 1991 and 1992 the limit on employment-based immigration more than doubled—from 59,000 to 140,000.[44] Another 8% of visas will be reserved for "diversity" immigrants, i.e., those from hitherto low admission countries of the world. The new diversity program excludes entirely already-high admission countries while reserving 55,000 immigrant visas for low admission regions. Within these selected regions are grouped eligible countries (both the regions and countries and the number of visas reserved for them may vary from year to year). Through a lottery system, would-be immigrants are selected to receive visas. There is a limit of 3,850 visas (7%) that can be issued to persons from any one country. While all of these policies have allowed for growing numbers of Africans to come to the U.S., the new Diversity Program promises to have a profound effect on future immigration from Africa. In 1995 alone, the new program allocated 20,200 visas for Africa (including North Africa), about 37% of the visas available.[45]

TABLE 1 Immigration to the U.S. from Africa: 1891 to 1970

Decade	Immigrants
1891–1900	350
1901–1910	7,368
1911–1920	8,443
1921–1930	6,286
1931–1940	1,750
1941–1950	7,367
1951–1960	14,092
1961–1970	28,954

Source: U.S. Immigration and Naturalization Service, *1989 Statistical Yearbook of the U.S. Immigration and Naturalization Service* (Washington, DC: U.S. Department of Justice, 1990), p. 3.

Immigration Trends: 1960s to 1990s

In Table 1 we observe that between 1961 and 1970 immigration from Africa doubled from the previous decade to almost 29,000. INS (Immigration and Naturalization Service) data reveal, however, that throughout the 1960s and early 1970s, most of this is accounted for by immigration from North Africa, especially from Egypt. In fact, between 1969 and 1971, over half the African immigrants were from Egypt. Morocco and South Africa were the next two largest sources of migration from Africa to the U.S. Indeed, North Africa continued to dominate until 1973–1974. From 1975 on, Sub-Saharan African migrants to the U.S. began to increase dramatically, while North African immigration has grown only modestly, as can be seen in Figure 1.

Logan remarks that during the 1980s the rate of increase for Sub-Saharan was in fact greater than for any other region in the world (in part due to its low initial numbers).[46] Although the number of African immigrants has grown steadily since the 1960s, as Wong shows, the percent of all U.S. immigrants who are African has been and remains quite small—only 1% in the 1960s and 2% during the 1970s.[47] However, the trend is upward; between 1980 and 1995, Africans increased their share to over 3% of all immigrants to the U.S.[48]

Data in Figure 1 support my analysis of the major factors influencing Sub-Saharan African immigration to the U.S. Although rising steadily in the 1960s and early 1970s, it is from the mid-1970s on that Sub-Saharan African migration begins its rapid increase. This coincides with the period of Africa's growing economic and political breakdown as well.

While this correlation is only suggestive, a look at a few of the characteristics of the migrants provides additional support for the impact of both globalization and internal economic and political problems on immigration. African migrants during the 1970s, when the upsurge began, were mainly young adult males, in contrast to female majorities from almost every other region.[49] This can be explained partly by the recency of most African

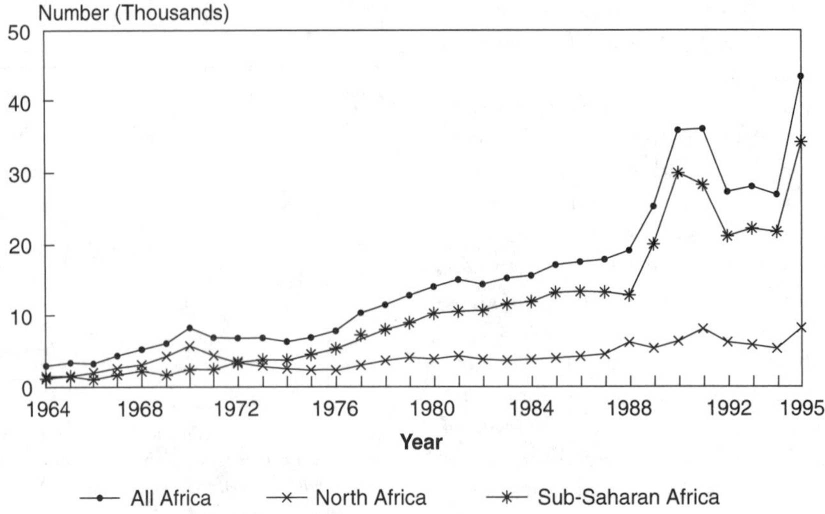

FIGURE 1 Immigration from North Africa and Sub-Saharan Africa: 1964–1995

Source: Based on computer data provided by the U.S. Immigration and Naturalization Service (Washington, DC: U.S. Department of Justice, 1995, 1996).

immigration. In many instances, female immigrants are arriving under family reunification provisions of post-1965 U.S. immigration laws. Relatively few Africans were here long enough to be naturalized, were the immediate relatives of U.S. citizens, or could get immigrant visas or permanent resident status which would allow them to bring over their families. In addition, most early African migrants were likely to be seeking an education and jobs, a selection factor that favors males over females. The educational level of African migrants is also revealing, supporting both the selective effects of such pull factors as the attraction of developed economies and the push factors of economic and political malaise on Africa's "best and brightest." Between 1960 and 1975, the average educational level of African immigrants to the U.S. was over 16 years.[50] This has declined somewhat in recent years in large part because more Africans are becoming permanent residents and naturalized citizens, which allows them to bring over their wives and children as immigrants. Dependents tend to lower the average educational level of a group, as Portes and Rumbaut point out.[51] Nonetheless, the average African immigrant continues to have 15.7 years of education, and a higher proportion of Africans than any other group in the U.S. (including white natives and white immigrants) have college degrees. Many have attended graduate school.[52] In 1980, Nigerians, along with Indians, Taiwanese, and Egyptians, were the four most educated groups in the U.S.; 96.4% of Nigerians were high school graduates, and almost 49% had at least a four-year college degree.[53] According to 1990 census data, 64% of foreign-born Nigerians aged 25 and older have at least a four-year degree, and 43% of all foreign-born Africans in the U.S. do.[54] Africans, along with Asians, were also more likely than any other immigrant group (or of the native U.S. population) to be highly skilled professional and technical workers. In 1975, for example, 22.6% of Africans and 17.8% of Asians were in this category.[55]

These data also attest to the influence of U.S. policy on both the quality as well as the number of African immigrants. Portes and Rumbaut observe that before 1965, U.S. policy

TABLE 2 Refugee Approvals: 1985–1992

Total from	1985	1986	1987	1988	1989	1990	1991	1992
Africa	3,000	3,000	2,000	3,000	2,000	3,500	4,900	6,000
E. Asia	50,000	45,500	40,500	38,000	38,000	38,000	38,800	33,500
E. Europe & Soviet Union	10,000	9,500	12,300	30,000	50,000	58,300	53,500	64,000

Source: U.S. Immigration and Naturalization Service, *1992 Statistical Yearbook of the Immigration and Naturalization Service* (Washington, DC: U.S. Department of Justice, 1993), p. 80.

made it difficult for Africans to come to the U.S. Because there were so few Africans here, the new emphasis on family reunification and occupational qualifications meant that mainly Africans with occupational credentials were eligible to immigrate.[56]

Another U.S. policy, the 1986 Immigration Reform and Control Act (IRCA), accounts for most of the dramatic surge and then decline in African immigration between 1986 and 1992 that appears in Figure 1. The INS reports that in 1992, after almost all eligible illegal aliens had applied for legal immigrant status, over 31,000 Africans had applied. In 1990, at the peak of African immigration, of the total 32,797 immigrants, 15,322 (about 46%) were the result of IRCA legalization. Most of these had entered the U.S. illegally or were students or visitors who had overstayed their original visas.

A final policy factor in African immigration to the U.S. is refugee policy. The 1980 Refugee Act, while ostensibly designed to depoliticize U.S. refugee policy, in reality continued to reflect Cold War politics and perceived U.S. national interests, thus favoring refugees from Marxist countries. It is not surprising, therefore, that despite the fact that a large and disproportionate number of the world's refugees were Africans in the 1980s, most of those admitted to the U.S. were from Communist Southeast Asia or Eastern Europe and the Soviet Union, as can be seen in Table 2. Only about 1% of the over 1 million refugees resettled in the U.S. since 1980 were from Africa.[57]

Of those who were admitted from Africa, the overwhelming majority were from Marxist Ethiopia. In 1983, for instance, there were 2,456 refugees from Africa; 2,209 were from Ethiopia. If there is any doubt that U.S. national security interests and politics were the deciding factors in admitting refugees from Africa, one need only observe that the next three countries with the most refugees to the U.S. were Sudan, Angola, and Zaire with 37, 37, and 24 refugees respectively.[58] Sudan and Zaire were both close Cold War allies of the U.S., while Angola was a Marxist state against which the U.S. government was covertly supporting civil war.

So far my analysis has focused on immigration from Sub-Saharan Africa or Africa in general. It is also important to look at which countries are sending most of the immigrants to the U.S. For this, two additional explanatory factors are necessary: Anglophone background and/or a history of political and economic ties to the U.S.

Table 3 gives the top 11 countries sending immigrants to the U.S. between 1974 and 1995. Together these countries account for 65% of all the immigration from Africa, including North Africa. During this period, over 421,000 Africans immigrated to the U.S., an average of more than 19,000 people per year. A superficial look at the country rankings is revealing. All but two countries—Cape

TABLE 3 African countries with the largest number of immigrants to the U.S.: 1974–1995

	Total	Avg. per Year	% of All African Immigrants
Nigeria	69,691	3,168	17
Ethiopia	55,838	2,538	13
S. Africa	36,761	1,671	9
Ghana	30,387	1,381	7
Liberia	16,976	772	4
Kenya	16,970	772	4
Cape Verde	16,962	771	4
Sierra Leone	10,235	465	2
Uganda	8,757	398	2
Tanzania	8,542	388	2
Sudan	6,728	320	1
All Africa	421,560	20,074	100

Source: Based on computer data provided by Michael Hoefer, U.S. Immigration and Naturalization Service (1995 and 1996).

Verde and Ethiopia—can be considered anglophone by virtue of colonial or historic ties to either Great Britain or the U.S. Another relevant fact is that the countries on the list—Nigeria (1), Ethiopia (2), South Africa (3), Sudan (5), Tanzania (6), Kenya (7), Uganda (8), and Ghana (9)—are among the ten most populous countries in Sub-Saharan Africa.[59] (Their population size rank is the number in parentheses.) Thus part of the reason these countries are the biggest source of immigrants is their relatively large population size compared with other Sub-Saharan countries.

Although they are not anglophone countries, Cape Verde and Ethiopia are not anomalous cases. Both had important historic ties to the U.S. before the 1970s. Cape Verdean immigration to the U.S. goes back to the late seventeenth century when captains of American whaling ships began recruiting them as sailors. Most of those who settled in the U.S. went to New England, where their ancestors and subsequent migrants continue to reside. Cape Verdean immigration was, therefore, quite substantial before 1974. Between 1900 and 1973, an estimated 20,000 Cape Verdeans came to the United States.[60] Ethiopia has long-standing political ties to the U.S. going back to World War II. During the 1950s and 1960s, the U.S. was the main ally of Ethiopia. Ethiopia provided the U.S. with a major communications base near Asmara while the U.S. made Ethiopia the major recipient of U.S. aid in Africa.[61]

The advantage of coming from anglophone ex-colonies is more than just the ability to speak English; it is also cultural. As already mentioned, a larger proportion of those who came to the U.S. were Africa's most educated. The "pioneers" were often the product of colonial education in their own societies or education abroad in England or the U.S. They were, therefore, highly Westernized, another factor in their willingness to migrate so far from home and also an asset in their ability to adjust to U.S. society and become successful. As Clausen and Birmingham observe,

> Colonialism has taught them [migrants] valuable lessons in their struggle for advancement. As individuals they had acquired mobility through colonial education. The value system in which they were indoctrinated was consistent with the individualism, capitalism, and self-determination available in American life.[62]

The trend for almost all of the leading immigrant countries is upward,[63] and all but South Africa experienced a large surge in immigration between 1988 and 1991, reflecting IRCA legalization. All of the countries producing the largest numbers of immigrants have been experiencing economic and political problems, but the countries with the greatest increase in immigration over the period (as shown in Table 4—Sudan, Ethiopia, Sierra Leone, Nigeria, and Liberia—have experienced

TABLE 4 Percent difference in immigration: 1974 vs. 1995

	1974	1995	% difference
Ethiopia	276	5960	2159
Sudan	43	1645	3826
Sierra Leone	61	919	1506
Liberia	191	1929	1010
Cape Verde	122	968	793
Nigeria	670	6818	1018
S. Africa	525	2560	488
Ghana	369	3152	854
Kenya	386	1419	368
Tanzania	243	524	216
Uganda	320	383	20

Source: Based on computer data provided by Michael Hoefer, U.S. Immigration and Naturalization Service (1995, 1996).

ruinous, recent civil wars or other political crises along with severe economic deterioration. Between 1965 and 1990, while the average annual per capita growth of GNP in all of Sub-Saharan Africa was an unimpressive .3%, the average for Sudan was −.1%; Ethiopia was −.1%; for Sierra Leone, .2%; for Nigeria, .2%; and for Liberia, −1.6%.[64]

Consequences of African Immigration to the U.S.

There is no consensus among researchers on whether migration from Africa to developed countries such as the U.S. is more positive than negative. A major concern is that because the migrants tend to be young, skilled, and educated, a large-scale "brain drain" is occurring that will hinder African development efforts. For example, Amin has argued that when impoverished regions lose migrants, it reinforces traditional survival strategies and prevents needed socioeconomic change. This in turn reinforces push factors on the remaining population and encourages more emigration. The result is the development of a "degenerated, agrarian capitalism corrupted and poor."[65] Furthermore, as Papademetriou argues, labor migration from poor to rich economies does not help poor economies transform themselves nor does it address the underlying weaknesses in the socioeconomic structure of rich economies. It is mainly profitable for private capital and the international economy by removing national boundaries for labor. Poor economies' loss of their meager supply of skilled and productive people is not compensated for by the often marginal gains acquired from the skills and remittances of the emigrés.[66]

Others argue that international migration encourages economic development and benefits both sending and receiving countries. Obviously, developed economies benefit by improving their global competitiveness through importing both the skilled and unskilled labor they need.[67] Another view is that in Africa's stagnating and deteriorating economies, emigration contributes to development by relieving unemployment and providing remittances from abroad that increase the supply of needed foreign exchange.[68] Skinner points out that the flows between African and developed countries do not go just one way. Africa is also the recipient of highly skilled labor migrants from developed countries from such sources as the Peace Corps, USAID, the World Bank, the UN, and the staffs of multinational corporations. These foreign workers may actually promote much needed pan-African and regional development because, as strangers, they are not bound by parochial loyalties or perspectives.[69]

Indeed, African sending countries often encourage labor migration. Relieving unemployment, providing remittances, and introducing savings for local investment are all forms of resource transfers that can benefit local economies. The impact of such resource transfers are not insubstantial. As the World Bank reports, globally migrants remit about $75 billion a year—about a third of the net capital flows going to developing countries each year. In Africa, remittances amount to between 10% and 50% of GNP in Lesotho and 25% and 50% of the value of exports in Egypt, Malawi, Morocco, and Sudan. Moreover, due to large international wage differentials, the amounts remitted are often a multiple of what migrants could earn at home.[70] Studies of Cape Verdeans reveal how resources gained in the U.S. can benefit the folks back home. From the beginning, Cape Verdeans maintained close ties to their homeland, often retaining rights to land to which they eventually returned to retire. Such individuals bought land, built homes, and provided money and gifts to needier families.[71] Remittances amounted to 40% of Cape Verde's trade deficit in 1979, and 11% of GDP in 1988, and the government of Cape Verde views emigrant capital as an important source of investment in new fishing and industrial enterprises.[72] The Cape Verdean-American community, while "enthusiastic Americans," has also built up considerable political clout at the state and Congressional levels of government, which has been used to garner substantial U.S. technical assistance and project funding for the islands. For instance, the U.S. supported Cape Verde in negotiations with the IMF and World Bank and funded school projects and a desalinization plant.[73] Gmelch argues, however, that more typically migrants invest in nonproductive things like housing, consumer goods, or unproductive, redundant businesses that do little to promote development back home.[74]

Although speculative at this point, the work and business experience and contacts as well as the capital Africans acquire in the United States could be a major *boon* to African development—if African governments provide an environment friendly to private investment and entrepreneurship.[75] Currently, such an environment exists only in a few African countries. Instead, statist policies, political corruption, mismanagement, and bureaucratic obstacles have made Africa unattractive to private investment from any source. Such obstacles to returning home or investing back home may be a major reason that Africans have among the highest rates of naturalization of any immigrant group.[76] This is especially true of the most skilled "PTKs" (professional, technical, and kindred workers), many of whom would return home if conditions improved.[77] Instead, such migrants often have little recourse but to stay in the U.S. As Logan remarks, "It can safely be argued that when P.T.K.s decide to apply for permanent residence or citizenship, they have already made the decision not to return home, at least not during their productive years."[78]

Another, less tangible, result for Africa of international migration is growing cultural as well as economic globalization and integration. Migration inevitably opens up, even for remote villages, a window to the larger world—albeit mainly a Western world. As Amin foresaw, modern international labor migration is part of the larger process of transformation of economic, political, and community life in Africa, largely stimulated by outside forces.[79] Perhaps overly idealistic, Cape Verdean poet/writer Eugénio Tavares in 1918 argued for the benefits of emigration to America for his countrymen, then living in a poor, stagnant, feudal society. Those who go to America, he wrote, gain more than just food and money. They gain enlightenment and new ideas, which they bring back when they return. They gain now horizons, ideas of progress, and higher expectations. The migrant is no longer constrained by "the narrow limits of his hut and his 'cachupa'." He is no longer willing "to bear the tyrannical constraints of humiliating, ill-paid work." His "aspirations are not confined to chewing." Finally, emigration provides an escape from poverty, hunger, and "wretched conditions" at home.[80]

Any discussion of the consequences of African international migration to the U.S. must also consider its impact on the U.S. Obviously, with African immigrants only little over 3% of all immigrants, the numerical impact is small. However, we can consider the impact of African immigration within the context of the overall impact of Third World immigration, both real and perceived. As I have already discussed, Third World immigration has become a hot political issue in both Europe and the United States. There are growing fears that there are too many immigrants, that many of them are racially and culturally unassimilable, and that they take jobs from the native population.[81] In the U.S. such concerns have been heightened as recession, restructuring, and deindustrialization have resulted in the loss of millions of jobs and stagnant incomes for an estimated 80% of families. Another worry is that the large number of new migrants threatens the cultural integrity of U.S. society; i.e., they don't speak English, they don't join the "melting pot," they are too "different."[82]

The World Bank tends to discredit such concerns as largely exaggerated. For one thing, international migration from less developed countries relative to their population size is no greater now than in the early 1970s—about 1 emigrant per 1,000 population. Only about 2% of the people born in low- to middle-income countries live outside their country of birth. About 2 to 3 million new Third World migrants leave each year (both legal and illegal), with only about half going to industrial countries. This amounts to 1.5 new immigrants per 1,000 population per year—the same as in 1970. However, migration between developed countries has fallen from 2.5 to 1.5 migrants per 1,000 population, and the foreign-born share of the population is rising in developed countries to an average of about 5%. This is due largely to the low fertility in developed countries not to a huge, new influx of foreigners.[83] In 1990, the foreign-born population in the U.S. grew to 8%; but, as Martin and Midgley point out, 15% of the population was foreign-born in 1910.[84]

This does not mean that immigration is having no significant demographic effect in Western countries. In Europe, for example, of the 13 million foreigners in the EU (Economic Union) in 1990, 8 million were from outside the EU—half were from North Africa, Yugoslavia, and Turkey—but a growing proportion are from Sub-Saharan Africa and Asia. In France alone, an estimated 25% of the population is of foreign nationality or has foreign ancestry of no more than two generations back.[85]

The Bank also contends that foreign migrants do not take many jobs from native workers. Rather they often complement the labor force by filling jobs unwanted by natives (this accounts for as much as 70% of recent migrant flows) or jobs that would otherwise disappear due to high labor costs. Migrant workers may have some negative effect on wages, the Bank concedes, but mainly in unskilled jobs.[86] Martin and Midgley report similar findings. Research on immigrants in the U.S. indicates that immigrants do not have a significant negative effect on the overall earnings or employment opportunities of native Americans. However, there may be a negative impact in particular industries and areas where immigrants have become concentrated.[87]

Prospects for African Immigration

Two variables will determine the scale of future African immigration to the U.S.:

1. what happens in terms of economic and political development in African countries, and
2. U.S. immigration and refugee policies.

These are both interrelated, so will be discussed together.

Henderson maintains that the best antidote to migration from the Third World is helping poor countries achieve more peaceful societies, freer and more democratic political systems, and higher economic growth. This would necessitate in many cases higher levels of aid and investment from the rich, industrial nations so alarmed by the influx of unwanted immigrants. As long as the global economy continues to mainly benefit the already rich, many people in stagnant, politically unstable Third World countries will continue to have no recourse but to emigrate, illegally if not legally.[88] African countries are, for the most part, facing the worst prospects for development of any world region. With population growth rates averaging 3% per year, it will be impossible for African economies to absorb the number of job seekers without a huge infusion of new job-producing investment. This is unlikely to occur. As Brittain concludes:

> Virtually no industrial investment comes to Africa's urban centers—there are no telecommunications, transportation infrastructure, or political or social stability to attract foreign business, despite the cheapness of African labor. In fact, it costs 50 percent more to run a business in Africa than in Asia, and the profits in Asia are nine times greater, according to a recent American report. In the 1980s, three quarters of all investment in developing countries went to just 10 countries—none in Africa. The 1990s will be no different.[89]

Both the push factors at home and the pull factors of jobs and opportunities in the U.S. are likely to increase the pressures on Africans to migrate to the U.S. Logan adds that few African countries are fully using their present quotas; this could easily change if conditions worsen while the number of Africans with higher education grows. Moreover, as Asian economies improve, the brain drain from there will decline relative to that from Africa.[90] I have already mentioned that U.S. refugee quotas for Africa are slowly increasing, and in 1995 the new diversity (DV-1) program allocated 20,200 visas to Africans. The latest program (DV-97) made 20,623 visas available for Africans.[91] U.S. immigration policies that favor those with needed skills and family reunification are also working to the African migrant's advantage. A sizable African community of nearly a half million now resides in the United States. As permanent residents, naturalized citizens, and native-born citizens, they are eligible to bring their spouses, children, and parents to the U.S. Like many immigrant communities before them, Africans are at a stage where both the reasons to migrate and the networks are well enough established for "chain migration" to occur. That is, primary migrants arrive first. After becoming residents and citizens, they bring their families over. Those family members in turn become residents and citizens and many bear children who are citizens. This encourages even more of their countrymen and countrywomen to come, and so the process continues.

Recent census bureau projections support this conclusion. The bureau's estimates are that between 880,000 immigrants per year will come to the United States between 1993 and 2050; 7% of these immigrants are expected to be black.[92] To be sure, not all of these new black immigrants will be from the African continent. But unless there is a dramatic political and economic revival in Africa or U.S. policy becomes so anti-immigrant as to sharply reduce the number of legal migrants, the number of Africans coming to the U.S. in the foreseeable future will surely continue to grow.

NOTES

1. Hal Kane, *The Hour of Departure: Forces That Create Refugees and Migrants.* Worldwatch Paper 125 (Washington, D.C.: Worldwatch Institute, 1995), pp. 32–35.
2. David Henderson, "International Migration: Appraising Current Policies." *International Affairs* 70 (January 1994), p. 98.

3. Alejandro Portes and Ruben G. Rumbaut, *Immigrant America* (Berkeley: University of California Press, 1990), pp. 12–13.
4. Kane, *The Hour of Departure,* pp. 6–7.
5. *Ibid.*, pp. 18, 21.
6. Demetrios G. Papademetriou, "International Migration in a Changing World." *International Social Science Journal* 36 (1984), pp. 415–417.
7. A.G. Champion, "International Migration and Demographic Change in the Developed World," *Urban Studies* 31 (1994), p. 657.
8. World Bank, *World Development Report* (New York: Oxford University Press, 1995), p. 68.
9. *Ibid.*, p. 65. Also see Sarah Collinson, *Beyond Borders: Western European Migration Policy Towards the 21st Century* (London: Royal Institute of International Affairs, 1993); Jacques Barou, "In the Aftermath of Colonization: Black African Immigrants in France" in *Migrants in Europe: The Role of Family, Labor and Policies*, Hans Christian Buechler and Judith-Marie Buechler (eds.), (New York: Greenwood Press, 1987).
10. Judith-Marie Buechler, "A Review-Guest, Intruder, Settler, Ethnic Minority, or Citizen: The Sense and Nonsense of Borders" in *Migrants in Europe: The Role of Family, Labor, and Politics*, Hans Christian Buechler and Judith-Marie Buechler (eds.), (New York: Greenwood Press, 1987), pp. 288–291.
11. Louise Lamphere, "Introduction: The Shaping of Diversity" in *Structuring Diversity: Ethnographic Perspectives on the New Immigrants*, Louise Lamphere (ed.), (Chicago: University of Chicago Press, 1992), pp. 7–8; Portes and Rumbaut, Immigrant America, p. 23.
12. Reginald T. Appleyard, "South-North Migration." *International Migration Review* 25 (1991), p. 61.
13. Barry Chiswick, "The Economic Progress of Immigrants: Some Apparently Universal Patterns" in *The Gateway: U.S. Immigration Issues and Policies*, Barry Chiswick (ed.) (Washington, D.C.: American Enterprise Institute, 1982), p. 156.
14. Douglas S. Massey et al., "Theories of International Migration," *Population and Development Review* 19 (September 1993), pp. 431–466.
15. Champion, "International Migration," p. 658.
16. Portes and Rumbaut, *Immigrant America*, pp. 18–19.
17. *Ibid.*, p. 230.
18. Edwin Clausen and Jack Bermingham, *Chinese and African Professionals in California* (Washington, D.C.: University Press of America, 1982), pp. 42–43, 94.
19. Barou, "In the Aftermath of Colonization," pp. 78–79.
20. Buechler, "A Review-Guest," p. 284; also A. Sivandon, "Race, Class, and the State: The Black Experience in Britain." *Race & Class* 27 (1976), pp. 350–367.
21. Kristen F. Butcher, "Black Immigrants in the United States: A Comparison of Native Blacks and Other Immigrants." *Industrial and Labor Relations* 47 (January 1994), p. 278; Vernon Briggs, *Immigration Policy and the American Labor Force* (Baltimore: Johns Hopkins University Press, 1984), p. 123.
22. Barou, "In the Aftermath of Colonization," p. 79; Buechler, "A Review-Guest," pp. 286–287; World Bank, *World Development Report*, p. 65.
23. Naomi Chazan et al., *Politics and Society in Contemporary Africa* (Boulder, CO: Lynne Rienner Publishers, 1992), pp. 314–315.
24. World Bank, *World Development Report*, p. 60.
25. "Recovery from War's Trauma." *Africa News* 34 (July 15, 1991), pp. 6–7.
26. Kane, *The Hour of Departure*, pp. 23–24.
27. Arthur Helton, "The Kindness of Strangers," *Africa Report* 39 (March/April, 1994), pp. 33–35.
28. World Bank, *World Development Report*, p. 65.
29. John Salt, "The Future of International Labor Migration," *International Migration Review* 26 (1992), pp. 1077–1106; Elliott P. Skinner, "Labor Migration and National Development in Africa" in *African Migration and National Development*, Beverly Lindsay (ed.), (University Park: Pennsylvania State University Press, 1985), p. 19; Appleyard, "South-North Migration," p. 613.
30. Salt, "The Future of International Labor Migration," p. 1094; Skinner, "Labor Migration and National Development," pp. 35–36.
31. Victoria Brittain, "The Continent That Lost Its Way" in *Global Studies: Africa,* F. Jeffress Ramsay (ed.), (Guilford, CT: Dushkin Publishing Company, 1995), p. 195. Reprint from

World Press Review, July 1994; Appleyard, "South-North Migration," p. 613.

32. Kane, *The Hour of Departure*, p. 39.
33. Skinner, "Labor Migration and National Development," p. 35.
34. Bernard, Logan, "The Reverse Transfer of Technology from Sub-Saharan Africa to the United States," *Journal of Modern African Studies* 25 (1987), p. 598.
35. Godwin Matatu, "Multitudes Move from Nigeria," *Africa* 138 (February 1983), pp. 10–18; Susan Kalish, "International Migration: New Findings on Magnitude, Importance." *Population Today* 22 (March 1994), pp.1–2; World Bank, *World Development Report*, pp. 65.
36. World Bank, *World Development Report*, pp. 16–18.
37. Chazan et al., *Politics and Society*, pp. 268, 313–314; Kane, *The Hour of Departure*, pp. 40–41.
38. George Ola-Davies. "The Paris Conference," *West Africa* (November 7–13, 1994), p. 1907.
39. Colm, Foy, *Cape Verde: Politics, Economics and Society* (New York: Pinter Publishers, 1988), p. 15.
40. Basil Davidson, *The Fortunate Isle: A Study in African Transformation* (Trenton, NJ: Africa World Press, 1989), p. 13.
41. Foy, *Cape Verde*, p. 14.
42. Collinson, *Beyond Borders*, pp. 36–37.
43. Unless otherwise indicated, the sources for the discussion of U.S. immigration and refugee policy are the 1990 and 1992 *Statistical Yearbook of the Immigration and Naturalization Service* (Washington, D.C.: U.S. Department of Justice, 1991 and 1993).
44. Salt, "The Future," pp. 1077–1106.
45. U.S. Department of State, *VISA Bulletin* No. 35 (Vol. 7). Washington, D.C.: "Diversity Immigrant: Visa Lottery (DV-1) Results" (October 19, 1995).U.S.Department of State: Office of the Spokesman.
46. Logan, "The Reverse Transfer of Technology," p. 605.
47. Morrison G. Wong, "Post-1995 Immigrants: Demographic and Socioeconomic Profile" in *Urban Ethnicity in the United States: New Immigrants and Old Minorities*, Lionel Maldonado and Joan Moore, (eds.), Vol. 29. Urban Affairs Annual Reviews (Beverly Hills: Sage, 1985), p. 53.
48. Computer data provided by Michael Hoefer, U.S. Immigration and Naturalization Service (INS), 1995 and 1996.
49. Marion F. Houstoun et al., "Female Predominance in Immigration to the United States since 1930: A First Look." *International Migration Review* 18 (1984), p. 929.
50. Butcher, "Black Immigrants," p. 281.
51. Portes and Rumbaut, *Immigrant America*, p. 62.
52. Butcher, "Black Immigrants," pp. 267–268.
53. Portes and Rumbaut, *Immigrant America*, p. 62.
54. *1990 Census of the Population. Ancestry of the Population of the United States* (Washington, D.C.: Bureau of the Census, 1993).
55. Portes and Rumbaut, *Immigrant America*, pp. 123–125.
56. *Ibid.*, p. 62.
57. Helton, "Kindness of Strangers," p. 34.
58. U.S. Immigration and Naturalization Service, *1983 Statistical Yearbook of the Immigration and Naturalization Service* (Washington, D.C.: U.S. Department of Justice, 1983), p. 85.
59. United Nations Development Programme (UNDP)/World Bank, *African Development Indicators* (Washington, D.C.: UNDP/World Bank, 1992), p. 11.
60. Foy, *Cape Verde*, p. 15; Antonio Carreira, *The People of the Cape Verde Islands: Exploitation and Emigration* (Hamden, CT: Anchor Books, 1982), p. 43.
61. Patrick Gilkes, "Ethiopia: Recent History" in *Africa South of the Sahara 1995* (London: Europa, 1995), p. 377.
62. Clausen and Bermingham, *Chinese and African Professional*, p. 112.
63. Uganda is the exception; its immigration numbers have been declining steadily during the 1990s.
64. UNDP/World Bank. *African Development Indicators*, p. 11.
65. Samir Amin, *Modern Migration in Western Africa* (Oxford: Oxford University Press, 1974), p. 102–103.
66. Demetrios G. Papademetriou, "International Migration," pp. 410–414.
67. Salt, "The Future," pp. 1077–1106.
68. Logan, "The Reverse Transfer of Technology," p. 598.

69. Skinner, "Labor Migration and National Development," pp. 37–38.
70. World Bank, *World Development Report*, pp. 53–66.
71. Carreira, *The People of the Cape Verde Islands*, p. 55; Foy, *Cape Verde*, p. 15.
72. Jonathon Grepne, "Cape Verde: Economy" in *Africa South of the Sahara 1995* (London: Europa, 1995), pp. 250–253.
73. Foy, *Cape Verde*, pp. 181–182.
74. George Gmelch, "Return Migration" in *Annual Review of Anthropology*, B. Siegel (ed.), (Menlo Park, CA: Annual Reviews, 1980) pp. 135–159.
75. World Bank, *World Development Report*, p. 66.
76. U.S. Immigration and Naturalization Service, *1991 Statistical Yearbook of the Immigration and Naturalization Service* (Washington, D.C.: U.S. Department of Justice, 1992), p. 152.
77. World Bank, *World Development Report*, p. 66.
78. Logan, "The Reverse Transfer of Technology," p. 611.
79. Amin, *Modern Migration in West Africa*, p. 19.
80. Quoted in Carreira, *The People of the Cape Verde Islands*, pp. 63–64.
81. For instance, see Martin Baldwin-Edwards and Martin A. Schain, "The Politics of Immigration: Introduction." *West European Politics* 17 (April 1994); also "Immigration Debate Centers on Economic Impact." *Population Today* 22 (October 1994), pp. 1–2.
82. See Lamphere, "Introduction: The Shaping of Diversity," pp. 1–34.
83. World Bank, *World Development Report*, p. 53.
84. Philip Martin and Elizabeth Midgley, "Immigration to the United States: Journey to an Uncertain Destination," *Population Bulletin* 49 (September 1994), Population Reference Bureau, p. 4.
85. Champion, "International Migration," pp. 660, 667.
86. World Bank, *World Development Report*, p. 66.
87. Martin and Midgley, "Immigration to the United States," pp. 30–31.
88. Henderson, "International Migration," pp. 109–110.
89. Brittain, "The Continent That Lost Its Way," p. 196.
90. Logan, "The Reverse Transfer of Technology," pp. 610–611.
91. U.S. Department of State. *VISA Bulletin* (October 1996), p. 6.
92. Martin and Midgley, "Immigration to the United States," p. 9.

Return Migration

✦ GEORGE GMELCH,[1] *State University of New York*

International migration today differs from that of the last century. Then migration was largely a one-way movement with major streams of migrants leaving Europe and Asia for North America. It was generally assumed that those who left the Old World never returned. As early as 1885, however, Ravenstein (1885) had noted the principle of return migration in his renowned list of migration laws: "Each main current of migration produces a compensating counter-current." Nevertheless, the view of migration as a once-and-only phenomenon which arose from the nineteenth-century transatlantic experience dominated migration studies. The thousands of migrants who returned to their homelands, including an estimated one quarter of the 16 million Europeans who arrived in the United States during the early decades of this century, were barely noticed by social scientists. In a migration bibliography published as recently as ten years ago by Mangalam (1968), only ten of the 2051 titles listed were studies of return migration. There were actually several times that many studies, but still a trifling effort.

Rhoades (1979) has suggested several other reasons for the neglect of return migration. The massive urbanization occurring in most parts of the world led to a "rural-urban" analytical framework in which geographical movements were viewed as occurring in one direction only—rural to urban. The nature of traditional anthropological fieldwork which involved research for a limited period of time (customarily one year) in a limited space (a single village) may also have led to a view of

[1]I wish to thank Richard Felson, Sharon Gmelch, Donald Hill, Robert Rhoades, and Walter P. Zenner for their helpful comments on an earlier draft, and John Cullen at the Irish Foundation of Human Development and Conor Ward at University College, Dublin, for their support and services which enabled me to undertake this review.

Gmelch, George. 1980. "Return migration." *Annual Review of Anthropology,* 9:135–59. Reprinted with permission from *Annual Review of Anthropology,* Volume 9, © 1980, by Annual Reviews, www.AnnualReviews.org.

migration as a static event. Finally, return is the most difficult aspect of the migration cycle to quantify. While most countries gather information on incoming aliens, the same does not apply for returning citizens.

In the last fifteen years, however, anthropology and its sister disciplines have begun to treat migration as a system, examining both stream and counter-streams; and working at both ends—sending and receiving societies. In this essay I will review the findings of the now growing literature on return migration, attempting to pull together the insights made by fieldworkers and to arrive at some generalizations. Treated will be typologies of return migrants, reasons for return, adaptation and readjustment of returnees, and the impact of return migration on the migrants' home societies.

Before proceeding, I should make clear what is meant by return migration. Perhaps reflecting the subject's recent emergence as an area of inquiry, there has been much terminological sloppiness. A wide variety of terms has been used to describe return migration: *reflux migration, homeward migration, remigration, return flow, second-time migration, repatriation*, and at a recent AAA meeting one speaker suggested *retromigration*. Following its usage in most of the works reviewed here, *return migration* is defined as the movement of emigrants back to their homelands to resettle. Migrants returning for a vocation or an extended visit without the intention of remaining at home are generally not defined as return migrants, though in some settings it is difficult to distinguish analytically the migrants returning home for a short visit or seasonally from those who have returned permanently. A related concept is *reemigration*. This refers to people who move back to their homelands and then emigrate a second time. The frequent movement between two or more places, such as in seasonal labor migration, is referred to as *circular migration*.

In this review I am primarily concerned with international return migration in which the returnees cross cultural boundaries. I will not be concerned with the return movements of migrants within a single cultural system such as African wage laborers going from the city back to rural villages. This type of domestic return, which frequently comes under the heading of circular migration, has been treated elsewhere (see, for example, Graves and Graves [1974] and Petersen [1978].) Most of the return migration literature deals with persons who originally migrated to urban-industrialized countries or regions, notably in northern Europe and northeastern North America, who have returned to their homelands in less developed areas, particularly the southern and eastern fringes of Europe and the Caribbean, but also to rural hinterlands within industrialized regions, such as the west of Ireland.

Data on the sociodemographic characteristics of return migrants are limited but do permit us to make some generalizations about *who* returns. Most return migrants originally emigrated from rural areas and small towns in developing regions. Their decision to leave was voluntary, yet motivated by economic necessity—high unemployment, decline in the amount of available agricultural land, the fragmentation of family holdings, and so forth. More men than women left, most while in their late teens or early twenties and still single. Most went to major urban-industrial centers where they obtained unskilled jobs which nevertheless paid far more than they could have earned at home. They followed a pattern of chain migration, going to places where their kinsmen or friends had already become established. Among the married couples, the men usually went first, sending for their wives and children later, once a home had been set up. Upon returning many settled in large towns and cities but many also went home to their rural place of origin. Few, however, resumed the agricultural occupations they had held before emigration.

Typologies of Return Migrants

Most typologies of return migration have dealt with two dimensions along which there is considerable diversity: the length of time migrants intended to remain abroad and their reason(s) for returning. In each scheme a basic distinction is made between those migrants who intended their emigration to be *temporary* and those who intended it to be *permanent*. The former usually returned to their country of origin after accomplishing the specific objective(s) they had set out to achieve, most often to accumulate a sum of money. By returning they are merely fulfilling their original plans. The second type, on the other hand, had intended, or at least hoped, their emigration to be permanent—that they would be able to create a better life abroad. But for various reasons they decided or were forced to return. King, (1977) Lianos, and Cerase (1967) categorize two or more subtypes among these "permanent" migrants according to the cause of their return. First are those who were forced to return due to some outside factor, either family circumstances, such as the need to look after an ill or elderly parent, or faltering economic conditions in the host country. These migrants were satisfied with their situation abroad and would have preferred to remain had they been able to do so. Second are those who failed to adapt to the way of life in the host society, perhaps because of the strangeness of the language, people, and customs or because they could not bear the psychic costs of being separated from close friends and the familiar environment of home.

The core features of the various classifications can be abstracted into the following composite typology:

1. Returnees who intended temporary migration. The time of their return is determined by the objectives they set out to achieve at the time of emigration.

2. Returnees who intended permanent migration but were forced to return. Their preference was to remain abroad but because of external factors they were required to return.

3. Returnees who intended permanent migration but chose to return. Failure to adjust and/or homesickness led to their decision to return.

The typologies reviewed here do help clarify basic types of return migrants. Nevertheless there are problems, especially in attempting to categorize migrants according to their intentions at the time or emigration, i.e., temporary versus permanent. Most migrants simply do not have definite plans. They go on a trial basis, letting their decision of whether or not to return and when to return be guided by the opportunities they find in the new society. It is Brettell (1979) who shows that the Portuguese migrants she studied, even after many years away, retain an "ideology of return." That is, most, no matter how settled, keep open the possibility that they will one day go home. They take action to that end in sending remittances and maintaining close contacts with people at home. An ideology of return and perpetually postponing a decision on permanent settlement has been described among other migrant groups as well.

Motives for Return Migration

Why do migrants return to their homelands? Why are many willing to give up a comparatively high standard of living in one of the advanced industrialized nations of the world in order to return to a less developed society? In reviewing the evidence on the reasons for returning I will concentrate on those migrants who either intended permanent emigration or lacked definite plans. I am not concerned with the forced repatriation of refugees during or following war when obviously little choice is involved, nor with circular labor migration.

A few writings point to unfavorable economic conditions in the host society, such as recession or layoffs and unemployment within a single industry, as the primary cause of return migration. Hernandez-Alvarez (1967) reports that many Puerto Rican migrants in the United States returned to Puerto Rico in the 1960s as a result of being displaced from their jobs by automation and mechanization. Kayser (1967, 1972), King (1978), and Rhoades (1978, 1979, 1979) have documented the massive return flows of European guestworkers or *Gastarbeiter* from Germany and other industrialized northern European nations due to recent economic recessions (1966–1967 and 1972–1973) which had their most serious impact on those sectors of the economy—factory and construction—in which most migrant workers are employed. Most studies, however, report noneconomic factors as the primary reasons for return migration. Most frequently mentioned are strong family ties and the desire to be in the company of one's own kin and longtime friends. The desire to return often surfaces during vacation trips home. Perhaps not entirely satisfied with factory work and city life, and exalted by open space, blue sky, clean air, an easygoing pace of life, and the friendliness of people at home, the migrant begins to seriously consider a new life at home. Many Newfoundland returnees indicated that they had made the final decision to return while in Newfoundland on holidays, and although they had always thought about returning, made the actual decision suddenly (Gmelch et al., in preparation). Some returned to their homes in Toronto, Montreal, and other Canadian mainland cities just long enough to pack their belongings and put their houses up for sale.

Ailing or elderly parents obligate some migrants, particularly the eldest children, to return. They go back to look after a sick relative and to run the family business or farm. Initially they may have intended to reemigrate to the host country once affairs at home were sorted out, but after settling in again they soon gave up thoughts of leaving. The importance of family ties in return migration is reflected, I believe, in the sizable numbers of migrants who return to their home communities in rural areas. One might expect all but retired and independently wealthy returnees to settle instead in urban areas where employment opportunities are greater and the attractions of city life, to which they had become accustomed, are present. Yet in studies where data are available on the place of resettlement, from one-third to one-half of the migrants returned to rural areas or small towns.

Feelings of loyalty or allegiance to the home society is also cited as an important consideration among many migrants. In several studies where a series of reasons for return were scaled and quantitatively measured, "love of homeland" or a similarly worded concept was cited as the most important factor in the decision to return. This was particularly true among Israeli, Irish, and Newfoundland migrants. For many of these returnees the social and cultural advantages of life in their native society outweighs the economic costs—the expense of moving and the decline in earning power—of returning. This is less often the case, however, in the poorer developing nations where the home economy cannot provide many returnees with adequate employment and a comfortable standard of living. Only in the hinterlands of the industrialized world are the economic costs of return small enough to be affordable.

In some cases the decision to return was also influenced by negative or "push" factors in the host country. Jamaican migrants in Britain encountered painful experiences of racial prejudice and discrimination. This was also reported to be a factor in the return of some Puerto Rican migrants from the United States. Emigrants from the warmer climates of south Asia and the Caribbean had difficulty adjusting to the comparatively severe European and northern North American winters.

And, as previously mentioned, poor economic conditions force some migrants to return.

Overall, however, the attractions or positive attributes of the home society—"pull" factors—have more influence in return migration decisions than factors inherent in the host societies. This was conclusively demonstrated by several quantitative studies of migration in which the relative influence of push and pull factors as motives for return were compared.

The most common method used to elicit migration motives in these studies has simply been to ask migrants directly why they returned (*standard motive*). There are several potential problems in this approach. For one, it implicitly assumes that migrants know what motivated them and that they will state those factors when asked. Moreover, as Taylor (1969) points out, there is a tendency for people to reduce the wide variety of factors that influenced their decision down to one or two overriding reasons. This is done to reduce the cognitive dissonance or psychological discomfort that results from having to make a decision where there are two or more alternatives. Also, the reason migrants give may vary with the identity of the interviewer and the context in which they are asked. A second problem arises in ordering and classifying the wide array of reasons given by migrants into a set of meaningful and manageable dimensions. Nina Toren (1975) tackles both problems in a methodologically sophisticated study of Israeli returnees from the United States. Rather than ask returnees directly to explain their motives for returning, she presented them with a scale or "accounting scheme" of eighteen reasons and asked them to indicate on a five-point scale the degree to which each influenced their decision to migrate. The eighteen motives were grouped into three broad categories: (a) economic and occupational; (b) patriotic and social; and (c) familial and personal. Within each category there were three reasons which indicated pull factors (positive features associated with the homeland) and three indicating push factors (negative factors associated with the host country). In effect, Toren operationlized the push–pull model of migration motives.

A modified version of this method was adopted by Taylor (1976) among Jamaicans and by Gmelch in separate studies of Irish and Newfoundland return migrants. All four studies using this technique found pull factors (the attractions of the place of destination) to be far more significant than push dimensions in promoting return migration. Push factors had surprisingly little effect on the decision to return. Consistent with the previously discussed findings, social-patriotic and familial-personal reasons were stated by the migrants to have greater influence on their decision to return than did economic-occupational factors. However, we must be cautious in interpreting these findings as it has not been demonstrated conclusively that the migrants' ratings of the various motivational factors accurately reflects the real reasons for their return. The economic dimension may be more important than many returnees are willing to admit. For instance, when controlling for socioeconomic status, Toren found the more successful Israeli migrants to be influenced more by occupational opportunities back home, while the less successful were primarily influenced by patriotic attachments and loyalty to the home country. For government bodies concerned with return migration, this means that higher status returnees may not be a good investment as they may leave again should better job opportunities open up elsewhere. The lower status migrants, in contrast, are more inclined to perceive their homecoming as the end of the journey.

Success or Failure

A question posed by some researchers is whether returnees were basically "successes" or "failures" as emigrants. Do they return because they have failed to adapt to their surroundings or achieve the "good life" they had expected? Or did they fare reasonably well, choosing to return not because of discontentment but because they felt there were important advantages to living in their homeland which were not available abroad? In other words, is return migration usually the consequence of a positive or a negative selection process? This question is of obvious importance for understanding the effects of return migration on sending societies.

The data suggest that most returnees were clearly not failures, but neither were they great successes. In her study of Israeli returnees, Toren found that return migration was nonselective: return migrants resembled those who remained behind both in level of education and in occupational position. Hernandes-Alvarez (1967) found that the Puerto Rican returnees had a small educational advantage over those who remained in the United States but had earned less money. They also had a higher rate of unemployment (16.7%). Most Irish returnees appear to be drawn from the middle ranges of the socioeconomic ladder in the overseas Irish community: return migrants at both the top and bottom are underrepresented. It has been suggested that among various European migrant groups the unsuccessful are disinclined to return because they do not wish to admit having failed. Moreover, many of those who do not fare well simply cannot afford the expense of a return trip home. The very successful are often not interested in returning because it would mean giving up secure, well-salaried positions that cannot be equaled in the homeland. Returning may also mean costly obligations to share one's wealth with less well-off kinsmen at home.

Until more is known about the characteristics of the migrants who remain abroad, however, it will be difficult to know for certain the relationship between economic success and the decision to return. Unfortunately, there have been very few systematic attempts to compare returnees with their compatriots who remain behind.

Adapation and Readjustment of Return Migrants

There are two perspectives from which the question of readaptation can be approached. The first approach examines the actual economic and social conditions of returnees: whether or not they have found jobs and adequate housing, developed personal relationships, participated in community organizations, and so forth. Success or failure in adaptation would depend upon the degree to which the migrant has satisfied these objective criteria. The second approach focuses upon the migrant's own perceptions of his or her adjustment and the extent to which he feels the homeland has filled self-defined needs and given him a sense of well-being. The literature approaches readaptation from both perspectives, etic and emic, to some degree. But the emphasis is clearly on the latter approach in which readaptation is analyzed as a form of personal adjustment and measured in terms of the degree of "satisfaction" or "dissatisfaction" expressed by the migrants. Plans to reemigrate are interpreted as a sign of dissatisfaction or maladjustment.

DaVanzo (1976) suggests that because return migrants are familiar with their destination and are likely to have friends and relatives there, the barriers to and psychic costs of returning will be lower than for individuals arriving for the first time. Moreover, if there is a degree of learning-by-experience associated with migration, then persons who had emigrated at least once should find it easier to move again. The data, however, present a very different picture. Some migrants do readjust quickly and encounter few problems; even after many years' absence they appear to pick up where they left off as though they had never been away. But many migrants are unhappy and disillusioned. They are often economically better off than their neighbors, yet they are disappointed and sometimes bitter about life in the homeland. Kenny (1972) and Rhoades (1978) note that younger Spanish migrants replace their *Heimwich* (homesickness) of Germany with *descontento* (dissatisfaction) in Spain's villages. King (1977), Bernard and Vouyoucalos (1976) and Kenny (1972) report "reverse culture shock" among Italian, Greek, and Spanish returnees, respectively. Taylor (1976) reports that 61% of the Jamaican returnees he interviewed were dissatisfied although his measures of adjustment are less than satisfactory. Paine (1974) notes that Turkish migrant workers back from Germany are so dissatisfied with conditions at home that a majority say they would like to reemigrate. And one-fifth of the 600 Irish returnees interviewed by Gmelch and his associates (1979) said they would be more satisfied back in the host society (United States or Britain) then they are at home.

Many migrants are ill-prepared for their return. They do not realize how much they or their communities have changed during their absence. Those returning from highly urban, industrialized nations to the Third World no longer share many of the basic notions that underlie their traditional culture. Relatives and former friends no longer share the same interests, and seem narrow, overly provincial, and, in some cases, backward. On the other hand, local people have developed new friendships during the absence of their migrant friends and relatives and are not always enthusiastic about resuming old relationships. A few migrants, the extreme cases, feel they have been so changed by their emigration experience that they now have more in common with people of the host society than with their own rural countrymen.

Some migrants encounter envy and suspicion among their less prosperous neighbors. Believing that all migrants are wealthy, locals sometimes take advantage of migrants by expecting higher payment for services and overcharging for goods. As one Newfoundland migrant explained, "When a Newfoundlander asks his neighbors to help him repair his roof or fix his boat, they say, 'Sure, just let me know.' But when someone who has been away asks, they say, 'Sure, how much are you going to pay me?'" (Gmelch et al., in preparation).

Many returnees are unhappy with the "way things are done" at home. A typical complaint concerns the lack of efficiency and punctuality. In contrast to the fast pace of the urban, industrial host societies, everything happens slowly at home. It seems to take forever to get things done. Clerks and cashiers move at a snail's pace, plumbers, electricians, and other repairmen fail to arrive at the appointed time or do not come at all. A meddling, insensitive, and inefficient government bureaucracy is a source of considerable frustration for some. Dahya (1974) reports that the correspondence columns of the Pakistani immigrant press are filled week after week with complaints about the country's bureaucrats, including charges of bribery, corruption, and nepotism. The returnees compare this with the efficiency and fair play they experienced in the hands of British civil servants. Such complaints are not unique to migrants in the developing nations. Norwegian returnees also complained bitterly about the lack of services and the interminable delays, such as a one-year wait to have a telephone installed.

Although most migrants do not return home in hopes of getting rich, economic conditions are sometimes worse than anticipated. Jobs are harder to find, wages lower, and working conditions poor to abysmal. Some Irish pub owners found they had earned more money tending someone else's bar in New York or Boston than they could running their own in Ireland. Taylor (1976) reports that the Jamaican returnees he studied were unwilling to take jobs at their preemigration economic level because they would lose esteem among their neighbors and relatives who expected them to be upwardly mobile.

For many migrant women who held jobs while away, problems of readjustment are heightened by their early and usually involuntary retirement. With few employment opportunities for women in the rural areas at the periphery, many migrant women are confirmed to home. Women returning to their husband's home community rather than their own, as is often the case among couples who met overseas, experience more difficulty establishing meaningful relationships than their husbands. Unfortunately, very little attention has been given to the special problems of female migrants. Clearly more research is needed on sex differences in migrant readjustment. The same is also true of the readjustment of children in migrant families. R. L. King, in one of the few studies that even mentions children, reports that the problems associated with return migration to Italy are "most acute for children of school age and teenagers." Unlike preschoolers, this age group had already started their education in the host country, England. Return migration for them meant leaving behind their friends and English, the language of instruction. In Italian schools at home they have difficulty because they cannot read or write Italian and "the behavior of the village children seems strange to them." Language is similarly a problem with some Spanish school children who return to Spain with better German than Spanish (R. Rhoades, personal communication). Jamaican migrants in Britain who intend to return avoid these problems by sending their children back to the island to be raised by relatives.

With time migrants learn to cope with many of the problems discussed here. Several studies discern a period of adjustment of from one to two years. Among Irish returnees, for example, the percentage who expressed dissatisfaction with their lives in Ireland dropped from 51% among migrants who had been back one year or less to 21% of those who had been home two or more years (Gmelch, 1979). And among those who had been back for more than five years, the number who were discontented dropped to 17%. Not included in these figures, however, are the estimated 5% to 10% who were so unhappy that they reemigrated. Bernard and Vouyoucalos (1976) describe readjustment as a process in which the strong allegiances and preferences for traits and institutions found abroad is blurred with time. "Less concious of the lost advantages of this former host country, but also less aware of his homeland's shortcomings, he or she settles down." This is not unlike the "reverse culture shock" or short-term readjustment problems many Peace Corps volunteers experience on their return to the United States.

Why do so many migrants experience problems in readjusting to the cultures in which they were socialized? A theme that runs through these studies is that migrants have unrealistic expectations of what the home society would provide. The process of adjustment is not just a function of the actual conditions—environmental and social—of the area, but a function of the expectations held by migrants. For a variety of reasons these expectations are often unrealistic. Their memories of home are nostalgic ones, with positive experiences standing out while negative aspects have receded from memory. Home, after all, was the place where the migrants spent the formative years, their youth, a time when they were healthy and relatively free from the annoying responsibilities of adult life. Vacation trips home did little to correct this idealistic image since they were usually made during the summer when the weather was good and the atmosphere festive. For the two or three weeks they were home social activity was intense, as it could be for a short period of time to celebrate the return of a relative. Letters from home were also a contributing factor. In hopes of encouraging the migrant to return, relatives exaggerated the benefits of life at home while underplaying or even ignoring unemployment and inflation. Together these factors raised the returnees' expectations higher than the reality of life in the homeland could satisfy, thus producing a sense of relative deprivation among otherwise successful migrants.

Some problems of readjustment are attributable to differences in the scale of the communities in which migrants have lived. Most returnees left large metropolitan areas, e.g., New York, Munich, Paris, London, where the density of population, heterogeneity of lifestyles, and wide range of choices in shopping, food, and entertainment provided much stimulation. Those who lived in "ethnic villages" within the city were somewhat sheltered from these influences but only partially. The migrants return, then, to a developing society—to a remote village or small town in the Mezzogiorno or Andalucia or to a quiet fishing outport with unpaved roads on the coast of Newfoundland. At home there is a certain uniformity in the work and outlook of the people. There are differences, of course, but they are small compared with what one experienced in the city. The pace of life is relaxed and there is seemingly little to do with one's free time other than play cards or join a few men in a game of *bocci* or *boules*. The contrast may be a bit exaggerated but many migrants would not disagree. The point is that many of the complaints migrants have about home, the slow pace, the provincial interests of local people, and so forth, are due to basic differences between urban and rural life. And to some degree returnees would experience many of the same adjustment difficulties if they moved to a rural area within the industrialized host society—to a village in the English Peaks district, say, or a farming community in Vermont.

For those who do not readjust, who do not settle in, reemigration is one solution, at least temporarily. Little is known about the numbers of migrants who reemigrate. However, several surveys asked returnees about their future intentions. The results show that 25% of Greek, 20% of Irish, 64% of Italian, and 85% of rural and 65% of urban Turkish migrants expressed a desire to reemigrate to the host countries from which they had returned. These figures require an important qualification. They do not distinguish returnees who wish to reemigrate because of dissatisfaction from those who wish to go abroad again in order to earn more money and who intend to return home. Some individuals become "shuttle migrants," cultural commuters who move back and forth between home and host societies, never fully satisfied with where they are.

Impact of Return Migration on Home Societies

The consequences of emigration for the sending societies has been the subject of much debate. Proponents of emigration argue that among other things, returning migrants bring back valuable industrial work experience and skills as well as capital needed for the economic development of their homelands. This position has been summarized by Arnold Rose (1969):

> The migrant workers are getting training and experience in modern techniques of production, which many bring back to their native lands; the cost of unemployment payments or social assistance to the unemployed are avoided; there may be less of a housing shortage; the migrants send some of their savings to their relatives in the home country, which provides foreign exchange to the governments of emigrant countries, and the returning migrants bring the rest of their savings home for investment in presumably productive enterprises (quoted in Rhoades, 1978).

Empirical studies of return migration, however, do not support these claims. In this section I will review the literature on the impact of return migration in terms of the introduction of new skills, returnee investment of capital, the introduction of new ideas and attitudes, changes in social structure resulting from return migration, and the influence of return migration in encouraging further emigration.

Introduction of Work Skills

Because the great majority of migrants work at unskilled jobs while abroad, few return with work experience that can be considered important to the development of the home economy. Paine reports that less than 10% of the Turkish workers returning from Germany had received any training while away. The pattern is similar for Greek, Spanish, Irish, Italian, Mexican, and other returnees. Of the migrants who do obtain better jobs while living away, most are only semiskilled. This, as Castles and Kosack (1973) note, usually means "nothing more than a brief introduction in how to carry out a specific operation in a specific factory."

Even for the few migrants who do acquire technical or industrial skills there is a good chance they will not be able to apply them at home. Rural areas from which most migrants originate lack the infrastructure needed to make effective use of their skills. Moreover, migrants generally have little desire to continue in industrial employment upon return. Among Turkish returnees, for example, just 3% of those returning to rural areas and 20% of those returning to cities were willing to consider wage employment. The dream of most return migrants is to be independent and self-employed, which usually means setting up a small business such as a grocery shop or taxi service, not returning to the assembly line.

In a study of Algerian migrants, Trebous (1970) offers a striking example of the inappropriateness of foreign acquired skills to the economy of the sending society. Nearly two-thirds of all Algerian workers in France worked in a single industry—the building trades. With limited activity in this sector of the economy in Algeria, the workers who returned were likely to find themselves unemployed. Similarly, migrants who worked in the rural, agricultural sector of the host society and resettled in rural areas in the home society may not be able to make use of their foreign work experience because of differences in the scale of the two economies. Raymond Wiest (1978) provides an illustration of this in an excellent study of Mexican wage-labor migration. The skills Mexican braceros learn while working in large-scale agriculture (mainly fruit picking) in the United States have little relevance to small-scale (mainly cereal) agriculture in Mexico.

Before leaving this topic two exceptions to this pattern should be noted. In a national survey of Puerto Rican returnees, Heranandez-Alvarez (1967) found that over 40% were white-collar and that as a group they represented a middle sector bordering on the nation's educational, financial, and occupational elite. His survey was conducted in 1960, however, at a time of rapid expansion of the Puerto Rican economy, which attracted many professionals home from the United States. Heranandez-Alvarez correctly predicted that the white-collar job market would quickly reach a saturation point making it difficult for future skilled migrants to find work. The second case concerns Filipinos who had been away for a long period working at various jobs on Hawaiian sugar plantations. MacArthur (1979) credits them with introducing many useful skills as cooks, carpenters, welders, heavy equipment operators, and the like.

In drawing conclusions about the role of return migrants in introducing work skills, an important qualification needs to be made. The bulk of field research has been done in rural areas, while a majority of return migrants in many countries have resettled in towns and cities. In an urban context the influence of the returnee might be different. There they have the opportunity of finding industrial or office work which would make use of their foreign acquired skills.

Investment of Savings

After years of hard work and saving, many migrants return with sizable amounts of capital. In addition to their savings account deposits, cash is obtained from the sale of their overseas assets. As Appleyard (1962) notes in a largely economic study of British returnees from Australia, "emigration to a distant overseas country and return are about the only occasions when a person liquefies the bulk of his assets." Most of the possessions—furniture, car, consumer durables, and house—accumulated during the migrant's residence abroad are sold prior to departure and the money transferred to a bank in the home country. Rhoades (1978) has been successful in estimating returnee capital by examining the bank deposits of Spanish return migrants. With this exception, however, there is little statistical data on how much money the average returnee brings home. But it is clear that many are well off by local standards and may even rival the purchasing power of local elites.

The key question, however, is not how much migrants return with, but how they invest their earnings at home. Do they invest in enterprises, such as new types of businesses, new farming techniques, or cooperatives, that will raise the productive capacity of the region and generate further capital? Or is their money spent on consumerism, to raise the living standards and social status of the individual returnee? The empirical evidence suggests the latter.

Housing or the purchase of a building plot for a house is the most common form of investment. Over two-thirds (69%) of returning Yugoslav workers surveyed said they intended to spend their earnings on a house. In the Philippines the type of investment varies somewhat with the length of time the migrant has been away, but housing and land are always the preferred form. The migrant who has been away a short time builds a traditional house, while the "old timer" with more money to spend builds a larger two-story cement and wood house. More lavish yet are the homes built by *pensionados,* retirement returnees, who paint their houses bright colors and equip them with modern appliances such as stereo and television sets, gas stoves, electric refrigerators, and showers that require the construction of an elevated tank outside to provide sufficient water pressure.

It is not uncommon for better-off migrants to built lavish, well-appointed structures. The intent appears to be as much to show off to one's neighbors as to live comfortably. Dahya (1973) describes this phenomenon in Pakistan where the brick and cement houses built by returnees, in contrast to the local mud structures, are intended mainly to impress.

> "It has more rooms than the needs of the family justify and at the most two rooms of the *pakka* house may be occupied by the family. The rest of the house which could be three stories high is kept empty, furnished but unoccupied. But none the less, the *pakka* structures, with their trellised balconies and loggias, multi-colored glass windows, and surrounding fields, stand out for miles to vindicate to one and all the migrant's and his family's achieved status."

It could be argued that such behavior is not only for "show" but raises the status of returnees and gives them better access to village resources, i.e., the show has an economic payoff in the end.

Investment in housing does have some benefit for the community. In places where a considerable portion of the local population has worked abroad, the presence of many new or renovated houses has given the areas a look of prosperity. In the Mezzogiorno of Italy, the explosion of migrant-financed building is described as "one of the most dramatic features of the changing rural landscape." The health of returnees living in new housing is probably improved by the higher level of sanitation afforded by indoor plumbing, heating, and tile or flagstone floors where there was once dirt. The new construction and renovation does increase local employment. But the jobs created are usually of a temporary nature, with their continuation depending upon a regular flow of return migrants with capital to invest in housing. Also, widespread home construction requires expenditures by the local authority for the expansion of services such as roads, water, and electricity. The limited funds available to local authorities could be better allocated in more viable growth areas.

Returnee investment in agricultural land is disappointing. Only where new lands are put into production or new, more efficient farming techniques are used do such investments contribute to rural development. But many migrants are no longer attracted either psychologically or economically to agriculture. Greek migrants are typical in this respect. While almost 30% worked in agriculture before their emigration, less than 8% intended to return to agricultural occupations. As a result, lands purchased by returnees from small peasant proprietors often stand idle, out of production, in some cases used only as summer retreats. Because of this as much as 20 to 30% of the land in some Spanish villages studied by Rhoades (1978) had been taken out of production.

After housing and land, consumer goods make up the next largest expenditure. The homes of returnees are often better equipped with modern appliances than those of nonmigrants. In a few instances the reported desire of migrants for consumer goods is excessive. In Spain, Rhoades (1978) notes, "The home of the typical long-term *aleman* (returnee) is lavishly furnished and decorated with virtually everything modern mass consumer markets offer. It is no exaggeration to define the situation as 'conspicuous consumption run amok' . . . nor to describe returnees as rabid Germanophiles in their consumption desires . . . " Such expenditures on consumer goods bring little benefit to the local economy. Most are purchased outside the immediate area, in large towns and cities. And the major items, from appliances to automobiles, are imports not even manufactured within the country.

With strong preference for self employment, a distaste or disinterest in both agriculture and wage labor, it is not surprising that migrants with sizable savings invest in small business. In Ireland almost a third (31%) were able to set up businesses of their own. However, the Irish businesses, like those reported for Spain, Yugoslavia, Italy, Monserrat, Carriacou, and elsewhere, are traditional ones, notably small shops, bars, and cafes. In many instances these businesses are redundant, adding to an already saturated market. In one Irish village of just 300 inhabitants, for example, there are five pubs. All but one are owned by returnees. Investing in businesses of this type does little to increase the productive capacity of the community. But as I will discuss in the next section, the cause for this does not rest solely with the return migrants.

New Ideas and Attitudes: Innovation or Conservatism

Migrants who have spent a number of years working in the metropolitan area of a foreign society may learn alternative and more efficient ways of doing things and to varying degrees develop an urban ethos. An important question is the extent to which migrants introduce these foreign-acquired ideas into their home communities. Bovenkerk (1974) phrases the question in terms of innovation versus conservatism, that is, is return migration an innovative influence promoting social change or a conservative force serving to maintain the status quo?

The writings on this issue are divided. Some analysts report that returnees play a positive role as innovators, while others find they have very little influence. The most frequently mentioned innovations are in the areas of material culture and house design. In one village in India, returnees introduced home ventilation and separate kitchens and bathrooms. On the Caribbean island of Carriacou they introduced the first motor vehicles. In Ireland returnees from the United States who had purchased pubs were credited with introducing padded seating, which has now widely replaced the former hardwood benches. Similarly, in the early 1960s, returnees is western Ireland were said to have been the first to install showers in their homes. In an Ilocos farming community in the Philippines, McArthur (1979) found that "short time" migrants followed the traditional, conservative pattern, while the "old timers" who spent many years in Hawaii were innovators. They were the first farmers to plant new fast-maturing varieties of rice and to use fertilizer, LPG (liquid petroleum gas) stoves, and transistor radios. The example they set was widely imitated by other villagers. In Greece, Saloutos (1956) reports that returnees introduced more orderly and efficient work habits and created a general atmosphere for advancement. In several studies migrants are not credited with making specific innovations, but are said to be more receptive to change—more willing, for example, to experiment with new varieties of crops. In societies where most adults have migrated at one time or another, such as in some Caribbean nations, it is difficult to separate changes induced by migration from other sources.

Apart from these examples, there is little evidence that returnees bring about significant change in the productive techniques or attitudes and values in their home communities. This point is clearly made in Cerase's (1974) typology of return migrants. Only one of the four types of migrants he identifies, the "return of innovation," strives to develop new enterprises and make things more efficient. These migrants aim to demonstrate that the old ways are not always the best. But they are frustrated from the very start. The local power structure opposes any attempts by aspiring returnees to start new businesses, such as building a small hotel, which would compete with already established local interests. Also they often discover that the available material resources are too limited to develop the enterprises they had in mind. In the end, Cerase remarks, the innovative returnee is bitterly disappointed.

How can we account for the limited innovative influence of returnees? In the case of Ireland, I have argued that many migrants have the potential to introduce change but do not largely because of the nature of the conservative, Catholic society they return to. Ireland, like certain other emigration societies, has traditionally been slow to accept change. In order to gain acceptance at home, Irish returnees have found that they cannot push their ideas or foreign experiences on local people. They particularly must not make unfavorable comparisons between Ireland and the country to which they had emigrated. Many migrants hold different attitudes toward the church, family planning, divorce, and politics, but they keep their opinions to themselves. Those who do not risk being ignored and labeled a "Yank." Schrier (1955) writing about an earlier generation of Irish returnees (pre-1950), suggests that the migrants transferred very little of their American experience to Ireland because they were not viewed by the Irish as "genuine Americans." "A group of strangers, if they do not represent a threat to a community, are generally respected for their differences, and over a period of years some of their customs or ideas might even infiltrate and become accepted by the society in which they have settled. But the returned Yank was at best an adapter, a hybrid whose roots were essentially in Irish soil, and he was not respected as the true barer of new gifts." It is conceivable that in a society in which people are receptive to new ideas, returnees might play a significant role in bringing about change.

Bovenkerk (1974) notes a number of other factors that may influence the innovative potential of return migrants. One is the absolute number of migrants who return. Large numbers of returnees in a community or region may provide the critical mass needed to organize and bring about needed reforms. Small numbers of returnees are likely to have little influence and be easily reabsorbed. On a similar note, the concentration of returnees in time could have an effect. Many migrants returning about the same time will have a greater impact than if the same number were to trickle home over a long period of time. The duration of the migrants' absence may also be a factor. Migrants who have been away a short period of time will not have experienced enough of the host culture to have much of an effect at home. At the other extreme, those who have been away for a long period may be alienated from their home society or may be too old to care or exert much influence. The social class of the migrants may have an effect in that returning professional people or graduate students are more likely to be listened to and held in high esteem than returning laborers. The differences between the country of emigration and the home society also need to be considered. Migrants returning from the metropolitan, industrial world to traditional, agricultural communities will have fewer skills or knowledge that are transferable than migrants returning to urban centers at home. Finally there is the nature of the acquired training and skills. The chances for innovation will be greater among migrants who have learned general skills. Highly specialized education or work skills have less chance of being useful in the home society due to the limited technology and relative lack of economic specialization in the developing regions. Finally, it should be noted that return migrants may be more of an innovative force than the field research has so far credited them. Rural peoples in most parts of the world today are influenced by many external forces, e.g., radio and television, government programs, and tourism, and it is not always easy to separate the influence of return migrants from other factors promoting change. None of the studies reviewed here attempt to analyze systematically the diffusion of ideas or techniques from migrants to the larger community. Rigorous research in this area may lead to a different set of conclusions.

Chain Migration

Some researchers have suggested that returnees, either by direct encouragement or by their example, encourage further emigration. A major cost of emigration to young people trying to reach a decision is the separation from family and friends that movement to another land necessitates. The returnee is a living demonstration to young adults in the community that it is possible to go abroad, see a part of the world, obtain a better paying job, save, and return to the homeland, reunited with family and friends and with enough capital to achieve a comfortable standard of living. As Kenny (1972) notes for Spain, "the *indiano's* triumphant return and ostentatious generosity incite the youth of the village to emulate his example."

The opposite effect is also possible if migrants return unfulfilled. Hofstede shows this to have been the case for Dutch emigrants to Australia and Canada whose unhappy return had a depressant effect on further emigration. It is unlikely, however, that this occurs often since unsuccessful migrants are less inclined to return, especially to their home communities where they would have the most influence on others. Moreover, the natural tendency among migrants upon return is to extoll the benefits of life in the host society in order to present their own migration experience in a favorable light.

Impact on Social Structure

While there is ample evidence of social mobility among individual returnees, there is no evidence that return migration causes any significant change in the social structure of home communities. There are occasional vague references to increased "fluidity" or "flexibility" in social structure brought about by the mobility of the local population, but otherwise there is no evidence of return migration having an effect of this kind. The few scholars who discuss the issue argue strongly that return migration has failed to bring about any significant change in the social order, the desired change being a reduction of inequality. On the contrary, Raymond Wiest (1978) believes that return of large numbers of *braceros* to the Mexican town he studied actually increased the social and economic differences between the migrants and their nonmigrant neighbors. The migrants were better off economically in the first place, and their newly acquired wealth only served to heighten inequality and social tensions, resulting in growing resentment against the returnees.

In a macroscopic study involving both host and donor societies, Rhoades (1978) examines an entire migratory system built around German industrial capitalism. Unlike synchronic studies, which view migration at one point in time and are characteristic of most return migration literature, the migration of workers from Europe's agrarian "periphery" to German cities is examined during three major eras of German history. From the founding of the Reich in 1871, an ideology of migration as equally beneficial to the European industrial core and the agrarian periphery went unquestioned by both the host and donor societies. In theory the cyclical flow of manpower would enable industrial Europe to sustain "miracle" growth through additional labor supplies while simultaneously assuring the on-the-job training of unskilled Mediterranean peasants and promoting the flow of wealth into impoverished sending regions.

Rhoades (1978) seriously questions this interpretation of functional interdependence, which has been labeled "the equilibrium model." Very few of the benefits for sending societies that proponents of migration claimed would occur actually materialized. It is true that sending societies have acquired much-needed foreign currency for their economies and that individual migrants have improved their own living standard. But emigration did not bring the predicted economic boost to the periphery regions. The unequal relationship between core and periphery regions has not by any measure been lessened. Contrary to the notion that cyclical migration provides migrant workers with important work experience and technical skills, which upon their return upgrades the home labor force, there has been instead a "rural/working class brain drain." The migrants recruited by German employers have been young, healthy, and most of them gainfully employed at the time of emigration. They have also been better educated and trained than the population left to manage the economy at home. The economic productivity of the sending societies has been damaged rather than helped by this extraction of its most vital manpower. And the industrial countries, as we have seen elsewhere, have not returned workers with new skills and valuable work experience. The industrial countries benefit, of course, from a "ready-made" workforce which has been reared, trained, and educated at the sending societies' expense. And when workers are no longer productive, through illness, accident, or old age, they return home with their maintenance costs again being absorbed by the sending society. Rhoades concludes that the purported benefits of emigration for sending societies are components of a "migration ideology" fostered by West European employers and governments to justify and maintain a migratory labor system that favors and facilitates the acceptance of their manpower policies.

Rhoades' conclusions are supported by the other studies reviewed here, and appear to be more general than the European migratory system which has been the concern of many of these writings.

Conclusions

The studies of return migration reviewed here vary widely in scope and method. Some are village studies based on participant-observation and informal interviews. Many are surveys, involving structured interviews with selected migrants from an entire region; a few are large questionnaire surveys with respondents being drawn from national samples. Two studies are based on interviews with returning migrants on board passenger ships enroute to their homelands.

The writings are largely descriptive. The tendency has been to treat each return migrant population as a special entity with unique experiences. Investigators have given little attention to the similarities between their subjects and other return migrant groups in order to distinguish the unique features of each case from what is generic to set of cases. One of the characteristics of the literature is a neglect, if not ignorance, of other writings on return migration. This is evident in the opening paragraphs of many articles in which the authors bemoan the dearth of literature. The literature is small, particularly when compared with the entire corpus of migration studies, but as this review demonstrates, there is enough to allow comparisons and some attempt at model building. Apart from the work Rhoades, (1978, 1979) Swanson, (1979) and Wiest, (1978, 1979), who are primarily concerned with the development impact of return migration, little theory has been applied to return migration cases, though this true of the migration literature in general. To some extent this must be expected in a new field of inquiry. The research is interesting in its own right, but it will only become useful in addressing general questions with the development of some general models. It is clear to this reviewer that more comparative research in which there is a systematic search for the uniformities, if not universals, in return migration phenomena is needed. Perhaps in no other area of population studies are the similarities in behavior so striking, yet so little effort has been made at comparison.

More specific directions for future research have also become evident in the course of this review, and others have been suggested by Bovenkerk (1974) and Wiest (1979). The processes of selection (age, sex, marital status, occupation, education) in return migration are not well understood. Reliable statistical data are needed on the demographic characteristics of return migrants and on how they differ from their compatriots who do not return. Not until this type of data are available will we and the home societies know what type of people they are receiving and what the returnees' contribution is likely to be. Most of the writings on return migration concern peasants and other "have-nots" of the developing world. We need to balance this view with more information on the return of the middle and upper-strata migrants. The influence of these groups on the development of their home regions may prove to be altogether different from what has been documented for returning laborers. While most migrants resettle in cities, the bulk of research has been in rural areas. It is vital that we also examine those who return to urban areas, whose readjustment and impact is likely to be altogether different from that of their rural counterparts. Questions of readaptation have been addressed with aggregate data that may mask important sources of variance. The adjustment involved in returning to one's native community, for example, needs to be compared with return to an entirely new community. Returnee adjustment must also be examined in relationship to the significant social and environmental variables (e.g., community size, kin support, employment status) in order to better understand their effect. More information is needed on the special readjustment problems of women and children; our knowledge here is particularly limited. We need to look at the innovative potential of returnees more systematically and determine under what conditions migrants' ideas and skills, however minimal, can be used constructively to the benefit of the home society.

To address these issues adequately we will need a multimethod approach. Statistical survey data are needed to establish the basic dimensions of the problem as well as to understand the range of variation and the co-variation of factors. But equally important will be the intimate knowledge and insight that comes through participant-observation which will allow us to move from description to explanation.

Filling in Some Holes: Six Areas of Needed Immigration Research

✦ HERBERT J. GANS, *Columbia University*

The only sensible way to write about the future is to eschew predicting what might be and to propose what should be—but that is also the personally most satisfying assignment. I will, however, fill it modestly, limiting myself to the presentation and discussion of six research "holes"—to borrow Rubén Rumbaut's metaphor—that deserve filling. As a sociologist, I see mainly sociological holes, and to keep the list from expanding into double digits, I stay within a favorite topic of sociological immigration research, the adaptation of immigrants and their descendants.

I use *adaptation* loosely in what follows, emphasizing both positives and negatives, including attempts to hold back acculturation, which is positive to some and negative to others. I also treat adaptation processes and all their conflicts as directly affected by macroeconomic and macrosociological factors that affect immigrants so that these processes and conflicts are by their very nature different for different immigrants.

EMIGRATION AND IMMIGRATION

The first hole that should be filled is an old one that Charles Hirschman has called the selectivity question: who comes and who does not come to America. The traditional answer, which surely reflected the nationalism of some early American immigration researchers, was that the immigrants were the most ambitious and energetic people, whereas their lesser fellow-nationals stayed home.[1] I was never convinced that this answer was accurate, and I remain unconvinced today, but it is worth raising the old question again. This time, the question should be specified to determine whether and how immigrants are selected or self-selected and by what criteria, including

Gans, Herbert J. 1999. "Filling in some holes: Six areas of needed immigration research." *American Behavioral Scientist,* Volume 42, Issue 9:1302–1313. Reprinted by permission of Sage Publications, Inc.

skills, and whether they actually use these skills after arrival.

Today, the selectivity question is also complicated by the fact that many, but by no means most, immigrants come as transnationals and that others come at least with the intention to be temporary, that is, sojourners. Whatever their future plans at arrival, a significant number participate in the remittance culture, which keeps them in America but which also becomes a factor in encouraging and holding back some potential immigrants.

Sociologists must also pay more attention to how people manage (and mismanage) the attempts to emigrate and immigrate, particularly considering the political, bureaucratic, and financial obstacles in their old countries, and of course in the United States, that now stand in their way. In addition, we need to learn more about what shapes success and failure in illegal immigration and, subsequently, the influence of illegal immigration on adaptation (Corcoran, 1993). But then researchers interested in adaptation still need to ask whether and how the ability and willingness to take leave of an old culture, not to mention family and friends, affect emigration and immigration.

More researchers should also apply the distinction between mainly economic immigrants and political refugees. Another category is needed, too: politico-economic refugees, people fleeing from the failed or sabotaged attempts to correct the economic problems of their home countries.

Sociologists have not done sufficient research on political refugees in the past, even though these bear some resemblance to other kinds of involuntary immigrants. Moreover, some remain involuntary all their lives, whereas others are so eager to become Americans that their refugee status plays only a minimal role in their adaptation.

Today's research on political refugees must distinguish between poor ones, for example, the Hmong and many Latinos; those who have achieved a moderate- or middle-income status, notably Korean refugees; and especially, the ex-dictators and their friends, from several countries, who are often adapting under luxurious conditions.

Yet, perhaps in some way, the most intriguing question in the adaptation of political refugees is how those who were well off in the old country managed sharp economic and social downward mobility when they first arrived here.[2] The findings might also be useful in helping native-born Americans who suffer from downward mobility due to downsizing or other upheavals of postindustrial and global capitalism.

The First and Second Generations

The second hole is, ironically enough, knowledge about the immigrants themselves. Although immigration research was a centerpiece of the Chicago school, the University of Chicago sociologists and their colleagues elsewhere actually did not conduct as much research among the immigrants themselves as is now thought and seem frequently to have been more interested in the second generation.[3] For one thing, immigrants were hard to study because many of them did not speak English, and the researchers often spoke nothing but. Besides, by the time empirical research was fully under way, a large, English-speaking second generation was already available for study and more accessible to under-staffed and underfunded researchers than immigrants were.

In addition, many sociologists were actually more interested in how America affected the immigrants, which also attracted them to the second generation. This pattern may be repeating itself, for the second generation has already become a major research topic today even though there are still few second-generation adults in the post-1965 immigration.

A full-scale review of the old immigration research literature badly needs doing, although it is not easy because the first generation of empirical researchers said little about their research methods, much less whom they interviewed, if anyone. For example, neither of Park's two books, *Old World Traits Transplanted* (Park and Miller, 1921) and *The Immigration Press and Its Control* (Park, 1922) are fully empirical studies. The first consists mostly of quotes from other authors, few of whom were social scientists or researchers, whereas the second is drawn from newspaper stories and interviews with three or four immigrant press editors. In fact, the major Chicago study that actually obtained data from immigrants was Thomas and Znaniecki's (1918–1920) *The Polich Peasant*, for even Wirth's (1928) *The Ghetto* appears to have been based largely on data from the second generation.[4]

The principal later books, by Ware (1935) and Warner and Srole (1945), were based on multigenerational studies undertaken at a time when the second generation was already demographically dominant. Warner and Srole, who conducted their empirical work in the mid-1930s, say virtually nothing about where and how they got their data, but Ware, who researched her book in the 1920s, hired local residents to interview others. Although she never indicated the generational status of her interviewees, she reported that "younger residents were especially sought . . . [and] the sample was biased . . . partly by design in the direction of those who were . . . more Americanized" (p. 192). Moreover, both Ware and Warner and Srole were interested in acculturation and assimilation more than in immigration.[5]

Judging by the scarcity of systematic empirical data on the immigrants, I now suspect that some of the original theorizing about the European immigrants used data from the second generation and then reasoned or imagined backward to a first generation coming to America with an old-country culture they sought eagerly to preserve. From there, it was easy to proceed to what was later called "straight-line theory," in which unacculturated immigrants were succeeded by acculturating second generations and by socially assimilating third and fourth generations.[6]

Today's immigrants are being studied not only by sociologists but also by anthropologists, whose traditional preoccupation with preindustrial cultures makes immigrants especially attractive to them.[7] The major sociological contribution to immigrant research so far has been to study the post-1965 immigrants' economic adaptation, which also corrects the almost total failure of students of the European immigrants and their descendants to look at economic behavior.

Research conducted among the post-1965 immigrants has emphasized their economic activities, especially entrepreneurial ones, with many studies dealing with the storeowners and shopkeepers as well as the owners of enclave enterprises including garment sweatshops.[8] More research is needed on the workers, particularly the immigrants who have gone to work for big and small employers in the larger economy. They may constitute the majority of immigrant workers. Although there are occasional journalistic and other studies of their exploitation, the details of their economic adaptation are still virtually unknown.

A large proportion of the other sociological studies of the immigrant generation is demographic or based on closed-ended survey questions, which supply more data on the answers to these questions that are reified as attitudes than on behavior. Also, too many studies are concerned with proving the inaccuracy of straight-line theory and the immigrants' resistance, however it is conceptualized, to acculturation. Whatever the ideological and other impulses for these studies, they make little sense from a research perspective because straight-line theory can only be tested among the adults of the second and later generations.

Instead, sociologists need to research how much contemporary immigrants actually practice the cultures and maintain the social structures with which they come over, as well as how much they themselves want to, or must, Americanize in order to survive—and if they are upwardly mobile,to succeed.

The study of today's immigrant adaptation should also include some analysis of what I call *anticipatory acculturation*. Because globalism and transnationalism have become popular buzzwords, many observers assume the immigrants' familiarity, while still prospective emigrants, with American culture, including exported mass media fare. Although our movies and television programs do not, and are not intended to, give an accurate picture of life in America, immigrants often learn from them and in ways not anticipated by the creators of media fare. Evidently, immigrants often see the substructure of standard American culture patterns that is taken for granted in all American popular culture and that holds up the superstructure of entertainment.[9]

Furthermore, an anticipatory acculturation study should look at the role of fantasies about America from the mass media and other sources. Fantasies already played an anticipatory role in the European immigration, for example, the notion of streets paved with gold, and the resulting disappointment may explain why some European immigrants returned home, particularly before World War I. Whether such disappointments exist today and affect immigrant return deserves examination.

As long as second-generation research continues, by necessity, to deal with children and adolescents, additional work should be done on immigrant children as school overachievers. This question is important not only to understand the dynamics of successful school performance, perhaps for the benefit of "Anglos" more than anyone else, but also to understand why the second- and third-generation immigrants often do more poorly than immigrant students. Because many of the descendants of European immigrants performed better in school with each succeeding generation, we need to ask whether, and if so why, acculturation and becoming American now lead to educational decline.

If so, the data are relevant also for the selectivity question, for if immigration to America recruits the smarter and more ambitious, their underperforming children may merely be behaving more normally. However, other factors could explain the decline in school performance, such as the low qualities of schools serving the poor and the limited occupational opportunities for poor immigrants' children, particularly those with dark skin, in today's economy.[10]

Once second-generation adults exist in large enough numbers, researchers can go to work to test straight-line theory, if they are still so motivated. In addition, however, researchers should look more closely at differences in second generations among the various immigrants, gather empirical data on the comparative role of class opportunities and restraints, and see what difference race, ethnicity, and other factors make in the second generation, if any. Other researchers should follow Waldinger and Perlman's lead (e.g., 1998) in comparing the second generations of the European and the current immigrations.

The racial diversity of the post-1965 immigration has already stimulated research on the role of race, particularly in immigrant economic adaptation. Other studies should be done on how Anglo constructions of race affect the adaptation of non-White immigrants of various socioeconomic levels, comparing particularly Black immigrants with Asian and other non-Black newcomers. The differential fates of West Indians and Hispanics, depending on their skin color, must also be studied and compared with the extent to which some or perhaps many Asian Americans appear to become "honorary Whites," some as early as the second generation.

A related study should be undertaken on the ever increasing intermarriages of Asians and Whites, focusing particularly on which Whites find officially still "non-White" mates attractive as marriage partners. Such a study might also provide clues about the future possibilities of a dramatic shift in White constructions of, and reductions in, prejudicial attitudes towards at least some non-White races.

In addition, the study of the second generation should include an analysis of the adaptation of what Rumbaut has called the 1.5 generation, which was not undertaken during the European immigration. More important, a study of this cohort, as well as of the so-called 1.25 and 1.75 generations, should be used to determine what factors in childhood abroad and here play what roles in the adaptation processes and conflicts of these generationally interstitial Americans. We know a little about how age of arrival affects the retention of foreign accents, but we know almost nothing about how it affects retention or rejection of old-country social, structural, cultural, emotional, and other patterns.

Conversely—and this is a plug for an old research wish—we need also to look at what is left from the sixth and later generations of the earliest nineteenth-century European immigrants, for example, among the Irish, Germans, and Scandinavians. Later in the twenty-first century, researchers can look at equivalent generations among the Eastern and Southern Europeans, as well as the California Chinese and Japanese, if only to see how the long-run adaptation process might be modeled and to compare generational adaptations to the very different Americas experienced by the descendants of the various "old" (read *European*) and the current "new" immigrations.[11]

Sometime in the twenty-first century, enough time may even have elapsed to begin to test classic straight-line theory systematically and determine the accuracy of its predicted outcome of total Americanization and the disappearance of ethnicity among Whites and other races.

Macro Factors in Immigration

A good deal of immigration research, particularly that oriented toward adaptation, has emphasized microsocial factors, although the study of economic adaptation, and of the behavior of transnationals, has brought in macrosocial and macroeconomic issues. This is a constructive trend, for we need to understand how the nature of and changes in the American economy, polity, and society affect immigrant adaptation.

However, we need to know even more, and with as much specificity as possible, how economy, polity, and society affect the adaptation of, and opposition by, Anglos to immigrants and their children. A related issue is trends in the construction of ethnicity and race, as manifested, for example, in the extent to which macro factors shape whether and which immigrants become scapegoats or valued newcomers and in the conditions that turn ethnic cultures from threats into leisure-time experiences and tourist sites.

Ultimately, sociologists should be able to understand all the macro factors that influence immigration and immigrants. This understanding might spur coordination with general macrosociology, which could in turn help reduce the marginality of immigration research in the discipline and aid its integration into the sociological mainstream.[12]

Insiders and Outsiders

The fourth area deserving of further work is the applicability of the insider-outsider dichotomy to immigration research. This dichotomy was first developed by Robert K. Merton (1973) to deal with the question of whether the ghetto could only be studied by Blacks, that is, insiders, or should also be studied by White outsiders. In an earlier article (Gans, 1997), I applied Merton's dichotomy to current immigration research, defining it in terms of researchers' backgrounds but also attitudes toward sociocultural preservation of the immigrant group.

I borrowed Merton's (1973) dichotomy after I had noticed much of the sociological research on today's immigrant groups was being conducted by researchers from these groups, who thereby constituted a new set of insiders (Gans, 1997). I also noted that many of the writings of these researchers reflect their unhappiness with the concept of acculturation as well as their stated or unstated desire to preserve their ethnic and racial groups or traditions.

Much more conceptual and empirical work needs to be done in this area, although a giant empirical step has been taken by Rumbaut (1998, 1999) in his research. My original hunch was tested on about 150 immigration researchers who were applicants for Social Science Research Council (SSRC) dissertation and postdoctoral grants, but Rumbaut's work is based on about 750 respondents in five different researcher populations.

For the purpose of this article, I need mention only that Rumbaut's analyses also support my initial suspicion that the insider-outsider dichotomy is particularly relevant to sociology. That discipline not only attracts more demographic insiders than the other disciplines do but also allows them to pursue insider topics. Conversely, political scientists, being virtually limited to the study of politics and government, are thereby drawn to research on subjects relevant to all immigrant groups, for example, the politics of immigration policy. Perhaps for that reason, political science does not recruit as many immigrants as does sociology.[13]

Historians are also discouraged from studying the recent immigration because it is too new, archival material is sparse, and disciplinary norms discourage work on recent topics for other reasons as well. In theory, anthropologists should be similar to sociologists, but judging by Rumbaut's (1998, 1999) data, anthropology recruits few immigrants and, after history attracts or recruits the highest proportion of third or later generation ethnics.[14]

Rumbaut's (1998, 1999) findings suggest again that the insider-outsider dichotomy is an especially important area for future work by sociologists of immigration. To begin with, such work must adapt Merton's (1973) original race-based dichotomy to the more complex situation of contemporary immigration research and the diverse origins of today's researchers. For example, although the Anglo constructions of race classify all newcomers from Southeast Asia as "Asian," one can debate whether a Korean American studying Japanese Americans is an insider or not, not only because of ancestral national differences but also because of the long Japanese oppression of Korea and Koreans.

Furthermore, today's politics of the researcher-researched relation is more complex than the Black-White issue facing researchers of the 1960s and discussed by Merton, for now class, gender, ethnicity, religion, identity politics, and other factors may come up as well. Thus, one must ask whether an affluent Dominican American studying poor Dominican newcomers is an insider or an outsider on class as well as generational grounds. And, if a Lebanese American Christian woman is doing a study of Syrian Jewish immigrants, she may confront concurrent issues of gender, religion, nationality—and Arab-Israeli politics.

To be sure, not all of these demographic differences between researcher and researched are new. DuBios and Frazier, two of the great African American researchers of the Black community, both came from upper-middle-class families, and their pejoratively tinged observations about poor Blacks reflected the class conflicts that stratified the Black community of their times. Nonetheless, their class antagonism was little noticed when these men wrote—if only because their White readers shared their biases toward poor Blacks. Meanwhile, the latter may never have had access to any social science research, whether by Whites or Blacks. Such class-related issues were not picked up when Merton was writing, because in that moment in political time, the insider-outsider issue was defined solely as racial.

As for the normative aspect of the insider-outsider question, sociology's conventional wisdom holds that professional researchers should be able to detach themselves sufficiently to conduct objective studies. Professional researchers are generally trained to keep their explicit values out of their research, but other values and feelings sometimes sneak in nonetheless. Besides, values enter into the selection of topics, as well as of hypotheses and concepts, whether researchers are insiders or outsiders.

It would, however, be wrong to assume that all insiders seek to preserve their communities. Many are sufficiently acculturated to have left them, which may have influenced their becoming social scientists. Insiders can also be hostile, using their research to attack or reject their own ethnic or racial groups.[15]

Furthermore, like all other people, immigrant researchers participate in disciplinary and other peer networks, some of whom may ask fellow researchers to share the prevailing attitude toward ethnic and racial preservation. Other pressures may come from funding sources when these are organizations dedicated to the preservation of the immigrant group.

The outsider concept carries its own complications. In Merton's (1973) original analysis, the White outsider was assumed to be not only a detached researcher but to have no interests or values relevant to the Black community. This was perhaps a justifiable assumption given the formulation of the issue when Merton wrote, and it was surely a rhetorically justifiable one in terms of the political arguments Merton was confronting. Nonetheless, not all White researchers were detached, many being integrationists. Although not overtly opposed to the preservation of the ghetto community, they did not always share the positive feelings of its residents, or those of Black Power advocates.

More significant, some researchers perceived themselves as detached but appeared to the ghetto residents they studied as prejudiced, although I suspect that their prejudice was often as much a matter of class as of race and thus not altogether different from the class biases found in the work of DuBios and Frazier.

Immigrant research raises some different issues. Although there have always been detached nonimmigrant researchers, others, particularly in the early WASP-dominated cohorts of immigrant research, favored Americanization, and some even supported the legislation that ended the European immigration in 1924. Yet others were appalled by the behavior and values of poor immigrants, particularly peasants or orthodox Jews, and expressed their class—and religious—biases in their research.

Today's outsiders are not likely to repeat these normative errors, for there are few advocates of rapid acculturation among sociologists of immigration. There are also few who openly express class antagonisms or who want to end immigration because of the imagined moral imperfections of the immigrants or their possible economic threats of African Americans. Actually, the more likely danger these days is the opposite, among both insiders and outsiders: too much romanticization of immigrant *Gemeinschaften*, tight-knit families, and intergrated cultures.

In any case, a simple insider-outsider dichotomy is not applicable to immigrant research. In the short run, it must become more qualified, but in the long run, it may no longer be relevant. Meanwhile, it is worth looking at the backgrounds, values, and conceptual-theoretical schemes of all immigrant researchers—as well as their question wording in surveys and interview studies—to see whether how and in what ways the researchers influence their findings. The researchers themselves must, however, take the leading role in this process, engaging in more reflexivity and giving up the simple-minded positivism that still prevails too often in empirical immigration research.

There remains a last insider-outsider question, which is particularly important for empirical researchers: whether insiders have easier and better access to the people being studied. In this case, the dichotomy is being applied by the people being studied, but often immigrants are more open to coethnics or coracials, and sometimes they will talk freely only with them. Nonetheless, at times, they talk freely only with an outsider, particularly a depth interviewer who comes once and never returns. Conversely, some immigrant groups do not seem to take ethnicity very seriously and are more concerned that researchers are insiders with respect to gender, age, and other criteria.

Who will talk freely with whom and about what subjects are empirical topics. Researchers could even now share their experiences about these matters as a stopgap until systematic research is undertaken on them.

The Sociology of Immigration Research

The fifth area is closely connected to the previous one, for individual (and peer) reflexivity needs to be supported by a sociology of immigration research that draws its theory and concepts in large part from the sociology of knowledge.

A beginning research program for such an area is easy to write, for it should aim to determine the reasons for the choices and omissions in immigration research topics and immigrants, past and present. For example, much of the research among the European newcomers was conducted on Jews and Italians, but far less on equally numerous groups, such as the Polish and other Slavic groups. And why did no sociologist ever look systematically at the later descendants of the Irish, Scandinavian, German, and other populations that began to arrive in the middle of the nineteenth century?

Actually, a sociology of research is needed in all fields of the discipline and in the rest of the social sciences. Although some postmodernist theoreticians have already moved in this direction, a revival of the older, Mannheimian tradition of the sociology of knowledge would make sure that the sociology of sociological research becomes more empirical and moves beyond the postmodern emphasis on textual analysis.

The Role of the Funders

A sociology of immigration research has to include an economic component: its funding and sources of funds and their effects on the shape of immigration research. At times, what funders decide to approve and reject may have more effects on research than the researchers themselves do, because without funds, much of the research can never be done.

The funders include not only the federal agencies and the foundations but ethnic and racial organizations, including activist ones, that fund research only occasionally. Such research should include studies on where the funders get their money, what topics and disciplines they fund and fail to fund and why, and whether they are more likely to support insiders than outsiders.

This area of study must of course include the SSRC and the funders to which its immigration research is indebted, notably the Mellon and Russell Sage foundations. SSRC International Migration Program decisions as to which applicants and projects to support have aided many of today's young immigration researchers but thereby also left others unfunded. Understanding the program's choices will help future sociologists understand why American immigration research at the turn of the millennium took the form it did.

Notes

1. Their answer to the selectivity question did not stop uncharitable Americans, including researchers, from complaining about the physical and moral faults of the newcomers once they had arrived.
2. The same question can be raised about immigrants, although many accept downward mobility for themselves as one cost of ensuring their children a better life.
3. Many of the Chicago researchers, Robert Park included, were actually more curious about Black-White relations and the American Black community. Martin Bulmer suggests in a personal communication (March 1998) that this is evident from the sparsity of immigrant studies in his list of Chicago studies (Bulmer, 1984, pp. 3–4), and it is also implied by Persons (1987).
4. Indeed, the Chicagoan with the most interest in immigrants may have been W. I. Thomas, who was also the real author of *Old World Traits Transplanted.* Park hired him to do the study because he was jobless, having been fired from the University of Chicago for sexual transgressions.
5. Ware's (1935) book was actually a community study of New York's Greenwich Village, but it was subtitled "A Comment on American Civilization in the Post-War Years."
6. In the Chicago school version of this theory, the second generation was beset with marginality. For a comprehensive account, see Persons (1987, chap. 6).
7. After World War II, historians also began to study the European immigrants, and by now there must be more historical than sociological studies about them.
8. Whether these immigration are truly entrepreneurs deserves discussion, although I would also argue for more research attention to entrepreneurs working with more capital and/or taking larger risks, including those who are turning the material culture of the new immigration into consumer goods for the larger American population.
9. A study of the role of overseas American mass media in anticipatory acculturation could also provide media researchers with another site for media affects research.
10. Yet other explanations include demographic and other differences between the old and new immigration, and the peer pressures against high school performance, called "acting White" among poor Black and Hispanic adolescents. It would be useful, for example, to look at the European immigration data again to see whether the poor children of the time pressed their peers to avoid the equivalent of acting White.
11. Needless to say, such a study would also provide a marvelous opportunity to see how race distorts long-term acculturation and assimilation, assuming that there is no basic change in White America's racial constructions in the meantime.
12. I write this with some hesitation because the mainstream is often the most official and therefore conventional, and the exciting research, like other creative work, is often done elsewhere. Moreover, once immigrants are no longer perceived as a problem to mainstream society, funds for studying immigration may dry up.
13. This will change if political scientists look for informal politics in immigrant groups, and it will surely change once the immigrants and their children vote in large enough numbers in American elections.
14. This observation is derived from special unpublished cross-tabulations, "Discipline of Highest Degree: Generational Cross-Tabulations," which Rumbaut and his assistants calculated for Gans on June 17, 1998. Using SSRC data (Gans, 1997), Gans compared specific countries of research and origin. He limited himself to first and second generation researchers and was unsure whether acculturation might have turned third-generation researchers into outsiders. These differences suggest that more research on the making of insiders and outsiders is needed.

15. For example, Louis Wirth's (1928) study of the poor Eastern European Jews of Chicago's West Side, *The Ghetto*, appears to have been hostile towards the people he studied, particularly those who were pursuing upward mobility in less than polite, or at least academic, middle-class, ways. However, whether Wirth was even an insider could be debated, for aside from the class differences between him and the people he studied, he was a German Jewish immigrant studying Eastern European Jews—and the two populations had disagreed with and fought each bitterly for generations.

Immigration Research: A Conceptual Map

✦ SILVIA PEDRAZA-BAILEY*

A veritable boom in immigration research has taken place in the last fifteen years. The purpose of this article is to provide a conceptual map, a way of presenting the issues and approaches that pertain to the topic, to guide us through the vast territory immigration research now encompasses. As this boundless growth in immigration research has occurred across the social sciences, this review of the literature is not intended to be exhaustive but merely illustrative of what sociologists, historians, and anthropologists have contributed. Since America is the quintessentially immigrant society, the focus is on American immigration, but the theoretical issues this review highlights can be applied equally well to other societies with histories of immigration and racial or ethnic relations, such as Great Britain or Brazil. Increasingly, immigration research is one of the topics where sociologists and historians meet (research on revolutions is another), although they meet in much the same fashion that one sometimes arrives at a party and is much surprised to find out who else is there. Our common research interests increasingly bring us together, although not without a fair amount of surprise and trepidation.

As Alejandro Portes (1978a) has repeatedly stressed, the study of immigrants was closely

*Silvia Pedraza-Bailey is assistant professor of sociology and American culture at the University of Michigan. Within the Program in American Studies, she is director of Latino (Hispanic-American) Studies. She is also a research associate of the Center for Research on Social Organization (CRSO), Department of Sociology, University of Michigan. Earlier versions of this paper were presented at the lecture series of the Program in American Culture and at the lecture series of the Program on the Comparative Study of Social Transformations (CSST). The author expresses her gratitude to two anonymous reviewers and to Jeffery Paige, Charles Tilly, and Martin Whyte for their comments and criticisms; and to William Sewell Jr., for his encouragement.

Pedraza-Bailey, Silvia. 1995. "Immigration research: A conceptual map." *Social Science History,* 14:1

wedded with the beginnings of social science in America. Immigrants and their plight were the focus of vivid studies from the early days of social science (Park and Burgess, 1921; Park, 1928, 1950c; Thomas and Znanieckic, 1927; Hansen, 1940a, 1940b; Handlin, 1959, 1973; Higham, 1955; Jones, 1960; Gans, 1962). Among historians, for whom the past never ceases to be and for whom immigration has always been one of the defining characteristics of American history, research on immigration has been more constant than among sociologists. As Maldwyn Allen Jones (1960) pointed out, "Most historians of immigration have been reluctant to consider its wider implications" (p. 326), yet the dominant influence was Frederick Jackson Turner's (1920) thesis of the significance of the frontier in American history. In essence, Turner argued that the frontier had exerted a transforming influence that had rendered European cultural values and institutions peculiarly American and that, in always presenting the opportunity for westward expansion, had served to preserve democracy and equality and to prevent the ossified social stratification that had been part of the European feudal past. Thus, in his analysis of American immigration. Marcus Lee Hansen (1940a, 1940b) underscored the intimate relationship between immigration and expansion, as without the influx of millions of Europeans there would not have been "the kind of frontier that produced the now accepted historical consequences" (p. 65). While serving to gain acknowledgment for the distinctive nature of American values and institutions, the frontier thesis also restricted the nature of historical research. As Robert Ostergren (1988) recently underscored, " Generations of historians grappled with and tried to reconcile themselves to the notion that the frontier was the crucible of American individualism and egalitarianism. That paradigm had no room for the notion of peasants reestablishing a communal past, rather than merging into an atomized or highly individualistic American society" (p. 19). Thus by the mid-twentieth century the dominant interpretation had become Oscar Handlin's (1973) notion of the uprooted peasant bewildered and alienated in the New World, unable to reestablish the past. Only recently have historians shifted the analytical focus from a view of immigrants as "the uprooted" to a view of them as "the transplanted" (e.g., Bodnar, 1985), thereby emphasizing the continuity of social forms from the premigration experience and highlighting the immigrants' attempts to recreate, within the new American context, the culture and institutions they had left behind (see Ostergren, 1988).

In sociology, the pattern of immigration research is more intermittent but quite clear. The leading influence was that of the Chicago school, whose work on immigration, ethnic, and urban studies laid the very foundations of American sociology. Despite varying emphases among the scholars who constituted the Chicago school of ethnic studies in the early part of the twentieth century overall, they shared the expectation that the outcome to the process of integrating those who arrived at America's shores would be a process of assimilation. Yet from the outset there was ambiguity in the idea. "It is not always clear," wrote Robert E. Park (1950d), "what assimilation means. Historically the word has had two distinct significations. According to earlier usage it meant 'to compare' or 'to make like'. According to later usage it signifies 'to take up and incorporate'" (p. 204). That ambiguity remained until Milton Gordon (1964) distinguished among types of assimilation. But the fundamental characteristic of assimilation theory was already evident: assimilation was expected to be a natural evolutionary process that would yield an inevitable outcome as time passed. To untangle the idea, Gordan first described the competing ideologies of assimilation that had taken root in American soil: Anglo-conformity, the melting pot, and cultural pluralism. Despite their differences, they all were more prescriptive of what immigrant assimilation should be rather than descriptive of what it actually was. To understand what the assimilation process was actually like, Gordon argued, it was crucial to distinguish between cultural behavior and social structure. Based on Park's awareness of the difference, Gordon set apart cultural and structural assimilation. Cultural assimilation entailed a process of acculturation on the part of the immigrants, of becoming "like" in cultural patterns, such as language, behavior, and values. Structural assimilation, as Gordon defined it, resulted only when the immigrants had been "taken up and incorporated" (p. 80). Specifically, structural assimilation entailed full integration of the immigrants and their descendants into the major institutions of the society (educational, occupational, political) and into the social cliques and clubs that led to intimate primary relationships, including intermarriage. This distinction aimed to provide a more exact conceptual tool to gauge the reality of the assimilation of immigrants and racial minorities in America. To this day, the distinction typifies the contrasting emphases of social science research on race and ethnic relations: that of ethnic identification (its absence or strength) and that of tangible outcomes (such as occupation, education, and income).

While the Chicago school failed in the early part of the century to clearly define its notion of assimilation (see Persons, 1987) and to distinguish among types of assimilation, it emphasized the "natural history" of ethnic relations, as best expressed in Park's race relations cycle. Park (1950b) conceived this cycle as stages of interaction through which immigrant or racial groups progressed irreversibly: contact, competition, and accommodation culminating in eventual assimilation. Because at the root of his thinking lay the ecological emphasis on race relations as spatial relations that defined the Chicago school of urban sociology. Park expected that the notion of assimilation and the stages of the race relations cycle could be extended to immigrants and racial minorities alike. From his point of view, both European immigrants and American blacks came from rural, peasant backgrounds and, upon migration to the urban ghetto, confronted a similar clash of cultures. Thus immigration and race and ethnic relations could both be viewed within the same frame of reference. Moreover, as Stow Persons (1987) underscored, the rural-urban axis of historical and cultural development was central to Chicago thinking, as it both epitomized the cultural or behavioral evolution that concerned the school and provided the perspective from which to approach the problems of urban sociology. This perspective was clearly apparent in another of the classics of the Chicago school: Thomas and Znaniecki's (1927) study of Polish immigrants.

Drawing from the work of Thomas, Park (1928) also was responsible for disseminating the theory of the "marginal man." Park stressed that marginal human beings—those who, as a result of migration, ended up by living simultaneously in two separate worlds—were not only marginal, never fully belonging to one world or the other, but also enormously creative and intelligent, as experiencing more than one social world had sharpened their vision and sensibilities. Again Park extended the concept of the marginal man from its origins in the notion of the human being caught between two cultures—the immigrant, the mixed-blood person (Eurasian, mestizo, or mulatto), the outcast and stranger (Jew)—to encompass the experience of American blacks, who shared the same national culture but lived at the margins of society in social, rather than cultural or ethnic, marginality. Thus, it was left to E. Franklin Frazier (1957a, 1957b), student of the Chicago school and black sociologist, to demarcate the difference between race relations and ethnic relations, when he underscored that American blacks had achieved cultural but not social assimilation. When Frazier applied Park's race relations cycle to the experience of American blacks, he emphasized the successive forms of economic subordination (slavery, the plantation society, Jim Crow laws) as well as the lack of final assimilation into American society, with the outcome of extensive cultural assimilation and complete social and institutional segregation. In his assessment of ethnic studies at Chicago, Persons (1987) noted that "Park had admitted that Americans had been able to assimilate all ethnic types except where color differences were involved, but without acknowledging that the admission undermined his theory. Frazier took the exception seriously, and in so doing restored in effect the distinction between ethnic relations and race relations" (p. 75). In the early part of the twentieth century, then, sociologists were concerned with what the experience of immigration had done to the immigrants' lives themselves, and with the outcomes to the process of integrating those who arrived at America's shores, outcomes that were usually conceptualized as acculturation and assimilation—becoming *like* the dominant population, which at the turn of the century clearly meant conforming to Anglo-Saxon ways (Gordon, 1964).

Research on immigrants and the eventual outcomes of the processes of immigration, therefore, was at the very foundations of American sociology. But that emphasis began to wane until, in the 1960s, it all but disappeared. Several different trends promoted its disappearance. First, the Immigration and Nationality Act of 1924 cut the massive waves of European immigration to the United States. Second, under the pressures of Anglo-conformity, the children of these European immigrants went on to assimilate in American society at a time when the price of success was often one's ethnicity and identity. *An Orphan in History* exemplifies this well as Paul Cowan (1982), whose real name was Saul Cohen, goes on a personal search for the Jewish past he lost as a result of his parents' great American success. Third, as Portes (1978a) stressed, the arrival of racial demands and militancy during the civil rights movement caused the analytical focus of research to shift to racial and ethnic relations. All-encompassing, these analytical perspectives arrived at general theories of race and ethnic relations. For example, in Donald Noel's (1968) theory, the competition of ethnocentric groups with differential power for the same scarce resources lay at the origin of ethnic inequality. Or, according to Edna Bonacich (1972), labor markets of higher- and lower-priced labor split along ethnic lines led to ethnic antagonism and efforts to control the lower-priced labor through exclusion or caste. Even more generally, R. A. Schermerhorn (1978) defined ethnic groups as all those who shared "a real or putative common ancestry" (p. 12). In the process, what is really distinctive about immigrants was lost. To be sure, they have their own ethnic identity and culture, but new immigrants form a distinct social category in two senses: at the micro level of the individual and at the macro level of the societies they exit and enter.

At the micro level, the immigrants' preparation for adult roles in society takes place in their country of origin, although they will live these roles (in whole or in part, depending on their age and circumstances) in the new society to which they have migrated. Furthermore, as Portes (1978a) maintained, immigrants, unlike ethnic minorities, "are decisively influenced not only by events in the United States but by experiences of a whole life in a different country. While the point was evident in classic studies of immigration, the tendency at present has been towards de facto fusion of new immigrants with native-born ethnic Americans" (p. 242). At the macro level, the state in two societies permits the immigrants to exit and enter. As gatekeeper, the state regulates and directs migration through a body of law. Those laws can establish quotas for different countries or areas (for example, the Western Hemisphere quota) and preference criteria for categories of persons (for example, occupational restrictions or family reunification preferences), depending on national purposes.

From the theoretical vantage point of studies of immigrant assimilation or integration, immigrants are also distinct in that they bring a whole host of social resources with them (their social class, education, occupation, culture, values) from another society, and their outcomes in American society will be a function partly of those initial resources, partly of the nature of their migration (as political or economic immigrants, victims of genocide, settlers, or sojourners), and partly of the social context that greets them, of the amount of opportunity available to them in the new society (in jobs, in the particular cities and industries where they become concentrated, in the nature of the discrimination or exclusion they face afterwards). Indeed, the major questions in immigration research can be summarized briefly as follows: What leads people to make the decision to move—what "push" and "pull" factors impel them to displace and uproot themselves (see Lee, 1966)? What is the nature of the crossing—not only the literal crossing but the more abstract crossing of government policy, the policies of two governments that can, in societies that have developed long histories of emigration and immigration, result in their developing systems of economic and political migration (see Pedraza-Bailey, 1985)? What can they attain afterwards? How do we best describe that process—as assimilation, adaptation, integration, incorporation (see Gordon, 1964; Portes, 1981)? Is that process invariant over time across immigrant or racial and ethnic groups (as theorists of assimilation expected it to be), or do we need to describe it in essentially different ways for different immigrant or racial and ethnic groups (as theorists of internal colonialism stressed)?

After this brief historiography of immigration research, let us now turn to the east-west coordinates of our conceptual map, coordinates which can be said to be constituted by the changing nature of migration and of American society itself. The most commonplace statement is also the truest: With the exception of the Native American, every American is an immigrant. As Muller and Espenshade (1985) pointed out, immigration to American can be broadly understood as consisting of four major waves: that of northwestern Europeans who immigrated up to the mid-nineteenth century; that of southern and eastern Europeans at the end of the nineteenth and beginning of the twentieth centuries; that of black Americans, Mexicans, and Puerto Ricans from the South to the North, precipitated by two world wars; and that of immigrants mostly from Latin America and Asia from 1965 on (see D. M. Reimers, 1983, 1985). Not only has each wave been characterized by a different racial or ethnic composition, but profound changes in the very nature of American society have been taking place over this time span. The immigrants of the first wave came to a essentially colonial, agrarian society; the immigrants of the second and third waves, to an urban society where they provided the cheap labor essential to industrialization and expansion in America; the immigrants of the fourth wave are coming to an increasingly postindustrial, service-oriented society.

If we superimpose the major theoretical questions in immigration research onto these four waves of American immigration and take into account the changes in the very foundation of American society that have simultaneously been taking place, we will then want to ask a number of key comparative questions: Have the descendants of the southern and eastern Europeans "caught up" to the level of achievement of the northwestern Europeans (see Greeley, 1982, Chiswick, 1985)? Is the experience of the racial and ethnic minorities different, as Thurgood Marshall (1978) argued, not only in degree but also in kind from that of the southern and eastern Europeans (see Lieberson, 1980)? And can those who are now the "new immigrants" (Latin Americans and Asians who have immigrated since 1965) hope to duplicate the experience of those who once upon a time were called the "new immigrants" (the southern and eastern Europeans)? Or has the society itself essentially and fundamentally changed, in the process of its transformation from an industrial to a postindustrial economy, in the amount of opportunity it now provides?

In sociology, the major challenge to assimilation theory came from the proponents of the internal colonialism model, the theoretical effort to delineate the ways in which the experiences of the racial minorities (blacks, Puerto Ricans, Mexicans, Native Americans—some of America's oldest immigrants and its indigenous sons and daughters) differed significantly from the experiences and eventual assimilation of he white European immigrants at the turn of the century. The internal colonialism model underscored that the experience of the former groups differed in that they had suffered a process of internal colonization due to the place and role in the system of production that they came to occupy because of their color and race (Blauner, 1969; Barrera, 1979). An important corrective to the assimilation model, the internal colonialism model itself suffered from stretching the colonial analogy too far, not recognizing the essential differences between the domestic situation of race relations in the United States and what happened in Africa and Asia. The shortcomings of both the assimilation and the internal colonialism models can be transcended by focusing on the varying ways in which different ethnic groups were *incorporated* into the society. As Joe Feagin (1978) argued, race and ethnic theorizing needs to develop a more comprehensive incorporation theory that takes into account that "in the process of incorporation there has been considerable variation in group access to social resources and rewards," by paying attention to "the initial and continuing placement and access of various groups" (p.47) within the economic, political, and educational institutions of the society.

As a result of the fourth wave of American immigration, which we are still living through, sociology has refocused its research on immigrants as a social category distinct from racial and ethnic minorities and on immigration as an international process that reshuffles persons and cultures across nations, until we now find ourselves amidst a veritable explosion of immigration research conducted by sociologists (who attend most to contemporary flows in the developed nations), anthropologists (who attend most to flows in the underdeveloped nations), and historians (who attend to past flows). In all cases there is a fair amount of searching for one's "roots" (e.g., Cinel, 1982; Gabaccia, 1983; Sancher-Korrol, 1983; Morawska, 1985; Pedraza-Bailey, 1985; Portes and Bach, 1985; Bukowczyk, 1987; Kamphoefner, 1987).

While the east-west of immigration research is the time line of the four major waves of immigration and the changes that have taken place in the economic foundation over the course of American history, the north-south can be said to be constituted by the different levels of analysis. What is often referred to as the traditional approach focused on individual-level variables; the newer approach focused on structural-level variables. The difference is, of course, the one between micro and macro levels of analysis.

In sociology, the traditional, individual, micro approach was best developed by Everett S. Lee (1966). His theory focused on the individual migrant's reasons for migration, the factors that "hold and attract or repel people" (p. 50). Unlike many economists, Lee went beyond a simple cost-benefit calculus of perceived advantages and disadvantages at the origin and destination. He stressed both the role of intervening obstacles that prove more of an impediment to some individuals than to others—such as distance, physical barriers, immigration laws, and cost—and the influence of personal traits, such as stage in the life cycle, information, contact with earlier migrants, personality, and the effect of such transitions as marriage or retirement. Still, the decision to migrate was the focus of this theory, although, as Lee said, "not all persons who migrate reach that decision themselves. Children are carried along by their parents, willy-nilly, and wives accompany their husbands though it tears them away from environments they love" (p. 51). Subsequent studies concentrated on the individual characteristics of the migrants.

In history, the traditional approach concentrated not only on the nature of the personal or familial decision to migrate but, particularly, on the impact that the experience of immigration had on the lives of the immigrants themselves. It has already become a commonplace that the classic of a generation ago, Oscar Handlin's (1973) *The Uprooted,* has now been replaced by John Bodnar's (1985) *The Transplanted,* already the classic of our times (see Gabaccia 1988b). Both studies moved away from the predominant approach of a case study of an ethnic group to a synthesis of the European immigrant experience. Both studies focused on the impact of immigration on the lives of the immigrants themselves. As his title suggests, Handlin underscored the profound clash of cultures that left the immigrants uprooted, bewildered, and in pain, having left the best of themselves and their lives forever behind them. Thus, Handlin (1973) caught the sadness, despair, and nostalgia of everyone who has ever been uprooted:

> Yesterday, by its distance, acquires a happy glow. The peasants look back . . . and their fancy rejoices in the better days that have passed, when they were on the land and the land was fertile, and they were young and strong, and virtues were fresh. And it was better yet in their fathers' days, who were wiser and stronger than they. And it was best of all in the golden past of their distant progenitors who were every one a king and did great deeds. Alas, those days are gone, that they believed existed, and now there is only the bitter present. (p. 97)

In Bodnar's eyes, the immigrants were in less pain; as his title indicates, he saw them and painted them as more resilient. The immigrant struggle, he emphasized, was shaped by capitalism, in the form of the arrival first of commercial agriculture in the Old World and then of industrial capitalism and urbanization in the New World. Transplanted by forces beyond their control, the immigrants were indeed the children of capitalism. But they in turn sought to gain some measure of control over their lives by effectively using the institutions they brought with them, particularly the core institution of "the family-houshold," and by developing new institutions—unions, churches, and schools that responded to their needs as members of a class (working class or middle class) and as ethnics (Germans, Italians, Poles, Jews).

The most recent approach to the study of immigration focused on structural-level variables. As the link between migration and world patterns of unequal development became increasingly evident, not only in North America—the magnet that today as yesterday continues to attract the world's poor—but also in Western Europe—where the periphery countries of Spain, Italy, Greece, and Turkey became suppliers of labor to the industrialized core countries of France, Germany, and Switzerland—a new set of structural, macro perspectives emerged. This type of immigration theory stressed the increased significance of immigrant workers in developed capitalist societies. To counteract the traditional perspective that focused on the migrants' reasons for migrating and its personal consequences, a structural perspective developed. In essence, this perspective argued that a system of economic migration had arisen from the flow of labor between developed and underdeveloped nations. The essential question now became, what functions did the system of labor migration perform for both the developed and the underdeveloped nations? Arguing independently but in a similar vein, Manuel Castells (1975), Michael Burawoy (1976), and Alejandro Portes (1978b) reformulated the problem by examining the structural sources and social and economic implications of labor migration. In a nutshell, they agreed that migrant labor—as immigrant and as labor—had structural causes and that it performed important functions for the developed capitalist nation that received it. Defining migrant labor institutionally, Burawoy stressed that migrant labor is a system that separates the functions of renewal and maintenance of the labor force, physically and institutionally, so that only the function of renewal takes place in the less developed society (such as Mexico or Turkey), while only the function of maintenance takes place in the developed world (such as the United States or France). Both Castells and Portes defined migrant labor as cheap labor, whose function in capitalism is to maintain the rate of profit. As a Marxist, Castells judged that migrant labor serves to counteract the tendency of the rate of profit to fall under capitalism. Not a Marxist, Portes saw migrant labor as less necessary to capitalism but more vital to small and medium-sized enterprises for whom alternatives (such as the overseas relocation of multinationals) do not exist. While replacement labor provided countries such as the United States and France with a dependable source of cheap labor, it also provided countries such as Mexico and Turkey with a "safety valve" as emigration became the solution to their inability to satisfy the needs of the poor and lower-middle classes.

Extending this approach, Pedraza-Bailey (1985) sought to explain refugee flows by adding that just as it was possible for the economic functions played by emigration and immigration to generate a system of labor migration between sending and receiving countries, it was possible for the political functions played by emigration and immigration to generate a system of political migration between sending and receiving societies, such as Cuba and the United States. In the Cuban case, she argued that while the loss of such large numbers of the professional and skilled classes proved erosive to the Cuban revolution, the exodus also performed an important political function: it lessened the capacity of those politically disaffected by the revolution to undermine it. In effect, the Cuban government controlled dissent by externalizing it. As a result, the revolution grew stronger. At the same time, in America, all the political migrations that took place during the peak years of the cold war—those of the Hungarians, Berliners, and Cubans—served an important symbolic function. In the historical period of the cold war, West and East contested the superiority of their political and economic systems. Political immigrants who succeeded in their flight to freedom became touching symbols around which to weave the legitimacy of foreign policy.

Despite their differences, explicit or implicit, the structuralists essentially argued that the notion of assimilation ought to be replaced by that of incorporation, embracing the varying ways in which immigrants or ethnic groups have become a part of American society. The concept of assimilation assumed that, irrespective of the initial placement of an ethnic group within the larger social structure, all immigrant and racial or ethnic groups would, in a natural and evolutionary way, become like the dominant group, adopting the core culture and eventually arriving at institutional party in income, education, occupation, and political participation, as well as in intimate primary relations, social life, and marriage. The concept of incorporation does not assume eventual parity but seeks to explain the persistent inequality of certain immigrant and racial or ethnic groups over time as a function of their initial and continuing placement within the larger social structure, which has left them with a continuing differential access to the economic, political, and educational institutions of their society.

After the boundaries drawn by the north-south and east-west of immigration research at present, let us now turn to a few of the blue highways, the secondary roads that take us away from the rapid main highways and that, if we have the time to follow them, can provide us with more interesting and beautiful pathways. Again, we will attempt not to draw all possible blue highways on the map but to point to a few as illustrative of topics in immigration research that have now taken on a life of their own. Cutting across the blue highways lie various unpaved roads, those areas where we have still done too little research. Overall, the types of research we need to do in immigration studies ought to be guided by the following criteria.

Regarding the relative integration of the new immigrants into American society, we need to consider the immigrants' patterns of labor market incorporation (e.g., in industrial labor, farming, the garment industry, or small business) and their attendant social mobility; the immigrants as social types (e.g., refugees versus economic immigrants, "brain drain" migrants versus unskilled migrants, women versus men, black immigrants as both racial minorities and ethnics) and its consequences for their social incorporation and mobility; and the immigrants' patterns of political participation (e.g., in social movements, political machines, or ethnic coalitions). Regarding the impact of emigration on sending societies, we need to consider the economic impact of emigration on sending villages and regions as well as on the households and family units of those who have left; the emigrants as social types (again, as refugees versus economic immigrants, "brain drain" versus unskilled migration) created by economic and political conditions at home; and the political impact of long-standing emigration when it has served either as a safety valve for economically produced discontent or to externalize the dissent produced by political conditions. Moreover, while focusing on either immigration or emigration, it remains important also to consider the total process of migration at both levels of analysis: as a totality at the structural, macro level of the functions those systems of migration performed for each of the societies involved, and at the micro level of individual agents whose decisions to migrate set in motion transcontinental chain migrations of kin and friends that ultimately transformed the very societies whose structures shaped those decisions. In all cases, the criteria are those which Max Weber (1978) pointed to so long ago regarding the dimensions of social stratification as class, status, and party.

To illustrate the immigrants' patterns of labor market incorporation, one blue highway is the research literature that has grown around the question of why immigrants (and not the native-born) become concentrated in petit-bourgeois small business enterprises, and what the source of the disparity between the foreign-born and the native-born, as well as among foreign-born groups themselves, is (Light, 1972, 1979, 1984; Bonacich, 1973; Bonacich and Modell, 1980). Intuitively, we all know that the epitome of ethnic enterprise is the Jew, throughout Europe for centuries and afterward in the immigrant generation in the United States and Latin America. Precisely because at other times and other places other immigrant groups have occupied a similar place in the social structure, the people among whom they lived often recognized the parallel. Thus the Chinese in Southeast Asia were often called "the Jews of the East," Asians in East Africa "the Jews of Africa," and, most recently, Cubans "the Jews of the Caribbean." The central question in research on ethnic enterprise is why some groups are overrepresented in this type of enterprise (among first-generation Koreans and Jewish immigrants the rates were as high as a third to a half), while other groups (black Americans, Mexicans, Filipinos) have consistently shown such minimal representation. Most explanations for the over- or under-representation of different ethnic groups in small business enterprises stress either the differential resources immigrants brought with them or the social context that greeted them (see Waldinger et al., 1985). More than anyone else, Light (1979, 1984) underscored the immigrant nature of ethnic enterprise. In essence, Light pointed out that the experience of immigration produces a reactive solidarity among immigrants, that is, one that did not exist prior to migration, which becomes an ethnic resource that helps foster small business development. Light (1984) suggested that there are really three separate labor forces, white, immigrant, and native minority, with the proportion of self-employment significantly higher in the immigrant labor force than in the white or native minority labor force. Aldrich et al. (1984) have also proposed that immigrants develop ethnic enterprises as a response to the "occupational closure" they face in the new labor market. Historically, ethnic enterprises were often a refuge for groups that, due to discrimination or other reasons, faced occupational closure, because immigrants draw on the resource of cheap family and ethnic labor. Unpaid family labor, donated by women (wives, mothers, aunts, daughters), is what allows immigrants to amass profits, save them, and reinvest them in their businesses, which continue to live and grow.

To illustrate the need to look at immigrants as a social type, yet another blue highway lies in the topic of women and migration, the social consequences of gender. On this topic, the historians, whose intent has been to write the unwritten history of women, as Louise Tilly (1988) stressed, and the anthropologists, whose concern with kinship is at the very root of their discipline, have both done a great deal more than the sociologists, among whom research on the topic is just beginning. Because most studies have addressed labor migration, the implicit assumption has been that of the male pauper model. Studying women is important not only because there are female paupers equally impelled to move and work, but also because we need to see in what ways, if any, the causes and consequences of migration differ between women and men. For example, Donna Gabaccia's (1988a) study of the regional variation in Italy regarding patterns of emigration showed that, in large part, large-scale emigration was a response to a decline in household production. Among the questions pertinent here is how gender is related to the types of jobs immigrant women can obtain. For example, among yesterday's immigrants as well as today's, women became incorporated in the garment industry because, first, it depended on a traditional skill that defined womanhood throughout much of the world, and, second, because it depended on home work and subcontracting, which allowed women to stay at home to care for their children (and also led them to accept low wages and abysmal, exploitative conditions [Waldinger, 1986]). Yet another question concerns the causes and consequences of a migration flow that was predominantly male (as the Italian one was) or female (as the Irish one was). Thomas Kessner (1977) argued that a predominantly male migration seemed to result in temporary settlement, large amounts of remittances sent back home, and a large amount of return migration. By contrast, Hasia Diner's (1983) study of Irish immigrant women argued the consequences of a predominantly female flow. Changes in landholding and inheritance patterns in Ireland led to the predominantly female nature of the migration. As the immigrants had no family obligations, they were able to concentrate in domestic service, particularly as live-in help, and to accumulate savings at an impressive rate. These savings went to bring over other relatives, especially other women; to pay for the lands mortgaged back home; to support their favorite devotions in the Catholic church; to provide a nest egg for marriage; and to finance their own upward mobility into nursing or stenography, allowing them to eschew marriage to a poor Irishman altogether. In the final analysis, this implied a more thorough and enthusiastic "Americanization." This leads to the question of how the experience of migration compares for a woman and a man. Nancy Foner's (1978) study of Jamaican women in London, for example, noted that, difficult as the experience of immigration was for everyone, it was often far more positive for women than for men, as it allowed women to break with traditional roles and patterns of dependence and assert a new-found (if meager) freedom. Other studies, however, have argued that immigrant women took on the burden of working outside the home as an extension of the traditional woman's role. While her place was no longer in the home, it was still by her husband's and children's welfare, implying no necessary change in values and family roles (Ferree 1979).

To illustrate the impact of emigration on sending communities, another blue highway takes us to the village level. Among the questions it covers are: What is the impact of remittances—do they become channeled into consumption alone, or are they productively invested (Cinel, 1982)? Are those who leave sojourners who will soon return or settlers, forever lost to the life of the village? This distinction has consequences not only for the immigrants themselves, insofar as they make different types of investments in jobs or personal relationships (see Kessner, 1977), but also for the communities that they leave behind, affecting family structure and family roles. For example, the anthropologist Caroline Brettell (1987), in *Men Who Migrate, Women Who Wait,* pointed out that the emigration of men from Portuguese villages to Brazil was so massive and went on for so long that it produced a new type of family structure, as three generations of women would come together to form new households and new families. Indeed, she noted that when the women of the village she was studying saw her living alone, they quickly invited her to join one of their matriarchal families. In their study of several Mexican villages with histories of substantial emigration to the United States, Douglas Massey et al. (1987) noted that the impact of migration on sending communities depends on when it takes place in the life cycle of the family (in the beginning years of family building and child raising, all must go to consumption, while later on in the family life cycle, savings can be productively invested) as well as when it takes place in the life cycle of a community with or without a history of emigration. As a result of his study of a community with a long history of migration (Aguililla, Mexico) to a particular city in the United States (Redwood City, California), Roger Rouse (1988) argued that the process is so long-standing, communication among people at both ends so interwined, and the flows of capital and labor so regular that the very image of a community from which people depart or go to is compromised. Instead, Rouse (1988) proposed that we reconceptualize it as a "transnational migrant circuit" (p. 9).

James Watson's (1975) study of San Tin, a single-lineage village in rural Hong Kong where all males are directly descended from the same founding ancestor and bear the surname Man, showed the links between the emigration of peasants and the Chinese lineage. Traditionally, the lineage functioned to protect villagers from bandits and hostile neighbors and was held together by the economic bonds of shared property in the ancestral estates. During the 1950s and 1960s, the collapse of the agricultural economy "pushed" the peasants at the same time that a nucleus of fellow lineage members who had already become established abroad "pulled" them, turning the village into an emigrant community. The resources of the lineage, material and nonmaterial, were mobilized to facilitate the emigration to Great Britain. Once in London, during the boom of the restaurant industry, the lineage also served to provide the capital, labor, and expertise with which to render Chinese restaurants profitable. Also though the lineage, a portion of the emigrants' wages were remitted back to the village, improving the lives of families back home and contributing to village public works and celebrations. Thus the lineage functioned as one of the "auspices of migration," as Charles Tilly and C.H. Brown (1967) called them: "the social structures which establish relationships between the migrant and the receiving community before he moves" (p. 142). Watson underscores that emigration had such a profound impact on the life of the village that, first, San Tin went from a center of production to a community of consumption and, second, it modified some of the central features of its traditional culture, such as marriage. The system of arranged marriages changed to a more modern one that relied on an unusual combination of traditional (intermediation) and modern (courtship) practices. Emigration, despite the modernizing changes that took place in the emigrants' lives and in the village, ultimately reinforced the traditional institution of the Chinese lineage by becoming intertwined with it.

Let us now turn to those areas where social scientists have done too little, the unpaved roads of immigration research. To illustrate the need to look at immigrants as social types, an unpaved road lies ahead in the need to do more studies of brain drain—the immigration of educated, middle-class professionals (doctors, scientists, accountants, nurses) from third world countries to the first world. Brain drain is an increasingly large component of the wave of migration that we are presently living through: it defines most of the Asian immigration and a large part of the Latin American immigration. Yet with the exception of accounting studies (so many moved from here to there, in the style of the H.O.), virtually the only theoretical work done on this topic is Portes and Ross's (1976) study "Modernization for Emigration: The Medical Brain Drain from Argentina." We also need to consider the various patterns of incorporation of refugees and economic immigrants and of different types of refugees. Zolberg et al. (1989) propose that, among refugees, we distinguish activists, targets, and victims (see also Rumbaut, 1982). It is ironic that there is so little research on the refugee as a social type when modern migration flows are increasingly composed of refugees. And we also need to consider the various patterns of incorporation of back immigrants—Jamaicans, Haitians, black Cubans, who are simultaneously ethnics and immigrants of color—to a society where color has always been a principle of exclusion, while they themselves feel an identity, like all immigrants, with the countries they left behind (Dixon, 1988; Halter, 1988). More studies of black immigrants would also serve to collapse the division that has now grown between studies of racial minorities and studies of immigrants.

Still other unpaved roads lie in our need to do more comparative studies that move beyond the confines of documenting case studies without arriving at syntheses of all migrations of certain type. That is to say, we need more studies that compare a small number of immigrant experiences in depth along a couple of key variables—what Robert Merton (1968) called "theories of the middle range." For example, we could fruitfully study the different patterns of labor market incorporation and social mobility among Jewish and Italian immigrants in New York City at the turn of the century (amplifying Kessner, 1977) or among blacks and Hispanics in Chicago in the 1980s; further, we could study old immigrants and new immigrants by contrasting the patterns of social and economic incorporation among immigrants to an industrial society at the turn of the century with those among contemporary immigrants to an increasingly postindustrial, service society. It would also be illuminating to study the different patterns of political participation exhibited by the Irish and Germans at the beginning of the twentieth century, as Walter Kamphoefner is doing, or those exhibited by blacks and Latinos at the end of the twentieth century, not to mention the role of political machines in immigrant political incorporation then and now.

A very rough unpaved road lies in our need to do studies that link the micro and macro levels of analysis more tightly. The recent macro approach was an important corrective to the traditional micro approach, which failed to take into account that since the advent of the industrial revolution, all individual decisions to move have accumulated into migration flows that move in only one direction. The danger of the structural emphasis, however, lied in its tendency to obliterate people, to lose sight of the individual migrants who do make decisions. The theoretical and empirical challenge now facing immigration research is to capture individuals as agents and social structure as both delimiting and enabling (see Sewell, 1989). We need to consider the plight of individuals, their propensity to move, and the nature of the decisions they make. We also need to consider the larger social structures within which that plight exists and those decisions are made. As Massey et al. (1987) underscored in their analysis of Mexican migration to the United States, international migration originates historically in transformations of social and economic structures in sending and receiving societies, but once begun, migrants' social networks grow and develop, supporting and channeling migration on a continuously widening scale. Thus, the migration that was initially propelled by an external, structural dy-namic and logic increasingly acquires an internal dynamic and logic of its own. "In this sense, migration comes to fuel itself" (p.252), particularly as families make it part of their survival strategies and use if during stages of the life cycle when family dependence is greatest. Thus individual motivations, household strategies, and community structures are altered by migration, making further migration more likely. As Tilly (1986) underscored, by and large, the effective units of migration are "neither individuals nor households but sets of people linked by acquaintance, kinship, and work experience who somehow incorporated American destinations into the mobility alternatives they considered when they reached critical decision-points in their individual or collective lives (p.3)."

Despite their disagreements, both Coleman (1986) and Sewell (1987) agree that for sociology to develop a theory of action, it needs to take into account the problem or moving from individual to macro social levels. However, only Sewell emphasizes that the crucial theoretical problem to be solved is Janus-headed: to determine not only how individual actions combine to produce (usually unanticipated) social consequences (micro to macro relations)—the problematic that "rational choice" theorists such as Coleman focus on—but also how individuals' values and orientations are historically and culturally produced by the manifold structural relations in which they are embedded (macro to micro relations).

As we have seen, the questions immigration research poses lie at the very roots of social science. The topic is as rich and as vast as our history and our present, in this as well as in myriad other multiracial and multiethnic nations. While much has already been done, much remains to be done in immigration research. It is hoped that this conceptual map will help to chart the course of that research.

IMMIGRATION, ETHNICITY, AND ETHNIC RELATIONS

The six readings in Part II examine changes in the economy and immigration and their effect on the new structures of ethnicity in the United States. This part begins with a classic essay by Max Weber titled "Ethnic Groups." In this short essay, Weber discusses how subjective and objective aspects of race and ethnicity can function as sources of attraction and repulsion among ethnic groups. Weber believes that ethnic identity and ethnic membership can facilitate the formation of political groups. What strengthens ethnic identity, however, is a common language through which political memories and memories of migration are perpetuated.

"The New Immigration and Ethnicity in the United States," by Douglas S. Massey, follows Weber's analysis. Massey argues that the new immigrants differ from the European immigrants in several crucial respects. These differences significantly reduce their prospects for assimilation.

The third reading, "Immigration and Ethnic and Racial Inequality in the United States" by Mary C. Waters and Karl Eschobach, examines the impact of economic restructuring, racial discrimination, and immigration on the current patterns of racial inequality in the United States.

Robert L. Bach's "Immigration: Issues of Ethnicity, Class, and Public Policy in the United States" argues that given the historical similarities among socioeconomic experiences of the working class, African Americans, women, and immigrants as members of a secondary labor market in America, the incorporation of immigrants can best be understood in the context of recent theoretical debates over the changing character of racial and gender inequality.

The fifth article in this section, Michael J. Piore's "The Shifting Grounds for Immigration," discusses the new developments in the migration process. The author calls for the modification of the notion of "circular migration" based on the job opportunities in developed nations, in light of such new developments as ethnic enclave economies and immigrant entrepreneurship.

Part II closes with Jeffrey S. Passel and Michael Fix's illuminating essay, "Myths About Immigrants," in which they lay bare the misconceptions, misperceptions, and misunderstandings about immigration and adaptation of immigrants entering the United States. The authors distinguish among refugees, legal immigrants, and illegal immigrants. Each group is governed by a unique set of rules, immigrates through distinct social and bureaucratic networks, is motivated by separate goals, and has idiosyncratic demographic characteristics.

Ethnic Groups

✦ Max Weber

"Race" Membership[1]

A problematic source of social action is "race identity": common inherited and inheritable traits that actually derive from common descent. Of course, race creates a "group" only when it is subjectively perceived as a common trait: this happens only when a neighborhood or the mere proximity of racially different persons is the basis of joint (mostly political) action, or conversely, when some common experiences of members of the same race are linked to some antagonism against members of an *obviously* different group. The resulting social action is usually merely negative: those who are obviously different are avoided and despised or, conversely, viewed with superstitious awe. Persons who are externally different are simply despised irrespective of what they accomplish or what they are, or they are venerated superstitiously if they are too powerful in the long run. In this case antipathy is the primary and normal reaction. However; this antipathy is shared not just by persons with anthropological similarities, and its extent is by no means determined by the degree of anthropological relatedness; furthermore, this antipathy is linked not only to inherited traits but just as much to other visible differences.

If the degree of objective racial difference can be determined, among other things, purely physiologically by establishing whether hybrids reproduce themselves at approximately normal rates, the subjective aspects, the reciprocal racial attraction and repulsion, might be measured by finding out whether sexual relations are preferred or rare between two groups, and whether they are carried on permanently or temporarily and irregularly. In all groups with a developed "ethnic" consciousness the existence or absence of intermarriage (*connubium*) would then be a normal consequence of racial attraction or segregation. Serious research on the sexual attraction and repulsion between different ethnic groups is only incipient, but there is not the slightest doubt that racial

Weber, Max. 1978. "Ethnic groups" in: *Economy and Society,* Volume I, pp. 385–398, University of California Press: Los Angeles. Reprinted with permission of University of California Press.

factors, that means, common descent, influence the incidence of sexual relations and of marriage, sometimes decisively. However, the existence of several million mulattoes in the United States speaks clearly against the assumption of a "natural" racial antipathy, even among quite different races. Apart from the laws against biracial marriages in the Southern states, sexual relations between the two races are now abhorred by both sides, but this development began only with the Emancipation and resulted from the Negroes' demand for equal civil rights. Hence this abhorrence on the part of the whites is socially determined by the previously sketched tendency toward the monopolization of social power and honor, a tendency which in this case happens to be linked to race.

The *connubium* itself, that means, the fact that the offspring from a permanent sexual relationship can share in the activities and advantages of the father's political, economic or status group, depends on many circumstances. Under undiminished patriarchal powers, the father was free to grant equal rights to his children from slaves. Moreover, the glorification of abduction by the hero made racial mixing a normal event within the ruling strata. However, patriarchal discretion was progressively curtailed with the monopolistic closure, by now familiar to us, of political, status, or other groups and with the monopolization of marriage opportunities; these tendencies restricted the *connubium* to the offspring from a permanent sexual union within the given political, religious, economic and status group. This also produced a high incidence of inbreeding. The "endogamy" of a group is probably everywhere a secondary product of such tendencies, if we define it not merely as the fact that a permanent sexual union occurs primarily on the basis of joint membership in some association, but as a process of social action in which only endogamous children are accepted as full members. (The term "sib endogamy" should not be used; there is no such thing unless we want to refer to the levirate marriage and arrangements in which daughters have the right to succession, but these have secondary, religious, and political origins.) "Pure" anthropological types are often a secondary consequence of such closure; examples are sects (as in India) as well as pariah peoples, that means groups that are socially despised yet wanted as neighbors because they have monopolized indispensable skills.

Reasons other than actual racial kinship influence the degree to which blood relationship is taken into account. In the United States the smallest admixture of Negro blood disqualifies a person unconditionally, whereas very considerable admixtures of Indian blood do not. Doubtless, it is important that Negroes appear esthetically even more alien than Indians, but it remains very significant that Negroes were slaves and hence disqualified in the status hierarchy. The conventional *connubium* is far less impeded by anthropological differences than by status differences, that means differences due to socialization and upbringing (*Bildung* in the widest sense of the word). Mere anthropological differences account for little, except in cases of extreme esthetic antipathy.

The Belief in Common Ethnicity: Its Multiple Social Origins and Theoretical Ambiguities

The question of whether conspicuous "racial" differences are based on biological heredity or on tradition is usually of no importance as far as their effect on mutual attraction or repulsion is concerned. This is true of the development of endogamous conjugal groups, and even more so of attraction and repulsion in other kinds of social intercourse, i.e., whether all sorts of friendly, companionable, or economic relationships between such groups are established easily and on the footing of mutual trust and respect, or whether such relationships are established with difficulty and with precautions that betray mistrust.

The more or less easy emergence of social circles in the broadest sense of the word (*soziale Verkehrsgemeinschaft*) may be linked to the most superficial features of historically accidental habits just as much as to inherited racial characteristics. That the different custom is not understood in its subjective meaning since the cultural key to it is lacking, is almost as decisive as the peculiarity of the custom as such. But, as we shall soon see, not all repulsion is attributable to the absence of a "consensual group." Differences in the styles of beard and hairdo, clothes, food and eating habits, division of labor between the sexes, and all kinds of other visible differences can, in a given case, give rise to repulsion and contempt, but the actual extent of these differences is irrelevant for the emotional impact, as is illustrated by primitive travel descriptions, the Histories of Herodotus or the older prescientific ethnography. Seen from their positive aspect, however, these differences may give rise to consciousness of kind, which may become as easily the bearer of group relationships as groups ranging from the household and neighborhood to political and religious communities are usually the bearers of shared customs. All differences of customs can sustain a specific sense of honor or dignity in their practitioners. The original motives or reasons for the inception of different habits of life are forgotten and the contrasts are then perpetuated as conventions. In this manner, any group can create customs, and it can also effect, in certain circumstances very decisively, the selection of anthropological types. This it can do by providing favorable chances of survival and reproduction for certain hereditary qualities and traits. This holds both for internal assimilation and for external differentiation.

Any cultural trait, no matter how superficial, can serve as a starting point for the familiar tendency to monopolistic closure. However, the universal force of imitation has the general effect of only gradually changing the traditional customs and usages, just as anthropological types are changed only gradually by racial mixing. But if there are sharp boundaries between areas of observable styles of life, they are due to conscious monopolistic closure, which started from small differences that were then cultivated and intensified; or they are due to the peaceful or warlike migrations of groups that previously lived far from each other and had accommodated themselves to their heterogeneous conditions of existence. Similarly, strikingly different racial types, bred in isolation, may live in sharply segregated proximity to one another either because of monopolistic closure or because of migration. We can conclude then that similarity and contrast of physical type and custom, regardless of whether they are biologically inherited or culturally transmitted, are subject to the same conditions of group life, in origin as well as in effectiveness, and identical in their potential for group formation. The difference lies partly in the differential instability of type and custom, partly in the fixed (though often unknown) limit to engendering new hereditary qualities. Compared with this, the scope for assimilation of new customs is incomparably greater, although there are considerable variations in the transmissibility of traditions.

Almost any kind of similarity or contrast of physical type and of habits can induce the belief that affinity or disaffinity exists between groups that attract or repel each other. Not every belief in tribal affinity, however, is founded on the resemblance of customs or of physical type. But in spite of great variations in this area, such a belief can exist and can develop group-forming powers when it is buttressed by a memory of an actual migration, be it colonization or individual migration. The persistent effect of the old ways and of childhood reminiscences continues as a source of native-country sentiment (*Heimatsgefühl*) among emigrants even when they have become so thoroughly adjusted to the new country that return to their homeland would be intolerable (this being the case of most German-Americans, for example).

In colonies, the attachment to the colonists' homeland survives despite considerable mixing with the inhabitants of the colonial land and despite profound changes in tradition and hereditary type as well. In case of political colonization, the decisive factor is the need for political support. In general, the continuation of relationships created by marriage is important, and so are the market relationships, provided that the "customs" remained unchanged. These market relationships between the homeland and the colony may be very close, as long as the consumer standards remain similar, and especially when colonies are in an almost absolutely alien environment and within an alien political territory.

The belief in group affinity, regardless of whether it has any objective foundation, can have important consequences especially for the formation of a political community. We shall call "ethnic groups" those human groups that entertain a subjective belief in their common descent because of similarities of physical type or of customs or both, or because of memories of colonization and migration; this belief must be important for the propagation of group formation; conversely, it does not matter whether or not an objective blood relationship exists. Ethnic membership (*Gemeinsamkeit*) differs from the kinship group precisely by being a presumed identity, not a group with concrete social action, like the latter. In our sense, ethnic membership does not constitute a group; it only facilitates group formation of any kind, particularly in the political sphere. On the other hand, it is primarily the political community, no matter how artificially organized, that inspires the belief in common ethnicity. This belief tends to persist even after the disintegration of the political community, unless drastic differences in the custom, physical type, or, above all, language exist among its members.

This artificial origin of the belief in common ethnicity follows the pattern of rational association turning into personal relationships. If rationally regulated action is not widespread, almost any association, even the most rational one, creates an overarching communal consciousness; this takes the form of a brotherhood on the basis of the belief in common ethnicity. As late as the Greek city state, even the most arbitrary division of the *polis* became for the member an association with at least a common cult and often a common fictitious ancestor. The twelve tribes of Israel were subdivisions of a political community, and they alternated in performing certain functions on a monthly basis. The same holds for the Greek tribes (*phylai*) and their subdivisions; the latter, too, were regarded as units of common ethnic descent. It is true that the original division may have been induced by political or actual ethnic differences, but the effect was the same when such a division was made quite rationally and schematically, after the break-up of old groups and relinquishment of local cohesion, as it was done by Cleisthenes. It does not follow, therefore, that the Greek *polis* was actually or originally a tribal or lineage state, but that ethnic fictions were a sign of the rather low degree of rationalization of Greek political life. Conversely, it is a symptom of the greater rationalization of Rome that its old schematic subdivisions (*curiae*) took on religious importance, with a pretense to ethnic origin, to only a small degree.

The belief in common ethnicity often delimits "social circles," which in turn are not always identical with endogamous connubial groups, for greatly varying numbers of persons may be encompassed by both. Their similarity rests on the belief in a specific "honor" of their members, not shared by the outsiders, that is, the sense of "ethnic honor" (a phenomenon closely related to status honor, which will be discussed later). These few remarks must suffice at this point. A specialized sociological study of ethnicity would have to make a finer distinction between these concepts than we have done for our limited purposes.

Groups, in turn, can engender sentiments of likeness that will persist even after their demise and will have an "ethnic" connotation. The political community in particular can produce such an effect. But most directly, such an effect is created by the *language group,* which is the bearer of a specific "cultural possession of the masses" (*Massenkulturgut*) and makes mutual understanding (*Verstehen*) possible or easier.

Wherever the memory of the origin of a community by peaceful secession or emigration ("colony," *ver sacrum,* and the like) from a mother community remains for some reason alive, there undoubtedly exists a very specific and often extremely powerful sense of ethnic identity, which is determined by several factors: shared political memories or, even more important in early times, persistent ties with the old cult, or the strengthening of kinship and other groups, both in the old and the new community, or other persistent relationships. Where these ties are lacking, or once they cease to exist, the sense of ethnic group membership is absent, regardless of how close the kinship may be.

Apart from the community of language, which may or may not coincide with objective, or subjectively believed, consanguinity, and apart from common religious belief, which is also independent of consanguinity, the ethnic differences that remain are, on the one hand, esthetically conspicuous differences of the physical appearance (as mentioned before) and, on the other hand and of equal weight, the perceptible differences in the *conduct of everyday life.* Of special importance are precisely those items that may otherwise seem to be of small social relevance, since when ethnic differentiation is concerned it is always the conspicuous differences that come into play.

Common language and the ritual regulation of life, as determined by shared religious beliefs, everywhere are conducive to feelings of ethnic affinity, especially since the intelligibility of the behavior of others is the most fundamental presupposition of group formation. But since we shall not consider these two elements in the present context, we ask: What is it that remains? It must be admitted that palpable differences in dialect and differences of religion in themselves do not exclude sentiments of common ethnicity. Next to pronounced differences in the economic way of life, the belief in ethnic affinity has at all times been affected by outward differences in clothes, in the style of housing, food and eating habits, the division of labor between the sexes and between the free and the unfree. That is to say, these things concern one's conception of what is correct and proper and, above all, of what affects the individual's sense of honor and dignity. All those things we shall find later on as objects of specific differences between status groups. The conviction of the excellence of one's own customs and the inferiority of alien ones, a conviction that sustains the sense of ethnic honor, is actually quite analogous to the sense of honor of distinctive status groups.

The sense of ethnic honor is a specific honor of the masses (*Massenehre*), for it is accessible to anybody who belongs to the subjectively believed community of descent. The "poor white trash," i.e., the propertyless and, in the absence of job opportunities, very often destitute white inhabitants of the southern states of the United States of America in the period of slavery, were the actual bearers of racial antipathy, which was quite foreign to the planters. This was so because the social honor of the "poor whites" was dependent upon the social *déclassement* of the Negroes.

And behind all ethnic diversities there is somehow naturally the notion of the "chosen people," which is merely a counterpart of status differentiation translated into the plane of horizontal co-existence. The idea of a chosen people derives its popularity from the fact that it can be claimed to an equal degree by any and every member of the mutually despising groups, in contrast to status differentiation, which always rests on subordination. Consequently, ethnic repulsion may take hold of all conceivable differences among the notions of propriety and transform them into "ethnic conventions."

Besides the previously mentioned elements, which were still more or less closely related to the economic order, conventionalization (a term expounded elsewhere) may take hold of such things as a hairdo or style of beard and the like. The differences thereof have an "ethnically" repulsive effect, because they are thought of as symbols of ethnic membership. Of course, the repulsion is not always based merely on the "symbolic" character of the distinguishing traits. The fact that the Scythian women oiled their hair with butter, which then gave off a rancid odor, while Greek women used perfumed oil to achieve the same purpose, thwarted—according to an ancient report—all attempts at social intercourse between the aristocratic ladies of these two groups. The smell of butter certainly had a more compelling effect than even the most prominent racial differences, or—as far as I could see—the "Negro odor," of which so many fables are told. In general, racial qualities are effective only as limiting factors with regard to the belief in common ethnicity, such as in case of an excessively heterogeneous and esthetically unaccepted physical type; they are not positively group-forming.

Pronounced differences of custom, which play a role equal to that of inherited physical type in the creation of feelings of common ethnicity and notions of kinship, are usually caused, in addition to linguistic and religious differences, by the diverse economic and political conditions of various social groups. If we ignore cases of clear-cut linguistic boundaries and sharply demarcated political or religious communities as a basis of differences of custom—and these in fact are lacking in wide areas of the African and South American continents—then there are only gradual transitions of custom and no immutable ethnic frontiers, except those due to gross geographical differences. The sharp demarcations of areas wherein ethnically relevant customs predominate, which were not conditioned either by political or economic or religious factors, usually came into existence by way of migration or expansion, when groups of people that had previously lived in complete or partial isolation from each other and became accommodated to heterogeneous conditions of existence came to live side by side. As a result, the obvious contrast usually evokes, on both sides, the idea of blood disaffinity (*Blutsfremdheit*), regardless of the objective state of affairs.

It is understandably difficult to determine in general—and even in a concrete individual case—what influence specific ethnic factors (i.e., the belief in a blood relationship, or its opposite, which rests on similarities, or differences, of a person' s physical appearance and style of life) have on the formation of a group.

There is no difference between the ethnically relevant customs and customs in general, as far as their effect is concerned. The belief in common descent, in combination with a similarity of customs, is likely to promote the spread of the activities of one part of an ethnic group among the rest, since the awareness of ethnic identity furthers imitation. This is especially true of the propaganda of religious groups.

It is not feasible to go beyond these vague generalizations. The content of joint activities that are possible on an ethnic basis remains indefinite. There is a corresponding ambiguity of concepts denoting ethnically determined action, that means, determined by the belief in blood relationship. Such concepts are *Völkerschaft*, *Stamm* (tribe), *Volk* (people), each of which is ordinarily used in the sense of an ethnic subdivision of the following one (although the first two may be used in reversed order). Using such terms, one usually implies either the existence of a contemporary political community, no matter how loosely organized, or memories of an extinct political community, such as they are preserved in epic tales and legends; or the existence of a linguistic or dialect group; or, finally, of a religious group. In the past, cults in particular were the typical concomitant of a tribal or *Volk* consciousness. But in the absence of the political community, contemporary or past, the external delimitation of the group was usually indistinct. the cult communities of Germanic tribes, as late as the Burgundian period (sixth century A.D.) were probably rudiments of political communities and therefore pretty well defined. By contrast, the Delphian oracle, the undoubted cultic symbol of Hellenism, also revealed information to the barbarians and accepted their veneration, and it was an organized cult only among some Greek segments, excluding the most powerful cities. The cult as an exponent of ethnic identity is thus generally either a remnant of a largely political community that once existed but was destroyed by disunion and colonization, or it is—as in the case of the Delphian Apollo—a product of a *Kulturgemeinschaft* brought about by other than purely ethnic conditions, but which in turn gives rise to the belief in blood relationship. All history shows how easily political action can give rise to the belief in blood relationship, unless gross differences of anthropological type impede it.

Tribe and Political Community: The Disutility of the Notion of "Ethnic Group"

The tribe is clearly delimited when it is a subdivision of a polity, which, in fact, often establishes it. In this case, the artificial origin is revealed by the round numbers in which tribes usually appear, for example, the previously mentioned division of the people of Israel into twelve tribes, the three Doric *phylai* and the various *phylai* of the other Hellenes. When a political community was newly established or reorganized, the population was newly divided. Hence the tribe is here a political artifact, even though it soon adopts the whole symbolism of blood-relationship and particularly a tribal cult. Even today it is not rare that political artifacts develop a sense of affinity akin to that of blood relationship. Very schematic constructs such as those states of the United States that were made into squares according to their latitude have a strong sense of identity; it is also not rare that families travel from New York to Richmond to make an expected child a "Virginian."

Such artificiality does not preclude the possibility that the Hellenic *phylai,* for example, were at one time independent and that the polis used them schematically when they were merged into a political association. However, tribes that existed before the *polis* were either identical with the corresponding political groups, which were subsequently associated into a *polis,* and in this case they were called *ethnos,* not *phyle;* or, as it probably happened many times, the politically unorganized tribe, as a presumed "blood community," lived from the memory that it once engaged in joint political action, typically a single conquest or defense, and then such political memories constituted the tribe. Thus, the fact that tribal consciousness was primarily formed by common political experiences and not by common descent appears to have been a frequent source of the belief in common ethnicity.

Of course, this was not the only source: Common customs may have diverse origins. Ultimately, they derive largely from adaptation to natural conditions and the imitation of neighbors. In practice, however, tribal consciousness usually has a political meaning: in case of military danger or opportunity, it easily provides the basis for joint political action on the part of tribal members or *Volksgenossen* who consider one another as blood relatives. The eruption of a drive to political action is thus one of the major potentialities inherent in the rather ambiguous notions of tribe and people. Such intermittent political action may easily develop into the moral duty of all members of tribe or people (*Volk*) to support one another in case of a military attack, even if there is no corresponding political association; violators of this solidarity may suffer the fate of the (Germanic, pro-Roman) sibs of Segestes and Inguiomer—expulsion from the tribal territory—even if the tribe has no organized government. If the tribe has reached this stage, it has indeed become a continuous political community, no matter how inactive in peacetime, and hence unstable, it may be. However, even under favorable conditions the transition from the habitual to the customary and therefore obligatory is very fluid. All in all, the notion of "ethnically" determined social action subsumes phenomena that a rigorous sociological analysis—as we do not attempt it here—would have to distinguish carefully: the actual subjective effect of those customs conditioned by heredity and those determined by tradition; the differential impact of the varying content of custom; the influence of common language, religion, and political action, past and present, upon the formation of customs; the extent to which such factors create attraction and repulsion, and especially the belief in affinity or disaffinity of blood; the consequences of this belief for social action in general, and specifically for action on the basis of shared custom or blood relationship, for diverse sexual relations, etc.—all of this would have to be studied in detail. It is certain that in this process the collective term *ethnic* would be abandoned, for it is unsuitable for a really rigorous analysis. However, we do not pursue sociology for its own sake and therefore limit ourselves to showing briefly the diverse factors that are hidden behind this seemingly uniform phenomenon.

The concept of the "ethnic" group, which dissolves if we define our terms exactly, corresponds in this regard to one of the most vexing, since emotionally charged, concepts: the *nation*, as soon as we attempt a sociological definition.

Nationality and Cultural Prestige[2]

The concept of "nationality" shares with that of the "people" (*Volk*)—in the "ethnic" sense—the vague connotation that whatever is felt to be distinctively common must derive from common descent. In reality, of course, persons who consider themselves members of the same nationality are often much less related by common descent than are persons belonging to different and hostile nationalities. Differences of nationality may exist even among groups closely related by common descent, merely because they have different religious persuasions, as in the case of Serbs and Croats. The concrete reasons for the belief in joint nationality and for the resulting social action vary greatly.

Today, in the age of language conflicts, a shared common language is preeminently considered the normal basis of nationality. Whatever the "nation" means beyond a mere "language group" can be found in the specific objective of its social action, and this can only be the *autonomous polity*. Indeed, "nation state" has become conceptually identical with "state" based on common language. In reality, however, such modern nation states exist next to many others that comprise several language groups, even though these others usually have one official language. A common language is also insufficient in sustaining a sense of national identity (*Nationalgefühl*)—a concept that we will leave undefined for the present. Aside from the examples of the Serbs and Croats, this is demonstrated by the Irish, the Swiss, and the German-speaking Alsatians; these groups do not consider themselves as members, at least not as full members, of the "nation" associated with their language. Conversely, language differences do not necessarily preclude a sense of joint nationality: The German-speaking Alsatians considered themselves—and most of them still do—as part of the French "nation," even though not in the same sense as French-speaking nationals. Hence there are qualitative degrees of the belief in common nationality.

Many German-speaking Alsatians feel a sense of community with the French because they share certain customs and some of their "sensual culture" (*Sinnenkultur*)—as Wittich in particular has pointed out—and also because of common political experiences. This can be understood by any visitor who walks through the museum in Colmar, which is rich in relics such as tricolors, *pompier* and military helmets, edicts by Louis Philippe, and especially memorabilia from the French Revolution; these may appear trivial to the outsider, but they have sentimental value for the Alsations.[3] This sense of community came into being by virtue of common political and, indirectly, social experiences, which are highly valued by the masses as symbols of the destruction of feudalism, and the story of these events takes the place of the heroic legends of primitive peoples. *La grande nation* was the liberator from feudal servitude, she was the bearer of civilization (*Kultur*), her language was *the* civilized language; German appeared as a dialect suitable for everyday communication. Hence the attachment to those who speak the language of civilization is an obvious parallel to the sense of community based on common language, but the two phenomena are not identical; rather, we deal here with an attitude that derives from a partial sharing of the same culture and from shared political experiences.

Until a short time ago most Poles in Upper Silesia had no strongly developed sense of Polish nationality that was antagonistic to the Prussian state, which is based essentially on the German language. The Poles were loyal if passive "Prussians," but they were not "Germans" interested in the existence of the *Reich;* the majority did not feel a conscious or a strong need to segregate themselves from German-speaking fellow-citizens. Hence, in this case there was no sense of nationality based on common language, and there was no *Kulturgemeinschaft* in view of the lack of cultural development.

Among the Baltic Germans we find neither much of a sense of nationality amounting to a high valuation of the language bonds with the Germans, nor a desire for political union with the *Reich;* in fact, most of them would abhor such a unification. However, they segregate themselves rigorously from the Slavic environment, and especially from the Russians, primarily because of status considerations and partly because both sides have different customs and cultural values, which are mutually unintelligible and disdained. This segregation exists in spite of, and partly because of, the fact that the Baltic Germans are intensely loyal vassals of the Tsar and have been as interested as any "national" Russian (*Nationalrusse*) in the predominance of the Imperial Russian system, which they provide with officials and which in turn maintains their descendants. Hence, here too we do not find any sense of nationality in the modern meaning of the term (oriented toward a common language and culture). The case is similar to that of the purely proletarian Poles: Loyalty toward the state is combined with a sense of group identity that is limited to a common language group within this larger community and strongly modified by status factors. Of course, the Baltic Germans are no longer a cohesive status group, even though the differences are not as extreme as within the white population of the American South.

Finally, there are cases for which the term *nationality* does not seem to be quite fitting; witness the sense of identity shared by the Swiss and the Belgians or the inhabitants of

Luxemburg and Liechtenstein. We hesitate to call them "nations," not because of their relative smallness—the Dutch appear to us as a nation—but because these neutralized states have purposively forsaken power. The Swiss are not a nation if we take as criteria common language or common literature and art. Yet they have a strong sense of community despite some recent disintegrative tendencies. This sense of identity is not only sustained by loyalty toward the body politic but also by what are perceived to be common customs (irrespective of actual differences). These customs are largely shaped by the differences in social structure between Switzerland and Germany, but also all other big and hence militaristic powers. Because of the impact of bigness on the internal power structure, it appears to the Swiss that their customs can be preserved only by a separate political existence.

The loyalty of the French Canadians toward the English polity is today determined above all by the deep antipathy against the economic and social structure, and the way of life, of the neighboring United States; hence membership in the Dominion of Canada appears as a guarantee of their own traditions.

This classification could easily be enlarged, as every rigorous sociological investigation would have to do. It turns out that feelings of identity subsumed under the term *national* are not uniform but may derive from diverse sources: Differences in the economic and social structure and in the internal power structure, with its impact on the customs, may play a role, but within the German *Reich* customs are very diverse; shared political memories, religion, language, and, finally, racial features may be source of the sense of nationality. Racial factors often have a peculiar impact. From the viewpoint of the whites in the United States, Negroes and whites are not united by a common sense of nationality, but the Negroes have a sense of American nationality at least by claiming a right to it. On the other hand, the pride of the Swiss in their own distinctiveness, and their willingness to defend it vigorously, is neither qualitatively different nor less widespread than the same attitudes in any "great" and powerful "nation." Time and again we find that the concept "nation" directs us to political power. Hence, the concept seems to refer—if it refers at all to a uniform phenomenon—to a specific kind of pathos that is linked to the idea of a powerful political community of people who share a common language, or religion, or common customs, or political memories; such a state may already exist or it may be desired. The more power is emphasized, the closer appears to be the link between nation and state. This pathetic pride in the power of one's own community, or this longing for it, may be much more widespread in relatively small language groups such as the Hungarians, Czechs, or Greeks than in a similar but much larger community such as the Germans 150 years ago, when they were essentially a language group without pretensions to national power.

Notes

1. On race and civilization, see also Weber's polemical speech against A. Ploetz at the first meeting of the German Sociological Association, Frankfurt, 1910, in GAzSS, 456–62. Two years later, at the second meeting of the Association in Berlin, Weber took the floor again after a presentation by Franz Oppenheimer. Among other things, Weber said:
   "With race theories you can prove and disprove anything you want. It is a scientific crime to attempt the circumvention, by the uncritical use of completely unclarified racial hypotheses, of the sociological study of Antiquity, which of course is much more difficult, but by no means without hope of success; after all, we can no longer find out to what extent the qualities of the Hellenes and Romans rested on inherited dispositions. The problem of such

relationships has not yet been solved by the most careful and toilsome investigations of living subjects, even if undertaken in the laboratory and with the means of exact experimentation." (p. 489)

2. Cf. the related section on "The Nation" in chapter 9, p. 5.
3. See Werner Wittich, *Deutsche and französische Kultur im Elsass* (Strassburg: Schlesier und Schweikhardt, 1900), 38ff; for a French transl., see "Le génie national des races francaise et allemande en Alsace." *Revue international de Sociologie*, vol. X, 1902, 777–824 and 857–907, esp. 814ff. Cf. also Weber, GAzRS, I, 25, n. I; GAzSS, 484. "Outsiders," in contrast to the pre-1914 custodian who showed Weber his greatest treasures, cherish the Colmar museum for one of the most powerful works of art of the late Middle Ages, Grünewald's "Isenheim Altar."

The New Immigration and Ethnicity in the United States

✦ DOUGLAS S. MASSEY

As anyone who walks the streets of America's largest cities knows, there has been a profound transformation of immigration to the United States. Not only are there more immigrants, but increasingly they speak languages and bear cultures that are quite different from those brought by European immigrants in the past. The rapidity of the change and the scale of the movement have led to much consternation about what the "new immigration" means for American society.

Some worry about the economic effects of immigration, although quantitative analyses generally show that immigrants do not compete with native workers and do not have strong effects on U.S. wage rates and employment levels (Borjas, 1990; Borjas and Freeman, 1992; Borjas and Tienda, 1987). Others worry about the social welfare burden caused by immigrants, but studies again suggest that, with the exception of some refugee groups, immigrants do not drain public resources (see Blau, 1984; Borjas, 1994; Simon, 1984; Tienda and Jensen, 1986; but Rothman and Espenshade, 1992 show that local fiscal effects may be significant). Observers also express fears of linguistic fragmentation, but research indicates that immigrants generally shift into English as time passes and that their children move decisively into English if they grow up in the United States (Grenier, 1984; Stevens, 1985; Veltman, 1988).

Despite this reassuring evidence, however, considerable disquiet remains about the new immigration and its consequences (see Espenshade and Calhoun, 1993). Indeed, an immigrant backlash appears to be gathering force. English-only amendments have passed in several locales; federal immigration law has grown steadily more restrictive and punitive; and politicians, led by Governor Pete Wilson of California, have discovered the political advantages that may be gained by blaming immigrants for current social

Massey, Douglas S. 1995. "The new immigration and ethnicity in the United States." *Population and Development Review* 21:631–652. Reprinted with permission from *Population and Development Review.*

and economic problems. Given the apparent animus toward immigrants and the imperviousness of public perceptions to the influence of objective research findings, one suspects that deeper forces are at work in the American psyche.

This consternation may have less to do with ascertainable facts about immigration than with unarticulated fears that immigrants will somehow create a very different society and culture in the United States. Whatever objective research says about the prospects for individual assimilation, the ethnic and racial composition of the United States is clearly changing, and with it the sociocultural world created by prior European immigrants and their descendants. According to demographic projections, Americans of European descent will become a minority in the United States sometime during the next century (Edmonston and Passel, 1991), and this projected shift has already occurred in some urban areas, notably Los Angeles and Miami. In other metropolitan areas, such as New York, Chicago, Houston, and San Diego, the transformation is well under way.

This demographic reality suggests the real nature of the anti-immigrant reaction among non-Hispanic whites: a fear of cultural change and a deep-seated worry that European Americans will be displaced from their dominant position in American life. Most social scientists have been reluctant to address this issue, or even to acknowledge it (nonacademics, however, are not so reticent—see Brimelow 1995; Lamm and Imhoff 1985). As a result, analyses by academic researchers have focused rather narrowly on facts and empirical issues: how many undocumented migrants are there, do they displace native workers, do they drive down wage rates, do they use more in services than they pay in taxes?

Answers to these questions do not get at the heart of the matter, however. What the public really wants to know (at least, I suspect, the native white public) is whether or not the new immigrants will assimilate into the Euro-American society of the United States, and how that society and its culture might change as a result of this incorporation. While social scientists have analyzed the state of the trees, the public has worried about the future of the forest, and no amount of empirical research has quieted these anxieties. In this article, I assess the prospects for the assimilation of the new immigrant groups and judge their likely effects on the society, culture, and language of the United States.

I begin by placing the new immigration in historical perspective and pointing out the distinctive features that set it apart from earlier immigrations. I then appraise the structural context for the incorporation of today's immigrants and argue that because of fundamental differences, their assimilation is unlikely to be as rapid or complete as that achieved by European immigrants in the past. I conclude by discussing how the nature of ethnicity is likely to change as a result of a new immigration that is linguistically concentrated, geographically clustered, and temporally continuous into an American society that is increasingly stratified and unequal.

The New Immigration in Historical Perspective

The history of U.S. immigration during the twentieth century can be divided roughly into three phases: a *classic era* of mass European immigration stretching from about 1901 to 1930; a *long hiatus* of limited movement from 1931 to 1970; and a *new regime* of large-scale, non-European immigration that began around 1970 and continues to the present. The cutpoints 1930 and 1970 are to some extent arbitrary, of course, but they correspond roughly to major shifts in U.S. immigration policy. The 1924 National Origins Act, which imposed strict country quotas, took full effect in 1929; and the 1965 amendments to the Immigration and Nationality Act, which repealed those quotas, took effect in 1968 (see Jasso and Rosenzweig 1990, pp. 26–97).

Information on the size and composition of immigrant flows during the three periods is presented in Table 1. Actual counts of immigrants by region and decade (the data from which the table was largely derived) are presented in the Data Appendix. In both tables, the figures refer to legal immigrants enumerated upon entry; they do not include undocumented migrants (see Massey and Singer, 1995, for recent annual estimates), nor do they adjust for return migration, which studies have

TABLE 1 Patterns of immigration to the United States in three periods of the twentieth century

	Classic era 1901–30	Long hiatus 1931–70	New regime 1971–93
Whole period			
Region of origin (percent)			
Europe	79.6	46.2	13.0
Americas	16.2	43.6	49.6
Asia	3.7	8.6	34.5
Other	0.5	1.6	2.9
Total	100.0	100.0	100.0
Total immigration (thousands)	18,638	7,400	15,536
Annual average (thousands)	621	185	675
Peak Year	1907	1968	1991
Peak immigration (thousands)	1,285	454	1,827
First ten years			
Region of origin (percent)			
Europe	91.6	65.9	17.8
Americas	4.1	30.3	44.1
Asia	3.7	3.2	35.3
Other	0.6	0.6	2.8
Total	100.0	100.0	100.0
Total immigration (thousands)	8,795	528	4,493
Annual average (thousands)	880	53	449
Last ten years			
Region of origin (percent)			
Europe	60.0	33.8	10.2
Americas	36.9	51.7	54.0
Asia	2.7	12.9	32.7
Other	0.4	1.6	3.1
Total	100.0	100.0	100.0
Total immigration (thousands)	4,107	3,322	9,293
Annual average (thousands)	411	332	929

Source: U.S. Immigration and Naturalization Service 1994: Table 2.

shown to be significant in both the classic era (Wyman 1993) and the new regime (Warren and Kraly 1985; Jasso and Rosenzweig 1990).

The classic years 1901–30 are actually part of a sustained fifty-year period of mass immigration that began sometime around 1880. During this period some 28 million immigrants entered the United States and, except for two years at the end of World War I, the yearly total never fell below 200,000, and in most years it exceeded 400,000. The largest flows occurred in the first decades of the twentieth century. From 1901 to 1930 almost 19 million people arrived on American shores, yielding an annual average of 621,000 immigrants (see Table 1). The peak occurred in 1907 when some 1.3 million immigrants arrived. Until recently, these numbers were unequaled in American history.

The vast majority of these people came from Europe. Although the composition shifted from northern and western Europe to southern and eastern Europe as industrialization spread across the American continent (see Massey 1988; Morawska 1990), the composition throughout the first three decades of the century remained overwhelmingly European, averaging 80 percent for the entire period. As a result, the United States became less black, more white, and more firmly European in culture and outlook.

This period of mass immigration gave rise to some of the nation's enduring myths: about the struggle of immigrants to overcome poverty, about the achievement of economic mobility through individual effort, about the importance of group solidarity in the face of ethnic prejudice and discrimination, and about the inevitability of assimilation into the melting pot of American life. In the words of an influential social scientist at midcentury, the first decades of the century offer "The Epic Story of the Great Migrations that Made the American People" (Handlin, 1951). Although a reaction against the melting pot myth later arose in the second and third generations, this was largely a symbolic opposition by people who had watched their parents and grandparents suffer under "northern European" dominance, but who by the 1960s had largely penetrated arenas of power, prestige, and influence and wanted to let the world know about it (see Glazer and Moynihan, 1970; Greely, 1971; Novak, 1971).

The classic era of mass immigration was followed by a forty-year hiatus during which immigration fell to very low levels and the predominance of European immigrants came to an end. From 1931 to 1970, average annual immigration fell to 185,000 and the share arriving from the Americas increased substantially, eventually equaling that from Europe. Over the entire hiatus period, 44 percent of immigrants came from the Americas, compared with 46 percent from Europe and 9 percent from Asia (the last region, according to the Immigration and Naturalization Service, includes the Middle East, which has contributed a small number of immigrants over the years, compared with such countries as China, Korea, the Philippines, and Japan). By the last decade of the hiatus, 52 percent of all immigrants were from the Americas and only 34 percent came from Europe; the peak year of immigration occurred in 1968, when 454,000 people were admitted for permanent residence.

As I have already noted, the dividing points of 1930 and 1970 are somewhat arbitrary and were chosen partly for convenience, since decennial years are easy to remember and correspond to the decennial tabulations favored by demographers. Evidence of the coming hiatus was already apparent in the last decade of the classic era, when immigration levels were a third below their 1901–30 average (411,000 rather than 621,000) and about half the average that prevailed in the first decade of the century (880,000). Moreover, by the end of the classic era, immigrants' origins were already shifting toward the Americas. Whereas 92 percent of all immigrants in the first decade of the century were European, by the 1920s the percentage had dropped to 60 percent. Although it was not recognized for many years, the era of massive European immigration was already beginning to wind down.

The termination of mass immigration around 1930 is attributable to many factors. The one that scholars most often credit is the passage of restrictive immigration legislation. In response to a public backlash against immigrants, Congress passed two new "quota laws," in 1921 and 1924, that were designed to limit the number of immigrants and shift their origins from southern and eastern Europe back to northern and western Europe (where they belonged, at least in the view of the nativist voters of the time—see Higham 1963 and Hutchinson 1981).

Although the national origins quotas, combined with earlier bans on Asian immigration enacted in 1882 and 1917, did play a role in reducing the number of immigrants, I believe their influence has been overstated. For one thing, the new quotas did not apply at all to immigrants from the Western Hemisphere, leaving the door wide open for mass entry from Latin America, particularly Mexico. Indeed, beginning in the decade of the 1910s, employers in Northern industrial cities of the United States began to recruit extensively in Mexico, and immigration from that country mushroomed from 50,000 in the first decade of the century, to 220,000 in the second, to 460,000 in the third (see Cardoso, 1980). Were it not for other factors, the change in immigration law would, at most, have shifted the national origins of immigrants more decisively toward the Americas in the 1930s, but it would not have halted immigration per se.

More than any change in legislation, however, the outbreak of World War I in 1914 brought a sudden and decisive halt to the flow of immigrants from Europe. During the first half of the decade, the outflow proceeded apace: 926,000 European immigrants arrived in the United States in 1910, 765,000 in 1911, and just over I million came in both 1913 and 1914. During the first full year of the war, however, immigration dropped to 198,000 and it fell every year thereafter to reach a low point of 31,000 in 1918. As a result, during the 1910s total immigration was halved compared with the prior decade (Ferenczi, 1929).

During the 1920s, European immigration began to revive, despite the restrictive immigration quotas. Some 412,000 immigrants arrived from Germany during 1921–30, 455,000 came from Italy, 227,000 from Poland, and 102,000 from Czechoslovakia. These entries supplemented large numbers arriving from European countries that were not limited by the new quotas: 211,000 from Ireland, 340,000 from Britain, and 166,000 from Norway and Sweden combined. One country, however, is notably absent from European immigrant flows of the 1920s: Russia, or as it was now known, the Soviet Union (U.S. Immigration and Naturalization Service, 1994).

Prior to World War I, immigration from Russia had been massive: 1.6 million Russian immigrants entered the United States during the first decade of the century, and 921,000 managed to get in during the subsequent decade despite the outbreak of war in 1914. The great majority of these people were Jews escaping the rampant anti-Semitism and pogroms of Czarist Russia (see Nugent 1992, pp. 83–94); but with the Bolshevik Revolution of 1917 and the consolidation of the world's first Communist state, the Russian Pale was abruptly disconnected from the capitalist West and emigration was suppressed by a new state security apparatus. As a result, immigration from Russia fell to a total of only 62,000 in the 1920s and to just 1,400 during the 1930s. The flow of Russian immigrants did not exceed 2,500 again until the 1970s (U.S. Immigration and Naturalization Service, 1994).

Just as immigration from non-Russian Europe was gaining ground during the 1920s, another cataclysmic event virtually halted all international migration: the Great Depression. From a total of 241,000 immigrants in 1930, the flow dropped to 23,000 three years later. With mass unemployment in the United States, the demand for immigrant workers evaporated and during the 1930s total immigration fell below 1 million for the first time since the 1830s. Only 528,000 immigrants entered the United States from 1931 to 1940, yielding an annual average of only 53,000.

Before the Great Depression had ended, World War II broke out to add another barrier to international movement. During the war years the flow of immigrants to the United States fell once again. From a Depression era peak of 83,000 in 1939, the number of immigrants fell to only 24,000 in 1943; and during six years of warfare, the number of immigrants averaged only 40,000 per year, lower even than during the Depression years of 1930–39 (U.S. Immigration and Naturalization Service, 1994).

With the termination of hostilities in 1945, immigration from Europe finally resumed; but by 1945 the face of Europe had changed dramatically. The Cold War had begun and the boundary line marking the area of Communist dominance had shifted westward. In addition to the Soviet Union, eastern Europe was now cut off from the capitalist economy of the West. Countries such as Czechoslovakia, Hungary, Romania, and Yugoslavia, which had sent large numbers of immigrants before the Depression, contributed few after 1945. Although 228,000 Polish immigrants came to the United States during the 1920s, only 10,000 entered during the 1950s.

Just as the avenues for emigration from eastern Europe were blocked, the countries of western Europe began to seek workers to rebuild their war-shattered economies. The wave of investment and economic growth triggered by the Marshall Plan created a strong demand for labor that, by the 1950s, began to exceed domestic supplies of most countries (Kindleberger, 1967). As the postwar economy expanded and the pace of growth quickened, Germany, France, Britain, Belgium, and the Netherlands not only stopped sending migrants abroad, they all became countries of immigration themselves, attracting large numbers of immigrants from Southern Europe and then, as these sources dried up, from the Balkans, Turkey, North Africa, and Asia (see Stalker, 1994). The era of mass European migration to the United States was finally and decisively over.

Although immigrants were no longer available in large numbers from Europe, the postwar boom in the United States nonetheless created a strong demand for labor there. With eastern Europe cut off and western Europe itself a magnet for immigration, this new demand was met by Latin Americans, whose entry was unregulated under the quotas of the 1920s. The number of Mexican immigrants rose from 61,000 in the 1940s to 300,000 in the 1950s and 454,000 during the 1960s. This expansion of immigration was not limited to Mexico. During the last decade of the hiatus period, some 200,000 Cubans entered the United States, along with 100,000 Dominicans and 70,000 Colombians. A new era of non-European immigration was clearly on the rise (U.S. Immigration and Naturalization Service 1994).

It has become conventional to date the emergence of the new regime in U.S. immigration from the passage of the 1965 amendments to the Immigration and Nationality Act, which were phased in and implemented fully in 1968. In keeping with the spirit of the times, this legislation abolished the discriminatory national-origins quotas and ended the ban on Asian entry. It put each nation in the Eastern Hemisphere on an equal footing by establishing a uniform limit of 20,000 entrants per country; it set an overall hemispheric cap of 170,000 immigrants; and it established a "preference system" of family and occupational categories to allocate visas under these limits. The amendments exempted immediate relatives of U.S. citizens from the numerical caps, however, and nations in the Western Hemisphere were subject only to a hemispheric cap of 120,000 immigrants, not a 20,000-per-country limit.

Although this legislation contributed to the creation of the new immigration regime, it was neither the sole nor the most important cause of the increase in numbers or the shift in origins. As with the national-origins quotas, I believe scholars have generally overstated the role of the 1965 amendments in bringing about the new immigration. The Immigration and Nationality Act was in no way responsible for the drop in European immigration, for example, since this trend was clearly visible before 1965 and followed from other conditions described earlier.

Nor did the 1965 act increase the level of immigration from Latin America. On the contrary, by placing the first-ever cap on immigration from the western hemisphere, the legislation actually made it more difficult for Latin Americans to enter the United States. Since 1965, additional amendments have further restricted entry from nations in the western hemisphere, placing them under the 20,000-per-country limit, abolishing the separate hemispheric caps, eliminating the right of minor children to sponsor the immigration of parents, and repealing the "Texas Proviso" that exempted employers from prosecution for hiring undocumented migrants. Rather than promoting the shift toward Latin American origins, then, the 1965 act and its successor amendments actually inhibited the transformation. The shift in origins occurred in spite of the legislation, not because of it.

The one effect that the 1965 act did have was to remove the ban on Asian entry and thereby unleash an unprecedented and entirely unexpected flow of immigrants from Korea, Taiwan, China, the Philippines, and other Asian countries (see Glazer, 1985). At the time, the legislation was seen as a way of redressing past wrongs that had been visited upon eastern and southern Europeans and of mollifying the resentment of their children and grandchildren, who had risen to wield powerful political influence in the Democratic Party, which dominated the U.S. Congress. Rather than opening the United States to immigration from, say, Italy and Poland, however, as legislators such as Peter Rodino and Dan Rostenkowski had intended, its principal effect was to initiate large-scale immigration from Asia.

As Table 1 shows, the percentage of Asians rose from under 10 percent of immigrants during the classic and hiatus eras, to around 35 percent under the new regime that began after 1970. Whereas only 35,000 Chinese, 35,000 Indians, and 34,000 Koreans were admitted as immigrants during the 1960s, by the 1980s these numbers had become 347,000, 251,000, and 334,000, respectively (U.S. Immigration and Naturalization Service, 1994). As a result of this sharp and sudden increase in Asian immigration, the percentage of Asians in the U.S. population began rising for the first time in more than a century.

Yet by themselves the 1965 amendments cannot explain the remarkable surge in Asian immigration. Another key factor was the loss of the Vietnam War and the subsequent collapse of the U.S. backed governments in Indochina. With the fall of Saigon in 1975, the United States faced new demands for entry by thousands of military officers, government officials, and U.S. employees fearful of reprisals from the new Communist authorities. As economic and political conditions in Vietnam deteriorated during the late 1970s and early 1980s, larger numbers of soldiers, minor officials, and merchants took to the seas in desperate attempts to escape.

For both political and humanitarian reasons, the United States had little choice but to accept these people outside the numerical limits established under the 1965 act. Although only 335 Vietnamese entered the United States during the 1950s and 4,300 arrived during the 1960s, 172,000 were admitted during the 1970s, and 281,000 arrived during the 1980s. In addition to the Vietnamese, the U.S. misadventure in Indochina led to the entry of many thousands of Cambodian, Laotian, and Hmong refugees, an influx that collectively totaled 300,000 by 1990. In all, about a third of Asian immigrants since 1970 can be traced to the failed intervention of the United States in Indochina (U.S. Immigration and Naturalization Service, 1994).

For different reasons, therefore, immigration from Asia and Latin America has surged over the past two decades. According to official statistics, the total annual flow of immigrants averaged 675,000 during the period 1971–93, an influx that in absolute terms exceeds the 621,000 observed during the classic era from 1901 to 1930. Unlike the entrants during the earlier period, these 15.5 million new immigrants were overwhelmingly non-European: about half came from Latin America and over a third originated in Asia; 13 percent were from Europe. The peak year was 1991, when 1.8 million persons were admitted for permanent residence in the United States.

As large as the annual flow of 675,000 immigrants is, both absolutely and relative to earlier periods in U.S. history, it nonetheless constitutes an underestimate of the true level of immigration, for it does not capture the full extent of undocumented migration to the United States, a category that became increasingly important during the 1970s and 1980s. Although the figures summarized in Table 1 include 3.3 million former undocumented migrants who legalized their status under the 1986 Immigration Reform and Control Act (IRCA), they do not include other illegal migrants who failed to qualify for the amnesty program or who entered after 1986.

Woodrow-Lafield (1993) estimates that about 3.3 million additional undocumented immigrants lived in the United States as of 1990, bringing the total number of immigrants for the period 1971–93 to around 854,000 per year. This figure still understates the true size of the inflow, however, because her estimate does not include immigrants who entered illegally and subsequently died, or those who subsequently emigrated. Full incorporation of all undocumented migrants into the figures of Table 1 would boost the relative share of Latin Americans even more, given the predominance of Mexicans in this population. Among undocumented migrants counted in the 1980 census, estimates suggest that 55 percent were Mexican (Warren and Passel, 1987), and of those legalized under IRCA, 75 percent were from Mexico (U.S. Immigration and Naturalization Service, 1991).

Whatever allowance one makes for undocumented migration, it is clear that around 1970 the United States embarked on a new regime of immigration that marks a clear break with the past. The new immigration is composed of immigrants from Asia and Latin America, a large share of whom are undocumented and who are arriving in substantially larger numbers compared with earlier periods of high immigration. Although the 1965 amendments to the Immigration and Nationality Act played some role in creating this new regime, ultimately the effect of U.S. immigration policy has been secondary. The dramatic change reflects more powerful forces operating in the United States and elsewhere in the world.

The New Immigration and the Future of Ethnicity

No matter what one's opinion of the melting pot ideology, the remarkable amalgamation of European immigrants into the society and culture of the United States is a historical fact. The disparate groups that entered the country in great numbers between 1880 and 1930—Italians, Poles, Czechs, Hungarians, Lithuanians, and Russian Jews—were not only quite different from prior waves of immigrants from northern and western Europe, they were also quite different from one another in terms of language, literacy, culture, and economic background. After several generations of U.S. residence, however, the differences are largely gone and the various groups have to a great extent merged together to form one large, amorphous class of mixed European ancestry.

By 1980, most people reporting ancestry in southern or eastern Europe were in their third or fourth generation of U.S. residence, and as a result of extensive intermarriage in earlier generations, they were increasingly of mixed origins. Over half of those reporting Polish, Russian, Czech, or Hungarian ancestry in the 1980 census were of mixed parentage; and the rate of intermarriage was 60 percent for women of Italian and Russian origin, 70 percent for Polish women, 83 percent for Czech women, and 88 percent for Hungarian women. For all women, the odds of intermarriage rose sharply as one moved from older to younger cohorts, and intergroup differences with respect to income, education, and occupation had all but disappeared (Lieberson and Waters, 1988).

As a result of rapid growth in the population of mixed European ancestry, white Americans are gradually losing contact with their immigrant origins. Research by Alba (1990) shows that such people do not regularly cook or consume ethnic foods; they report experiencing little or no ethnic prejudice or discrimination; they are largely uninvolved and uninterested in ethnic politics; they are unlikely to be members of any ethnic social or political organization; and they tend not to live in ethnic neighborhoods.

Although most white Americans identify themselves ethnically, the labels are growing increasingly complex and the percentage who call themselves "American" or "nothing at all" is rising (Lieberson and Waters, 1988; Alba 1990). In the late twentieth-century social world of European Americans, where intermarriage is pervasive, mixed ancestries are common, economic differences are trivial, and residential mixing is the norm, ethnicity has become symbolic (Gans, 1979), a choice made from a range of "ethnic options" that are loosely tied to ancestry (Waters, 1990).

Compared with the ascriptive ethnicity of the past, the descendants of European immigrants are moving into the "twilight of ethnicity" (Alba, 1981), and rather than signaling a lack of assimilation, the use of ethnic labels proves how far assimilation has come. The amalgamation of European ethnic groups has proceeded to such an extent that expressions of ethnic identity are no longer perceived as threats to national unity. On the contrary, the use of ethnic labels has become a way of identifying oneself as American (Alba, 1990).

It is natural to view the process of European assimilation as a model for the incorporation of Asians and Latin Americans into U.S. society. Present fears of ethnic fragmentation are assuaged by noting that similar fears were expressed about the immigration of Italians, Poles, and Jews. Nativist worries are allayed by showing that today's immigrants appear to be assimilating much as in the past. According to available evidence, income and occupational status rise with time spent in the United States; patterns of fertility, language, and residence come to resemble those of natives as socioeconomic status and generations increase; and intermarriage becomes increasingly common with each succeeding generation and increment in income and education (Jasso and Rosenzweig, 1990; Massey, 1981).

Focusing on individual patterns of assimilation, however, ignores the structural context within which the assimilation occurs. By focusing on micro-level analyses of immigrant attainment, we forget that the remarkable absorption of European immigrants in the past was facilitated, and to a large extent enabled, by historical conditions that no longer prevail. Compared with the great European immigrations, the new immigration differs in several crucial respects that significantly alter the prospects for assimilation and, hence, the meaning of ethnicity for the next century.

The first unique historical feature of European immigration is that it was followed by a long hiatus when few additional Europeans arrived. Although nearly 15 million European immigrants entered the United States in the three decades between 1901 and 1930, for the next sixty years the flow fell to the functional equivalent of zero. Compared with an annual average of 495,000 European immigrants from 1901 to 1930, only 85,000 arrived each year from 1931 through 1970, and most of these were not Poles, Italians, or Russian Jews, the big groups before 1930. Although overall immigration revived after 1970, the flow from Europe remained small at around 88,000 per year.

Thus, after the entry of large numbers of Europeans for some fifty years, the influx suddenly stopped and for the next sixty years—roughly three generations—it was reduced to a trickle. The cutting off of immigration from Europe eliminated the supply of raw materials for the grist mill of ethnicity in the United States, ensuring that whatever ethnic identities existed would be predominantly a consequence of events and processes operating within the United States.

Without a fresh supply of immigrants each year, the generational composition of people labeled "Italians," "Poles," and "Czechs" inexorably shifted: first, foreigners gave way to the native-born, then first-generation natives yielded to the children of natives, and more recently the children of natives have given way to the grandchildren of natives. Over time, successive generations dominated the populations of European ethnic groups and came to determine their character. With each generational transition, ethnic identities and the meaning of ethnicity itself shifted until finally most groups moved into the "twilight of ethnicity."

This pattern of assimilation was undoubtedly greatly facilitated by the long hiatus in European immigration. In essence, it gave the United States a "breathing space" within which slow-moving social and economic processes leading to assimilation could operate. The hiatus shaped and constrained the meaning of ethnicity by limiting the generational complexity underlying each group's ethnic identity: the ending of European immigration in 1930 meant that for all practical purposes, ethnic groups would never include more than three generations at any point in time.

In addition to generational change, the other engine of immigrant assimilation is social mobility, and a second historical feature of European immigration is that it was followed by a sustained economic expansion that offered unusual opportunities for socioeconomic advancement. From 1940 through 1973, incomes rose, productivity increased, unemployment fell, income inequality diminished, poverty rates declined, rates of college attendance grew, and housing improved as the U.S. standard of living seemed to rise effortlessly each year (Galbraith 1963; Levy 1987, 1995). First-and second-generation immigrants from southern and eastern Europe rode this wave of prosperity to achieve full economic parity with northern and western Europeans by 1980.

Thus, two structural conditions—the long hiatus in immigration and the economic boom that accompanied it—are primarily responsible for the remarkable assimilation of European immigrants into the United States. Were either of these factors lacking, the story of immigrant arrival, adaptation, and ultimate absorption would have had a very different conclusion than movement into the twilight of ethnicity or the emergence of symbolic ethnicity. On the other hand, neither of these two structural conditions is likely to hold for the new immigrants from Asia and Latin America, and the patterns and outcomes of assimilation are likely to be quite different as a result.

Rather than having the opportunity of a sixty year "breathing space" within which to absorb and accommodate large cohorts of immigrants, the United States will more likely become a country of perpetual immigration. Unlike the European ethnic groups of the past, today's Latin Americans and Asians can expect to have their numbers continuously augmented by a steady supply of fresh arrivals from abroad. Rather than being a one-time historical phenomenon, immigration has become a permanent structural feature of the post- industrial society of the United States.

Although the relative influence of the different causes is a matter of debate (Massey et al., 1993), international migration clearly stems from a complex interplay of forces operating at several levels (Massey et al., 1994). Wage differentials between poor and affluent countries provide incentives for individuals to migrate to reap higher lifetime earnings at the destination (Todaro, 1976; Todaro and Maruszko, 1987). Households send migrants to work in foreign labor markets as a means of self-insuring against risk and overcoming capital constraints created by market failures at home (Stark, 1991). A demand for immigrants arises in postindustrial societies because market segmentation creates a class of jobs with low pay, little status, and few mobility prospects that native workers will not accept (Piore, 1979); and the penetration of market forces into developing societies itself creates a mobile population disposed to international movement (Sassen, 1988). The effect is amplified by rapid population growth in the developing world.

Once begun, migratory flows acquire a momentum that is resistant to management or regulation (Massey, 1990a). Networks of social ties develop to link migrants in destination areas to friends and relatives in sending regions (Massey et al., 1994). Branch communities eventually form in the receiving society, giving rise to enclave economies that act as magnets for additional immigration (Logan, Alba, and McNulty, 1994; Portes and Bach, 1985; Portes and Manning, 1986). Large-scale emigration causes other social and economic changes within both sending and receiving societies that lead to its cumulative causation over time (Massey, 1990b).

Thus, current knowledge about the forces behind international migration suggests that movement to the United States will grow, not decline. None of the conditions known to play a role in initiating international migratory flows—wage differentials, market failures, labor market segmentation, globalization of the economy—is likely to end any time soon. Moreover, the forces that perpetuate international movement—network formation, cumulative causation—help to ensure that these flows will continue into the foreseeable future.

To a great extent, these forces are beyond the immediate reach of U.S. policy, particularly immigration policy. Despite the passage of more-restrictive immigration laws and the enactment of increasingly punitive policies, illegal migration from Mexico (and elsewhere) has continued to grow and shows no signs of diminishing (Donato, Durand, and Massey, 1992; Massey and Singer, 1995). Although politicians call for even stronger measures (Lamm and Imhoff, 1985), the forces producing and perpetuating immigration appear to be of such a magnitude that the new regime of U.S. immigration may continue indefinitely.

The belief that immigration flows can be controlled through legislation stems from a misreading of U.S. history. Although the cessation of European immigration in 1930 is widely attributed to the implementation of restrictive quotas in the early 1920s, I argue that the cutoff actually occurred because of a unique sequence of cataclysmic events: World War I, the Bolshevik Revolution, the Great Depression, and World War II. A similar string of destructive and bloody events might arise to extinguish the powerful migratory flows that have become well established throughout Latin America and Asia, but for the sake of the world we should hope they do not.

In all likelihood, therefore, the United States has already become a country of perpetual immigration, one characterized by the continuous arrival of large cohorts of immigrants from particular regions. This fact will inevitably create a very different structure of ethnicity compared with that prevailing among European immigrant groups in the past. Changes in the size of populations from Latin America and Asia will be brought about not only through assimilative processes such as generational succession and intermarriage, but also through the countervailing process of net immigration. In contrast to European ethnics, the ranks of Latin American and Asian ethnics will be augmented continuously with new arrivals from abroad.

Rather than creating relatively homogenous populations spanning at most three generations, the new regime will therefore produce heterogeneous ethnic populations characterized by considerable generational complexity. Processes of social and economic assimilation acting upon earlier arrivals and their children, when combined with the perpetual arrival of new immigrants, will lead to the fragmentation of ethnicity along the lines of class, generation, and ancestry. Rather than a slow, steady, and relatively coherent progression of ethnicity toward twilight, it will increasingly stretch from dawn to dusk.

Moreover, because the social and economic forces that produce assimilation operate slowly, while those promoting immigration work quickly, the rate at which ethnic culture is augmented by new arrivals from abroad will tend to exceed the rate at which new ethnic culture is created through generational succession, social mobility, and intermarriage in the United States. As a result, the character of ethnicity will be determined relatively more by immigrants and relatively less by later generations, shifting the balance of ethnic identity toward the language, culture, and ways of life of the sending society.

The future state of ethnicity in the United States is now seen most clearly in the Mexican American population. Upon the annexation of northern Mexico into the United States in 1848, fewer than 50,000 Mexicans became U.S. citizens (Jaffe, Cullen, and Boswell, 1980). Virtually all Mexican Americans today are descendants of immigrants who arrived in the 100 years between 1890 and the present. During this time, the United States experienced continuous immigration from Mexico except for a brief, ten-year span during the 1930s, thereby establishing a pattern that will probably characterize other streams of immigration in the future (Hoffman 1974; Cardoso 1980; Massey et al., 1987).

Owing to the long history of immigration from Mexico, Mexican Americans are distributed across a variety of generations, socioeconomic classes, legal statuses, ancestries, languages, and, ultimately, identities (Bean and Tienda, 1987). Rather than the relatively coherent identity that characterized European ethnic groups, Mexican identity is rife with internal divisions, conflicts, contradictions, and tensions (Browning and de la Garza, 1986; Nelson and Tienda, 1985). The fragmented state of ethnicity is reflected in the fact that the U.S. Bureau of the Census must use three separate identifiers in its Spanish Origin question—Mexican, Mexican American, and Chicano—each of which corresponds to a particular conception of Mexican identity (García, 1981).

Not only will continuous immigration create a new, complex, and fragmented kind of ethnicity, but the new immigrants and their descendants are likely to encounter a very different economy from the one experienced by the European immigrants and their children. Rather than rising prosperity and occupational mobility, current economic trends point in the opposite direction. In the United States since 1973, wages have stagnated and income inequality has grown (Phillips, 1990; Levy, 1995); the long decline in poverty rates ended (Smith, 1988); and mobility in the occupational structure has decreased (Hout, 1988). Moreover, just at the point when public schools used by immigrants have fallen into neglect, the importance of education in the U.S. stratification system has increased (Hout, 1988; DiPrete and Grusky, 1990; Levy, 1995), particularly for Hispanics (Stolzenberg, 1990).

Thus, not only will the United States lack the opportunity of an extended period within which to absorb and integrate an unprecedented number of new immigrants, but one of the basic engines of past assimilation may be missing: a robust economy that produces avenues of upward mobility for people with limited education. Continuous immigration will strengthen the relative influence of first-generation arrivals in creating ethnic culture, while the rigidification of the U.S. stratification system will slow the rate of socioeconomic advancement among the second and third generations, making them look more like the first. Both of these structural conditions will increase the relative weight of the sending country's language and culture in defining ethnic identity.

The new immigration also differs from European immigration in other respects likely to influence the creation and maintenance of ethnicity in the United States. Although the flow of immigrants from 1971 to 1993 is actually smaller relative to the size of the U.S. population than the flow during the classic era, it is more concentrated in terms of national origins and language. As Table 2 shows, the rate of legal immigration (3.0 per thousand population) is presently less than half that observed during the classic era (6.3 per thousand); and even making an allowance for undocumented migration (raising the total annual flow to 830,000) does not erase the differential (it increases the rate only to 3.8 per thousand population). But whereas the largest nationality of the classic era (Italians) represented only 19 percent of the total flow of immigrants, the largest group under the new regime (Mexicans) constitutes 24 percent of the flow. Moreover, whereas the language most often spoken by immigrants in the classic era (Italian) was confined to immigrants from one country, the most important language among the new immigrants (Spanish) is spoken by migrants from a dozen countries who together constitute 38 percent of all arrivals.

Thus, although European immigrants were relatively larger in number, they were scattered across more national-origin groups and languages, thereby reducing their salience for native white Americans and limiting the possibilities for linguistic segmentation in the United States. For European immigrants during the classic era, the only practical *lingua franca* was English; but since nearly 40 percent of the new immigrants speak the same language, Spanish becomes viable as a second language of daily life, creating the possibility of a bilingual society.

The new immigrants are not only more concentrated linguistically, they are also more clustered geographically. In 1910 the five most important immigrant-receiving states of the United States—New York, Pennsylvania, Illinois, Massachusetts, and New Jersey—took in 54 percent of the total flow, whereas the five most important urban destinations (New York, Chicago, Philadelphia, Cleveland, and Boston) received 36 percent of the flow. By 1990, in contrast, the five most important immigrant-receiving states—California, New York, Texas, Illinois, and Florida—absorbed 78 percent of the flow, and the five most important urban areas (Los Angeles, New York, Chicago, Anaheim-Santa Ana, and Houston) received

TABLE 2 Indicators of the relative size and concentration of immigration to the United States in two periods of the twentieth century

	Classic era 1901–30	New regime 1971–93
Rate of immigration (per 1,000 population)	6.3	3.0
Rate of immigration (including undocumented migrants)	6.3	3.8
Share of largest national group (percent)	19.4	23.6
Share of largest linguistic group (percent)	19.4	38.4
Share of the five most important destination states, 1910 and 1990 (percent)[a]	54.0	78.2
Share of the five most important urban destinations, 1910 and 1990 (percent)[b]	35.6	47.9

[a]In 1910 the five most important destination states were New York, Pennsylvania, Illinois, Massachusetts, and New Jersey; In 1990 they were California, New York, Texas, Illinois, and Florida.

[b]In 1910 the five most important urban destinations were New York, Chicago, Philadelphia, Cleveland, and Boston; in 1990 they were Los Angeles, New York, Chicago, Anaheim-Santa Ana, and Houston.

Sources: U.S. Immigration and Naturalization Service 1991, 1993, Tables 2, 17, and 18; U.S. Bureau of the Census 1913, Tables 15 and 16.

nearly half of all entering immigrants. The metropolitan areas receiving these immigrants—notably New York, Chicago, and Los Angeles—were the most important centers of communication and mass media in the country, guaranteeing that the new immigration would be a visible presence not only in the cosmopolitan centers of the East and West coasts, but in the country at large.

The increasing concentration of Spanish-speaking immigrants in a few metropolitan areas will inevitably change the process of assimilation itself. Through the new immigration, large communities of Spanish speakers will emerge in many U.S. urban areas, lowering the economic and social costs of not speaking English while raising the benefits of speaking Spanish. As a result, the new immigrants from Latin America are less likely to learn English than were their European counterparts at the turn of the century (Jasso and Rosenzweig, 1990). The emergence of immigrant enclaves—a process already well advanced in many areas—also reduces the incentives and opportunities to learn other cultural habits and behavioral attributes of Euro-American society.

Conclusion

The new immigration to the United States from Asia and Latin America that has become increasingly prominent since 1970 has several features that distinguish it from the older European immigration of the early twentieth century. First, the new immigration is part of an ongoing flow that can be expected to be sustained indefinitely, making the United States a country of continuous immigration rather than a nation of periodic entry. Second, the new immigrants will likely enter a highly stratified society characterized by high income inequality and growing labor market segmentation that will provide fewer opportunities for upward mobility. Third, national origins and geographic destinations of the new immigrants are highly concentrated, creating large foreign-language and cultural communities in many areas of the United States.

That these distinctive conditions will prevail in the coming decades and beyond is, of course, conjectural—other scenarios are also possible. I would argue, however, that the conditions I described are the most likely outcome of existing and well-established trends. If so, the experience of European immigrants provides a poor model for the assimilation and incorporation of new immigrants from Asia and Latin America. Rather than relatively homogenous ethnic groups moving steadily toward assimilation with the American majority, the new immigration will create complex ethnic groups fragmented along the lines of generation, class, ancestry, and, ultimately, identity. Rather than ethnic populations moving toward the twilight of ethnic identity, ethnicity itself will be stretched out across the generations to reach from dawn to dusk.

The uninterrupted flow of immigrants from Latin America will also increase the prevalence and influence of the Spanish language and Latin culture in the United States. Large Spanish-speaking communities have already emerged in the gateway cities of New York, Los Angeles, Houston, and Chicago, and Latinos have become the majority in Miami, San Antonio, and in most cities along the Mexico–U.S. border. The combination of continuous immigration and high regional and linguistic concentration will produce more such communities and will move the United States toward bilingualism and biculturalism. Assimilation will become more of a two-way street, with Euro-Americans learning Spanish and consuming Latin cultural products as well as Latins learning English and consuming Anglo-American products. Increasingly the economic benefits and prospects for mobility will accrue to those able to speak both languages and move in two cultural worlds.

Since these trends will occur in an increasingly rigid and stratified society, growing antagonisms along class and ethnic lines can be expected, both within and between groups. Given the salience of race in American life, the acceleration of black immigration from Africa and the Caribbean, and the history of racial conflict and hostility in the United States, the relationship between native blacks and the new immigrants is likely to be particularly conflict-ridden (see Portes and Stepick, 1993; Portes and Zhou, 1993).

Although these trends are now most apparent with respect to Latin Americans, especially Mexicans, the potential for immigration and ethnic transformation is probably greater in Asia, where migration to the United States has just begun. The potential for Chinese immigration alone is enormous. Already the Chinese make up 7 percent of all legal immigrants, not counting the ethnic Chinese from various Southeast Asian countries, and Chinatowns have arisen and expanded in many U.S. cities. Since theory and empirical evidence suggest that large-scale emigration is created by economic development and market penetration (Massey, 1988; Hatton and Williamson, 1992), China's movement toward markets and rapid economic growth may contain the seeds of an enormous migration.

Even a small rate of emigration, when applied to a country with more than a billion people, would produce a flow of immigrants that would dwarf levels of migration now observed from Mexico. Social networks linking China and the United States are now being formed and in the future will serve as the basis for mass entry. Immigration from China and other populous, rapidly developing nations in Asia has an unrecognized potential to transform America's ethnic composition and to further alter the meaning and conception of ethnicity in the United States.

DATA APPENDIX Immigrants to the United States from major world regions: Numbers by decade 1901–90 and for 1991–93 (thousands)

	Region of origin				
Years	**Europe**	**Americas**	**Asia**	**Other**	**Total**
1901–10	8,056	362	324	53	8,795
1911–20	4,322	1,144	247	23	5,736
1921–30	2,463	1,517	112	15	4,107
1931–40	348	160	17	3	528
1941–50	621	356	37	21	1,035
1951–60	1,326	997	153	39	2,515
1961–70	1,123	1,716	428	55	3,322
1971–80	800	1,983	1,588	122	4,493
1981–90	762	3,615	2,738	223	7,338
1991–93	466	2,104	1,032	103	3,705
1901–93	20,287	13,954	6,676	657	41,574

Source: U.S. Immigration and Naturalization Service 1994, Table 2.

Immigration and Ethnic and Racial Inequality in the United States

✦ MARY C. WATERS, *Harvard University*

✦ KARL ESCHBACH, *University of Wisconsin*

ABSTRACT

This review examines research about current levels and recent changes in ethnic and racial stratification in the United States. Research about ethnic inequality emphasizes that economic stagnation and restructuring are troubling impediments to progress toward equality, and it shows evidence that employers may still use racial and ethnic queues in hiring. A number of issues arise with respect to the incorporation of the new waves of immigrants who have arrived since immigration law reform in 1965. We discuss patterns of adaptation of new immigrants, including available evidence on the ethnic enclave economy and substitution in the labor market of immigrants for native minorities. We summarize new theories and hypotheses about the fate of the children of recent immigrants, and we point to topics in this area needing further research.

KEYWORDS

stratification, race and ethnicity, inequality, economic conditions, immigration

The half century since the close of World War II has seen numerous changes to the face of racial and ethnic inequality in the United States, while the problem of inequality has endured. When Myrdal published *An American Dilemma* (1944), the segregationism tolerated by Plessy v. Ferguson was the law of the land, and caste-like barriers separated blacks from whites. Myrdal's chief task was to comprehend the vicious circle that perpetuated these rigid

Waters, Mary C. and Eschbach, Karl. 1995. "Immigration: Issues of ethnicity, class, and public policy in the United States." *Annual Review of Sociology,* Volume 21:419–446. With permission, from *Annual Review of Sociology,* Volume 21, © 1995, by Annual Reviews, www.AnnualReviews.org.

distinctions between the races. By contrast, when Warner and Srole (1945) described the ethnic structure of a representative American city, they described the patterned relationships among its various European national descent groups. The variable these authors used to explain the unequal standing of these groups was the relative lapse of time since each group had migrated to the United States—time for initial distinctions among European descent populations to be erased through homogenization of the social positions of members of different groups.

In the intervening five decades, ascriptive inequality has been transformed by several interrelated events. The economic growth of the postwar decades formed the backdrop for a period of both legal and substantive changes in racial and ethnic inequality in the United States. The formal disabilities of Jim Crow separatism were dismantled by court decisions and by legislative action. Differences between blacks and whites on education and income narrowed. These changes, together with rising general levels of prosperity, created for the first time a substantial black middle class. At the same time, the open opportunity structure created by the expanding economy eased the incorporation of the children and grandchildren of members of the waves of migrants who had flooded to the United States from Europe before and during the early decades of the century.

Yet the story of changing inequality is not a Pollyanna-ish tale. At the close of the twentieth century, group differences have changed shape rather than disappeared. The background of these changes is the changed economic position of the United States. The rapid pace of economic growth in the immediate postwar period could not be sustained after the 1960s, stalling further progress toward racial equality. The export of manufacturing employment has put particular pressure on workers at the lower end of the education distribution where members of racial minority groups are overrepresented. An era of diminished expectations has thrown into relief the continuing relevance of race to economic opportunity.

The new global order has changed the racial and ethnic map of the United States one further way. Immigration has had a very large impact on American society since the 1960s, and most especially it has increased the diversity of the nonwhite population of the United States. In 1990 7.9% of the U.S. population was foreign born. The 19.8 million foreign-born people in the United States is the largest number in U.S. history. The sources of immigration flows have also shifted as a consequence of changes in immigration law and in the international pattern of migration flows. In 1990, 25.2% of the foreign-born population was Asian, 42.5% Latin American, 22% European, and 10.3% from other countries. The decade of the 1980s produced a large number of immigrants; 44% of the total 1990 foreign-born population arrived in that decade (Bureau of Census, 1993).

In this paper, we review recent literature assessing the impact of three factors—economic restructuring, racial discrimination, and immigration—on the current patterns of racial inequality in the United States. Because of the enormous impact of immigration on the composition of America's nonwhite populations, we stress the importance of combining analyses of the economy and of racial and ethnic discrimination, along with the new evidence we have about immigrant absorption and change.

Racial and Ethnic Categories

Scholars who study ethnicity are in general agreement that racial and ethnic categories are social constructions rather than natural entities that are simply "out there" in the world. This constructed character of ethnic groups has several implications for research. One is that the categories the analyst uses are bound to be arbitrary. For example, Office of Management and Budget (OMB) Directive 15 specifies whites, blacks, Hispanics, Native Americans, Asians, and Pacific Islanders as racial and ethnic categories for purposes of enforcement of civil rights legislation. In fact, this is an arbitrary classification scheme which may owe its high level of recognition to Directive 15 itself. Each aggregation includes subpopulations that are themselves diverse, both in the social and cultural organization of sending countries and in the average experiences of group members in the United States. For example the term *Asian* covers the experiences of so-called model minorities like the Japanese and Koreans who have high socioeconomic standing in the United States, as well as Southeast Asian populations that have experienced more difficulties.

There are no easy methodological solutions to this problem of classification, except for the recognition of the arbitrariness of any set of ethnic categories. We concentrate on the OMB minority groups in this paper—paying close attention to the distinct subpopulations that make up each aggregation. We do not survey the important literature on white ethnic group inequality because of space limitations. (For a good overview, see Alba, 1990; Lieberson, 1980; Lieberson and Waters, 1988; Hirschman, 1983.)

For most racial and ethnic populations in the United States, classification problems also arise because of the progress of amalgamation and assimilation. The significant exception remains African Americans. Because of the rigidity of the boundary between blacks and whites, few definitional problems arise: rates of intermarriage between blacks and others have historically been low. Even with recent increases, in 1983–86, only 5% of African American males had marriages involving white spouses, and 2% of African American females had white spouses (Kalmijn, 1993). Further, the common use in the United States of the rule of hypodescent (the one-drop rule) to classify persons of remote black African descent as African American reduces ambiguity about the boundaries of this population (Davis 1991).

At the other extreme, white ancestry groups have experienced extremely high rates of intermarriage with one another, so that many members of the conventional European national descent populations are of mixed ethnic descent. Scholars have debated whether the patterns of intermarriage and ambiguity about identity among white ethnics mean that assimilation theory accurately portrays the fate of the European descent ethnicities (Greeley, 1974; Gans, 1979; Alba, 1990).

Intermarriage may be especially important in the future evolution of ethnic categories that are neither European nor African. As we discuss in this review, current conditions of incorporation may sustain the structural segregation and the social significance of ethnic descent for these other groups that on average are much greater than for European Americans, but much less than for African Americans.

American Indians, for example, remain the most disadvantaged of major American ethnic categories on census measures of poverty and educational attainment. The persistence of the social significance of a Native American ethnic category 500 years after Columbus's voyage is evidence that ethnic distinctions may in some cases be durable. Yet one of the mechanisms that has sustained the distinctiveness of American Indian communities has been the spinoff of many migrants from these communities into the general American population. Because of the subsequent amalgamation and assimilation of many of these off-reservation migrants and their descendants, far more of the descendants of the inhabitants of North America self-identify as whites rather than as American Indians (Snipp, 1989; Eschbach, 1995). Thus the assimilation process walks hand in hand with the maintenance of ethnic boundaries.

New immigrant populations from Asia and Latin America may well experience processes of incorporation into the United States that will create considerable confusion about who is a member of a given ethnic population. Data from 1990 showed that because of intermarriage "about one quarter of the 2 million children with at least one Asian parent, and of the 5.4 million with at least one Hispanic parent live in inter-racial households with a white parent or step parent" (Harrison and Bennett, 1995, p. 40). These percentages will be likely to increase in subsequent generations of descendants. Available evidence suggests that Americans do not consistently use the rule of hypodescent to classify persons of part-Hispanic or part-Asian descent with the 'minority' component of their descent (Davis, 1991); ethnic self-identification is inconsistent in these mixed descent populations (Harrison and Bennett, 1995).

These facts suggest the need for considerable caution in making comparisons of different racial and ethnic populations. At any given cross-section, different immigrant-ethnic populations will be at different stages of incorporation into the United States population and will be different in the degree to which they are composed of ethnically mixed stock. Differences in the process of amalgamation and subsequently in the formation of ethnic identity may form an important component of the explanation of the size and socioeconomic composition of different groups (Hout and Goldstein, 1994). The social scientific analyst of patterns of ethnic inequality is ill-advised to overlook the transitory quality of the most basic ethnic categories.

Basic Data on Inequality

With this caveat in mind, Table 1 provides information, based on data from the 1990 census, on median family income, labor force participation, and poverty rates for the major minority groups and whites in the United States. These data show the continuing inequality among American minority groups, when compared with whites. Of the major racial/ethnic minorities in the United States, only Asians have a higher median family income than do whites, with an income of $41,583, compared with $37,630 for non-Hispanic whites. American Indians have the lowest median income with $21,750, followed closely by blacks and Hispanics. Data on unemployment follow this general pattern, with blacks and American Indians the worst off, followed by Hispanics. Asians have unemployment rates comparable to whites. Poverty rates also follow this general pattern, with blacks showing a poverty rate for individuals that is three times the rate for whites.

Measurement Issues

These simple rankings mask a more complex picture. The most important variables used to decompose these overall patterns are subethnic groups, gender, and family and household composition. Panethnic groupings such as black, Hispanic, and Asian mask very important differences among subgroups, which we explore further in this review.

There are also important gender differences in relative success of members of these groups—in general, women from minority groups look better in comparison with white women than do minority men compared with white men. So too, family structure is an important variable affecting the levels of success or poverty that a group experiences. For instance, while rates of unemployment and income are much less favorable for blacks and Puerto Ricans than for whites, some of those differences lessen when only husband-wife families are compared across the groups; but because blacks and Puerto Ricans have more families headed by single females, they have lower overall income and success rates. Asians tend to have households with more workers in them than whites; thus when household and family incomes are compared, Asians look better off than when per capita income is compared.

TABLE 1 Selected socioeconomic indicators for groups in the United States, 1990

Ethnic racial groups	Median family income, 1989	Percentage persons in poverty	Labor force participation[a] (%)
White not Hispanic	$37,630	10	65
Black	22,430	29.5	63
American Indian[b]	21,750	30.9	66.1
Hispanic	25,064	25.3	67.5
Mexican	24,119	26.3	68.3
Puerto Rican	21,941	31.7	60.4
Cuban	32,417	14.6	65.0
Asian	41,583	14.0	67.4
Japanese	51,550	7.0	64.5
Chinese	41,316	14	65.9
Filipino	46,698	6.4	75.4
Korean	33,909	13.7	63.3
Asian Indian	49,309	9.7	72.3
Vietnamese	30,550	25.7	64.5
Cambodian	18,126	42.6	46.5
Hmong	14,327	63.6	29.3
Laotian	23,101	34.7	58.0

[a]Persons 16 years and over in labor force.

[b]Includes Eskimos and Aleuts.

Source: U.S. Census of Population, 1990, Social and Economic Characteristics CP-2-1, Washington, DC: U.S. Government Printing Office, 1993.

Because of the differences in overall demographics of the groups, as well as differences in the levels of education and other human capital that groups have because of differential migration or the legacy of past inequality and discrimination, sociologists and economists interested in understanding the causes and consequences of racial/ethnic inequality also look at the net returns to human capital for different groups. Using statistical controls, they ask whether a given person with the same background characteristics, such as level of education, region of residence, gender, marital characteristics, has the same earnings as a statistically equivalent person from a different ethnic/racial group. The difference in these returns of earnings for human capital characteristics are variously interpreted as proof of some sort of market inequality or, often, as evidence of discrimination.

In addition to measuring income differences, an important difference across groups involves labor force participation, as well as unemployment. Researchers who focus only on earnings or income differences across groups miss differences in overall socioeconomic outcomes that come about because laborers are discouraged in the labor market or are unable to participate. Thus comparing income and earnings between groups will miss some of the causes of black poverty, given that black men have a labor force participation rate 8% lower than that of whites, and their participation is appreciably lower than that of all other groups except for American Indians. The labor force participation rate includes in the denominator individuals who are actively employed, who have a job but are not currently at work, and those who are looking for work. It can be affected by different cultural norms and values regarding women working outside the home, the age structure of a population, the overall health and disability prevalence across a population, and other factors not necessarily measuring "willingness to work." However, as a gross indicator, it tells us something about attachment to the labor force and the discouragement of workers.

In addition, monetary inequality is not the only measure of the lack of equality of outcomes in our society. There are other ways to measure inequality among racial and ethnic groups that we do not have the space to review here, including health and demographic measures such as infant mortality rates, life expectancy, morbidity, and disability. Ethnic and racial groups also differ in rates of home ownership, residential segregation, overall wealth, exposure to crime and toxic pollutants, and in access to power in the upper reaches of our society. In this article we concentrate on income inequality, recognizing that this does not tell a complete story.

The Situation of Black Americans

How has this current pattern of inequality emerged? The story is somewhat different for the different ethnic categories, because of the varying histories of the groups. For black Americans, the removal of formal legal segregation in the 1960s, along with the rising economic prosperity in that decade, brought rises in weekly or hourly earnings and increased education and returns to education. However, these promising trends have been coupled with changes in family structure that have led to the deterioration of household income for women and children in single-parent families. Growing rates of black male joblessness mean that rising earnings are distributed over a narrowing portion of the potential labor force. Recent developments raise no particular optimism that the wage gains that occurred into the 1970s will quickly eradicate group differences. Economic restructuring in the context of global competition helps to create structural barriers to improvement of the situation of persons with the least education and fewest skills to offer to employers. In addition, evidence suggests that racial discrimination remains an obdurate problem for African Americans regardless of social and economic class.

In 1940, 92% of blacks were poor; by the early 1970s the black poverty rate had declined to 31% (Farley, 1993). The relative black/white odds of being in poverty fell from more than 6:1 in 1930 to less than 4:1 in 1985 (Jaynes and Williams, 1989). Smith and Welch (1989) estimated that the annual earnings in constant 1987 dollars for a full year, full-time black male worker, inferred from weekly earnings, rose from just under $5,000 in 1940 to more the $20,000 in 1980, and that black male wages rose from 43% to 73% of white male wages in this same period. The ratio for actual annual earnings, given differences in labor supply, in 1980, however, was somewhat less at 62% (Farley and Allen, 1987).

Economic growth was a primary engine for improving the economic status of both blacks and whites from the end of the Depression through the early 1970s (Jaynes and Williams, 1989; Smith and Welch, 1989; Farley, 1993). Decompositions of changes in black-white differences show that the lion's share of the explanation for the narrowing of the wage gap for males is attributable to the narrowing in the education gap between blacks and whites, and to declines in the racial disparity in earnings as returns to schooling (Smith and Welch, 1989; Farley and Allen, 1987). Concentration in the south also had a smaller depressive effect on black earnings in 1980 than in 1940, because of redistribution of the black population from the south, but even more because of declining regional wage disparities and racial disparities within the south (Smith and Welch, 1989). White and black distribution to occupations also became more similar across this period. Jaynes and Williams (1989) reported that from 1950 to 1982, because of shifts in the American occupational structure, the percentage of white men in professional or managerial positions increased from 20% to 32%, and for black men from 6% to 20%.

The story about transformations affecting women is different. In 1940, black women had higher rates of labor force participation and employment than did white women. Using census data Farley (1993) estimates that, based on 1940 employment rates, black women have been employed for 14.5 of their forty years between ages 25 and 64, compared with just 8.8 years for white women. Increases of labor force participation by both black and white women led to increases in years in employment for both groups thereafter. By 1991, Bureau of Labor Statistics data showed that white women's years in employment during these ages would be 24.4 years, compared with 23.7 years for black women. By 1980, earnings ratios had closed for women in most education categories; for women with college degrees the earnings of black women exceeded those for white women (Farley, 1993). However preliminary analysis of CPS data for the years 1969 to 1987 by Corcoran and Parrott (unpublished paper) found that white women's wages grew more rapidly than black women's wages after 1977. Corcoran and Parrott suggest that as the labor force participation of white women increases, advantages of black women deriving from unmeasured differences in labor force attachment may disappear, unmasking a racial wage gap among women.

The economic gap between blacks and whites seems unlikely to close soon because the American economy seems to have stalled well short of the mark that would allow full equality. The impact of economic restructuring is particularly acute for those at the bottom of the education and skill distribution where blacks are overrepresented. Many scholars point to declines of middle-level jobs (Harrison and Bluestone, 1988), the redistribution of manufacturing jobs away from the central cities where many jobless blacks live (Sassen, 1988), and the rise of earnings inequality among workers of all races (Danziger and Gottschalk, 1993) as causes for pessimism about the prospect for rapid future narrowing of the racial gap.

One manifestation of these changes may be that gains in earnings have been offset by a growing racial disparity in joblessness (unemployment and non-participation in the civilian labor force) between black and white men (Moss and Tilly, 1991). In part, this increased joblessness reflects the substitution by young black men of "good" activities such as military service and education for work (Mare and Winship, 1984; Smith and Welch, 1989). Yet there is a trend toward relatively high rates of joblessness and nonparticipation in the labor force for African American males even at older ages (Jencks, 1991; Smith and Welch, 1989). Changes in the social fabric of some African American communities, partly a consequence of the narrow opportunity structure for many African Americans, help to perpetuate structural barriers to improvement in the well-being of African Americans. Growing rates of female headship in African American families have increased racial disparity in incomes and may create difficulties in the socialization of the next generation.

Female headship has been increasing for both black and white families, but especially for blacks. In 1940, 20% of black families with children under 18 were headed by women; by 1990 this figure had increased to 52%. For white families over the same period, families headed by women increased from 8% to 17% (Farley, 1993). Because female headship is associated with high rates of poverty, this increase in female headship for blacks has expanded somewhat the disparity in poverty rates for white and black families. Farley estimates that if the 1960 distribution of family type had held in 1980, black poverty rates would then have been 26% rather than the observed 33%. Bane (1986) estimated that in 1983 differences in household composition accounted for 44% of the difference in overall poverty rates between blacks and whites. However, Bane also cautioned that such decompositions could partially be artifacts of selection into household type, and particular caution was advised in the interpretation of trend data.

One important line of research associated with William Julius Wilson (1987) has focused in particular on the effects of these changes on African Americans who live in areas of concentrated poverty in the central city core of metropolitan areas. On the employment side these subpopulations suffer from a lack of education and skills and a mismatch between their urban location and the relocation of employment opportunities outside of cities (Kasarda, 1985; Wilson, 1987). On the social side, Wilson suggests that neighborhood concentrations of the most disadvantaged black populations have propagated destructive attitudes and behaviors that perpetuate the disadvantage, such as high rates of teenage childbearing, female family headship, drug use, illegal market activity, and detachment from the labor force.

A large research literature attempts to model the impact of these "neighborhood" effects—net of personal characteristics—on destructive behaviors and poor social and economic outcomes. These studies have shown inconsistent and generally relatively minor effects (Brooks-Gunn et al., 1993; Crane, 1991). (For a good overview see Jencks and Mayer, 1990.)

While the emphasis in much of the literature on the social and economic impacts of economic restructuring on the most disadvantaged blacks has considerable justification, Jencks (1991, 1992) reminds us that the population that suffers from the full range of problems associated with the concept of the urban underclass is relatively narrowly circumscribed.

Despite the gains that have been made by some middle class and working class blacks in recent decades, there is a strong body of evidence that discrimination remains an important part of the explanation of black-white inequality. Farley and Allen (1987) show that for a black male there is still an earnings disadvantage at all levels of economic attainment. From studies testing the reaction of employers to job applicants of different races, Kirschenman and Neckerman (1991) find strong evidence of direct racial discrimination at the point of hiring by white employers. Feagin and Sikes (1994) show that the experience of racial hostility is routine for African Americans across social classes. These studies suggest that the fact that a particularly heavy share of the burden of current economic changes is borne by poor African Americans is not simply an artifact of the uncompetitive labor market position of many black workers; the civil rights revolution has by no means eradicated racial discrimination in American social and economic life.

American Indians, Hispanics, and Asians

Questions sometimes arise about the prevalence and importance of discrimination to the employment and earnings of Hispanics or Latinos, Asians, as well as native North Americans. Peoples in these categories are often categorized together with Americans of African descent as peoples of color, or racial minorities, though this attribution is particularly ambiguous for many Latino and Indian Americans given the large volume of intermixing between European and indigenous American peoples. What are the patterns of earnings inequality compared to the white population, and what costs does ascriptive discrimination impose, given the historical importance of color consciousness in the United States?

Studies of the labor market experiences of Hispanics as a whole, and of the different subgroups, find that while Hispanics are disadvantaged in the labor market compared to whites, only Puerto Ricans are as severely disadvantaged as blacks and American Indians. Although, overall, Asians have a higher median family income than do American whites ($41,583 versus $37,630) in 1990, there is a great deal of variation among the subgroups. They range from the severely distressed Hmong population with a median family income of $14,327, a poverty rate of 63.6%, and a labor force participation rate of 29.3% to the successful Japanese with a median family income of $51,550 and a poverty rate of only 7%. The longer established Chinese, Japanese, Filipino, and Asian Indians are doing well—better than the white non-Hispanic average. However the Southeast Asian refugees from Laos, Cambodia, and Vietnam are not achieving as well.

What explains this pattern of variation? Multivariate earnings models suggest some evidence of wage and employment discrimination against Hispanics, Native Americans, and Asians, but that it is less important factor than in the case of blacks. For many Asian groups, of course, there is no pattern of net disadvantage to explain; though this result is compatible with the finding of discrimination in returns to education and other human capital attributes. For many Latino groups, problems in the United States reflect in part the attributes of the migrant pool. At a migrant's destination, his/her poor human capital characteristics interact with the effects of American economic restructuring to perpetuate disadvantages. For Asians and Latinos, the characteristics of immigrants and their absorption into the country are an integral part of the story. The regional concentrations and different modes of incorporation of the different subgroups as well as their differing times of arrival and social class backgrounds also help to explain variations in outcomes (Bean and Tienda, 1987; Nelson and Tienda, 1985; Portes and Truelove, 1987). We turn now to an examination of these groups in detail.

American Indians

The poorest of all the groups in the United States is also the group least influenced by immigration. In 1990, the Census counted 1.96 million American Indians and Alaskan Natives, which makes this the smallest of the four conventional minority categories in the United States. It was also among the poorest—a condition that has been noted by researchers historically (Brophy and Aberle, 1966; Levitan and Hetrick, 1971; Meriam, 1928). This poverty has been associated with the underdevelopment of many reservation communities because of their geographical isolation, lack of resources, and political domination by federal authorities (Cornell and Kalt, 1990, Snipp, 1986, Trosper, 1994, White 1983).

Earnings models for Indians confirm sharp wage disparities between Native Americans and white Americans. These are primarily attributable to large differences in human capital. Scholars disagree about whether the data show discrimination effects (Gwartney and Long, 1978; Sandefur and Scott, 1983; Trosper, 1974).

One difficult theoretical and policy question about Indian reservation communities concerns the impact of residence on reservations on earnings disadvantages. Standard migration models would anticipate labor outflows exceeding those observed from these resource-poor rural enclaves. For other ethnic populations, concentrations of disadvantaged group members such as those found on reservations might be considered evidence for the existence of imposed barriers to exist; for Indian tribes these are taken as an expected consequence of sovereignty. However, using data from the question as to place of residence five years ago on the 1980 census, Snipp and Sandefur (1988) could not find consistent earnings returns to migration from reservation areas.

Hispanics

In 1990, persons of Mexican origin formed the largest Hispanic group, numbering nearly 13.5 million persons. Puerto Ricans were the second largest with 2.7 million living on the mainland. There were slightly more than 1 million persons of Cuban origin. There were 5.1 million persons in the composite "Other Hispanic" category, including mostly Central and South Americans and other Caribbean people. Dominicans were the largest group within this category with over 500,000 people.

The outstanding theme characterizing the heterogeneity of Latinos is that Puerto Ricans do exceptionally badly in terms of employment and income, and Cubans do exceptionally well. Puerto Ricans are legally U.S. citizens; they are concentrated in the industrialized northeast and work in industrial jobs. They have the highest proportion of persons living in poverty, show increasing withdrawal from formal labor markets, and have the highest rates of any Latino group of welfare dependency and family disruption (Morales and Bonilla, 1993).

Mexicans have high labor force participation rates, but partly because of their lower overall educational attainment, they work for very low wages. Some of them are illegal immigrants, thought to be a docile and pliable work force, and so preferred by employers.

Many of the Cubans are political refugees, and a large number of them are concentrated in the city of Miami where they have created an enclave economy that provides employment opportunities for other Cubans, even those who speak little English or who are new arrivals (Portes and Bach, 1985).

DeFrietas (1985, 1991) shows that unemployment and earnings differentials between Hispanics and non-Hispanics depend mostly on differences in worker characteristics. Both Reimers (1985) and Abowd and Killingsworth (1985) conclude that unequal educational attainment is the major determinant of the observed wage gap. The evidence on educational attainment shows Latinos doing poorly relative to other groups. Comparing college completion rates, Morales and Bonilla (1993) note that between 1980 and 1990 the white population increased college enrollment from 31% to 39%, African Americans from 28% to 33%, while Latinos remained level at 29%. However, Harrison and Bennett (1995) argue that the popular press reports of a crisis in education for Hispanics are overblown. They argue that "native born Hispanics are almost as likely to complete high school as blacks and American Indians; the very low percentage of Hispanic immigrants with high school diplomas reduces the completion rates of the group as a whole."

Standard multivariate studies of economic attainment of Hispanic men and women do show evidence of discrimination. Stolzenberg (1990) found, using the 1976 Survey of Income and Education (SIE), that Hispanics who speak English well and who have completed high school have returns to schooling about equal to white non-Hispanics. However, he did find that less educated Hispanics do have less return to their education than do statistically comparable non-Hispanic men. DeFrietas (1991) used 1980 census data on income in 1979 and found a gap of 10% or more between Hispanics and non-Hispanics after controlling for age, education, English language ability, nativity, and State/Metro residence. The Urban Institute found additional evidence of discrimination against Hispanic job applicants in an audit study of employers in Chicago and San Diego (Kenney and Wissoker, 1994).

According to Morales and Bonilla (1993) changes in the American economy in the last few decades have hit Latinos particularly hard because of their low educational attainment and their labor market positions. Earnings for Latino men, controlled for inflation, actually dropped in the period between 1978 and 1987; in constant dollars they earned an average $49 per year less in 1987 than in 1978. Morales and Bonilla attribute part of this decline to the erosion of the minimum wage and the fact that 23.8% of Latino men were minimum wage workers.

Carnoy et al. (1993), using 1980 census and Current Population Survey data from 1982, 1985, and 1987, found a decline in Latino relative incomes for both males and females in the 1980s. They argue that the relatively favorable trends in convergence between Latino and white earnings in the 1960s and 1970s were due to educational increases and a shift in employment from agriculture to manufacturing. They attribute the recent declines to increased numbers of immigrants with low education and English ability and the concentration of Latinos in low-paid service jobs and to the decline of higher-paid manufacturing jobs. Harrison and Bennett (1995) used a 1990 census data to find that some Hispanic men continue to earn less than comparably educated white men. Hispanic men with less than an associate degree earned only 76% of what white males with equivalent education earned.

The recent trends for women Hispanics as with other women minorities are better than the trends for men. Harrison and Bennett (1995) found that among all education levels, except among selected cohorts either without high school diplomas or with associate degrees, Hispanic and non-Hispanic white women have achieved parity in earnings. More detailed analyses should be done with 1990 census data for specific Hispanic groups because studies done with earlier data show strong differences by national origin. Reimers (1985), using 1976 SIE data, found that Central and South American men received wage offers 36% below those for white non-Hispanic men; the differential was 18% for Puerto Rican men, 12% for Other Hispanics, and 6% for Mexicans. Cubans, by contrast, showed a 6% advantage over white non-Hispanics with a similar background.

Scholars have paid particular attention to the puzzle of high poverty rates and declining labor force participation among Puerto Ricans, despite the "advantage" of U.S. citizenship. The concentration of Puerto Ricans in declining manufacturing jobs, and the possibility of more virulent discrimination against Puerto Ricans of darker complexions are possible explanations, along with the availability of means tested transfer payments, the growth of households headed by women, and the growth of circular migration (Bean and Tienda 1987; Tienda et al., 1992).

Because in 1990 35.8% of Hispanics were foreign born, the question of how the new immigrants are affecting the overall standing of Hispanics as a whole and of the different subgroups is an extremely important one. Factors such as changing migration streams, the proportion of workers who are undocumented, and particular economic strategies of the foreign-born affect the overall profile of the different groups.

In the 1980s the group "Other Hispanic" grew at a fast pace through immigration. This growth also contributed greatly to the heterogeneity of the Hispanic population. Many Central Americans from countries like El Salvador, Guatemala, and Nicaragua as well as Caribbean immigrants from the Dominican Republic tend to have limited educations, high poverty rates, and low median family incomes. South American immigrants from countries like Colombia, Peru, and Bolivia have much higher educational attainment, lower poverty rates, and higher incomes.

Undocumented workers, who are disproportionately Latin American, differ from legal immigrants in ways that also reinforce the low income profile of the group. Borjas and Tienda

(1993) examined the employment experiences and wages of undocumented workers who applied for and received legalization under the 1986 IRCA amnesty program. They found that the legalized immigrants had higher rates of labor force participation than did the foreign-born populations as a whole, exceeding those rates by 5% for men and 17% for women. Undocumented workers earned lower wages than legal immigrants—they earned 30% less than their legal counterparts from the same regional origins.

Asians

Asian Americans are the fastest growing minority group in the country. The Asian American population doubled in size in the 1980s and now totals 6.9 million, an increase from 1.5% to 2.9% of the total U.S. population. This growth was due in great part to immigration. Of Asian Americans 66% were foreign born in 1990, and 28% of all Asian Americans entered the United States between 1980 and 1990. Southeast Asians from Vietnam, Laos, and Cambodia had the highest percentages of foreign-born, around 79%. Japanese had the lowest at 32.4% (Bureau of Census, 1993).

Those people classified as Asian in the census and other sources come from a number of different countries with different cultures, languages, and histories. Within national origin groups there are also differences in social class background, timing of arrival, and labor market opportunities (Yamanaka and McClelland, 1994).

Part of the explanation of Asian socioeconomic achievement lies in their greater-than-average educational attainment. The lower incomes and higher poverty of Southeast Asians are largely attributable to the much lower average educational attainment of members of these groups. While 23.3% of the total U.S. male population had a college degree or higher, 48.7% of Asian Indian men, 41.6% of Filipino men, and 35% of Chinese men were college graduates; among Cambodians, Hmong, and Laotians, only 3% of men had a college degree or higher. Harrison and Bennett (1995) report that Asians were about two-thirds more likely to have completed college than whites.

This high educational attainment is partly a result of Asian immigration selectivity. Many Asians enter under highly selective immigration criteria. Harrison and Bennett report that native-born Asians are still substantially more likely to complete college (32%) than are whites and other groups, but the differential is smaller than for foreign-born Asians.

Though the relatively high education and earnings of many Asian groups mean that these groups do not suffer the same magnitude of disadvantages as many other groups, there is some evidence that returns to education are lower for Asian Americans than for whites, though this pattern may be changing (Hirschman and Wong, 1984; Wong, 1986). Asian men and women needed more education to receive the same income as whites. This can be attributed to discrimination in the higher end of the occupational structure (the glass-ceiling effect) or to other unobservable human capital differences in things like quality of schooling or English language skills.

Hirschman and Wong (1984) analyzed 1960 and 1970 census data and 1976 SIE data for Japanese, Chinese, and Filipinos, as well as for other non-Asian groups. They found a marked decline in the direct negative effect of ethnicity on earnings (except among Chinese). They speculate that perhaps Chinese Americans do worse than others because the enclave of Chinatown serves as a funnel that directs Chinese Americans into low paying jobs. (This hypothesis is revisited when we review the more recent debate about the effects of ethnic enclaves on returns to education.) However, Hirschman and Wong found that there still were costs associated with Asian ethnicity—when adjusted for background variables, all groups except the Japanese had incomes somewhat less than comparable whites. Japanese men actually earned more than comparable white men in 1976. In a similar study, Wong and Hirschman (1983) found that Asian women had higher incomes overall than whites because they had higher amounts of education, lived in higher income areas, and were younger overall than whites.

In a multivariate study of income by education and by occupation, Barringer et al. (1993, p. 265) found that when other factors were controlled, "whites earned more than Asian Americans in almost all occupational categories except in the professions, where Asian Americans had much higher incomes, but even there they bested whites only among the self employed." They conclude that Asian Americans are highly educated and convert that education into high status occupations, but nevertheless they are paid less than whites for the same or comparable positions (Barringer et al., 1993, p.266).

Recent evidence from the 1990 census shows that Asian returns to education are approaching those of non-Hispanic whites at upper levels of education. Compared with other minorities, Asians are approaching parity in their ability to convert their educational status into income and occupational standing, at 92% and 97% of comparable whites for the annual and hourly earnings of Asians with graduate degrees (Harrison and Bennett, 1995). However, these analyses were not broken down by specific national origin groups.

Much of the literature on Asian Americans concerns the question of whether Asians' success makes them a "model minority" whose high education and income are due to cultural factors and hard work, which allow them to rise above adversity (Kitano, 1976). The academic achievement of Asian American children, and the more stable family structure of Asian Americans, compared with other groups in America, are cited as examples of the ways their overall cultural values lead to success. Researchers critical of the success model of understanding Asian Americans stress:

1. The heterogeneity of the Asian population, the economic distress of Southeast Asian refugees, and the existence of unskilled workers employed` in the low end of the split labor market (Poston 1988, 1994; Hein 1993; Lee 1989). These authors stress that there are dangers in viewing all Asians as successful, because the extreme poverty of Southeast Asians and the poverty of low skilled members of other groups will then not receive the public policy interventions that are needed.

2. The extra effort and household strategies Asian Americans are forced to use to overcome continuing discrimination, and the costs of that effort (Caplan et al., 1989; Kwang, 1989; Rumbaut, 1989; Espenshade and Ye, 1994; Kibria, 1994; Yamanaka and McClelland, 1994). These researchers stress the fact that many Asians avoid extreme poverty or welfare dependence through hard work and long hours that take physical and psychic tolls on individuals and families. Also families survive by dispatching many workers into the economy and by combining wage labor, government transfers, and other creative strategies to get by.

3. The specific problems faced by Asian enterpreneurs (Min, 1990). These include long hours and combining many family workers in one household, as well as facing the physical dangers of crime in shops in inner city neighborhoods, and the racial tensions, boycotts, and even riots such as those faced by Korean shop owners in black neighborhoods. While all of these criticisms of the blind equation of Asian Americans with socioeconomic success are valid, the fact remains that many Asian Americans are doing as well, or better than, whites. Southeast Asians are not doing well overall—however, these refugees came with little formal education and little preparation for their move to the United States. The question of what will happen to their children—the second generation—is a very

important one for this debate. Caplan et al. (1989, 1991) cite the educational success of the children of the boat people as a hopeful sign that there will be a great deal of economic mobility. In fact they cite the educational success of children of boat people as "truly startling and extraordinary" (although their study did not include the severely distressed Cambodians and Hmong). If the children of the Southeast Asian boat people do show enormous socioeconomic mobility and high educational attainment in the future, this will indeed call forth the model minority descriptions, and it will be up to analysts to revisit the debate.

New Immigrants and Native Minorities

Perhaps the most perplexing question about the current pattern of racial and ethnic inequality in the United States is how—given the economic restructuring and loss of manufacturing jobs that have occurred—some new immigrants manage to do well in the labor force compared with native minorities? Portes and Zhou (1992, p. 498) describe this as the "peculiar American paradox of rising labor market marginalization of native-born blacks and Puerto Ricans, along with growing numbers and employment of third world immigrants" (see also Sassen, 1988). This is related to the important policy question of whether the foreign-born take jobs from native minorities. Another question that motivates research in this area is why some immigrants seem to do better than others—how to explain the relative success of Cubans or East Indians compared with Puerto Ricans or Vietnamese?

The classic economic approach to understanding the incorporation of immigrants has been to measure individual level data on human capital endowments such as education, language ability, and the like, and then assess the returns of wages and earnings to those human capital characteristics. The standard model (such as in Chiswick, 1979) finds that the longer immigrants are present in the United States labor force, the more their initial earnings disadvantage is overcome. Chiswick found that the crossover point when the foreign-born equal or surpass the native-born is fifteen years.

The current debate about immigrants and their human capital skills revolves around the argument of Borjas (1990, 1991) that the average skill levels or "quality" of immigrants has declined over time. This is important for understanding the assimilation process of immigrants because of the frequently used assumption that convergence between foreign-born and native-born wages and earnings equals assimilation. If it is assimilation, recent immigrants would be expected to catch up to or cross-over the earlier immigrants and natives. However, if recent immigrants are of lower overall quality than earlier immigrants, then the progress seen in cross-sectional data is illusory, and more recent immigrants would be expected to have lower earnings than natives permanently.

Borjas' conclusions have been criticized on a number of points, including a failure to take into account emigration by the less successful foreign-born, (Jasso and Rosenzweig, 1990) and the confusion of "immigrant quality" with national origin differences and differences in contexts of reception and modes of incorporation. As Tienda (1983b) points out, the standard human capital approach, with its emphasis on individual differences, does not explain why, after extensive controls for various determinants of earnings, there persist differences in the rate at which foreign workers of differing national origins reach income parity with the native-born population. For instance Poston (1994), in an analysis of economic attainment among foreign-born men, finds that men from European origins do much better than those from other regions of the world. He also finds that refugees-turned-immigrants from places such as El Salvador, Guatemala, Haiti, Honduras, Laos, Nicaragua, Panama, and

Vietnam are not doing as well as economic immigrants from other countries in terms of their economic attainment.

Tienda (1983b) and Portes and Rumbaut (1990) argue for an analysis based on looking at the mode of incorporation or context of reception that different national origin groups face. The very evaluation of worker characteristics by employers is often not done on an individual basis but is affected by things like the degree of ethnic concentration of particular groups, and the degree of prejudice toward those groups present in American culture. The national origin differences Borjas finds in returns to human capital may be due to some unobservable individual characteristic that is a measure of "quality," or it may be due to some group-level characteristics, such as the effects of ethnic networks on economic incorporation, or discrimination in the form of hiring queues, lesser pay for equal work, or some other sort of differential reaction on the part of American society based on something other than individual characteristics. Lieberson (1980) showed that greater concentrations of particular ethnic groups in a particular labor market increased the chances for competition and discrimination against those groups (see also Tienda and Wilson, 1992). Later cohorts by definition face greater concentrations of their group as they join earlier migrants from their ethnic groups.

An approach that emphasizes the social as well as the economic context of the reception of immigrants includes an analysis of community level variables that condition the kinds of achievement individuals experience (Portes and Zhou, 1992). An example of this approach is the discussion of the ethnic enclave as a pathway for mobility for immigrants.

The Enclave Debate

When immigrants enter a new society they often face barriers to full inclusion in the economic activities of the host society. Besides through outright discrimination, this occurs, for example, because of the absence of network ties necessary to gain access to or to succeed in certain kinds of activities, because of barriers to entry to professional or internal labor markets that have the effect of excluding those with foreign credentials, because the skills of immigrants are concentrated in specific occupations, and because the skills may not be well matched to the needs of the employers in the host society.

An immigrant group's economic standing depends in part on the way in which it overcomes these barriers to become incorporated into the economy. Often entrepreneurism has been an avenue. A consistent finding in the examination of immigrant earnings and employment is the overrepresentaion of immigrants in entrepreneurial activities, and a positive relationship between self-employment and income (Portes and Zhou, 1992). The involvement of immigrants in small business has been investigated by a number of scholars including Light (1973), Bonacich (1973), Light and Bonacich (1988), Waldinger (1986, 1989), and Waldinger et al. (1990). The ethnic enclave (first defined by Wilson and Portes, 1980, and Portes and Bach, 1985) is a particularly important avenue of mobility for Cuban Americans. The enclave is defined as a "concentration of ethnic firms in physical space—general metropolitan area—that employ a significant proportion of workers from the same minority" (Portes and Jensen, 1992, p. 418).

Portes and his associates have argued that the enclave allows immigrants to find employment that brings better returns to their human capital than would be found in the secondary labor market outside of the enclave, and that it is therefore beneficial for workers as well as employers. They cite the Cuban enclave in Miami as an example of the use of an enclave as an unorthodox mobility path that in part explains the relative success of Cubans compared with other Hispanics. This view of the ethnic enclave has direct implications for long-held assumptions about assimilation. The argument is that people who stay within the ethnic enclave do better than those who leave it for employment, which is of course in direct contradiction to an assimilation model that would posit greater success for those leaving the ethnic concentration.

The enclave hypothesis has engendered a great deal of debate. While Portes and Jensen (1987, 1989) see the enclave as offering opportunities for economic mobility, Sanders and Nee (1987, 1992) see it as an ethnic mobility trap. These authors conducted an analysis of census data on Cubans in Miami and Chinese in California and concluded that while employers may be better off in the enclave economy, workers were not better off and may be exploited by their co-ethnic employers.

One difficulty with the debate about the impact of enclaves is that limitations of the census data that have formed the basis of many of the studies make it difficult to operationalize theoretical concepts directly. Different researchers have also used different definitions of the enclave, defining it by place of work (Portes and Jensen, 1989, 1992) or place of residence (Sanders and Nee, 1987, 1992). Zhou and Logan (1991) operationalized the enclave in three different ways, as place of residence, place of work, and place of industry. Using place of residence as the definition of the Chinese enclave in New York, they found positive returns for human capital for workers both inside and outside the enclave. Zhou and Logan also raise the possibility that some enclave economies provide better opportunities than others and that there may be gender differences in the operation of enclave effects.

Logan et al. (1994) point out that the ethnic enclave is a relatively rare phenomenon, characterizing the Cubans in Miami, Los Angeles, and Jersey City, Mexicans in Los Angeles and Houston, Chinese in New York, San Francisco, and Los Angeles, Koreans in Los Angeles, and Japanese in Los Angeles, San Francisco, San Jose, Anaheim, and Honolulu. Many other cities have large numbers of minorities without a spatial overrepresentation of an ethnic group corresponding to an ethnic enclave. This uneven pattern of enclave development across different cities and different ethnic groups is an intriguing one, worthy of further research investigating the mechanisms by which enclaves become established.

Research about the structuring and impact of ethnic enclaves constitutes an important part of the agenda for the study of the incorporation of immigrant ethnic groups. While we do not agree with Waldinger (1993) that the term ethnic enclave should be abandoned because of the difficulty of definition and measurement, we do believe that many of the central questions about its operation are dependent not on further analyses of census data, but on gathering new data with direct measurements of theoretically relevant variables of the sort gathered by Portes and Bach (1985).

Implications of Immigration for Native Minorities

Another important set of questions about immigrants concerns their impact on native minorities. Immigrants have higher rates of entrepreneurship and labor force participation than do blacks and Puerto Ricans in the nation's cities, and lower rates of unemployment. Do immigrants take jobs from native minorities? Jackson (1983) cites the possibilities for increased interethnic tensions if immigrants succeed and leave America's longtime resident minorities behind. Some of the popular media suggested the stress caused by competition for jobs was one reason behind ethnic tensions that surfaced in the 1992 Los Angeles uprising (Muller, 1993).

Despite these expectations, at the aggregate level, econometric studies show that immigrants do not compete with native workers and do not decrease their wages or employment levels (Borjas and Tienda 1987; Borjas 1990; LaLonde and Topel; 1991). Muller (1993) argues that middle-class blacks in gateway cities such as New York, Chicago, and Los Angeles experience upward mobility into professional and managerial sectors at rates higher than they do in cities without immigrants. However, certain industry case studies and local area studies have found substitution and competition (Waldinger, 1986; Bailey, 1987; Waters, 1994).

Various explanations have been advanced to account for the finding that immigrants do not take jobs from native minorities. The bimodal distribution of skills among immigrants means that some immigrants arrive with high education and skills. These immigrants do not compete with those members of native minorities who are overrepresented at the lower end of the skill distribution, and they may even begin businesses that then create jobs for native workers. Simon (1989) also argued that consumption by immigrants stimulates the economy, because immigrants upon arrival begin consuming before they are employed, thus increasing demands for goods and services even if they do not find employment. However, the effect is likely negligible at best.

Waldinger's (1994) work on immigrants and natives in New York City shows that the establishment of ethnic networks and the decline in the population of native whites leads to the establishment of ethnic niches in employment and job vacancies that defuse immigrant native competition.

One important line of research studies the effect of unskilled immigrants on the employment of unskilled natives. Many reason that illegal immigrants accept lower wages and worse working conditions because of their need to work and avoid detection by immigration authorities, and because conditions of employment considered substandard in the United States exceed those available at the margin in many countries of origin.

In the economics literature, a standard approach to the study of the effect of immigrants on native workers is to treat different analyses of cities within the United States as distinct labor markets and to compare labor market outcomes across cities with higher and lower immigrant densities. Using this approach, Butcher and Card (1991) examine whether the declines in the 1980s of the real earnings of the least skilled workers in the U.S. economy were related to immigration. They found that while the rise in wage inequality in the 1980s was bigger in cities with relatively bigger immigrant inflows, immigration was more associated with growth in wages at the high end for workers than in decline of wages at the low end.

Muller (1993) finds a negative correlation between blacks' income and the percentage of immigrants and between black youth unemployment and immigration. He concludes that either immigrants create economic growth, which in turn improves job prospects for blacks, or that Mexicans and Asians as well as blacks are all attracted to urban areas where employment opportunities are growing.

One possibility is that unskilled native workers migrate out of cities where immigrant workers are arriving. Filer (1992) analyzed population movements between 1975 and 1980 and found that intercity migration decisions of natives were sensitive to immigrant growth, and that immigrant arrivals are almost completely offset by native outflows. However, Butcher and Card (1991) find the opposite in their analysis of native migration and immigrants in the 1980s. These authors conclude that there is a positive link between immigrant inflows and net native in-migration.

Although these aggregate comparisons across cities do not show effects on unskilled native minorities of a rise in immigration, this does not mean that there are not substitution effects in particular occupations, industries, or work sites. Many black Americans believe that they are losing jobs to immigrant workers

(Waters, 1994). In a survey of hiring practices among Chicago area employers, Kirschenman and Neckerman (1991) found strong employer preferences in hiring decisions for immigrants over inner-city blacks (see also Muller, 1993, p. 179). Substitution of immigrants for blacks in unskilled work sites might take place in ways that are difficult to measure directly. For instance large numbers of immigrants available to do contract work or working in small enterprises might affect the ability of cities and industries to hire nonunion contractors to do work previously done by unionized workers. Blacks who had been employed in unionized public work sectors could suffer as a result (Muller, 1993).

These aggregate studies based on correlations between presence of immigrants and black employment and earnings in specific cities do not make clear whether blacks might have done better had immigrants not been present, and had there been economic growth. Employers may have been forced to raise wages for low-skilled jobs, which might have made them more attractive to native workers.

Given the stagnation of movement toward closing the wage gap between blacks and whites, the fact that many immigrant groups do better than native populations, and the historical tendency of native labor to look warily on immigrant competition, questions about the role of immigrants on disadvantaged native minorities seem likely to generate continuing interest. One important area for research in the future is reconciling the perception by many unskilled minority workers that immigrants take jobs from them with the econometric findings that substitution is not occurring.

The Second Generation

Because new immigrants are predominantly nonwhite, the success of some new immigrants relative to native minorities leads to an intriguing question about the future of the children and grandchildren of the immigrants. Will they follow some of the more hopeful patterns of success and mobility that seem to characterize their parents? Or will they experience downward social mobility as they join America's native nonwhite minority in disproportionate poverty, low-skilled work, and unemployment? While there have been no wide-scale studies of the second generation of the post-1965 immigrants, recent years have produced a number of case studies and a few thoughtful and important hypotheses about the experiences of the second generation.

Gans (1990) suggests that in contrast to the children of European immigrants early in this century, the second generation of post-1965 immigrants may well experience socioeconomic decline relative to their parents because of the much changed opportunity structure in the American economy. He outlines several scenarios of possible socioeconomic and social integration of this new second generation. He hypothesizes that some of the children of the immigrants might "Americanize" by adopting the negative attitudes of many American youths toward the low-level, low-pay jobs to which they, like their parents, appear to be confined. On the other hand, some may remain tied to their parents' ethnic community and values; by rejecting the negative attitudes toward school, opportunity, hard work, and the "American dream" that some among the native poor have adopted, these children may end up doing better. If this is true, the ironic result may well find "the people who have secured an economically viable ethnic niche acculturating less than did the European second and third generations" (Gans 1990, p. 188), and those without such a niche may become American but experience downward social mobility and reclassification as "undeserving members of the so-called under class" (Gans 1990, p. 183).

Portes and Zhou (1993) make a similar argument. They argue that the mode of incorporation of the first generation creates differential opportunities and cultural and social capital in the form of ethnic jobs, networks, and values that create differential pulls on the allegiances of the second generation.

For immigrant groups who face extreme discrimination in the United States and who are close in proximity to American minorities who have faced a great deal of discrimination, "reactive ethnicity" emerges in the first generation. For groups who come with strong ethnic networks, access to capital, and with fewer ties to minorities in the United States, "linear ethnicity" develops. Groups with linear ethnicity may resist acculturation in the United States and end up providing better opportunities for the second generation through the "social capital" created through ethnic ties. The second generation of those with reactive ethnicity, by contrast, are likely to develop the "adversarial stance" toward the dominant white society that American minorities such as poor blacks and Hispanics hold. They conclude: "Children of nonwhite immigrants may not even have the opportunity of gaining access to middle class white society, no matter how acculturated they become. Joining those native circles to which they do have access may prove a ticket to permanent subordination and disadvantage" (Portes and Zhou 1993, p. 96). These hypotheses rest on notions of network ties, community resources, and social capital that require in-depth study among both native minority groups and the second generation. Because the census no longer asks a question about birthplace of parents (last asked in the 1970 census) the second generation disappears statistically into the native minority population. This is a serious problem in assessing overall trends of assimilation and success for the post-1965 immigrant cohort, as well as in measuring negative or positive impacts of immigrants on native-born minorities. Determining which of the scenarios outlined by these analysts actually will occur will be dependent on careful ethnographic research in these communities, on gathering detailed and expensive survey data, and on reinstituting the census question on parental birthplace.

Conclusion

The research literature on ethnic inequality reviewed here shows that progress in narrowing the gap between minorities and whites and among white ethnics was made when the economy was expanding through the mid-1970s. After that, for many groups, the progress slowed, stopped, or reversed. The restructuring of the American economy in the last few decades has hit many unskilled minority workers hard. In addition, the evidence indicates that direct discrimination is still an important factor for all minority subgroups except very highly educated Asians. The large numbers of immigrants entering the United States in recent decades have had mixed success, but there are some intriguing ways in which immigrants seem to have achieved mobility in spite of hard economic times and nonwhite status.

In addition to the questions and data needs described in the earlier discussions of the second generation and of the ethnic enclave, we see some additional important avenues for further research. These include the unraveling of the separate and interactive effects of gender and race/ethnicity, an analysis of the involvement of immigrants in affirmative action programs, and the effects any such involvement may have on native minorities. In addition a sustained look is needed at the question of what continues to cause direct labor market discrimination by employers in favor of whites and immigrants over blacks in hiring decisions.

Acknowledgments

We are grateful to Sarah Song for research assistance, and to Lynne Farnum and Victoria Kent for secretarial assistance.

Immigration: Issues of Ethnicity, Class, and Public Policy in the United States

✦ ROBERT L. BACH

ABSTRACT

This article argues that the incorporation of immigrants into the advanced industrial states may be best understood in the context of recent theoretical debates over the changing character of racial and gender inequality. Specifically, it attempts to draw parallels between the conditions of working-class minorities and women born in the advanced economies and the economic progress of new immigrant groups. Shifting from a focus on individualized discrimination, emphasis is placed on the structural divisions within each immigrant group. For example, the bifurcation of the black community, resulting from the relative success of its middle class and the persistent decline of the underclass, is mirrored in the differentiation of immigrant and refugee groups. In contrast to the success stories of a few immigrant entrepreneurs or reconstituted fragments of an uprooted capitalist class, the majority within these immigrant and refugee groups are forming part of a restructured working class found throughout the advanced industrial states. This emphasis on the restructuring of the working class identifies grounds for a political framework based on a broad coalition of interests among those of various backgrounds who work for low and modest wages.

Bach, Robert L. 1986. "Immigration: Issues of ethnicity, class, and public policy in the United States." *The Annals of the American Academy of Political and Social Science,* Volume 485:130–152. Reprinted by permission of Sage Publications, Inc.

Robert L. Bach is an associate professor of sociology at the State University of New York at Binghamton. With Alejandro Portes, he recently wrote the book Latin Journey: Cuban and Mexican Immigrants in the United States *(1985). He is currently engaged in three research projects: U.S.-Cuban Relations and Cuban Migration; The Incorporation of Southeast Asian Refugees in the United States; and Women in the Garment and Electronic Industries.*

NOTE: Research upon which part of this article is based was funded by grants from the Rockefeller Foundation and the Ford Foundation. The opinions expressed are solely those of the author.

Since World War II, the world has been witness to an unprecedented movement of people from less developed regions to the advanced industrial states. Throughout most of this period, the expectation was that many—perhaps a majority of those who were not refugees—would return to their countries of origin. In Europe an expectation accompanying the widespread use of guest-worker programs was that when labor was no longer needed the migrants would depart. In the United States, immigration law and policy are based far more on the assumption that immigrants come to stay. Still, even here the possibilities of return have been promoted through a guest-worker program—the Bracero Program, terminated in 1964; and the circulatory nature of much of the illegal flow and the significant rates of return migration even among those presumed to be permanently resettled have worked in this direction.

In the 1970s, however, following economic crises in both the United States and Western Europe, it came to be generally recognized that large numbers of immigrant groups were not going to return home. They were becoming large, new, seemingly permanent ethnic minorities. Recognition of this transition from immigrant to ethnic group fostered both a revival of old views and efforts to develop new perspectives on immigrant adaptation. In the United States, the theoretical shifts are now fairly well known. Older theories of assimilation, though severely criticized for years, were resurrected under the guise of neoclassical labor market theories. Other observers focused on the characteristics of the new groups, emphasizing their distinctive cultural or ethnic traits, to discover the differences between them and the native-born population. Still others focused on the structural conditions of the labor market, identifying separate economic functions for immigrant as opposed to native-born workers.

The purpose of this article is not to review these familiar, if controversial, views of immigrant adaptation. Rather, the object is to advance a conceptual framework that brings together a variety of similar, yet disconnected, observations on the conditions in the United States faced by both immigrants and native-born blacks and women. Many writers have noted a general similarity in the conditions of immigrants, blacks, and women—especially as members of a secondary labor market. The commonality is deeper than generally observed, however, and it provides a basis for a conceptual framework that integrates the political and economic interests of each group. My aim is to make explicit what many researchers have reported in a variety of ways, namely that there has been a convergence of views on the nature of inequality in the United States that requires a reconceptualization of the role of discrimination in the current period. This conceptual shift supports a reorganization of the way in which we think about the incorporation of immigrants into their host societies.

Links Between Immigration and Racial and Gender Inequality

There are several reasons for constructing a framework for a discussion of immigration that takes as its point of departure a commonality between immigrants and minorities in the U.S. economy. The most important may be historical. A few years ago, William Julius Wilson (1980) noted that civil rights supporters were puzzled by recent developments in the black community. Despite gains in antidiscrimination legislation and the promotion of affirmative action programs, the situation of black Americans was deteriorating, and politically they were being abandoned even by their liberal white allies.

A similar concern has puzzled those engaged in the age-old debate over the economic progress of immigrants: Why do some immigrant groups advance economically more rapidly and further than others? In fact, why do some of these newcomers surpass even native-born minority groups? The puzzle is actually a paradox. On the one hand, a prestigious literature on immigration has argued that newcomers advance quite rapidly and even surpass their respective native-born ethnic groups within the first generation.[1] This literature had great influence on the Select Commission for Immigration and Refugee Policy, leading it to accept the premise that the nation did not have to worry that immigration would lead to long-term divisions in the population. This argument has never been reconciled with an impressively large, if politically less influential, set of research results that details the multiple problems, constraints, and barriers that immigrants face as they enter the United States. In particular, it did not mesh with studies that demonstrated that immigrants entered the lowest sectors of the labor market, where their opportunities for advancement were structurally limited.

The reasons for the puzzle in both literatures are the same. There have been profound shifts in the nature of inequality in the United States and a realignment of political and intellectual views of the importance of racial, ethnic, and gender discrimination. In Wilson's view, a careful examination of the issues shows that this puzzlement is due to the lack of an appreciation of the variations in the black experience, especially the differences that emerged during the 1960s and 1970s between blacks in the middle class and those among the working poor or underclass. The changes in inequality and in views of discrimination had a similar impact on ethnic and gender inequality, specifically posing an alternative to both the conservative and liberal understanding of discrimination.

As is well known, the conventional conceptualization of discrimination as an explanation for the subordinate, unequal positions of minorities focuses attention primarily on the individual. Discrimination exists in those situations where individuals with equal characteristics and experiences receive unequal rewards. These rewards are typically measured either by earnings or by promotions and hirings. The primary controversy between the liberal definition of discrimination and the conservative one is whether unequal outcomes are sufficient to establish the existence of discrimination, or whether intention and conspiracy to discriminate have to be manifest. In recent years, of course, conservatives appear to have triumphed: the prevailing view seems to be that discrimination exists only in cases where one person intentionally rewards another unequally, based on sex, race, ethnicity, age, or nativity.

While this debate raged, a very different conceptualization of the nature of discrimination and inequality was developing. Part of the reason for this conceptualization was the increasing difficulty of establishing—and finding—individuals who had similar or equal backgrounds. As advances were made by relatively small numbers of middle-class blacks, professional women, and immigrants in gaining some protection against the worst excesses of individualized discrimination, the outstanding feature of inequality became the very different locations in the economy occupied by these groups. For example, the debate on gender inequality—once totally dominated by classical concerns over individualized discrimination, or equal pay for equal work—became a much more complex and compelling argument about the differential job structures for men and women. Simply stated, few working women occupied the same jobs that men did and, therefore, few were even subject to individualized forms of discrimination.[2]

For blacks, economic transformations made a similar structural or compositional argument possible. Decline in Rust Belt manufacturing, increase in the demand for skills requiring access to education unavailable to many working-class blacks, and concentration in the central cities have separated a major portion of the black population from jobs in which they could compete for equal pay. As a result, individualized discrimination could become a problem for only a comparatively small segment of the population.

The connection between immigration and the shifting conceptualization of inequality and opportunity for minorities and women can best be traced through the history of the debate over immigration policy reform. The last major reforms of U.S. immigration law took place in the 1960s, when the struggles of the civil rights movement against discrimination were extended to the nation's doorsteps and provoked a significant realignment on the issue of who should be able to enter the United States.

The 1965 amendments to the immigration law were equally swayed by anti-discrimination sentiments. The primary objective of these amendments was to end the National Origins Quota Act, which included a virtual ban on immigration from the Pacific region and clearly discriminated against non-European immigrants. In fact, as I have argued elsewhere, the reform of the immigration law in 1965 followed quickly—and was fundamentally linked with—the passage of the Civil Rights Act.

Like the spectacular gains served by the civil rights legislation, however, these long-awaited immigration reforms faced a far different and more complex set of circumstances in the second half of the 1960s. The change in the composition of the immigrant population added considerable heterogeneity to both the class composition and the national origin of the influx. After 1968, the proportion of both Latin American and Asian immigrants rose rapidly and soon surpassed the traditional European flow. The occupational backgrounds of Latin Americans were generally lower than those of earlier European immigrants. The new emphasis on family reunification added a strong working-class component to the influx. The heterogeneity of occupational origins made background experiences and skills a new source of differentiation among the various nationalities and became an important source of subsequent uneven economic progress in the United States.

Two additional changes in the structure of immigration added to this heterogeneity. First, in the 1970s there was a large, self-sustaining influx of undocumented workers. The movement of Mexican workers to the United States became a silent invasion of persons arriving in a precarious, politically defenseless position. This undocumented influx was not limited to the Mexican flow. By the 1980s, there was a rapid increase in the diversity of national origins of those being apprehended by the Immigration and Naturalization Service.

Second, by the late 1960s, the Cuban refugee flow had reached an unprecedented volume. Refugee resettlement on so large a scale brought the goals of foreign policies directly into established communities where minorities and whites coexisted. Broader, more encompassing political realities began to influence and separate groups at a local level. Special government interest in the Cuban population created the possibility, and certainly the perception, that the Cubans in America were receiving preferential treatment.

The experience with Cubans served as the basis for theoretical and programmatic insights into refugee resettlement until 1975. Then, the fall of American-backed regimes in Southeast Asia produced a new wave of refugees. The diverse national and class origins of this new influx added considerable complexity to the immigrant population and changed the perception of what constituted a resettlement effort. In particular, the program had to change significantly to accommodate the Southeast Asians' very different social and class origins.

Another major change in this post-reform period resulted from the economic crisis of the 1970s and the restructuring of the U.S. economy. Inflation, housing, education, and employment became problems and reshaped the context for the reception of immigrants. New restrictionist pressures at the national border coincided with increased interest in differential group progress in the United States. For example, some writers on the topic advocated a strategy of economic selectivity at the border, to ensure the most productive and efficient integration of newcomers into the labor market.[3] Instead of civil rights concerns over equitable access or family reunion, the overriding principle became economic efficiency and reduced costs to social welfare programs. The new immigrant-related policy converged with increased pressures on the working class and the poor.

By the late 1970s, many observers still committed to social reform continued to concentrate on earlier battles over constitutional rights and did not fully recognize the newer forms of discrimination and inequality. As support for affirmative action programs for blacks declined and pressure for an Equal Rights Amendment for women waned, well-meaning interest in immigration reform remained restricted to broad legislative changes. The Select Commission on Immigration and Refugee Policy, for instance, still accepted as one of its primary charges the task of ridding the United States of all vestiges of a discriminatory admissions policy.

A primary consequence of this legacy of antidiscrimination battles over control of the border was that, while each new wave of immigrants posed novel legislative problems, the condition faced by immigrants in the United States lost its political attractiveness. For example, the treatment of Cuban and Haitian newcomers met with criticism in 1980. The unequal treatment and the policy ambiguity that accompanied the influx of Cubans and Haitians fit well the traditional, liberal concern over constitutional rights, legislative reform, and human dignity. Once these entrants settled, however, there was a noticeable drop in agitation and even in attempts to service them as they encountered severe difficulties in entering the local labor market, locating shelter, and gaining access to assistance programs (Portes & Stepick 1980). More attention was devoted to the immediate problems of individual rights at the border than to the less tractable problems of unemployment, underemployment, institutional racism, and abuse in the minority ghettos of major U.S. cities.

Community Perspectives

In the 1970s, the changing conditions of inequality produced a switch in emphasis to group solidarity and achievement. Black scholars turned to a black perspective, which focused on black achievements, racial solidarity, militancy, and hostility to whites. The feminist movement was similarly radicalized, and came to target economic and political equality with men as its goals.

Some immigrant groups adopted similar positions. For example, segments of the Cuban-American community transformed their economic and political goals into chauvinistic expressions of separatist pride and self-aggrandizement. From this Cuban-heritage view, the Cuban community in Miami is not an ethnic minority group but a community in temporary exile. While in such a state, it will maintain relatively distinct economic activities strongly defended by political and ideological boundaries.

Much of this kind of community or nationalistic argument served an important purpose—to counter the subtle racism of individualistic assimilationist views that stressed the breakup of community, the lack of skills, and the weakness of certain groups. The racism was replaced by a new affirmation of ethnic viability and pride that also de-emphasized the internal differentiation of the community—in particular, social class. For example, a Mexican-heritage view—stressing solidarity of persons with a common Mexican heritage—obscured the class divisions within the Chicano community. In the Cuban-American community of Miami the interests of a reconstituted upper class had effectively captured and defined the political orientation of all Cubans there, despite the considerable heterogeneity of economic and social conditions among them. In the Asian communities on the West Coast, entrepreneurial middlemen and highly educated professionals and technicians cast a generalized image of an aggressive, upwardly mobile population.

Overall, these community views pitted artificially—and erroneously—constructed homogeneous groups against each other. The analytical discussion was formulated in comparative group terms, black as opposed to white, men to women, and immigrants to native born. Little attention was devoted to inequalities inside each community or to problems with the economy that stratified each community. The result was the same, even when the economy was an explicit concern. This is best illustrated by the dual-labor-market perspective to the study of immigration.

Applied to immigration, this perspective has two fundamental premises: that the development of modern industry leads to a division of the labor market into primary and secondary jobs, and that immigrants constitute the best labor force for the secondary jobs. The first premise has made a major contribution to understanding the structural differentitaion of job opportunities. The second, however, reinforces the mistakes of the community perspective. The important element in the thesis is explicit reliance on a contrast between the motivations of immigrants and those of the native born. Native-born workers are said to resist accepting dead-end, low-wage jobs because they have career goals and rely more on the social ranking of their jobs for a definition of their self-worth. In contrast, it is averred, immigrants take marginal jobs that produce only supplemental earnings. The reason given is that labor migrants are target earners, whose primary motivation is simply to maximize temporary earnings and then return home. As immigrants settle, however, these motivations change, and the immigrants develop goals that more closely resemble those of the native born.

Even from this brief summary it is clear that the primary analytic contrast places immigrants, conceived to be a homogeneous group with shared motivations, against the native-born population, similarly viewed as an undifferentiated group. Such a view not only embodies the group perspective, but reverts to even earlier, orthodox assumptions and stereotypes of groups' characteristics. For example, as I have argued elsewhere (Bach, 1979), Piore (1979) draws explicitly upon sociological theories of racial inequality deeply rooted in outmoded concepts of the culture of poverty. He writes that for immigrants "the hallmark of the culture of poverty becomes the absence of culture and community."[4] Moreover, he argues that in the transition from migrant to settled ethnic minority, the migrants' culture of poverty "is an autonomous process that occurs within the immigrant community independently of whatever contact that community has with the larger cultural environment." The result is that these migrant subcultures create problems that retard economic advancement, through deviant forms of social adaptation, unstable households, or inflated consumer expectations.

This perspective suffers from at least two shortcomings. The first constitutes an act of commission, the second, an act of omission. Piore likens immigrants' motivations to those of housewives, students, and peasants, who are seen as seeking only supplemental earnings. This trivializes the contribution of immigrant workers, not only to the economy but to their households and places of origin. Ironically, given his focus on the functions of immigrants for the economy, it also misrepresents the magnitude of immigrants' contributions and roles in specific sectors of the economy.

Second, and more important for the argument here, this motivational perspective ignores the socioeconomic heterogeneity of both immigrant and native born groups; and the fact that a large portion of the immigrant flow simply does not correspond at all to the image of the secondary labor market worker is overlooked. As Portes and Bach (1985) have argued, the majority of legal immigrants represent a middle-class influx, composed of professionals, technicians, and those with above-average education. In addition, although motivations certainly change as immigrants remain in the United States—for surely whenever material conditions in one's life change, goals and motivations also change—it is the heterogeneous character of each group and the very conditions of resettlement that are the important factors in determining how immigrants' perceptions change and whether these new perceptions, in turn, have an effect on economic progress.

The overall problem with the dual-labor-market conception is that it fails to explain the paradox of immigrants' economic progress. Those who argue that the primary contrast is between immigrants and the native-born encounter problems in explaining the apparently remarkable progress of some immigrant groups and especially the success of a relatively small segment of each group. This is especially true when the successful immigrant group is nonwhite and when broad charges of individualized discrimination are hard to substantiate.[5]

The increased significance of refugee flows for the progress of the immigrant population as a whole also creates problems for a community perspective. For the most part these problems come about because research on refugees falls victim to the now-familiar orthodox views of their collective character. Refugees are presumed to be different from labor immigrants because they have different motivations: labor migrants are target earners, while refugees are permanent settlers. Such broad, gross stereotypes have been advanced not only by orthodox economists but also by those who have focused on the administrative necessity of finding a way to distinguish migrants from refugees.

The critical point, however, is that such a view reproduces the entire problem with group comparison based on overall characteristics. First, comparisons are based on group traits, and there is no empirical evidence that motivation, based on such undifferentiated group membership, exists. Second, since the motivations among members of each group are heterogenous, large segments of both the labor-migrant and refugee populations share reasons for migrating and set similar goals in the United States. Third, the emphasis on motivation advances a group-psychology view in total isolation from the material conditions faced by these groups in the United States. As biased as the first two tendencies are, the third is inexcusable. Such views are based on a lack of the requisite thorough appreciation of these structural conditions and, thus, are unsupportable. They are tantamount to assuming that once a group is labeled refugee it becomes isolated from the prevailing pressures that all workers face in the receiving economy.

Structural Diversities

By the early 1980s, the diversity of minority groups and the vastly different conditions they faced in the United States had produced another switch in perspective among many students of racial, ethnic, and gender inequality. It became clear to observers of the black community that civil rights legislation had benefited primarily middle-class blacks. For the black majority, the situation in ghettos and working-class neighborhoods was not improving. Inadequate schooling, substandard and overcrowded housing, lack of access to jobs and job training created a new form of segregation—segregation by class.

For working-class women, the situation was similar. Entry into the labor force was far from the panacea that had been promised by the forecast of equal rights. In fact, working women were faced with increasing obligations in the labor force, which they now had to combine with obligations in the household.[6]

As students of these group experiences pursued their respective concerns, they independently derived comparable expressions for the idea that class differentiation within communities was the primary source of differences between communities. Here, specifically, the literature on blacks and immigrants converged. As students of the black experience began addressing the differential modes of adaptation, researchers of the immigrant experience focused on differential modes of incorporation. In sharp contrast to individualistic perspectives that blame the victim and promote a culture of poverty—popular among some researchers of the black experience—and assimilation theory and the concept of inadequate human capital—among immigration researchers—the focus became the structural conditions that gave rise to observed differences in circumstances and behavior.

Attempts to establish these modes of adaptation or incorporation focused attention primarily on class alignments—above all, the restructuring of the working class. Considerable care was taken, however, not to de-emphasize the clear importance of ethnic and community rules of affiliation in determining the unique social combinations found in specific locations in the U.S. economy. Analytic attention was focused on how class and ethnicity interacted, including the nature of the regional economy, the social composition of the community, the degree of job segregation, the housing market, and institutional discrimination.

Perhaps most important, sources of change were uncovered within the community itself that had little to do with presumed group motivations. Instead, they were found to be structurally rooted in the availability of material resources. Within structural constraints, segments of immigrant communities have been able to mobilize resources through a variety of means. Some bring resources with them or create a critical mass through pooling dispersed resources from familial or kinship networks. Others gain access to political and economic power by serving as clients to established groups or the government. And still others, who have only their own ability to work, attempt to trade that ability for a sufficient personal and household income. This last, the largest group, has few resources for advancement, since it lacks both access to capital resources and political leverage. In fact, until immigrants become a regularized political constituency by gaining citizenship, they have virtually no political influence with which to attract economic benefits.

The Wage Labor Force

Based on this intertwining of class and ethnic resources, the incorporation of immigrants usually falls into three interrelated modes or patterns. The most prevalent, as previously noted, involves integration into the wage labor force. Facing the generalized pressures of the labor market, immigrant workers are subject to a variety of constraints and sources of competition. As predicted by dual-labor-market theories, these wage workers are disproportionately located in the sector of secondary jobs. A significant share, however, succeeds in gaining access to the primary sector and, as anticipated, acquires considerable monetary benefits. Portes and Bach (1985) have shown, for example, that among both Mexican immigrants and Cuban refugees access to the primary sector increases both occupational prestige and earnings. The primary mechanism for advancement, however, appears to be simply gaining access to the primary sector. Only in a limited sense are immigrants able to translate their skills or training into greater rewards once they are located in either sector of the labor market.

For these working-class immigrants, ethnicity is an important factor in differentiating their labor market outcomes. The secondary sector is characterized by antagonistic ethnic relations, in which the newcomers are segregated with members of their own group and native-born ethnic minorities. The primary sector exposes these immigrants to an Anglo labor force comprised almost totally of native-born workers. Without access to alternative resources, these wage workers must rely on networks within the community to locate jobs. Ethnically segregated job structures are reproduced through these organized social networks. Problems may arise when immigrants attempt to utilize existing working-class organizations to help secure better jobs. With few exceptions, the unions and working-class organizations in most cities are dominated by older, more settled groups outside the new groups' ethnic networks.

Working-class immigrants also face the full consequences of structural shifts in the U.S. economy. Unable to garner sufficient resources through training or access to primary-sector jobs to create alternatives, they succumb to the vagaries of an economy under rapid transformation. The original premise of the dual-labor-market thesis fairly accurately identifies the nature of this shift in the structural changes in the job structure. In the 1960s and 1970s, working-class immigrants were incorporated into the economy on the basis of mass production. As O'Connor (1973) argued in the early 1970s, monopoly firms engaged in standardized production encouraged the proliferation of peripheral firms whose dependence on low wages required highly competitive labor conditions. As Piore and Sabel (1984) have argued recently, later in the 1970s and in the 1980s the rise in new technologies—which are based more on small batch production and on customized instead of standardized goods and which are more sensitive to fluctuations in market demand—has created a more dynamic job structure. But this reorganization of productive relations has had only a limited effect on the immigrant wage workers. In fact, as Bach and Tienda (1985) have shown, the more pervasive tendency among working-class immigrants has been an increased segregation in operative and laborer jobs within the manufacturing sector at a time when other major groups in the working class are moving out.

Another important feature of the structural constraints facing the immigrant wage worker is the match between changes in regional economies and unevenly distributed geographical patterns of resettlement. The incorporation of many new Asian immigrants into the electronics industry in Southern California provides an example. Although working-class immigrants and refugees are consigned to lower positions in this industry, in many cases the strength of economic growth in the region has provided employment opportunities and sufficient stability to establish a good household income.

But incorporation into the electronics industry has been uneven. The industry has had several recessions in the last ten years, and each time the immigrants or refugees have been among those who lost their jobs. The electronics industry has also spawned a network of underground assembly operations, located primarily in garages and employing significant numbers of women. With few exceptions, this type of work offers only the best of a bad situation for wage workers.

Entrepreneurs

Exceptions to the limited progress in the electronics industry are important, however, for they highlight a second mode of incorporation. The opportunities made available for immigrant workers by industrial transformation have allowed for an apparent proliferation of entrepreneurial activities. Immigrant Asian entrepreneurs, for example, are frequently glamorized by the press and applauded by public officials. But they are relatively rare, fail at nearly as high rates as they succeed, and, more important, require the labor of an ethnic or immigrant working class to both build and maintain their operations. This mode of incorporation, which Bonacich (1980), Light (1980), and others have analyzed so well, involves the growth of a middleman entrepreneurial class. It emerges in the interstices of economic networks, often providing services to the larger economy while offering employment to fellow immigrants or other, native-born, ethnic workers. Those who have capitalized beyond small restaurants or food markets generally employ workers at low wages and offer few opportunities for advancement. In terms of the entire immigrant group, however, they constitute a significant segment of the community that provides examples for those searching for immigrant success.

Ethnic Enclaves

Another mode of incorporation has been identified as an ethnic enclave. This form is based specifically on the experiences of the Cuban community in Miami and the historical experiences of Jewish and Japanese immigrants. It requires a highly differentiated class structure, concentration in a relatively small geographical area, and a commitment by members of the capitalist class to hire fellow immigrants as workers in their firms. Unlike the middleman minority pattern, however, an important exchange occurs. The capitalist class offers employment to each wave of newcomers and, primarily through a subcontracting, self-employment mechanism, offers them opportunities for economic mobility. In exchange, these workers refrain from labor militancy and, in general, support the ethnically defined boundaries of the community. Although this enclave pattern can be observed in only a few historical instances, there are many situations in which similar principles of class and ethnic relations work on a more limited scale.

Southeast Asian Refugees

A final structural pattern may be developing in the context of the resettlement of nearly 800,000 Southeast Asian refugees. Although each of the three patterns described earlier can be observed in this group, the resettlement of these refugees has involved the state and, especially, public assistance programs more than in the other cases. The relationship of the Cuban community to a succession of governments has been a very important instrument of their collective advancement, but the principles of this kind of relationship are much different for Southeast Asians. Unlike any other group of immigrants, these newcomers have been resettled in direct contact with the Anglo community through the mechanism of refugee sponsorship. The outcomes of this pattern are still unclear, but it is already evident that the sponsorship relationship serves at least as a primary source of social and economic differentiation within the refugee community. Whether it promotes economic progress or not relative to other immigrant groups is still an open question.

The general point is that the progress of immigrant and refugee groups is greatly influenced by various sources of differentiation. In most accounts of the process, however, only a few attributes of the immigrant group are offered as explanatory factors. Assumptions of differential motivations, skills, and abilities are then substituted for a thorough examination and explanation. Instead, the multiple modes of incorporation described previously, which may coexist within one community and, on occasion, may overlap, explain the progress or lack of progress among immigrants.

The Immigrant Ideology and Public Policy

Profound and rapid transformations of the economy tend to be associated with major shifts in political alignments. Groups and individuals once constituting the mainstream of political and intellectual thought switch their positions as they confront new problems and search for new solutions. Given such shifts of viewpoints, it would be remarkable if the issues of immigration reform and the economic progress of immigrants in the United States were not also associated with such intellectual realignments. The emergence of a common base for understanding problems facing the largest minorities in the United States requires a reconceptualization of the role of discrimination in determining social inequality.

The recognition of the centrality of diverse but shared structural positions suggests, perhaps surprisingly, certain political strategies. For example, Wilson (1980) quotes Bayard Rustin's astute observation on the dilemma facing black progress: "What is the value of winning access to public accommodations for those who lack money to use them?" Echoing this theme, women ask themselves of what value equal rights are if they mean simply being allowed to work in low-wage, gender-segregated jobs. The need to expand the notion of equal rights to include comparable levels of involvement in all spheres, including political power and employment, is evident. To achieve that, it is necessary to restructure the U.S. economy, in order to gain control over the determination of not only the distribution of economic wealth but the conditions under which it is produced.

These issues underly the arguments about social inequality and highlight the significance of ideology and the support it provides for particular public policies. As many observers have noted, immigrants not only provide an additional, flexible work force and lessen the demand for social expenditures; they also undermine the political logic of the welfare state. It focuses attention on invidious comparisons between highly unequal groups rather than pointing out the real sources of inequality and subordination. For example, the highly touted comparative success of Asian-Americans can be explained largely by their differential incorporation into job and industrial sectors and by the region of their concentration. In fact, to the extent that research on migration accepts as the critical contrast the contrast between immigrants and the native born, it reinforces the tendency of migration to reduce the power of organized labor by dividing working-class interests into competitive camps. It also adds to the tendency of migration to join with other factors in making visible the association between public assistance and race or ethnicity.

This is the importance of the immigrant ideology—it takes vastly different groups and, by comparing them, makes a negative statement about those who are worse off. For example, it is simply not true—as William Raspberry writes—that Southeast Asian refugees with large families are not worse off than others. Even in the study he cites, that was not the case. And certainly in other studies, household size creates economic problems in several predictable ways.

Ironically, however, Raspberry has hit upon an important point. Ideology and group myths are important, as Raspberry has pointed out, but not in the way that he uses them. Given the structural divisions that separate large groups of workers within the black community, among working women, and amid the diverse groups of immigrants, there is a basis for a common understanding of the problem these people encounter. It is the articulation of these common problems and concerns that, if it is used as a new theoretical perspective, can provide a basis for political action and advancement. This newer perspective, rather than the myths of group attributes favored by those who are clearly in power or who fail to examine critically the nature of systemic constraints, will provide the common values for a critical mythology. Interestingly, one possible direction for this mythology is to replicate the experiences of working-class immigrants at the turn of the century: they found labor organization, political agitation, and shared values with others from the working class as the conditions for their collective economic progress.

Notes

1. For example, see Barry R. Chiswick, "The Economic Progress of Immigrants: Some Apparently Universal Patterns," in *Contemporary Economic Problems,* ed. W. Fellner (Washington, DC: American Enterprise Institute, 1979), pp. 357–399.
2. The National Research Council defines the problem as follows: "A second type of wage discrimination . . . arises when the job structure within a firm is substantially segregated by sex, race, or ethnicity, and workers of one category are paid less than workers of another category when the two groups are performing work that is not the same but that is, in some sense, of comparable worth to their employer." Donald J. Treiman and Heidi Hartmann, *Women, Work, and Wages: Equal Pay for Jobs of Equal Value* (Washington, DC: National Academy Press, 1981), p. 9.
3. Pastora San Juan Cafferty, Barry R. Chiswick, Andrew M. Greeley, and Teresa A. Sullivan, *The Dilemma of American Immigration: Beyond the Golden Door* (New Brunswick, NJ: Transaction Books, 1983).
4. Piore, *Birds of Passage*, p. 77.
5. See, for example, Morrison G. Wong and Charles Hirschman, "Labor Force Participation and Socioeconomic Attainment of Asian-American Women," *Sociological Perspectives,* *26*(4): 423–446 (Oct. 1983).
6. Among working-class immigrant women, conditions were doubly difficult. Monica Boyd has observed, for example, that the lower occupational status of immigrant women in Canada seems to be due not only to their being women, but to their being foreign-born as well. Monica Boyd,"At a Disadvantage: The Occupational Attainments of Foreign Born Women in Canada," *International Migration Review,* *18*(4):1113, 1985).

The Shifting Grounds for Immigration

✦ MICHAEL J. PIORE

ABSTRACT

This article is addressed to the theory of the international migration of workers to low-wage sectors of developed industrial economies from underdeveloped regions. Its starting point is the framework of analysis originally put forward in *Birds of Passage*, a framework built around the notion of circular migration through the secondary sector of a dual labor market. It then discusses how that theory might be amended in light of recent developments in migration patterns to encompass enclave economies, immigrant entrepreneurship, and the settlement process.*

This article provides some components of a conceptual framework for the analysis of changes in the size and composition of immigration and its impact on industrial economies. Its starting point is *Birds of Passage* and the conceptual apparatus developed there, which grew out of the attempt to understand the large flow of workers between underdeveloped and developed areas in North America and western Europe that was apparent throughout much of the 1960s and the 1970s, as well as, in the United States at least, in the late nineteenth and early twentieth century. After summarizing the principal features of that framework, the article then goes on to discuss how it might be modified in the light

**Michael J. Piore is a professor of economics at the Massachusetts Institute of Technology. He specializes in labor economics and industrial relations. The bulk of his work has focused on the structure of labor markets, particularly those for low-income and minority groups. His most recent book, coauthored with Charles Sabel, is* The Second Industrial Divide *(1984).*

Piore, Michael J. 1986. "The shifting grounds of immigration." *The Annals of the American Academy of Political and Social Science.* Volume 485, 23–33. Reprinted by permission of Sage Publications, Inc.

of the major shifts affecting immigration in the last ten years. I take these to be (1) the increasing role of so-called refugees in the gross flows, (2) the growing numbers of people involved in the immigration process and the increasing length of time over which that process is being played out, and (3) possible changes in the economic structures, particularly the job structures.

Temporary Migration and Secondary Jobs

The central argument of *Birds of Passage* is that large-scale migration between developed and underdeveloped regions has to be understood in terms of the structure of job opportunities in developed areas and the peculiar motivation of migrant workers relative to the motivation of workers born and raised in the area in which they work. The understanding of the job structure was based upon the dual-labor-market hypothesis. The hypothesis is that, for a variety of reasons we do not fully understand, developed industrial economies generate two distinct types of jobs. One of these sets of jobs, found in what is termed in this hypothesis the *secondary sector*, is characterized, relative to the other set of jobs, by low wages, menial social status, and considerable employment instability or, at least, uncertainty. National workers, because they are interested in long-term career prospects and normally expect a job to support their families and define their social position, shun such work. It is accepted, if it is accepted by national workers at all, only by those—such as students, retired workers, housewives, peasant workers, farm owners, among others—whose labor force commitment is marginal and who have other defining social roles. These people are frequently pulled away from industrial work by their other commitments, so that their labor force commitment is more commensurate with the instability of secondary jobs. Moreover, they tend to view their earnings as supplementary to those of other family members or designed basically to complement or facilitate their primary social activity. Housewives work for appliances, students work for tuition, peasants work to finance additional land purchases, and so forth. When such marginal native workers are limited in number or tied down geographically by their primary commitments, the society has a problem filling secondary jobs. Migrants are one solution to this problem.

Migrants are a solution because they typically view their migration as temporary. Their notion is to come to the developed area for a short period of time, earn and save as much money as possible, and then return home to use their savings to facilitate some activity in their place of origin. Often such migrants are themselves peasants and what they are seeking are funds with which to purchase additional land, livestock, or farm equipment. But sometimes they are planning to open a small commercial enterprise or some kind of manufacturing facility. In any case, because they view their stay as temporary, they are undeterred by the lack of career prospects in the secondary labor market or by the short-run instability of the employment. Since they are only working temporarily and in any case derive their social status from their roles in their home community, they are also untouched by the menial, even demeaning, character of the work. They frequently come from areas where wages, and the general price level, are so low relative to those of the immigrant-receiving industrial country that the work seems much better paying than it does to national workers. But even when the wage differential is small, the way in which they live in the industrial area and their peculiar motivation for coming enable them to save a great deal more of their earnings than they would be able to do at home. For all of these reasons, the very jobs that are repugnant to primary national workers are acceptable, even attractive, to migrants;

that acceptance is viewed in *Birds of Passage* as the engine of the migration process.

The difficulty with temporary migrants as a solution to the problem of filling secondary jobs is that they do not remain temporary. While many, maybe even most, actually return home, a significant number end up staying longer than originally intended. They then tend to bring their families from home or to form new families, and as a result many of their children grow up in the country of destination. Even if the original migrants eventually do return, the children tend to be attached to the destination. They view that place as their permanent home and are thus essentially national workers, with the same aspirations toward stable jobs that provide for the support of a family and confer status and dignity on those who hold them. As these children mature, therefore, they come into competition with national workers for primary employment opportunities while at the same time re-creating a vacuum in the secondary sector. Finally, when a significant portion of a given migrant stream begins to settle in this way, it tends to create opportunities for more permanent migrants moving from the country of origin and planning to remain on a long-term basis with relatives at the destination. This afterwave of the first migrant stream also tends to compete with national workers for primary jobs.

This view of the migration process tended to minimize the problems that it posed for the developed country. It stressed the advantages both for the migrants themselves and to the place of origin, especially relative to other ways of managing a dual labor market. It pointed public policy away from efforts to curtail the migration process altogether and toward ways of managing the process and controlling the size of the secondary sector toward which it was targeted. It stressed in particular policies and procedures for facilitating the return of the migrants, for smoothing the upward mobility of their children who stayed, and for limiting the size of the secondary sector through minimum wages and other forms of labor legislation.

More Conventional Economic Theories

This view of the migration process may be contrasted with the view conventional in economics. The latter is one in which migration is driven by an income differential between industrial areas and less developed countries or regions. People are assumed to be motivated almost entirely by income and as a result move toward industrial areas where the income is higher. The movement lowers the supply of labor in the area of origin, driving up wages there, and increases the supply of labor at the destination, forcing down its wages. Eventually, the wages in the two areas will equalize, bringing the migration to a halt. The basic model is, of course, modified to allow for costs such as transportation, job search, and the like. These costs are treated as an investment that the individual makes in order to obtain the higher income at the destination, and they must be deducted from the income there in order to determine the net returns from migration. When they are taken into account, wages in the two areas may not completely equalize, but since such costs are small, the wages will still be close. Models like these lie behind predictions that the population growth rates in Latin America will lead to a flood of immigrants. The notion is that the growth in population will swell the labor force, driving down wages and increasing the size of the income differential; as the income differential increases, the flow of migrants will rise.

As an explanation of the patterns of immigration that we actually observe, this model clearly does not work. In the American case, for example, it fails to explain the chief paradox of historical migration patterns: the American labor market drew first on distant

European countries for labor and only lately has tapped domestic labor reserves in the rural South and those of its close neighbors in Latin America and the Caribbean, despite the fact that transportation costs for the latter were clearly less than for the former and the cultural and linguistic differences that would seem to determine other costs of migration were also less extreme. Patterns of recent migration into Europe cannot be explained by the income differential either.

That the economic model survives at all under these circumstances is explainable by the fact that one can almost always find some plausible imperfection—cost—in the form of information, transportation, or the like to introduce into the model to get the desired effect. The problem is that these costs tend to be introduced in an ad hoc fashion. The explanations that are generated may or may not be valid but they are not coming out of the economic model, and the latter—by being used to explain immigration in this way—is rendered tautological. The framework of *Birds of Passage* can be understood in these terms as an effort to add enough additional technological and sociological structure to the conventional model to make it once more a genuine theory. The result is nonetheless disturbing to most economists, because almost all actual migration processes to which the theory is applied are driven by the technological and sociological variable and not by cost differentials. I point that out merely to clarify the conceptual issues here. I happen to think that the process is actually driven by the technological and sociological variable.

The dual-labor-market model is sometimes characterized, especially by economists, as sociological, and hence it is useful to distinguish it from other sociological approaches. There are various explanations of migration that link the sociological characteristics of the workers at their place of origin to the roles they assume at the destination, but generally the linkages are different for each ethnic group. For example, religion and the experience of oppression are used to explain Jewish success, family structure and the experience of oppression to explain the lack of black success, and so on. Most such theories, it should be added, are not designed to explain the migration process itself. Rather, they are addressed to the issue of assimilation or what is called, in the framework of *Birds of Passage*, settlement.

The dual-labor-market hypothesis attempts to identify a single set of factors common to all migrants and to relate those factors systematically to the economic structure of industrial and preindustrial societies. As a type of theory, it is thus closer to Marxism, although the structural factors that it makes responsible for movement are not those upon which classical Marxism focuses.

Enclave Economy

Among structural theories that share this ambition, the major alternative in the migration literature to the dual-labor-market hypothesis is the notion of the enclave economy. The term *enclave economy* was coined by Alejandro Portes (1981) to explain the differences in the employment patterns of Mexican and Cuban immigrants to the United States. His argument is that the Mexican pattern conforms closely to the dual-labor-market hypothesis: circular migration through low-wage menial jobs attached to job hierarchies in which higher-level opportunities were held by American nationals. Jobs held by Mexicans were also located in enterprises owned and managed by native workers. The Cubans, however, succeeded in creating in Miami a whole economy composed of Cuban-owned enterprises. Even when Cuban immigrants were holding low-level jobs, they tended to work in enterprises in which there was an integrated job hierarchy. They were able to work their way up from bottom-level jobs and, often, eventually became managers and entrepreneurs in their own right. In this way, immigrants were able to obtain stable jobs and advancement in the first generation. First-generation immigrants still remained cut off from the mainstream of American society—remaining in the enclave economy, so to speak—but the integration of their children involved only lateral transfer out of the enclave and into positions of similar social status in the mainstream. In contrast, Mexican children had not only to move out of the ethnic community to integrate, but they also had to move across social and labor market barriers at the same time.

The Cuban economy in Miami is unique in the American, postwar immigrant experience; indeed, it is difficult to find a comparable historical example. But a number of immigrant groups have managed to gain control over a significant segment of a regional industry so that social mobility of the kind envisaged in the enclave hypothesis is possible. Jews and Italians established such footholds in the New York City garment industry; the Irish and Italians have held similar positions in the construction industry in a number of cities. The Irish position in local government should have worked to similar effect. Most recently, Asian immigrants have advanced in a similar way.

Tom Bailey and Roger Waldinger (1983) have attempted to explore modified versions of the enclave hypothesis in contemporary New York—Bailey (1983) in the restaurant industry and Waldinger (1984) in the garment industry. In both industries there is substantial immigrant entrepreneurship. The findings are complex. Entrepreneurship does not lead automatically to an enclave economy as Portes (1981) uses the term. Immigrant employers, like employers in general, often prefer to mix different ethnic groups, reserving higher-level positions for their own family and avoiding the paternalistic obligations that the employment of their compatriots seems to entail. But there are ethnic enclaves in these New York industries—particularly among the Chinese, less so among Hispanic groups. Thus it seems meaningful to speak of the dual labor market and the enclave labor market as two distinct economic patterns associated with immigration. Once these two patterns are established, one is led to ask a series of analytical questions about when one or the other might prevail.

With regard to this distinction I find existing research too limited, and not sufficiently focused, to provide meaningful answers to this type of question, but it does suggest several observations. First, enclave economies appear to require immigrant entrepreneurship and, hence, bring to the fore the question of why some immigrant groups engage in significant entrepreneurial activities and others do not. Second, entrepreneurship is not sufficient to establish such activities for at least two reasons. One of these is that, as we have just seen, some immigrant employers do not like to employ members of their own ethnic group. The other is that many small business activities do not provide many supplementary employment opportunities. Almost every immigrant community seems to provide minimal business opportunities for its own members—ethnic food stores, travel and moving agencies involved in the immigration process itself, legal and medical services—but none of these are big employers. For the latter, the immigrant entrepreneurs have to gain a foothold in the larger market, as the examples of garment, construction, and government services suggest.

The two patterns of dualism and enclavism and the observations about the latter, limited though they are, are growing in significance because they appear to shed some light on the principal changes presently occurring in the immigrant process, namely, the shift toward settlement among the older immigrants and toward refugees as a principal source of new immigration.

Refugees

The major difference between refugees and other migrants is that refugees appear to see their immigration from the very start as permanent. They may entertain dreams of returning to their home and engage in extensive political activity designed to permit them to do this, but they seem to see their economic future as dependent upon the ability to establish a secure position and advance within the economy of the destination. They are not, moreover, in a position simply to leave and return home when economic conditions turn bad at the destination, as are temporary migrants.

One of the results of this distinction is that where there are the two types of migrants moving into a single, and limited, set of employment opportunities, the refugees are likely to displace the temporary migrants. Because the temporaries have an overwhelmingly economic motivation, they do not remain unless it is profitable to do so. Undocumented migrants in the United States frequently say that there is no point in staying unless they can hold down two jobs, and very few are willing to wait around if they cannot find any jobs at all.

Refugees, on the other hand, have no place to go, and hence they are likely to be more persistent in getting and keeping whatever jobs are available. It is true that because they are permanent, they may be more concerned about the social character of their jobs than temporary migrants are, but unlike national workers, they generally have few economic alternatives. This is so in part because they often lack access to transfer payments and other social services. But the exclusive emphasis on governmental aid in policy debates on this subject seems to me to miss the major point. Most aid in an established community comes from other members of the community, especially close family members, and governmental aid is—historically, at least—better seen as an institutional expression of community rather than an artificial intrusion upon private affairs. If the aid enables people to refuse secondary jobs and hold out for higher stakes and better jobs, it is because job characteristics reflect upon the family and larger community of which the worker is a part. Refugee families are not in a position to protect their status in this way. Sometimes they manage to preserve status structures from their communities of origin as a substitute for status that is unavailable in the place of refuge, but that does not prevent—in fact, it may even facilitate—their acceptance of low-status, low-wage jobs.

This is particularly important in the United States at the moment. It implies that widely expressed fears that the refugees will be added to a labor force already overbloated with undocumented migrants are unfounded. To the extent that the refugees have been flowing into the secondary sector of a dual labor market, they have probably displaced temporary migrants and cut back the undocumented migration flow, albeit maybe not on a one-for-one basis.

The other likelihood is that the refugees are more apt to form economic enclaves. The enclaves will affect not only the process of integration and social mobility but possibly the total number of available economic opportunities.

The Settlement of Temporary Migrant Streams

The other factor making the enclave hypothesis increasingly significant is the settlement of previously temporary streams of migrants. The new migration began in Europe in the early 1960s and in the United States in the latter half of that decade. It has now been going on in a number of places for over twenty years. Even if most of the migrants went home eventually, the period of time and the numbers involved imply a substantial residue of settled people, and direct observation suggests that there are indeed stable communities that are being joined by new, permanent settlers from families that initially remained behind. This has become the central problem of migration policy in Europe, where, because the migration in the 1960s and 1970s was designed to be temporary, it has come as something of a shock.

We seem to know very little about the capacity of such initially temporary migrant streams to develop enclave-type structures. Perhaps, if a careful investigation were possible, it would prove that only refugees actually do so, although the prevalence of such structures among the Italians, Portuguese, and Greeks in the United States and northern Europe as well as the Jews and Irish among the nineteenth-century immigrants to the United States implies that this is not the case.

Job Structures

The other half of the framework of analysis originally developed in *Birds of Passage* centered on the job structure. Two types of developments in this aspect of the problem in recent years are affecting the migration process. First, the actual employment structure—certainly in Europe and possibly in the United States as well—appears to have become less conducive to international migration in the last decade. This development is readily understood in terms of the original framework. Second, the forces guiding that structure appear to be in the process of change. This does not necessarily imply that the particular hypotheses about the job structure upon which the original analysis rested were wrong, but it does suggest that they are likely to become increasingly irrelevant. One must then ask what the new forces imply for the evolution of the migration process.

The Evolution of Actual Employment

In western Europe, the principal trends have been a stagnation in the overall level of employment, a precipitous rise in the level of unemployment, and a shift in the composition of employment opportunities away from manufacturing toward services and within manufacturing out of heavy, so-called smokestack industries. There has also been a vociferous demand on the part of European employers for more flexibility in employment commitments and an attempt to make greater use of part-time and temporary workers.

U.S. employment levels have varied more radically over the business cycle than those of western Europe, but there has been, in marked contrast to Europe, a large increase in the number of jobs. Overall levels of unemployment have also increased in the past decade but relatively less than in Europe. The structure of employment opportunities has changed as well. The shift in the structure has paralleled that of Europe. There have been relative declines in smokestack industries and in manufacturing as a whole; relative increases in services, although because aggregate employment expanded, the structural shift involved a much larger absolute expansion of the service section; a smaller decline in heavy industry; and a slight expansion in overall manufacturing employment. In the United States, traditional light industry, such as shoes, garments, and textiles, also exhibited declining employment between 1981 and 1985, although unlike other employment changes, this seemed to be less a trend than a reflection of the temporary overvaluation of the dollar.

The net effect of these changes was probably a decline in the demand for migrants relative to national workers. This decline is clearly evident in western Europe, where it can be documented statistically. In Europe, in fact, there has been a net outflow of migrants in most recent years. Since those who returned home were probably the least attached to the country of destination, the effect was to make the migrant population a more permanent and more settled one. This was in addition to the effects of refugees and of the mere passage of time on settlement. Data are not available to document these effects in the United States, since such a large portion of the transient migrants is clandestine, but the changing composition of employment opportunities may not have reduced the level of migration or contributed significantly to settlement because the absolute level of employment did not decrease.

Most of these changes in the composition of employment are readily understandable within the framework of the dual-labor-market hypothesis. The secondary sector, into which the migrants are recruited, exists in this hypothesis in large part because the jobs held by nationals in the primary sector are secured by institutional arrangements from the flux and uncertainty of a capitalist economy. The flux and uncertainty themselves continue, however, and lead the employers to create a secondary sector that can absorb them. It is not surprising, therefore, that when the instability and uncertainty that the secondary sector was designed to handle materialized with a vengence in the late 1970s and early 1980s, it should hit migrant employment hardest and the migrants should respond by going—or being sent—home. That the most temporary should leave first, and the residual migrant population should become increasingly stable, also follows from the theory. If in the United States migration has fallen off less than in Europe, it is because U.S. employment levels, after declining in 1981 and 1982, recovered and then went on to expand whereas in Europe they did not recover.

The increasing reliance on national workers in the secondary sector can be understood in similar terms. If uncertainty and instability remain once the temporary migrants have been sent home, employers must obviously look for other sources of labor to absorb them. The future of temporary migration may, however, come to depend upon whether employers can find the flexibility they are still looking for at home in other labor force groups. In Europe, the focus at the moment is on changes in the institutional structures securing employment that would let employers use nationals more flexibly, that is, more as they treated migrants in the past. Managers do not seem to doubt that they will be able to find national workers who are willing to be used in this way if they can obtain the legal reforms that such use would require.

These legal barriers do not exist in the United States, and employers have relied heavily on the postwar baby boom, which bloated the youth age cohort, and on women to provide a flexible national labor force. The baby-boom cohorts are, however, becoming adult and the female labor force may be approaching the limit in terms of both its size and its willingness to accept part-time and/or unstable work. The focus in public policy is then likely to shift—indeed, it has already begun to do so—to the retired work force and those aspects of pensions and social security that determine whether retirees need, and can easily take, postretirement jobs. A political impasse on this question would force greater reliance upon migrants if the dual-labor-market structure persists. Other developments, however, suggest that the underlying structure of the labor market may be shifting as well.

The End of Mass Production

The dual-labor-market structure emerged in a world that had two critical characteristics. First, the technology was dominated by mass production, and the labor market institutions were structured by that technical form. Second, production was oriented largely toward domestic demand.

The dominance of mass production led to the division of the economy into a technologically progressive core, which focused on mass production, and a subordinate, relatively backward periphery. In the core, efficiency was achieved through the progressive division of the productive process into increasingly narrow, highly defined tasks and through the development of specialized resources specifically tailored to the peculiarities of the particular operation to which they were assigned. These specialized resources consisted first of narrowly trained workers—called, in the United States, semiskilled and called simply, in Europe, specialized—and then of dedicated pieces of capital equipment. The job structure of the core was composed of the semiskilled workers on the one hand and of managers and engineers who designed, directed, and coordinated the otherwise isolated and independent work stations, on the other.

Mass production was efficient, however, only for markets that were large enough to support the extensive division of labor and stable enough to keep the specialized resources fully employed. Hence, it was surrounded by a more flexible periphery that produced products with inherently small markets such as luxury goods, specialized equipment for mass production, and new products. This peripheral sector also met the unstable portion of the demand for mass-produced goods. The periphery typically used much more general resources: tools or multipurpose equipment and a job structure that relied on broad craftsmen supplemented wherever possible by unskilled workers doing simple tasks to economize the time and talent of the highly trained.

In Europe, some of the immigrant employment was found in the most rudimentary and monotonous jobs in the mass-production core. But more often in Europe and typically in the United States, the immigrants took the unskilled jobs in the periphery, and the highly skilled professional managerial and craft jobs in both sectors were reserved for natives. In some of the oldest peripheral industries that never developed true mass production—construction, high-fashion garments, restaurants—immigrants took over high-skilled jobs as well, apparently because they brought the high skills with them.

The argument of *Birds of Passage* implies that technological progress through the division of labor is somehow basic or natural and the resultant job structure is thus a permanent and inevitable characteristic of industrial society. But recent industrial history suggests this presumption is wrong. Over the last decade, the technological dynamic has shifted away from mass production. New technologies seem now to favor small-batch production characteristic of what used to be the periphery of the economy. The computer is emblematic of this technological trend. In manufacturing, for example, economies of production once possible only through the physical dedication of the equipment to a particular make and model of a specific product can now be obtained through the software attached to general machinery; the design, and even the basic product under production, can be altered by changing the software without touching the equipment itself. Other technologies work in the same direction. The laser is a completely general cutting tool. Photocopying reduces economies of scale in printing; bioengineering has a like effect in the production of organic products. As a result of such developments, small firms, producing in batches, have come into their own technologically and no longer operate solely as an adjunct of mass production.

At the same time, the economy as a whole, and producers in the periphery in particular, have become much less dependent upon the domestic market. Because they produce in small batches, firms can often find a niche for their product in the international market, whatever the state of domestic demand. For an economy composed increasingly of small-scale producers, economic opportunities are thus much less scarce.

These developments would tend by and large to create a favorable environment for permanent migration. Small-scale batch production lends itself to entrepreneurial activity and enclave economies, as is suggested by the role of immigrant entrepreneurs in the industries that exemplify this type of structure.

The ethnic community also appears to provide a good vehicle for the development of craft skills and for the creation and maintenance of the industrial infrastructure that the small firms composing such a community seem to require. The internationalization of markets suggests that these new enclaves could absorb demand that would otherwise go to other countries; the enclaves could thereby develop without taking jobs away from nationals, even indirectly. Thus, fortuitously, the structure of the economy seems to be moving in the very same direction as the structure of immigration. Things seem to be working out very neatly.

Too neatly, perhaps, in at least one respect. The kicker here is the technology. The older technologies of industries like garments and construction were virtually stagnant. Their nature had not really changed in 100 years and that is one of the reasons that immigrants were capable of moving into even the skilled jobs. The current dynamism of small-scale production derives from the latest technologies, primarily computers but also such developments as photo printing, laser cutting, and biotechnologies. Developments in computer technology suggest that their innate sophistication need not block access by the relatively unschooled, but whether the developments that are promoting the growth of the types of jobs previously dominated by immigrants are really accessible to them remains to be seen.

12

Myths about Immigrants

✦ JEFFREY S. PASSEL ✦ MICHAEL FIX

In November 1990, President George Bush signed the Immigration Act of 1990, an expansive law that increased legal immigration by 40%. He declared that the law was "good for families, good for business, good for crime fighting, and good for America." In 1994, however, immigration has reemerged as a pivotal issue. It now defines political conflict over the basic values of American society—much like race, taxes, and crime—and evokes racial, cultural, and economic anxieties. Unfortunately, as the public debate intensifies, it is increasingly characterized by disagreement over facts as well as policy. The immigration issue, like other "wedge" issues, encourages rhetorical excess, often involving serious misperceptions and misinterpretations of historical fact and contemporary research. James Clad's article (1994) falls victim to much of the misinformation and misperceptions so common in the field of immigration today. Agreement about facts does not imply agreement about policy, but a generally accepted factual base and framework is essential for rational assessment of policy alternatives.

The structure and goals of U.S. immigration policy are frequently misunderstood. U.S. immigration policy needs to be viewed as not one, but three fundamentally different sets of rules: those that govern legal immigration (mainly sponsored admission for family and work), those that govern humanitarian admissions (refugees and those granted asylum), and those that control illegal entry. The distinction is important because each category is governed by different legislation, involves different networks of bureaucracies, is guided by different goals, and results in immigrants with largely different characteristics.

The attention given to the failure to stop undocumented immigrants has led journalists, the public, and many politicians to conclude that U.S. immigration policy, as a whole, has failed. Our research and that of others indicates that this is not the case. However, the focus on undocumented immigration has blurred the "bright line" between legal and illegal policy and eroded the legitimacy of legal and humanitarian admissions.

Passel, Jeffrey S. and Fix, Michael. 1994. "Myths about immigrants." *Foreign Policy*. Issue 95: 151–156. Reproduced in its entirety with permission from *Foreign Policy* #95 (Summer 1994).

The failure to recognize those distinctions also leads to the common misunderstanding that U.S. immigration policy is driven almost entirely by economic goals. In fact, legal immigration policy serves many goals. It is also intended to serve the important social goal of unifying families (principally of U.S. citizens) and the cultural goal of promoting diversity in the U.S. population and immigrant stream. Refugee policy is intended to serve the moral goal of promoting human rights. Most assessments of U.S. immigration policy do not acknowledge the power and value of noneconomic goals.

Finally, the number, characteristics, and adaptation of immigrants entering the United States as refugees, as legal immigrants, and as illegal immigrants all differ in important ways. The differences are seldom understood and often ignored in research and in policy debates.

Magnitude of Immigrant Flows

The composition of the immigrant population and flow are generally misperceived. The vast majority of immigrants in the United States are here with the country's express consent. Of the nearly 20 million immigrants counted in the 1990 census, only about 15% were here illegally. In fact, fully one-third of the immigrant population has made the effort to naturalize, swearing allegiance to the United States by becoming citizens. That figure is surprisingly high, representing about half of all immigrants who have lived in the country long enough to be eligible for citizenship. While the number of foreign-born persons in the United States is at an all-time high, the share of the population that is foreign-born—8% in 1990—is much lower than it was throughout the 1870–1920 period, when close to 15% of the total population was foreign-born.

The size and composition of the annual immigration flow is also often misinterpreted. Approximately 1.1 million immigrants arrive in the United States each year. About 700,000 are legal permanent residents, with family-based admissions accounting for almost three-quarters of the total. A large majority of the family immigrants are close relatives of U.S. citizens, not distant relatives of recently arrived aliens. Refugees and other humanitarian admissions add another 100,000 to 150,000 each year. Undocumented immigration contributes about 200,000 to 300,000 people annually, less than 30% of the immigrant flow.

As can be seen in Table 1, immigrant admissions remained relatively constant through the 1980s and then rose about 25% through fiscal year 1992 as a result of the 1990 act. That trend is consistently misinterpreted by the news media and the public because Immigration and Naturalization Service (INS) data on immigrants are unclear. The INS data on "immigrants" represent the number of persons becoming "permanent resident aliens." As a result of the Immigration Reform and Control Act of 1986 (IRCA), more than 2.7 million formerly illegal immigrants were granted legal status. That process involved becoming a "temporary resident alien" for several years before acquiring permanent resident alien status. Those several million individuals entered the country before 1985, with most arriving before 1982. However, they appear in INS data as "immigrants," beginning with small numbers in 1987 and peaking at more than 1.1 million in 1991. As a result, the official figures on "immigrants admitted" erroneously appear to have tripled between 1987 and 1991, followed by a 50% drop in 1992, the most recent year for which the INS has published a yearbook. The IRCA group masks the actual trend, which is a steady, incremental rise in admissions.

The amount of undocumented immigration is invariably overstated. The most informative measure of illegal immigration is growth in the population that enters and stays—200,000–300,000 a year. That figure, though not insignificant, is far below the more than 1 million stopped at the border each year; they are largely temporary labor migrants who are

TABLE 1 Legal immigration reported by INS: 1985–1992

Fiscal Year	Total Immigrants	IRCA Legalizations[1]	Other Legal Immigrants
1985	570,009	N.A.	570,009
1986	601,708	N.A.	601,708
1987	601,516	8,060	593,456
1988	643,025	39,999	603,026
1989	1,090,924	489,384	601,540
1990	1,536,483	885,005	651,478
1991	1,827,167	1,125,444	701,723
1992	973,977	164,635	809,342

Source: 1992 Statistical Yearbook of the Immigration and Naturalization Service.

[1]Includes provisions of Immigration and Naturalization Act, Section 249, 1972 Registry. IRCA is the Immigration Reform and Control Act of 1986.

N.A. = not applicable.

often apprehended multiple times, make multiple trips to the United States, and often leave the country uncounted and largely unnoticed.

The character of illegal immigration is also misunderstood, as it is associated almost wholly with Mexico. Although Mexicans represent the largest component of the illegal population, more than one-half of undocumented immigrants enter legally but overstay the duration of their temporary visas. Consequently, the undocumented population is more ethnically diverse than is commonly assumed (only about one-third is Mexican) and control measures will require more than improved enforcement and barriers along the U.S.–Mexican border.

Pace and Diversity of Immigration

One of the most striking features of contemporary immigration has been the rapid shift in the origins of immigrants, resulting largely from legislative changes in 1965. Europe, which accounted for two-thirds of legal immigrants in the 1950s, sent only 15% in the 1980s. The increase in Asian immigration has been the most dramatic, up from 6% in the 1950s to 45% in the 1980s. Latin America increased its share of legal immigrants to about 40% in the 1960s, but its share has not grown since then, although the absolute numbers have increased. Another indicator of the increased diversity is that the number of countries with at least 100,000 foreign-born residents in the United States grew from 20 in 1970 to 27 in 1980 and 41 in 1990 (data from censuses).

The force of immigration is also intensified by its pace. Almost one-half of immigrants in the United States today were not here a decade ago. By contrast, only 29% of the 1970 immigrant population had arrived in the previous decade. Because immigrants' incomes tend to rise with time in the United States, as does their knowledge of English and other dimensions of adaptation to their new country, the recency of arrival of today's immigrants fosters a misperception of their potential for integration into American society.

Characteristics of Immigrants

The shift in origins of immigrants has led to a broad perception that their "quality" has declined over the past several decades. Our research indicates that quality is related to legal status. Despite widespread belief to the contrary, when U.S. census data are disaggregated, they reveal that recent legal immigrants actually exceed natives on conventional measures of "quality." On the most conventionally used criterion, education, the credentials of legal immigrants—which are high to start with—actually increased during the 1980s. About one-third of the legal immigrants age 25 and over had college degrees, compared with only 20% of U.S. natives. Only one-quarter of the legal group had less than a high school diploma, a figure just marginally greater than that for the native population.

The educational credentials of people from countries that sent large numbers of illegal immigrants account for the perception of declining immigrant quality. Dramatically low numbers (less than 5%) have college degrees, while more than 75% are high school dropouts. The educational profile of refugees is intermediate.

An even better measure of "quality" may be household income. Recent legal immigrants have average household incomes that fall only 7% below those of natives. For those who arrived before 1980, both legal immigrant households and refugee households have average incomes that significantly exceed those of natives. Again, the recent refugees and immigrants from countries sending large numbers of illegals both have low incomes; they account for the perceived "low quality" of recent immigrants. The pattern of improving incomes with increased time in residence in the United States, together with the large percentage of newly arrived immigrants, suggests the need for any policy review to take a dynamic view of immigration, not a static one.

In addition to the scale of current immigration, its pace, and diversity, several other factors must be taken into account when assessing the impact on the United States.

Geographic Concentration

Unlike most other social issues in the United States, immigration exerts its most pronounced effects in only six states. About three-quarters of immigrants entering in the 1980s went to California (which received nearly four of every ten), New York, Texas, Florida, New Jersey and Illinois. In addition, immigration is an overwhelmingly urban phenomenon. More than 93% of immigrants settle in metropolitan areas versus only 73% of natives. The combination of geographic concentration and the general decline of urban institutions such as schools complicates the country's ability to integrate newcomers and distorts perceptions of immigrants' impacts.

Economic Impacts

Recent worries over the economic impact of immigrants have been exacerbated by the failure of the U.S. economy to expand employment between 1989 and 1992. During that period, when net job creation amounted to 250,000, several million new immigrants arrived. (In contrast, during 1986–1989 7.7 million jobs were added.) Of course, since 1992 the economy has grown rapidly and 1.7 million jobs were added in 1993 alone, so the view of immigration's effects may improve in the near future.

Our review of the economic literature indicates that despite claims that immigrants take the jobs of native workers, studies using aggregate statistics drawn from census data indicate that immigration had no meaningful job displacement effects. The studies also indicate that immigrants have only a small effect on wages, varying from place to place depending on the vitality of the local economy. In strong local economies, immigrants increase economic opportunities for natives; in weak ones, they have a small negative effect on the economic opportunities of low-skilled workers.

Those results may seem counterintuitive. However, many commentaries overlook the positive, but often indirect, benefits of immigration. Immigrants are slightly more likely than natives to be self-employed. Their businesses employ both natives and immigrants. Further, the incomes that immigrants earn, save, and spend ripple through the country's economy in ways that are only rarely credited to immigrants. According to the 1990 census, immigrants earned more than $285 billion in 1989, or about 8% of total income, almost exactly the same as immigrants' share of the total population.

Public Sector and Fiscal Impacts

Perhaps the most hotly contested question in current debates on U.S. immigration policy is whether immigrants use more in public services than they pay in taxes. The best recent research using a variety of data sources and modes of inquiry estimates that all immigrants arriving after 1970 pay a total of $70 billion in taxes to all levels of government, thereby generating $25 billion to $30 billion more than they use in public services. That finding is sharply at odds with a number of seriously flawed studies done by groups advocating cuts in legal immigration or by governments seeking "reimbursement" for their expenditures. The impacts, however, vary considerably by legal status and level of government.

Immigrants represent a net fiscal plus. From a fiscal standpoint, most of the surplus accrues from legal immigrants; illegal immigrants seem to generate more expenses than revenues across all levels of government. The U.S. structure of fiscal federalism often obscures the positive aspects of immigration. Studies consistently find that immigrants represent a net gain to the federal government; that their impacts vary at the state level, depending on the structure of state services; and that immigrants, like natives, use more in services than they pay in taxes at the local level. That pattern of differing impact is exacerbated by geographic concentration of immigrants.

A particularly contentious area of fiscal impacts has been immigrants' use of public assistance. Here again, a full understanding requires distinguishing among immigrant groups on the basis of when they arrived in the country and what their legal status was at that time. In doing so, welfare use among immigrants is found to be concentrated among refugees to a degree that is largely unrecognized. Refugees, alone among immigrants, are eligible for benefits from the time they arrive in the country. The other group of immigrants with disproportionate use of welfare is elderly immigrants, who have come to the country at such advanced ages that they cannot accumulate sufficient work experience to qualify for Social Security benefits. Welfare use among nonrefugee, working-age immigrants (ages 15–64) is extremely low and, contrary to popular perception and some current research, falls well below that of natives. Welfare use among illegal immigrants seems undetectable.

Advantages of Immigration

Current calls for immigration reform emphasize two areas of concern: anxiety over the integration of immigrants into American society and immigrants' perceived negative economic impacts. Yet the weight of evidence indicates that the economic consequences of immigration are largely positive. Also, most immigrants are integrating socially and economically, and they are doing so without broad negative effects on their new communities. Some issues do require action. However, in considering reforms, it is essential to look beyond narrow economic calculations and keep in mind the multiple purposes of U.S. immigration policy, including social, cultural, and moral goals. Further, the different domains of policy—legal immigration, humanitarian admissions, and illegal immigration—each require their own policy responses. For example, reducing legal immigration and changing admission requirements for legal immigrants will not constrain humanitarian flows or illegal immigration. In fact, such actions may even have the opposite effect. One conclusion supported by the evidence is that measures undertaken to control illegal immigration have been largely unsuccessful. Illegal immigrants are disproportionately poorly educated and low-skilled, tend to have low incomes, and generate net fiscal costs, particularly for local governments. Those findings, in turn, point to a need for altering the policies for controlling illegal immigration, not to a major overhaul of the country's legal admissions policy. Since the majority of illegal immigrants are not clandestine entrants crossing the southern border, but visa overstayers, increased border enforcement will be insufficient. One strategy might be to coordinate enforcement efforts for labor, tax, and immigration laws, focusing on the informal sector of the economy.

The concentration of immigrants in six states and in already-stressed urban areas raises questions about institutional capacity and fiscal fairness. The overall effects of immigrants, particularly legal ones, tend to be positive. In the short run, however, immigrants' adaptation to U.S. life may burden local governments since most revenues from immigrants (and natives) flow to the federal government, whereas the provision of services is the responsibility of local and state governments. That disparity has intensified over the past decade with cuts in the very few federal programs targeted on immigrants and their communities. Consequently, the issue of intergovernmental fiscal equity—an important aspect of immigrant policy—will require attention. Several options are available. Distribution formulas for federal grant programs could be more responsive to the presence of immigrants. Another, perhaps complementary, approach could involve reimbursement of state and local costs associated with immigrants or even an immigrant block grant tied to the size of a specific population, such as recently arrived people who have limited English proficiency.

High levels of immigration give the United States underappreciated advantages in the world economy: America has a substantial population with familial, ethnic, and language ties to some of the most dynamic economies in the world. With increasing ease of communication and travel, those ties may be crucial for enabling American companies to become active and successful actors in an increasingly interrelated global market. It is time the immigration debate turns on facts rather than emotions. Erecting barriers (physical as well as legal) and pulling up the figurative drawbridge to protect American society are likely to dissipate those advantages that the United States has acquired over the last generation.

PART III

IMMIGRATION, GLOBALIZATION, AND TRANSNATIONALISM

As we have seen, Part II elaborates on the effects of globalization and the restructuring of the United States economy on the lives of new immigrants, their families, and their community. The essays in Part III explore the impact of globalization on the process of incorporation of immigrants into American society. In the first reading, "Globalization and the Revalorizing of Ethnic Places in Immigration Gateway Cities," Jan Lin explains how, through transnational capital and trade, immigrant entrepreneurs have rejuvenated the declining central zones of the immigrant gateway cities such as Houston, New York, and Miami both economically and culturally.

In the second essay, "Globalization, Immigration, and Changing Social Relations in U.S. Cities," Glenda Laws indicates that globalization has increased the mobility of capital and labor and has functioned as a labor supply system. Moreover, it has reorganized the nature and distribution of jobs leading to a polarized labor market in which some immigrants do not find jobs and become marginalized. Exclusion from the labor market, Laws points out, leads to socio-spatial segregation, poverty, and inadequate housing and health care.

The third reading, "Transnationalism: A New Analytic Framework for Understanding Migration," by Nina Glick Schiller and her colleagues adopts a transnational perspective on migration. In an increasingly global world a new category of migrants is emerging: "transmigrants" are those whose lives cut across national boundaries. According to Schiller, the networks, activities, and patterns of life for this new kind of migrating population encompasses multiple familial, economic, social, religious, and political relations in both host and home societies.

Expanding on the theme of transnationalism, Alejandro Portes, in the final reading of this part titled "Global Villagers: The Rise of Transnational Communities," discusses the forces that have facilitated the formation of transnational communities in the United States. He further illustrates the implications of transnational immigration for globalization, American society, the migrant's home society, ethnic enclaves, immigration policy, and national identity and citizenship. This process is facilitated by the global expansion of capitalism and through free-trade laws, improved communication, and better transportation. Members of transnational communities, Portes argues, have dual lives, move between different cultures; maintain homes in two countries; and pursue economic, political, and cultural interests in both communities. Transnational migrants often use their own networks to form political communities.

Globalization and the Revalorizing of Ethnic Places in Immigration Gateway Cities

✦ JAN LIN, *Occidental College*

ABSTRACT

Immigration cities have counterbalanced deindustrialization and urban decline by acting as gateways of labor, capital, commodity, and cultural exchange in the new global economy. Ethnic places are emblematic transnational spaces that both constitute and convey broader processes of economic and cultural globalization. Ethnic entrepreneurs, community activists, and artists have revalorized spaces in the zone-in-transition, places from which they were historically restricted, evicted, or displaced. These rejuvenated ethnic places serve as "polyglot honeypots" for urban managers pursuing growth machine strategies in the postindustrial symbolic economy. Contradictions and conflicts are presented by globalization as much as opportunities.

The phenomenon of globalization in American cities is a complex set of transformations that suggest contrasting scenarios of promise and peril. These contradictions are manifest considering the vicissitudes of boom and bust buffeting U.S. localities and regions within the machinations of the increasingly interdependent and competitive global economy.

AUTHOR'S NOTE: An earlier version of this article was presented at the annual meeting of the American Sociological Association, August 1997, in Toronto, Canada. The research was funded in part by a Miner D. Crary Summer Fellowship from Amherst College. I thank Leland Saito, Sharon Zukin, Dennis Judd, and the anonymous referees for their suggestions and encouragement.

Lin, Jan. 1998. "Globalization and the revalorizing of ethnic places in immigration gateway cities." *Urban Affairs Review*. Volume 34, Issue 2:313–339. Reprinted by permission of Sage Publications, Inc.

Transnational capital, world trade, immigration, and cosmopolitan culture are all trends associated with the emergence of "world cities,"[1] which represent one vaunted route out of de-industrialization and urban decline. The dystopic underside to the dynamism of world cities has been observed, however, with reference to displacement, loss of local autonomy, socioeconomic polarization, and interracial conflict (Friedmann and Wolff, 1982; Davis, 1987; Sassen-Koob, 1988). Immigration gateway cities such as New York, Houston, Miami, and Los Angeles may be alternately identified as pluralistic "gorgeous mosaics" or Malthusian "Noah's arks." Globalization must be conceptualized, thus, as a powerful but fundamentally problematical process.

As these transformations have progressed, ethnic places are increasingly conspicuous as emblematic "transnational spaces," which both constitute and convey broader processes of economic and cultural globalization in the immigration gateway cities. The Chinatowns, Koreatowns, and Little Havanas of the post-industrial city have rejuvenated warehouse districts, retail corridors, and residential quarters of the zone-in-transition, reversing the obsolescence threatened with the decentralization of jobs and people to the urban periphery. Associated with the economic recovery of ethnic merchants and place entrepreneurs are the cultural reclamation efforts of a range of community-based artists, historians, and activists in undertakings such as public arts projects, cultural festivals, heritage preservation of certain symbolic or sacred cultural sites, and ethnic history museums, initiated often through acts of political contestation or community insurgency. These combined maneuvers mark the repossession of central urban economic and cultural spaces from which these ethnic actors were historically restricted, evicted, or displaced.

The new central-city ethnic places are primary purveyors of transnational commerce as well as culture, articulating closely with the world trade functions characteristic of global cities; furthermore, they may be employed by local state actors to project an image of the multiethnic city as an investment environment conducive to transnational corporate capital. Local state actors have found it advantageous to link ethnic commercial and cultural districts with economic devices such as world trade centers, convention center promotion, sports franchise expansions, arts promotion, and urban tourism. Characterized variously as "growth machine" strategies (Logan and Molotch, 1987) or the post-industrial "symbolic economy" (Zukin, 1995), these schemes represent new frontiers of central-city growth amid the losses in manufacturing and commercial activity. Ethnic places, significantly, serve as "polyglot honeypots" in advancing these post-industrial functions in the transnational environment of the immigration gateway cities. Ethnic places (both commercial and cultural) thus may be seen alongside the producer services as leading edges of globalization.

Globalization presents a salubrious, yet slippery, terrain of new opportunities and potential hazards for ethnic entrepreneurs and culture producers, which I comparatively examine through a number of cases in the emergent global cities. Among the complications that emerge are intergroup conflicts over the character of ethnic place reclamation. Intragroup conflicts also may occur, especially between local and overseas factions within certain groups, such as the Chinese and the Japanese. More broadly, the repossession of ethnic commercial and cultural spaces may be critically conceptualized as a form of economic and symbolic revalorization that upgrades central urban space for higher, transnational uses antithetical to small-scale, local ethnic actors.[2] Across the topography of urban space, ethnic places may authenticate "difference" while reinforcing class distinctions, serving as arenas for the investment and further accumulation of transnational capital.

This article seeks to contribute to analytical bridgework between a political-economic discourse (Smith and Feagin, 1987; Sassen, 1988) and cultural-semiotic discourse regarding the nature of globalization (Appadurai, 1990; Featherstone 1990; Robertson 1992).[3] Such a linkage compels a conceptualization of the global economy as being composed of not just circuits of labor, capital, and commodities but also cultural products and symbolic repertoires.

The onset of a global dynamic in economic and cultural change may be traced to the fifteenth century, with the emergence of the modern European-dominated capitalist world system.[4] It can be noted, however, that technological innovations in transportation and communications (e.g., intercontinental air travel and containerized shipping; electronic, satellite, and fiber-optic media), as well as the proliferation of transnational corporations, have led to an acceleration in global processes in the past three decades (Waters, 1995).[5] Cross-border financial, population, and cultural exchanges have intensified and quickened in this latest phase of globalizations in a global economy knit by linkages of consumption as much as production. In this "emerging symbolic economy" (Zukin, 1995) or "economy of signs and space" (Lash and Urry, 1994), it is increasingly difficult to disentangle symbolic exchanges from actual material exchanges and processes.

Associated with the growth of symbolic exchanges is a debate regarding the prospects for peripheral or local cultures. McLuhan's (1964) triumphant proclamation of an emergent planetary consciousness through his concept of the "global village" has been followed by speculation on the displacement of the local through the hegemonic global reach of capitalist core culture in a process commonly dubbed Westernization or Americanization. The scenario of homogenization, however, has been refined with a more nuanced picture of global-local interaction and relativization through processes of indigenization (in which local culture is "retribalized" via the repudiation of global culture) or hybridization (in which local culture is creolized or syncretized) (Appadurai, 1990; Robertson, 1992; Barber, 1995; Hannerz, 1996; Huntington, 1996). Relativization may affect cities and sites in the core itself, in an inversion of traditional core-periphery relations.

Thus structural similarity in the process of globalization should not overdetermine the manner in which it takes place in the local context of American cities or ethnic enclaves. The onset of globalization processes since the 1960s has been differentially constituted in the various immigration gateway cities. Vociferous community insurgency has accompanied the reclamation of ethnic places in some cities, and revalorization efforts in other cities have involved greater cooperation between ethnic contenders and the local state. These contrasts reflect contingencies and variations in regional economies, the preceding history of local race and ethnic relations, traditions of community activism, and relations between local ethnics and overseas counterparts.

I begin with broad conceptual discussions on the relationships between globalization, immigration, and ethnic commerce, using quantitative data derived from the U.S. Department of Justice, Immigration and Naturalization Service (1991–1996) and the Survey of Minority-Owned Business Enterprises (U.S. Department of Commerce 1992a, 1992b).[6] This reading moves on to an examination of the changing disposition of ethnic places of the central city from the industrial to the post-industrial era with reference to urban sociological and race and ethnic theory. Finally, I critically assess the links between ethnic commerce and culture and the post-industrial growth agendas in a sample of the immigration gateway cities. The latter portion of the reading is based on field interviews conducted with ethnic business representatives, ethnic community activists and heritage preservationists, and city managers in Houston in 1992, New York in 1995, and Miami and Los Angeles in 1996.

Immigration Gateways, Ethnic Commerce, and the Zone-in-Transition

Recent immigration flows to the United States have been concentrated in cities, yet there has been a deficiency of comparative urban perspectives on immigration (Waldinger, 1989), despite numerous case studies on immigration in individual cities and communities (Kleniewski, 1994). Table 1 addresses this investigative lacuna by focusing on the fifteen major immigration gateway cities of the most recent period. These metropolitan areas received nearly three out of every five immigrant arrivals from 1990 to 1995. Amalgamating some cities into larger consolidated metropolitan statistical areas (CMSAs) results in a list of ten major immigration gateway centers.

These fifteen gateway cities received a majority (57.5%) of U.S. immigration in the 1990–1995 period. Significantly, one may observe that immigration gateways are also "world cities" that articulate domestic economic activities with the global economy (Waldinger, 1989; Muller, 1993). Sassen-Koob (1988) has focused on the mobility of labor and capital through these nodal cities,

TABLE 1 Recent Immigration Flows into Top 15 Gateway Cities, 1990–1995

Metropolitan Area	Number	%
Los Angeles–Long Beach	1,000,086	14.8
New York City	819,761	12.1
Chicago	287,054	4.2
Miami	218,732	3.2
Anaheim–Santa Ana	217,515	3.2
Houston	195,899	2.9
Washington, D.C.	174,958	2.6
San Diego	164,216	2.4
San Francisco	135,928	2.0
Riverside–San Bernardino	131,719	1.9
San Jose	127,369	1.9
Boston	116,834	1.7
Dallas	110,674	1.6
Oakland	104,338	1.5
Newark	83,524	1.2
15-city total	3,888,607	57.5
U.S. total	6,766,796	100.0
Los Angeles CMSA	1,349,320	19.9
New York CMSA	903,285	13.3
San Francisco Bay Area CMSA	367,635	5.4

Source: U.S. Department of Justice, Immigration and Naturalization Service (1991–1996).

Note: The data report the metropolitan area of intended residence for all legally admitted immigrants. Where relevant, data from the fifteen top cities also have been aggregated into the consolidated metropolitan statistical area (CMSA). The Los Angles CMSA comprises Los Angles–Long Beach, Anaheim–Santa Ana, and Riverside–San Bernardino. The New York CMSA is the sum of New York City and Newark. The San Francisco Bay Area CMSA represents San Francisco, San Jose, and Oakland.

which is evident with the proliferation of labor-intensive "downgraded manufacturing" (sweatshops and other informal sector activities) and producer services activities (especially connected with global finance and advanced corporate control functions). Abu-Lughod (1995) also has drawn attention to the predominance of foreign trade and shipping activities in world cities.

I conceptualize immigration gateway cities as a subset of world cities, which serve not only as command centers in the cross-border movement of capital and labor but also as critical nodes in processing flows of commodities and cultural products. The trade and transport firms concentrated in these cities facilitate the import and export of goods between the U.S. hinterlands and other global trading regions. Following this logic, we may observe that (1) New York and Boston are gateways to Atlantic Rim trade; (2) Miami, Dallas, and Houston are gateways to Latin American and Caribbean Rim trade; and (3) San Francisco and Los Angeles are gateways to Pacific Rim trade. Thus Los Angeles is dubbed the "capital of the Pacific Rim" (Rieff, 1991) and Miami the "capital of Latin America" (Rieff, 1987). Attention to the distributive and trade sectors thus augments one's understanding of economic globalization beyond the producer services as a leading edge of growth under postindustrialism.

Table 2, which reports on the sectoral distribution of Asian and Hispanic firms, as compared with all U.S. firms, in the fifteen major immigration gateway cities, confirms that Asian and Hispanic enterprises are overconcentrated in both the transport and retail trade sectors, relative to all U.S. enterprises. The Asian overconcentration is especially pronounced in retail trade, composed of some 20.5% among Asian firms, as compared with an 11.7% proportion in retail trade among all U.S. firms. Interestingly, Asians are underrepresented (4.5%) in the construction sector, and Hispanics are overrepresented (12.2%) as compared with all U.S. firms (8.2%). With reference to Miami, Portes and Stepick (1993) report that Cuban entrance into the construction trade was achieved only after persistent efforts to fight the exclusionary practices of white-dominated union locals. The Hispanic overrepresentation in construction is balanced by an underrepresentation in the finance, insurance, and real estate (FIRE) sector.

Returning to the matter of the distributive and retail sectors, I follow Bonacich (1973) and

TABLE 2 Sectoral Distribution of Ethnic Enterprises Compared with All U.S. Enterprises in Top 15 Immigration Gateway Cities, 1992 (%)

	Asian	Hispanic	All United States
Agriculture, forestry, fishing, and mining	1.5	3.7	2.2
Construction	4.5	12.2	8.2
Manufacturing	3.3	2.6	2.7
Transport, communications, and utilities	4.8	7.0	4.2
Wholesale trade	3.6	2.4	3.3
Retail trade	20.5	12.6	11.7
Finance, insurance, and real estate	11.7	6.4	12.8
Services	45.2	45.6	50.0
Other	4.9	7.7	4.9

Source: U.S. Department of Commerce (1992a, 1992b). Published data and special tabulating.

Note: Numbers may not add up to 100 due to rounding.

Portes and Manning (1986) in drawing the distinction between immigrant enclaves (which are spatially distinct ethnic commercial places serving a largely captive or coethnic market, such as Chinatown in San Francisco and New York, Koreatown in Los Angeles, and Miami's Little Havana) and middleman minorities (which are dispersed ethnic firms serving nonethnic clientele, such as Korean greengrocers in New York or Korean merchants in south-central Los Angeles, who have experienced intergroup hostility). The distinctions become somewhat muddled considering that enclaves such as New York and San Francisco's Chinatown also commonly serve nonethnic consumers. Furthermore, interracial hostilities directed initially at middleman minorities (e.g., Koreans in south-central Los Angeles) may extend to ethnic enclaves (e.g., Los Angeles's Koreatown), as occurred during the Los Angeles riots of 1992. It is important also to distinguish immigrant niches from enclaves and middleman minorities, such as Filipino and South Asian Indian concentrations in the health services industry, or South Asians in the convenience store and motel industry—niches in which immigrants do not serve primarily coethnics or minority clientele.

Another discussion surrounds the question of where the initial sources of income arise, which then lead to the expansion of ethnic enclave economies (Logan, Alba, and McNulty, 1994). With reference to New York's Chinatown, Abeles Schwart, Haeckel, and Silverblatt (1983) and Zhou (1992), assert that apparel manufacturing was the major initial source of "export earnings," which subsequently were multiplied through forward and backward linkages (to coethnic suppliers and retailers) and consumption linkages (as the wages of ethnic workers were spent at the establishments of coethnic retailers). Regarding the Cuban enclave of Miami, Wilson and Martin (1982) identify manufacturing and construction as the source sectors generating the greatest degree of interindustry multiplier effects. Logan, Alba, and McNulty (1994) observe that Miami's Cuban enclave is unusually large and sectorally differentiated as compared with other ethnic economies, but they also cite other enclaves that have become successful through agriculture or retail trade functions (e.g., Koreans and Japanese in various cities).

These conceptual debates on the finer dynamics of ethnic enclaves notwithstanding, there is general agreement in the literature on the affirmative job and revenue-generating capacities of ethnic subeconomics. Table 3 addresses the matter of revenues by presenting the top-industry receipt leaders for Asian and Hispanic firms in 1992. Retail trade, services, and wholesale trade were the top revenue-generating sectors among both Asians and Hispanics. FIRE was the next leading sector among Asians, and construction was the next leading sector among Hispanics. The retail and wholesale trade sectors accounted for 45.4% of the total receipts among Asians; the comparable proportion among Hispanics was 41.5%. In the five-year period from 1987 to 1992, receipts among Hispanic firms increased by 195%, from $24.7 billion to $72.8 billion, and Asian firm receipts increased by 159%, from $40 billion to $104 billion. These growth rates greatly surpass the 61% increase among all U.S. firms, which rose from $2.0 trillion to $3.3 trillion in total receipts.

These insights on the economic contributions of ethnic enterprises connect with recent debates on the positive versus negative impacts of immigration in the United States (Muller, 1993; Heer, 1996; Fix and Passel, 1994). The negative impacts usually identified include (1) increased competition between lower-skilled immigrant workers and lower-skilled native workers (especially noncollege-educated African Americans) and (2) stress on local and state finance through immigrant use of a range of services, including health, education, and welfare. The affirmative impacts commonly identified include (1) growing opportunities for the higher-skilled, college-educated

TABLE 3 Top-industry Receipt Leaders for Asian and Hispanic Firms, 1992 (in millions of dollars)

Industry Sector	Asian	Hispanic
Retail trade	28,768	17,731
Food stores	7,037	3,338
Miscellaneous retail	6,567	2,849
Eating and drinking places	6,457	3,954
Automotive dealers and service stations	5,475	5,475
Services	25,595	16,787
Health services	8,851	4,131
Business services	4,235	3,457
Hotels and other lodging places	3,316	475
Engineering and management	2,505	1,828
Personal services	2,459	1,758
Wholesale trade	18,533	12,489
Nondurable goods	9,304	6,483
Durable goods	9,229	6,006
Finance, insurance, and real estate (FIRE)	8,988	4,832
Real estate	7,384	3,661
Construction	5,165	8,212
Total	104,100	72,824

Source: U.S. Department of Commerce (1992a, 1992b).

Note: A sectoral breakdown on receipts among ethnic firms in just the top fifteen immigration gateway cities was not possible because some data on industry sectors were suppressed at the level of the metropolitan area. These data represent all U.S. cities.

native workforce because of the entrance of low-wage immigrants into lower levels of the labor market and (2) positive immigrant contributions to urban economies and governmental revenue streams, through the public finance payments that immigrant workers and business owners make for sales taxes, personal and business income taxes, and property taxes. Property taxes, it should be noted, are a major source of revenues for urban governments. The contentious debates among academics, policy makers, and public officials regarding the net fiscal cost/benefit impacts of immigration are ongoing, but the data presented here suggest that ethnic enterprises can contribute considerably to municipal revenues.

The notion of globalization and ethnic commerce as leading edges of post-industrial urban growth revises an argument struck among urbanists in the 1970s that the real consequence of deindustrialization was an interregional job and population shift from northeastern (Frostbelt) to southwestern (Sunbelt) cities as manufacturing firms were lured by lower wages, lower land costs, and anti-union and preferential business climates of the Sunbelt. The refined argument counterbalances scenarios of decline and deindustrialization with the dynamism of globalization and immigration to explain the continued economic vigor of some older centers (e.g., New York City, Boston, and Chicago) in the 1990s (Waldinger, 1989). Sassen-Koob (1988) similarly observes that the booming first-order American global cities of the contemporary era represent both the declining Frostbelt (New York City) and the ascending Sunbelt (Los Angeles).

The function of ethnic enclaves in the global city may be more clearly understood through an urban spatial perspective that recognizes the role that ethnic enterprises have played in reviving industrial, warehousing, and retailing districts of the central city, which were declining with the departure of manufacturing and commercial activities to peripheral locations. Macy's and Bloomingdale's abandoned their downtown locations to anchor the new shopping malls and "gallerias" of the suburban cloverleafs. Kresge's retooled and entered the suburban periphery to become Kmart, but the once ubiquitous Woolworth five-and-dime stores clung persistently to their downtown locales, finally closing their last 400 stores in July 1997. Pakistani immigrants have filled some of this niche in the demand for low-end retail niche with the opening of 99-cent and dollar discount stores in New York City (Kershaw, 1997). But the new immigrant impacts on urban economies can be seen much more clearly across the geography of urban space.

New York City's midtown wholesaling district (from 14th to 34th Streets) is a case in point. Previously dominated by white ethnic entrepreneurs (including Jewish and Italian immigrants), the district steadily lost economic vitality from the 1920s to the 1960s with the decentralization of manufacturing and retailing functions to the suburban and exurban periphery. Since the 1960s, however, new Asian, Latin American, and Caribbean entrants have filtered into the same built environment, renewing the economic dynamism of the district and giving it a new transnational atmosphere (a similar ethnic succession has occurred in the proximate Garment District). The New York Chinese Businessmen's Association purports to represent some 2,500 enterprises, mainly engaged in import-export wholesaling in the midtown area. A Korean business district of wholesalers, restaurants, and banks can be found in a rectangular area from 24th to 34th Streets between Fifth and Sixth Avenues. In October 1995, it was officially recognized by the city of New York with the posting of "Koreatown" signage at the intersection of 32nd Street and Broadway (Min, 1996). Underneath the Broadway street sign can be found an accompanying sign designating the corridor as "Korea Way."

New York's Chinatown has grown expansively since the 1960s from its location in lower Manhattan, succeeding Jewish and Italian outmovers in proximate blocks of the Lower East Side. Dominicans have established a commercial and residential presence in the Washington Heights district of upper Manhattan. South Asian Indians, though residentially decentralized, retain a commercial and cultural district in the Jackson Heights area of Queens, which serves as the "symbolic heart" of the dispersed community (Lessinger, 1995). Chinese, Koreans, and other new immigrant groups have succeeded white ethnic outmovers, establishing a multiethnic "Asiantown" in the Flushing area of Queens.

In Houston, Chinese and Mexican merchants have given new life to the deteriorating near-city warehousing and industrial districts to the east of the central business district (CBD). The downtown Chinatown wholesalers import food and restaurant products through the port of Houston for distribution in the metropolitan area as well as throughout the South and Midwest. A "Little Saigon" of Indochinese merchants has emerged in the disused midtown area to the immediate south of the CBD. New Asian and Latino commercial activity also has emerged in the suburban west and southwest economic corridors of the metropolis. Mexican activity can be found in Houston Heights, Chinese along Bellaire Boulevard, South Asians along Hillcroft, and Koreans in the Harwin wholesaling corridor as well as in retailing and restaurants on Long Point Road. The entrance of new ethnic merchants was expedited largely by the availability of low commercial rents and high vacancy rates during the 1980s, when Houston experienced a severe regional recession because of the tumble in petroleum prices associated with the oil glut on the world market. The emergence of ethnic commercial activity thus can be interpreted to have contributed toward the stabilization of the local economy.

In Los Angeles, the nation's largest Koreatown has emerged in an approximately 20 square-mile area west of downtown, which was formerly more than 90% white. Businesses in the area are primarily Korean, but Koreans make up less than 15% of the residents, who are primarily Hispanic (mainly Mexican) (Min, 1996). The old Chinatown north of downtown has been enhanced with the emergence of Indochinese merchants along the north Broadway corridor. Latino merchants now burgeon along south Broadway. East of the CBD, Little Tokyo has experienced some revival in the decades following the internment debacle. Beyond the central city, a suburban Chinatown, "Little Taipei," occupies Monterey Park. Southward in Orange County, Vietnamese merchants now proliferate along Bolsa Avenue in Westminster.

In Miami, Cubans settled initially in the old Riverside-Shenandoah section of Miami (between Flagler Street and the Tamiami Trail), a historically Jewish residential enclave. The Tamiami (Tampa-Miami) Trail, otherwise known as Highway 41 or SW 8th Street, was from the 1930s to the 1950s the major commercial spine for the Jewish community. Postwar prosperity led to residential outmovement of upwardly mobile Jewish-Americans into the Dade County suburbs, and the scene was set for the entrance of the Cubans in the 1960s, who redubbed SW 8th Street "Calle Ocho" (Eighth Street) as the surrounding district became known as Little Havana. Like the Jewish-American merchants who preceded them, the Cuban arrivals experienced discriminatory exclusions from the Anglo merchant establishment of Flagler Street, the main downtown commercial corridor. By the 1980s, Cubans themselves began filtering into the suburbs of Dade County, as Nicaraguans followed in their wake into the commercial and residential space of Little Havana. Though increasingly integrated residentially, the Cuban cultural and commercial presence remains conspicuous throughout the metropolis.

Although the new ethnic commercial enclaves are not exclusively located in central-city or near-city zones of the city—particularly in newer sunbelt automobile-centered cities such as Miami, Houston, and Los Angeles, where immigrant enterprises have penetrated the suburban commercial corridors of feeder roads and strip malls—some of the more prominent (Chinatowns, Koreatowns, and Little Havanas) still occupy central locations. I now turn to examine more specifically the historical transformations of the ethnic spaces of the zone-in-transition in the city center.

Ethnic Places from Urban Village to Global Village

The massive immigrations of the industrial era (1840–1920) drew primarily from the "new stock" nonwhite Anglo-Saxon Protestant (WASP) European immigration (Catholic, Jewish). Industrial core cities of the Northeast and Midwest (NE-MW) drew the bulk of the foreign immigration to the United States (Ward, 1971). The Chicago School of Sociology viewed urban ethnic places (such as the Jewish "ghetto," Kleindeutschland, Little Italy, and Greektown) as "decompression chambers" for newly arrived immigrants, which facilitated their economic adaptation and cultural assimilation into American life (Ward, 1989, 170). Burgess (1967) codified the human ecological supposition that the immigrant quarters of the zone-in-transition that surrounded the CBD eventually would wither away with the outward expansion of the CBD and the upward mobility of latter-generation ethnics into the outer-concentric residential zones of the suburbs. Harvard University scholar Oscar Handlin similarly inferred that the ethnic communities of the huddled masses were transitional phenomena by which the "uprooted" mitigated the shock of transoceanic passage.

The invasion-succession paradigm of the human ecologists privileged the invisible hand of the free market in determining urban land patterns and neglected political variables, including racial/ethnic discrimination and the interventions of the WASP-dominated state. Immigrant minorities were relegated to the zone-in-transition by the formal and de facto restrictions, exclusions, and covenants of Anglo powerbrokers as much as by the market barriers presented by high rents in the CBD. The restrictions experienced by nonwhite minorities (e.g., Asians, Latinos, African Americans) were even greater than those experienced by white ethnic immigrants (e.g., Irish, Italians, Jews), especially in the cities outside of the NE-MW core region. Thus African Americans and Latinos were restricted by Jim Crow or Jim Crow–type segregation laws and Asian-Americans by restrictive covenants and Alien Land Acts. Thus, in turn-of-the-century Los Angeles, Mexicans, African Americans, and Chinese occupied fallow real estate around the Olvera Street Plaza north of the Anglo-controlled CBD centered on Broadway. The Mexican barrio became known as the Sonora or "Dogtown." The Chinese mixed with African Americans on a corridor known as "Calle de los Negros" or "Nigger Alley" (Pearlstone, 1990, 72). A Japanese colony appeared nearby at the intersection of East First and San Pedro Streets. In Houston, Mexicans and African Americans formed an approximate ring around the Anglo CBD. A Chinese merchant colony arose on the eastern periphery of the CBD, serving primarily African Americans.

If ethnic settlements were shunned, excluded, or otherwise ignored during the industrial period of American urban growth, city managers and the federal government actively began bulldozing ethnic places under slum clearance policies of the interwar period, and more actively under urban renewal in the postwar period, to make room for expressway arterials, middle-class housing, or expansion of the CBD and government office buildings. Ethnic places were deemed unsanitary public health hazards, congested visual eyesores, and contagious mediums of vice and other social pathologies to middle-class urbanites. Chinatowns, Little Italies, and Mexican barrios were regarded as obstacles to modernization and cultural assimilation. In Manhattan's Lower East Side, riverfront tenements were cleared to make way for the East River Drive and public housing. The Cross-Bronx Expressway severed a huge Jewish tenement community. Houston's Chinatown was relocated to facilitate expansion of the CBD, and in Los Angeles, Chinatown was relocated to facilitate the construction of the Union Railway Station. These are some prominent cases in ethnic communities, but many observers have noted that the predominant victims of urban renewal programs were African-American communities.

Gans's (1962) seminal study, *The Urban Villagers*, heralded the emergence of a new academic and policy perspective that challenged pejorative assumptions regarding ethnicity and urban ethnic places by portraying the affirmative, social organizational functions of the Italian-American "peer group society" in resolving everyday problems of urban poverty. The book is also memorable for its forceful critique of federal slum clearance policies on a number of counts, including (1) lack of community input in the renewal process, (2) lack of financial compensation to minority property owners in the eminent domain process, (3) the absence of or inadequate relocation assistance to displaced families, and (4) the evaluative, rather than analytic, utility of terms such as *slum* in labeling ethnic places as undesirable and dysfunctional.

The Hart-Cellar Immigration Act of 1965, passed during the liberal political environment of the civil rights era, overturned decades-long restrictive immigration quotas, auguring the arrival of a new wave of Latin American, Caribbean, and Asian immigration. The demographic, political, and cultural changes accompanying the civil rights movement and Hart-Cellar Act marked the passing of assimilation discourse as a battery of new conceptual paradigms emerged, which interpret ethnicity as an adaptable phenomenon that accompanies social change, rather than being a static, primordial status of premodernity; these include ethnic plural politics (Glazer and Moynihan, 1963), emergent ethnicity (Yancey, Ericksen, and Juliani, 1976), symbolic ethnicity (Gans, 1979), ethnic enclave economies (Portes and Manning, 1986; Zhou, 1992), and panethnicity (Espiritu, 1992). Most recently, a fertile new terrain has arisen around concepts of globalization and transnationality.

Studies of ethnic transnational communities draw attention to the binational cultural and economic networks in which new immigrants interact. These frequent interactions between home and host societies are enabled by innovations in communications and transportation technologies, which have shrunk the barriers of geographical, economic, and cultural borders between constituent nations of the global system of states. A reciprocal circuitry of political and economic relations occurs through monetary remittances, seasonal labor migrations, circular migrations within the life cycle, dual residence, and binational investment practices (Rouse, 1991; Rodriguez, 1995). As Pessar (1995) reports, Dominican-Americans experience New York City like a "waiting room," as they forge livelihoods *aqui y alla* (here and there). Chinese cosmopolitans from Hong Kong (the former) and Taiwan send their children (*xiao liuxuesheng,* "little foreign students," or more popularly "parachute kids") to study in U.S. schools and prospectively gain permanent residency while their parents (*kongzhong feiren* "trapeze artists," or *taikongren*, "astronauts") frequently shuttle the transoceanic distances (Wong 1995, 7). Lessinger (1995) describes how the Indian government encouraged binational economic activity among South Asian Indian Americans by offering them continuing status as nonresident Indians. Finally, Portes (1996) deploys McLuhan's concept of the electronic "global village" to express the cosmopolitan affiliations of the new transnational citizens in charting a brave new world of diminishing cultural and geographic borders.

These new immigration studies furrow some terrain remarkably similar to that cultivated by new perspectives in critical cultural studies (Appadurai, 1990; Rouse, 1995), particularly Appadurai's concept of "ethnoscapes," which purports to release ethnicity like "a genie [previously] contained in the bottle of some sort of locality" (p. 15). In privileging semiotic over material exchanges in international capitalism, Appadurai overdetermines the notion of "deterritorialization"through a reading of globalization as fractals-chaos-uncertainty, thereby obliterating the tangibility of "place" or "community" with an alternative cartography of rootless, diasporic networks of nomads, refugees, expatriates, tourists, and economic and artistic cosmopolitans. Preferring radical revisionism to iconoclasm, I would assert that traditional comprehensions of geographic places and territorial communities in the world system have not disappeared but have become problems, and the physical distances and temporal spans between places and localities have been increasingly compressed but not finally annihilated. Ethnic global villagers may be nearly freed from place-bounded restraints in their commercial and cultural pursuits, but ethnic spaces of the city are still highly salient as processors and distributors of ethnic products, durable and nondurable, in their cuisinary, commodity, and communicative forms (including mediums of print, cassette, disc, video, and live performance).

Thus, in the post-industrial environment of the world cities, American ethnic places as global villages are now more ethnically polyglot with nonwhite immigrants, who interact in sustained transnational networks of association, rather than provincial urban villages resistant to and marginalized by the pressures of cultural assimilation. Through the combined window of opportunity created by a domestic social upheaval in civil rights and external developments in global capitalism, ethnicity has a greater resilience and gravity in arenas of economic, political, and cultural interaction. But as discussed earlier, globalization may be as pernicious as it is auspicious, and the merchants, place entrepreneurs, and cultural practitioners have encountered risks as well as advantages.

Transnational Capital, Polyglot Honeypots, and Post-Industrial Growth Coalitions

The promoters of growth in post-industrial cities have had to contend with a variety of economic and fiscal crises associated with postwar deindustrialization and suburbanization, dual trends that have deprived central cities of employment, residents, and a vital tax base. The fiscal impoverishments accompanying these structural transformations were further deepened with the curtailment of federal revenue-sharing programs under the Reagan administration. Increasingly left to their own devices, the localities responded in part by working in greater partnership with the private corporate sector to foster economic growth (Fainstein et al., 1986; Judd and Swanstrom, 1994). In a number of cities, international capital has been a critical component of this new growth. Local planners and city managers have been active agents in promoting the globalization of metropolitan economies (Smith and Feagin, 1987), facilitated through devices restructuring the central-city built environment, such as the erection of world trade centers and the enlargement of port and airport facilities, convention centers, and tourist complexes.

In Miami, a Downtown Action Committee began a publicity project in 1975 for a "New World Center," which envisioned Miami as center of the hemispheric past and future. One of the resulting projects, the Omni International Complex (containing a luxury hotel, shopping mall, theaters, restaurants), helped key Biscayne Boulevard's emergence as the "Fifth Avenue of the South" (Parks, 1991, 168). Biscayne Bay became not only an exclusive resort for the idle rich but also a vital hub for the transshipment of tourists and commodities in the Latin American and Caribbean Rim. The port of Miami became the largest cruise ship port in the world. A free trade zone was created near Miami International Airport. *Fortune 500* companies began making Coral Cables the site of their Latin American headquarters. There was a massive metropolitan building boom in the 1980s.

In New York City, Chase Manhattan Bank president David Rockefeller formed a Downtown-Lower Manhattan Association in 1956, which commissioned studies recommending the razing and restructuring of the preindustrial built environment for global capital through the construction of a World Trade Center (WTC). The Port Authority of New York–New Jersey (which operates New York's port, airports, and major bridges and tunnels) assumed the WTC project in 1964, which, when completed between 1975 and 1980, became the world's largest office complex, helping to spur New York's recovery from the fiscal crisis of 1975. Now the material edifice and symbolic landmark for New York City's position as a command center and headquaters complex for global capitalism, the WTC has helped to offset losses in *Fortune 500* corporation headquarters from the regional economy and has stimulated redevelopment in Lower

Manhattan, including the World Financial Center and high-income residential projects at Battery Park City.

These shifts have been paralleled in Houston with the fading power of a local Anglo power elite, the "8F crowd" (so named because of the Lamar Hotel suite at which they traditionally met), in the wake of the entrance of transnational oil and gas industry firms in the regional economy. The George R. Brown Convention Center, designed like a postmodern ocean liner to recognize Houston's importance as a port city, was built in 1987. The city's global aspirations were touted with the Bush administration's choice of Houston as the site for the 1990 Economic Summit of the advanced industrialized Group of Seven (G-7) nations. Los Angeles similarly experienced the steady entrance of the transnational corporate presence into its CBD, a process encouraged by long-time mayor Tom Bradley in the 1970s and 1980s.

Globalization is an incomplete characterization of the shifts taking place under postindustrialism if related changes are not identified. Urban growth machines, constituted of coalitions of place entrepreneurs (rentier capitalists) and public officials committed to local economic development, have been endemic to American cities since the era of westward expansion, but as Logan and Molotch (1987, 57–85) observe, growth machines of the modern era are alliances of a more "multifacted matrix" of interests that include the local media, utility companies, universities, arts institutions, professional sports, organized labor, and small retailers. Judd and Swanstrom (1994) describe corporate center strategies, tourism, and sports franchise expansion as the centerpieces of contemporary urban redevelopment schemes. Zukin (1995) suggests a more diverse repertoire (somewhat overlapping with Logan and Molotch's menu) of "culture industries"—including arts promotion, media, advertising, tourism, and museums—that she congregates under the concept of a "symbolic economy." In its full analytic context, Zukin's argument in effect supersedes that of Logan and Molotch when she shows how cultural production and consumption have merged with land-use and investment practices.

Urban tourism efforts are predicated upon the strategy of assembling clusters of attractions or cultural "honeypots" near revivified railroad termini and hotel and convention center complexes, providing urban tourists, conventioneers, and business visitors with easy walking or transportation access (Law, 1993, 128). Having reached an advanced stage in European cities—which possess significant inventories of monuments, buildings, sites, and districts of architectural, historic, antiquitous, or sacred significance—urban tourism similarly has been fabricated in the American context through the much-vaunted prototypes of the Rouse Corporation's waterfront "festival marketplaces" and the Disney Corporation's heritage-facsimile theme parks. I focus here on those experiments in which strategies of economic globalization are linked with schemes to recover the urban multiethnic inheritance.

The Tricky Political Geography of Ethnic Place Reclamation

The linked civil rights and ethnic power movements of the 1950s and 1960s helped to initiate and reinforce parallel projects of community action and heritage reclamation in American race and ethnic places. Cultural reclamation efforts in ethnic communities were given further impetus during the years surrounding the American bicentennial activities of 1976, a period of cultural restoration during the nadir of the post-Watergate recessionary 1970s, which augmented the significance and respectability of ethnic heritage recovery. Manhattan's Lower East Side now contains a number of ethnic museums and preserved heritage sites, including the Chinatown History Museum, the Eldridge Street Synagogue, and the Lower East Side Tenement Museum. Cultural and community insurgency often was linked. Activists associated with the Chinatown Basement Workshop assembled an initial trove of artistic and material cultural artifacts that eventually were transferred to the Chinatown History Museum; this museum became a reality after agitations for preservation surrounded the proposed auction of a public school building that had fallen into city possession. The Little Italy Restoration Association unsuccessfully fought to acquire an abandoned police headquarters for an Italian cultural center; the spectacular Beaux-Art–style edifice instead was converted to a luxury condominium complex (Conforti, 1996).

In Los Angeles, opposition to a police center expansion and a municipal plan to demolish some historical sites in the process of widening East First Street in Little Tokyo spurred an activist movement in Little Tokyo, which eventually gained National Historic Landmark status for a city block that holds thirteen buildings of particular merit, including a number of historic storefronts.[7] The Hompa Hongwangi Buddhist Temple (built in 1925) was converted to the Japanese American National Museum. An "artistic sidewalk" wraps around the block, a multihued walkway of rose, white, and gray concrete afloat with images of *tsutsumi*, a Japanese custom of "wrappings" such as baskets, folded cloths, and suitcases. Quotes are also inscribed—warm memories of early neighborhood life in brass and harsh memories of internment in stainless steel. Sheila Levrant de Brettville, the designer of the Omoide no Shotokyo (Remembering Old Little Tokyo) walkway, said, "Buildings are like people. A portion of the story of the proprietors in each building is depicted. . . . To evoke their personal narrative is to evoke the larger community in which they lived."[8] An antiquated housing barrack and watchtower (preserved and transferred from their original location at a Los Angeles processing center for Japanese-Americans awaiting relocation to wartime internment camps in the desert) sits starkly across the street surrounded by barbed wire.

Also in Los Angeles, Mexican historians and community activists have been seeking to repossess Chicano history at the Olvera Street Plaza. The plaza, which was the nucleus of II Pueblo de Nuestra Senora la Reina de Los Angeles (the original agricultural settlement built by Mexican labor under the aegis of the Spanish crown in 1781), passed into Mexican rule in 1822 until being conquered by the United States in 1847. The site faded from significance as Anglo attentions were fixed on shifting CBD growth to Pershing Square south of the old center. Chinatown was razed to make way for the Union Railway Station in the 1930s, however, and other portions of the district were cleared to make way for highways and government building expansions in the post–World War II era. The site was finally recognized as El Pueblo de Los Angeles Historical Monument by the L.A. Recreation and Parks Commission in the late 1980s under persistent Chicano pressure. The ideological struggle has continued, however, with the emergence of a vociferous intergroup conflict over the character of the heritage recovery effort. A restoration centered on the "prime historical period" of 1920–1932, when a plurality of ethnic groups existed at the plaza (but Mexican influence at the plaza was at its weakest), has been endorsed by the Euro-American-led Recreation and Parks Commission, but the Mexican Conservancy and other Chicano interests have favored a sequential history that recognizes the fundamental role of Native Americans and Mexicans in founding the settlement. The appointment of a diverse slate of board members representing all ethnic communities by Mayor Riordan somewhat resolved the conflict, but intergroup tensions persist.[9]

Cuban heritage reclamation efforts in Miami center on the "Freedom Tower" and the Tower Theater intersection on Calle Ocho in Little Havana. The so-called Freedom Tower, which is located on Biscayne Boulevard near harbor tourist amenities, was built in 1925 in the Spanish Renaissance architectural style, modeled after the Giralda Tower in Sevilla, Spain. For its first 32 years, it housed the offices of the *Miami Herald*. It later became the processing point for some 150,000 Cuban refugees airlifted to Miami on more than 3,000 "Freedom Flights" from 1965 to 1973. In the collective memory of Cuban émigrés, the Freedom Tower occupies an urban iconographic position similar to the fusion of New York City's Ellis Island and Statue of Liberty. The vacant building is now held by Saudi investors, but the Miami Office of Community Development and local preservationists have won historic designation for the site while they prepare proposals for its future disposition.

At a more advanced level of restoration is the Tower Theater site at the intersection of SW 8th Street (Calle Ocho) and SW 15th Avenue, the "heart" of the Little Havana commercial corridor. The theater is notable among Cuban-Americans as the first to begin screening American films dubbed in Spanish, giving many immigrants their most durable introduction to American culture. It is slated for conversion into a Latino film and performing arts center, with an interpretive museum of Cuban-American culture, and associated restaurants and retail shops. Also on the intersection is Maximo Gomez Park, a favorite spot for domino tournaments, where elderly Cubans are especially known to congregate, smoking cigars and engaging in political discourse and reminiscing about Cuba. Star-shaped plaques on the sidewalk commemorate renowned celebrities such as Gloria Estefan and the "Queen of Salsa," actress/singer Celia Cruz. City planners now refer to Little Havana as the "Latin Quarter" to recognize the greater diversity of members of the Latino diaspora, such as Central Americans, who now occupy the district. The SW 8th Street corridor is also the site of the Calle Ocho street festival; drawing up to 1 million people every year in March, the event is vaunted by its promoters as the "world's largest block party."[10]

In Houston, Mexican merchant interests affiliated with the East End Chamber of Commerce have sought to promote the development of a promenade/bike trail and urban historical park along the length of the Buffalo Bayou from Allens Landing to the ship *Turning Basin*, to be marked at intervals with sites of natural, historical, and ethnic significance. Although the plan seems somewhat incongruous within the industrial environment of Houston's east side, proponents are quite serious about their proposal, brandishing the model of San Antonio's highly successful Riverwalk. Near the Our Lady of Guadalupe Church (the major spiritual and community center of the original Mexican settlement of the second ward of Houston) are a cluster of newer sites, including the palm-lined Guadalupe Plaza for civic gatherings and the partially constructed Mercado del Sol, intended as a Latino festival marketplace in an abandoned mattress factory.

The reclamation of ethnic place culture in Houston and Miami, although predicated upon an affirmative expression of ethnic pride, has less of the air of cultural insurgency and critical historical revisionism advanced by purveyors of ethnic heritage recovery in Los Angeles and New York. These differences extend somewhat from variations in the character of the preceding history, experienced by each group in their respective locales, and in the inventory of historians and community activists. To illustrate, the strongly anticommunist Cubans, who are largely refugees/immigrants of the more liberal postwar civil rights period, were the beneficiaries of significant U.S. government assistance during their relocation and settlement, despite some real initial discrimination on the part of Miami property owners and employers. In Houston (where Mexicans experienced conquest and dispossesion), although place-based community development is strong in the east end Mexican community, place-based cultural restoration activities are still incipient. By contrast, Los Angeles efforts have emphasized the atrocities of Anglo conquest and the stark historical experiences of ethnic eviction, displacement, and internment. In New York City, heritage activities have centered on the salvaging of quotidian artifacts of tenement life and documenting the quiet but noble struggles of immigrant progenitors as pushcart peddlers, laundry workers, and garment workers in the promising but punishing crucible of the Lower East Side. The Chinatown History Museum recently changed its name to the Museum of the Chinese in the Americas in an attempt to move its scope and operations beyond local provincialities to encompass and promote new transnational, diasporic approaches to the study and dissemination of migration history.

The Japanese- and Chinese-American places of New York and Los Angeles also have been the arena of contentious struggles between local and overseas interests. Overseas interests gradually have made investment inroads into Little Tokyo in Los Angeles as the commercial and cultural reclamation of the district has proceeded in the past three decades, a trend that has been encouraged by the L.A. Community Redevelopment Agency (CRA). Little Tokyo community activists, fearing displacement of elderly residents and mom-and-pop merchants, launched an unsuccessful effort to block construction of a hotel (the New Otani)[11] and shopping center (Weller Court) financed by overseas Japanese capital in the early 1970s. The "antieviction task force" decried public subsidies granted by the CRA to large investors via "tax increment financing" schemes, which reduced short-term land acquisitions costs, through the expected guarantee of long-term incremental increases in tax liability (opponents viewed the short-run subsidies as a "land grab" on the part of overseas capital). Local interests were placated in the ensuing years by long-awaited CRA projects supporting smaller merchants (Japanese Village Plaza) and senior housing needs (Little Tokyo Towers and Miyako Gardens Apartments). Overseas Japanese capital was, in fact, aggressively courted by the boards of the Japanese-American National Museum in its recent capital campaign, which will finance a gargantuan new pavilion across the street. Akio Morita, founder and chairman of the Sony Corporation, dedicated one of his executives to raising an initial nest egg of some $9 million among the Keidenren of Japan (the major Japanese business federation). In a revealing hyperbole, Morita has triumphantly saluted local Japanese-American communities for the "inroads" they have made for Japanese corporate investments in the United States.[12]

New York's Chinatown has been the site of similar conflicts between local ethnics and their overseas counterparts. Encouraged by commercial dynamism in the district, the city in 1981 introduced revised zoning rules permitting high-density development near the entrance ramps of two bridges where there was a surplus of abandoned city-owned property (the Special Manhattan Bridge District). Community opposition quickly materialized, however, with the announcement of two major high-rise condominium projects to be financed by overseas Chinese capital. Protracted legal battles led to the revoking of one building permit, and the other project eventually was found culpable (with reference to the Mount Laurel doctrine) of inadequate "environmental impact review," where *environment* was given a wide latitude of meaning, including potential displacement of local residents and business and a negative impact on the community (Lin, 1998).

The opposition between local and overseas Chinese interests has not been so antithetical in downtown Houston, however, where the Houston Chinatown Council actively has sought backing of overseas investors in their efforts to market Chinatown as a tourist amenity for delegates at the nearby George R. Brown Convention Center. A six-block mixed-use development is envisioned with restaurants offering world cuisines (including Chinese, Vietnamese, Korean, Thai, Mexican, Italian, and Texas-style barbecue), a farmer's market, community center, theater for Chinese opera and other performances, and housing. Representatives of Shenzhen, China (Houston's sister city), will donate a gigantic Chinese gate with guardian lions.[13]

The Future of Ethnic Places

Some observers may be too quick to proclaim the obsolescence of concepts such as place, community, and locality with the locomotive onrush of globalization, technological advance, and urban spatial change. Urban decentralization and the continuing growth of nonplace-based or electronic networks of commerce and communication—including catalog shopping, television, cable, video, and the Internet—suggest the continued diminishing salience and power of central urban places as marketplaces of commodities and cultures. But this reading has found that central ethnic places are not only resilient but growing in significance, contributing to the cultural and commercial revalorization of the central spaces of immigration gateway cities.

The renewal of ethnic places in the zone-in-transition and central city has contributed to the rejuvenation of the economy as well as to the public culture of the city. As new marketplaces of cultural and economic products and sites of landmarks, representation, fetes, and artistic performance; these places play a major role in urban collective life, much as the agoras of ancient Greece. To the Greeks, the agora was not only the commercial marketplace but the "public hearth" or *hestia Koine*, the center of the community:

> So now come to the dynamic center of the Greek city: the agora. . . . The agora can be property called a marketplace, its oldest and most persistent function was that of a communal meeting place. As usual, the market was a by-product of the coming together of consumers who had many other reasons for assembling than merely doing business. . . . But in its primitive state, the agora was above all a place for palaver; and there is probably no urban marketplace where the interchange of news and opinions did not, at least in the past, play almost as important a part as the interchange of goods. (Mumford 1961, 148–149)

Similar roles have been played by the Arab *suq*, the Latin American *mercado* or *feria*, the Chinese *ziyou shichang*, and the other various marketplaces, emporiums, bazaars, and public commercial places of the globe. A comparable communal and commercial role was played by Main Street in the many small towns of the American heartland.

The zone-in-transition truly merits its moniker in the postindustrial era as a spatial locus of new commercial and cultural transformations that, along with growth in the producer services complexes of the urban core, constitute the evolving spatial and economic apparatus of the evolving world city. The putative repossession and revalorizing of these central urban spaces from which ethnic actors were previously restricted or evicted is an outwardly auspicious process fraught with many latent dilemmas, revealing fundamental complexities regarding the links between space, capital, and power in the postindustrial immigration gateway cities.

The involvement of ethnic actors in the economic and cultural revalorization of ethnic places ultimately has incorporated them into the intricate dynamics of broader political-economic relations with local states and global capital. Community contenders are drawn into negotiation with state agencies, possibly becoming incorporated into the state apparatus itself, thus involving them in intergroup struggles within the state bureaucracy. As polyglot honeypots, ethnic places may serve as multicultural tourist attractions and conduits of international trade and services, contributing both to the livelihood of ethnic contenders and municipal programs of globalization. But the revalorization of ethnic places also implicates them in broader strategies of gentrification and transnational capital accumulation, which ultimately may displace local ethnic residents and commercial merchants.

Notes

1. I employ the term *world city*, while noting the considerable debate surrounding the comparative relevance and analytical utility of both the term *world city* and the related concept of the *global city* (which is essentially a world city with first-order command functions in the global hierarchy of cities). See *Urban Affairs Review* (vol.33, no. 4, March 1998) for a trenchant exchange between James W. White, Saskia Sassen, and Michael Peter Smith on the global city concept, particularly regarding the incidence of class and racial/ethnic polarization, and the question of political variables. I continue to deploy the world city concept because of its utility in linking urbanization to global processes. I downplay the aspect of socioeconomic polarization while retaining a sense that globalization is a problematical process that may raise contradictory social and economic consequences in the urban milieu. On the matter of political variables, my argument accounts for the significant role of community contenders as well as local state actors in affecting the pace and direction of globalization and the revalorizing of ethnic places.
2. Similarly, Mele's (1995) study of the Lower East Side of New York offers an incisive analysis of the artistic and countercultural pioneers who culturally revalorized the neighborhood, only to be subsequently displaced via gentrification and subcultural appropriation by corporate agents of the global cultural economy.
3. Some theoretical bridgework already has been erected in the more recent writings of Sassen-Koob (1996), Smith and Feagin (1987), and King (1995).
4. Citing strong interregional trade links and world empires of global reach, Abu-Lughod (1989) and Chase-Dunn (1989) suggest there was evidence of global processes even before the era of European hegemony.
5. Robertson (1992, 43), in a related sense, suggests that the continuing modernization of the lesser developed world also may accelerate globalization.
6. The Survey of Minority-Owned Business Enterprises (SMOBE) and the Public Use Microdata Sample (PUMS) of the U.S. census both have been employed in previous investigations of ethnic enclave activity. I use the SMOBE in my research because, unlike the PUMS, it permits an analysis of the revenue-generating impacts of minority enterprises. The U.S. census draws these revenue data from the Internal Revenue Service.
7. Along with sites such as the Los Angeles Memorial Coliseum and the Watts Tower, the Little Tokyo National Historic Landmark became the 15th in Los Angeles County and the 2,147th in the nation. The designation compels an official review if federal funds or permits are involved in substantial alterations of the landmark but does not absolutely protect the district from future demolition (Gordon, 1995).
8. Words of the artist at Little Tokyo dedication ceremonies on 8 August 1996. Sheila Levrant de Brettville also designed "Biddy Mason: Time and Place," a commemorative wall documenting the struggles of a freed African American slave woman who journeyed the overland trails to Los Angeles and started a career as a midwife. This is part of an ensemble of public arts and architectural preservation projects called "The Power of Place" (which landmark sites of racial/ethnic, women's, and labor struggle), led by Dolores Hayden of the UCLA program in Architecture and Urban Planning (Hayden, 1995).
9. As interpreted by Suellen Cheng and William Estrada, curators with El Pueblo de Los Angeles Historical Monument, in August 1996 field interviews. The conflict is also discussed by Acuna (1996, 26–30).
10. The Calle Ocho festival was the brainchild of Leslie Pantin, a Cuban-American attorney, who

(with partners) borrowed the idea of the Calle Ocho "Open House" from the New Orleans Mardi Gras and Philadelphia ethnic festivals of the 1970s. Wildly successful from its first year, the event has become integrated with a broader "Carnaval Miami" festival staged throughout the city, which culminates on its second weekend with the Calle Ocho street festival.

11. The New Otani became the object of a vociferous labor struggle in 1996 when the Hotel Employees Restaurant Employees Union launched a nationwide boycott of the hotel after management fired three union leaders of a campaign targeting the hotel for labor law abuses.
12. As related by Bruce Kaji, first president of the Little Tokyo Redevelopment Association in the 1960s and founding president of the Japanese-American National Museum in the 1980s, in an August 1996 interview.
13. As discussed by Dan Nip, a Houston Chinatown seafood wholesaler and head of the Houston Chinatown Council, in an August 1992 interview.

Globalization, Immigration, and Changing Social Relations in U.S. Cities

✦ Glenda Laws

ABSTRACT

The current process of globalization, with deep historical roots, has had a significant impact on social problems in U.S. cities. My focus is the links between globalization, immigration, and urban social relations. At the heart of this linkage is an economic restructuring across societies and in the U.S. city that has potent social consequences for immigrant populations. Such people, induced to migrate by changing economic circumstances, find growing ghettoization, isolation, and cultural antipathies in their new settings. In the new globality, immigrant populations are commonly fingered as the other, the invading and ominous people threatening time-tested social norms and economic principles.

Globalization has a social and cultural impact on the lives of various social groups in several different ways. It is not simply an economic process.

Some people, including investors who have seen their profits grow and workers who have been employed because of expanding business opportunities, have benefited from

Glenda Laws was an associate professor of geography at the Pennsylvania State University. She was an urban social geographer with an interest in marginalized populations and political struggles around their well-being. Throughout her career, Dr. Laws focused on, among others, the mentally ill, the homeless, the poor, immigrant women, and the elderly. She was interested in social and economic restructuring and, specifically, the spatial implications of restructuring for those marginalized groups in urban areas. Dr. Laws died in June 1996 at age 37.

Laws, Glenda. 1997. "Globalization, immigration, and changing social relations in U.S. Cities." *The Annals of the American Academy of Political and Social Science*. Volume 55:89–104. Reprinted by permission of Sage Publications, Inc.

the growth of global markets, while others have not. Consequently, relations between people living and working in U.S. cities have changed during the latest round of global restructuring. Immigrant groups have been particularly affected. That is because, in many respects, immigrants and immigration levels are directly related to the globalization of the economy. People, for the most part, migrate in search of economic opportunities (for example, work or investments), and as the economy has globalized, people from around the world find that opportunities attractive to them might well cross international boundaries. Once arrived at their destination, however, immigrants often experience various forms of segregation. Before turning to a discussion of some of the ways globalization has contributed to the economic, social, political, and spatial segregation of immigrants, I want to start with several preliminary observations.

First, despite much attention being given to the idea of globalization as if it were a recent phenomenon, it would be naive to suggest that U.S. cities have only recently entered a global political economy. Ever since the first European settlements, cities in North America have been linked, to a greater or lesser degree, to the machinations of a global system. The term *globalization,* as it is currently used, suggests that linkages between places around the world are now more numerous and more intense than hitherto and that supranational organizations are assuming an ever-greater importance. In the context of economic activity, this involves the growth over the last few decades of multinational corporations, the expansion of international capital markets, and related changes in patterns of international trade. Each of these elements of globalization, however, has a history measured in centuries rather than decades. Because of its long historical antecedents, perhaps it is best to think of the current round of globalization, in its economic, political, and sociocultural guise, as a round of qualitatively different international relations, usefully characterized by Jan Nederveen Pieterse (Featherstone and Lash, 1995, p. 46) as inherently fluid, indeterminate, and open-ended.

Although these new and multiple forms of global interdependence have implications for localities (for example, U.S. cities and their suburbs), the global and the local, or globalization and localization, do not stand in simple opposition to one another. Rather, they are intimately related and it is not particularly useful to discuss either without the other.

Second, we should note the importance of focusing upon the political and sociocultural dimensions of globalization—in terms of both causes and effects. We witness, for example, the growth of international governing bodies such as the United Nations and the World Bank and of advocacy groups such as Amnesty International and the increasingly important role such organizations play in political decision making and developments in the global economy.[1] Further, in terms of sociocultural relations, globalization involves the migration of people and customs. In some instances, large-scale migrations have resulted in the loss or marginalization of some cultures as some immigrants come to dominate indigenous populations (for example, migrations from the so-called Old to the New World under colonial expansions). In other instances, the immigrants themselves are ostracized and segregated in their new locations. Such, in fact, is the situation in many U.S. cities as the twentieth century draws to a close.

Transformations in the global political economy have had a significant impact on relations between residents of U.S. cities. Since the social problem of residential segregation in U.S. cities has been around for some time, it is certainly not a product of the latest round of globalization. Likewise, it would be difficult to argue with any certainty that poverty among inner-city residents is directly related to globalization or that violence directed at minority groups is an outcome of globalization processes. However, the form and function of segregation under globalization might be changing. We need to ask what role urban or local segregation plays in a global economy that (seemingly) increasingly looks to supranational organizations. We must, however, bear in mind that if globalization could be used to explain everything, its analytical value for understanding specific manifestations of social problems would need to be questioned. Despite such caveats, I do believe that transformations in the global political economy have had a significant impact on social problems in U.S. cities, and I hope to tease out some of these links in the ensuing discussion. My focus here is on immigrants who have relocated as a result of changing conditions associated with globalization. Although a comprehensive examination of this topic would include consideration of the conditions in the places from which immigrants move, space does not permit coverage here. I will therefore concentrate on the experiences of and attitudes toward immigrants who have settled in the United States. To organize what follows, I begin by reviewing the links between globalization, immigration, and urban social relations. Then, at the risk of over-simplification, I consider some of the economic, social, and political experiences of recent immigrants living in U.S. cities. Finally, I will explore the implications of continued globalization for residents of U.S. cities.

Globalization, Immigration, and Urban Social Relations

In the contemporary global political economy, some countries function as labor-exporting nodes, for both long- and short-term migrants, while others act as labor-importing countries. Saskia Sassen describes "migration as a global labor supply system" (Sassen, 1988, pp. 31–36) that provides workers to both urban and rural labor markets in developed industrialized economies. This implies that both capital and, to a lesser extent, labor are mobile on a global scale. For both capital and labor, a "sentimental attachment to some geographic part of the world is not part of the [global economic] system" (Thurow, 1996, p. 115). Of course, many businesses (especially small firms) and people do find themselves attached, whether by choice or circumstance, to a particular place and, as a result, may find that they are not competitive in the global market. At various spatial scales, whether international, national, or local, some regions lose workers and capital investment while others gain.

Explanations for large-scale movements of workers and their families between nation-states are rooted in long and complex histories that surround the diffusion of capitalism. Colonial expansions prior to World War I depended on such migrations between the Old and New Worlds. With rapid economic growth since World War II, immigrant workers from less developed countries have become an increasingly important component of the labor forces of most developed countries. Sassen describes current trends as follows:

> Two features characterize labor migration: the growing use of immigrant labor in the tertiary sector of developed countries and the growing use of foreign and native migrants in the secondary sector of developing countries. . . . Unlike other labor-intensive components of industrialized economies, service jobs cannot easily be exported. Thus, the growing concentration of immigrant labor in the service sector of highly industrialized countries may be pointing to constraints in the historical transformation of the international division of labor, insofar as most service jobs must be performed *in situ*. This growing concentration of immigrant labor in service jobs in developed countries can be viewed as the correlate of the export of [manufacturing] jobs to the Third World (Sassen, 1998, p. 53).

At the local scale, U.S. cities, along with their counterparts in other developed economies, have played an important role in the global labor market. The hierarchical organization of multinational corporations has designated some cities as headquarters locations that act as sites for leadership, research and development, and interaction with politicians. These command points watch over the global empires of the largest corporations. More routine functions, like manufacturing, have moved offshore, taking with them many relatively well-paid blue-collar jobs. However, the loss of some, indeed many, manufacturing jobs has not seen the eradication of low-wage positions in U.S. cities. Although increasingly challenged by Japan and other Asian economies, the postwar dominance of the U.S. economy has created (and continues to create) incomes and consumption opportunities that require minimally paid positions. The following description of the local social geography and economy of one neighborhood, Lennox, near the Los Angeles international airport captures the links between globalization and the low-wage workforce:

> The proximity of [the airport] is not coincidental. Many [immigrants] were drawn by the lure of work in area hotels and restaurants, the low-wage service jobs now largely the domain of immigrants. Indeed Lennox is a kind of late-20th century company town, housing a Third World servant class of maids, waiters, and others whose cheap labor sustains an international transportation and tourism hub (Mc Donnell, 1995).

Left behind, too, are those manufacturing activities that can find a cheap enough labor force within the United States to make them competitive in the international market (as well as those manufacturers who require a relatively skilled labor force that cannot as yet readily be found outside the developed economies). Sweatshops (and other institutionalized forms of low wages), then, represent one way of maintaining competitiveness. In addition, those employed in the headquarters offices of multinational corporations require support staff (such as accounting and legal expertise, clerical assistants, and janitorial services), and this has created demands for a whole range of business and personal services. That is, multinational corporations, and the ancillary services that are generated in a region by their presence, are very much dependent on a large, international labor market. The domestic side of that labor market includes a significant number of immigrants.

Of course, this is not an especially new development in the evolution of the U.S. space economy. In the first decade of the twentieth century, nearly 8.8 million people moved from abroad to major U.S. industrial cities. This number translates into a rate of 10.4 immigrants for every 1,000 people living in the United States. Both the number and the rate fell off until the post–World War II economic boom, which created renewed demand for immigrant labor. In addition, changes to immigration laws in 1965 resulted in higher levels of migration related to family reunification. The new legislation also led to a change in the countries of origin of migrants, from mainly European sites to regions in Central and South America and Asia. Between 1981 and 1990, 7.34 million immigrants entered at a rate of 3.1 per 1,000 population. Between 1991 and 1993, amid growing calls for a slowdown in immigration, the rate had reached 4.8 per 1,000, and some 3.71 million immigrants were admitted. In addition, the Bureau of the Census estimates that there may be as many as 4.00 million undocumented immigrants (Bureau of The Census, 1995). In 1994, 8.7 percent of the U.S. population was foreign born, the majority of whom live in cities. More than 18 million foreign-born individuals lived in metropolitan areas in 1990, while only 1.3 million resided in nonmetropolitan areas.

Migrants change the character of the places in which they settle. They establish businesses, invest in housing and other aspects of neighborhood infrastructure, celebrate cultural festivals, and bring with them a variety of cultural practices. Sometimes this multicultural aspect of migration is greeted enthusiastically by host communities; more often it is welcomed with ambivalence. However, it takes only the most casual attention to the popular media to realize that there is a groundswell of opposition to continued immigration at what is popularly perceived to be a large scale. Despite this opposition, there remains a persistent demand for both legal and illegal migrant labor. Undocumented immigrants are able to find work in U.S. cities as local manufacturers meet the demand for cheaply produced goods. The products of sweatshops find markets in the United States. And these markets are not only found among struggling small businesses or in the informal economy. Large retailers purchase (knowingly or otherwise) and then sell clothing produced by illegal aliens in Los Angeles sweatshops (Swoboda and Pressler, 1995). Furthermore, affluence in the United States has created a demand among relatively well-off families for housekeepers and gardeners, many of whom are immigrants (Natali, 1991). Rural regions, too, exhibit a "dependence on an imported peasantry" (Schlosser, 1993, p. 80).

Domestic labor markets, then, offer opportunities for global migrants, even while simultaneously there is an almost continuous call for immigration reform. Despite such calls, there are, of course, many supporters of liberal immigration policies. Advocacy groups are joined by business interests that see migrant labor as one means of maintaining competitiveness. A recent advertisement on the Internet asked, "Will immigration damage your business?" and argued that a reduction in the number of employment-based immigrants and restrictions on the length of time temporary workers could stay in the country would be problematic for businesses. Tensions between those who support and those who oppose immigration is indicative of how globalization affects relations between urban residents.

Sassen, in a study of "the global city," examines the increasing social polarization evident in New York City, London, and Tokyo as economic restructuring not only widens the income gap between rich and poor but also accentuates the contrasts between the gentrified commercial and residential settings used by the most privileged urban residents and the sweatshops and crowded houses where poor people work and live (Sassen, 1991). She demonstrates that globalization has invoked not only new economic geographies but also new social geographies. Spatial segregation of different social groups has persisted under globalization even at the same time that it has promoted international, interethnic, and interracial contacts through global migration. Increasing social polarization is a question of social justice, and it begs the questions of how some groups are privileged by social processes and how others might be disadvantaged by those same processes (Young, 1992).

In what follows, I will focus primarily on discussions of the economic experiences of immigrants based on their labor force attachment; then I will turn to a consideration of some sociocultural experiences including the assimilation-versus-multiculturalism debate and the violence that sometimes arises from intolerance of cultural difference. I also consider the political powerlessness of immigrants. To illustrate the discussion, I draw upon popular sources, especially reports from newspapers, because these are the sites from which many people gather information to develop their opinions about the merits of, or problems associated with, immigration policy and immigrants.

Economic Segregation: Labor Market Positions and Experiences

"Economic segregation of immigrants" refers to the fact that many simply do not have access to the same resources as the U.S.-born population. One of the most important determinants of both individual and household resources is the positions that workers hold in labor markets. Occupational and sectoral concentrations mean that some groups of immigrants receive, on average, very low wages. Income levels clearly have implications for opportunities and experiences outside the workplace, such as housing, health care, and leisure. For both advocates and opponents, then, the links between immigration and domestic labor markets are critical.

Opponents suggest that by accepting low wages (because they are often high compared with those that immigrants received in their home countries), immigrants have two important potential impacts on local labor markets. First, wage rates are driven down. Second, immigrants are employed in jobs that would otherwise be filled by unskilled or low-skilled U.S.-born workers. For immigrants who had been in the United States for less than five years in 1990, average wages were almost 32% below those of U.S.-born workers (Borjas, 1995, Fix, Passel, and Zimmermann, 1996). It may seem unclear why immigrants should be castigated for the unfairness of this situation if we assume that employers should pay fair and reasonable wages to all workers, regardless of their immigrant status.

The sweatshop conditions in which many immigrant workers find themselves are also indicative of the intensity of exploitation found in some urban areas. On 2 August 1995, a raid on a factory in El Monte, California, exposed a "workshop that held immigrant workers in 'slave labor' conditions inside a barbed-wire compound and forced them to work seven days a week for as little as 50 cents an hour."[2] In February 1996, the factory's operators pleaded guilty to a number of charges including indentured servitude. In this particular case, the majority of workers were described as "illegal aliens," but a suit filed in April 1996 claimed that the operators were paying legal Latino immigrant workers only $1.63 per hour for as many as thirteen hours of work per day in another two factories in Los Angeles.[3] Textile and clothing sweatshops seem to be especially exploitative in their treatment of workers—and, important, women. At least part of the explanation for the atrocious conditions such workers find themselves in must relate to the erosion of organized labor with respect to its important watchdog role. Globalization has seen many textile activities move offshore. There has been a parallel decline in the number of unionized employees. The Garment Workers Unions suffered a serious membership loss from 314,000 members in 1979 down to 133,000 in 1993.[4] Unions need, for the sake of all workers, to ensure that foreign-born workers are paid wages equal to those of U.S.-born employees.

In September 1995, a letter to the editor of the *New York Times* by the president of the National Association of Manufacturers reveals an interesting business perspective on the links between attitudes toward immigration and the structure of labor markets:

> American manufacturing no longer has an interest in maintaining a mass influx of unskilled, low-wage immigrants. While a large number of unskilled laborers helped fuel the Industrial Revolution, the technology-driven plants and offices of today's competitive global economy require the expertise of skilled workers.
>
> The National Association of Manufacturers is interested in the immigration issue, but only to maintain the employment-based immigration that provides American companies with the essential technical expertise in short supply in the United States. The shortage of available expert workers is a growing concern of American business.[5]

The distinction drawn here between unskilled and expert workers means that Schlosser's "imported peasantry" (Schlosser, 1993, p. 30) is less valued than the class of "high-tech itinerants wandering the globe" (Helm, 1993). Interestingly, the representative of the National

Association of Manufacturers does not note that the service and agricultural sectors seemingly still rely on low-skilled immigrants. Lobbyists for the agriculture industry, for example, recently sought federal legislation that would have granted visas to 250,000 temporary foreign farm workers.[6] Furthermore, this perspective does not help us understand the persistence of sweatshop forms of manufacturing in those areas that are not so much "technology driven" as they are labor intensive.

Iris Marion Young argues that exploitation in the U.S. wage labor market may be at its most extreme in the case of the menial work performed by members (especially those classified as "minorities") from the so-called new service class (Young, 1992). Newspaper reports suggest that migrant workers, sometimes unaware of their legal rights, are especially susceptible to poor treatment. For example, in January 1996, the Service Employees' International Union charged that three immigrant workers were cheated out of wages to which they were entitled by a contractor with the Massachusetts Bay Transportation Authority. The landscape and property management contractor was accused of claiming that "the three full-time workers [were] part-time employees to avoid paying prevailing wages (Lewis, 1996).

Some immigrants simply cannot find a way into the labor market, especially the legal market, and constitute part of the category of people Young describes as suffering from marginalization; they are "people the system of labor cannot or will not use" (Young, 1992 p.53). Exclusion from the labor force then leads to deprivation in a number of areas of everyday life since a life of poverty does not allow individuals to find adequate housing, health care, and other resources for themselves and their families. This situation has been a cause of some of the most heated political debates over the last decade or so. Immigrants are accused of burdening an already overstretched welfare system in calling upon public assistance programs for basic goods and services. Although illegal immigrants are especially vulnerable to such accusations, the anit-immigrant rhetoric used tends to extend the debate to all foreigners. At times this demands that legal immigrants be denied Social Security and other benefits unless they take out U.S. citizenship.

But is it clear that immigrants are as much of a drain on public assistance as might be thought? According to George Borjas, the relative position of immigrants in the U.S. economy deteriorated between 1970 and 1990. During those two decades, the percentage of immigrants receiving welfare increased from less than 6% to just over 9% (Bojras, 1995). Important, these figures reveal that more than 90% of immigrants do not receive welfare. Fix, Passel, and Zimmermann further note that immigrants use welfare programs at about the same rate as U.S.-born residents, although there may be significantly higher usage among particular subsets of immigrants (such as refugees and elderly people) (Fix, Passel, and Zimmermann, 1996). Wages for immigrants have not kept up with those of U.S.-born workers.

Whereas in 1970, immigrants and U.S.-born workers were, on average, receiving almost equal wages, the wage differential in 1990 showed immigrants earning more than 15% less than the U.S.-born. Perhaps the growing visibility of the poverty experienced by some segments of the immigrant population over the last two decades might account for some of the opposition to continued migration. The degree to which immigrants might be a drain on a particular pool of resources, however, really depends on the spatial scale of analysis being discussed. Researchers at the Urban Institute in Washington, D.C., argue, for example, that "while immigrants generate a net fiscal surplus, the bulk of the taxes they pay are federal, while the obligations for providing them services remains with local and state governments. Hence, in some communities, immigrants generate a net deficit at the local level" (Fix and Passel, 1994). That is, in the overall operation of the U.S. economy, immigrants are a positive force; however, in particular communities and neighborhoods, immigrants might draw upon public resources more heavily than U.S.-born residents do.

Naturally, the restructuring of the U.S. economy, as noted in the letter from the representative of the manufacturers' association cited earlier, has created demands for highly skilled immigrant labor. The latest cohorts of immigrants tend to be more highly educated than either earlier immigrants or U.S.-born residents of comparable age.[7] In 1994, 147,012 employment-based immigrants were admitted to the United States. More than 40,000 of these were classified as priority workers or professionals with advanced degrees (Bureau of the Census, 1995). While there is evidence that these workers do relatively well when it comes to wages, in some cases even highly skilled immigrant workers find themselves in exploitative situations. One *Los Angeles Times* report describes the creation of high-technology sweatshops staffed by "skilled—and cheap—programmers" from abroad: "Legions of programmers, many working on dubious visas, are hacking away right now in cheap motel rooms, guarded hideaways, and corporate computer centers throughout America." The relationships to globalization are made explicit in the following description:

> These new high-tech itinerants wandering the globe in search of work are mirrored by a new breed of work wandering the globe in search of cheap labor. Linked to the United States by satellite and electronic mail often backed by government subsidies, overseas workers are providing quality programming at prices far below what it would cost here (Helm, 1993).

Despite their very high skill levels, then, foreign programmers often enter the United States (on short-term visas) to be paid less than the prevailing wage. Opponents have criticized the immigrants, saying they lower wages, but at least one anti-immigrant group has placed the blame on the corporations that allow their contractors to pay these low wages. Such a strategy places pressure on U.S. firms to pay immigrant workers at prevailing rates so that they are not as competitive with local workers.

The longer immigrants reside in the United States, the better their wages and labor market positions are likely to be. Immigrant labor markets are, however, polarized between the low wages of the unskilled who often find work only through informal contacts, and the highly paid positions held by in-migrating individuals whose professional skills are in high demand. Both segments of the immigrant labor market are the target of efforts to restrict the number of people migrating into this country. But where does that leave immigrants who are outside the labor market, and what, then, are their experiences?

Sociospatial Segregation

Accompanying globalization and the influx of migrants has been the growth in anti-immigrant sentiment, evident in any number of sources, including print media, talk radio, and political campaign speeches. By deliberate choice, many of the phrases used here (and elsewhere in this article) come from newspaper reports. It is such popular representations as these that fuel many of the debates about immigration and immigrants. They are the sources from which many people gather information to develop their opinions about the merits of, or problems associated with, immigration policy and immigrants. The extent of the necessity of migrant labor is not clear in the minds of many residents of the United States. Opponents to large-scale immigration complain that because of their supposed heavy use of public services, immigrants, especially (though not exclusively) undocumented workers and their families, are a burden to an economy that already has too large a deficit. At a time when politicians grapple with how to balance budgets at federal, state, and local levels, and when unemployment among some segments of the working-age population is very high, questions are asked about why more people are allowed to enter the country. Advocates of immigration argue that immigrants and their families contribute to both the cultural and economic development of the nation.[8] These debates about the relative merits of legal and illegal migration create tensions not only in federal policy debates but also in communities and neighborhoods where there are large concentrations of immigrants.

One suburban Los Angeles resident told a *Los Angeles Times* reporter, "What we have in Southern California is not assimilation—it's annexation by Mexico" (McDonnell, 1995). In another case, a man charged with assaulting an immigrant reportedly told an arresting officer in Glendale, California, "All of them should go back where they came from. . . . They take our homes, our jobs, they buy up everything, and look at me. I was born here. They don't belong here." (Ed Bond, 1994). U.S.-born (and some immigrant) residents argue that there are simply too many immigrants entering the country who have rejected assimilationist models and who favor a multicultural society that preserves cultural differences.

At the center of many debates is the resistance or inability of some immigrants to adopt English as their primary language. In some cases, immigrants, especially older people and recently arrived migrants, have limited English skills, and thus there has been a growing trend for government services to be provided in other languages. For example, to avoid claims of anti-Hispanic bias, the Chicago Housing Authority introduced a range of Spanish-language services.[9] Opposition to this trend has resulted in greater visibility for the English-only movement (Platt, 1990, Tatalorich, 1995, Crawford, 1992). Supporters of English-only initiatives—such as Arizonians for Official English, U.S. English, and English First—lobby at various levels of government for legislation that makes it illegal for government services to be provided in another language. By spring 1996, twenty-three states had adopted some measure that makes English the "official" language, and the Supreme Court agreed to take another look at the issue (Biskupic, 1996). Immigrant parents themselves are not always supportive of bilingual education. For example, a group of Latino parents in Los Angeles demanded that their children be placed in English-only classes because they want them to learn the dominant language (Pyle, 1996).

There is clear evidence that proficiency in English makes a difference to the range of job possibilities open to many immigrants. This in turn can affect the types of housing and other social necessities that are available to immigrant workers and their families. For the poorest immigrants, housing is a major problem. *Los Angeles Times* writer David Freed describes "cramped, decaying hovels" that "have slid into filthy disrepair over the years" and that have "crumbling walls and dripping ceilings." These are the homes of some of the least-skilled immigrants from Asia, Mexico, and South America (Freed, 1989). It is not just housing but also the communities in which immigrants live that face problems when low wages predominate. First-generation immigrants, especially those with low skills and thus low wages, often find themselves in communities where basic infrastructure is deteriorating.The situation in Washington Heights, a neighborhood of Dominican immigrants in New York City, exemplifies the material hardships faced by immigrant communities in the midst of global affluence:

> Washington Heights still has movie theaters and florists and other strong life signs gone from neighborhoods that have succumbed to urban blight, but it also has wall murals that serve as memorials to young men killed in the neighborhood's drug wars. Factory workers see jobs disappearing. Small-business owners are struggling to stay ahead of their rents and debts. Community organizations built on publicly funded programs are groaning under government budget cuts. Neighborhood community centers are threatened with closures and curtailed hours (Suro, 1995).

Related to the backlash against migrants are hate crimes in which they and their families are subject to violence targeted at individuals and the property they own. Hate crimes are directed at people on the basis of their immigrant status, race, ethnicity, or other attributes ascribed to a social group (L. A. County Commission on Human Relations, 1992, Cekola, 1994, Barnum, 1994, Bond, 1991, 1988). Specific statistical data are unreliable because of serious underreporting not only by the victims but also due to the reluctance of some agencies who are supposed to be reporting to the federal government to do so fully. Because of its racialized nature, violence directed toward immigrants spills over onto U.S. citizens and U.S.-born people who appear to be immigrants. The National Asian Pacific American League Consortium released a report in 1995 that found that often Asian Americans were told to "go home . . . as if they were not Americans" (Sun, 1995). Violence, as many people have noted, is an expression of perceived power relations. Immigrants are often the target of abuse and violence because they are believed to be receiving more than they deserve and at the expense of others. Perpetrators, for example, might believe that immigrants are taking jobs or using up resources to which they themselves are more entitled. This raises questions about perceptions of citizenship and what it means to be a citizen in one place but not in another.

Immigrants and Politics: Questions of Powerlessness

Powerlessness refers to the lack of control people have over their day-to-day lives. Young argues that the roots of powerlessness lie in positions held in the workforce. Those people with the most privileged and respected positions are more powerful than those who are not in such positions. Thus low-skilled immigrants usually end up in jobs in which they have little authority. Higher-skilled immigrants who are admitted on temporary work visas may not have any power to change jobs, regardless of how terrible the working conditions in which they find themselves might be. Social power can, however, be exercised in other areas of life, such as in the electoral process. Immigrants, legal and otherwise, low-skilled or high skilled, may find that they are relatively powerless in this respect. For example, a highly skilled immigrant engineer living in Silicon Valley may hold a position that is both privileged and much respected. But that same engineer may not be able to vote on legislation that affects the lives of immigrants in the United States. Thus this person is not powerless in the same sense as someone who is denied access to the labor market, but is in other ways—in this case, in terms of voting rights. Clearly, to speak of immigrants and their experiences is not to imply a homogeneous group of people who will all have identical experiences. Immigration, as a social attribute, intersects with many others—and race is perhaps the most critical factor.

There are attempts to extend voting rights to legal immigrants, at least at the local level. Within the Los Angeles Unified School District, criticism developed around a proposal to allow parents, regardless of their citizenship, to vote in school board elections. In Washington, D.C., in 1992, a council member introduced a bill that would allow immigrants to vote in some circumstances. In Takoman Park, Maryland, voting rights for legal immigrants were granted in the early 1990s (Jones, 1992, Sutner, 1992, Kaiman, 1991).

Globalization that encourages migration across international boundaries may well diminish the powerlessness faced by some people. Refugees, for example, who face political persecution in their home country might well find their position improved on being granted residency in a U.S. city. The period during which their case is being heard, however, is one in which their lives are still out of their control. Immigrants as a social group are clearly not totally powerless; they have relatively less power than some other groups.

Cutbacks in the welfare state may well be linked to the increasing integration of the U.S. economy into the global economy and its loss of dominance. The deficit is clearly a result of globalization, and it is linked to all kinds of cutbacks in domestic policy.

Conclusion: Political and Policy Implications

Rhetorical and often inflammatory statements about immigration and immigrants often have little relationship to the reality of the situation. The veracity of claims from both opponents and advocates of immigration is not easily determined. Despite the isolationist rhetoric of some conservative politicians in the United States, it is unlikely that the country can uncouple itself from the global political and economic structures that are now in place. Globalization gives businesses the choice of importing workers or exporting employment and production to other countries. Both create competition for U.S.-born workers living and working at home. Both also encourage, if not rely upon, significant global migration. Thus, despite calls for reform (read "restrictions") of federal immigration policy, it is unlikely that the United States can close its doors to all foreigners—even while immigration to the United States is not as open as some critics would claim.

While globalization is often defined in economic terms, its social consequences are great. This is not to imply that some global economic processes determine local social conditions without any reciprocity. Around the world, concern has been expressed about the extent to which global economic processes might be eradicating some local cultures. However, immigrants to U.S. cities also modify the social and cultural geographies of the places in which they live and work.

Just as more obviously multinational corporations and governments at all levels have developed strategies that simultaneously respond to and promote globalization, so groups of less privileged people also develop such strategies. Globalization has been described as a "new spatial geopolitics" (Featherstone and Lash, 1995, p. 3). The new urban geopolitics of U.S. cities pits localities against one another as they engage in bidding wars for foreign investment; social groups against one another as each group attempts to stake out a territory of its own; and businesses and the state against communities.

Notes

1. See Commission on Global Governance, *Our Globe Neighborhood* (New York: Oxford University Press, 1995).
2. Swoboda and Pressler, "US Targets Slave Labor Sweatshop."
3. See "39 Garment Workers File Suit to Recover $1.8 Million in Wages," *Los Angeles Times*, 5 Apr. 1996. See also Diane E. Lewis, "Sweatshop Workers Get Early Holiday Gift," *Boston Globe*, 10 Dec. 1995; *Sweatshops in New York City, A Local Example of a Nationwide Problem* (Washington, DC: General Accounting Office, 1989); *Garment Industry, Efforts to Address the Prevalence and Conditions of Sweatshops* (Washington, DC: General Accounting Office, 1994).

4. Bureau of the Census, *Statistical Abstract*, tab. 696. There is little doubt that globalization has eroded the power of unions in the United States. Business can escape union demands by moving operations to a foreign location. Increasing numbers of part-time and other nonunion jobs have undermined traditional sources of union membership. These trends have seen "unions do a u-turn on immigrant worker issue" as "an emerging generation of California labor leaders envisions poorly paid foreign-born workers—regardless of their immigrant status—as becoming a booming new base of support of U.S. unions." See Stuart Silverstein, "Unions for a U-turn on Immigrant Worker Issue," *Los Angeles Times*, 3 Nov. 1994.
5. Jerry J. Jasinowski, "What U.S. Business Wants from Immigration" (Letter to the editor) *New York Times*, 13 Sept. 1995.
6. The proposal was rejected by the U.S. House of Representatives on 21 Mar. 1996.
7. "Foreign-born Residents Highest Percentage of U.S. Population Since World War II, Census Bureau Reports" (Press release, CB95-155, U.S. Department of Commerce, Bureau of the Census, 25 Aug. 1995).
8. Advocacy groups like the Federation for American Immigration Reform (FAIR) are especially visible opponents of immigration. For details of the arguments against immigration, see Roy Beck, *The Case Against Immigration: The Moral, Economic, Social and Environmental Reasons for Reducing Immigration Back to Traditional Levels* (New York: W.W. Norton, 1996). See also V. Briggs, Jr., *Mass Immigration and the National Labor Market* (Armonk, NY: M.E. Sharpe, 1992); P. Brimelow, "Time to Rethink Immigration?" *National Review*, 22 June 1992, pp. 30–46. For a very brief overview of the benefits of immigration, see Fix and Passel, "Perspective on Immigration." The full study by Fix and Passel is reported in their *Immigration and Immigrants: Setting the Record Straight* (Washington, DC: Urban Institute, 1995).
9. "Hispancis and Housing Subsidies" (editorial), *Chicago Tribune*, 24 Apr. 1996.

Transnationalism: A New Analytic Framework for Understanding Migration

✦ NINA GLICK SCHILLER, *University of New Hampshire*
✦ LINDA BASCH, *Manhattan College Parkway*
✦ CRISTINA BLANC-SZANTON, *Columbia University*

Our earlier conceptions of immigrant and migrant no longer suffice. The word *immigrant* evokes images of permanent rupture, of the uprooted, the abandonment of old patterns and the painful learning of a new language and culture. Now, a new kind of migrating population is emerging, composed of those whose networks, activities, and patterns of life encompass both their host and home societies. Their lives cut across national boundaries and bring two societies into a single social field.

We argue that a new conceptualization is needed in order to come to terms with the experience and consciousness of this new migrant population. We call this new conceptualization "transnationalism" and describe the new type of migrants as *transmigrants*. We have defined *transnationalism* as the processes by which immigrants build social fields that link together their country of origin and their country of settlement. Immigrants who build such social fields are designated "transmigrants." Transmigrants develop and maintain multiple relations–familial, economic, social, organizational, religious, and political that span borders. Transmigrants take actions, make decisions, and feel concerns, and develop identities within social networks that connect them to two or more societies simultaneously (Basch, Glick Schiller and Blanc-Szanton, n.d.).[1]

Glick Shiller, Nina, Basch, Linda, and Blanc-Szanton, Cristina, 1992. "Transnationalism: A new analytic framework for understanding migration" in: *Towards a Transnational Perspective on Migration: Race, Class, Ethnicity, and Nationalism Reconsidered*, eds. Nina Glick Schiller, Linda Basch, and Cristina Blanc-Szanton, pp. 1–24. Annals of the New York Academy of Science. Reprinted with permission from Annals of the New York Academy of Science.

The following vignettes based on our observations of migrants from Haiti, the eastern Caribbean, and the Philippines now living in New York allow a glimpse of the complexities and intricacies of transmigrant experience and identity that, we believe, calls for a new analytical framework.

The ten men sat around a living room on Long Island. The occasion was a meeting of their regional association. Each member of the association had pledged to send $10.00 a month to support an older person living in their home town in Haiti. They came from different class backgrounds in Haiti, although all were fairly successful in New York. But one of the members, a successful doctor, expressed dissatisfaction—although he has a lucrative practice, a comfortable life style in New York, and a household in his hometown which he visits every year "no matter what." As he stated it, "I'm making money and I am not happy. Life has no meaning."

His speech about his emotional state was a preamble to his making an ambitious proposal to his hometown association. He called on his fellow members to join him in the building of a sports complex for the youth in their hometown. He indicated that he already had bought the land which he would donate and he would also donate $4,000–5,000 for the building and called on others to assist in the construction. He had given no thought to maintaining the building or staffing it.

The doctor was not alone in his aspirations to make a mark back home in a way that maintains or asserts status both in Haiti and among his personal networks in New York. There were more than twenty Haitian hometown associations in New York in 1988. Their memberships were composed of people who have lived in New York for many years. Many of them undertook large-scale projects back "home," projects which often are grand rather than practical. For example, an ambulance was sent to a town with no gasoline supply and no hospital.

These associations differ dramatically in the activities and audience from hometown associations of earlier immigrants whose main, if not only thrust of activity was to help the newcomers face social welfare issues in the new land. Russian Jewish immigrants in the beginning of the twentieth century, for example, founded "landsman" associations to provide their members with burial funds and assist the poor and orphaned in the United States. In contrast, the members of Haitian hometown associations, much as the participants in similar Filipino and Grenadian and Vincentian associations, are part of a social system whose networks are based in two or more nation states and who maintain activities, identities and statuses in several social locations.

Approximately 200 well-dressed Grenadian immigrants, mostly from urban areas in Grenada and presently employed in white collar jobs in New York, gathered in a Grenadian-owned catering hall in Brooklyn to hear the Grenadian Minister of Agriculture and Development. The Minister shared with Grenada's "constituency in New York," his plans for agricultural development in Grenada and encouraged them to become part of this effort.

By being addressed and acting as Grenadian nationals, these immigrants were resisting incorporation into the bottom of the racial order in the United States that categorizes them as "black," much as Haitians do when they construct hometown associations or meet as members of the Haitian diaspora to discuss the situation in Haiti.

By having their views elicited by a government minister from home, the Grenadians were exercising a status as Grenadian leaders, a social status generally unavailable to them in the racially stratified environment of New York. Their perceptions of themselves as Grenadian "leaders" were further activated by the minister's suggestion that these migrants have the power to convince their relatives at home that agricultural work, generally demeaned as a productive activity, is worthwhile and important.

But the Minister was also addressing the migrants as Grenadian ethnics in New York when he asked them to try to assist in introducing Grenadian agricultural goods to the United States market by using their connections in New York within the fledgling Caribbean American Chamber of Commerce to which many of them belonged. And of particular significance, the organizers of this meeting, who had each been in the United States a minimum of ten years, were as involved in the local politics of New York City as in Grenada. In fact, they were able to transfer—and build on—the political capital they gained in New York to Grenada, and vice versa. Grenada's ambassador to the United Nations has been a leader in the New York Caribbean community for twenty years. And so often did these political actors travel between Grenada and New York, that it became difficult for the anthropologist to recall where she had last seen them.

Well-established Filipino migrants are also periodically visited by representatives of the Philippines government urging transnational activities including strong encouragement to reinvest their American earnings into Philippine agriculture. The role of the Philippines state in contributing to the construction of transnational migrant fields extends even further.

At a desk, an employee was helping a customer close her box and complete the listing of items it contains. We were in the offices of a company in New Jersey (the only company where boxes can be delivered directly to the warehouse rather than being picked up for delivery). A regular flow of such boxes leaves every day from seven to eight major Filipino shipping companies. Anything can be sent back door-to-door and with limited taxes—appliances, electronic equipment and the like—as long as it fits the weight and size prescriptions defining a *balikbayan* box.

President Marcos had created the term *balikbayan* (literally homecomers) during a major national speech encouraging immigrants to visit their home country once a year during the holidays. He developed economic and legal means to facilitate their return and allowed each of them to bring yearly two *balikbayan* boxes duty-free. Mrs. Aquino restated her concern for the numerous silent "heroes and heroines of the Philippines." She then enabled them to purchase gifts of up to $1,000 duty-free upon entering the Philippines. Contracting for overseas labor and the system of sending remittances, so very important now for the country's economy, has been similarly institutionalized. The existence of transnational migration is thus officially sanctioned and highly regulated by the Philippine state.

We thus see how the transnational social field is in part composed of family ties sustained through economic disbursements and gifts. At the same time this field is sustained by a system of legalized exchanges, structured and officially sanctioned by the Philippine state.

As these examples show, transnational migrants arrive in their new country of residence with certain practices and concepts constructed at home. They belong to certain more or less politicized populations and hold particular class affiliations. They then engage in complex activities across national borders that create, shape, and potentially transform their identities in ways that we will begin to explore in this paper and in these conference proceedings. This is not to say that this phenomenon has not been observed by others. However, an adequate framework for understanding this phenomenon or its implications has yet to be constructed. Building on our own research with transmigrants from Haiti, the English-speaking Caribbean, and the Philippines[2] as well as the earlier observations of others, we seek in this paper to develop such a framework. This framework we argue allows an examination of how transmigrants use their social relationships and their varying and multiple identities generated from their simultaneous positioning in several social locations both to accommodate to and to resist the difficult circumstances and the dominant ideologies they encounter in their transnational fields. We start our analysis by identifying and developing six premises that situate transnationalism in time, space, world systems, and sociological theory.

The six premises central to our conceptualization of transnationalism are the following: (1) bounded social science concepts such as tribe, ethnic group, nation, society, or culture can limit the ability of researchers to first perceive, and then analyze, the phenomenon of transnationalism; (2) the development of the transnational migrant experience is inextricably linked to the changing conditions of global capitalism, and must be analyzed within that world context; (3) transnationalism is grounded in the daily lives, activities, and social relationships of migrants; (4) transnational migrants, although predominantly workers, live a complex existence that forces them to confront, draw upon, and rework different identity constructs—national, ethnic and racial; (5) the fluid and complex existence of transnational migrants compels us to reconceptualize the categories of nationalism, ethnicity, and race, theoretical work that can contribute to reformulating our understanding of culture, class, and society; and (6) transmigrants deal with and confront a number of hegemonic contexts, both global and national.[3] These hegemonic contexts have an impact on the transmigrant's consciousness, but at the same time transmigrants reshape these contexts by their interactions and resistance.

Social Science Unbound

For the past several decades descriptions of migrant behavior that could be characterized as transnational have been present in the migration literature, but these descriptions have not yielded a new approach to the study of migration. Students of migration did not develop a conceptual framework to encompass the global phenomena of immigrant social, political, and economic relationships that spanned several societies.

There was a certain recognition that the constant back and forth flow of people could not be captured by the categories of "permanent migrants," "return migrants," "temporary migrants," or "sojourners." In fact, Richardson, whose own work documents Caribbean "migration as livelihood" states that "students of the movements of Pacific islanders have found human mobility there so routine that they now employ the term circulation rather than migration" (1983, p. 176). Chaney astutely noted that there were now people who had their "feet in two societies" (1979, p. 209). Noting that many Garifuna "today have become United States citizens, yet they think of themselves as members of two (or more) societies," Gonzalez described migrants from Belize as forming " 'part societies' within several countries" (1988, p. 10).

In part, the recognition by social scientists that many migrants persist in their relationship to their home society, not in contradiction to but in conjunction with their settlement in the host society, did not develop beyond the descriptive level because migrant experiences in different areas of the world tended to be analyzed as discrete and separate phenomena rather than as part of a global phenomenon. For example, students of Caribbean migration noted the tendency of generations of migrants from the Caribbean to spend long periods away from home, yet support their families and often family landholdings or small enterprises with the money they sent home. They identified Caribbean nations as "remittance societies" and viewed this as a Caribbean phenomenon (Rubenstein, 1983; Wood and McCoy, 1985). Yet remittances are now part of the economies of nations in disparate parts of the world.

In all the social sciences, analyses of immigrant populations, their patterns of social relations, and systems of meaning have continued to be enmeshed within theories that approached each society as a discrete and bounded entity with its own separate economy, culture, and historical trajectory. That the study of immigrant populations should have been built upon such a bounded view of society and culture is not surprising considering that all social sciences had for decades been dominated by such static models.

Anthropologists, for example, were long constrained by the closed models of "structural functionalism" (Radcliffe Brown, 1952) that endowed populations, variously designated as "tribes," "peoples," "ethnic groups," or simply "cultures," with given, "natural," and group-specific properties. Each population was studied as a bounded unit, living in one place, bearing a unique and readily identifiable culture.[4] Sociology, meanwhile, had fastened on Parsons' emphasis on "social system" and the development of systems theory, and political scientists created models of "traditional" versus "modern" societies (Parsons, 1951). In the comparative study of "social systems," all fields of scholarship projected an ethnographic present in which the stasis of tradition was broken apart only by nineteenth and twentieth century European or American "contact," resulting in migration, urbanization, and acculturation. Anthropologists may have expressed uneasiness about the consequences of the very same processes that produced the political scientists' quintessential goal of modernization, but until the 1970s all disciplines remained constrained by their bounded categories of social analysis.

For the past two decades, such views have been subject to powerful critiques generated by several different analytical paradigms. But these critiques have yet to lead to new approaches to the study of immigrant populations. In anthropology, efforts to break free from bounded thinking have gone in two directions. Some analysts "deconstruct" culture, recognizing the artifice of the bounded unit of analysis by replacing conceptions of a single uniform "pattern" with multiple visions of individual, gendered, and particularized experiences. By and large, as Marcus has noted, "ethnographers of an interpretive bent—more interested in problems of cultural meaning than in social action—have not generally represented the ways in which closely observed cultural worlds are embedded in larger, more impersonal systems" (Marcus, 1986, p. 166). The emphasis is on the formulation of the ethnographic text as a product of the interaction between the individual ethnographer and the "informant" (Rosaldo, 1989). For those writers who, in their discussion of "text construction," acknowledge a global context the question becomes "once the line between the local worlds of subjects and the global world of systems becomes radically blurred, . . . [h]ow, . . . is the representational space of the realist ethnography to be textually bounded and contained in the compelling recognition of the larger systems contexts of any ethnographic subjects?" (Marcus 1986, p. 171).

Others, such as Wolf (1982; 1988) and Worsley (1984), building on a Marxist-influenced anthropology which decades earlier had expressed disquietude about the reification of the concept of "tribe,"[5] have called for a global level of analysis. Sectors of sociology and political science share this global vision and look to the "world capitalist system" as a unit of analysis. Wallerstein, a sociologist, developed a "world systems theory" in which different geographic regions of the world performed different and unequal functions in a global division of labor (Wallerstein 1974; 1982). World systems theory allowed social science to move beyond the examination of the structures of individual economies and to link the penetration of capital into previously non-capitalized sectors of production to the movements of people into the labor market.[6]

However necessary this global perspective, it has proved to be insufficient on several counts.[7] Little has been done by world systems theorists to explain the continuing significance of nation-states within these larger global processes, and world systems theorists have tended to ignore the legal, military, and ideological basis for the continuing existence of nations. In fact, the international flow of capital and distribution of labor takes place in a world that continues to be very much politically divided into nation-states that are unequal in their power, and which serve differentially as base areas of international capital. Wallerstein has addressed the constructed nature of nationalism and has recognized the significance of nationalism in the development of states. Nevertheless, a great deal more needs to be said about the fact that nation-states, although they exist within the world capitalist system, continue to control armies and nuclear weapons. Much world system analysis has focused on the economic rather than the political aspects of the system, especially in discussions of migration.[8]

Another shortcoming of world systems theorists who have built upon Wallerstein has been their tendency to view migrants as essentially units of labor. While the direction has been set by authors such as Portes and Bach (1985) and Sassen-Koob (1988), who acknowledge that a global perspective must include the social, cultural, and political dimensions of migrant experiences, this work has yet to be done. Our observations suggest that the transnational context of migrants' lives develops from the interplay of multiplex phenomena—historical experience, structural conditions, and the ideologies of their home and host societies.

In developing the concept of transnationalism we wish to provide those studying contemporary migrating populations with a framework in which global economic processes, and the continuing contradictory persistence of nation-states, can be linked to migrants' social relationships, political actions, loyalties, beliefs, and identities. At this juncture in the social sciences, it is essential that the study of migrating populations combine an emphasis on social relations, understood to be fluid and dynamic, yet culturally patterned, with an analysis of the global context. Such an approach is certainly necessary to elucidate the processes underlying the experience of those sectors of migrating populations who become transmigrants.

Transnationalism as a Product of World Capitalism

To analyze transnationalism we must begin by recognizing that the world is currently bound together by a global capitalist system. Such a perspective allows us to examine the economic forces that structure the flows of international migration and to place the migrants' responses to these forces and their strategies of survival, cultural practices, and identities within the world-wide historical context of differential power and inequality.

Because of the growing internationalization of capital, by the 1980s the structure of employment in the United States had undergone transformations often called "restructuring" or "deindustrialization" (Block, 1987, p. 136). Many stable industrial-sector jobs had been lost through the export of manufacturing industries and related jobs abroad, frequently to Third World countries. In many large urban areas in the United States well-paying, unionized, industrial employment was replaced by service sector and clerical employment. Sweat shops and home work proliferated. The newly created employment was characterized by low pay and little or no benefits or security.

At the same time, in the global restructuring of capital, the local economies of the Third World were disrupted by the intrusion of large scale agrobusinesses, the investment of transnational corporations in export processing industries, and tourism (Nash and Fernandez,1983). These economic shifts created a displaced, underemployed, labor force, not easily absorbed by the growing but still relatively small highly capitalized sector of the economy. The economic dislocations in both the Third World and in industrialized nations increased migration, yet made it difficult for the migrants to construct secure cultural, social or economic bases within their new settings. This vulnerability increased the likelihood that migrants would construct a transnational existence.

Understanding this global context has led to new perspectives on migration, perspectives that can contribute to an understanding that current migration is a new and different phenomenon. There is, however, no consensus among analysts on the character of the new migration. There are some who point to the invention of rapid transportation and communication systems, rather than the current state of world social and economic system, as the reason that modern-day migrants are more likely than their predecessors to maintain ongoing ties to their societies of origin (Wakeman, 1988). Others continue to view migrants within a classic "push-pull" model in which migration is seen as a product of separate and unrelated forces in the society of origin and the society of settlement (Lee, 1966). Using recent historiography that has revised our picture of nineteenth century immigrants, one might argue that there has been no major change in migration patterns. Apparently many earlier migrants were, in some sense, transmigrants who remained in communications with their home country and participated in its national movement (Vassady, 1982). We believe that current transnationalism does mark a new type of migrant existence and that only by more fully developing a global perspective on the transnational life experience of migrants, will social scientists be able to understand the similarities and differences between past and present migrations.

Transnationalism as Cultural Flow or as Social Relations?

The word *transnationalism* has recently become popularized in the realm of cultural studies with references made to "transnational phenomena" and "transnational research" (Wakeman, 1988, p.85). However, this usage of transnationalism stands conceptually apart from the entire bodies of literature on migration and on the world system. Instead, those who speak of "transnational phenomena" focus on flows of meanings and material objects in an effort to describe "transnational" culture, and put the discussion of culture in a world-wide framework.

Appadurai and Breckenridge (1988) seek to explain the recent development of a "public culture" in India, which they see manifested in public foods, entertainment, goods, and services that largely transcend national boundaries. Such a public culture, they argue, is a response to India's cultural interactions and exchanges with other nations. They highlight the complexities, the back-and-forth transferences, and the contradictions that characterize transnational flows of objects and cultural meanings.

A similar approach to global cultural trends has been taken by Hannerz (1989). Critiquing those who see diffusion of cultural goods and ideas only from powerful core nations to those on the economic periphery, Hannerz argues against notions of a "global village" or the "homogenization" of culture. Hannerz rightly emphasizes the constant tendency of people to creatively reinterpret, a process he calls "creolization." Focusing largely on movements of cultural items and flows of media images, he also emphasizes "cultural flows." The concurrent movement of peoples, and the activities, networks, relationships, and identities of transnational migrants have yet to be addressed.

In our task of developing a transnational framework that is of use in the analysis of migration, we can build on some groundbreaking work that has directed our attention to systems of social relations that are wider than national borders. In their 1975 description of Barbadian immigrants, Sutton and Makiesky-Barrow (1987) spoke of a "transnational socio-cultural and political system".[9] They posited that migration provides "an important channel for the bi-directional flow of ideas such that political events at home (e.g., independence) had an impact on the migrant communities abroad while migrant experiences were relayed in the opposite direction" (p. 114). Portes and Walton suggested that migration could be "conceptualized as a process of network building" (1981, p. 60). Rouse introduced the concept of "transnational migrant circuits" that encompass several societies (1988; 1989).

As the work of these authors and our own research makes clear, to understand current day migrants we must not only map the circulation of goods and ideas, but understand that material goods are embedded in social relations. If someone sends home a barbecue grill to Haiti, the grill does not stand in and of itself as an item of material culture that will change the material culture of Haiti. While it is interesting to talk about the new development of cultural forms around imported items, something else needs to be said. The grill is a statement about social success in the United States and an effort to build and advance social position in Haiti. It will be used in a fashionable round of party-going in which status is defined and redeemed in the context of consumption.

When someone from a small town in Haiti, St. Vincent, or the Philippines who now lives in New York sends home a cassette player, how are we to interpret this flow? The player can be used along with imported cassettes to bring the latest musical forms and themes from around the world into the most remote rural area. But on this same cassette those sitting on a mountainside in Haiti, in a rural village in the Philippines, or on a family veranda in St. Vincent send messages, warnings, information about kith and kin "at home" that influence how people behave and what they think in New York, Los Angeles, and Miami (Richman, 1987). Connections are continued, a wider system of social relations is maintained, reinforced, and remains vital and growing.

Whether the transnational activity is sending the barbecue to Haiti, dried fruits and fabric home to Trinidad so these goods can be prepared for a wedding in New York, or using the special tax status of *balikbayan* boxes to send expensive goods from the United States to families back home in the Philippines, the constant and various flow of such goods and activities have embedded within them relationships between people. These social relations take on meaning within the flow and fabric of daily life, as linkages between different societies are maintained, renewed, and reconstituted in the context of families, of institutions of economic investments, of business, and finance, and of political organizations and structures including nation-states.

The Complex Identities of Transnational Migrants

Within their complex web of social relations, transmigrants draw upon and create fluid and multiple identities grounded both in their society of origin and in the host societies. While some migrants identify more with one society than the other, the majority seem to maintain several identities that link them simultaneously to more than one nation. By maintaining many different racial, national, and ethnic identities, transmigrants are able to express their resistance to the global political and economic situations that engulf them, even as they accommodate themselves to living conditions marked by vulnerability and insecurity. These migrants express this resistance in small, everyday ways that usually do not directly challenge or even recognize the basic premises of the systems that surround them and dictate the terms of their existence.

As transmigrants live in several societies simultaneously, their actions and beliefs contribute to the continuing and multiple differentiation of populations. The creolization observed by Hannerz is not only a product of intensified worldwide product distribution systems, but also of this dynamic of migration and differentiation.

In order for us to be able even to perceive, much less analyze, the role played by migration in the continuing differentiation of the world's population, we must add to the study of international migration an examination of the identities and aspirations of transmigrants. This perspective should accompany our understanding that such migrants compose a mobile labor force within a global economic system. This is a labor force that acts and reacts in ways that emphasize, reinforce, or create cultural differentiation and separate identities.

For example, the same individual may attend a meeting of U.S. citizens of the same "ethnic group," be called as a New Yorker to speak to the Mayor of New York about the development of "our city," and the next week go "back home" to Haiti, St. Vincent, or the Philippines and speak as a committed nationalist about the development of "our nation." A migrant may pray in a multiethnic congregation that identifies itself as a common community in Christ, attend rallies for racial empowerment that emphasize black or Asian identities, and dance at a New Year's Eve ball organized for members of the migrant's "own" ethnic community. This same person may swear allegiance to his or her fellow workers at a union meeting in the United States while sending money back home to buy property and become a landlord. Through these seemingly contradictory experiences, transmigrants actively manipulate their identities and thus both accommodate to and resist their subordination within a global capitalist system.

Transnational social fields are in part shaped by the migrants' perceptions that they must keep their options open. In the globalized economy that has developed over the past several decades, there is a sense that no one place is truly secure, although people do have access to many places. One way migrants keep options open is to continuously translate the economic and social position gained in one political setting into political, social and economic capital in another.

Sometimes the transnational field of relations extends to the leadership of nation-states. The Aquinos rallied political support among Filipinos in the United States and brought many of them back to the Philippines in Cory Aquino's first government. Some of these people were sent back to the United States in turn to pressure American politicians with regard to key issues such as economic aid and the United States military bases in the Philippines.

Social scientists are only now beginning to comprehend the significance of these developments and to develop an appropriate analytical framework. What is needed is a reconceptualization of culture and society, work that is only now beginning (Wolf, 1982, 1989; Worsely, 1984; Rollwagen, 1986). As a first step we must rethink our notions of nationalism, ethnicity and race.

Rethinking Class, Nationalism, Ethnicity, and Race

As we indicated earlier when we traced the link between transnationalism and world capitalism, transnational migrants are primarily proletarian in their placement within the host labor force if not in their class origins. At the same time each transmigrant population is class differentiated. The Chinese transmigrant population contains powerful elements of the Hong Kong capitalist class, for example, while the Indian, Caribbean, and Filipino populations have important petit bourgeois and professional strata.

The identity of the transmigrant population is contested terrain. Both the capitalist class forces within the dominant society and the leading class forces of the migrating population collude and compete in their interests and outlook with respect to the domination of the migrant workforce. Note those Grenadian leaders who defined the entire transmigrant population in terms that minimized class stratification, yet reinforce their class position by emphasizing Grenadian transmigrants as both citizens of the

Grenadian nation and members of a U.S. Caribbean ethnic group. Thus that sector of the migrant workforce that is proletarian whether in origin or in insertion is both subject/actor in a continuing discourse about not only how they should behave, but just as important, about who they are. Their loyalty and sense of self, both individually and collectively, are the subjects of hegemonic constructions that emanate both from the place of settlement, such as the United States, and from their home society. Hegemony is at its root a conceptualization about the process by which a relationship is maintained between those who dominate within the state and those who are dominated (Gramsci, 1971; Williams, 1977; Brow, 1988; Comaroff, 1991). While ultimately relations of domination are maintained by force, the social order is enforced by the daily practices, habits, and common sense through which the dominated live their lives, dream their dreams, and understand their world. By conceptualizing hegemony we are led to see, as Raymond Williams (1977) pointed out, that

> (Hegemony) is a lived system of meanings and values–constitutive and constituting—which as they are experienced as practices appear as reciprocally confirming. . . . It is . . . a culture which also has to be seen as the lived dominance and subordination of particular classes. (p. 110).

Hegemonic constructions and practices are constantly created, reenacted, and reconstituted. These conceptions and categories are in part internalized by both dominant and dominated alike and create a sense of common loyalty and legitimacy for the dominant classes. In the United States, hegemonic constructions speak little of class but much more directly of race, ethnicity, and nationalism. Simultaneously these constructions serve to discipline a "classless" public into capitalist subjects through practices of consumption, leisure, and work.

The socially constructed nature of our entire repository of terms used to define and bound identity—*nationality*, *race*, and *ethnicity*—has just recently begun to be scrutinized adequately by social scientists. And the implications of transnationalism for hegemonic constructions of identity have yet to be analyzed.

The different hegemonic contexts to which these transnational migrants relate must be examined. Within both the United States and the home countries the state and the dominant classes attempt to establish and perpetuate control over their populations. They do this by elaborating systems of domination based on hegemonic constructions and practices in a process that is closely related to nation-building. These emergent formulations will speak to and build on the experiences and consciousness of the transnational migrants, directing the migrants' incorporation into the class relations of the nation-states in which they are living—both home and host. As we have seen, the activities of the transmigrants within each state and across national boundaries are influenced by, but also influence, all aspects of this hegemonic process in each nation-state.

In the United States these hegemonic constructions, though not uniform, have certain basic themes. The possibility of class identities is not only negated but cross-cut by constructions of race and ethnicity. The racial categories of their new setting, in this case the United States, are imposed on those incoming populations, though this occurs in different ways and with different emphases if they are Caribbeans, Chicanos, or Asians, for example. At the same time, demands are placed on those same populations to identify "ethnically." The hegemonic context imposes a discipline on newcomers who develop self-identifications, if not broader collective action, in accordance with categories and related behaviors that are not of their own making. But transnational migrants, with variation linked to their class background and racial positioning, have their own notions about categories of identity and their own conceptions of the rules of the hegemonic game. People live in and create a new social and cultural space which calls for a new awareness of who they are, a new consciousness, and new identities. However, both the actors and analyst still look around them with visions shaped by the political boundaries of nation-states.[10]

Nationalism has been identified as an early nineteenth-century invention (Kedourie 1960; Kamenka 1973), resulting from the rapid replacement of existing absolute monarchies in Europe by units called nation-states and the subsequent establishment of such polities in other parts of the world. While the unifying content of nationalism varied from country to country, it was based on an ideology of the commonness of origins, purposes, and goals that allowed those in power to legitimate rule over large and diverse populations. Nationalism gave heterogeneous groups a sense of shared common interest, and carried a vision of a nation-state as a "people," each nation making up a separate, equal, and natural unit.

Intellectuals provided these new formulations with their own rationality, describing religion, ethnicities, and kinship as archaic, whereas the new nations were seen as moving towards a rational and scientific modernity—part of an unending spiral of forward-looking improvements. Nations were defined as the necessary outcome of commercialism, scientific culture, and industrial progress occurring in Europe. By the twentieth century the concept of nation-state embodied a series of ideological constructions including scientific rationality, the economic role of the state, the institutionalization of economic calculations, and modernism.

Only recently have intellectuals begun to approach the study of nationalism more critically, and a number of authors have conceptualized nationalism as a historically specific construction in which the country's leaders and populations play an active role (Anderson, 1983; Worsely, 1984; Chatterjee, 1986; Kapferer, 1988; Fox, 1990). Some writers link the construction of nationalism to the colonial venture. This work has provided the social sciences with an analysis of nationalism that highlights its construction, through shared symbolism, of an imaginary common interest that may occasionally galvanize rebellion to existing authority or more often allow such authorities to control their national populations most effectively.

Despite the internationalization of capital and the transnationalization of populations, nation-states and nationalism persist and must be the topic of further analysis. For out purposes, it is important to recognize that transnational migrants exist, interact, are given and assert their identities, and seek or exercise legal and social rights within national structures that monopolize power and foster ideologies of identity. At the same time, it is clear that the identity, field of action, ideology, or even legal rights of citizenship of transnational migrants are not confined within the boundaries of any one single polity. The development of transnationalism challenges our current formulations about nationalist projects. We must ask whether transmigrants will continue to participate in nationalist constructions that contribute to the hegemony of the dominant classes in each nation state as they live lives that span national borders (Basch, Glick Schiller, and Blanc-Szanton, 1992).

As with nationalism, the constructed, manipulated, variable, flexible nature of ethnicity is only now becoming clear. *Ethnicity* first emerged as a key concept in social science in the United States during the late 1960s. Until that time, despite the multitude of indicators that sectors of populations of immigrant descent continued to maintain or even develop separate identifications, often including some ties to their country or region of origin, social science maintained that the appropriate mode of analysis for the study of immigrant populations was "assimilation."

The assimilationist framework that envisioned the melting of the prior national identities of immigrants into a single new American nationality has been shown to be a construction reflecting and contributing both to a myth of social mobility (Omi and Winant, 1986) and to the construction of American nationalism. The assimilationist framework and its concomitant popularization as an ideology, with America cast as a "melting pot," promoted a consistent message: a universal promise of mobility and success based on individual motivation and effort in a society in which there were no class barriers.

The assimilationist model had little to say about race. Often African Americans were seen as a recently arriving immigrant group in the North, even though a section of this population had helped construct and then continued to live in these cities.[11] However, in the 1960s, as demands for civil rights and full assimilation changed to demands for Black Power, the entire nature of ethnicity in America was reexamined by social scientists. The result was the creation of new theoretical models. First, Glazer and Moynihan's (1963) effort to look "beyond the melting pot" took up and popularized pluralist ideology first articulated in the 1920s (Kallen, 1956). The enthusiastic reception of the notion of cultural pluralism several years later by media, academics, and white "ethnics" (Greeley, 1971; Novack, 1974) seems linked to the development of minority demands for empowerment. A structuralist approach which emphasized the role of the larger society in fostering ethnic difference developed soon after as a critique (Alba, 1985; Yetman, 1985). Neither approach provided insights into racial divisions in the United States, however. Both were products of and contributed to the continuation of paradigms that conceptualize populations as divided into discrete, tightly bounded groups, and explain persisting identities as products of forces contained within separate nation-states.

In the United States, the cultural pluralists focus attention on cultural differentiation which they maintain divides the populace into separate, but equivalent, "ethnic groups," each with its own history, culture, and political interests. Central to the entire paradigm of cultural pluralism is the fact of persisting cultural differentiation traced by some pluralists to primordial sentiments described as virtually a "tribal" instinct (Isaacs, 1975).

Pluralists have paid scant attention to differences within the populations labeled as ethnic. Jews and Italians, for example, are categorized as single ethnic groups, whereas in both cases they in fact originated from different classes, regions, or countries, arrived with profound internal cultural differences, and in the course of settlement, developed new internal differentiations of class, region, and outlook (di Leonardi, 1984; Gorelick, 1974). National loyalties that link incoming populations to ancestral homes may be acknowledged by pluralists, but such relations are believed to fade over time.

The structuralists focus more on the economic and social forces within the polity that foster divisions between ethnic populations and thus the persistence of ethnic groups (Alba, 1988; Glick, 1975). They pay more attention to the constructed and manipulated nature of ethnic boundaries and ethnic differentiation. The term '*ethnogenesis*' is sometimes used to distinguish a process of cultural differentiation that develops from forces found within the larger society (Gonzalez, 1988). In its extreme, all cultural differentiation is seen as not just "invented" but imagined, so that no actual cultural differences separate populations conceived to be culturally distinct. Bentley (1987) has labeled this the "empty vessel" approach to the study of culture to highlight the tendency of structuralist analysis to discount the role of the members of ethnically defined populations to actively employ ongoing cultural repertories.

The current critique of pluralist and structuralist arguments has called for an analysis of ethnicity that leaves room both for "cultural practice" and human agency. There is an understanding that ethnicity is a product of the dialectic between continuities of cultural behavior and social constructions that are defined or reinforced by a particular nation-state (Blanc-Szanton, 1985a, b; Basch, 1985). However, a growing tendency in writing on ethnicity to focus on individual choice reduces rather than expands our analytical horizons (Cohen, 1978). With the emergence of transnationalism the individual migrant is now embedded in a wider social field that spans two or more nations. A transnational perspective on ethnicity must be developed that includes an examination of culture and agency within this expanded social field.

Race is also a social construction but one with a different history and a different relationship to the growth of the global system. It is useful to recall that until recently race and nation often were used interchangeably, as in the construction "the British race," in order to make clear that race is no more a product of genetics than nationality or ethnicity.[12] Over time, however, in places like the United States, the set character of race was imposed by the insistence that biology rather than culture is to be determinative of differentiation. In other national settings, ethnic divides may be used as race is—in this sense both are social constructions used to order social and economic relations.

At the same time, the historical construction of race is so firmly entrenched within the structure of global capitalism, and in the structures of inequality of particular societies, that some argue that social organization on the basis of race is best described as a "racial order" (Greenberg, 1980), besides which ethnic categories seem ephemeral and fluid.

Eric Wolf (1982) has stressed the historical difference between the operation of ethnic and racial categories in the development of capitalism. "Racial designations, such as "Indian" or "Negro" are the outcome of the subjugation of populations in the course of European mercantile expansion" (p. 380). Formulations of cultural difference do not apply to race—as we saw in the 1990 census—when one could only be black, not African American, West Indian, or Haitian. While ethnic or national terms stress cultural difference, Wolf makes it clear that racial terms disregard "cultural and physical differences within each of the two large categories, denying any constituent group political, economic, or ideological identity of their own."

The analytical mandate here is urgent and complex. Because race permeates all aspects of the transnational migrant's experience, it is important to analyze its several components. First of all, migrant identity and experience are shaped by the position of their country within the global racial order just as they are affected by the social location of their racial group within the nation state. Secondly internal class differentiation exists within the racial group to which transmigrants are assigned. For example, all those designated black in the United States can hardly be said to share the same class position. Moreover, the population designated as black in the United States is culturally differentiated (Bryce-Laporte, 1972, 1980; Foner, 1983; Fouron, 1983; Basch, 1987; Charles, 1989; Glick Schiller and Fouron, 1990). Migrants coming from the Caribbean, for example, confront an African American population that shares several centuries of historical experience. At the same time the global construction of race provides the basis for affinity and communality.

Yet all of these factors do not encompass the complexity of the racial identity of migrants who are transnationals. An analysis of the conceptions of race of transnational migrants also must examine the constructions of race that persist "back home." Talking about "back home" emphasizes the necessity of examining how the several nation-states within which transmigrants reside influence constructions of identity that draw on race, ethnicity and nationalism and the manner in which transmigrating populations, with their own internal differences, process these constructions within their daily lives.

Conclusion

We have emphasized the constructed nature of the identities of nationality, ethnicity, and race, and stressed the necessity of looking beyond the boundaries of existing analytical categories of social science. To conceptualize transnationalism we must bring to the study of migration a global perspective. Only a view of the world as a single social and economic system allows us to comprehend the implications of the similar descriptions of new patterns of migrant experience that have been emerging from different parts of the globe. At the very same time, it is in terms of these bounded identity constructs that migrants frame their individual and collective strategies of adaptation. In forging a framework of analysis capable of comprehending the life experiences of transnational migrants, social scientists cannot merely dismiss categories of identity as artificial and reified constructions that mask more global processes.

A focus on transnationalism as a new field of social relations will allow us to explore transnational fields of action and meaning as operating within and between continuing nation-states and as a reaction to the conditions and terms nation-states impose on their populations. Migrants will be viewed as culturally creative but as actors in an arena that they do not control. Transnational flows of material objects and ideas will be analyzed in relation to their social location and utilization—in relation to the people involved with them. This approach will enable us to observe the migrant experience in process, analyze its origins, monitor changes within it, and see how it affects both country of origin and countries of residence. Such a perspective will serve as a necessary building block for the reformulation of such key social science concepts as society and culture.

Notes

1. The term *transnational* has long been used to describe corporations that have major financial operations in more than one country and a significant organizational presence in several countries simultaneously. The growth of transnational corporations has been accompanied by the relocation of populations. It therefore seems appropriate to use the term *transnational* as a description for both the sectors of migrating populations who maintain a simultaneous presence in two or more societies and for the relations these migrants establish. In 1986 the American Academy of Political and Social Science employed the term as the theme of a conference publication titled *From foreign workers to settlers—Transnational migration and the emergence of a new minority.* The conference papers dwelt more on the effect on public policy of this type of migration, but did so without developing the concept of transnational migration.
2. A fuller development of the themes in this reading can be found in our book, *Rethinking migration, ethnicity, race, and nationalism in transnational perspective* (Basch, Glick Schiller, and Blanc-Szanton, forthcoming). See also Glick Schiller and Fouron (1990) and Basch *et al.* (forthcoming).
3. The concept of hegemony, long embedded in Marxism but developed by Gramsci (1971), facilitates the discussion of the relationship between power and ideology.
4. While the concept of uniform patterns of culture (Benedict, 1959) has been thoroughly critiqued by numerous anthropologists it persists in the profession and is a basic building block of most introductory texts.
5. The authors represented in *Essay on the problem of the tribe* (Helm, 1975) and Morton Fried's (1975) insightful work on primordial state formation and the tribe made seminal contributions to the effort to move anthropology beyond the conceptualization of cultures as tightly bounded and discrete.

6. Important early work in a global analysis was carried out by André Gunder Frank (1966). Work to link world system theory to migration has been carried out by numerous authors including Bach (1980), Portes and Walton (1981), Pessar (1982) and Sassen-Koob (1988).
7. For efforts to both critique and build upon a world systems framework see Smith (1984), Lozano (1984), Porters and Bach (1985).
8. Zolberg (1983) has emphasized the political and legal structuring of international migration.
9. See also Sutton's (1987) more recent discussion of "the emergence of a transnational sociocultural system."
10. For a more complete explanation of these processes see Basch, Glick Schiller, and Blanc-Szanton, 1992; n.d.
11. Classic assimilationist works are those of Wirth (1928) and Park (1950d). This framework was extended to African Americans in the work of Myrdal 1962 (1944) and E. Franklin Frazier (1957). Critiques of this approach have been made by numerous authors. For writers who specifically compare the experiences of immigrants and African Americans, see Stanley Lieberson (1980) and Omi and Winant (1986).
12. Park (1950), whose writings contributed to the assimilationist framework, spoke of the "race-relations cycle" and used the terms "nationality" and "race" interchangeably, thereby side-stepping the historic separation in the United States between people of color and white America.

Global Villagers: The Rise of Transnational Communities

✦ ALEJANDRO PORTES

When the residents of Ticuani, a small farming community in the Mixteca region of Mexico, wanted a clean water supply, they turned to a private civic group, the Ticuani Potable Water Committee. As it had many times before, the committee delivered: It quickly raised $50,000, mostly in $100 donations, to purchase and install new tubing to bring clean water to Ticuani.

This story, reported by the sociologist Robert C. Smith, might seem to be an unremarkable tale of civic cooperation. The water committee, however, wasn't in Ticuani or even in Mexico. It was in Brooklyn, New York. Nor was this just a case of immigrants sending money back home; thanks to modern telecommunications and air travel, the committee was directly involved. After learning that the tubes had arrived, the committee members flew from JFK Airport on a Friday, conferred with contractors and authorities over the weekend, and returned in time for work Monday morning. The water project marked the twentieth anniversary of the committee's first transnational public project and for this occasion the committee unveiled its new seal, to be used in all future correspondence and public events. The seal says, "*Por el Progreso de Ticuani: Los Ausentes Siempre Presentes. Ticuani y New York*," which means, "For the Progress of Ticuani: the Absent Ones, Always Present."

The Ticuani-Brooklyn network is an example of a phenomenon of growing importance—communities that span national borders. A by-product of improved communications, better transportation, and free trade laws, transnational communities are in a sense labor's analog to the multinational corporation. Unlike their corporate siblings, however, their assets consist chiefly of shared information, trust, and contacts. As the members of these communities travel back and forth, they carry

Portes, Alejandro. 1996. "Global villagers: The rise of transnational communities." *The American Prospect*. Number 25: 74–77. Reprinted with permission of *The American Prospect*. Volume 7, Number 25: March 1–April 1, 1996. *The American Prospect*, 5 Broad Street, Boston, MA 02109.

cultural and political currents in both directions. Their emergence complicates our understanding not only of global trade but also of immigration and national identity.

Neither Here Nor There

Transnational communities create a variety of new economic relationships across national borders. In the Dominican Republic, for example, entrepreneurs who have spent time in the United States operate hundreds of small and medium-size factories, commercial ventures, and financial agencies. In a study of 113 such firms in the late 1980s, Luis Guarnizo and I found that approximately half survive thanks to periodic investments by family and friends who remained in the U.S. The men and women who operate these firms in the Dominican Republic are not "return immigrants" in the traditional sense of the term. Instead, they make use of their time abroad to build a base of property, bank accounts, and business contacts and then travel back and forth to take advantage of economic opportunities in both countries.

These Dominican entrepreneurs frequently travel abroad to find new immigrant investors, often with the help of Dominican-owned financial and real estate agencies in New York City. They also rely on global contacts for sales. Proprietors of small garment firms, for example, regularly travel to Puerto Rico, Miami, and New York to sell their wares and on their return fill their empty suitcases with supplies such as garment designs, fabrics, and needles. To the untrained eye, these travelers may appear as common migrants visiting and bearing gifts for their relatives back home, when they are actually engaged in trade.

We expect immigrants to come to the United States, make a living, and send money to relatives back home, but in transnational communities the money often flows in the other direction. For example, a study of Chinese immigrants in the New York area, conducted by sociologists Christopher Smith and Min Zhou, shows how Chinese immigrants troll for capital abroad in such places as Hong Kong and Taiwan to finance new banks in the Flushing area of Queens in New York City. These banks have made possible a surge in home buying by New York's Chinese immigrants, who often are unable to obtain credit from mainstream institutions. Although small by conventional standards, these banks have proliferated, and they now serve simultaneously the economic interests of the immigrant community and those of overseas investors.

As money and goods flow through transnational communities, so do cultural influences and even politics. Consider the indigenous Otavalan community in the highlands of Ecuador, which over the last 25 years has spawned a transnational community that reaches into the major cities of Europe and North America, where the Otavalans market their colorful clothing wares. Otavalans abroad do not make their living from wage labor or even local self-employment but from the sale of goods brought from Ecuador. They maintain constant communication with home to replenish supplies, monitor their *telares* or garment shops, and buy land. They have even discovered the commercial value of their folklore, and groups of performers have fanned through the streets of cities in Europe and the United States.

Sociologist David Kyle reports that after years of traveling abroad, the Otavalans have brought home a wealth of novelties, and many have taken European or North American wives. In the streets of Otavalo, it is not uncommon to meet these white women attired in traditional indigenous garb. The transnational community has shaken up the Otavalan social hierarchy. The sale of colorful ponchos and other woolens accompanied by the plaintive notes of the *quena* (flute) have been so profitable that Otavalo's native entrepreneurs and returned migrants make up much of the town's economic elite.

Ethnic enclaves in the United States are no less vulnerable to the social aftershocks of the transnational metamorphosis. Sociologist Timothy Fong reports that Chinese newcomers have transformed the city of Monterey Park, California, into the "first suburban Chinatown." Originally, many Taiwanese and Hong Kong entrepreneurs established businesses in the area less for immediate profit than as a hedge against political instability and the threat of a communist takeover. (Opening a new business in the United States helps in obtaining permanent residence permits.) But many of these entrepreneurs have brought their families along to live in Monterey Park, while they continue to commute across the Pacific to conduct business. The profitable activities of these "astronauts," as they are dubbed in Chinese because of their frequent air travel, have helped Monterey Park's Chinese ascend swiftly from marginal status to the city's business class.

In their most advanced forms, transnational networks have evolved into political communities. Alerted by the initiatives of immigrant entrepreneurs, political parties and even governments have established offices abroad to canvass immigrants for financial and electoral support. Not to be outdone, many immigrant groups organize political committees to lobby the home government or, as in the case of the Mexican community studied by Smith, influence the local municipality. To provide yet another example, Colombian and Dominican immigrants in New York City organized during the 1970s and 1980s to demand the right to vote in elections in their respective countries and obtain the support from their home governments to combat negative images of their communities in the United States.

The result of this process is the transformation of the original pioneering economic ventures into transnational communities that include an increasing number of people who lead dual lives. Members are at least bilingual, move easily between different cultures, frequently maintain homes in two countries, and pursue economic, political, and cultural interests that require a simultaneous presence in both.

The Sources of Transnationalism

What gave rise to these transnational communities? For the most part, it is the social and economic forces unleashed by contemporary capitalism—many of the same ones, in fact, that allow corporations to move manufacturing plants from one country to another.

If today's U.S.-bound immigrants faced the same economic and technological conditions as their European predecessors at the turn of the century, there would be no transnational communities. At that time, a relative abundance of industrial jobs spawned stable working-class ethnic communities. Most Poles and Italians in the United States became workers, not entrepreneurs, because the industrial job opportunities made this an attractive option. There were rags-to-riches stories, but it typically took more than one generation to go beyond working for wages. By contrast, today's uncertain, poorly paid service-sector jobs encourage immigrants to seek an alternative autonomous path. Just as migration abroad became the norm in certain regions of the Third World in the past, today participation in transnational enterprises is turning into "the thing to do" among some groups of immigrants.

Earlier in the twentieth century, the expense and difficulty of long-distance communication and travel simply made it impossible to lead a dual existence in two countries. Polish peasants couldn't just hop a plane—or make a phone call, for that matter—to check out how things were going at home over the weekend. Now, such communication is possible, and many use it to cope with the whims of the global marketplace.

Transnational communities do not, of course, thwart the operations of large corporations. As more common people become involved in transnational activities, however, they subvert one of the premises of globalization, namely that labor stays put and that its reference point for wages and working conditions remains local. Immigrant workers who become transnational entrepreneurs convey information about labor conditions and novel economic opportunities. The growth of sociopolitical and economic ties across borders also affords immigrant workers some protection from cultural isolation and inferior legal status in the First World. Flows of capital from newly industrialized countries of Asia to North American cities facilitate home and business ownership in the immigrant community.

The significance of transnationalization is already apparent in smaller countries that export labor. In the peripheral nations of the Caribbean Basin as well as those Asian countries with long ties to the United States—such as Taiwan, South Korea, and the Philippines—the twin processes of corporate globalization and immigrant transnationalization have remolded entire economies. Virtually every family has a relative abroad, and the back-and-forth movement of people, information, and investment has become integral to family strategies for upward mobility. Consumption patterns and lifestyles are shaped as much by the global media as by the activities of former immigrants who have become transnational entrepreneurs. Even governments get into the act by seeking, as in the case of President Aristide of Haiti, to tap the immigrant community for capital investments and political contributions.

Meltdown or Melting Pot?

The rise of transnational activities of all kinds—economic, social, and political—adds an interesting twist to the debate about immigration policy. Restrictionists have long argued that immigrants take jobs away from American workers. However, many of these are jobs that not even immigrants want, let alone natives. In the process of avoiding these jobs by mobilizing their social networks, immigrants can manage to create new sources of employment, not only for themselves but for later immigrants as well. The Cuban enclave economy of South Florida furnishes a good example. A large proportion of the Cuban-owned businesses in the area are in the import-export trade and other transnational sectors. They enabled their owners to bypass the low-wage labor market and have also been a major source of employment for more recent arrivals. In my study of the 1980 Mariel exodus from Cuba, I found, for example, that after six years in the United States, close to half of these refugees were either working for themselves or in firms owned by their co-nationals.

Cultural conservatives also seek to restrict immigration because of the damage it presumably does to American values and cultural patterns. But transnational entrepreneurs epitomize the very values commonly associated with success and achievement in America. Not coincidentally, the cities that have taken the lead in adapting to the process of globalization—New York, Los Angeles, and San Francisco—are also cities of high immigration. Miami, not New Orleans, became the center of U.S.-Latin American trade largely because of the linkages to the region its large immigrant population built.

More complicated is the question of how transnational communities transform our notion of citizenship. At a time when so much of the American public is disengaged from civic life—apparently to the detriment of the political system—what does it mean to have so many citizens who are, in a very real sense, neither here nor there? The answer pivots on how narrowly one wishes to construe the concept of civic community. From one perspective, these solitary groups of foreigners, concerned with their own economic and social ends, and generally indifferent to the broader issues in American society, represent a direct threat to its integration. This view is grounded in the belief that the past holds the most appropriate model for the future. But "society" and "community" are not static and the path of change has been already blazed by the increasing globalization of the American economy. In this context, transnationality and its political counterpart, dual citizenship, may not be a sign of imminent civic breakdown but the vanguard of the direction that new notions of community and society will be taking in the next century.

Regardless of the position one takes, attempting to suppress emerging transnational communities, whether in the name of citizenship or a state-centric social order, is probably futile. The existing global social networks are too strong, the growth of distance-shrinking technology too fast. Even advanced countries have not been able to control immigrant populations, so how could they hope to tame their economic and social initiatives?

This is what the American labor movement learned to its chagrin when it threw its weight behind anti-immigrant measures during the 1970s. Such measures did not arrest the flow, but instead alienated immigrant workers from union organizing drives to the benefit of employers. As political scientist Leah Haus shows, one union after another shifted away from this stance in the 1980s and 1990s, involving themselves in immigrant communities and adopting their goals. By becoming increasingly "transnationalized" themselves, unions increased their chances for survival through building ties to the fastest-growing segment of the labor force in low-wage industries and neutralizing employers' divide-and-rule tactics.

Fast-paced social change is full of surprises, not all of them pleasant. But the attempt to turn back the clock in the name of a more familiar and secure social order often ends up producing even worse, unintended consequences. The rise of transnational communities represents the most novel facet of contemporary immigration to the United States and, as such, is full of uncertainties. It is also full of energy and promise. Its development will be worth monitoring in the years to come.

PART IV

IMMIGRANTS AND MODES OF INCORPORATION

Part IV examines various modes of incorporation of immigrants into their new society. The first reading in this part is Robert Blauner's classic essay, "Colonized and Immigrant Minorities." Blauner compares immigration and colonization as the two major processes through which new groups gain inferior access to the resources of a society. In this connection Blauner coins the much-quoted term *internal colonialism,* which refers to the enduring disadvantage of certain populations in American society.

Manuel Castells's "Immigrant Workers and Class Struggles in Advanced Capitalism: The Western European Experience" examines migration dynamics from a Marxist point of view. He attributes migration to such macrostructural requirements of modern capitalism as nonunionized, highly flexible, low-wage labor. In this essay, Castells explains how immigrant labor helps the capitalist economy to cope with economic crises by accepting the lowest wages, working under dangerous conditions, and tolerating sudden unemployment without a murmur.

"Middleman Minorities and Advanced Capitalism" by Edna Bonacich discusses the apparent paradox of thriving early capitalist forms of enterprise in the midst of advanced capitalist societies. After a brief introduction of the concept of "middleman minority," first introduced by Blalock in 1967, Bonacich describes economic and political activities of middleman minorities in the host society. This group, Bonacich maintains, remains removed from the host country's economy and politics mainly due to the sojourning status of immigrants and the hostile reactions of members of the host society. Therefore, middleman minorities take up occupations and lifestyles that are easily transportable and that strengthen their ties and loyalties to their communities and to their homeland.

Ivan Light's article titled "Immigrant and Ethnic Enterprise in North America" endeavors to explain the over-representation of foreign-born populations in the small-business sector. After reviewing the classical "cultural" and "disadvantage" theories of ethnic entrepreneurship, Light describes migrants' active patterns of ethnic and class resource utilization in their economic ethnic enterprise.

Mohsen Mobasher's article, "Ethnic Resources and Ethnic Economy: The Case of Iranian Entrepreneurs in Dallas," illustrates many of the above theoretical issues in ethnographic detail. His work sheds light on several aspects of ethnic economy such as its link to immigrant community, market orientation, patterns of interethnic and intraethnic competition, and ethnic and class resource utilization.

Part IV closes with Barbara Schmitter Heisler's "The Sociology of Immigration." In this essay Heisler concentrates on the long-term consequences of immigration and modes of incorporation of successive generations of immigrants. She draws attention to new conditions and call for new theories of immigration, including patterns of transnational immigration and postnational citizenship.

Colonized and Immigrant Minorities

✦ ROBERT BLAUNER

During the late 1960s a new movement emerged on the Pacific Coast. Beginning at San Francisco State College and spreading across the bay to Berkeley and other campuses, black, Chicano, Asian, and Native American student organizations formed alliances and pressed for ethnic studies curricula and for greater control over the programs that concerned them. Rejecting the implicit condescension in the label "minority students" and the negative after-thought of "nonwhite," these coalitions proclaimed themselves a "Third World Movement." Later, in the East and Middle West, the third world umbrella was spread over other alliances, primarily those urging unity of Puerto Ricans and blacks. In radical circles the term has become the dominant metaphor referring to the nation's racially oppressed people.

As the term *third world* has been increasingly applied to people of color in the United States, a question has disturbed many observers. Is the third-world idea essentially a rhetorical expression of the aspirations and political ideology of the young militants in the black, brown, red, and yellow power movements, or does the concept reflect actual sociological realities? Posed this way, the question may be drawn too sharply; neither possibility excludes the other. Life is complex, so we might expect some truth in both positions. Furthermore, social relationships are not static. The rhetoric and ideology of social movements, if they succeed in altering the ways in which groups define their situations, can significantly shape and change social reality. Ultimately, the validity of the third-world perspective will be tested in social and political practice. The future is open.

Still, we cannot evade the question, to what extent—in its application to domestic race relations—is the third world idea grounded in firm historical and contemporary actualities? To assess this issue we need to examine the assumptions upon which the concept rests. There are three that seem to me

Blauner, Robert. 1987. "Colonized and immigrant minorities," in *From Different Shores: Perspectives on Race and Ethnicity in America*, ed. Ronald Takaki, pp. 149–160, Oxford University Press. Used by permission of Oxford University Press, Inc.

central. The first assumption is that racial groups in America are, and have been, colonized peoples; therefore their social realities cannot be understood in the framework of immigration and assimilation that is applied to European ethnic groups. The second assumption is that the racial minorities share a common situation of oppression, from which a potential political unity is inferred. The final assumption is that there is a historical connection between the third world abroad and the third world within. In placing American realities within the framework of international colonialism, similarities in patterns of racial domination and exploitation are stressed and a common political fate is implied—at least for the long run. I begin by looking at the first assumption, since it sets the stage for my main task, a comparison and contrast between immigrant and third world experience. I return to the other points at the end of the essay.

The fundamental issue is historical. People of color have never been an integral part of the Anglo-American political community and culture because they did not enter the dominant society in the same way as did the European ethnics. The third world notion points to *a basic distinction between immigration and colonization as the two major processes through which new population groups are incorporated into a nation.* Immigrant groups enter a new territory or society voluntarily, though they may be pushed out of their old country by dire economic or political oppression. Colonized groups become part of a new society through force or violence; they are conquered, enslaved, or pressured into movement. Thus, the third world formulation is a bold attack on the myth that America is the land of the free, or, more specifically, a nation whose population has been built up through successive waves of immigration. The third world perspective returns us to the origins of the American experience, reminding us that this nation owes its very existence to colonialism, and that along with settlers and immigrants there have always been conquered Indians and black slaves, and later defeated Mexicans—that is, colonial subjects—on the national soil. Such a reminder is not pleasant to a society that represses those aspects of its history that do not fit the collective self-image of democracy for all men.

The idea that third-world people are colonial subjects is gaining in acceptance today; at the same time it is not at all convincing to those who do not recognize a fundamental similarity between American race relations and Europe's historic domination of Asia and Africa. (I discuss how U.S. colonialism differs from the traditional or classical versions toward the end of the essay.) Yet the experience of people of color in this country does include a number of circumstances that are universal to the colonial situation, and these are the very circumstances that differentiate third world realities from those of the European immigrants. The first condition, already touched upon, is that of a forced entry into the larger society or metropolitan domain. The second is subjection to various forms of unfree labor that greatly restrict the physical and social mobility of the group and its participation in the political arena. The third is a cultural policy of the colonizer that constrains, transforms, or destroys original values, orientations, and ways of life. These three points organize the comparison of colonized and immigrant minorities that follows.

Group Entry and Freedom of Movement

Colonialism and immigration are the two major means by which heterogeneous or plural societies, with ethnically diverse populations, develop. In the case of colonialism, metropolitan nations incorporate new territories or peoples through processes that are essentially involuntary, such as war, conquest, capture, and other forms of force or manipulation. Through immigration, new peoples or ethnic groups enter a host society more or less freely. These are ideal-types, the polar ends of a continuum; many historical cases fall in between. In the case of America's racial minorities, some groups clearly fit the criterion for colonial entry; others exemplify mixed types.

Native Americans, Chicanos, and blacks are the third-world groups whose entry was unequivocally forced and whose subsequent histories best fit the colonial model. Critics of the colonial interpretation usually focus on the black experience, emphasizing how it has differed from those of traditional colonialism. Rather than being conquered and controlled in their native land, African people were captured, transported, and enslaved in the Southern states and other regions of the Western hemisphere. Whether oppression takes place at home in the oppressed's native land or in the heart of the colonizer's mother country, colonization remains colonization. However, the term *internal colonialism* is useful for emphasizing the differences in setting and in the consequences that arise from it. The conquest and virtual elimination of the original Americans, a process that took three hundred years to complete, is an example of classical colonialism, no different in essential features from Europe's imperial control over Asia, Africa, and Latin America. The same is true of the conquest of the Mexican Southwest and the annexation of its Spanish-speaking population.

Other third-world groups have undergone an experience that can be seen as part colonial and part immigrant. Puerto Rico has been a colony exploited by the mainland, while, at the same time, the islanders have had relative freedom to move back and forth and to work and settle in the States. Of the Asian-American groups, the situation of the Filipinos has been the most colonial. The islands were colonies of Spain and the United States, and the male population was recruited for agricultural serfdom both in Hawaii and in the States. In the more recent period, however, movement to the States has been largely voluntary.

In the case of the Chinese, we do not have sufficient historical evidence to be able to assess the balance between free and involuntary entry in the nineteenth century. The majority came to work in the mines and fields for an extended period of debt servitude; many individuals were "shanghaied" or pressed into service; many others evidently signed up voluntarily for serf-like labor. A similar pattern held for the Japanese who came toward the end of the century, except that the voluntary element in the Japanese entry appears to have been considerably more significant. Thus, for the two largest Asian groups, we have an original entry into American society that might be termed semicolonial, followed in the twentieth century by immigration. Yet the exclusion of Asian immigrants and the restriction acts that followed were unique blows, which marked off the status of the Chinese and Japanese in America, limiting their numbers and potential power. For this reason it is misleading to equate the Asian experience with the European immigrant pattern. Despite the fact that some individuals and families have been able to immigrate freely, the status and size of these ethnic groups have been rigidly controlled.

There is a somewhat parallel ambiguity in the twentieth-century movement from Mexico, which has contributed a majority of the present Mexican-American group. Although the migration of individuals and families in search of work and better living conditions has been largely voluntary, classifying this process as immigration misses the point that the Southwest is historically and culturally a Mexican, Spanish-speaking region. Moreover, from the perspective of conquest that many Mexicans have retained, the movement has been to a land that is still seen as their own. Perhaps the entry of other Latin Americans approaches more nearly the immigrant model; however, in their case, too, there is a colonial element, arising from the Yankee neocolonial domination of much of South and Central America; for this reason, along with that of racism in the States, many young Latinos are third-world oriented.

Thus the relation between third-world groups and a colonial-type entry into American society is impressive, though not perfect or precise. Differences between people of color and Europeans are shown most clearly in the ways the groups first entered. The colonized became ethnic minorities *en bloc,* collectively, through conquest, slavery, annexation, or a racial labor policy. The European immigrant peoples became ethnic groups and minorities within the United States by the essentially voluntary movements of individuals and families. Even when, later on, some third-world peoples were able to immigrate, the circumstances of the earlier entry affected their situation and the attitudes of the dominant culture toward them.

The essentially voluntary entry of the immigrants was a function of their status in the labor market. The European groups were responding to the industrial needs of a free capitalist market. Economic development in other societies with labor shortages—for example, Australia, Brazil, and Argentina—meant that many people could at least envision alternative destinations for their emigration. Though the Irish were colonized at home, and poverty, potato famine, and other disasters made their exodus more of a flight than that of other Europeans, they still had some choice of where to flee. Thus, people of Irish descent are found today in the West Indies, Oceania, and other former British colonies. Germans and Italians moved in large numbers to South America; Eastern Europeans emigrated to Canada as well as to the United States.

Because the Europeans moved on their own, they had a degree of autonomy that was denied those whose entry followed upon conquest, capture, or involuntary labor contracts. They expected to move freely within the society to the extent that they acquired the economic and cultural means. Though they faced great hardships and even prejudice and discrimination on a scale that must have been disillusioning, the Irish, Italians, Jews, and other groups had the advantage of European ancestry and white skins. When living in New York became too difficult, Jewish families moved on to Chicago. Irish trapped in Boston could get land and farm in the Midwest, or search for gold in California. It is obvious that parallel alternatives were not available to the early generations of Afro-Americans, Asians, and Mexican-Americans, because they were not part of the free labor force. Furthermore, limitations on physical mobility followed from the purely racial aspect of their oppression.

Thus, the entrance of the European into the American order involved a degree of choice and self-direction that was for the most part denied people of color. Voluntary immigration made it more likely that individual Europeans and entire ethnic groups would identify with America and see the host culture as a positive opportunity rather than an alien and dominating value system. It is my assessment that this element of choice, though it can be overestimated and romanticized, must have been crucial in influencing the different careers and perspectives of immigrants and colonized in America, because choice is a necessary condition for commitment to any group, from social club to national society.

Sociologists interpreting race relations in the United States have rarely faced the full implications of these differences. The *immigrant model* became the main focus of analysis, and the experiences of all groups were viewed through its lens. It suited the cultural mythology to see everyone in America as an original immigrant, a later immigrant, a quasi-immigrant or a potential immigrant. Though the black situation long posed problems for this framework, recent developments have made it possible for scholars and ordinary citizens alike to force Afro-

American realities into this comfortable schema. Migration from rural South to urban North became an analog of European immigration, blacks became the latest newcomers to the cities, facing parallel problems of assimilation. In the no-nonsense language of Irving Kristol, "The Negro Today Is Like the Immigrant of Yesterday."

The Colonial Labor Principle in the United States

European immigrants and third-world people have faced some similar conditions, of course. The overwhelming majority of both groups were poor, and their early generations worked primarily as unskilled laborers. The question of how, where, and why newcomers worked in the United States is central, for the differences in the labor systems that introduced people of color and immigrants to America may be the fundamental reason why their histories have followed disparate paths.

The labor forces that built-up the Western hemisphere were structured on the principle of race and color. The European conquest of the Native Americans and the introduction of plantation slavery were crucial beginning points for the emergence of a worldwide colonial order. These "New World" events established the pattern for labor practices in the colonial regimes of Asia, Africa, and Oceania during the centuries that followed. The key equation was the association of free labor with people of white European stock and the association of unfree labor with non-Western people of color, a correlation that did not develop all at once; it took time for it to become a more or less fixed pattern.

North American colonists made several attempts to force Indians into dependent labor relationships, including slavery. But the native North American tribes, many of which were mobile hunters and warrior peoples, resisted agricultural peonage and directly fought the theft of their lands. In addition, the relative sparsity of Indian populations north of the Rio Grande limited their potential utility for colonial labor requirements. Therefore Native American peoples were either massacred or pushed out of the areas of European settlement and enterprise. South of the Rio Grande, where the majority of Native Americans lived in more fixed agricultural societies, they were too numerous to be killed off or pushed aside, though they suffered drastic losses through disease and massacre. In most of Spanish America, the white man wanted both the land and the labor of the Indian. Agricultural peonage was established and entire communities were subjugated economically and politically. Either directly or indirectly, the Indian worked for the white man.

In the Caribbean region (which may be considered to include the American South) neither Indian nor white labor was available in sufficient supply to meet the demands of large-scale plantation agriculture. African slaves were imported to the West Indies, Brazil, and the colonies that were to become the United States to labor in those industries that promised to produce the greatest profit: indigo, sugar, coffee, and cotton. Whereas many lower-class Britishers submitted to debt servitude in the 1600s, by 1700 slavery had crystallized into a condition thought of as natural and appropriate only to people of African descent. White men, even if from lowly origins and serf-like pasts, were able to own land and property, and to sell their labor in the free market. Though there were always anomalous exceptions, such as free and even slave-owning Negroes, people of color within the Americas had become essentially a class of unfree laborers. Afro-Americans were overwhelmingly bondsmen; Native Americans were serfs and peons in most of the continent.

Colonial conquest and control has been the cutting edge of Western capitalism in its expansion and penetration throughout the world. Yet capitalism and free labor as Western institutions were not developed for people of color; they were reserved for white people and white societies. In the colonies European powers organized other systems of work that were noncapitalist and unfree: slavery, serfdom, peonage. Forced labor in a myriad of forms became the province of the colonized and "native" peoples. European whites managed these forced labor systems and dominated the segments of the economy based on free labor. This has been the general situation in the Western hemisphere (including the United States) for more than three out of the four centuries of European settlement. It was the pattern in the more classical colonial societies also. But from the point of view of labor, the colonial dynamic developed more completely within the United States. Only here emerged a correlation between color and work status that was almost perfect. In Asia and Africa, as well as in much of Central and South America, many if not most of the indigenous peoples remained formally free in their daily work, engaging in traditional subsistence economies rather than working in the plantations, fields, and mines established by European capital. The economies of these areas came within the orbit of imperial control, yet they helped maintain communities and group life and thus countered the uprooting tendencies and the cultural and psychic penetration of colonialism. Because such traditional forms of social existence were viable and preferred, labor could only be moved into the arenas of Western enterprise through some form of coercion. Although the association of color and labor status was not perfect in the classical colonial regimes, as a general rule the racial principle kept white Europeans from becoming slaves, coolies, or peons.

Emancipation in the United States was followed by a period of rapid industrialization in the last third of the nineteenth century. The Civil War and its temporary resolution of sectional division greatly stimulated the economy. With industrialization there was an historic opportunity to transform the nation's racial labor principle. Low as were the condition and income of the factory laborer, his status was that of a free worker. The manpower needs in the new factories and mines of the East and Middle West could have been met by the proletarianization of the freedmen along with some immigration from Europe. But the resurgent Southern ruling class blocked the political and economic democratization movements of Reconstruction, and the mass of blacks became sharecroppers and tenant farmers, agricultural serfs little removed from formal slavery. American captains of industry and the native white proletariat preferred to employ despised, unlettered European peasants rather than the emancipated Negro population of the South, or for that matter than the many poor white Southern farmers whose labor mobility was also blocked as the entire region became a semi-colony of the North.

The nineteenth century was the time of "manifest destiny," the ideology that justified Anglo expansionism in its sweep to the Pacific. The Texan War of 1836 was followed by the full-scale imperialist conquest of 1846–1848 through which Mexico lost half its territory. By 1900 Anglo-Americans had assumed economic as well as political dominance over most of the Southwest. As white colonists and speculators gained control (often illegally) over the land and livelihood of the independent Hispano farming and ranching villages, a new pool of dependent labor was produced to work the fields and build the railroads of the region. Leonard Pitt sums up the seizure of California in terms applicable to the whole Southwest:

> In the final analysis the Californios were the victims of an imperial conquest. . . . The United States, which had long coveted California for its trade potential and strategic location, finally provoked a war to bring about the desired ownership. At the conclusion of fighting, it arranged to "purchase" the territory outright,

> and set about to colonize, by throwing open the gates to all comers. Yankee settlers then swept in by the tens of thousands, and in a manner of months and years overturned the old institutional framework, expropriated the land, imposed a new body of law, a new language, a new economy, and a new culture, and in the process exploited the labor of the local population whenever necessary. To certain members of the old ruling class these settlers awarded a token and symbolic prestige, at least temporarily; yet with that status went very little genuine authority. In the long run Americans simply pushed aside the earlier ruling elite as being irrelevant.

Later, the United States' economic hegemony over a semicolonial Mexico and the upheavals that followed the 1910 revolution brought additional mass migrations of brown workers to the croplands of the region. The Mexicans and Mexican-Americans who created the rich agricultural industries of the Southwest were as a rule bound to contractors, owners, and officials in a status little above peonage. Beginning in the 1850s, shipments of Chinese workmen—who had sold themselves or had been forced into debt servitude—were imported to build railroads and to mine gold and other metals. Later other colonized Asian populations, Filipinos and East Indians, were used as gang laborers for Western farm factories. Among the third-world groups that contributed to this labor stream, only the Japanese came from a nation that had successfully resisted Western domination. This may be one important reason why the Japanese entry into American life and much of the group's subsequent development show some striking parallels to the European immigration pattern. But the racial labor principle confined these Asian people too; they were viewed as fit only for subservient field employment. When they began to buy land, set up businesses, and enter occupations "reserved" for whites, the outcry led to immigration restriction and to exclusion acts.

A tenet central to Marxian theory is that work and systems of labor are crucial in shaping larger social forces and relations. The orthodox Marxist criticism of capitalism, however, often obscures the significant patterns of labor status. Since, by definition, capitalism is a system of wage slavery and the proletariat are "wage slaves," the varied degrees of freedom within industry and among the working class have not been given enough theoretical attention. Max Weber's treatment of capitalism, though based essentially on Marx's framework, is useful for its emphasis on the unique status of the free mobile proletariat in contrast to the status of those traditional forms of labor more bound to particular masters and work situations. Weber saw "formally free" labor as an essential condition for modern capitalism. Of course, freedom of labor is always a relative matter, and formal freedoms are often limited by informed constraint and the absence of choice. For this reason, the different labor situations of third-world and European newcomers to American capitalism cannot be seen as polar opposites. Many European groups entered as contract laborers, and an ethnic stratification (as well as a racial one) prevailed in industry. Particular immigrant groups dominated certain industries and occupations: the Irish built the canal system that linked the East with the Great Lakes in the early nineteenth century; Italians were concentrated in road building and other construction; Slavs and East Europeans made up a large segment of the labor force in steel and heavy metals; the garment trades was for many years a Jewish enclave. Yet this ethnic stratification had different consequences than the racial labor principle had, since the white immigrants worked within the wage system whereas the third-world groups tended to be clustered in precapitalist employment sectors.

The differences in labor placement for third world and immigrant can be further broken down. Like European overseas colonialism, America has used African, Asian, Mexican, and, to a lesser degree, Indian workers for the cheapest labor, concentrating people of color in the most unskilled jobs, the least advanced sectors of the economy, and the most industrially backward regions of the nation. In a historical sense, people of color provided much of the hard labor (and the technical skills) that built up the agricultural base and the mineral-transport-communication infrastructure necessary for industrialization and modernization, whereas the Europeans worked primarily within the industrialized, modern sectors. The initial position of European ethnics, while low, was therefore strategic for movement up the economic and social pyramid. The placement of nonwhite groups, however, imposed barrier upon barrier on such mobility, freezing them for long periods of time in the least favorable segments of the economy.

Rural Versus Urban

European immigrants were clustered in the cities, whereas the colonized minorities were predominantly agricultural laborers in rural areas. In the United States, family farming and corporate agriculture have been primarily white industries. Some immigrants, notably German, Scandinavian, Italian, and Portuguese, have prospered through farming. But most immigrant groups did not contribute to the most exploited sector of our industrial economy, that with the lowest status: agricultural labor. Curiously, the white rural proletariat of the South and West was chiefly native born.

Industry: Exclusion from Manufacturing

The rate of occupational mobility was by no means the same for all ethnics. Among the early immigrants, the stigmatized Irish occupied a quasi-colonial status, and their ascent into a predominantly middle-class position took at least a generation longer than that of the Germans. Among later immigrants, Jews, Greeks, and Armenians—urban people in Europe—have achieved higher social and economic status than Italians and Poles, most of whom were peasants in the old country. But despite these differences, the immigrants as a whole had a key advantage over third-world Americans. As unskilled laborers, they worked within manufacturing enterprises or close to centers of industry. Therefore they had a foot in the most dynamic centers of the economy and could, with time, rise to semiskilled and skilled positions.

Except for a handful of industrial slaves and free Negroes, Afro-Americans did not gain substantial entry into manufacturing industry until World War I, and the stereotype has long existed that Asians and Indians were not fit for factory work. For the most part then, third world groups have been relegated to labor in preindustrial sectors of the nonagricultural economy. Chinese and Mexicans, for example, were used extensively in mining and building railroads, industries that were essential to the early development of a national capitalist economy, but which were primarily prerequisites of industrial development rather than industries with any dynamic future.

Geography: Concentration in Peripheral Regions

Even geographically the Europeans were in more fortunate positions. The dynamic and modern centers of the nation have been the Northeast and the Midwest, the predominant areas of white immigration. The third-world groups were located away from these centers: Africans in the South, Mexicans in their own Southwest, Asians on the Pacific Coast, the Indians pushed relentlessly "across the frontier" toward the margins of the society. Thus Irish, Italians, and Jews went directly to the Northern cities and its unskilled labor market, whereas Afro-Americans had to take two extra "giant steps," rather than the immigrants' one, before their large-scale arrival in the same place in the present century: the emancipation from slavery and migration from the underdeveloped semicolonial Southern region. Another result of colonized entry and labor placement is that the racial groups had to go through major historical dislocations within this country before they could arrive at the point in the economy where the immigrants began! When finally they did arrive in Northern cities, that economy had changed to their disadvantage. Technological trends in industry had drastically reduced the number of unskilled jobs available for people with little formal education.

Racial Discrimination

To these "structural" factors must be added the factor of racial discrimination. The argument that Jews, Italians, and Irish also faced prejudice in hiring misses the point. Herman Bloch's historical study of Afro-Americans in New York provides clear evidence that immigrant groups benefited from racism. When blacks began to consolidate in skilled and unskilled jobs that yielded relatively decent wages and some security, Germans, Irish, and Italians came along to usurp occupation after occupation, forcing blacks out and down into the least skilled, marginal reaches of the economy. Although the European immigrant was only struggling to better his lot, the irony is that his relative success helped to block the upward economic mobility of Northern blacks. Without such a combination of immigration and white racism, the Harlems and the South Chicagos might have become solid working-class and middle-class communities with the economic and social resources to absorb and aid the incoming masses of Southerners, much as European ethnic groups have been able to do for their newcomers. The mobility of Asians, Mexicans, and Indians has been contained by similar discrimination and expulsion from hard-won occupational bases.

Our look at the labor situation of the colonized and the immigrant minorities calls into question the popular sociological idea that there is no fundamental difference in condition and history between the nonwhite poor today and the ethnic poor of past generations. This dangerous myth is used by the children of the immigrants to rationalize racial oppression and to oppose the demands of third-world people for special group recognition and economic policies—thus the folk belief that all Americans "started at the bottom" and most have been able to "work themselves up through their own efforts." But the racial labor principle has meant, in effect, that "the bottom" has by no means been the same for all groups. In addition, the cultural experiences of third-world and immigrant groups have diverged in America, a matter I take up in the next section.

Culture and Social Organization

Labor status and the quality of entry had their most significant impact on the cultural dynamics of minority people. Every new group that entered America experienced cultural conflict, the degree depending on the newcomers' distance from the Western European, Anglo-Saxon Protestant norm. Since the cultures of people of color in America, as much as they differed from one another, were non-European and non-Western, their encounters with dominant institutions have resulted in a more intense conflict of ethos and world view than was the case for the various Western elements that fed into the American nation. The divergent situations of colonization and immigration were fateful in determining the ability of minorities to develop group integrity and autonomous community life in the face of WASP ethnocentrism and cultural hegemony.

Voluntary immigration and free labor status made it possible for European minorities to establish new social relationships and cultural forms after a period of adjustment to the American scene. One feature of the modern labor relationship is the of separation of the place of work from the place of residence or community. European ethnics were exploited on the job, but in the urban ghettos where they lived they had the insulation and freedom to carry on many aspects of their old country cultures—to speak their languages, establish their religions and build institutions such as schools, newspapers, welfare societies, and political organizations. In fact, because they had been oppressed in Europe—by such imperial powers as England, Tsarist Russia, and the Hapsburg Monarchy—the Irish, Poles, Jews, and other East Europeans actually had more autonomy in the new world for their cultural and political development. In the case of the Italians, many of their immigrant institutions had no counterpart in Italy, and a sense of nationality, overriding parochial and regional identities, developed only in the United States.

But there were pressures toward assimilation; the norm of "Anglo-conformity" has been a dynamic of domination central to American life. The early immigrants were predominantly from western Europe. Therefore, their institutions were close to the dominant pattern, and assimilation for them did not involve great conflict. Among later newcomers from eastern and southern Europe, however, the disparity in values and institutions made the goal of cultural pluralism attractive for a time; to many of the first generation, America's assimilation dynamic must have appeared oppressive. The majority of their children, on the other hand, apparently welcomed Americanization, for with the passage of time many, if not most, European ethnics have merged into the larger society, and the distinctive Euro-American communities have taken on more and more of the characteristics of the dominant culture.

The cultural experience of third-world people in America has been different. The labor systems through which people of color became Americans tended to destroy or weaken their cultures and communal ties. Regrouping and new institutional forms developed, but in situations with extremely limited possibilities. The transformation of group life that is central to the colonial cultural dynamic took place most completely on the plantation. Slavery in the United States appears to have gone the farthest in eliminating African social and cultural forms; the plantation system provided the most restricted context for the development of new kinds of group integrity.

In New York City, Jews were able to reconstruct their East European family system, with its distinctive sex roles and interlocking sets of religious rituals and customs. Some of these patterns broke down or changed in response, primarily, to economic conditions, but the changes took time and occurred within a community of fellow ethnics with considerable cultural autonomy. The family systems of West Africans, however, could not be reconstructed under plantation slavery, since in this labor system the "community" of workers was subordinated to the imperatives of the production process. Africans of the same ethnic group could not gather together because their assignment to plantations and subsequent movements were controlled by slaveholders who endeavored to eliminate any basis for group solidarity. Even assimilation to American kinship forms was denied as an alternative, since masters freely broke up families when it suited their economic or other interests. In the nonplantation context, the disruption of culture and suppression of the regrouping dynamic was less extreme. But systems of debt servitude and semifree agricultural labor had similar, if less drastic, effects. The first generations of Chinese in the United States were recruited for gang labor; they therefore entered without women and children. Had they been free immigrants, most of whom also were male initially, the group composition would have normalized in time with the arrival of wives and families. But as bonded laborers without even the legal rights of immigrants, the Chinese were powerlesss to fight the exclusion acts of the late nineteenth century, which left predominantly male communities in America's Chinatowns for many decades. In such a skewed social structure, leading features of Chinese culture could not be reconstructed. A similar male-predominant group emerged among mainland Filipinos. In the twentieth century the migrant work situation of Mexican-American farm laborers has operated against stable community life and the building of new institutional forms in politics and education. However, Mexican culture as a whole has retained considerable strength in the southwest because Chicanos have remained close to their original territory, language, and religion.

Yet the colonial attack on culture is more than a matter of economic factors such as labor recruitment and special exploitation. The colonial situation differs from the class situation of capitalism precisely in the importance of culture as an instrument of domination. Colonialism depends on conquest, control, and the imposition of new institutions and ways of thought. Culture and social organization are important as vessels of a people's autonomy and integrity; when cultures are whole and vigorous, conquest, penetration, and certain modes of control are more readily resisted. Therefore, imperial regimes attempt, consciously or unwittingly, either to destroy the cultures of colonized people or, when it is more convenient, to exploit them for the purposes of more efficient control and economic profit. As Mina Caulfield has put it, imperialism exploits the cultures of the colonized as much as it does their labor. Among America's third-world groups, Africans, Indians, and Mexicans are all conquered peoples whose cultures have been in various degrees destroyed, exploited, and controlled. One key function of racism, defined here as the assumption of the superiority of white Westerners and their cultures and the concomitant denial of the humanity of people of color, is that it "legitimates" cultural oppression in the colonial situation.

The present-day inclination to equate racism against third world groups with the ethnic prejudice and persecution that immigrant groups have experienced is mistaken. Compare, for example, intolerance and discrimination in the sphere of religion. European Jews who followed their orthodox religion were mocked and scorned, but they never lost the freedom to worship in their own way. Bigotry certainly contributed to the Americanization of contemporary Judaism, but the Jewish religious transformation has been a slow and predominantly voluntary adaptation to the group's social and economic mobility. In contrast, the U.S. policy against Native American religion in the nineteenth century was one of all-out attack; the goal was cultural genocide. Various tribal rituals and beliefs were legally proscribed and new religious movements were met by military force and physical extermination. The largest twentieth-century movement, the Native American Church, was outlawed for years because of its peyote ceremony. Other third-world groups experienced similar, if perhaps less concerted, attacks on their cultural institutions. In the decade following the conquest, California prohibited bullfights and severely restricted other popular Mexican sports. In the same state various aspects of Chinese culture, dress, pigtails, and traditional forms of recreation were outlawed. Although it was tolerated in Brazil and the Caribbean, the use of the drum, the instrument that was the central means of communication among African peoples, was successfully repressed in the North American slave states.

American capitalism has been partially successful in absorbing third-world groups into its economic system and culture. Because of the colonial experience and the prevalence of racism, this integration has been much less complete than in the case of the ethnic groups. The white ethnics who entered the class system at its lowest point were exploited, but not colonized. Because their group realities were not systematically violated in the course of immigration, adaptation, and integration, the white newcomers could become Americans more or less at their own pace and on their own terms. They have moved up, though slowly in the case of some groups, into working-class and middle-class positions. Their cultural dynamic has moved from an initial stage of group consciousness and ethnic pluralism to a present strategy of individual mobility and assimilation. The immigrants have become part of the white majority, partaking of the racial privilege in a colonizing society; their assimilation into the dominant culture is now relatively complete, even though ethnic identity is by no means dead among them. In the postwar period it has asserted itself in a third-generation reaction to "overassimilation" and more recently as a response to third-world movements. But the ethnic groups have basically accepted the overall culture's rules of "making it" within the system, including the norms of racial oppression that benefit them directly or indirectly.

The situation and outlook of the racial minorities are more ambiguous. From the moment of their entry into the Anglo-American system, the third-world peoples have been oppressed as groups, and their group realities have been under continuing attack. Unfree and semifree labor relations as well as the undermining of non-Western cultures have deprived the colonized of the autonomy to regroup their social forms according to their own needs and rhythms. During certain periods in the past, individual assimilation into the dominant society was seen as both a political and a personal solution to this dilemma. As an individual answer it has soured for many facing the continuing power of racism at all levels of the society. As a collective strategy, assimilation is compromised by the recognition that thus far only a minority have been able to improve their lot in this way, as well as by the feeling that it weakens group integrity and denies their cultural heritage. At the same time the vast majority of third-world people in America "want in." Since the racial colonialism of the United States is embedded in a context of industrial capitalism, the colonized must look to the economy, division of labor, and politics of the larger society for their individual and group aspirations. Both integration into the division of labor and the class system of American capitalism as well as the "separatist" culture building and nationalist politics of third-world groups reflect the complex realities of a colonial capitalist society.

The colonial interpretation of American race relations helps illuminate the present-day shift in emphasis toward cultural pluralism and ethnic nationalism on the part of an increasing segment of third-world people. The building of social solidarity and group culture is an attempt to complete the long historical project that colonial domination made so critical and so problematic. It involves a deemphasis on individual mobility and assimilation, since these approaches cannot speak to the condition of the most economically oppressed, nor fundamentally affect the realities of colonization. Such issues require group action and political struggle. Collective consciousness is growing among third-world people, and their efforts to advance economically have a political character that challenges longstanding patterns of racial and cultural subordination.

Conclusion: The Third-World Perspective

Let us return to the basic assumptions of the third-world perspective and examine the idea that a common oppression has created the conditions for effective unity among the constituent racial groups. The third-world ideology attempts to promote the consciousness of such common circumstances by emphasizing that the similarities in situation among America's people of color are the essential matter, the differences less relevant. I would like to suggest some problems in this position.

Each third-world people has undergone distinctive, indeed cataclysmic, experiences on the American continent that separate its history from the others, as well as from whites. Only Native Americans waged a 300-year war against white encroachment; only they were subject to genocide and removal. Only Chicanos were severed from an ongoing modern nation; only they remained concentrated in the area of their original land base, close to Mexico. Only blacks went through a 250-year period of slavery. The Chinese were the first people whose presence was interdicted by exclusion acts. The Japanese were the one group declared an internal enemy and rounded up in concentration camps. Though the notion of colonized minorities points to a similarity of situation, it should not imply that black, red, yellow, and brown Americans are all in the same bag. Colonization has taken different forms in the histories of the individual groups. Each people is strikingly heterogeneous, and the variables of time, place, and manner have affected the forms of colonialism, the character of racial domination, and the responses of the group.

Because the colonized groups have been concentrated in different regions, geographical isolation has heretofore limited the possibilities of cooperation. When they have inhabited the same area, competition for jobs has fed ethnic antagonisms. Today, as relatively powerless groups, the racial minorities often find themselves fighting one another for the modicum of political power and material resources involved in antipoverty, model-cities, and educational reform projects. Differences in culture and political style exacerbate these conflicts.

The third world movement will have to deal with the situational differences that are obstacles to coalition and coordinated politics. One of these is the great variation in size between the populous black and Chicano groups and the much smaller Indian and Asian minorities. Numbers affect potential political power as well as an ethnic group's visibility and the possibilities of an assimilative strategy. Economic differentiation may be accelerating both between and within third-world groups. The racial minorities are not all poor. The Japanese and, to a lesser extent, the Chinese have moved toward middle-class status. The black middle class is also growing. The ultimate barrier to effective third-world alliance is the pervasive racism of the society, which affects people of color as well as whites, furthering division between all groups in America. Colonialism brings into its orbit a variety of groups, which it oppresses and exploits in differing degrees and fashions; the result is a complex structure of racial and ethnic division.

The final assumption of the third-world idea remains to be considered. The new perspective represents more than a negation of the immigrant analogy. By its very language the concept assumes an essential connection between the colonized people within the United States and the peoples of Africa, Asia, and Latin America, with respect to whom the idea of *le tiers monde* originated. The communities of color in America share essential conditions with third-world nations abroad; economic underdevelopment, a heritage of colonialism and neocolonialism, and a lack of real political autonomy and power.

The insistence on viewing American race relations from an international perspective is an important corrective in the parochial and ahistorical outlook of our national consciousness. The economic, social, and political subordination of third-world groups in America is a microcosm of the position of all peoples of color in the world order of stratification. This is neither an accident nor the result of some essential racial genius. Racial domination in the United States is part of a world historical drama in which the culture, economic system, and political power of the white West has spread throughout virtually the entire globe. The expansion of the West, particularly Europe's domination over non-Western people of color, was the major theme in the almost five hundred years that followed the onset of "The Age of Discovery." The European conquest of Native American peoples, leading to the white settlement of the Western hemisphere and the African slave trade, was one of the leading historical events that ushered in the age of colonialism. Colonial subjugation and racial domination began much earlier and have lasted much longer in North America than in Asia and Africa, the continents ususally thought of as colonies' prototypes. The oppression of racial colonies within our national borders cannot be understood without considering worldwide patterns of white European hegemony.

The present movement goes further than simply drawing historical and contemporary parallels between the third world within and the third world external to the United States. The new ideology implies that the fate of colonized Americans is tied up with that of the colonial and former colonial peoples of the world. There is at least impressionistic evidence to support this idea. If one looks at the place of the various racial minorities in America's stratified economic and social order, one finds a rough correlation between relative internal status and the international position of the original fatherland. According to most indicators of income, education, and occupation, Native Americans are at the bottom. The Indians alone lack an independent nation, a center of power in the world community to which they might look for political aid and psychic identification. At the other pole, Japanese-Americans are the most successful nonwhite group by conventional criteria, and Japan has been the most economically developed and politicially potent non-Western nation during most of the twentieth century. The transformation of African societies from colonial dependency to independent statehood, with new authority and prestige in the international arena, has had an undoubted impact on Afro-Americans in the United States; it has contributed both to civil rights movements and to a developing black consciousness.

What is not clear is whether an international strategy can in itself be the principle of third-world liberation within this country. Since the oppression, the struggle, and the survival of the colonized groups have taken place within our society, it is to be expected that their people will orient their daily lives and their political aspirations to the domestic scene. The racial minorities have been able to wrest some material advantages from American capitalism and empire at the same time that they have been denied real citizenship in the society. Average levels of income, education, and health for the third world in the United States are far above their counterparts overseas; this gap will affect the possibility of internationalism. Besides which, group alliances that transcend national borders have been difficult to sustain in the modern era because of the power of nationalism.

Thus, the situation of the colonized minorities in the United States is by no means identical with that of Algerians, Kenyans, Indonesians, and other nations who suffered under white European rule. Though there are many parallels in cultural and political developments, the differences in land, economy, population composition, and power relations make it impossible to transport wholesale sociopolitical analyses or strategies of liberation from one context to another. The colonial analogy has gained great vogue recently among militant nationalists—partly because it is largely valid, partly because its rhetoric so aggressively condemns white America, past and present. Yet it may be that the comparison with English, French, and Dutch overseas rule lets our nation off too easily! In many ways the special versions of colonialism practiced against Americans of color have been more pernicious in quality and more profound in consequences than the European overseas varieties.

In traditional colonialism, the colonized "natives" have usually been the majority of the population, and their culture, while less prestigious than that of the white Europeans, still pervaded the landscape. Members of the third world within the United States are individually and collectively outnumbered by whites, and Anglo-American cultural imperatives dominate the society—although this has been less true historically in the Southwest where the Mexican-American population has never been a true cultural minority. The oppressed masses of Asia and Africa had the relative "advantage" of being colonized in their own land. In the United States, the more total cultural domination, the alienation of most third-world people from a land base, and the numerical minority factor have weakened the group integrity of the colonized and their possibilities for cultural and political self-determination.

Many critics of the third-world perspective seize on these differences to question the value of viewing America's racial dynamics within the colonial framework. But all the differences demonstrate is that colonialisms vary greatly in structure and that political power and group liberation are more problematic in our society than in the overseas situation. The fact that we have no historical models for decolonization in the American context does not alter the objective realities. Decolonization is an insistent and irreversible project of the third-world groups, although its contents and forms are at present unclear and will be worked out only in the course of an extended period of political and social conflict.

Immigrant Workers and Class Struggles in Advanced Capitalism: The Western European Experience

✦ Manuel Castells

Since the great social upheaval of May 1968 in France, class struggles in Western Europe seem to have reentered a period of progressive development, both through a strengthening of trade-union and traditional political practices and through the appearance of new issues and the mobilization of new social strata around these issues. Thus the "old mole" was far from dormant and its underground workings lead sometimes to explosions of mass rage, and sometimes to the consolidation of new bases of protest and opposition to the system.

Among these new developments, the issue of immigration and the mobilization of migrants are particularly prominent. As the major trump card in capitalist expansion, and as the bogy scapegoat of the bourgeoisie always ready to feed the fires of xenophobia and racism, as a pretext for a reluctantly renewed charity, as a myth in mobilizing the European left and as a source of confusion for trade-unions and left-wing parties, immigrant workers constitute both in the reality of their daily oppression and in their potential for social revolt, one of the most important and least known stakes in the newly emerging class struggles of advance capitalism.

In view of the complexity of the subject, the mass of fragmentary information and the scarcity of adequate economic and statistical data, any analysis of immigrant workers must start out from carefully defined objectives. The

An analysis based on materials collected with the assistance of Anne-Marie Metailee. Maison des Sciences de l'Homme. The original version of this paper was prepared for a conference on "Sources of Discontent and Institutional Innovation in Advanced Industrial Societies" held under the auspices of the Institute on Western Europe, Columbia University.

Castells, Manuel. 1975. "Immigrant workers and class struggles in advanced capitalism: The Western European experience." *Politics and Society* 5:33–66. Reprinted by permission of Sage Publications, Inc.

problematic we take as a starting point conditions all our efforts at interpretation, and provides a framework which organizes our approach to this reality. Our aim here is not to expose the scandal of the material conditions under which these workers live and work, nor to justify their presence in order to increase the tolerance of the indigenous population towards them. Our point of departure is rather the fact of the growing importance of immigrant workers in the wage-earning working population of every country in western Europe and the increase in political struggles and protest movements concerning them. For us the question is therefore to know the specific effect produced by immigrant workers on a class structure, and on the politics of the class struggle which result thus determined. In answering such a question we will at the same time be able to describe the class content of the struggles of immigrant workers themselves and thereby start to assess their political practices.

An analysis of class struggles must, of course, both be suggested by the practical expressions of these struggles and be able to account for them. But in order to arrive at such a result in an objective manner, it is necessary to start from the position of the immigrant labour force in the structure of social contradictions and from the role given to it by the historical development of the dominant element in this structure, namely, capital in its advanced monopolistic phase.

We shall start by recalling the fundamental structural tendencies of monopoly capitalism in Western Europe in order to locate the phenomenon of immigration within this specific social and economic logic. We will then draw out the implications for the class structure and for the trade-union and political practices which tend to flow from it. Finally we shall see how these different contradictions are articulated in the concrete history of newly emerging class struggles by referring more specifically to immigrant workers' movements in France. Our analysis remains at a fairly high level of generality and the small amount of statistical data used is illustrative rather than demonstrative in purpose. In fact a rigorous study of this subject within the problematic of the class struggle has yet to be undertaken. Thus the present paper does not claim to be the endpoint of research within this perspective but, rather, a point of departure. It is thus necessary to pose theoretically rigorous and historically concrete questions in order to obtain, by stages, answers which, instead of provoking pity for the lot of immigrant workers, will provide them with elements capable of clarifying their practice.[1]

1. Uneven Development and the Internationalization of the Labour Force

At first glance, migratory movements may be analysed as simply the result of two laws of the capitalist mode of production: *the submission of the worker* to the organization of the means of production dictated by capital (and, hence, to its spatial concentration in areas regarded as most profitable); and the *uneven development* between sectors and regions, and between countries, in accordance with inter-capitalist competition and the political relationships between the major blocs under bourgeois hegemony historically constituted in the various social formations.

Seen this way, migratory movements have existed throughout capitalist development, and rural exodus and the decline of regions whose productive structure has been weakened in favour of the most advanced capitalist forms are basic features of the social structure which constitutes monopoly capitalism. Furthermore, one can even say that a veritable whirlpool of geographical and occupational mobility is inevitable to the extent that capital can only develop by continually decomposing those sectors which are backward compared with the most profitable forms. This frees an even larger labour force whose members lose their existing jobs and move into new posts created in the most advanced sectors, a movement which is far from automatic and which necessitates increasingly costly retraining.

This uneven development does not, of course, derive from disparities in the distribution of natural resources but from the logic of capital and the division of labour it commands according to the imperatives of the rate of profit. Thus, for example, the French steel industry will close down its iron mines in Lorraine and leave the area to establish itself by the sea (Dunkerque, Fos) where it will use imported iron ore from Mauritania and Brazil . . . (Castells and Godard, 1974). Furthermore, in certain cases a political logic (dependent on the general interest of capital) rather than an immediately economic logic is at the source of uneven regional development. Thus, for example, the dichotomy between the highly developed North of Italy and the poverty-stricken Mezzogiorno derives from the particular forms taken by the political bargain underlying the constitution of the dominant class bloc in Italy as a whole: the banking and industrial bourgeoisie of the North accepts the maintenance of the social status quo in the South in order not to overturn the southern class structure which permits the domination of the traditional landed oligarchy. In exchange, the latter accepts bourgeois hegemony at the level of the State and guarantees the labour reservoir which has always been at the base of Italian capitalist growth (Centre de Coorinamento Campano, 1972).

This same mechanism operates at the international level where labour concentration is determined by the growth of capital. For a long period before the Second World War, the advanced capitalist countries made sporadic use of labour from their colonies and from the backward European countries (Italy, Spain, Poland, etc.). In 1936 there were proportionately more foreigners in France than in 1972 (2,198,000 compared with a little under 4,000,000) and even at the time of the 1929 crisis 7% of the French population were foreigners.

A brief analysis of the countries importing and exporting labour (see Table 1) is illuminating on this point: the lower a country's level of development (e.g., as measured by per capital G.N.P.) the higher the level of emigration, and vice versa.

At first sight, then, emigration/immigration is simply a product of the uneven development inherent in the capitalist mode of production which affects the labour force. It must be noted, however, that this is not the same as viewing migration simply as the product of a succession of economic conditions, and hence as capable of being absorbed into jobs created by economic growth within each country. On the contrary, uneven development is a structural tendency of the mode of production and the gaps between firms, sectors, trusts, regions, or countries tend to increase rather than diminish. For example, in recent years, despite having the highest growth rate in Western Europe, Spain has had a regularly increasing level of emigration, with small movements around this trend caused much more by recessions in the countries receiving immigrants than by any decline in requests to emigrate. Similarly, there are over two million Italian workers in other European countries despite Italy's high growth rate and production level. The reasons for such a permanent emigrant labour force are clear from the point of view of the sending country: decomposition of backward productive structures—especially in agriculture; structural unemployment in certain sectors; and the much higher nominal and real wages available in the advanced capitalist countries.

But though differences in levels of development explain the causes of emigration, immigration into the advanced countries is governed by much more deep-seated reasons which cannot be reduced simply to the manpower needs of the economy. If this were the cause, immigration would be a conjunctural phenomenon (and highly sensitive to the least sign of economic recession). While it is true that the employment situation is immediately reflected in increases and decreases in the level of immigration (thus, for example, the economic recession in Germany in 1967

TABLE 1 Immigration from Mediterranean countries towards selected European countries

Country of Emigration	Population (0) 1971 (millions)	Country of Immigration: Germany (1) 1971	France (2) 1971	Belgium (3) 1971	Luxembourg (4) 1971	Netherlands (5) 1971	Switzerland (6) 1969	Austria (7) 1971	Sweden (8) 1971	United Kingdom (9) 1966	All Countries (10)	$(11) = \frac{10}{0} = \frac{\text{Emigrants in Europe}}{\text{Total Population}} \times 100$
Mediterranean Europe												
Spain	33,290	270,000	589,925	51,485	1,700	19,810	97,860	270		34,510	1.065,560	3.2
Greece	8,892	395,000	10,125	14,050		1,905	8,000	550	14,000	8,520	452,150	5.1
Italy	53,667	590,000	588,740	188,430	11,000		531,500	1,510	8,000	96,660	2,015,840	3.7
Portugal	9,630	55,214[E]	694,550	4,280	6,300	1,366	2,000			5,420	769,130	7.9
Turkey	35,232	653,000	18,325	12,250		21,746	9,651	22,415		4,310	741,697	2.1
Yugoslavia	20,527	594,000	65,220	2,930	400	7,454	20,800	131,835	37,000	12,290	871,929	4.2
North Africa												
Algeria	14,012	1,985[E]	754,462	3,740							760,187	5.4
Morocco	15,525	10,921	194,296	24,560		20,582					250,359	1.5
Tunisia	5,137	9,918[E]	106,845	1,640		339					118,742	2.3
Population of Mediterranean origin (12)		2,580,038	3,022,488	303,365	19,400	73,202	669,811	56,580	59,000	161,710	7,045,594	3.6
Total foreign population		3,400,000	3,505,210	716,237	36,500	93,093	971,795	72,205	411,280	178,600	11,086,920	
Total population	195,912	61,281,000	51,004,300[A]	9,690,991	337,500[B]	12,878,000[C]	6,184,000[D]	7,391,000[F]	8,081,000	52,303,720		

Share of foreigners in total population (%)	5.55	6.87	7.39	10.81	0.72	15.71	2.3	5	3.4	
Foreign population of Mediteranean origin (13) Total foreign population %	76	86	42	53	78	69	90	14	9	63

(0) Source: IAM Publications, Saris Etudes of Documents, No. 6, April, 1973, *Yearbook of Mediterranean Countries.*

(1) Federal Statistical Office, Bonn.

E) Employed foreign workers, and June, 1971.

(2) Ministry of the Interiors, Paris. Total foreign population 31 December 1970, including refugees (99,160), exiles (4,082), seasonal workers, and illegal immigrants.

A) *Yearbook of Labor Statistics,* 1970. ILO (provisional statistics 1 January 1971).

(3) National Statistical Institute, Brussels. Total foreign population 31 December 1970, including children, refugees, and exiles. The data by nationality is drawn from the Administration for Public Safety, Brussels. Foreign population as of 31 December, 1972, except for children under 12 years.

(4) Migrant workers only. Source: EEC.

B) *Yearbook of Labor Statistics*. ILD (1969 population).

(5) Active foreign population. Source: Ministry for Social Affairs, the Hague. Data from 15 June, 1971.

C) Total population in 1969. Source: OECD, *Statistics on Active Population,* Paris 1971.

(6) Foreign population in December, 1969, except for seasonal workers and border workers. Source: Foreigners Police, Bern.

D) Total population 31 December 1969. Source: OECD *Statistics on Active Population,* Paris 1971.

(7) Migrant workers only. Official statistics in November, 1971 reported in *Disko-nische Information*. Sonderheft 2 Diakonische Werk. F. Austria.

F) Total population in 1970. Source: OECD.

(8) Source: The Swedish Institute, Stockholm, *Fact Sheets on Sweden,* December, 1971 . Population in October, 1971.

(9) Foreign population in England and Wales (statistics on Scotland where available. Source: Survey of birthplaces, 10% sample.

(10) Total emigrants in Europe by country of emigration.

(11) Share of emigrants in Europe as a percentage of total population of country of emigration.

(12) Foreign population of Mediterranean origin.

(13) Share of foreign population of Mediterranean origin as a percentage of total foreign population from countries of emigration.

TABLE 2 Departures (returns) of Foreign Workers from Germany

Year	Number	% of the number of foreign workers
1966–67	500,814	46.3
1967–68	207,859	21.3
1968–69	194,550	15.4
1969–70	277,579	16.3
1970–71	308,417	14.9
1971–72	332,520	14.7

Source: SOPEMI, OECD

resulted in the departure of a large number of immigrants, as shown in Table 2), it is also the case that the long-term trend is continued growth in immigrant labour, which in 1972 represented at least 10% of the working population in the advanced capitalist countries of western Europe (the Common Market countries, Austria, Norway, Sweden, and Switzerland). It might be argued that this is due precisely to the continuous economic growth of these countries, but this is completely tautological since immigrant labour is in fact one of the motors of this growth, rather than simply a result (Kindleberger, 1967).

Two facts seem to be particularly significant in this respect: first, the size of the immigrant labour force in the most productive sectors (especially in industry) and its position in the working population as a whole, make it impossible to regard it as a conjunctural phenomenon, even if one were to assume that it resulted simply from a super-abundant supply of labour.

Thus, in 1972 there were 2,354,200 foreign workers in *Germany,* representing 10.8% of all wage-earners. They constituted 25% of workers in the building industry and 80% in certain sectors of public works, but are also strongly represented in the metallurgical industry (11% of all wage-earners). In *France,* according to official statistics, there were 1,800,000 immigrant workers on 1 January 1973 (8% of the working population)— a figure which appears to be an underestimate since it takes little account of clandestine work. In building and public works they represent 27% of all workers (but this often rises to 90% on building sites in the Paris region), in metal industries 17%, and in extractive industry 16%. There are 530,000 immigrant workers in the automobile industry, of whom 200,000 in the Paris region, i.e., 46% of all semiskilled workers, work on the assembly line. In *Switzerland,* according to official figures for 1968, there were 817,000 immigrant workers representing 29.8% of the working population, but with a high concentration in the building, machine-tool, and hotel industries. Almost 40% of workers in Swiss factories are foreigners, and when one considers solely directly productive work, they already constitute a clear majority. In *Belgium* the 220,000 foreign workers employed in 1971 represented 7.2% of the working population, and were particularly concentrated in the mining, building and metallurgic industries, and this despite a marked recession in the Walloon region, which led to measures to restrict immigration. In the *Netherlands,* the figure of 125,000 employed persons in 1972 (3.2% of the working population) is lower than elsewhere due primarily to trade-union opposition to immigration. In *Denmark* the same phenomenon is found, foreign workers numbering only 30,000 in 1972. In *Great Britain,* the 1,780,000 immigrant workers in 1971, represented 7.3% of the working population in the building and machine-tool industries, commerce and service industries. Immigrant labour is thus a fundamental element in the economic structure of European capitalism, and not simply an extra source of labour in conditions of rapid growth.

But there is a second fact, which is particularly disturbing: namely, the appearance over the long term (1950–1970) of a parallel increase between unemployment and immigration in most of the countries, with the *possible* exception of Germany, where, for the most part, full employment seems to have been effectively achieved. A detailed analysis of changes in the levels of unemployment, immigration, and productivity, by country, sector, and type of firm, would be necessary in order to verify this tendency. However, certain indications may be obtained by examining the figures for unemployment and immigration in France (Table 3) and the interrelation of changes in them. A combination of two phenomena is apparent: in the short term, for each year, there is a correspondence between the increase in unemployment and the decline in immigration. But in the long term, *there is a tendency for both phenomena to increase together.* This is all the more significant in that the immigration statistics refer only to official entries (a smaller figure) which most closely follow changes in economic conditions.

In other countries, we find the following trends:

- In Belgium and in Netherlands, unemployment is *stable* and immigration rises moderately. (So, in fact, unemployment and immigration *coexist.*) (See Tables 4 and 5.)
- In Germany, unemployment is stable at a low level; at the same time, immigration arises at a high rate. So, immigration is not produced by a full-employment situation in the labour market but by *selective full-employment.* (See Table 6.)
- In Switzerland and Luxembourg a real full-employment labour market exists for native workers, with an increasingly strong percentage of immigrats (29.8% of the labour force in Switzerland and 27.8% in Luxembourg). In these countries we could analyse immigration as a matter of labour supply. But even here this interpretation must be linked to an explanation in terms of the specific characteristics of immigrant labour force.
- In Britain, a stable immigrant labour force coexists with an increasing high rate of unemployment. In fact there is no complementary and opposite evolution of two phenomena as liberal economic theory could expect. The explanation must be in the terms of the structural position of immigrant workers in British industry.

The case of Great Britain is extremely revealing in this respect, because the permanent settlement of a large proportion of the immigrant labour force has been accompanied by a gradual increase in unemployment (up to 3% in 1972) and by a considerable increase in the level of *emigration* by Britons, especially those with high skill to the United States. Thus there is no manpower shortage, but rather a reclassification of the characteristics required to carry out certain jobs.

We thus want to argue that immigration is not a conjunctural phenomenon linked to the manpower needs of expanding economies but a structural tendency characteristic of the current phase of monopoly capitalism. This structural tendency is supported by the discrepancies and disequilibria resulting from uneven development but it is explained primarily by the internal dynamic of advanced capitalist societies. While uneven development explains why people emigrate, it does not explain why capital is ready to provide jobs for migrant workers in the advanced countries occasionally even in conditions of unemployment. Neither does it explain why the dominant classes introduce a social and political element (immigrant labour) whose presence contradicts their ideology and necessitates more complex mechanisms of social control. In other words, the extent of immigration and the strategic role of immigration in the European economy has to be explained, not in terms of the technical demands of production, but by the specific interests of capital in a particular phase of its development.

2. Crisis of Capitalism, Counter-Tendencies of Economic Policy, and Structural Role of Immigration

What are the current requirements of capital? And how are they translated into manpower policy, especially as regards immigrant labour?

TABLE 3 Immigration, unemployment, and economic growth, France, 1960–1971

(Percentage of foreigners in total population; rate of growth of new immigrant workers; percentage of unemployment on total active population and rate of growth; Gross National Product and rate of growth—By year)

	a) Immigration			b) Unemployment			c) Economic Growth	
	Foreigners							
Year	Number (thousands)	(active and non active) Percentage of the total population	Rate of growth of new immigrant workers, by year	Number (thousands)	Percentage of active population	Rate of growth	Gross National Product (US $ per capita)	Rate of growth
60	2,178	4.7%	1.0 (1960–1959)	239,000	1.2		1,340	
61	2,306	4.9	1.5	203,000	1.0	0.84	1,450	1.08
62	2,448	5.2	1.5	230,000	1.2	1.13	1,590	1.09
63	2,574	5.3	1.1	273,000	1.4	1.18	1,750	1.10
64	2,721	5.6	1.1	216,000	1.1	0.79	1,920	1.09
65	2,828	5.8	0.9	269,000	1.3	1.24	2,040	1.02
66	2,873	5.8	1.0	280,000	1.4	1.04	2,200	1.07
67	2,941	5.9	0.8	365,000	1.8	1.30	2,350	1.06
68	2,951	5.9	1.0	428,000	2.1	1.17	2,540	1.08
69	3,122	6.2	1.3	337,000	1.6	0.78	2,790	1.09
70	3,338	6.5	1.2	336,000	1.7	1.07	2,910	1.04
71	3,608	7.0	1.0	456,000	2.1	1.25		

Source: a) Ministére de l'Intérieur and Office National d'Immigration; b) and c) OECD. 1.0 Means continuous stable new immigration; 1 Means decreasing new immigration; 1 Means increasing new immigration.

TABLE 4 Belgium

	Immigration			Unemployment			Economic Growth	
Year	Number of immigrant workers (thousands)	Percentage of all employees	Rate of growth	Number (thousands)	Percentage of active population (employees)	Rate of growth	Gross National Product (US $ per capita)	Rate of growth
1960							1,250	
1961	154,000	5.7		89,000	3.4%		1,320	1.05
1962	157,000	5.8	1.01	75,000	2.8	0.84	1,410	1.06
1963	166,000	6.0	1.05	62,000	2.3	0.82	1,500	1.06
1964	185,000	6.5	1.11	55,000	2.0	0.88	1,660	1.10
1965	200,000	6.9	1.08	63,000	2.2	1.14	1,800	1.08
1966	203,000	7.0	1.01	67,000	2.4	1.06	1,920	1.06
1967	200,000	6.9	0.98	92,000	3.3	1.37	2,050	1.06
1968	196,000	6.7	0.98	110,000	3.9	1.19	2,160	1.05
1969	201,000	6.7	1.02	88,000	3.0	0.80	2,380	1.10
1970	208,000	6.9	1.03	76,000	2.6	0.86	2,670	1.12

Source: E.E.C. and O.E.C.D.

TABLE 5 Netherlands

Year	Immigration			Unemployment			Economic Growth	
	Number of immigrant workers (thousands)	Percentage of all employees	Rate of growth	Number (thousands)	Percentage of active population (employees)	Rate of growth	Gross National Product (US $ per capita)	Rate of growth
1958	29,900	0.9%						
1959	21,200	0.6	0.70					
1960	24,100	0.7	1.13	50,000	1.2%		980	
1961	28,000	0.8	1.16	36,000	0.8	0.72	1,070	1.09
1962	32,000	0.9	1.14	35,000	0.8	0.97	1,140	1.06
1963	38,000	1.1	1.18	35,000	0.8	1.00	1,220	1.07
1964	51,600	1.4	1.35	32,000	0.7	0.91	1,420	1.16
1965	63,100	1.7	1.22	36,000	0.8	1.12	1,560	1.09
1966	76,300	2.0	1.20	46,000	1.0	1.27	1,670	1.07
1967	72,100	1.9	0.94	90,000	2.0	1.95	1,820	1.09
1968	80,300	2.1	1.11	84,000	1.8	0.93	1,990	1.09
1969	60,100	1.5	0.74	66,000	1.4	0.78	2,190	1.10
1970				56,000	1.2	0.84	2,400	1.09
1971				69,000	1.4	1.23		

Source: E.E.C. and O.E.C.D.

TABLE 6 Germany

	Immigration			Unemployment			Economic Growth	
Year	Number of immigrant workers (thousands)	Percentage of all employees	Rate of growth	Number (thousands)	Percentage of active population (employees)	Rate of growth	Gross National Product (US $ per capita)	Rate of growth
1958	127,000	0.7%						
1959	167,000	0.8	1.31					
1960	279,000	1.4	1.60	271,000	1.4%		1,300	
1961	473,000	2.3	1.60	181,000	0.9	0.6	1,470	1.10
1962	629,000	3.0	1.33	154,000	0.7	0.8	1,580	1.00
1963	773,000	3.6	1.21	186,000	0.9	1.2	1,670	1.06
1964	902,000	4.2	1.16	169,000	0.8	0.9	1,810	1.08
1965	1,119,000	5.1	1.24	147,000	0.7	0.8	1,950	1.07
1966	1,244,000	5.7	1.11	161,000	0.8	1.09	2,050	1.05
1967	1,014,000	4.8	0.81	459,000	2.2	2.8	2,070	1.01
1968	1,019,000	4.8	1.00	323,000	1.5	0.7	2,240	1.08
1969	1,366,000	6.2	1.34	179,000	0.8	0.5	2,520	1.12
1970	1,948,900	9.0	1.42	149,000	0.7	0.8	3,030	1.20
1971	2,240,700	10.3	1.15	185,000	0.8	1.2		
1972	2,354,200	10.8	1.05					

Source: E.E.C. and O.E.C.D.

In order to answer these questions we must introduce some elements of Marxist economic theory concerning the contradictory development of the capitalist mode of production. The basic structural contradiction demonstrated by Marx in volume 3 of *Capital* concerned the *tendency for the rate of profit to fall*, as a result of the increase in the organic composition of capital made inevitable by competition among capitalists, monopolistic concentration, and technical progress. If we consider only living labour, the labour force, as creating value, and hence surplus-value, and profit as deriving from it, given the increase in the organic composition of capital, then the rate of profit must fall since the variable capital used to pay the labour force grows more slowly than total capital (constant capital plus variable capital), and thus the source of value becomes proportionately smaller in relation to the mass of capital engaged in production. At the level of the system as a whole and in the long term, there is a tendency for the rate of profit to fall (even if the quantity of surplus-value increases) and hence for the system to move towards crisis to the extent that capital stops investing as investment ceases to be profitable.

However, even though certain studies suggest the validity of this analyis in past periods,[2] the tendencies identified are no more than *tendencies*, i.e., can be partly counteracted in the historical practice of capital by the more or less deliberate introduction of counter-tendencies through economic policy.[3] One of the main examples of such action is the devalorization or "putting to bed" of part of social capital, for which a lower or even nil rate of profit will be accepted, by placing it in the charge of the State. Moreover, this kind of action is combined with various subsidies and assistance from the State to the major private economic groups, drawing on collective resources, and thus removing a share from wages for purposes of accumulation. It may also be noted that State intervention extends to all fields, following the well-known Keynesian model, acting as regulator in every situation and *attempting* to establish a program for monopoly capital.

Beyond the measures involving capital itself, the basic counter-tendency introduced into the system is an increase in the rate of surplus-value, i.e., the quantity of surplus-value produced by a given variable capital. This increase is obtained in two complementary ways: by higher *productivity* through technical progress (which increases the excess labour in relation to the labour necessary to reproduce the labour force) and by the *reinforcement of exploitation*, either in intensity, in extensiveness, or by reducing the mass of variable capital necessary for a certain quantity of surplus-value.

Thus the first question to be examined is this: *What is the relationship between the massive use of migrant labour and the counter-tendency to the tendency of the rate of profit to fall, especially with regard to reinforcement of exploitation?*

There are other basic contradictions in the current phase of capitalism which, while related to the first, have relatively autonomous effects. On the one hand, there is the cyclical character of capitalist expansion with periodic recessions due to overaccumulation. Although the cyclical nature of crises was concealed during a long expansionary period, since 1967 Europe has again become used to the idea of sudden fluctuations in economic activity as a part of the functioning of the system. In order to avoid the disequilibrating effect of these fluctuations, due to the chain reactions they cause in the economy, advanced capitalism has set up a number of anti-cyclical mechanisms, one of the most important of which is precisely immigrant labour.

Finally, the excess of capitals seeking investment opportunities and the creation of a mass of floating capitals in the advanced economics, on the one hand, and the necessity for ever-faster growth inherent in monopoly capital, on the other, are the source of the *structural inflation* characteristic of capitalism today. We advance the hypothesis that immigration has a speific role as a basic deflationary factor in controlling these critical effects of inflation.While statistics and economics give little guidance on this subject, a number of suggestions are possible.

If we can determine the role of immigrant labour in the management of these key problems of advanced capitalism, we shall have simultaneously established its place in the structural contradictions and in the social interests underlying different immigration policies and underlying the protests of the workers themselves.

TABLE 7 Wages of foreign workers compared with all workers, France, 1968 (Employment Committee, VI Plan)

	Overall	Foreigners
Paris Region	1,441	1,190
Rhône-Alpes	1,051	878
Provence-Côte d'Azur	1,070	861
North	966	885
Lorraine	973	921
Languedoc	952	741
Alsace	989	892
France overall	1,095	973

(This does not take duration of work into account)

2.1. Immigration and the Reinforcement of Capitalist Exploitation

In order to increase the degree of exploitation and raise the rate of surplus-value, capital makes use of two methods, usually in combination: (1) paying a proportionately smaller value for the reproduction of the labour force, (2) increasing the duration and intensity of work. We have stated that in both cases immigrant labour represents a decisive trump card for capital. Let us now examine this in more detail.

As far as the first point is concerned, immigrant labour displays the following characteristics:

- It is the part of the labour force which receives the lowest wages. (See Table 7.)
- It is the part whose health conditions are best, contrary to widespread opinion. This is so for two very simple reasons: (1) immigrants are generally young and in the prime of their working life and (2) very rigorous health examinations ensure that immigrants who are not in good health are quickly replaced. This means that though the health of immigrants as individuals is more severely affected than that of nationals, as a group immigrants are more healthy since only the young and healthy are retained. . . and only for as long as they remain in that condition.
- It is the part of the labour force which works in the worst safety and health conditions, thereby permitting considerable savings in the organization of work, reducing still further the costs of reproduction.
- When considered from the point of view of capital as a whole, rather than from that of the individual capitalist, one of the essential effects of immigration is to enable considerable savings to be made in the costs of social reproduction of the labour force as a whole, thereby raising correspondingly the overall average rate of profit. This occurs by means of three main mechanisms:

1. First, because by recruiting immigrants primarily from among the young and productive (see Tables 8, 9, and 10) it is possible to avoid paying the costs of 'rearing' the worker, and the maintenance costs after his/her working life has ended. According to an O.E.C.D. estimate these costs amount to $10,000 per worker, which implies a figure for the free human capital represented by immigrants in Europe of about $50 million.

2. Second, given the restrictive measures governing immigration and the conditions in which immigrants live and work, the majority

TABLE 8 Rates of activity by nationality, Germany, September 1969

Nationality	Rate of Activity (percent)
Italians	68
Yugoslavs	80
Turks	76
Greeks	71
Spaniards	71
Portuguese	79
All foreigners	63

Sources: Wirtschaft und Statistik (No. 5, 1970), p. 246. *Ausländische Arbeitnehmer* 1969, p. 94.

TABLE 9 Rates of activity by country of birth, Great Britain, 1966

Country of Birth	Rate of Activity (percent)
Irish Republic	66
Commonwealth countries	58
Jamaica	73
Rest of Caribbean	68
India	59
Pakistan	72
Cyprus	54
Foreign countries	57
Poland	65
Germany	46
Italy	66
All immigrants	60

Source: 1996 Census, Great Britain Summary Tables, Economic Activity Tables, Part III.

are unmarried or "forced" bachelors (see Tables 11 and 12), and the costs of reproduction of families are not borne by capital, which thereby saves on the cost of collective facilities, public housing, schools, hospital beds, welfare benefits, etc. The savings are all the more significant in that outlays on such facilities are not profitable since demand for them has to be subsidised.

3. Third, the conditions of reproduction of the immigrants themselves as well as of the

TABLE 10 Rates of activity by nationality and sex, France, 1968

	Rate of Activity (percent)		
Nationality	Total	Male	Female
Algerians	52.5	70.2	4.8
Moroccans	64.0	78.5	13.1
Tunisians	45.2	66.2	16.5
Italians	42.3	63.5	14.7
Spaniards	40.9	60.4	24.8
Portuguese	63.9	74.6	23.9
Yugoslavs	66.6	77.8	48.2
Poles	35.2	50.7	20.0
All foreigners	47.1	64.8	19.8

Note: Figures are for crude rate of activity, i.e., the number of active persons as a percentage of the total number of people (including children) in each group.
Source: 1968 French Census, *Hommes et Migrations Etudes* (No. 113, 1969).

families who succeed in accompanying them are clearly below the average standards of indigenous workers. Their housing conditions are particularly bad.[4] Not only does social capital not bear these costs but also the "sleep merchants" profit from the discrimination, creating a parallel housing market for immigrants which becomes even more profitable provided legality is set aside and summary methods are used to maintain order in the hostels, furnished rooms, or slums.[5]

This is why, to mention but two examples, 32% of immigrants in Germany live in temporary dwellings according to official statistics, while 98% of shantytown dwellers in France are immigrants. (See Tables 13, 14, and 15.)

The effect of immigrant workers on wage levels concerns not only their own wages, but also those of wage-earners as a whole, since the possibility of appealing to the manpower of the dependent capitalist countries acts as a veritable world *reserve army* on the working class of the advanced capitalist countries. One cannot infer from this a conflict between the interests of the

TABLE 11 Family immigration to France and Germany

	France[1]				Germany[2]	
	Number of families / Total population	Couples / Married	Children / Total population	Children / Couples	Married migrants as % of total	Married migrants accompanied by wife as a percentage of married migrants
All foreigners	68.69	35.21	26.75	1.53	70	51
Spanish	79.38	43.5	30.45	1.40	74	60
Greek					78	78
Italian	81.18	40.32	29.57	1.41	64	54
Portuguese	65.98	32.8	29.74	1.71	78	44
Turks					82	34
Yugoslavs	52.65	40.40	14.31	0.66	76	34
Algerians	54.99	20.74	38.88	3.79		
Moroccans	40.77	16.10	21.45	2.76		
Tunisians	63.05	30.48	31.13	2.45		

[1]*Source: Hommes et Migrations,* Série <Documents> n° 829 of 15 June 1972. 1968 Census, April 1 poll.
[2]Bundesanstalt füi Arbeit, August 1970: Results of a special inquiry on the family situation of migrant workers.

TABLE 12 Females as a percentage of immigrants

	Portugal	Spain (assisted immigration)	Greece	Turkey	Finland
1969	42.3	16.2	43.6	20.0	47.6
1970	34.7	15.4	42.8	16.1	44.7
1971	42.0	13.0	45.0	16.1	43.5
1972	41.5	13.7	43.6	21.9	46.8

working class and those of immigrant workers, for once in the same boat together they can only get out of the vicious circle of their exploitation by joining together in opposition to capital. It remains true, *as a tendency*, that the very possibility of recourse to immigration causes a relative lowering of wages thus contributing to the structural countertendency which helps delay the fall in the rate of profit.

Finally, turning to the intensity of their exploitation, on average immigrant workers work much longer hours than nationals, occupy the worst jobs, and are subjected to the fastest speeds (to the extent that they work on assembly lines and are paid by piecework). The much higher rate of work accidents among immigrants is indicative both of their work conditions and of the speeds they are obliged to maintain.

All these empirically indisputable factors are however too obvious; acceptance of them is too automatic and even hides a sort of unconscious racist preconception. *Why*

TABLE 13 Socioeconomic status of foreign employees in Germany by nationality and sex, 1968

Socioeconomic Status	Nationality							
	Italy	Greece	Spain	Turkey	Portugal	Yugoslavia	Others	All Foreign
Men								
Nonmanual	–	–	–	–	–	–	35	8
Skilled manual	13	7	15	16	12	55	25	20
Semiskilled manual	37	53	44	38	43	27	22	36
Unskilled manual	48	37	38	43	43	14	12	34
Women								
Nonmanual	–	–	–	–	–	–	50	12
Skilled manual	–	–	–	–	–	–	–	3
Semiskilled manual	34	37	34	33	35	29	15	30
Unskilled manual	63	60	59	62	60	58	18	53

Note: Percentages do not add up to 100 due to omission of certain minor categories, like apprentices, and because of rounding.

Source: "Reprâsentativuntersuchung, Herbst 1968," *Auslandische Arbeitnehmer,* 1969, p. 86.

TABLE 14 Socioeconomic status of foreign and Swiss employees, 1960

Socioeconomic Status	Foreign Employees (percent)	Swiss Employees (percent)
Nonmanual	15.0	52.0
Skilled manual	25.0	18.5
Semiskilled manual	37.0	22.5
Unskilled manual	23.0	7.0
Total	100	100

Source: P. Granjeat, *Les migrations de travailleurs en Europe* (Paris: Institut International des Etudes Sociales, 1966), p. 82.

should immigrant labour accept what, for the indigenous working class, has become unacceptable? Because they are naturally submissive? Because of their extreme need? Even accepting the notion that the poverty experienced in their own countries makes immigrant workers willing to tolerate any and all conditions on their arrival, the problem is why this acceptance persists and especially, why it is possible to treat them as individual

TABLE 15 Foreign employees in France by socioeconomic status, by nationality, 1967 (percent)

Socioeconomic Status	Nationality							
	Spain	Italy	Poland	Portugal	Algeria	Morocco	Tunisia	All
Engineers and managers	0.5	0.8	0.8	0.1	–	0.4	1.1	1.2
Supervisory personnel and technicians	1.5	3.0	2.0	0.2	0.1	0.4	1.3	1.7
Non-manual workers	3.9	3.7	3.8	0.9	1.2	2.9	11.2	3.4
Skilled manual	31.5	41.1	24.5	28.8	11.5	14.9	16.1	25.2
Semi-skilled manual	36.5	35.4	42.3	35.1	38.0	46.0	32.0	36.6
Unskilled manual	26.4	16.0	26.6	34.9	49.2	35.4	38.3	31.9
Total	100	100	100	100	100	100	100	100

Source: "Enquéte effectuée par le Ministère d'Etat chargé des Affaires Sociales." op.cit.

wage-earners whereas the relationship of the indigenous working-class with capital is established collectively, through the labour movement. This is the key to answering the question. Though working conditions, wage levels, and social benefits have improved, and though European workers have bettered their living conditions, this has not come about through the goodwill of capital but through the new sociopolitical conditions which flow from the balance of power between the classes created by the labour movement. In other words, *the utility of immigrant labour to capital derives primarily from the fact that it can act towards it as though the labour movement did not exist,* thereby moving the class struggle back several decades. A twenty-first-century capital and a nineteenth-century proletariat—such is the dream of monoploy capital in order to overcome its crisis. How does this happen? Not because of any presumed submissiveness of immigrants, whose many struggles in recent years have shown a degree of combativeness, however sporadic and limited. Rather their legal-political status as foreigners and their political-ideological isolation lead to the basic point: *their limited capacity for organization and struggle and very great vulnerability to repression* (Gorz, 1970).Their status as foreigners deprives immigrants of political rights and, also, in practice, of their rights as trade-unionists. Their participation in class struggles, their level of organization under these conditions is thus restricted to a vanguard, which is cut off from the mass of immigrants and is often regarded with suspicion by the indigenous labour movement. It is all the more easily repressed. Moreover, since the permanence of immigrant workers in each country is only relative, and their degree of subjective identification weaker, their interest in participating in current struggles is limited, and generally concentrated in outbursts linked to their concrete living and working conditions.

Moreover, the racism and xenophobia diffused by the dominant ideology accentuate the cleavages derived from national cultural particularities[6] and determine the ideological isolation of immigrants. They are thus separated from their class and placed in a balance of power so unfavourable that often they fluctuate between an acceptance of the conditions of capital and pure individual or collective revolt. This cuts them off still more from the labour movement, in a sort of vicious circle which tends to reproduce the fragmentation and dislocation of the working class in advanced capitalism.

This brings us to the first result of our analysis, which should be underlined. Banal though it may be, some crucial implications for immigrant struggles follow from it: the advantage of immigrant labour for capital stems precisely from the specificity of their inferior position in the class struggle, which derives from the legal-political status of immigrants. From the *point of view of capital* this status can be modified in minor ways, but not transformed, because it is the source of the basic structural role of immigration. Thus the basic contradiction concerning immigrants is one which opposes them not directly to capital, but to the State apparatus of capital and to the political status given to them in its institutions. This has the following consequences:

- The position of immigrants in the class struggle is very specific compared with the rest of the labour movement.
- The contradiction in which they occupy the dominated pole is a basic contradiction of capitalism.
- The contradiction is immediately political in so far as it relates directly to the State apparatus.
- Given a basic, directly political, and very specific contradiction, reinforced in the ideological sphere by their cultural particularities and the xenophobic tones of the dominant ideology, immigrants find themselves in an extremely unfavourable balance of power which tends to reproduce their separation from the rest of the labour movement.

The circle is not completely closed, as we shall see, since immigrants' membership in the working class determines an objective basis of interests common to *workers as a whole*. And from this basis, a unified labour movement *can be constructed* on the basis of a working class which, though objectively fragmented, is not split.

This analysis also sheds light on a common argument about the causes of immigration which we have deliberately left aside in our discussion so as to be able to provide the answer once it was known. This is the idea that immigrants are necessary to carry out the arduous jobs rejected by the indigenous population. In fact, this is only a half-truth. While it is certain that immigrants do carry out the most arduous, the worst-paid, and the least-skilled jobs (see Table 6), it does not follow from this that these jobs, though necessary, have been given up by other workers. Such jobs are not given up because they are "dirty" and "soul-destroying"(since the jobs taken instead can hardly be said to be "fulfilling") but because they are less well-paid. Whenever arduous work is relatively well-paid (e.g., miners) nationals, in particular, are found doing it. It remains true, however, that these jobs are badly paid and are most arduous, but *in relation to what standard?* To the historical standard of the balance of power established by the labour movement in each country, to what would be unacceptable to a working class which had the necessary strength to impose better working conditions and higher wage levels. In brief, then, *immigrant workers do not exist because there are "arduous and badly paid" jobs to be done, but, rather, arduous and badly paid jobs exist because immigrant workers are present or can be sent for to do them.*

The building industry, for example, has remained largely small-scale in character because the employment of immigrants has made small fragmented capitals profitable without recourse to industrialized building methods. If immigrant labour were to disappear, *depending on the balance of power of the labour movement*, the building industry would be reconverted and modernized. But this is no more than a pious wish, because such a situation would considerably reduce the rate of profit, thus precipitating an economic crisis. This is why capital cannot do without the "arduous jobs" or the immigrant workers who do them. This is the "invisible structure"of the determination of capital of which one sees only the effects, sometimes combined with premature interpretations.

We now need to examine whether the political-ideological specificity of immigrants in the class struggle is also the basic feature which enables them to play a crucial role in the anticyclical and anti-inflationary policies of monopoly capital.

2.2. Economic Fluctuations, Inflation, Immigration

In spite of the systematic intervention of the State apparatus, in spite of the control mechanisms set up, the capitalist economy still undergoes cyclical fluctuations. They are of a new type in so far as the acceleration of technical progress, on the one hand, and the internationalization of capital on the other, have introduced distortions into the regularity of the cycles, while magnifying the effects of recessionary periods.

In this perspective immigrant workers are one of the basic elements preventing recessions from turning into crises. Instead of accepting the reality of unemployment, advanced capitalist economies have regulated with immigrant labour, temporarily limiting immigration (as in Belgium in 1971, and Germany in 1972), imposing new restrictive legislation (Switzerland, England, France), or simply to expelling—in a more-or-less disguised fashion—part of the immigrant labour force. Thus, the 1967 recession in Germany resulted in a very large reduction in the number of foreign residents, thereby exporting a considerable fraction of the total unemployment (see Table 2). There were still 459,000 unemployed in 1967 in Germany, and 353,000 in 1968, who naturally received unemployment benefits. It has been calculated that the expulsion of foreign workers enabled saving of over DM1,000 million in unemployment benefits alone[7].

This general trend, which has also been observed in France is often interpreted in the banal terms of the supply and demand of jobs. Its significance lies precisely in the ease with which one can be rid of this labour, due to its inferior legal-political status. This again reveals the basic role of the status of foreigner from the point of view of the functioning of the capitalist economy.

Something more specific is also involved, which requires closer analysis. The crises of capitalism today are not classical crises caused by overproduction, but crises produced primarily by inflation, which is itself the result of capital surpluses and financial movements linked to the activities of multinational firms, among other things (Levinson, 1971). What characterizes these crises is precisely the *combination of inflation and recession,* or "stagflation," as it has become known. The mechanism is quite simple: inflation results not from the play of supply and demand, but from structural features of the current phase of capitalism, which cannot be discussed in detail here (Dallemagne, 1972). These mean that a rise in product prices is not counteracted by a fall in demand since prices are determined by the cost of the capital invested, itself subject to inflationary pressures through financial mechanisms. Now and then prices will surge ahead of what demand can bear, thus causing relative overproduction which leads to a recession. This further reduces the level of effective demand, but without bringing about a proportionate fall in prices unless a dangerous fall in the average rate of profit is acceptable. Under these conditions, what are the characteristics of the ideal "worker-consumer" in order to counteract these periodic crises?

1. He/she must be very productive in the expansionary phase.
2. He/she must be excludable without difficulty in the recessionary phase when there is a danger of overproduction.
3. He/she must consume little, in order to reduce inflationary tensions in expansionary periods and especially to cushion the decline in demand in recessionary periods. This is possible since his disappearance as a wage-earner (and hence of his wage as purchasing power) has little effect on the overall level of effective demand. In this way productive capacity can be reduced with little change in effective demand, thereby avoiding the chain of events which can follow from applying brakes to growth. In this way, fluctuations can be prevented from turning into crises.

The central role of immigrant labour as a regulator for capitalist crises is too often ignored, hidden by interpretations phrased in terms of the economic situation (adjustment of supply and demand) without attention to the determinants of these adjustments or discrepancies. Two conditions must be met in order for immigrant labour to play this role:

1. The status of foreigner, which is weak in political and ideological terms, must be maintained.
2. The immigration of families must be limited as much as possible and, at most, be restricted to a narrow and higher section of immigrants whose ideological integration acts as an adequate guarantee.

These then are the reasons for the current orientation of immigration policies in all the European countries towards the so-called German solution: immigration limited to "unmarried" workers, rigorously controlled, for a limited period, and with a high rate of turnover, in return for an improvement in material living conditions for the limited time during which their services are provided. The British Immigration Act, the new Swiss measures, and, most of all, the Fontanet-Marcellin circular in France, all point in this direction.

It must be mentioned, in passing, that from the point of view of a purely economic logic of capital, the same aims (raising of the rate of profit by excess exploitation, counter-cyclical control) could be achieved by productive investments in the countries from which immigrants come—provided of course that a similar balance of power could be imposed on the workers there, i.e., through police states. Such an approach can be found in various schemes drawn up by large European, and especially French, business. However, in the short term it is unlikely that a policy of this type will emerge since it ignores two basic features of immigration: its position in the various fractions of capital; and its fragmenting, and hence weakening, effect on the working class. This means, in turn, that such a tendency could only emerge once three conditions are met: the final unification of capital around monopolies; the incorporation of the labour movement so that it ceased to constitute a great danger for captial which would thus no longer need to weaken it; finally, and most important, a strong development of immigrant struggles which threatens the social equilibrium constructed at their expense. This latter development is already taking place in Switzerland, while it appears far off in France; Germany is an intermediate case.

This question, however, is significant in that it enables us to establish the limits of a purely economic analysis based on the logic of capital. We must now turn to an analysis of the relationship of immigrants to existing social classes.

3. Immigration, Social Classes, and Class Fractions

Immigrants are not just foreigners. The vast majority are foreign workers (98% in France), i.e., (1) *workers,* (2) *foreigners.* As soon as either of these two features, which define both their class situation and their specificity as a class fraction, is forgotten one ceases to be able to understand the significance of immigrants for capital, and, beyond that, for the transformation of society.

The specific class situation of foreign workers has to be related to the class struggle and existing class interests in order to uncover current alliances and contradictions and hence, to deduce appropriate tactics and strategy, given the specific aims of these classes and fractions.

Thus, although the general interests of advanced capitalism concerning immigration may be those we have indicated, they are varied and specific for each fraction of capital, and, in particular, they diverge according to whether we are dealing with monopoly capital or capital invested in industries or sectors with lower rates of profit or smaller quantities of surplus-value. For big capital, the primary aim is to preserve the basic characteristics of the immigrant labour force, while stablizing* it in its production phase, e.g., by providing minimal material conditions for its reproduction. Hence big capital desires the "regularization" of immigration provided that this does not go too far and cause outbursts of trouble nor interfere with the maintenace of the labour force. Thus, for example, measures concerning housing may be taken (France), the consultation of immigrant representatives by local authorities may be proposed (Belgium), or certain social security measures taken (Germany), always of course in a totally inadequate and fragmented way.[8] Big firms may even agree to job security for a small elite group of immigrants, thus offering a carrot to the "good immigrant" to improve his job. More concretely: for big capital the basic concern is to avoid political and trade-union rights for immigrant workers, and hence to lessen their capacity to engage in struggle. Hence is policy of control and minor modification concerning immigration, sometimes paternalist in the economic sphere, always repressive (dissuasive) in the political sphere.

Conversely, for many small and medium-sized firms (especially in the building, textile and service industries) the immigrant labour force is crucial to their *day-to-day survival*, because of the excess exploitation that they can carry out given the lack of rights and of organization of these workers. For these firms, immigrants are a source of the excess profit necessary to compensate for their below average rate of profit. They thus violate bourgeois social legality by hiring *clandestine* immigrants, in order to exploit the immigrant illegally, avoid paying social security contributions, and impose sub-human working conditions on them. In the case of small and medium firms, then, extreme violation of legal rights is added to the legal and controlled violations, regularized once the long term, demanded by large capital. This is why France, the most backward† of the receiving countries, and the one with the highest proportion of small and medium-sized firms, tolerated without complaint up to 1972 a level of clandestine immi-

*Stabilizing the labour force, but not, as a rule, the individual worker.

†One must not use terms such as "small" or "large" capital but refer to the organic composition and dynamism of capital. Some large monopolies in the building industry also exploit clandestine immigrants.

gration which at that time represented almost 80% of all entries. For these firms any improvement in the living conditions of immigrants would be unacceptable, since it would affect their necessary excess profits. This argument applies *a fortiori* to speculative capital which profits from the destitute condition of immigrants in order to create a new source of accumulation ("sleep merchants" and others). The two factions of capital, however, agree on one basic point: the structural need for the systematic political repression of immigrants, and the complete elimination of their ability to defend themselves. Having obtained satisfaction on this basic point, large capital can afford to fall back on "humanitarian" arguments when immigrant struggles oblige it to retreat, whereas for backward firms the excess exploitation of immigrants is a matter of life and death. These differences must be borne in mind in order to understand the variety of capitalist immigration policies. But this fragmentation of interests of capital presupposes a basic agreement on the maintenance of immigrants in a position of social and political "apartheid."

The *objective* political weakness of immigrant workers is not only an important counter-tendency used by capital to avert the impact of its own contradictions, but it also is a major trump card for the bourgeoisie in its struggle against the working-class. The very presence of immigant workers constitutes a permanent source of fragementation within the working class, both inside and outside the firm. While immigrant and indigenous workers share the same historic interests and some immediate interests, they diverge on other immediate interests, e.g., working and housing conditions, and, in particular, freedom of association, a basic issue for immigrants but superfluous for indigenous workers.

This fragmentation is a permanent and objective obstacle to the struggle and organization of *all* workers, since it places a substantial fraction of them in an inferior position, making participation in the struggle much more difficult and dangerous for them. This is too often forgotten, impressed as we are by the violence and audacity of certain immigrant struggles. On the rare occasions when such struggles do take place, they do so in spite of the initial disadvantages and considerable risks of repression incurred by the immigrants involved. This explains why only a small minority of immigrants takes part in these struggles and why they only develop at the price of very heavy sacrifices which clearly distinguishes them from the rest of the labour movement. For immigrants, then, every struggle puts their embryonic organziation in danger. This fragile stake had been overcome by the labour movement in advanced capitalism. The fragmentation of the working class represented by a permanent fraction of immigrant workers is, thus, a basic factor in maintaining immigration as a unified interest of the dominant classes.

This is all the more true since this split does not rest solely on the inferior political status of immigrants, but also on the racist and xenophobic reactions of the bourgeoisie (Windisch, 1971). The success of Powell and the National Front in England; the very large popular vote for the xenophobic bill known as the "Schwarzenbach initiative" in Switzerland; the wave of racist assassinations (especially in Marseille) in Autumn 1973, are symptoms of the ultimate weapon for dividing the working class: racism. These reactions occur even within the working class, not only among the indigenous population against immigrants, but also in the opposite direction.

This objective and subjective split between indigenous and immigrant workers, is often reinforced by the corporatism and blindness of trade unions which, under the pretext of defending the jobs of nationals, fail to understand the real strategy of capitalism in this matter they collaborate, in fact or in intention, with big capital in its policy of regularizing and controlling (ultimately with police help) immigration. Trade unions are sometimes afraid to counteract the xenophobic attitudes of part of the labour force (under the influence of the dominant ideology), and end up reinforcing the situation which they themselves denounce, or give lip service to denouncing. However it is obvious that trade unions cannot be considered as a unit, and that their attitudes will depend partly on their general orientation to the class struggle, and partly on the pressure which immigrants are able to exercise on them. Thus, in France, trade unions attempt immediately to work towards working class unity (Gani, 1972) whereas in Switzerland they collaborate with the bourgeoisie. But trade unions no longer have a free hand in this respect, since they increasingly have to take account of the weight of immigrants among their membership. This is perhaps the key to the whole problem since indigenous trade unions are often reinforced by the suspicion and anti-unionism of many immigrants (due not to excessive consciousness, but to a lack of consciousness!) in a sort of vicious circle which risks reproducing the fragmentation of the working class with catastrophic consequences for the labour movement in advanced capitalism.

This vicious circle can only be broken by the common discovery by immigrant and indigenous workers of their basic identity of interests, and identity which must not be interpreted solely in terms of a distant historical destiny, but in relation to the present conditions of the class struggle. Immigrants will never succeed in imposing their basic demand (equal rights) without a generalized battle supported by the labour and democratic movement as a whole. Indigenous workers must avoid at all costs a rupture in the working class which could lead to a major defeat which would strengthen, perhaps decisively, the balance of power in favour of the bourgeoisie.

This discovery of a concrete community of class interests can only occur through common struggles against capital. And these common struggles will come about through the participation of immigrants and indigenous workers in each other's specific struggles. In other words, the dynamic of social relations, while determined by the class structure, is organized in terms of the historically specific development of the practices of the struggle. This is the subject to which we shall now turn, with special reference to the particularly rich example of France, before drawing some more general conclusions about the role of immigrants in the class struggle.

4. Immigrant Workers and Class Struggles: The French Example

The resurgence of social struggles in France since 1968 has had a profound effect on immigrant workers. For some time, though they were publicly defined as a "social problem," there were not, strictly speaking, any specific separate struggles of immigrant workers. Up to 1972 there were two basically different types of action concerning immigrant workers—on the one hand, an ideological exposure of the "scandal" of immigrant conditions, led primarily by the left-wing movement in their usual role as revealers of contradictions rather than as a political force; on the other, a series of working-class protest struggles in factories with high proportions of immigrant workers which indicated the concrete potential for mobilizing of this stratum of workers. It may be noted that the most important struggles ("Grosteel" at Le Bourget: "Penarroya" at Lyon, both in 1972) were protest struggles led by trade unions, especially the C.F.D.T., even though the style of action was quite innovative (primarily because of the severity of the struggles in the face of the intransigence of the employers, which they finally overcame). The struggles by semiskilled workers at Renault-Billancourt and at Renault-Flins, where there was a high degree of immigrant participation, allowed a new form of working-class struggle to develop outside trade-union channels, due to a certain degree of Maoist penetration among the immigrants, concurrently with powerful trade-union action. What characterizes this set of struggles, however, is that they are working-class struggles involving immigrants but in no case advancing demands specific to immigrants. To this extent the incorrect initial social base persists and the mass of immigrants remains cut off from the struggle of the labour movement, at the same time as the trade unions rarely go beyond the level of pious wishes with regard to demands for equal rights for all workers. But with the entry into force on 18 September 1972 of new regulations regarding immigration (the Fontanet-Marcellin circular) things are starting to change. These regulations represent a true offensive by large capital to regularize the field of immigration, giving prime emphasis to the repressive and police features of immigration control. The three main measures in the circular can be summarized as follows:

1. No immigrant worker will be able to work or live in France without passing through the legal channels of the Office National d' Immigration. Illegal immigrants will no longer be able to regularize their position (up till then 80% of immigrants were clandestine).
2. Work and residence permits will be linked and granted for the same period. The length of this period will be determined by the work contract, which means that the right to stay in France of an immigrant worker will depend on the goodwill of his employer.
3. Before the issue of a residence permit, an immigrant worker must have a "decent dwelling." But since the causes of the housing crisis are not being touched, this measure may be regarded as a pious wish. In reality, it has a very great but different significance, since the description "decent" will depend on the judgement of the police. It thus indtroduces an arbitrary element into the granting of residence.
4. Finally, in order to deal with all aspects of the administration of immigrants together, the dossiers will be brought together into a single file in the care of the local police station which will thus be able to carry out repressive operations at leisure.

This set of measures is justified, according to the circular, by the need to "regularize" immigration. In fact it is a regularization which reflects very closely the interests of big capital. It represents:

1. The hegemony of monopoly capital over backward capitalism, in the field of immigration policy.
2. A drastic attempt to nip in the bud the rudimentary immigrant workers' movement which was starting to develop out of several woring class struggles.

The circular thus has two features: the capitalist rationalization of immigration, and the political repression of immigrants. Initially, labour unions saw only the first feature and were thus not terribly opposed to it (especially the C.G.T.), since they agreed it was necessary to regularize immigration in order to avoid the worst abuses. But they were not aware of the economic impossibility of such a regularization. At the same time they underestimated the importance of the feature of the circular concerning the establishment of arbitrary employer and police power over immigrants as a whole (except for those entering under special agreements: Algerians, black Africans, E.E.C. nationals).

On the other hand, it quickly became evident to immigrants, from their everyday experience that something basic had changed. The police headquarters and local police stations stepped up their administrative checks, and deportations began. The measures taken were carefully thought out and selective: Arab workers were the first to be hit (mainly Tunisians and Moroccans, unprotected by any special status), whose political-legal isolation is well-known, given the widespread anti-Arab racism among the indigenous population. In the face of this intimidation, immigrant workers mobilized in disorder, to a large extent spontaneously. Two tendencies soon appeared within this movement. One tendency started from the specificity of immigrant workers, organizing them into a Defence Committee for Immigrants Rights to Live and Work (C.D.V.T.I.), on the fringe of the trade-union movement and had as a central plank the demand for a guaranteed legal status which would eliminate the arbitrary powers of police and employers and guarantee the presence of immigrants in the country under satisfactory conditions, even while accepting the inferior status of immigrant, and the regularization of immigration. The other tendency preached the class unity of all workers and demanded equal rights through a common struggle by workers of all nationalities, organized, for example, into French-Immigrant Unitary Committees (C.U.F.I.). Both tendencies were instigated by revolutionary groups although the C.U.F.I. also contained trade-union militants. The trade unions, for their part, demanded the repeal of the circular without, however, launching any major battles on this subject. As deportations increased, semi-spontaneous actions were set off. The demands of the C.U.F.I. were too ambitious for an immigrant movement to use from the outset: they could only be imposed through trade-union action within firms and the trade-unions had difficulty because of the unresponsiveness of French workers. On the other hand, the "defence of human rights" line of the C.D.V.T.I., which was specific to immigrants, gained the support of many of those who were primarily demanding not to be deported, as well as support from prominent liberal and charitable figures (e.g., the Church played a major role). As a form of struggle they chose the *hunger strike* by those threatened with deportation, the first of which was launched in Valence at Christman 1972. Following the success of this first strike (the position of those involved was regularized "because of the date") a veritable wave of hunger strikes by clandestine immigrants shook the whole of France. Supported by public opinion and with a very high level of mobilization of extreme left militants, almost all of the hunger strikes brought success to the participants, but (a) the circular was not withdrawn, (b) *in particular* no mass movement was organized since the strikes mostly involved the persons directly affected, and (c) unity with the labour movement was only at the level of declarations. Parallel to this, the C.U.F.I. *gave support* to these initiatives and spent most of their time organizing neighbourhood committees containing immigrants of various nationalities and French political militants. They succeeded in achieving national *coordination* between the almost one hundred local committees which sprang up semi-spontaneously throughout France.

As soon as the deportation campaign came to an end so did the hunger strikes, thus showing their highly defensive and individual character. Nothing changed at the general level and these struggles did not lead to the creation of any social force.

Immigrant working-class struggles, however, linking labour demands and demands specific to immigrants appeared during the same period (Spring 1973) within certain factories, led primarily by the left wing of the C.F.D.T. and by independent groups of immigrants. A new strike at Renault, the Margoline's strike at Nanterre, the strike of Spanish women workers in the "Claude-St. Cyr" clothes firm, are tough, exemplary, and victorious battles which are starting to link together working-class and immigrant struggles, through the *simultaneous* support of labour unions and nationally organized independent immigrant organizations (Association of Moroccans in France, Coordination of Spanish Workers in the Paris Region, and later the Arab Workers Movement, etc.).

The 1 May 1973 was "Immigrants 1st May" which saw a procession including thousands of immigrant workers, both inside and outside the trade-union contingents, linking their specific demands to those of the working-class as a whole. And the trade unions are again taking up their demands.

This created a new balance of power. The government reacted with both integration and repression. On the one hand, the circular was made more "flexible," (for example by giving a three-months grace period after the expiry of a contract to enable a new job to be found) and it was suspended for four months in order to regularize the position of clandestine workers (which was not in fact done). But, on the other hand, the main provisions remained unchanged, and deportation orders were served *for political reasons* on the leaders of the new immigrant movement which had developed on the fringes of the trade-union movement. Finally, and most important of all, a racist campaign developed (officially disapproved of by the government), which included mass racist demonstrations in Marseille and a wave of assassinations of Arabs whose authors were never traced. This activity reached such a pitch that Algeria suspended emigration to France. The trial of strength between the immigrant movement and capital, which requires a certain status for immigrants, has started. It will be long and hard. All the more since the immigrant movement is starting to escape its isolation and gradually to find its place again in the trade-union movement through a reciprocal discovery of common class interests through common struggles (Pinet, 1973).

This said, a basic problem has been posed, without yet having really emerged in the practice of the immigrant worker movement: insofar as the class struggle does not stop at protest struggle but is basically pulled together at the political level, what is the relation between immigrants' struggles and the political struggle between classes?

5. Immigrant Struggles, Working-Class Struggles, and Political Struggle between Classes

We know (Poulantzas, 1973) that no class struggle *of any consequence* takes place without raising the question of power and hence seeking the destruction-transformation of the State apparatus, the instrument by which the interests of the dominant classes as a whole are realized. Class struggles are thus concentrated within the political struggle between classes, which has as its objective the capture of power and, then, the transformation of social relationships, by ending to the exploitation of man by man.

In the case of immigrant worker' struggles one question immediately arises: which States are involved? Which capture of power is being referred to, that in the sending country, or that in the receiving country? This question is by no means unreal, particularly if we bear in mind the whole series of ultra-internationalist interpretations. These argue from the facts of immigration and the internationalizational of capital and advocate an international revolution, that is, they deny the possibility of any revolutionary process which operates at less than a European scale, at the very least. According to this view, one should speak of a single international working-class since an international proletariat is not only a goal but a reality already present in the relations of production.

Nothing could be further from the truth.

To speak in this way has meaning only in the context of an exclusively trade-union and economistic strategy. Certainly, it is necessary for trade unions primarily concerned with obtaining the best possible negotiating conditions to develop an international trade-union federation in opposition to the international grouping of employers. But to do no more than this is to forget that the interests of the working-class are realized *politically*, that the political process concerns the State, and that the State has forms and patterns of change specific to each nation created by the bourgeoisie. Each state represents a particular system of interests and alliances, and it oppresses in a specific way a section of workers which is relatively united by history and mode of life. The confrontation of each State requires a separate strategy to develop class alliances and class struggle at the political level. It is obvious that there is a Holy Alliance of international capital. But the idea of an international struggle is no more than an idea. Today there is no united world proletariat confronting a single opponent. The unity of the proletariat will be built in the struggle, through the convergence of interests uncovered in the practices of the struggle. Given the uneven development of the class struggle in relation to each state, each proletariat must necessarily develop its own strategy. To talk of an international working class "on the Common Market level" is either an ideological position, expressing a desire without helping concretely to bring it about, or else an economistic position which identifies the context of negotiations with the Europe of big capital. In neither case, is it a political position connected with the strategy of classes engaged in a struggle for power.

To which revolutionary processes, then, does the class faction, immigrant workers, belong? In relation to which political struggle are they defined? In our view, immigrant workers as a class fraction are defined within the class struggle of the receiving country. Nevertheless, as a labour movement, they have a two-fold definition since *within each country there is a multinational working class which corresponds to a multinational labour movement* and which is doubly linked: as a multinational entity it is directed *politically* towards the struggle whose goal is the State apparatus in the receiving country; and as a national component of such an entity it is part of the labour movement in the sending country, since, in practice, it continues to retain a close relation with the struggles in the sending country.

Such an analysis raises the problem of whether this multinational labour movement should not have a corresponding multinational political leadership. But such a measure would contradict the class alliances necessary in the revolutionary process in each country, in so far as classes other than the working class are not multinational. This is a real "contradiction within the people." But before it can be resolved politically from the point of view of the proletariat, there must first be unity of the multinational proletariat today fragmented within each country. The frequent preference for welding class alliances at the cost of the unity of the proletariat implies an acceptance from the outset of the submission of working-class interests to those of the intermediate strata. This then is an attempt to explain the strange passivity of the labour movement towards its immigrant faction. The persistence of this fragmentation may be both a basic reason for the political weakness of the labour movement and the result of a strategy of alliances engendered by the interests of other classes. The link between immigrant workers and the political class struggle is thus both close and problematic.

Notes

1. This paper does not attempt to synthesize all the data available on immigration, but simply to put forward certain ideas. The best work available on the subject, Stephen Castles and Godula Kosack, *Immigrant Workers and Class Structure in Western Europe*, London, Oxford University Press, 1973, collects together the basic data, and also includes a select bibliography of material relating to a number of countries. Periodical information on the subject of immigration is available in the O.E.C.D. Bulletins (Sopemi-Service) and in the journal *Hommes et Migrations*.
2. See the works of Boccara.

3. *Le capitalisme monopoliste d'Etat* (2 vols.), Paris, Editions Sociales, 1970.
4. See *Le logement des migrants,* Droit et Liberté, 1973, and the bibliography of German and English works in Castles and Kosack.
5. See P. and J. Calame, *Le travailleurs erangers en France,* Paris, Les Editions Ouvrières, 1972.
6. See the journal *Hommes et Migrations* ("documents" series), and Clifford S. Hill, *How Prejudiced Is Britain?,* London, Panther Books, 1967.
7. M.D. "Les effets économiques de la Migration sur les pays d'accueil: tentative de bilan," *Economie et Humanisme*, July–August 1971.
8. See *Espaces et Societes,* No. 4, 1971.

Middleman Minorities and Advanced Capitalism

✦ EDNA BONACICH, *University of California-Riverside*

ABSTRACT

Serveral theories contend that middleman minorities should disappear within advanced capitalism, but they have not, a phenomenon which needs to be explained. Middleman firms are essentially petit bourgeois. Their viability lies in cheapness, especially of labor. Certain minorities have the cultural wherewithal to succeed in small business, while they perform important services within the context of advanced capitalism: the pioneering of labor-intensive lines and the decentralization of industries which otherwise come under tight governmental and labor union control.

In attempting to account for the middleman minority phenomenon, several theorists contend that they are the product of certain kinds of society. One common theme (e.g., Hamilton, 1978; Jiang, 1968) is that a minority specialty in middleman activities (or "pariah capitalism") is likely to arise in societies with "traditional" values, including a low esteem for commerce and the trader. Another theme is that they arise in societies with "status gaps" between dominant and subordinate elements in the society (e.g., Blalock, 1967; Loewen, 1971; Rinder, 1958–59; Shibutani and Kwan, 1965). Such a gap is found in feudal societies between the aristocracy and peasants, in slave societies between free persons and slaves, in colonial societies between the colonizers and the colonized, and in racist societies between dominant and subordinate racial groups.

In contrast to theories which assume that the middleman phenomenon arises, in part, from characteristics of the minorities themselves

Bonacich, Edna. 1980. "Middleman minorities and advanced Capitalism." *Ethnic Groups*. Volume 2, 211–219. University of California Press: Los Angeles. Reprinted with permission of University of California Press.

(e.g., Bonacich, 1973; Light, 1972; Stone, 1974; Weber, 1968), these "contextual" theories tend to assume that, when the context changes, middleman minorities will disappear. In particular, they predict that advanced capitalism is not conducive to the middleman form, since trade is not only socially acceptable but has become the dominant mode of interaction, and status has become normally distributed with an enlarged "middle class." Thus, according to Hamilton (1978):

> Nowhere in this phenomenon of pariah capitalism do we find, in terms of power, a middle ranking group. And when we do find middle ranking groups, as in Europe from the Middle Ages on, we do not find pariah capitalism. Historically speaking, such middle ranking capitalists tend to be indigenous to the society in which they work, and as such, their social roles are not easily ethnicized.

The demise of middleman minorities in advanced capitalism is assumed to take two forms. Either they become largely assimilated, as in the case of the Jews in the United States, or they are destroyed, by expulsion (Indians in Uganda) or genocide (Jews in Europe). For instance, according to Leon (1970): "The Jews lived within the pores of feudal society. When the feudal structure started to crumble, it began expelling elements which were, at one and the same time, foreign to it and indispensable to it"(p.225). The Jews became victims of modernization.

Despite the prediction that middleman minorities will disapear in advanced capitalism, there are many contrary examples, including Asians in Britain (Aldrich, 1977; Dahya, 1974), Koreans in Los Angeles (Bonacich, Light and Wong, 1976), Iraqis in Detroit (Sengstock, 1974). Chinese and Japanese in the U.S. (Bonacich, 1975; Wong, 1977), and Jews in the U.S. (Frauman, 1941; Koenig, 1942; Meyer, 1940; Platkin, 1972; Zenner, 1977). Although such commerical minorities may not attain the same degree of economic power as is possible when they monopolize the field, they still retain many of the hallmarks of middleman minorities: concentration and over-representation in trade and independent small business, a distrinctive and relatively solidary ethnic community, and a somewhat hostile relationship with the surrounding society. The persistence of middleman minorities within advanced capitalism needs to be explained, and their role within it explicated.

Before considering the role that middleman groups play within modern capitalism, we need to settle a more fundamental question, namely, what relationship does the middleman economic form bear to modern capitalism? Two views can be distinguished: that middleman minorities are modern capitalists, and that their form is premodern. The former view is associated with Somebart (1951) in the case of the Jews, and with authors (such as Stone, 1974) who see a connection between a Protestant ethic religious value system and economic behaviour. The general argument is that these groups represent the forefront of commerce. They herald a new age of rational economic calculation, bringing with them urbanity, knowledge of money, and international linkages.

In the opposite camp are those who would argue that the middleman form does not represent modern capitalism, but instead is a premodern form. Weber (1968), for example, states:

> The Jews were relatively or altogether absent from the new and distinctive forms of modern capitalism, the rational organization of labor, especially production in an industrial enterprise of the factory type. The Jews evinced the ancient and medieval business temper which had been and remained typical of all genuine traders, whether small businessmen or large-scale moneylenders, in antiquity, the Far East, India, the Mediterranean littoral area, and the Occident of the Middle Ages: the will and the wit to employ mercilessly every chance for profit . . . But this temper is far from distinctive of modern capitalism, as distinguished from the capitalism of other areas. Precisely the reverse is true.(p. 614)

Marx (1959) would concur: "Nothing could be more absurd than to regard merchant's capital, whether in the shape of commercial or money-dealing capital, as a particular variety of industrial capital" (p. 318). He goes on to point out that merchant's capital long predates the capitalist mode of production. As for Weber, the essence of the capitalist mode lies in the organisation and extraction of surplus value from free wage labor, a feature which is by no means necessary to the trader, who is indifferent to the means by which the goods he exchanges are produced.

Another essential feature of modern capitalism, according to Weber, is the use of "rationality," or the dictates of the marketpalce, to determine economic decisions. Such factors as family ties, or ethnic heritage, should not interfere with market considerations. Weber (1968) contrasts the Jews and Protestants by pointing to the fact that the latter established industries employing other Protestants, while the Jews failed to evolve this form, presumably because their religion, like most traditional value systems, forbade the "exploitation" of in-goup members. The uniqueness of the Protestant mentality was that it no longer drew a circle of protection around the community.

Whether or not we believe that Protestantism played a part in the development of modern industrial capitalism, an important point is being made by Weber. The "double standard" or "dual ethic" of middleman groups is a characteristic which is different from modern capitalism. The special treatment afforded members of the ethnic community represents a "traditional" value system not strikingly different from that of the peasant and colonial societies in which these groups resided in centuries past.

Put another way, middleman groups are essentially "petit bourgeois" in orientation. They do not engage in the kind of activity that epitomizes modern industrial capitalism, namely, the hiring of contracted wage labor from which profits are extracted. Instead, they tend to work as a single unit in which the distinction between owner and employee is blurred. Their shops depend on the use of ethnic and familial ties, not on impersonal contracts.

One consequence of the difference in organization between middleman petit bourgeois shops and modern industrial bourgeois factories is that they grow in different ways. Because of their reliance on impersonal contracts, there is no limit on the growth of the industrial plant. Armies of workers can be employed. In contrast, the petit bourgeois shop depends upon personal ties and loyalties, mutual trust and obligation. As such it is imperative that people know each other well and in many contexts. This puts a major limit on the growth of the firm. It can only encompass as many workers as the employer can know well enough to trust. Thus there is a tendency for such firms to grow by splitting off and setting up new versions of themselves with new owners who can have personal ties with their workers.

It is sometimes pointed out that middleman shops are small because they lack capital. Indeed, as objects of societal antagonism, it is not unusual for many members to be impoverished or able to command only small sums for investment. But it is also the case that occasionally considerable wealth may be amassed by members of these groups. Yet (with exceptions) they still show a proclivity to concentrate in small commercial establishments. Their social form dictates this; limiting the size and nature of the firms they establish.

The first position, that middleman minorities are the harbingers of modern capitalism, has an element of truth, however. For, although they treat members of their own ethnic community in terms of "traditional" values, they do treat outsiders in rational economic terms (e.g., Blalock, 1967; Fallers, 1967; Toennies, 1971; Foster, 1974). Thus, when located in a traditional setting, they represent the most "modern" economic position. They know how to use money, how to haggle in the marketplace, and how to make a good deal.

We can, perhaps, distinguish three types of economic orientation. There is a "traditional" approach in which everyone is treated mainly in nonmarket terms; there is the modern capitalist approach, in which everyone is treated in terms of the market; and there is the petit bourgeois middleman approach, in which in-group members are treated according to traditional values, while outsiders are treated in terms of the market. Depending on which "face" of the middleman group the observer examines, he will conclude they are modern of premodern. But because they are at least partially premodern, we must conclude that they are different from the modern industrial capitalist.

Given that middleman minorities are at least partially premodern in their economic orientation, how can we account for their apparent persistence in advanced capitalist countries? This question has been addressed by Light (1972), who points out that, paradoxically, the ascribed ties of a strong ethnic community can, in some ways, be more efficient than the contractual ties of modern, voluntary relations. Bonacich (1973) develops this theme, trying to show how middleman groups have been able to use communal resources to cut costs in innumerable directions. Despite their tendency not to let the market dictate all business practices, these minorities are able to undercut "modern" businesses, admittedly only in a limited number of spheres, such as retailing and services, which are not highly developed. But many lines within modern capitalism are not highly evolved and can be pursued more cheaply by middleman groups.

The basis for the economic advantages of middleman firms lies in their ability to mobilize communal resources resting on trust, not contract. Multiple resources are invloved in the development of small business, but perhaps the most important is the ability to keep down the cost of labor. Middleman minority small business is able to operate cheaply in large measure because it is able to utilize "cheap labor." The cheapness of middleman labor derives from several conditions, including discrimination by the surrounding society, standard of living in the homeland, and perhaps a sojourning orientation. Not least among the causes, however, is the social economic organization of these minorities. The petit bourgeois organization of their firms places ethnic loyalty above class consciousness as employees. Since everyone working in the business is either a relative of the owner, or plans to set up a business of his own shortly and is working for someone else in order to receive on-the-job training. The whole group is geared, not to improving wages and work conditions, but to saving and reinvesting capital. This characteristic makes the middleman firm almost immune to labor unions, and gives the owner access to a "docile" and hardworking labor force the likes of which no industrialist can command.

While we can see that there are internal forces within middleman minorities which continue to operate whatever the setting of these groups, and which can therefore help to account for their over-representation in small business even in advanced capitalist societies, the contextual question remains. Does advanced capitalism encourage the perpetuation of a minority petit bourgeoisie, or does it merely tolerate such a specialty? Is the middleman role of use to modern capitalism? There do appear to be certain "functions" which a petit bourgeoisie serves within modern capitalism, suggesting that indeed such a minority specialty may be tolerated and perhaps encouraged. These functions can be divided into two main themes: pioneering and decentralization.

By "pioneering" I mean that middleman minorities are useful for entering sections of an economy that are not well-advanced. Because of their inexpensive utilization of labor, they are useful in labor-intensive fields which have not undergone the rationalization, centralization, and mechanization that requires considerable capital. When an industry becomes capital-intensive, the importance of cost of labor declines, and the relative advantage of middleman groups declines, too.

The second theme, "decentralization," concerns the idea that, within advanced capitalism, there are centrifugal as well as centripetal forces. The larger the plant, the more likely is there to be class consciousness among workers, and the more it is likely to come under state scrutiny regarding such matters as taxation, pollution, and labor standards. Thus while the secular trend in modern capitalism is toward the concentration of capital and the establishment of large scale plants, there is also a countertendency to create smaller plants and outlets which have the advantage of being able to avoid close public scrutiny. The persistent tendency to sub-contract garment production to small sweatshops is a case in point. U.S. capital can take advantage of entrepreneurial minorities and their ability to keep labor costs down by arranging various types of dependent relationship with them. Franchising is one example, subcontracting another. Even a steady distribution in a location which capital finds "unprofitable" to service, such as urban ghettos with high crime rates, may be a useful purpose to which middleman groups can be put.

In conclusion, some groups (but not others) have a proclivity to engage in small business and are likely to be good at it, at least in part because they are able to use communal solidarity to keep their costs, especially labor costs, down. This feature can be useful within advanced capitalism, both to the groups themselves, since they are able to compete effectively in certain lines, and to elements of the capitalist class, who are able to make use of middleman enterprise. Thus, we would argue that there is, at least at present, a place for a petite bourgeoisie within advanced capitalism, and that a minority group with a petit bourgeois specialty is probably better equipped to fill this place anyone else.

Immigrant and Ethnic Enterprise in North America

✦ IVAN LIGHT, *University of Califonia, Los Angeles*

In the decade 1820–30, 80% of free white Americans owned their own means of livelihood (Corey, 1966). This decade was the high-water mark of self-employment in America, and subsequent trends have shown an almost uninterrupted decline. Generations of sociologists have declared that business self-employment in the modern United States has become an economic anachronism which is in the process of disappearance (Light, 1979). Following Marx on this point, they have observed that the progressive concentration of capital reduced the once numerous class of free enterpreneurs that existed in the last century. Indeed, three decades ago C.W. Mills (1951) already showed the steady decline of agricultural and nonagricultural self-employment in the United States between 1870 and 1950:

> A larger number of small businesses are competing for a smaller share of the market. The stratum of urban entrepreneurs has been narrowing, and within it concentration has been going on. Small business becomes smaller, big business becomes bigger. (Mills 1951, p. 24).

After Mills wrote this evaluation, the decline of self-employment in the American labor force unambiguously continued until 1973. In that year a slim majority of American farmers continued to be self-employed, but less than 7% of non-farm workers were self-employed (Ray, 1975). Given these trends, government and business analysts agreed that the probability of self-employment had become poorer than in the past and its rewards correspondingly more meagre (Cingolani, 1973, Special Task Force, 1973) In this economic context, social scientists generally concluded that small business self-employment was incompatible with capitalist economic concentration and could be expected to slide into oblivion for this reason (Bottomore, 1966; O'Connor, 1973; Horvat, 1982; Auster and Aldrich, 1981).

Light, Ivan. 1984. "Immigrant and ethnic enterprise in North America." *Ethnic and Racial Studies*. Volume 7, Number 2:195–211. Reprinted with permission of Taylor & Francis Ltd., www.tandf.co.uk/journals.

However, on the cultural side, sociologists had to explain the atavistic persistence of entrepreneurial values and ambitions in the American labor force (Chinoy, 1952; Walker and Guest, 1952) as well as the extent of self-employment among the wage-earning population (Lipset and Bendix, 1959). Given the USA's *laissez-faire* traditions (Meyer, 1953) it was easy to understand entrepreneurial ambitions and frustrated aspirations as cultural residuals of an economoically bygone era (Vidich and Bensman, 1960). Thus, Risman (1950) juxtaposed the "inner-directed" old-fashioned individualism of yesteryear's entrepreneurs with the god-handed "other-direction" of corporate executives, finding in this contrast a shift in the modal personality from the former to the latter. In a similar exercise, Miller and Swanson (1958) found that achievement imagery in the American middle class had shifted away from self-employment toward bureaucratic careers in corporate hierarchies. Bell's (1976) analysis of the "cultural contradictions of capitalism" identified the Puritan tradition as a self-destructive rationality whose adolescent heirs had discarded the disciplines of planning and work in favor of "voluptuary hedonism."

Entrepreneurship's protracted decline provided a neat illustration of cultural lag, the belated adjustment of superstructure to changes in production relations (Aronowiz, 1973). A small business economy needed entrepreneurial motivations in its labor force. When the economic basis of small business deteriorated, socialization lagged behind, continuing to produce entrepreneurial ambitions and values in lifelong wage workers (Lynd and Lynd, 1937). The temporary result was a glut of disappointed aspirants for small business self-employment, a situation of imbalance between supply and demand (O'Connor 1973). Ultimatley, the market's surplus of aspiring entrepreneurs reached back into the socialization system, causing reallocation of motivational resources away from this over-populated occupation in diminishing demand. As salaried workers corrected their aspirations for realistic prospects, the social origins of American small business owners declined (Newcorner, 1961; Meyer, 1947, Mills, 1966). By 1952 the "creed of the individual enterpriser" had become "a working class preoccupation" (Lipset and Bendix, 1964, p. 462).

Ethnic and Immigrant Enterprise in America

Taken very generally, cultural lag still offers a satisfactory explanation of what happened to entrepreneurial individualism in twentieth-century America. However, the cultural lag orthodoxy encounters two serious objections, one empirical, the other conceptual. First, as Giddens (1973) has observed, the *rate* of decline in self-employment was never so rapid as Marxists had expected even though the direction of change was mostly negative. Moreover, in the specific period "the number of self-employed Americans rose by more than 1.1 million, reversing decades of steady decreases" (Fain, 1980, p. 3). This stabilization suggests that a plateau in self-employed population firmly supports an ideology of entrepreneurship among a minority (see Table 1). This conclusion is particularly appealing since Boissevain (1984) has reported that in 1978 "Common Market countries registered a net increase in the number of entrepreneurs and family workers" thus reversing their postwar trend of decline.

Second, cultural lag orthodoxy depends upon a simplifying, inaccurate assumption of homogeneity in economy and labor force. A homogeneous economy means uniformity in industrial conditions among the various sectors as well as a uniform rate of capitalist concentration in each. Labor force homogeneity means all workers are identical in values, attitudes, skills, employment access, and return on human capital. Both assumptions

TABLE 1 Self-employed and unpaid family workers in the United States, 1948–79 (in thousands)

1948	1948	1958	1968	1972	1979
Non-agricultural industries					
Total employed	51,975	56,863	72,900	78,929	94,605
Self-employed	6,109	6,102	5,102	5,332	6,652
Percent of total	11.8	10.7	7.0	6.8	7.0
Unpaid family workers	385	588	485	517	455
Percent of total	0.7	1.0	0.7	0.7	0.5
Agriculture					
Total employed	6,309	4,645	3,266	3,005	2,993
Self-employed	4,664	3,081	1,985	1,789	1,580
Percent of total	73.9	66.3	60.8	59.5	52.8
Unpaid family workers	1,318	943	549	466	302
Percent of total	20.9	20.3	16.8	15.5	10.1

Source: T. Scott Fain, "Self-Employed Americans: Their Number Has Increased," *Monthly Labor Review* 103 (1980): Table 1; p. 4.

are unrealistic. The U.S. economy actually consists of a plurality of sectors which differ in respect to industrial conditions, capitalist concentration, and rates of change. O'Connor's (1973) distinctions between competitive, monopoly, and state sectors need attention, and this tripartite division could easily be augmented in the interest of exactitude (reviewed in Kallenberg and Sorenson, 1979). Additionally, the U.S. labor force consists of unequally situated groups which differ in cultural heritages. At the very least, one must distinguish the immigrant, the nonwhite, and the native white labor force sectors. Workers in these sectors experience differential returns on human capital, rates of under- and unemployment, welfare and legislative support, and career opportunities.

Given variation in the economy and labor force, uneven resolution of cultural lag follows. On the one hand, some business sectors retain contrary-to-trend compatibility with entrepreneurial activities. On the other, some working populations retain atavistic aspirations for business self-employment. In point of fact, immigrant and nonwhite workers cluster heavily in the economy's competitive sector within which, by definiton, a small business milieu persists (Waldinger, 1982; Zenner, 1982; Auster and Aldrich, 1983). Thus, on structural grounds alone, there is reason to predict that old-fashioned entrepreneurial ideology should remain among immigrant and minority sector workers long after native white workers have resigned themselves to salaried and wage employment in the monopoly and state sectors.

This situation is not really novel. In actual fact, the foreign-born have been overrepresented in American small business since 1880 and probably earlier (Light, 1980; Higgs, 1977). Two explanations seem plausible. The first is disadvantage in the labor market. Such disadvantage causes foreigners to concentrate in small business because they suffer under- and unemployment as a result of poor English, unvalidated educational credentials, discrimination, and so forth (Reitz, 1980). Anyone who is disadvantaged in the labor force derives from this unfortunate situation a special incentive to consider self-employment, and the greater his disadvantage, the greater his incentive. The unemployed apple vendors of the Great Depression epitomize the resourcefulness of workers who, unable to find wage-earning jobs, turn to any and every pitiful self-employment from economic desperation.

However, labor markets' disadvantage cannot be the whole explanation of this phenomenon, because some immigrant and ethnic minority groups have higher rates of urban self-employment ("entrepreneurship") than do others (Goldscheider and Kobrin, 1980; Boissevan, 1984; Jenkins, 1984). Given equal disadvantage why do some foreign groups have higher rates than others, and why should the foreign-born in general have higher rates of business self-employement than disadvantaged native minorities, especially blacks (Handlin, 1959)? Native blacks are more disadvantaged than native whites, yet the blacks' rates of business self-employment have been and remain lower than the native whites' rates and much lower than the foreign-born rates despite presumptively higher disadvantage of the blacks (Light, 1972, 1979; Wright et al., 1982).

Orthodox and Reactive Cultural Contexts

The orthodox answer to this issue has fastened upon transplanted cultural endowments of various ethnic minority groups. Derived from Max Weber, this model of entrepreneurship has claimed that individuals introject cultural values in the course of primary socialization. When a group's values and motivations encourage business enterprise, cultural minorities produce socialized adults who prosper in business. The prototype is Weber's (1958) Protestant sectarians who espoused the values of diligence in a calling, thrift, profit, and individualism. These values and attendant motivations caused adult sectarians to prosper in business. With appropriate adjustments, this model might account for the anomalous and persistent over-representation of selected cultural minorities in self employment. American examples include Jews, Chinese, Japanese, Greeks, Macedonians, West Indians, Dominicans, Gypsies, Iraqi Christians, Lebanese, Koreans, and Arabs.[1] In all such cases, cultural theory has explained business over-representation and/or success in term of intact, unmodified cultural heritages. A fine example is the migration of Gypsy fortune-tellers. Before debarkation in New York City, the Gypsies already knew how to tell fortunes, and their cultural baggage included ready-to-use skills (crystal balls, tarot cards, palmistry) other groups simply lacked. Gypsy practice of these skills in the United States only involved the utilization of a cultural tradition for the specific purpose of self-employment (Sway, 1983).

This view has merit but research in ethnic enterprise has disclosed its inadequacy. In reality, immigration and alien status release latent facilitators which promote entrepreneurship independent of cultural endowments (Turner and Bonacich, 1980). Three facilitators are especially important. The first is psychological satisfaction arising from immigration to a high-wage country from a low-wage country. Immigrants in the United States have recurrently proven willing to accept low money returns, long hours of labor, job-related danger, and domestic penury in order to maintain business self-employment. Relative to their countries of origin, even adverse conditions look good to immigrants and, until fully adapted to the American standard of living, immigrants obtain satisfaction from squalid proprietorships that would not attract native-white wage earners. This is *relative satisfaction.*

A second, much-documented reaction is enhanced social solidarity attendant upon cultural minority status. Chain migrations create immigrant communities with extraordinarily well-developed social networks. Numerous studies have shown that these social networks create resources upon which immigrant co-ethnics can draw for business purposes (Light, 1972; Bonacich, 1973, 1975; Bonacich and Modell, 1980; Wilson and Portes, 1980)."The cornerstone of an ethnic subeconomy is the communal solidarity of a minority group" (Hraba, 1979, p. 374). Insofar as reactive solidarity encourages immigrant entrepreneurship, a situation has brought out a collective response which is not cultural in the orthodox sense (Young, 1971). A concrete example is the influene of immigrant *Landsmannschaften* upon business enterprise. Immigrant *Landsmänner* belong to a primary group which did not exist as such in their country of origin. Thus, among the Japanese of Los Angeles *Hiroshimakenjin* formed a solidaristic subgroup within the metropolitan population – all the brothers hailed from Hiroshima. On the other hand, contemporaneous residents of Hiroshima did not share the sense of local solidarity so the immigrants had obviously created a solidarity abroad that did not exist in Hiroshima, their city of origin (Modell, 1977). This is a *reactive* solidarity which required alien status to liberate, and as such is quite different from the practice of fortune-telling by immigrant Gypsies.

The third endowment is sojourning (Siu, 1952). Sojourning arises when immigrants intend to repatriate, and derive from this intention a desire to amass as much money as possible as quickly as possible. As Bonacich (1973) has shown, sojourning implies a battery of entrepreneurial motivations which give middleman minorities an advantage in business competition over nonsojourners. Admittedly, the cultural status of sojourning is uncertain, and the phenomenon arguably arises liturgically as well as situationally (Light, 1979). Nonetheless, sojourning is a frequent (but not invariant) accompaniment to international immigration, and its presence provides an economic edge to the foreign born in small business enterprise (Zenner, 1982; Portes, Clark, and Lopez, 1981–82).

Light's (1980) distinction between reactive and orthodox cultural contexts of entrepreneurship is a new one necessitated by the rapidly growing literature on this topic, but anticipated by earlier writers (Young, 1971). Orthodox and reactive contexts in Light's rubre correspond closely to what Turner and Bonacich (1980) elsewere identified as cultural and situational variables. In both cases, authors responded to the tendecy of ethnic business researchers to "talk past" real issues on the one hand or, on the other, to engage in "unnecessary and wasteful polemics" about pseudo-issues (Turner and Bonacich, 1980, pp. 145, 147). Authorities agree that, however named, the conceptual distinctions identified do not necessitate an empirical repugnance because different variables can contribute to the entrepreneurship of the same ethnic groups. Old-fashioned cultural analysis (Belshaw, 1955) stressed only orthodox etiologies, thus creating the erroneous implication that only culturally intact transmission affected entrepreneurship (Freedman, 1959). Conversely, Bonacich's (1973) model of "middleman minorities" ignored orthodox contributions, focusing only upon reactivities. In Light's (1972) treatment of prewar blacks and Asians in the USA, the over-representation of Asians in business proprietorships is credited to reactions arising from relative satisfaction and immigrant solidarity *as well as* to rotating credit associations, culturally transmitted institutions fitting the orthodox model (see also Woodum, Rhodes and Feagin, 1980).

Orthodox, reactive, or mixed entrepreneurship arises when only-orthodox, only-reactive or mixed orthodox and reactive components of entrepreneurship figure in an empirical analysis. On the face of the available evidence, some groups belong in one, other groups in another category. The crucial evidence arises from two comparisons. On the one hand, the foreign-born in general have been over-represented in American small business since at least 1880 and are still over-represented. On the other hand some foreign-born groups have higher rates of business self-employment than do others. For example, Jews have been and remain extraordinarily entrepreneurial, whereas Irish have been lower than the foreign-born average (Goldscheider and Kobrin, 1980). The general over-representation of the foreign-born betokens a situationally induced responsiveness to self-employment. This responsiveness is *prima facie* evidence for a reactive model. On the other hand, the higher-than-average rates of selected foreign-born groups suggest unique cultural endowments. Unique endowments imply cultural heritages transmitted intact, the orthodox cultural model. The best fit of theory and evidence occurs when theory acknowledges the additive possibilities of orthodox and reactive components. On this view, the foreign-born in general experience the reactive entrepreneurship arising from their alien situation, but middleman minorities (Jews, Chinese, Greeks, etc.) add to this reaction their culturally intact heritages of sojourning entrepreneurship (Bonacich and Modell, 1980). As a result, rates of entrepreneurship are higher among middleman minorities than among the foreign-born in general, and higher among the foreign-born than among the native-born whites.

Ethnic and Class Resources

Efforts to explain ethnic and immigrant entrepreneurship invariably turn up batteries of special causes. That is, the immigrants developed higher than average rates of entrepreneurship because they drew upon special resources which native groups lacked. In Barth's (1962) terminology these facilities constitute entrepreneurial "assets," but the term *resources* is more general and does not lend itself to confusion with financial assets (Light, 1980). *Ethnic resources* are any and all features of the whole group which coethnic business owners can utilize in business or from which their business benefits (Reitz, 1982; Wallman, 1979a: ix; 1979b: 10). Thus, ethnic resources include orthodox cultural endowments, relative satisfaction, reactive solidarities, sojourning orientation, and these four encompass all types of ethnic resources empirically described in the existing literature (cf. Turner and Bonacich, 1980). As such, ethnic resources should be distinguished from class resources. *Class resources* are cultural and material. On the material side, class resources are private property in the means of production and distribution, human capital, and money to invest. On the cultural side, class resources are bourgeois values, attitudes, knowledge, and skills transmitted intergenerationally in the course of primary socialization (Di Maggio, 1982). An established bourgeoisie equips its youth with appropriate class resources, and, having them, the youth are well endowed to prosper in a market economy. Class resources exist, and sociological theory has amply and basically acknowledged their importance. An analytical dispute has arisen, however, when studies of ethnic entrepreneurship have sought to distinguish ethnic resources from class resources. The mainstream view ignored ethnic resources, assuming that only class resources do or even can exist. On this view, an ethnic bourgeoisie is just a bourgeoisie rather than a bourgeoisie which has unique access to ethnic resources.

In principle, class and ethnic resources might occur singly or in combination. This compatibility yields four basic etiologies: class-only, ethnic-only, class-ethnic mixed, and no resources. A class-only etiology explains ethnic minority or immigrant entrepreneurship strictly on the basis of class origins, property, money, and human capital. Class-only explanation is type 1 in Table 2. Ethnic-only analysis omits the above, focusing explanation wholly upon ethnic resources such as cultural heritages, reactive solidarities, sojourning, and relative

TABLE 2 Ethnic and class resources of entrepreneurship

	Resource Basis			
	Ethnic		Class	
	Orthodox	Reactive	Material	Cultural
1. Class-only	O	O	X	X
2. Ethnic-only	X	X	O	O
3. Mixed	X	X	X	X
4. Mixed: class predominant	x	x	X	X
5. Mixed: ethnic predominant	X	X	x	x
6. No resources	O	O	O	O

O = none
x = some
X = much

satisfaction. Ethnic-only explanation is type 2 in Table 2. Mixed analysis combines elements of ethnic and class analysis to suit empirical cases of entrepreneurship. Mixed explanation is type 3 in Table 2. Since class-only analysis is most compatible with a macro-theory of the economy, the mixed and ethnic-only analytic possibilities signal a newly discovered frontier of theoretical controversy. If the latter types exist, class macrotheory needs adjustment to take into account complexities currently ignored.

The North American literature contains no examples of class-only or ethnic-only resourse mobilizing entrepreneurial subgroups. All the empirical cases are mixed. The evidence thus reduces the theoretical polarities to ideal types. Admittedly sone cases of ethnic minority or immigrant entrepreneurship weigh more heavily on one side or the other of this class/ethnic balance. Especially in the past immigrant entrepreneurship seems to have depended more heavily upon ethnic resources than it currently does. Turn-of-the century Chinese and Japanese immigrants in California are the best-documented illustrations. Disadvantaged in the general labor market, they turned in extraordinary proportion to self-employment, apparently mobilizing ethnic resources very effectively to this end (Light, 1972; Modell, 1977; Bonacich and Modell, 1980). Post-1970 Asian immigrants in North America continue to mobilize ethnic resources to support business ownership, but the balance has shifted toward money, human capital, and bourgeois culture. Thus, all cases of Asian entrepreneurship have been mixed, but in the last half-century the balance has appreciably swung from ethnic toward class resources (Thompson, 1979).

In contemporary American and Canadian society, immigrant entrepreneurship still combines ethnic and class resources, thus creating an empirical problem of sorting out each contributor and assessing its contribution. Thorny as is this measurement problem, the empirical dualism is clear especially in the important cases of political refugees from the third world. To a substantial extent, Korean, Vietnamese, Taiwanese, Hong Kong, Cuban, and Iranian immigrants now in the United States derived from property-owing upper classes in their countries of origin.[2] Fearing or experiencing sociopolitical turmoil in their homelands, these refugees entered the United

States with human capital, money to invest, and bourgeois cultural values. Accordingly, it is no surprise that their involvment in small business has been extensive, their success in it remarkable, and their achievements much celebrated in popular media (Ramirez, 1980). On a class-only model the small business success of these refugees reflects only the class resources they brought with them, and any group of wealthy refugees would have created as many small businesses. Ethnicity conferred nothing: this is the null hypothesis.

Class resources indisputably help, but empirical research suggests that a class-only explanation is inadequate. An immigrant bourgeoisie utilizes ethnic resources in supplementation of class resources. The two best-studied examples are Cubans in Miami, and Koreans in Los Angeles.[3] Wilson and Portes (1980; Portes, 1981; Wilson and Martin, 1982) found that about one-third of Cubans in Miami were employed in Cuban-owned business and another fragment were self-employed. For the Cubans returns on human capital were more favorable among the self-employed than among those employed for wages in the competitive sector. Indeed, returns on human capital were equivalent to those in the primary sector. Explaining this success, Wilson and Portes (1980) conclude:

> Immigrant enterpreneurs make use of language and cultural barriers and of ethnic affinities to gain privileged access to markets and sources of labor. . . . The necessary counterpart to these ethnic ties of solidarity is the principle of ethnic preference in hiring and of support of other immigrants in their economic ventures. (p. 315)

Since these resources would be unavailable in Cuba, the Cuban immigrant bourgeoisie acquires access to ethnic resources in Miami where they are members of a cultural minority. To a substantial extent, these reactive resources permit the Cubans to thrive in small business and even to out-perform the native whites in this sphere despite the material advantages of the latter.

Bonacich, Light, and Wong (1977, 1980; see also Light, 1980; Bonacich and Jung, 1982) have looked into the entrepreneurial success of 60,000 Koreans in Los Angeles. In 1980, approximately 40% of employed Korean men headed small firms (Yu, 1982).[4] An additional 40% of Koreans worked in these firms so only about 20% of Korean immigrants found employment in non-Korean-owned firms or government agencies. Admittedly, the Korean immigrants were highly educated: on one account nearly 70% of men had college degrees compared with only 15% of Los Angeles County residents in general. Additionally, the Koreans brought with them sums of capital, rarely less than $25,000 and sometimes millions. On the other hand, these class resources supplemented ethnic resources; they did not exclude them. As among the Cubans in Miami, Koreans in Los Angeles made effective business use of language and cultural barriers distinguishing co-ethnics from the general population, reactive social solidarity, nepotistic hiring, and formal and informal mutual support networks. Additionally, Koreans made some use of rotating credit associations,[5] nationalistic appeals for labor peace, vertical and horizontal integration of firms, informal and formal restraints of trade,[6] and political connections with City Hall developed by leading Korean business organizations. In all these respects, Korean entrepreneurship drew upon ethnic resources not merely upon class resources.

Collectivist and Individualist Styles of Entrepreneurship

Textbook treatments of entrepreneurship have long begun with the economistic assumption that small business owners are individualists. Indeed, the term *entrepreneurial individualism* remains in general currency as a reflection of this persisting assumption. Underlying the microeconomic theory of the firm are the class resources of the bourgeoisie which provide facilities for individual business owners. In Schumpeter's famous image, these entrepreneurs behave like spectators in a crowded stadium during a rainstorm. Feeling rain, each spectator independenty decides to raise his umbrella, and decides to put in away when the sun once again comes out. In this analogy, the material resource is the umbrella, and the cultural resource is the trained wisdom to utilize it properly. But each entrepreneur thinks and acts independently albeit in utilization of class-linked resources.

Accepting Schumpeer's (1934) class-only model of entrepreneurship,[7] sociology has, however, parted company with neoclassical economics on the issue of consciousness. Insofar as a resource-transmitting bourgeoisie develops self-consciousness, this consciousness becomes a class resource capable of affecting the economic success of members.Thus, elitist studies of the American upper class have long claimed that debutante cotillions, preparatory schools, swank vacation resorts, exclusive suburbs, and stuffy downtown clubs reflect and forge upper-class consciousness (Useem, 1980). Group consciousness enhances the chances of individual bourgeois to monopolize access to material and status rewards. For instance, clubs provide a private place to concoct business and political deals or to arrange marriage. Admittedly the importance of bourgeois group consciousness has not been so systematically examined in its economic as in its political ramifications. However class-only theories of the bourgeoisie have acknowledged the development of a entrepreneurial collectivism which enhances the competitive chances of the individual members of the bourgeoisie. Evaluating two generations of social research on the American business elite, Useem (1980) finds "internal cohesion" strikingly in evidence. "Unity is far more extensively developed at the top than anywhere else in the class structure" (p. 58).

A similar evolution has characterized sociological studies of ethnic business (Jenkins, 1984). Classical sociologists called attention to cultural endowments which governed the style of business ownership, and explained in historical context the transition from merchant to bourgeois. The prototype was, of course, Weber's (1958) Protestant sectarians whose economic style reflected religio-cultural values. Their disciplined lifestyle caused them to prosper in business, but they were expected to do so as noncooperating individuals standing or falling on individual merits. Of course, there is no denying that under some cultural or situational conditions, small business owners can be individualistic nor that introjected values of hard work, thrift, and economic rationality encourage business survival and success.[8] Bechofer et al.'s (1974) study of Scottish business owners in Edinburgh depicts individualistic business conduct. Jarvenpa and Zenner (1979) reported the same individualism among Scots in the Canadian fur trade. On the other hand, even Weber overstated the extent of individualism among Protestant sectarians and, aware of this error, was more careful (1958b) in some writings. Historical research among Puritan business owners in seventeenth-century New England has not disclosed the expected individualism. On the contrary, Bailyn (1955), Hall (1977), and Griffen and Griffen (1977) concluded that observantly Calvinist business owners in New England were active participants in commercial networks knit together on the basis of extended kinship and friendship, these networks actually linking ports of origin in the British Isles and New England cities.

In the same sense, cultural treatments of middlemen minorities in North America began with the assumption that cultural subgroups acted out their values in enterprising individualism based upon hard work, thrift, rationality, and self-denial (Auster and Aldrich, 1983). In this model, immigrant entrepreneurs drew upon a cultural tradition, then fanned out into the economy in individualistic search of profitable opportunities. Equipped with cultural resources, co-ethnics knew how to make the most out of such business opportunities as they encountered—but each did so as an isolated individual.

There is, of course, no question that ethnic values and motivations do affect individual behavior. However, ethnic research has shown there exists a largely ignored dimension of collective action which goes beyond individualistic value or motivational effects, important as those are (Leff, 1979). This is the dimension of entrepreneurial collectivism in the ethnic minority (Young, 1971; Cummings, 1980). Collective styles of entrepreneurship depend upon group resources in which business owners only participate insofar as they maintain active, adult participation in community life (Herman, 1979). For example, a rotating credit association requires cooperators to establish a reputation for trustworthiness in the ethnic community, and this reputation depends in turn upon active involvement (Light, 1972). Similarly, an immigrant or ethnic informational network confers benefits upon business owners, but to obtain these benefits an owner needs to belong to the network. Isolates cannot share network information so this ethnic resource only benefits participants in ethnic community network. Finally, trade guilds may regulate and control internal competition, but the benefits of collusion in restraint of trade accrue to members. Isolates suffer the consequences of collusion by others.

In principle, class and ethnic resources both confer potentialities for individualist or collectivistic styles of business managment. As before, however, all empirical cases in the literature have been mixed. For instance, Koreans in Los Angeles have utilized both class and ethnic resources, and these resources have here supported individualistic and there collectivistic entrepreneurship. Taken together, Korean entrepreneurship in Los Angeles is a pastiche of ethnic and class resources and individualist and collectivist styles. On the other hand, the balance of individualism and collectivism in immigrant entrepreneurship appears to have shifted in three generations. Chinese and Japanese immigrants in California at the turn of the century utilized entrepreneurial strategies which were more collectivistic than those currently utilized by Chinese immigrants in Toronto (Chan and Cheung, 1982). In the same manner, Polish, Finnish, Irish, Mormon, and Jewish entrepreneurship appears to have undergone a shift in this century away from an immigrant-generation dependence upon collective resources toward a native-born generation dependence upon individual resources.[9]

Two related changes explain this shifting balance. On the one hand, the competitive sector has become smaller in size and the price of admission higher in response to capitalist concentration. Ethnic collectivism may be less adequate than in the past. On the other hand, upward social mobility has conferred class resources upon native-born ethnics whose progenitors did not have them. Specifically, native-born descendants of immigrant business owners enter the business sector with money, education, and skills their forebears lacked. Possesing class resources, immigrant and ethnic minority entrepreneurs become more individualistic in style. Thus, impoverished immigrants needed to combine their small amounts of capital in rotating credit associations in order to assemble a sum large enough to finance small business. Dependent upon kinsmen and landsmen for initial capital, immigrant business owners could not thereafter operate their businesses as if they were isolated individualists. With personal money to invest, the descendants of these immigrants and contemporary "new" immigrants no longer need to borrow from kin and friends (Kim, 1977). Therefore, they establish their business enterprises without rotating credit associations, and operate them in a more individualistic manner.[10] Similarly, poor immigrants did not understand inventories or balance sheets so they turned to kin and friends for advice in business management. Equipped with MBAs, their descendants and North America's new immigrants possess the business skills they need as class resources. Therefore, they do not need to turn for management advice to informal, ethnically linked agencies, and they are free to operate their business enterprises as if they were isolated individuals. In this manner, access to class resources may obviate collectivism in ethnic enterprise—but not exclude it altogether. In Toronto, Thompson (1979) reports, a bipolar business class has actually emerged as a result of these processes. On the one side are the old-fashioned, ethnic-dependent mom-and-pop-store owners; on the other, Hong kong millionaires operating investment corporations. "The new stratum of entrepreneurial elites differ in both origin and lifestyle from the traditional merchant elites who for years controlled the [Chinese] ethnic community" (Thompson, 1979, p. 311).

In principle, ethnic and immigrant small business ought to run out of solidarity to exploit because cultural assimilation and higher education undercut the ascriptive solidarities from which immigrant-generation business owners derived the resources to power their business network (Turner and Bonacich, 1980). Much evidence suggests that over generations ethnic resources do decay for this reason (Bonacich and Modell, 1980; Borhek, 1970; Goldscieider and Kobrin, 1980; Montero, 1981). "Over the long run," Reitz (1980, p. 231) observes, "there is a progressive trend toward abandonment of ethnic group ties for all groups in which long-term experience can be measured." However, the rate of deterioration has been much slower than sociologists once expected (Wilensky and Lawrence, 1979). The indisputable profitability of ethnic capitalism is an apparent cause of this retardation. Especially relative to equally qualified members of the same ethnic group in the general labor market, owners of ethnic sector business enterprises earn high incomes in business. Big profits make ethnic business attractive (Wilson and Portes 1980; Sway, 1983; Reitz, 1982; Bonacich and Modell, 1981). Ethnic business owners identify with their ethnic community and participate actively in it. They provide the leadership for ethnic institutions. Ethnic attachments also persist more strongly among wage workers whose workplace is a coethnic firm whose language is that of the homeland, not English (Bonacich and Modell, 1980; Reitz, 1980; Woodrum, Rhodes, and Feagin, 1980). These two classes often account for 40% to 80% of the total ethnic population. Ethnic-owned businesses "help prop up other institutions which recuit and maintain ethnic membership" (Reitz, 1980; p. 233). Ethnicity supports the ethnic economy, and the ethnic economy supports ethnic perpetuation (Bonacich and Modell, 1981).

No Resources Entrepreneurship

The preceding analysis offers a satisfactory account of why equally disadvantaged ethnic and immigrant minorities display unequal rates of entrepreneurship: survival and success depend upon group resources. Groups with more resources outperform groups with less; and groups with class resources are individualistic whereas groups with ethnic resources are collectivistic. On this view, entrepreneurship is highest when disadvantaged immigrant minorities are well endowed with class and ethnic resources; endowment with one or the other is intermediate; and neglible endowment in both class and ethnic resources implies correspondingly low rates of entrepreneurship.

Behind this conclusion lies the assumption that immigrant minorities' rate of business ownership is a fair measure of their entrepreneurship. The rate of business ownership has been operationally defined as self-employed per 1000 in the urban labor force.[11] A major objection to this definition, it is increasingly clear, arises from the inadequacy of published statistics (Karsh, 1977; Light, 1979: 39–40; U.S. Small Business, 1980). "The Census has a completely nonsociological way of defining "self employment'" (Wright et al., 1982, p. 712n). U.S. statistics routinely exclude petty traders without fixed business premises, no-employee firms, illegally operated firms in legitimate industries, and firms producing unlawful goods or services. Since minorities and immigrants bulk is very large in such firms, their exclusion from official tabulations results in undercounts of minority-owned business enterprise as well as theoretical misperception of the whole phenomenon of ethnic entrepreneurship. No one knows how many untabulated firms exist nor what is their distribution among various sectors of the laborforce.

The case of native-born black Americans is instructive because blacks are disadvantaged but native-born. All statistical and ethnographic sources have uniformly reported that rates of business self-employment among urban blacks have been and remain lower than ever among native-white, let alone the foreign-born (Light, 1972, 1979, 1980). At the same time, ethnographic sources have stressed the importance of "hustling" as an economic activity among underclass urban blacks (Valentine, 1978; Glasgow, 1980; Light, 1977b). Hustling involves piecing together a livelihood by operating a variety of legal, semi-legal, and sometimes illegal business activities. Legal enterprises of urban blacks include street corner and door-to-door peddling of trinkets, objets d'art, junk, salvage, and fire-damaged merchandise. Unlawfully conducted legal enterprises include unlicensed taxicabs, unlicensed pharmacies, unlicensed medical services, welfare cheating, tax-evading labor services, and so forth. Illegal enterprise includes gambling administration, pimping, prostitution, narcotics vending, and other victimless crimes (Light 1977a, 1977b). Predatory crimes include armed robbery, burglary, shoplifting, and all similar activities. All these self-employed activities are entrepreneurial in that they involve risk and uncertain return (Harbison, 1956). Although comprehensive statistic are lacking, there seems little doubt that urban blacks are as over-represented in marginal legal and unlawfully operated self-employment as crime statistics indicate they are in illegal enterprise and predatory crime. Taken together, this package suggests much higher than average self-employment among economically marginal blacks in unmeasured business at the same time that official statistics reveal much lower than average self-employment in measured business.

Given the presumptively high rates of black self-employment in these undocumented industries, it is improper to conclude that native blacks are less entrepreneurial than other economically disadvantaged immigrants and ethnic minorities. It rather appears that native-born blacks have elaborated an alternative, heavily illegal, highly individualistic style of coping with protracted economic marginality. Compared with the foreign-born in general, and middleman minorites in particular, native-born blacks are low in ethnic resources of entrepreneurship, but share economic disadvantage (Wong, 1977; Light 1972; Venable, 1972). Compared with native whites, native blacks are high in economic disadvantage, low in class resources of entrepreneurship, but similar in respect to ethnic resources of entrepreneurship. Table 3 documents these contrasts. Low on ethnic resources of entrepreneurship but high in economic disadvantage, native-born blacks were compelled to depend upon class resources in which they have been under-endowed for centuries. As an overall result, marginal black enterprises have not broken into the circle of legal, officially enumerated small business enterprises. Their problem has been nonpromotion of their very large class of petty but invisible enterprises such that a visible minority enjoy upward social mobility within the legitimate, competitive sector (Glasgow, 1980). It is in the assistance of upward mobility that ethnic and class resources make themselves appreciably manifest (Gelfand, 1981). Given labor force disadvantage, chronic unemployment or both, any ethnic or immigrant minority

TABLE 3 Profiles of entrepreneurship

	Comparison groups			
	Middleman minorities	**Foreign born**	**Native blacks**	**Native whites**
Rotating credit associations	+			
Precapitalist commercial background	+			
Landsmannschaften	+	+		
Extended kinship	+	+		
Relative satisfaction	+	+		
Sojourning	+			
Unpaid family labor	+	+		
Labor force disadvantage	+	+	+	
Ineligible for public welfare	+	+		
Language barrier	+	+		
Special consumer demands	+	+		

resorts to self-employment, but only resources make possible the promotion of marginal enterprises into small businesses whose long-term profitability brings along the social mobility of proprietors, their kin, and their heirs (Wilson and Martin, 1982).

Summary and Conclusion

Uneven development has created economic enclaves within which small business can still be profitable. Success in small business requires, however, a combination of class and ethnic resources with some evidence indicating the former have increased their importance in the last generation. Nonetheless, ethnic resources persist, and immigrant and ethnic minority groups are over-represented in small business in large part because their access to ethnic resources permits them to outcompete native workers. In this comparative respect native whites and blacks are similar but the native blacks lack class resources and additionally suffer labor market disadvantage which gives them a motive to seek self-employment income. Underclass blacks do find this income in the form of hustling, but hustling has by and large failed to create firms that are large and legal enough to achieve visibility in government statistics.

Ethnic resources of enterpreneurship often depend upon premodern values and solidarities. So long as these survive in the ethnic community, coethnic business owners are able to utilize them in business, achieving advantage over fully proletarianized, native-born workers among whom blacks are conspicuous. In theory, ethnic capitalism and cultural assimilation should first undercut and then demolish precapitalism solidarities, thus eliminating an ethnic group's competitive edge in small business. In the perspective of history, this self-destruction probably occurs. However, its rate should not be exaggerated. Ethnic enterprises still earn handsome financial returns, and these substantial rewards prop up the ethnicity upon which owners depend for resources. Profitability brakes the rate of deterioration of ethnic solidarity, supports the persistence of ethnic-owned firms in the competitive sector, and perpetuates the whole competitive sector.

NOTES

1. See Gelfand, 1981; Chs. 4, 5; Goldscheider and Kobrin, 1980; Light, 1972, Ch. 5; Light and Wong, 1975; Wong, 1977; Sassen-Koob, 1981, p. 30–1; Modell, 1977; Bonacich and Modell, 1981; Lovell-Toy, 1980,1981; Chock, 1981; Sway, 1983; Sengstock, 1967; Bonacich, Light, and Won, 1977, 1979; Blackistone, 1981; Herman, 1979, p. 90; Zenner, 1982; Waldinger, 1982; Yu 1982; Bonacich and Jung, 1982.
2. "Most of the refuges are ethnic Chinese, most of whom were shopkeepers or businessmen who had little future under a communist system," "Bleak outlook for Vietnam refugees," *East/West* (San Francisco), June 20, 1979: 1. See also: Rogg, 1971, p. 480; Thompson, 1979; Wilson and Portes, 1980; Chan and Cheung, 1982; McMillan, 1982.
3. But two recent studies have produced important new documentation. In New York City's garment industry, Waldinger (1982) reported extensive and critically important utilization of ethnic networks among Dominican entrepreneurs. In Los Angeles's taxi industry, Russell (1982) documented the mutual assistance common among Soviet Jews seeking to break into the occupation.
4. A similar situation apparently exists in New York City, site of the second largest Korean settlement in the United States. See Illsoo Kim, 1981, p. 110; see also "Faced with prejudice and language difficulties, New York Koreans turn to private business," *Koreatown* (Los Angeles). December 14, 1981: 8–9.
5. "$400,000 *Kye* broce." *Joong-ang Daily News* (Los Angeles: in Korean), February 20, 1979; Kim, 1981, p. 210–11.
6. "Markets agree to cut down on competition," *Korea Times English Section* (Los Angeles), November 23, 1981: 1. "KCCI asks bizmen for more cooperation," *Korea Times English Section,* February 6, 1980; "Fifteen Korean chambers unite," *Koreatown,* November 17, 1980; "Prosperity of shops leads community development," *Korea Times English Section,* November 22, 1976.
7. Schumpeter's (193) views are endorsed in Beveridege and Oberschall, 1979, p. 207, 225, 229; criticized in Jones and Sakong, 1980, p. 211; reviewed in Hagen, 1968, p. 221–227.
8. "When individuals go into business they must be prepared to lower standards of living and make personal sacrifices until their firms begin to prosper," Cingolani, 1972.
9. See Chs. 4–10 in Cummings (ed.), 1980.
10. In the wake of extremely high interest rates, white Californians began to utilize the *Pandero,* a Brazilian rotating credit association, for purposes of home purchase. In this situation, a class-based, individualistic style reverted to old-fashioned collectivism as class resources became inadequate because of high interest rates. See DeWolfe, 1982.
11. Gerry and Birkbeq (1981) and Portes (1981) argue that marginal self-employed of the third world are 'timely disguised wage workers' because of their indirect economic dependencies upon big firms. However, Aldrich and Weiss (1981) have shown that a linear relationship exists between employment size and business owners' incomes, and linearity persists in the USA when nonemployer firms are introduced. "Owners without employees are simply the 'poorest of the poor' among small capitalists. This group . . . should be assigned to the owner class in future research."

Ethnic Resources and Ethnic Economy: The Case of Iranian Entrepreneurs in Dallas

✦ MOHSEN M. MOBASHER

ABSTRACT

The main objective of this essay is to provide an ethnographic account of Iranian ethnic economy and entrepreneurship in Dallas, Texas. It relies on ethnographic information to show (a) the various mechanisms though which the strong interrelationship between the Iranian community and the Iranian ethnic economy is created and sustained, (b) the extent to which many first generation Iranian immigrants in Dallas utilize the ethnic resources of their community to establish and operate their own businesses, and (c) the ways in which Iranian entrepreneurs utilize ethnic media in interethnic and intraethnic competition. The data presented in this article are part of a larger study on ethnic, gender, and class resource utilization by self-employed Iranian immigrants in Dallas. Data were gathered mainly through participant observation between September 1993 and August 1995. In addition, data were gathered from 485 questionnaires completed by the community members, fifty-seven questionnaires completed by Iranian business owners, and forty-five in-depth face-to-face interviews with self-employed Iranian men and women.

INTRODUCTION

The large volume of studies on the ethnic enterprise, or what Light and Gold (2000) have pertinently called "ethnic ownership economy" in advanced countries of Europe and the United States is a consequence of the recent growth of new ethnic populations and the impact of the fundamental economic and technological restructuring of American society on the employment opportunities and economic activities of immigrants and ethnic minority groups. As a result of these structural, economic, and industrial changes, some immigrants and ethnic groups have been relegated to jobs with low wages, harsh working conditions, and little or no opportunity for job mobility in the secondary sector, whereas others responded by establishing their own businesses and creating their own economy. There are significant differences, however, between the levels of entrepreneurship among different immigrant groups that cannot be explained simply by constraints in the labor market. For example, while some ethnic groups such as Koreans, Chinese, Arabs, Greeks, and Iranians demonstrate a high rate of entrepreneurship, others, such as Mexicans, Vietnamese, and Puerto Ricans, have had below-average rates of entrepreneurship (Light and Karageorgis, 1993b).

Emergence of ethnic entrepreneurship and entrance of ethnic minorities into self-employment is influenced by labor disadvantages and discrimination inflicted by members of the host society (Light, 1972, 1979, 1984), as well as cultural values of ethnic minorities such as work ethnic, frugality, future orientation, and an emphasis on profit-seeking and individual orientation (Bonacich et al., 1980; Light, 1972; Min, 1987; Wong, 1977). Sojourning status is another reason for entrance of immigrants into self-employment (Bonacich and Modell, 1980). Sojourning, Bonacich and Modell argue, awakens hostilities in the host population and enhances the formation of a separate community whose members concentrate in marginal petit bourgeois businesses—notably trade, petty finance, and money handling.

Entrance into and success in small business depends upon the use of class and ethnic resources (Bonacich, 1975; Thompson, 1979; Light, 1984; Chan and Cheung, 1985; Kim and Hurh, 1985; Min and Jaret, 1985; Portes and Bach, 1985; Portes, 1987; Wong, 1987; Zimmer and Aldrich, 1987; Light and Bonacich, 1988; Min, 1988; Waldinger, 1988; 1989; Yoon, 1991; Lee, 1992; Light et al., 1993; Tseng, 1994), as well as access to networks of contacts and ethnic institutions (Light, 1972; Boissevain and Grotenbreg 1987; Portes, 1987; Zimmer and Aldrich, 1987; Aldrich and Waldinger, 1990; Waldinger et al., 1990).

Light (1984) defines class resources as "private property in the means of production and distribution, human capital, and money to invest" (p.201). In their definition of class resources Light and Karageorgis (1993) distinguish between cultural and the material endowment of the bourgeoisie. By material endowment of class, they mean private property, wealth, capital to invest, and human capital. The cultural endowment, however, includes the vocational culture of the bourgeoisie as well as its status culture. Whereas class resources are available only to a segment of an ethnic group whose social and economic position in society has enabled them to invest in human capital or to inherit these resources from their parents, ethnic resources are available to every member of an ethnic group who shares the common origin and culture. Kinship and marital systems, trust, social capital, cultural assumptions, religion, language, rotating credit associations, entrepreneurial values and attitudes, reactive solidarities, acculturation lag, sojourning orientation, social networks, ethnic solidarity ideology, a middleman heritage, and underemployed and disadvantaged coethnic workers are among some of the typical ethnic resources identified by researchers (Light and Karageorgis, 1993; Light and Bonacich, 1988). Ethnic resources are used in all aspects of the business establishment and operation from raising capital, to recruiting labor, to dealing with customers and clients. Access to ethnic resources is much easier among ethnic groups with stronger ethnic ties (Bonacich, 1973; Goldscheider and Kobrin, 1980; Kim and Hurh, 1985; Light, 1972, 1980; Lovell-Troy, 1980, 1981; Min, 1988; Waldinger, 1984, 1989).

There is growing evidence that self-employment has played an important role in the economic adaptation of the newly arrived Iranian immigrants in the United States. Like several earlier immigrant groups in the United States, such as Jews, Chinese, Italians, Greeks, and others, Iranians' proportionately higher involvement in entrepreneurial activities differentiates them from much of the native population. According to Waldinger et al.(1990), Iranians are among the top twenty-five immigrants with high self-employment rate. In Los Angeles, the percentage of Iranians in self-employment is about 56.8 percent (Light et al., 1993). Similarly, close to 56 percent of the working Iranian men and women in Dallas are self-employed and run some kind of business (Mobasher, 1996). Like most other immigrant groups, Iranians often rely on ethnic and class resources to establish an enterprise. This essay provides an ethnographic overview of Iranian ethnic economy with emphasis on ethnic resources. Particular attention is given to the Iranian ethnic media and its significant role in introducing the ethnic businesses to the ethnic community, integrating and expanding the Iranian ethnic economy through advertising for ethnic business products and services as well as employment and business opportunities, linking the Iranian ethnic economy and the Iranian community, and functioning as a crucial tool for ethnic entrepreneurs in their interethnic and intraethnic competition.

Iranian Migration Trends to the United States

Immigration of Iranians to the United States has a relatively short history and Iranians are among the most recent new immigrant groups in this country. Although the earliest data reported for Iranian immigrants by the Immigration and Naturalization Service (INS) are for the fiscal years 1921–1930, all available published reports from the INS indicate that Iranian immigration to the United States before 1950 was negligible. Between 1921 and 1950 a total of 1,816 Iranian residents immigrated to the United States. This number increased to 13,727 between 1951 and 1970. Between 1971 and 1979, the average number of Iranian immigrants who were admitted to the United States was 3,563 per year. In 1980 alone, 10,410 Iranian immigrants were admitted to the United States. During the fiscal years 1981–1990, the average annual number of Iranian immigrants doubled, reaching 12, 624 per year. In general, the Iranian migration to the United States could be said to have occured in three phases:

1. The prerevolutionary period (1950–1977)
2. The revolutionary period (1978)
3. The postrevolutionary period (1979–present)

The first period was characterized by a heavy concentration of Iranian professionals and students. This was followed by a rise in religious minorities and high-ranking officers during the revolutionary period, and by refugees and immediate family members of the naturalized citizens in the postrevolutionary period. Overall, compared with the prerevolutionary and the revolutionary immigrants, the postrevolutionary Iranian immigrants were a more heterogeneous group with diverse sociocultural backgrounds, religious affiliations, political orientations, family situations, and age distribution. As a result the Iranian community in the United States changed from a population composed of dispersed Iranian sojourners and temporary migrants (students, interns) to a community of nonreturnee middle- and upper-class professionals, refugees, and entrepreneurs. This set the stage for the gradual emergence of a number of ethnic institutions such as the ethnic media, ethnic language classes for the second generation, and professional associations.

Geographically, Iranians in the United States are concentrated in a few states and metropolitan areas. According to the 1980 census, more than 50 percent of Iranians reside in

California. The second and the third largest concentrations of Iranians are in New York and Texas respectively. Although these areas contain the majority of the Iranian population in the United States, Iranians tend to be dispersed widely throughout all states: Virginia (7,957), Maryland (7,924), Illinois (5,189), Florida (4,753), New Jersey (4,053), Massachusetts (3,895), and Washington (2,742) ranked fourth through tenth respectively as recipients of Iranian immigrants (Bureau of Census, 1990).

Iranian Immigrants and Iranian Community in Dallas

Much like other Iranian communities in the United States, the Iranian community in Dallas has a relatively short history and is only about quarter of a century old. The exact number of Iranians in Dallas is unknown. Likewise, the earliest data for Iranian migration to Dallas is unascertainable. The bulk of Iranian immigrants, however, have come to Dallas in four waves. The first wave occurred between 1976 and 1978 and was composed of students who came directly from large cities in Iran. The second wave came from 1980 to 1983. Like those in the first-wave, most second-wave Iranians who came to Dallas were students. However, unlike the first-wave immigrants who came directly from Iran, most second-wave Iranian immigrants came from colleges in small cities of Texas and the adjacent states. The third wave of Iranian immigrants arrived in Dallas from 1983 to 1987 and was composed mostly of refugees who had emigrated from Iran shortly after the revolution and lived in another country for several years prior to their entrance. Finally, the fourth wave of Iranian immigration to Dallas started in 1986 and continues today. Unlike the first three groups who came to Dallas primarily as students and refugees, Iranian immigrants of the fourth wave are parents, siblings, fiancees, or spouses of naturalized Iranian immigrants.

Being latecomers, Iranians in Dallas, much like Iranians in other major cities in the United States, are largely young and foreign-born. Nevertheless, despite the dispersion and lack of an Iranian enclave or "Little Iran," Iranians in Dallas have developed modern forms of associations and institutions through which they can express their ethnic identity and maintain their nonspatial community. Through the Internet and similar computer networks, Iranians of various ages, professional, religious, and political groups have been able to create a symbolic community within which cultural, economic, and political news about Iran and Iranian immigrants are circulated and discussed. Other institutions and cultural symbols such as the Iranian media; the Iranian Yellow Pages and Directory of Texas; Persian language programs; informal and professional associations; Persian concerts, plays, lectures, and poetry reading nights; Persian feasts and celebrations such as "Now-Ruz" or the Spring Festival; film festivals; and religious organizations constitute some important means for facilitating social interaction among the dispersed Iranian immigrants in Dallas. Moreover, these ethnic institutions, as well as the numerous social and cultural activities, help Iranian immigrants to fulfill some of their needs, express their ethnic identity, and preserve their culture. In summary, these ethnic institutions indicate that despite the absence of an Iranian neighborhood there is an Iranian ethnic community in Dallas.

Iranian Ethnic Economy, Market Orientation, and Utilization of Ethnic Resources by Iranian Entrepreneurs in Dallas

The Iranian ethnic economy in Dallas is a relatively recent phenomenon. Until 1986 there were only a handful of Iranian businesses in the city. In the early stages of its development in the 1980s, other than an Iranian grocery store and a few small restaurants that served Persian food on weekends, the Iranian ethnic economy was largely limited to a small number of nonethnic restaurants and Persian rug stores scattered throughout the city. With the exception of the Iranian grocery stores, most of the Iranian businesses were oriented toward the larger market of the American society. Moreover, due to their nature, these businesses never generated a community network. Community networks are more likely to develop through ethnic restaurants and grocery stores where community members interact with one another and exchange community news. With the demographic expansion of the Iranian community and its ethnic institutions, and with the growth of more ethnic establishments such as grocery stores and ethnic restaurants, a community began to emerge. The emergence of Iranian ethnic community, ethnic institutions, and networks during the last decade has generated the infrastructure and resources for development and expansion of Iranian-owned businesses in Dallas. Today, the Iranian business community encompasses more than 500 small and large businesses, in all types of activities, from multimillion dollar Oriental rug stores with tens of employees to individually operated photo shops, accounting firms, and engineering companies. A large number of these business establishments have an ethnic market orientation and serve predominantly Iranian clienteles. Others are oriented exclusively toward non-Iranian clienteles. Still others have a mixed market and serve both Iranian and non-Iranian clienteles. The use of ethnic resources, particularly the Persian language media by Iranian entrepreneurs, is largely affected by the type and market orientation of the enterprise and its link to the Iranian community.

Enterprises with ethnic clientele. Enterprises in this category provide what Light (1972) calls a "protected market." Ethnic grocery stores, ethnic restaurants, tax accountants, translation agencies, entertainers, and educational businesses that offer Persian language and Persian music classes are some examples of businesses with ethnic clientele. As indicated before, enterprises with ethnic clientele were among the first businesses established at the early stage of the formation of the Iranian community in Dallas. Thus, the origin and popularity of these enterprises is linked to demographic and cultural factors. Without exception, the history of establishment of these enterprises throughout the United States parallels the immigration of thousands of Iranian immigrants into the United States during the postrevolutionary period. Furthermore, these enterprises provide goods and services specifically directed toward ethnic taste, need, and unique features of the Iranian culture that American enterprises do not provide.

Businesses with ethnic clientele have more attachment to the ethnic community, rely on and use more ethnic resources for their operation, and interact more with coethnics. Consequently, they have access to a wider network for community news and information. Moreover, for advertising and hiring purposes, these businesses are strongly woven into a network of ethnic institutions, particularly the ethnic media.

During the first stages of the development of the Iranian community during the 1980s, when major ethnic institutions and community centers were underdeveloped, Iranian businesses with ethnic clientele, particularly, ethnic grocery stores and restaurants, played a significant role in the development of the Iranian community and provided a multitude of cultural, social, and economic services throughout the community in Dallas. In addition to providing ethnic items, Iranian ethnic grocery stores have been the nucleus of the Iranian community in many other ways. Virtually every cultural and social event in the Iranian community, whether major, such as the New Year celebration concert, or minor, such as a small poetry reading night, is promoted and publicized in these stores. Promoting a particular event, however, depends on the relationship between the store owner and the event's sponsor. Moreover, the ethnic grocery stores have helped many newly arrived immigrants to find housing and employment. They also have functioned as an information center, providing names and telephone numbers of immigration attorneys, major government institutions, and community specialists such as entertainers, religious leaders, and advisers. In addition to their social services, ethnic grocery stores have been providing many commercial services, such as exchanging money and sending immigrants' remittances to Iran.

Provision of these services has not been limited to the ethnic grocery store. Iranian restaurants also have played significant social, cultural, and economic roles in the community life of Iranian immigrants. These establishments are the arenas for social exchange between widely scattered people and groups. At lunchtime, the patrons receive and pass on news regarding community events, businesses, and so on. For many self-employed Iranians, these restaurants are convenient places to meet friends and clients and discuss business. Although the Iranian grocery stores and restaurants in Dallas have had a different history of establishment, and differ in their level of involvement with the Iranian community, all of them have a vested interest in the community affairs and play a significant role in the political, cultural, social, and economic occurrences within the community.

One of the major characteristics of the Iranian business with coethnic orientation in Dallas is the prevalence of severe intraethnic competition. This competition is more conspicuous among Iranian grocery stores and restaurants. It results mainly from the heavy dependency of the few Iranian restaurants and grocery stores on a limited pool of Iranian customers in the community. One way to cope with this competition in the ethnic market is regular extensive advertisement in the local Iranian mass media. Another way is horizontal integration between Iranian grocery stores and restaurants and other ethnic institutions such as professional associations. This horizontal integration is formed through direct participation of business owners in such community events as the new year celebration and the lecture series sponsored by professional associations. By donating money and time to these community events, Iranian grocery stores and restaurants find an opportunity to proclaim monetary and moral support of the community and gain respect, reputation, and customers in the community. This is evident in one of the ads that was printed in an issue of one of the local Iranian magazines. Although the magazine is printed in Persian, the entire ad was in English. The ad is reprinted as it appeared in the local magazine. (Notion of "xxx" in the following ads is used to replace specific names of businesses that the author chooses to suppress.)

> "xxx". Established 1980. FOR THOSE WHO CARE FOR QUALITY, SERVICE AND SELECTION.
>
> We cater to and care for Iranian and Iranian-American community with many years of experience.
>
> We have participated financially and morally in more than 300 Iranian community events from seminars to educational, cultural, fund-raisers, art, music, sport, special occasions, new year, seezda-be-dar and. . . . Still doing the same with more energy and understanding which constitutes the backbone of this small institution. We are best known for our quality, flavor and flair. What makes "xxx" different and apart from others, it's not the price of cheese, it is the understanding that we have for the very articulate and advanced Iranian and Iranian-American community. As we are getting close to the New Year we take pride in wishing you a happy new year and merry Christmas.

Like the Iranian magazines, the local Iranian radios are ethnic resources that are exclusively used by Iranian businesses. The following commercials are representative of business commercials broadcast by local radio stations. Despite the variation in tone and length they reveal how ethnicity is used as a medium for interethnic competition in economic activities. The business commercial from an ethnic grocery store follows:

> "xxx", the little house of *Iran* welcomes your arrival. "xxx" with 15 years of experience in the *Iranian community*, gatherer of the best food supplies, with the highest quality, is always ready to serve you. All seasonal fruits, fresh daily, with the most suitable prices: slender *Iranian* eggplant priced at .99 cent per pound, best quality dried cherries, top quality barberries, $7.99 per pound. Visit "xxx" and become familiar with our daily prices. Here are some our prices: pita bread, two for .99 cents, Royal rice, 11 pound bag $6.55, Bulgarian feta cheese $2.60 per pound, Ice cream .50 during the week, cooking ware and wedding and other gift items made in Italy. "xxx" is the largest distribution center of *Iranian* publications, cassettes, compact discs, and *Persian* videos in Dallas. Social services of "xxx" in *Iranian community* include exchange of money at no charge and the best rate without mediator in the shortest time. Wedding ceremonial table spread, gold coin, and organizer of your gatherings and meetings at the best hotels in Dallas, and the best floral decorations for your ceremonies. Work hours from Monday through Saturday 9:00 AM to 9:00 PM. Sundays, 11:00 AM to 7:00 PM

As illustrated in this commercial, the ethnic media provides an opportunity for ethnic entrepreneurs to advertise their goods and services as well as their commitment and loyalty to the immigrant community. Moreover, Iranian customers are constantly reminded of how the atmosphere of these places help to revive pleasant memories of Iran.

In addition to competition with coethnic competitors, Iranian entrepreneurs engage in interethnic competition with other non-Iranian entrepreneurs who are in the same line of business. This competition is most apparent in the ethnic grocery business. Between 1986 and the more recent time when the number of Iranian-owned grocery stores and restaurants began to grow there was very minimal competition between Iranian and non-Iranian entrepreneurs. Today, however, with the expansion of the Iranian community both quantitatively and qualitatively, there is a considerable hostility between the Iranian grocery stores/merchants and non-Iranian merchants who sell the same ethnic products engendered primarily by economic competition for the Iranian dollars. A large Indo-European whole food mart owned by a Pakistani is located about 5 miles to the east of a cluster of Iranian grocery stores and offers a stock of products that overlap with the Iranian store's offerings. Consequently, the owners of the Iranian grocery stores fear a substantial decline of business. To increase demand the new non-Iranian entrepreneurs have lowered prices, and are conducting vigorous advertising campaigns in the Iranian community through the Iranian media. This has caused several of the well-established Iranian grocery stores to do likewise in order to keep pace. The new non-Iranian entrepreneurs are considered by the Iranian grocery owners to be ignorant of the Iranian community as a whole, preoccupied with their large-scale enterprises, and unconcerned with the general welfare of the community. One strategy adopted by the Iranian merchants to compete against the non-Iranian merchants is to expand their community participation beyond the realm of economic activities and exercise power in the social and political spheres of the community life. As such, the owners of Iranian businesses resort to such means of social control as gossip to delegitimize and destroy the reputation of non-Iranian business owners in the eye of the general Iranian population. As indicated in the following ad, to win the economic competition, Iranian business owners emphasize common ethnicity and nationality in their ads, and use that to encourage Iranians to buy their ethnic supplies from the Iranian businesses.

> As previously announced, our dear fellow compatriots do not have to shop at non-Iranian food marts for lower prices. The best items at a very low price in an entirely Iranian atmosphere, at the heart of Dallas are available to dear fellow Iranian citizens at "xxx" everyday. . . . "xxx" supermarket is the center for the distribution of the most reputable Iranian publications printed world wide, Iranian audio cassettes, CDs, videos, fresh pastries, ice cream and the best cook wear. "xxx" better than any place, cheaper than any place. Working hours are every day from 9:00 AM to 10:00 PM.

In sum, Iranian businesses in Dallas are not immune from the other competitors who are in the same line of businesses. The existence of other ethnic competitors who provide the same ethnic goods and services with lower prices has caused many Iranian enterprises to lose a significant number of their coethnic clients.

Enterprises with nonethnic clientele. In addition to enterprises that mainly cater to Iranian immigrants, the Iranian ethnic economy in Dallas consists of enterprises that go beyond the boundaries of the ethnic community for their survival. Since the main pool of customers for these businesses are non-Iranian populations, the use of ethnic resources by these enterprises is very selective and minimal. The only ethnic resources that are commonly used by enterprises in this category are coethnic employees and ethnic networks for partnership arrangements. In general, compared with businesses with ethnic clientele, businesses with nonethnic clientele are more likely to rely on class resources such as capital, personal skills, and educational or professional training than ethnic resources for business start up and operation.

Unlike ethnic enterprises with ethnic customers that are strongly present and visible in the ethnic community, ethnic enterprises with nonethnic clientele tend to be removed from the ethnic community and its affairs. Ethnic enterprises with nonethnic clients can be divided into subcategories considering the nature of the enterprise and individual skills of the entrepreneurs: (1) white-collar enterprises such as various engineering firms, and (2) blue-collar enterprises such as nonethnic restaurants, gasoline stations, convenience stores, and cab companies. Although similar in market orientation, these two enterprise subcategories are extremely different in operation, and in the demographic characteristics of their proprietors. Whereas self-employed Iranians who own a white-collar firm put in fewer hours and enjoy the luxury of a two-day weekend rest from work, proprietors of blue-collar ethnic firms put in more hours and work much harder. Compared with self-employed Iranians in blue-collar ethnic firms, white-collar entrepreneurs have higher levels of education and language skills. Moreover, they usually establish a firm after obtaining a college degree in the United States and working for another firm in the primary sector of the market. Whereas the blue-collar enterprises turn into self-employment mainly because of low educational skills, insufficient qualifications for a white-collar job, and language barrier, owners of the white-collar ethnic enterprises turn to self-employment mainly because of blocked mobility in the primary sector of the labor market. Finally, because the owners of the white-collar firms possess such class resources as educational and occupational skills, use of ethnic resources for operation of these firms is irrelevant and insignificant.

Ethnic enterprises with mixed customers. Iranian enterprises in this category are typical American small businesses such as photo labs, print shops, mechanic shops, jewelry stores, beauty-care salons, and repair shops. These mixed-customer oriented business enterprises constitute the largest portion of the Iranian ethnic economy in Dallas. This is the only sector of the Iranian ethnic economy in which the proprietors seem to have had some previous experience before emigration from Iran. In addition to proprietors with previous experience, this sector of the Iranian ethnic economy is also dominated by immigrants who immigrated to the United States as students, who were unable to find a desirable job in their respective educational fields.

In general, proprietors of these enterprises rely on both ethnic and class resources for their survival. Nevertheless, the significance of the ethnic and class resources changes over the course of business development. Due to their reliance on both the nonethnic and the coethnic customers, these enterprises advertise in the ethnic community as well as in the host community. However, advertising in the ethnic community tends to be sporadic and is often done through various ethnic media sources. Nevertheless, many of the business owners whom I interviewed indicated that they get most of their ethnic customers through word of mouth and referrals by networks of friends. Advertising in the host community, however, is done mainly through the local business guides and coupon books for various business enterprises.

Compared with ethnic enterprises in the first two categories, ethnic enterprises in this category have a stronger desire to hire nonethnic employees for customer relations and marketing positions. In almost all of the enterprises within this category that I surveyed there was at least one full-time American employee. Results of interviews with owners of these enterprises confirmed my field observations.

Conclusion

Like most other immigrant groups, Iranians often rely on ethnic and class resources to establish an enterprise. The analysis of ethnic resource use by Iranian entrepreneurs reveals two major findings. First, use of ethnic resources is affected by the type and market orientation of the enterprise. Second, Iranian entrepreneurs rely considerably less on traditional ethnic resources, such as rotating credit associations, in their business activities. Instead, they rely significantly on such modern ethnic resources and institutions as the ethnic media. With the exception of a few studies (Kim, 1987; Light and Bonacich, 1988), the interrelation between the ethnic media and the ethnic economy is largely unexplored in the literature of ethnic entrepreneurship. As is indicated in the case of Iranian immigrants in Dallas, the ethnic media may be considered as a crucial ingredient of immigrant communities and ethnic economies. Iranian ethnic mass media not only contributes to ethnic cohesion and cultural maintenance, it is also used as a marketing tool for ethnic entrepreneurs in their interethnic and intraethnic competition.

Information about the type and location of Iranian businesses conveyed through the local ethnic media sources helps to expand and strengthen the ethnic economy in many ways. First, it increases the participation of the business in the community by publicizing its services, and by calling attention to its importance in the community. Second, it increases the interaction between coethnics and the business owners. Third, it facilitates employment opportunities within the ethnic economy. Finally, it facilitates the potential economic advancement of ethnic entrepreneurs.

This ethnographic case study suggests that ethnic entrepreneurs with businesses that are oriented toward the ethnic market play a decisive role in linking the ethnic economy to the ethnic community. They maintain and reinforce this link mainly through participation in community activities and extensive reliance on ethnic media sources. These ethnic media sources have not only been instrumental in strengthening the ethnic economy and linking it to the ethnic community, but also in promoting and enhancing the significance of Iranian ethnic identity and Iranian culture in exile. In almost every business ad and commercial such words as *Iran, Iranian,*

Persian, Iranian community, Iranian compatriots, Iranian nationality, and *Iranian culture* are used and manipulated as an important basis for economic transaction between the business owners and the coethnic customers.

The tie between the ethnic economy and the ethnic community has economic, social, and political consequences for owners of ethnic businesses. For one thing, it increases their access to a protected ethnic market and a pool of coethnic labor. Moreover, by using patriotic lingo (words such as *dear fellow citizens* and *compatriots*) in business ads, ethnic businesses promote and strengthen ethnic identity, ethnic culture, and group consciousness in diaspora. In turn, increased ethnic identity and consciousness promotes support of the ethnic businesses when competing with noncoethnic business owners. Finally, through participation in activities that are sponsored by ethnic institutions such as professional associations, ethnic entrepreneurs advertise their business, secure their status within the community, and gain advantage over rival owners inside and outside of the ethnic community. Table 1 summarizes the link between ethnic economy, ethnic community, and use of ethnic resources based on market orientation of Iranian businesses. As indicated in Table 1, the white-collar Iranian businesses that are oriented toward non-Iranian customers are less likely to rely on coethnic workers, ethnic institutions, and coethnic customers than ethnically oriented businesses such as ethnic restaurants.

TABLE 1 Diversity of Iranian businesses in Dallas-Fort Worth metropolitan area

			Non-Ethnic Clientele	
	Ethnic Clientele	**Mixed Clientele**	**White Collar**	**Blue Collar**
Example	ethnic grocery stores and restaurants, educational and social services	photo labs, repair shops, beauty salons, insurance agencies, beauty-care salons	engineering firms, medical and financial services	nonethnic restaurants, convenience stores, gasoline stations, and cab companies
Community Attachment & Integration	high	moderate	low	low
Reliance on Coethnic Workers	high	low	low	high
Reliance on Coethnic Customers	high	moderate	low	low
Reliance on Ethnic Institutions	high	moderate	low	low

The Sociology of Immigration: From Assimilation to Segmented Integration, from the American Experience to the Global Arena

✦ BARBARA SCHMITTER HEISLER

Theory and research in international migration have centered on two basic sets of questions: Why does migration occur and how is it sustained over time? What happens to the migrants in the receiving societies and what are the economic, social, and political consequences of their presence? Historically sociologists have focused primarily on the second set of questions, leaving the first to economists and demographers. More recently, beginning roughly in the 1980s, however, sociologists have also paid increasing attention to the first set.

Immigration theory and research have a long history in sociology, compared with other social sciences. Harking back to the beginnings of the discipline in the United States, immigration and its consequences were among the central themes pursued by the Chicago School of Sociology.[1] Indeed, the assimilation perspective, pioneered by members of the Chicago School in the 1920s and 1930s and refined by their students in the following three decades, remained the dominant sociological paradigm until the late 1960s. Postulating assimilation as the eventual outcome of "all the incidental collision, conflict, and fusions of peoples and cultures" resulting from migration (Park, 1928), the assimilation perspective could not explain the "resurgence" of ethnicity and the persistence of racial inequality and conflict that were becoming increasingly apparent at that time.[2]

While earlier research by Reeves-Kennedy (1944, 1952), Herberg (1956), and, in particular, Glazer and Moynihan

Schmitter Heisler, Barbara. 2000. "The sociology of immigration: From assimilation to segmented integration, from the American experience to the global arena" in *Migration Theory: Talking Across Disciplines,* eds. Caroline B. Brettell and James F. Hollifield, pp. 77–95. Routledge: New York. Reproduced by permission of Routledge, Inc., part of the Taylor & Francis Group.

(1963) had raised some questions concerning the Chicago School's optimistic contention that new immigrants would eventually move up the occupational hierarchy, lose their cultural distinctiveness, and blend into the dominant culture, it was not until the late 1970s and early 1980s that sociologists seriously challenged the dominant assimilationist trajectory. As immigration has become a pressing issue around the world, the past two decades have witnessed a virtual explosion of theory and research. Until the mid-1980s, however, most theoretically informed work focused on the United States, the *sine qua non* of immigration countries. Responding to the recognition that migration had become a worldwide phenomenon involving transformations on a global scale (Castles and Miller, 1998), more recent work has increasingly included comparative, transnational, and global perspectives.

Although sociologists have not developed an encompassing theory of immigration, today the field is characterized by considerable theoretical vigor. Yet, a casual survey of the rapidly growing body of work produced by sociologists reveals a rather persistent, albeit gradually narrowing, division of labor between scholars who study American immigration and those who engage in more comparative research. As was the case for the Chicago School, scholars of American immigration are located at the center of the sociological enterprise, and although these scholars have developed a variety of new theories and models, the basic questions guiding their research do not differ substantially from those asked by the sociologists who first devoted systematic attention to immigration. On the whole, scholars who follow a more comparative research agenda have asked different questions, questions that have led them to make increasing contact with other social sciences, in particular, political science and anthropology; that is, they are much more likely "to talk across disciplines."

The purpose of this chapter is to provide a broad overview of the development and current state of sociological theory.[3] Given that the field is characterized by considerable diversity, I organize my discussion around the major theoretical perspectives. My discussion is informed by the conviction that a fuller understanding of the multifarious and increasingly important issues raised by international migration and its consequences calls for increased comparative and cross-disciplinary theory and analysis.

American Exceptionalism? Immigration and Immigrant Incorporation in the United States

As sociological theory of immigration and immigrant incorporation has moved away from the assimilation perspective in the 1970s, the models and concepts have changed considerably since Robert Park first formulated his race relations cycle (Park and Burgess, 1921)[4] and W. I. Thomas and Florian Znaniecki wrote their seminal work *The Polish Peasant in Europe and America* (1927). Yet, the primary focus of research and the main questions asked by these students of American immigration still inform current work.

While more recent work has been more deliberately policy oriented, research and theory on immigration remain rooted in the social-problems-oriented approach associated with the Chicago School, which has been a persistent theme in American sociology. Thus, the driving research questions continue to center on the processes of immigrant incorporation (or nonincorporation, as the case may be). What has changed are the conceptualizations and understanding of these processes, from a single process leading to the eventual assimilation of all immigrants to the dominant American culture to what

Alejandro Portes has called "segmented assimilation" (1995a; Portes and Zhou, 1993), referring to assimilation into different existing cultures.[5] The main laboratories for empirical observations, which had already moved from Chicago to New York in the 1950s and 1960s, now include the new centers of immigration, Los Angeles and Miami.

More important for the discussion at hand, in the past twenty-five years we can identify several conceptual and analytic shifts in the study of immigrant incorporation in the United States: (1) a shift from focusing on immigrants and their efforts to adapt to their new environment, toward focusing on the interaction between immigrants and the structure of American society; (2) a shift from an undifferentiated and amorphous conceptualization of the latter to one that takes into account existing economic (in particular, labor market), ethnic and class structures and inequalities; (3) a shift from focusing primarily on cultural variables to emphasizing structural/economic variables, that is, the conditions of labor markets and the skills of immigrants; and (4) a shift from a single model identifying various steps or stages in the process of incorporation (i.e., assimilation) to the coexistence of several models, projecting a variety of conditions and possible outcomes.

These changes represent responses to the apparent failure of the assimilation model to explain the "resurgence" of ethnicity and the persistence of racial inequality and conflict in the late 1960s and early 1970s. Part of the failure can be attributed to the assumptions built into the assimilation model in particular the assumption of what Herbert Gans has called "straight-line assimilation" (Gans, 1973; 1992).[6] Rejecting the assimilation model as ideologically rooted in Anglo conformity, naïve images of the melting pot and out of touch with contemporary realities (Alba and Nee, 1997),[7] sociologists responded by developing several new models of immigrant incorporation. These models are decidedly more structural, focusing less on the immigrants themselves (e.g., on "the anguish of becoming American" [Agueros et al., 1971]), but on the process of interaction between host society institutions and structures and the characteristics of newcomers.

Although the claims made by the newer models have tended to be more modest and less sweeping, the question asked did not change substantially. What changed fundamentally were the images of the host society. While the assimilation perspective portrayed American society as a rather amorphous, homogeneous entity, an absorbent sponge, the newer theories gave shape to this amorphous entity. They pointed out that the sponge is structured and that the structure itself is subject to change.

Although Milton Gordon's (1964) influential multidimensional assimilation model identified several barriers to the assimilation process, the barriers identified were those associated with primary group affiliations. The larger institutional structures (e.g., labor markets, political and educational institutions), identified as crucial barriers by the postassimilation models, were hardly considered important. Gordon also took for granted what immigrants were assimilating to—namely, middle-class American cultural patterns—which, in turn, remained largely unaffected, barring some minor changes at the margins, such as food or recreational patterns (Alba and Nee, 1997).[8] In line with the then-dominant functionalist perspective on social mobility, Gordon perceived eventual assimilation and upward mobility as the movement of individuals, not groups. Thus, Gordon's model did not consider the possibility that entire groups may be moving or that ethnic boundaries themselves may be shifting over time.

While recognizing these obvious shortcomings of the assimilation model, recently several scholars have called for its rehabilitation

(Alba and Nee, 1997; Morawska, 1994). Discarding the model's ideological baggage, and in particular the proposition that assimilation is a universal outcome, Alba and Nee have argued persuasively that the assimilation model remains useful for studying social processes that occur spontaneously. As part of "the theoretical tool kit" (p. 863), this model allows for the recognition that American culture is mixed and that elements of minority cultures are absorbed into the mainstream.[9]

The Renaissance of Ethnicity and the New Immigration: Enclaves and Niches

While the idea of the single "melting pot" suggested by the assimilationist perspective had been questioned by the research of Reeve Kennedy and Herberg in the 1940s and 1950s and subjected to further empirical analysis in the early 1960s (Glazer and Moynihan, 1963), the more recent literature on immigrant incorporation suggests the existence of multiple "melting pots," or rather multiple processes, or modes of incorporation. Unlike the "triple melting pot" identified by Glazer and Moynihan in the 1960s, more recent conceptualizations of the processes of incorporation are not defined in religious/cultural terms, but rather in terms of economic activity, industry, labor markets and socioeconomic position. While the newer models differ from each other, their common essence is best captured by the concept "ethnic communities."

Taking their initial cues from the experiences of Asian immigrants, Edna Bonacich's middleman minority model (Bonacich, 1973; Bonacich and Modell, 1980) and Ivan Light's (Light, 1972; Light and Bonacich, 1988) ethnic entrepreneur/ethnic economy model represent the pioneering work in this area. More recent models are the ethnic enclave economy model and the ethnic niche model. Although "ethnic community" models are rooted in different theoretical perspectives and thus identify somewhat different types of ethnic community structures, they all recognize the ethnic community as a distinct mode of immigrant incorporation.

While the fact that some immigrant groups (in particular Chinese, Japanese, and Jews) were over-represented in small-business activity had long been recognized, the middleman minority theory provided systematic answers to this fact. Eschewing a more obvious cultural explanation, Bonacich identifies the systematic exclusion of some immigrants from mainstream employment as the main cause for their position as small-scale traders and merchants. Positioned between mainstream producers and consumers, middleman minorities occupy a distinctive class position "that is of no special use to the ruling class," and act as a go-between to more subordinate groups (Bonacich, 1980, pp. 14–15). Although Bonacich linked the success of middleman minorities to their social solidarity, as a Marxist she was more concerned with their distinctive class position. Using the model in their study of Japanese Americans, Bonacich and Modell (1980) found that the social solidarity that had helped to establish success in the first generation was eroding in the second generation as many Japanese moved into the professions, suggesting that ethnic solidarity was primarily a temporary and situational phenomenon.

Less indebted to a Marxist perspective, Light's immigrant (ethnic) entrepreneur model (1979, 1984) more directly underlines the immigrant nature of ethnic enterprise, where the very experience of immigration produces a reactive solidarity (that did not exist before immigration) that becomes a resource for members of the group. Here, the sociocultural and demographic features of a group (e.g., entrepreneurial heritage, values, and attitudes), a multiplex of social networks and underemployed and disadvantaged coethnic workers, manifest themselves as ethnic resources that provide advantages to the group (Light and Rosenstein, 1995).

Based on extensive research in the Cuban community in Miami, Alejandro Portes and his colleagues and students (Portes and Bach, 1985; Portes and Manning, 1986; Portes and Rumbaut, 1990; Wilson and Portes, 1980) developed the ethnic enclave economy model in the late 1980s. In contrast to the previous two models, the ethnic enclave economy model is rooted in dual or segmented labor market theory, which postulates the existence of two separate and distinct labor markets, a primary labor market of good jobs, decent wages, and secure employment and the secondary labor market of unskilled jobs, poor wages, and insecure employment (Edwards, Reich, and Gordon 1975; Piore 1979). Lacking the necessary skills for primary labor market employment and facing discrimination, immigrants are typically confined to employment in the secondary labor market where they are exploited as cheap labor and, in stark contrast to the assimilation perspective, have few opportunities for social mobility. For some immigrant groups, however, the ethnic enclave economy provides an alternative to the secondary labor market. Employment in the enclave economy offers some protection from the vicissitudes of the secondary labor market and a variety of advantages in terms of language and training opportunities (Portes and Bach, 1985).[10]

The characteristics of the ethnic enclave economy differ from those associated with middleman minorities and immigrant entrepreneurs. Unlike the previous two models, an ethnic enclave economy is characterized by the spatial concentration of the immigrant group and by considerable within-group stratification. These characteristics give rise to clustered networks of businesses owned by group members. While ethnic business initially serves the culturally defined needs of coethnics, it branches out to serve the larger community. The key elements of ethnic enclaves are spatial clustering (Portes and Jensen, 1989) and sectoral specialization (i.e., Cubans in Miami were found to be in five manufacturing sectors). Thus, unlike middlemen minorities or ethnic enterprise, the ethnic enclave economy is economically diversified, including all types of business, trade, and industrial production. Not all immigrations produce ethnic enclave economies. Indeed, studies suggest that they are rather difficult to create (Logan et al., 1994). Success depends on the size of the ethnic group, the group's level of entrepreneurial skills, capital resources, and the availability of less skilled coethnics.

Building on Lieberson's (1980) pioneering historical study of ethnic succession in urban labor markets, Roger Waldinger and his associates developed the ethnic niche model (Waldinger, 1996; Waldinger and Bozorghmer, 1996). This model is based on the observation that concentrations of immigrant employment are not limited to trade (as is the case for middleman minorities), or trade and small business (as is the case for ethnic enterprise), or trade and a variety of businesses (as is the case for the ethnic enclave economy), but can also be found in public-sector employment. In short, the existence of ethnic niches does not require immigrant entrepreneurs.

As is the case for the previous models, occupational ethnic niches develop from the interaction between the immigrant group and the larger society. Ethnic niches emerge when an ethnic group is able to colonize a particular sector of employment in such a way that group members have privileged access to new job openings, while restricting the access of outsiders. Ethnic niches emerge in every market economy where jobs are ranked according to the principles of desirability and availability.[11] In the United States, such rankings have been strongly influenced by a racial and ethnic pecking order, creating a queue. Immigrants are typically located at the bottom of the queue. Changes in the economy affect the queue, creating vacancies for social mobility and new spaces for new immigrants. Waldinger's research in New York and Los Angeles seems to demonstrate the continued importance of ethnic niches as a dimension of immigrant employment (Bailey and Waldinger, 1991; Waldinger, 1994).

In contrast to economic models of immigrant insertion into the labor market, the focus on immigrant networks, immigrant niches, and enclave economies give testimony to a fundamental sociological proposition: economic behavior is shaped by the overarching social relations and structures in which people are embedded (Weber, 1965). To capture the fact that social expectations changed and even subverted the original intent of economic transaction, Granovetter (1985), used the term *embeddedness*.[12] The additional distinction between "relational embeddedness," referring to personal relationships among actors, and "structural embeddedness," referring to networks of social relations in which actors participate (1990), allows for the conceptualizations of relational and structural resources within social organization and for analyzing networks that may differ in size and density. Such embeddedness is the basis for the existence, creation, and reinforcement of social capital. First introduced into sociology by James Coleman (1988) and Pierre Bourdieu (1980), the concept of social capital has become a central component of recent theories. Broadly conceived, "social capital refers to the capacity of individuals to command scarce resources by virtue of their membership in social networks or broader social structures" (Portes, 1995b, p. 12). Applying these principles to immigrants, Portes and Sensenbrenner (1993) identified two main sources of social capital in immigrant communities: "bounded solidarity" and "enforceable trust." The former refers to principled group behavior that emerges specifically from the situational circumstances in which immigrants may find themselves in host societies. It is independent of earlier shared values. The latter refers to the ability of group goals to govern economic behavior based on expectations of higher community status and the fear of collective sanctions.

While ethnic entrepreneurship, ethnic enclaves, and ethnic niches illustrate the importance of group characteristics and the uses of ethnicity as a potential resource (in terms of networks and the social capital they generate), each of these models outlines a specific mode of incorporation. Indirectly these models also attest to the extraordinary diversity of contemporary immigration and the structural differentiation and flexibility of American society, generating a variety of new adaptations, processes, and outcomes.

To more fully capture the possible variations, Portes has developed a more inclusive and systematic model of immigrant incorporation that identifies twelve distinct outcomes, depending on the interaction of host society and immigrant characteristics (1995a; see also Portes and Rumbaut, 1990). Moving from the macro- to the midlevel of the social structure, the model identifies three levels of immigrant reception: the level of government policy, the level of civil society and public opinion, and the level of the immigrant community. The first level identifies three possible policy responses, labeled "receptive," "indifferent," and "hostile." The receptive category applies to refugees who receive resettlement assistance; legal immigrants fall into the indifferent category; and the hostile category applies to populations whose entry and residence meets active opposition (i.e., undocumented immigrants). At the second level, each of the three government reception categories are divided into "prejudiced" and "nonprejudiced" reception, where prejudiced reception is accorded to nonwhite groups (the majority of recent immigrants), while white immigrants enjoy nonprejudiced reception. At the third level, Portes distinguishes between strong and weak ethnic communities. Strong communities are characterized by geographic concentrations and more diversified occupational structures including significant numbers of entrepreneurs (i.e., ethnic enclave economies), whereas weak ethnic communities are either small or predominantly composed of manual workers.

The model yields twelve distinct contexts of immigrant incorporation. The location of an immigrant group in a specific context shapes the limits and possibilities of individual and group action. Thus, for example, the context of legal Mexican immigrants is shaped by indifferent policies of government reception, prejudiced responses from civil society, and public opinion and a weak ethnic community. Like Mexicans, Korean immigrants confront indifferent government reception and prejudiced responses from civil society, but they benefit from strong ethnic communities. As immigrant destinies depend on the specific context of incorporation, this model helps explain why Mexican immigrants (and most immigrants from Central America and the Caribbean) tend to occupy low socioeconomic positions and are less likely to be upwardly mobile.

Citizenship, Globalization, and Transnationalism

The mass migration to Europe and the increased salience of international migration as a worldwide and global phenomenon (Castles and Miller, 1998) gave impetus to new ways of thinking and a variety of new theories. Less concerned with the process of immigrant incorporation in one country (e.g., the United States) than with explaining the causes and consequences of immigration beyond the confines of a single country, these theories represent responses to the recognition that mass migration is self-perpetuating, transforming, systemic, and increasingly driven by global forces.

Although the permanent settlement of newcomers and the simultaneous loss of home country ties were never historical realities (Foerster, 1919; Hoerder, 1985; Piore, 1979), the empirical realities of post-1965 immigration to the United States and the new mass migration to the advanced European countries first pointed to a new and growing semisettlement and an emerging transnationalism. The maintenance of home country ties and the semisettled condition of immigrants seemed hardly surprising in the European case, where most host countries did not encourage (and often actively discouraged) the permanent settlement of workers presumed to be temporary (Heisler and Schmitter-Heisler, 1986) and where many sending states actively supported the maintenance of ties in order to ensure the continued flow of valuable remittances (Schmitter-Heisler, 1985). In the United States, pioneering research by Massey et al. (1987) was among the first to identify the persistence and growing importance of economic, social, and political ties between Mexican immigrants and their Mexican communities of origin.

Citizenship: National and Postnational

The largely unanticipated migration and settlement of large numbers of migrant workers in Europe's advanced industrial countries gave rise to comparative studies of citizenship and new theorizing about citizenship, nationhood, and the inclusion or exclusion of immigrants (Brubaker, 1989; 1992; Faist, 1995; Heisler and Schmitter-Heisler, 1991; Schmitter, 1979). This topic had been of little concern in the United States where immigration had long been part of the "founding myths" and naturalization was relatively easy for legal immigrants and the children of immigrants became citizens by virtue of their birth on American territory (the principle of *jus soli*).[13] Characterized by different principles of citizenship, based primarily on descent (*jus *sanguinis*), many European countries imposed significant (albeit varying from country to country) barriers to naturalization and restriction on birthright citizenship.

Sociological work on citizenship and inclusion has drawn on T. H. Marshall's seminal essay on citizenship and social class (1964). In addition to distinguishing between three types of citizenship—civil, political, and social—and tracing their respective historical trajectory in the British case, Marshall advanced the proposition that the development of citizenship rights has important consequences for social inequality and social cohesion: citizenship rights have served to attenuate inequalities of social class and helped to integrate previously excluded segments of society. Taking Marshall's proposition that citizenship rights are crucial to fostering the integration of previously excluded groups as her starting point in a comparative study of Germany and Switzerland (both countries with significant barriers to political citizenship), Schmitter argued that the more extensive social citizenship rights extended to immigrants in Germany would foster their greater economic and social and eventual political integration (1979). In her analysis, differences in social citizenship rights embedded in the welfare state facilitated migrants' integration into host society institutions, in particular labor markets and housing, and served as a resource for mobilization to gain more political rights.

In contrast, comparing Germany and France, Brubaker identified political citizenship as the crucial variable for immigrant incorporation. Conceptualizing the state as membership association, Brubaker argued that the starkly contrasting historical legacies of citizenship and nationhood in France (expansive, a territorially based community, and state-centered, assimilationist) and Germany (restrictive, a community of descent, ethnocultural, and "differentialist") led to differences in the civic incorporation of immigrants in these two countries. While Schmitter and more explicitly Hammar (1985, 1990) saw partial membership (Hammar uses the concept "denizenship" to denote the substantial social, civil, and even political rights accorded to long-term noncitizen residents in most advanced industrial democracies) as a possible alternative to full membership in the state, and hence a distinct "mode of incorporation," Brubaker identified such "partial membership," as characterized by the German case, as a deviation. Focusing on tracing the historical differences of citizenship and nationhood in the two countries, Brubaker paid little attention to the fact that these differences did not seem to affect the degree of integration into economic (labor market) and social institutions (housing, schooling).

In the context of expanding and deepening European integration and an increasing convergence in citizenship laws in France and Germany (Weil, 1998), for members of European Union states, political citizenship in the countries in which they may reside has become largely irrelevant. While it continues to present some barriers to citizens of nonmember states, even in this case, long-term residency has been associated with substantial rights. The expansion of rights for noncitizens has been the focal point for postnational citizenship theorists (Bauböck, 1994; Jacobson, 1996; Soysal, 1994). Postnational citizenship theorists have attributed such expansion to the development of international human rights standards, as laid down in bodies like the UN, the ILO, and the WTO, that guarantee a range of civil and social rights for noncitizens. Thus, Soysal (1994) has argued that refugee and human rights conventions signed by states have codified an international system based on the inviolability of the rights inherent in the "modern person" independent of rights inherent in the state. Legitimized by an international human rights discourse, rights and identities become increasingly decoupled from national citizenship, and the rights component of citizenship becomes reconfigured as the universal right of personhood, which is independent of nationality. Similarly, Jacobson (1996) has identified the international human rights regimes as a major force of change. For Jacobson, the lessening sovereign agency of states has been accompanied by a new regime of rights that reaches across national borders, and states are becoming an institutional forum for a larger international and constitutional order based on human rights.

Like Schmitter and Hammar, postnational citizenship theorists argue that full political citizenship and inclusion in the nation-state may not be a necessary precondition for the protection and well-being or integration of long-term noncitizen residents. But rather than locating the extensive rights accorded to long-term noncitizen residents to the characteristics of Western democracies (e.g., the welfare state, the human rights clauses enshrined in their constitutions), they locate these rights beyond the individual nation-state. Indeed, postnational citizenship theories are part of a larger set of theories that attempt to explain international migration and settlement patterns in the context of global transformations.

Globalization, Transnationalism, and State Sovereignty

The concepts of globalization, and in particular transnationalism and associated terms such as transnational community and transnational circuits, have gained increased prominence in all social sciences and hence are at the center of interdisciplinary concerns (see chapters by Brettell and Hollifield, 2000). Here, I limit myself primarily to the contributions made by sociologists.

Anthropologists have derived their understanding of transnationalism primarily in the context of kinship and network theories (Brettell, 2000). Thus, Basch and her collaborators defined transnationalism "as the process by which immigrants forge and sustain multi-stranded social relations that link their societies of origin and settlement" (1994, p. 6). The pioneering research by sociologist Massey and his collaborators (Massey et al., 1987) also clearly identified the persistence and growing importance of economic, social, and political ties between Mexican immigrants and their communities of origin. An increasing number of empirical ethnographic studies by sociologists and anthropologists (Goldring, 1992; Kyle, 1995; Mahler, 1995; Portes and Guarnizo, 1991; Smith, 1995) have identified similar ties, indicating that immigrant networks and the associated social capital are no longer confined to activities located primarily in the host society. Reaching across political borders, they are increasingly located in transnational spaces (Faist 1998; Pries 1997), where transnational social spaces "are combinations of social and symbolic ties, positions in networks and networks of organization that can be found in at least two spaces" (Faist, 1998, p. 217).

Working deductively from the perspective of world systems, and more recent and related globalization theories (Morawska, 1990; Petras, 1981; Portes and Walton, 1981; Sassen-Koob, 1988, 1991), some sociologists have linked the new global migrations and their consequences to the increasing penetration of the capitalist mode of production into more peripheral countries accompanied by new demands for cheap labor in core countries and the rapid globalization of economic and financial markets. Although the causes of migration may be primarily economic, in a globalized economy, once set in motion migration patterns are sustained and perpetuated by "well-established regional networks of trade, production, investment and communication" (Massey et al., 1998). The technological revolution, which has facilitated travel and communication across national borders, also supports the maintenance and expansion of transnational social networks created by the migrants themselves.

Although recent scholarship shows that immigrants coming to the United States did not cut their ties and "immigrant nationalisms did not simply go to the grave with the members of the migrating generation" (Jacobson, 1995, p. 5), theorists of transnational social spaces argue that current transnational practices differ significantly from those previous practices. They not only differ in terms of the frequency and quality of contacts and connections, they also differ structurally and politically. They are an integral part and supported by systems of increasingly dense commercial, financial, and cultural networks between sending and receiving countries that are embedded and part of a larger global system. In short, the new transnationalism is another manifestation of globalization.

Returning to questions of immigrant incorporation, what are the implications of transnational communities, or transnational social spaces for immigrant incorporation in receiving countries? Several scholars have suggested that transnational communities or transnational social spaces may represent a "strategy of survival and betterment" (Faist, 1998, p. 217), a separate and distinct mode of incorporation (Pries, 1997). Referring specifically to the second generation, Portes suggests that the children of nonwhite immigrants who are over-concentrated in urban areas, lacking access to mobility ladders, may join an increasingly multicultural underclass, "a ticket to permanent subordination and disadvantage" (Portes, 1998, p. 52). "In this context, remaining ensconced in dense immigrant communities, especially those that have gone transnational in their strategy for economic adaptation, may not be a symptom of escapism, but rather a rational strategy for capitalizing on the moral and material resources that only these communities can make available" (Portes, 1998, p. 52). However, in his conclusion Portes strikes a cautionary note concerning the long-term implications of transnational communities, which, as he argues, cannot be assessed fully at this time. Whatever their long-term implications, the emerging work on transnationalism and transnational communities gives testimony and provides new insights into the extraordinary complexity of immigration processes at the end of the twentieth century.

While propositions concerning the emergence of transnational communities have been relatively uncontroversial and have been supported by a growing body of empirical research, the significant political consequences for core countries and for the traditional system of nation-states postulated by globalization theorists have generated considerable debate. This is particularly the case for the argument that globalization has significantly undermined state sovereignty and transformed the system of nation-states. Globalization theorists have argued that in a world of economic interdependence and globalization, supported by technological advances, states are becoming less and less able to control the flow of capital and labor. Bringing together both strands of the argument made by globalization theorists—the decline of state sovereignty and the rise of an international human rights regime—Sassen-Koob (1996) has argued more recently that the forces of globalization have undermined the traditional nation-state that had been built on the congruence between nation and state. As nation (defined in terms of belonging) and state (defined in terms of territory) become increasingly decoupled, national belonging and identity become increasingly detached from their historic moorings (Sassen-Koob, 1996).[14]

Although theorists working from the theoretical framework of world systems and globalization have tended to give precedence to economic forces, and theorists of post-national citizenship have drawn on theories of citizenship and on the increasing role of international organizations, they arrive at similar conclusions. This is particularly the case for the new transnationalism. "Transnationalism is clearly in the air," as the editors of a recent volume on the topic have noted (Guarnizo and Smith, 1998, p. 3). Yet, I can only agree with Guarnizo and Smith's statement that "the very popularity and prominence in a variety of disciplines captured by this concept poses the risk of it becoming an empty conceptual vessel" (p. 4).

Conclusion

Although the preceding review is far from comprehensive, it demonstrates the considerable diversity and vitality in the area of immigration. Sociologists have built on previous work and, responding to changing world conditions, explored a variety of new directions. The latter have led to increased interdisciplinary contacts with other social sciences (in particular, anthropology and political science) moving in similar directions. Yet, overall the field is far from unified. I would agree with Alejandro Portes that the different components that have made up the field are "so disparate that they can only be unified at a highly abstract and probably vacuous level" (Portes, 1997).[15]

While each of the theories and models discussed preceding has been subject to theoretical, conceptual, and empirical criticisms, in this chapter, I have purposely refrained from critiquing them. Instead, I would like to conclude with a constructive note by asking the question of how we might advance from here.

First, I would argue that sociologists build more bridges across the division of labor between "Americanists" and the "Comparativists/Globalists," that is, sociologists should talk more within their discipline. An obvious and recent bridge has been the recognition that immigrant communities have come to include significant transnational dimensions, which serve to create new forms of social capital (Smith, 1998).[16] Yet, because recent work on transnationalism emerged from different theoretical roots than the more traditional approaches associated with models of immigrant incorporation and ethnic communities, so far there have been few attempts to use the theoretical and empirical insights of the former to elucidate and inform the latter, to develop a more comprehensive model of immigrant incorporation. For example, are transnational communities an additional and distinct mode of immigrant incorporation as some scholars have cautiously suggested (Faist, 1998; Portes, 1998; Pries, 1997)? How do we relate transnational communities to other modes of incorporation—assimilation, ethnic enclave economies, ethnic niches, and ethnic entrepreneurs—with which they apparently coexist? Are transnational communities confined to migrants of the first generation or do they reach beyond into succeeding generations as Portes seems to suggest (1998)?

While theorists of transnationalism and globalization tend to identify global transformations as key causes for the newly emerging patterns of international migration and settlement, by relegating the state to the margins, they fail to consider the possible role played by sending countries as purposive actors attempting to shape the spaces of their transnational citizens. There has been a tendency to see transnational communities as created primarily from below, by migrants attempting to carve out new social spaces. Yet, as Robert Smith (1998) has argued, the role of sending countries should not be overlooked. Many sending states are actively promoting the reproduction of transnational subjects (the passage of dual citizenship laws by Mexico and the Dominican Republic are just one of many examples). The roles of sending states in shaping both transnational communities and postnational citizenship only beg for more detailed and, in particular, more comparative analysis. While there is nothing new about sending countries trying to influence the patterns of migration and the settlement of their citizens abroad (Schmitter, 1984), the importance of "the home state—in its local, state, and national incarnations—in creating transnational forms of political and social life, and in maintaining local, ethnic, and national identities linked to the home country, has not diminished, but increased" (Smith, 1998, p. 200).

Building more bridges between Americanists and Comparativists automatically leads to more cross-disciplinary discourse as Comparativists and Globalists have tended to be more interdisciplinary. For example, there is an ongoing dialogue across disciplines among scholars working within globalization, transnational, and postnational perspectives. In the case of transnationalism, the dialogue is mostly among sociologists and anthropologists. While sociologists have been more inclined to examine transnationalism through macrosociological lenses and anthropologists have been far more concerned with micro- and midlevel processes, there is little disagreement on the growing importance of the transnational sphere in understanding the processes of migration and settlement.

As for the globalist and postnational perspectives, the dialogue is among sociologists and political scientists. Here, there is less agreement as political scientists have, by and large, been critical of the central claims made by postnationalists and globalists that the international human rights regime and economic globalization have substantially undermined state sovereignty, making states increasingly marginal actors in the process of migration and settlement (Freeman, 1995; Joppke, 1998; Hollifield, 1998, 1999, 2000).

Finally, as European societies have displayed different histories, it is in this context that we could test some of the broad tenets of assimilation theory, devoid of its ethnocentric, American-centric context. A similar case could be made for the various ethnic community models.[17] Yet, such an endeavor must be approached cautiously. Just as the assimilation perspective did not pay much attention to the structural characteristics of American society, we cannot assume that the structural characteristics of American society are identical with those found in other advanced industrial societies. While the globalization perspective pays little attention to political and social differences between core countries subject to the same forces of globalization, the immigrant community models discussed above take the structural characteristics of American society as given. I suggest that applications of these models in different contexts could provide additional opportunities for refinement, modification, and innovation of these models. Along these lines, I have recently attempted to adapt Portes's model of immigrant incorporation (1995b) to the German context (Schmitter-Heisler, 1998). By taking account of the structural differences between German and American society, I conclude that the United States offers more and more diverse contexts for immigrant incorporation and with it more opportunities and fewer constraints than Germany.

NOTES

1. We may also mention Max Weber's research on the conditions of rural peasants and Polish migrant workers east of the Elbe River in Germany. For a summary, see Bendix, 1962, pp. 14–30.
2. In a 1993 article, Nathan Glazer argues, "The failure of assimilation to work on blacks as on immigrants, owing to the strength of American discriminatory and prejudiced attitudes and behavior toward blacks, has been responsible for throwing the entire assimilatory ideal and program into disrepute" (p. 122).
3. I am using the term *theory* rather loosely to include typologies and models that may not meet the strict definition of theory. For a good discussion of these issues, see Portes, 1997.

4. The race relations cycle was based on the idea that immigrant groups, and, by implication, ethnic and racial groups more generally, typically go through several phases—contact, competition and conflict, accommodation, assimilation—where the end product is a melting with the larger society. In the final phase, group members acquire "the memories, sentiments, and attitudes of other persons or groups, and, by sharing their experience and history, are incorporated with them in a common cultural life" (Park and Burgess, 1921, p. 735).
5. Assimilation may be a path into the white middle class, into the inner-city underclass, or into the ethnic immigrant community.
6. Critics of the straight-line assimilation assumption have argued that ethnicity may go through periods of re-creation (Greeley, 1977; Yancey, Erikson, and Juliani, 1976). In a later article, Gans introduced the concept "bumpy-line ethnicity," which suggests that the movement toward assimilation is punctured by periods of stagnation (1992).
7. Park's original model was fleshed out by his students Lloyd Warner and Leo Srole (1945) and further elaborated and extended by Milton Gordon (1964) to include several steps toward assimilation (the presumed outcome).
8. Gordon's seven-stage model had the advantage of lending itself to operationalization, but as Alba and Nee (1997) point out, the focus on primary group integration overlooks the larger social processes.
9. Several historians have argued that assimilation theory is useful in understanding past processes. See, in particular, Morawska, 1994. See also Kazal, 1995 and Barkan, 1995. Anticipating criticisms that assimilation may have become a reality for European ethnic groups of the past, but hardly applies to new immigrants confronting different circumstances today, Alba and Nee (1997) make three important points. First, it is difficult to project the future of migration patterns. Second, we do not know whether assimilation would have taken place in absence of a halt to further mass immigration between the 1920s and 1965. Third, as they are socially constructed, racial distinctiveness and perceptions change over time. South Asians and people from the Caribbean Islands are examples.
10. Empirically, there is considerable debate concerning the claim made by ethnic enclave economy theorists that employees fare better in the enclave economy than in the secondary labor market. For a review of the empirical studies, see Light et al., 1994.
11. Waldinger defines ethnic niches as "an industry, employing at least one thousand people, in which a group's representation is at least 150 percent of its share of total employment" (1996, p. 95).
12. The concept was first introduced by Karl Polanyi and colleagues (1957).
13. This is not to say that American scholars did not study citizenship, but that the topic has been treated primarily by legal scholars. See Hollifield, 2000.
14. Political scientists such as Freeman (1996) and Joppke (1998) tend to disagree with the two theses underlying the globalization perspective: the thesis of declining sovereignty and the thesis of pervasive restrictionism.
15. How far these two strands are removed from one another was demonstrated to me recently as a member of a jury to decide the Thomas and Znaniecki prize for the best book in international migration given by the ASA's section. I was the only member of the jury who included a comparative, transnational book among my top six choices from among the books submitted.
16. While there are also signs of such talking at the level of international conferences, so far these conferences tended to be confined to comparing country studies, rather than to generating new theoretical propositions.
17. This is not to say that scholars have not used these models. Existing applications, in particular of the immigrant entrepreneur model which is the most easily transferable across societies, have generally been uncritical in that they have simply transferred the model and sought to confirm it in a different context. From a theoretical perspective, it is more fruitful to explore possible deviations from the model.

Immigration, Gender, and Family

Part V addresses the increasingly significant issues of gender and migration. Despite the fact that women now make up a significant proportion of the total migrating population, the theoretical work on economic activities and productive roles of immigrant women around the world has attracted the attention of migration scholars only in recent years. (Brettell and Simon, 1986). As the female proportion of the total migrating population increased significantly, more social scientists began to explore various dimensions of female migration. Instead of treating women as passive characters who simply follow a male migrant, female migrants were seen as active participants in the labor force who search for new wage labor opportunities in the advanced industrial countries.

The last part of this volume examines the link among migration, labor force participation of immigrant women, and gender roles within the immigrant families. In the first essay of this section, "Anthropology and the Study of Immigrant Women," Caroline B. Brettell and Patricia A. deBerjeois review the contributions of anthropologists to the study of immigrant women in the United States, focusing on wage-earning roles of immigrant women and its impact on the status of women and their domestic and familial roles, the role of kinship and other social relationships in the adaptation process of immigrant women, the effects of migration on the mental and physical health of immigrant women, and the role of the government in the lives of immigrant women.

In the second article, "Immigrant Women: Nowhere at Home?," Donna Gabaccia explores the marginal status of women and the absence of scholarly research on immigrant women. In the author's view, the marginalization of studies on immigrant women is not the result of a dearth of research, but rather the discordant and conflicting questions, methods, and categories used in disciplines that study immigrant women.

The third reading of this section: Yen Le Espiritu's "Gender and Labor in Asian Immigrant Families" explores the impact of migration on patriarchal family relations among Asian immigrants and the ways in which labor-force participation of these women has transformed gender relations among professional, self-employed, and wage-laborer Asian couples. Women's access to economic and social resources coupled with men's relative loss of status in both public and private arenas have caused severe pressures on the traditional gender relations among Asian immigrants in the United States.

The fourth reading, "Marital Relations" by Pyong Gap Min, reveals the same pattern of gender-role reversal among Korean immigrants in New York. The book from which this essay is selected demonstrates how the increased economic role of Korean women together with limited economic success of Korean men has created tension, marital conflict, violence, and divorce within the Korean immigrant families in the United States.

This part concludes with "Benefits and Burdens: Immigrant Women and Work in New York City." In this reading, Nancy Foner demonstrates that labor force participation of Jamaican women in New York has improved their status in the household and has given them greater bargaining power, personal autonomy, independence, and self-esteem. These gains, Foner points out, have created new challenges, demands, and pressures for immigrant women both on the job and at home. Many women work long hours in demanding, low-paying, dead-end positions with no benefits. In addition, they have to deal with the demands of child care and the burden of household work.

Anthropology and the Study of Immigrant Women

✦ CAROLINE B. BRETTELL AND PATRICIA A. DEBERJEOIS

In 1970, the meeting of the American Ethnological Society focused on the topic "Migration Anthropology" (Spencer, 1970). In his introduction to the volume of proceedings, Leonard Kasdan rightly observed that although migration had long been recognized as an important factor of change in a number of social science disciplines, anthropology had not defined it as a topic of research with high priority. However, changes in the world in the 1950s and 1960s brought migration onto the center stage of the discipline. In a range of areas where ethnographers had traditionally worked among native or peasant populations, for example, Africa, Latin America, and Asia, they began to document the process of outmigration from the villages of the rural countryside to the growing urban centers where new employment opportunities were expanding rapidly (Butterworth, 1962; Cohen, 1969; Eames, 1954; Mangin, 1969). The interest in migrants and immigrants grew in conjunction with the development of both peasant studies and urban anthropology.

By 1975, two of the volumes that were published in the series that emerged from the Ninth International Congress of Anthropological and Ethnological Sciences treated migration and its relationship to processes of urbanization, development, and ethnic group formation (Du Toit and Safa, 1975). Though the chapters in these volumes deal with a number of issues in a wide variety of migratory contexts, only passing references, if any, are made to the role of women in migration. Indeed, there is no entry in either index for "women" or "female." As numerous scholars have pointed out, the assumption was that women, if they left their home society at all, did so as passive followers rather than as

Brettell, Caroline B. and deBerjeois, Patricia A. 1993. "Anthropology and the study of immigrant women" in: *Seeking Common Ground*, ed. Donna Gabaccia, 41–63. Reproduced with permission of Greenwood Publishing Group, Inc., Westport, CT.

active initiators. Furthermore, the modernization theories that were still prevalent at the time stressed emigration or outmigration as matters of individual choice rather than as household strategies with which women were intimately involved.[1]

Stimulated, no doubt, by the publication in 1974 of Rosaldo and Lamphere's pathbreaking *Women, Culture, and Society*, a book that brought gender as an analytic concept into the mainstream of anthropology, the journal *Anthropological Quarterly* published a special issue, "Women and Migration," in January of 1976. In each of the papers in the volume, migrant and immigrant women are not only viewed as actors in the migration process but also are set into networks of exchange of people, goods, services, and information. The authors demonstrate that women are as influenced as men by the forces of colonialism, socialism, and capitalism.

Despite Leeds's claim in the closing essay of this special issue that women were being spuriously reified as a unit of analysis, from this point on a number of anthropologists chose to address the experiences of migrant and immigrant women in a range of receiving societies, including Europe and the United States (Leeds, 1976; Bhachu, 1985; Brettell, 1995; Buechler, 1981; Foner, 1978; Gilad, 1989; Goodman, 1987). Using a variety of research methods (participant observation, the collection of life histories and case studies, in-depth interviews, etc.) to access how the women themselves understand their lives and the challenges posed by migration, they focused on how these experiences might differ from those of men and how geographical mobility, both within and across national boundaries, might alter not only culturally rooted understandings of what it means to be a woman, but also various other aspects of culture that individuals and families bring with them as they migrate or emigrate.

In this chapter, we will review the anthropological contribution to the study of immigrant women, addressing ourselves in particular to research on a range of immigrant populations in the United States.[2] Taking our lead from some of the analytic models that have emerged in feminist anthropology, we first discuss the work roles of immigrant women, how these intersect with domestic and familial roles, and the implications of this intersection for changes in the status of women. From there we move to a consideration of the significance of kinship and other social relationships that are instrumental in the process of adaptation for immigrant women. We then deal with research that broadly treats the question of culture change. After a brief overview of the factors that continue to tie a given migrant population to its ethnic roots over generations, we turn our attention to the wealth of studies within medical anthropology that have contributed to our understanding of immigrant women in the United States. Finally, we address the impact of the state on the lives of immigrant women.

Public and Private, Production and Reproduction: Balancing Work Roles and Domestic Roles

As a result of their inquiry into the question of whether women are universally subordinate to men, cultural anthropologists have contributed the domestic/public model to feminist theory. Embedded in this model are the notions that male activities in the public sphere are more highly valued, that men have formal authority over women while women exert informal influence and power within the domestic domain, and that women's status is lowest where these spheres are highly differentiated and where women are isolated from one another.[3] A parallel model emanating from Marxism analyzes the interrelationship between production and reproduction (Meillassoux, 1981; Rubin, 1975). Feminist theorists have stressed that the way in which women's reproductive labor intersects with their productive labor is crucial to their position in society.

Although these models have been subjected to rigorous criticism for their lack of historical or cultural specificity, they have nevertheless influenced anthropological study of immigrant women in the United States (Edholm et al., 1977; Harris, 1981; Moore, 1988; Rogers, 1978; Rosaldo, 1980; Yanagisako and Collier, 1987). They have led researchers to explore whether wage earning serves to enhance the power and status of immigrant women within their households and to investigate whether greater sharing of household activities emerges as a result of the work obligations of women. While the latter question obviously pertains to all wage-earning women, the notion is that immigrant women often not only face a clash of cultures, but may also be deprived of the support networks of kinship and community that existed in the countries they left behind.

Chai explicitly applies the conceptual scheme of domestic/public to an analysis of Korean immigrant women in Hawaii.[4] Middle-class and well-educated, Korean immigrant women were relegated to the domestic sphere in their home society. In Hawaii they must adjust to the economic demands of immigrant life by taking waged work outside the home. Husbands offer more help in the household than they did in Korea, but this is in part a function of age cohorts, and in many cases husbands retain ultimate authority over family decision making. However, some Korean women, according to Chai, begin to question their husbands' right to dominate them. "Women's wage earning," she concludes, "may lead to a more flexible division of labor, decision-making, and parental responsibility, as well as to less sex segregation in social and public places.[5] She also observes that as Korean immigrant women tire of the menial jobs to which they are relegated in the public domain of the larger society, they revert to working in family-owned businesses and construct their own public domain with its own ladder of achievement within the Korean ethnic community. Workplace and home are combined and permit these women to spend more time raising successful children who will achieve social and political status within the majority culture.

The decision to combine work roles with domestic roles, and thereby fuse the reproductive with the productive, has been documented for a number of other immigrant women in North America. Meintel, for example, shows that Portuguese women with young children tend to turn to work as cleaning women or to do home piece work because the hours and conditions of work are both more flexible and less stressful (Meintel, 1987). She observes, however, that such an option is possible only if these women are in stable marital relationships with partners who earn a good income. Another option is described by Lamphere for Colombian and Portuguese immigrant families in New England (Lamphere, 1987; Simon and Brettell, 1986). Given the constraints of the local economy, wives and mothers are forced into the productive sphere of waged work in textile factories. As a result, reproductive labor within the household is reallocated and husbands take on many household chores that are normally defined as female tasks. In addition, husbands and wives work different shifts in order to accommodate child care. Nevertheless, some cultural conceptions, such as the belief that the male should remain the head of the household, are more resistant to change despite the economic contributions of women.

A similar disjunction between norms and behavior has been described for Haitian immigrant women in New York. Cultural definitions and expectations for sexual roles have changed less rapidly than the economic gains made by women. Furthermore, the financial independence of women exacerbates antagonism between the sexes. Haitian immigrant women put in a double day, working eight hours on the job and then coming home to housekeeping, cooking, and child care. If their husbands help, it is with reluctance because the *foye* (home) is the domain of women and it is there that a woman's primary responsibilities are located. The world of men is the *lari*—the street and beyond.[6]

If Haitian women have not experienced a dramatic reallocation of household tasks as a result of the demands made upon them by waged work, Dominican women, who are largely employed in the New York garment industry, have. Pessar describes a definite move to a more egalitarian division of labor and distribution of authority within the Dominican household (Pessar, 1998, 1987, 1986). She quotes one Dominican woman who comments that "we are both heads." Dominican immigrant men are willing to help out with household chores, especially child care and shopping, although their role decreases as a daughter becomes old enough to help her mother. The more cooperative domestic arrangements that emerge within many Dominican immigrant households, as well as the fact that migration does not rupture the social sphere in which women are self-actualized, are the major factors influencing the greater desire of Dominican women, in comparison with men, to remain in the United States (Pessar, 1986).

Within many immigrant Dominican households, income pooling, something that rarely occurs in the Dominican Republic, means that no distinction is made between the "essential" earnings of the male and the "supplementary" earnings of the female. However, this is not always the case. For example, Mexicana farm workers differentiate the "important" crops harvested by men from secondary "women's crops." Mexicana women "never express that their agricultural work is economically equivalent to men's." Instead when women work with their husbands, they define it as "*ayudandole a el*."[7] It is in this "helping" context that women's waged work is ideologically acceptable. This is particularly the case when the household rather than the individual is defined as the basic productive (as well as reproductive) unit of the immigrant family.[8] Chavira argues that Mexicana women's roles in subsistence as well as their manipulation of the subsidy programs and other bureaucratic resources that are made available to them give them a position of power within their families.

Pessar cautions us to be aware of variations in household culture and organization that will influence individual attitudes toward women's work in the immigrant context, the sharing of domestic responsibilities, and the desire to remain abroad or return to the home country. Some Dominican immigrant men are reluctant to modify their patriarchal attitudes and behavior (Pessar, 1987). This intransigence is the major cause of marital breakdown. Nevertheless, a significant proportion of Dominican immigrant women feel they are better off. They perceive waged work positively because it brings both economic and personal benefits. This is a conclusion also reached by Foner in her work on Jamaican women in New York (Foner, 1986). Independence and financial control are viewed as definite advantages and are a strong deterrent to return migration.

Although they are dealing with a seasonal Mexican female migrant population, Guendelman and Perez-Itriago document similar positive subjective assessments of life abroad that are rooted in the contrast between family roles in California and those that pertain in Mexico. As one of their informants put it, "in California my husband was like a *mariposa*, meaning a sensitive, soft, responsive butterfly. Back here in Mexico he acts like a distant macho."[9] Many of the seasonal migrant women express an interest in returning to the United States in order to resume more cooperative relationships. Yet some, according to Fernandez-Kelly, are constrained by the pressures of caring for many children, especially if migration means facing the vagaries of undocumented illegal status in the United States.[10]

The anthropological research on immigrant women that has been stimulated by the analytical oppositions between domestic and public arenas or between production and reproduction indicates a set of complex and varied responses to the necessity of balancing work life with home life. In some cases greater equality between men and women is the result and in others it is not, and the differences must be explained by a close exami-nation of cultural factors and economic constraints. Meintel and associates observe that "when changes in task-sharing and decision-making occur in conjunction with women's wage earning, they are likely to be found in areas which are most directly affected by women's employment: e.g., child care as opposed to housework, and financial decisions as opposed to those concerning freedom of movement and contraception" (Meintel, 1984; Ortner, 1984). It is common for anthropologists to emphasize the disjunction between behavior and norms, a disjunction that seems to have a powerful influence in the pace of change in various spheres of life for immigrant families. Cultural norms that continue to label men as principal providers and women as housekeepers and dependents are powerful deterrents to more egalitarian domestic arrangements. Nevertheless, in some situations immigrant women, like women elsewhere around the world, are able to exercise informal power.

If a number of immigrant women in the United States assess their increased earning capacity, their improved standard of living, and their greater opportunities to work and achieve upward mobility positively, they perceive other facets of immigrant life negatively. For many, the most negative results of migration are the temporary or permanent loss of a kinship support system and the absence of leisure time. It is thus to the social world of immigrant women both within and beyond the domestic sphere that we now turn.

Husbands, Wives, and Immigrant Social Networks

"Strategy" and "process" have replaced "structure" as underlying concepts within anthropology (Ortner, 1984). Social networks, first examined with seriousness by ethnologists working in urban Africa in the late 1960s and the 1970s, have thus become a key focus of research on social organization. Anthropologists recognize the value of networks to migrants. These networks consist of friends or relatives of the migrant who are already in the destination area or those who are return migrants (Gonzalez, 1975). They serve as communication links between the sending and receiving communities. This seems especially important in international migration where the distances involved make adequate information harder to obtain.

There are two general types of networks. One serves the purpose of chain migration, where individuals channel their efforts to reunite extended family groups (Graves and Graves, 1974). The other type is community based and operates to support newcomers as they adjust to the demands of their new environments (Benson, 1990; Gold 1989). Immigrant women are frequently found at the center of these networks. They both initiate and maintain them. They are the "nodes" that connect people, and generally they do it so subtly and unobtrusively that the significance of their actions is sometimes little recognized even by themselves (Smith, 1977).

Though deeply embedded in migration processes around the world, kin-based migration networks that foster chain migration have proliferated as a result of the United States Immigration Act of 1965, which had as its aim the reuniting of families. The new law made it possible for individuals to "call over" other family members one at a time. Chavez, for example, writes of an unmarried EI Salvador woman who first called her niece and two years later her mother and her nephew.[11]

There are two distinct problems with the reunification policy. It takes a long time to bring over an entire family, and in many cases the definition of family that the law proscribes is not broad enough to fit the concept of family held by certain ethnic groups. As a result, complex strategies to bypass the laws and restrictions that perpetuate family separation have been devised and carried out (Fjellman and Gladwin, 1985; Garrison and Weiss, 1979). In many cases these include marriages of convenience or the adoption of children. Often the migrations can only be managed in stages, with the newcomer first going to Canada or Mexico or to U.S. cities other than their final destination. Women have an active part in the decision process that determines the order of migration of absent members, and they hold down jobs that fund the moves. Stafford tells us that women continue to play an important role in Haitian chain migration schemes, helping themselves and others through the difficult adjustment process.[12]

Community-based networks take shape in both sending and receiving areas. Mexican men from the Nayarit region who leave their wives behind make sure that a network of wife helpers (usually drawn from among the husband's kin) is in place to help with short-term loans, repairs to the household, bills, the care and sale of animals, the purchasing of materials, and other tasks normally carried out by the husband.[13] When a man returns, part of what he has earned will be spent on gifts for members of this help network. This cements the obligation. However, as time passes and the woman becomes more self-sufficient, she relies less and less on these help networks. She becomes a *mujer fuerte* and gains esteem and social prestige while her husband is absent.

A substantial number of Dominican immigrant women are single parents who want to provide a better life for their children than is possible in their home countries. They must make use of networks at both ends of their migration trail. If they have young children who must be cared for, they may choose to leave them behind with their maternal grandmother. Once in this country, women usually live in extended family groupings that are composed of blood or marital kin who provide one another with financial and emotional support. Forming networks within their own groups, these women belie the stereotype of the passive Latin woman. They are not patiently waiting to be helped by husbands or brothers but are assuming active leadership roles, taking charge of their own lives and helping kinswomen do the same.[14]

Korean immigrant women in Hawaii also spend a period of coresidence with kin and, contrary to tradition, it is usually the relatives of the wife rather than those of the husband.[15] Laotian women, accustomed to carrying out daily tasks on a communal basis, form networks with kin and nonkin living nearby to help them cope with the loss of the support systems they had in Laos.[16] These networks are cooperative in nature and without accurate record-keeping succeed in remaining balanced. Whether employed outside the home or not, the women share in caring for each other's children. They plan and carry out food shopping and preparation together. They provide for each other's social needs and serve as channels of community information.

Women have social license not available to men to share their personal concerns and worries with each other. These discussions take place informally as women gather at social and religious functions, or around a common worktable on the job. While outsiders may view these as gossip sessions, they actually serve as occasions for passing on valuable information and widening the range of an individual's contacts. O'Connor, for example, writes about the female-centered networks that emerge among Mexican immigrants, many of them undocumented, in Santa Barbara as a result of their labor force participation in local nurseries.[17] Based on the idea of *confianza* that is traditionally characteristic of kin and fictive kin relations in Mexico, these networks within the workplace provide the framework within which immigrant women seek help from formal agencies or mobilize themselves for social action. According to O'Connor, this represents a dramatic change from Mexico, where "women rarely work outside the subsistence economy, . . . have little knowledge of formal political or legal entities beyond local municipal affairs, . . . and participate in the social networks of their husbands and fathers [rather than] instigate network relationships of their own."[18]

While the bulk of research on the networks of migrant and immigrant women deals with the larger kin group or the workplace, some studies consider how the role changes experienced by male and female immigrants are related to changing patterns in their social relationships. According to a theory proposed by Bott, couples share a social network and perceive each other as companions in direct proportion to how they normally divide conjugal tasks. If conjugal roles are separate, so also are social and kin networks. When roles overlap or become cooperative in nature, social and kin networks do also (Bott, 1971). An instance that might lend support to this theory can be seen in the experience of Korean women in Hawaii.

In Korea the lives of men and women run on separate but parallel tracks. Labor is strictly divided, with men performing economically related tasks outside the home and women responsible for motherhood and other tasks inside the home. Each has distinct networks with which they interact and socialize on a daily basis. In Hawaii women must hold jobs outside the home and many couples have made adjustments in the ways domestic duties are assigned. Men and women both are separated from their customary social and support ties and need to rely on each other. They spend more time together both in domestic tasks and in social activities. A majority of women, though by no means all, report enhanced marital relationships.[19]

A similar situation is reported by Lamphere, Silva, and Sousa in their work on Portuguese immigrants in New England. The realignments in household division of labor resulting from women's work outside the home have drawn nuclear families closer, while ties to extended families and friends become less important (Lamphere et al., 1980). Conversely, Bloch argues that the economic pursuits of Polish immigrants divide family members, sending each off in a different direction every day. The family unit becomes fractionalized as its members develop distinct sets of friends and a variety of interests, returning home at night too tired to reconnect with each other. Polish women express feelings of isolation, feel that they are overworked, and fear that they have lost touch with their children. They seem at a particular disadvantage compared with women of other ethnic groups because they are unable to draw support from friends and kin. Bloch reports that they operate on a basis of suspicion and competitiveness with both family and nonfamily members. Where other groups see increased opportunity for all flowing from information exchange and cooperative efforts, the Poles see in these behaviors only the possibility of losses of personal advantages. They therefore are fearful and secretive in their dealings with those from whom others draw support.[20]

A different outcome is experienced by middle-class Cuban women. These women view the role of wife as primary. Children are valued and loved, but the focal point of a Cuban woman's life is her husband and her relationship to him. In the United States, Cuban women are entering the workforce in increasing numbers, and operating within it competently and aggressively, but they have not let this influence their interactions with husbands inside the home. What they have done, however, is to take on an additional role, one that was carried out by a man's mistress in Cuba, where showing off a beautiful mistress gave status to a man and did not dishonor his wife. Since United States customs do not provide the same approbation for such behavior, the Cuban wife fills it and thereby earns her husband the status he would otherwise be denied. Women who in Cuba were able to become slightly plump must diet in the United States to maintain the image of youth and beauty necessary to fulfill this role.[21]

Anthropological research has demonstrated that the balance contained within male-female relationships is upset by the migratory experience. Both men and women must adjust to the demands of changing roles inside and outside the home. Relationships with children change also. In some cases prolonged separation of children from parents becomes necessary, and in others parents find that the demands of operating and financing households in the United States leaves little time and/or energy for the sort of interaction with children that would have taken place in their home communities. New social networks may be forged or old ones sustained. These networks may or may not be shared by husband and wife. The networks of immigrant women are crucial for disseminating information not only about employment opportunities, but also about various institutions of the host society. One of these institutions is the health care system, and it is to these issues that we now turn.

Health, Illness, and the Immigrant Woman

The study of how cultures change is fundamental to anthropology, and a number of processes by which this occurs have been delineated. Culture change is clearly of central importance in the study of immigrants, although research in this area often analyzes a group or population according to their participation in traditional practices. Considered are things such as the meanings involved in continuing to serve symbolic foods and whether or not these foods are prepared with traditional ingredients or with the use of substitutes that maintain the symbolic value but may lose authentic taste quality. Native language use and the efforts that are made to teach the original language to succeeding generations provide another arena for assessing change. Language is often at the core of expressions of ethnic identity (Buchanan, 1979). Of interest also are the methods used to hand down traditional songs and dances. (Schuchat, 1981). Studies measure the number of ethnically based voluntary associations that are active within the community and the rate of participation in them by its members. Religious practices conducted in the ethnic vernacular and social activities that bring together the ethnic group are yet another indicator of cultural cohesion (Baskauskas, 1977). Many of these studies are not primarily focused on women, but they deal with domains of family life that are centered on women. Thus the way that immigrant women respond to cultural difference is of utmost importance to any understanding of how immigrant families adapt to a new way of life. One female-centered domain where both cultural differences and adaptation are significant is that of family health.

Major contributions to the study of health issues among immigrants have been made by medical anthropologists. Medical anthropology emerged as a subfield of the discipline in the mid-1960s, although the issues that scholars in this field address (ethnomedicine, cultural conceptions of disease, human reproduction, etc.) have a longer history within anthropology, many of them subsumed within ethnographic studies of religion, research on culture and personality, or investigations of international public health systems (Johnson and Sargent, 1990). In directing their attention to the adaptation of immigrants in the United States, medical anthropologists have demonstrated that the health of migrants is worse than that of nonmigrants (Baker et al., 1986; Hackenberg et al., 1983), and that many suffer from significant stress disorders that are not necessarily alleviated over time (Dressler and Bernal, 1982; Westermeyer et al., 1984). Clearly the impact of migration on health issues has a gender component. Research on gender and health can be subdivided into three areas: studies of the relationship between ethnomedical and biomedical orientations toward sickness and healing, studies of mental health and stress, and studies of the use of the health care system.

Indigenous Health Beliefs and U.S. Health Care

Immigrants and refugees, even those who have been in the United States for some time, either continue folk healing methods or juxtapose their own medical beliefs and practices with those of the United States (Rubel, 1960; Smith, 1972). Scholars who have conducted research in this area emphasize that health care professionals must adopt a transcultural perspective.

Bell and Whiteford show that Tai Dai women hold different concepts of illness causality than do Euro-Americans.[22] They emphasize food, temperature changes, and supernatural forces to a greater degree. Samoan migrants in Los Angeles retain a belief in the concept of *aitu*, the ghost spirit who punishes the living by bringing on a variety of physiological and mental illnesses (Lazar, 1988). For Samoan immigrant women, *M'ai aitu* is a culturally appropriate and patterned way to cope with anxiety and stress. DeSantis shows that while Cuban immigrant women in Florida have a biomedical orientation to illness and health care that is similar to that of Western health-care professionals (illnesses and their associated symptoms are identified by their biomedical names), Haitian women are more ethnomedically oriented and tend to "give folk interpretations of biomedical explanations regarding pathophysiological processes." She associates these differences with (1) the educational and health-care systems in the countries of origin, (2) the socioeconomic and political situation that affects immigrants in the localized receiving community, (3) household structure and function, and (4) beliefs about child behavior (the study focused on children's illnesses).[23]

Many immigrant and refugee women combine orientations and therefore remedies. Thus, the Cuban women discussed by Kirby use prescription tranquilizers in conjunction with herbal teas and other home remedies in their search for a cure for "*nervios*."[24] Cohen claims that Latina women frequently seek consultations with native pharmacists from their home country to supplement the care that they receive from the U.S. system (Cohen, 1979). Sargent, Marcucci, and Ellison show that Khmer women increasingly seek prenatal care at U.S. hospitals and clinics and tend to deliver their babies in hospitals. However, they also continue to follow traditional postpartum protective measures and to consult the indigenous midwife (*chmop*).[25]

Scholars in a number of disciplines have studied fertility patterns among immigrant women, mostly demonstrating a decline after migration.[26] Anthropologists have tended to focus on the cultural factors that influence attitudes toward childbirth, pregnancy, and other female health issues.[27] Morse and Park document cultural variations in perceptions of the pain that is associated with childbirth and explain them according to whether or not childbirth is viewed as natural or not.[28] In another article on the Khmer community in Dallas, Sargeant and Marcucci demonstrate how pregnancy is culturally and socially constructed. The Khmer, like many other cultural groups, believe in humoral concepts and use them to diagnose pregnancy, treat symptoms, and control diet during pregnancy.[29] Similar humorally based attitudes are described for Indochinese women in California. They influence their preference for formula over breast milk.[30] Korean immigrant women in Honolulu have trouble communicating their anxieties about *naeng*, a folk illness rooted in ideas about a cold womb, to clinicians. Frequently, humoral and cosmopolitan lore are synthesized as an explanation for personal afflication.[31] Finally, Engle, Scrimshaw, and Smidt have worked on sex differences in attitudes toward newborns among Mexican immigrants in the Los Angeles area. Although they discovered an absence of preference among mothers (especially by comparison with fathers), they also suggest that "the more acculturated women express less positive attitudes toward their newborns," and the relationship was slightly stronger for girls than boys.[32]

Mental Health and Stress

A certain amount of stress is associated with the experience of immigration. A number of scholars, both sociologists and anthropologists, have examined variations in mental health by gender.[33] Friedenberg and associates show that Argentine immigrant women in New York are more demoralized across socioeconomic strata than are males, especially those who are nonworking or without household help to assist in child care (Friedenberg et al., 1988). In a study of Hmong refugees in Minnesota, Westermeyer and associates show that men experience greater stress during the initial phase of migration because of a loss in power and status and an inability to cope adequately with the public domain. However, as their employment situation and linguistic capabilities improve, their symptoms decrease. By contrast, women in the initial phase experience less psychological distress than men because they continue in their traditional domestic roles and do not have to deal with the obligations of financial support. The exceptions are women who become employed: "They reported more Phobic Anxiety symptoms . . . due to the new and relatively nontraditional roles as wage workers outside the Hmong community."[34] However, mental illness and stress increase for women over time, particularly as they become concerned about the Americanization of their children. Women heading their own household experience constant stress, a fact also noted by Cohen for single Latina immigrant women who have settled on the East Coast of the United States.[35]

Vega and associates also focus on the initial migration phase, and argue that depression symptom levels of Mexican immigrants are higher among those who have been in the United States for less than five years.[36] They find a positive correlation between depression and disrupted marital status, serious life events, poor physical health, and being a single head of household. Depression is negatively correlated with educational and income levels, and there seems to be no relationship according to the number of children. They argue that for women in particular "family structure and normative expectations are unstable and deeply conflicted. . . . The effort to maintain traditional cultural role expectations within the context of a highly urbanized and affluent social system could be expected to increase stress and economic marginality.[37] When migrant women maintain contact with their support network of kin in Mexico, they are much better adjusted.[38]

The conflicts between motherhood and breadwinner roles create significant stress for a number of immigrant women in the United States. Among Latin American women in San Francisco, illness, whether mental or physical, validates a claim to maternal identity.[39] Korean women in Hawaii complain of a variety of health disorders from insomnia to chest pain, to loss of appetite and frigidity. Chai suggests that many of these complaints are psychosomatic and are an informal strategy used by these women to legitimize and reaffirm their roles as good wives and mothers in a situation where their inadequate English, limited knowledge of American culture, employment in degrading jobs, and the double burden of waged and domestic work leads to declining authority over their children.[40]

Finally, Kirby describes the solace from stress that Cuban women in South Florida find in increased use of minor prescription tranquilizers. This stress is a result of the conflict between the ideal sex roles defined by Cuban culture and the economic realities of immigrant life—particularly the need to take on waged employment and to juggle work, child care, and other household responsibilities.[41] Tranquilizers alleviate ailments associated with *nervios*—a mental health ailment described by other scholars of immigrant women in North America,[42] one that is commonly attributed to poor working conditions, low wages, and gender relations (Dunk, 1989). Use of tranquilizers, in Kirby's view, "may be indicative of an adaptive strategy for dealing with culture change, and not merely as an example of illicit drug abuse."[43]

Access to and Use of the Health Care System

A number of anthropologists have focused on the access to and use of the health-care system by various immigrant and refugee groups in the United States. For many, contact with the system is minimal. In a study of Laotian Tai Dam female refugees in Iowa, Bell and Whiteford show: (1) that two thirds of Tai Dam women do not use and have never used birth control because of insufficient knowledge a cultural norms, (2) that language creates problems of communication with doctors, (3) that a quarter of Tai Dam women are not covered by insurance, and (4) that close to a quarter have never seen a dentist and almost half do not have a personal physician.[44] Mexican immigrant women tend to underutilize health facilities even for prenatal care (Chavez, 1985). Illegal status and both the lack of insurance and fear associated with it provides one explanation. Work factors may also be important. Fifty-five percent of a sample of Mexican immigrant women in one study had at least one illness episode during their stay in the United States, and more working than nonworking women reported illness.[45] This may not be the result of the harsh conditions of work per se but of the increased access to medical care through work, which may influence the reporting of illness.

Other research shows that women immigrants seek medical attention and assistance as a way to alleviate tension and stress—being sick is a culturally appropriate means of gaining sympathy and support. For Latin American immigrant women in San Francisco, "illness may provide the opportunity for involvement in one of the few truly recreational activities available to women—going to the doctor."[46] When immigrant women do seek access to the U.S. health-care system, it is largely through their own social networks.[47]

Chavira characterizes their role as "subsidy providers" as one of the more important among Mexicana migrants in the midwestern United States. "Women always carry, handle, and store all the family's documents and handle all bureaucratic matters affecting the family. In these ways, women are responsible for the family's health and other business. They function, as well, as cultural brokers as they introduce the family to the medical bureaucratic culture."[48] By becoming the health experts, women gain prestige and authority in vital decisions about geographical movement.

Through their dealings with the health care system, immigrant women come into contact with one aspect of state bureaucracy. In the final section of this chapter we explore other aspects of this interaction as well as the significance of social class.

Immigrant Women, Social Class, and the State

The political economic perspective has attuned anthropologists to the way in which global processes and class relations influence everyday lives. Within feminist anthropology this has resulted in a rich body of data on the impact of national and international development projects on women and in an exploration of how the social position of women is affected by the social, economic, and political policies of states. Research has emphasized not only how national immigration policies influence the demography of international female migration, but also their insertion in the receiving society. A model that addresses a threefold oppression or a "triple invisibility" according to gender, class, and ethnicity has emerged from these concerns.[49] One scholar has described a fourth oppression stemming from internalized self-perceptions whereby an exploited position is accepted as normal and natural (Morokvasic 1983, 1984, 1988).

Class is experienced in the context of a transnational division of labor that is in turn linked to local and generally segmented occupational structures that funnel immigrant women into a few sectors of the economy, the garment industry and domestic service in particular (Chavez, 1987) Safa, for example, argues that the job market explains why Hispanic immigrant women outnumber men in the New York area.[50] A decline in these jobs in recent years has forced them to scramble to find other ways to support themselves. Alternatively, Fernandez-Kelly and Garcia show how local and federal agencies, operating within the framework of capitalist government policies, contribute to the growth of an informal or underground economy that employs numerous Hispanic women in Los Angeles and Miami.[51]

While these macro political and economic concerns have occupied the attention of some anthropologists, others have focused more closely on internalized perceptions of class and particularly the experience of downward mobility that is voiced by immigrant women who defined themselves as middle class prior to their arrival in the United States. Brazilian women in New York who were used to employing servants are now employed as servants. They cope with this change in social position by defining their situation as short-term and temporary.[52] Haitian women who held professional or white-collar positions in their home country express enormous resentment about their loss of social status and the fact that their education and skills are not valued in a predominantly English-speaking society. One Haitian woman who found herself working in a leather goods factory in the United States commented, "The job I do is for an animal. It's the same day after day. . . . I used to be a schoolteacher in Haiti. Now I'm doing a job that doesn't even require me to think."[53] High-status middle-class Korean women who were not employed outside the home prior to emigration generally work at menial jobs that are not commensurate with their education once they arrive in the United States (Chai, 1987). They are forced to take on these jobs because of the discrimination faced by their husbands. Professionals, managers, and white collar workers in Korea, these men find themselves working as janitors, gardeners, painters, and dishwashers in the United States. The same is true among Soviet Jews and Vietnamese refugees (Gold, 1989).

Interestingly, it is the studies of middle-class female immigrants that show waged work failing to enhance women's status. The major motive for international migration among Colombians is the proletarianization of the middle class; they face increasing unemployment and poverty in their own country.[54] Perhaps because they had waged employment in their home country, Colombian immigrant women do not gain self-esteem and autonomy in relation to their spouses because of their earnings. In the "least attractive categories in the labor market" of the United States, they are insecure about their position as workers and earn less than their husbands.[55] According to Boone, Cuban women in Washington, D.C., do not value labor in and of itself because it is an extension of their domestic roles and is expected of them.[56] Alternatively, another study argues that Cuban mores restricted women's activities to the home and that women gained prestige and high standing by remaining within the domestic domain.[57] This status is lost as a result of the necessity of employment in the United States. The meaning of this loss of status is perhaps best expressed in a statement made by a Cuban respondent in a study conducted in Hudson County, New Jersey. "I used to work as a doctor's secretary in Cuba. I could dress well and it was a respectable job. Here I have to do factory work. . . . Instead of improving myself in coming to the United States, I feel like I'm going backwards every day."[58] The contradictions in the research on Cuban immigrant women's attitudes toward work emphasize most blatantly the need to be precise about the social class background of immigrants.[59] This is nowhere more apparent than in a comparison between Cuban entrepreneurs in Miami and proletarianized Mexican women in Los Angles. In one case, home work becomes a strategy to maximize earnings and reconcile the cultural and economic demands placed upon women; in the other it is an avenue to increasing vulnerability.[60]

While social class is significant, anthropologists are quick to emphasize that the exploitation and discrimination that immigrant women experience may result more from their foreignness and/or femaleness. Foner notes a number of factors that divide Jamaican women from other immigrant or working-class women and, conversely, unites them with Jamaican men in a common cause.[61] Among Dominican women, "the identification and satisfaction with improvements in life-style dampen the collective sentiments and solidarity that are potentially nurtured and ignited in the workplace."[62] These women view themselves as middle class and measure themselves against where they were when they left their home country. Their orientation, according to Pessar, is individualistic rather than collective, and as a result they shun unions, legislative processes, and collective community action.

Pessar's observations draw attention to the pitfalls of ascribing our own concepts of liberation and oppression to immigrant women, who either feel the inevitability of their situation or have a different set of standards by which to evaluate their success. Both these factors explain their comparatively low level of political consciousness. Although there are a few exceptions, generally where anthropologists and other social scientists have even acknowledged the stirrings of group-based political expression, they describe it as incipient or weak.[63] The fact that community and social organizations tend to be male-oriented explains, in Gordon's view, the low level of collective action among Caribbean immigrant women.[64] Their social world is the interpersonal world of kin and neighbors. Another factor is the basic division in the working class along ethnic lines. Lamphere describes some of this resentment between older (Italian, Irish, French, Canadian) and newer (Portuguese, Latin American) female immigrant factory workers in a New England apparel plant. Much of it centers on accusations of "rate busting." The perception is that new immigrants work too fast and the piece rate is lowered such that all workers have to increase their output to make the same pay. Despite these divisions and tensions, a culture of resistance that crosses ethnic lines can develop, according to Lamphere, when unions base their organizational activities on the informal networks that are established among women who bring their social and familial roles to the workplace.[65] This humanized work culture may not emerge in every situation, but where it does it can provide a powerful base for collective action by immigrant women.[66] Certainly more research is necessary to unravel the possibilities for political consciousness among immigrant women more generally.

CONCLUSION

Anthropology is a diverse and holistic discipline that encompasses within it a wide variety of theoretical perspectives and an unlimited number of research problems that are both interesting and important. This breadth is reflected in the scholarship on immigrant women in the United States. While much of this research is carried out at the micro community level, today it is rarely without some recognition of the significance of macro-economic and political forces. While feminist models have suggested new questions to address, the emphasis within anthropology on the insider's interpretation of events has meant that universal dichotomies are not applied categorically. What is perhaps less apparent in studies of immigrant women, though fundamental to the anthropological imagination, is the comparative perspective. Ethnologists have tended to focus on single cultural groups and as a result lose the context within which to delineate how culture as opposed to some other factor, such as class, influences the lives and experiences of immigrant women. However, from the perspective of anthropology, social classes also have culture. It is the concept of culture that leads us to appreciate the multiple voices of immigrant women.

NOTES

1. For examples of studies that use the household as the major unit of analysis, see Janet E. Benson, "Households, Migration and Community Context," *Urban Anthropology* 19, 1 (1990): 9–29; Elizabeth K. Briody, "Patterns of Household Migration into South Texas," *International Migration Review* 21, 1 (1987): 27–47; Ina Dinerman, "Patterns of Adaptation among Households of U.S-Bound Migrants from Michoacan Mexico," *International Migration Review* 12 (1978): 485–501; Patricia Pessar, "The Role of Households in International Migration and the Case of U.S.-Bound Migration from the Dominican Republic," *International Migration Review* 16, 2 (1982): 342–364; Charles Wood, "Structural Change and Household Strategies: A Conceptual Framework for the Study of Rural Migration," *Human Organization* 40, 4 (1981): 338–343.
2. In this chapter we use migrant and immigrant interchangeably, though we are always talking about women who are crossing an international boundary. In general, we are dealing with the literature on relative newcomers to the United States, but occasionally studies of second- or even third-generation ethnic groups are included. We have included some research on refugee groups. These populations are the focus of increasing attention by anthropologists, and they often experience problems similar to those of economic migrants. Finally, where we thought it relevant, we have made reference to some studies of immigrant women in Canada.
3. Rosaldo, *Women, Culture, and Society,* pp. 17–43.
4. Chai, "Adaptive Strategies of Recent Korean Immigrant Women in Hawaii," and "Freed from the Elders but Locked into Labor."
5. Chai, "Freed from the Elders but Locked into Labor," p. 299.
6. Stafford, "Haitian Immigrant Women," p. 186.
7. This concept of helping—women help men outside the home and men help women within it—has been described for other immigrant groups. See Goody, "Introduction to Female Migrants and the Work Force"; Alicia Chavira, "Tienes Que Ser Valiente: Mexican Migrants in a Midwestern Farm Labor Camp," in Melville, *Mexicans at Work,* pp. 64–73, here, p. 69.
8. Briody, "Patterns of Household Migration."
9. Guendelman and Perez-Itriago, "Double Lives," p. 268.
10. Fernandez-Kelly, "Mexican Border Industrialization."
11. Chavez, "Coresidence and Resistance."
12. Stafford, "Haitian Immigrant Women."
13. Ahern, Bryan, and Baca, "Migration and La Mujer Fuerte."
14. Cohen, "The Female Factor in Resettlement."
15. Chai, "Adaptive Strategies of Recent Korean Immigrant Women in Hawaii," and "Freed from the Elders but Locked into Labor."

16. Muir, *The Strongest Part of the Family.*
17. O'Connor, "Women's Networks," p. 82.
18. *Ibid.*, p. 85. See also Lamphere, "Bringing the Family to Work," and Zavella, "Abnormal Intimacy," for additional discussions of how networks affect women's consciousness among migrant and immigrant populations.
19. Chai, "Adaptive Strategies of Recent Korean Immigrant Women in Hawaii," and "Freed from the Elders but Locked into Labor."
20. Bloch, "Changing Domestic Roles among Polish Women."
21. Boone, "The Uses of Traditional Concepts."
22. Bell and Whiteford, "Tai Dam Health Care Practices."
23. DeSantis, "Health Care Orientations of Cuban and Haitian Immigrant Mothers," pp. 76, 79.
24. Kirby, "Immigrants, Stress and Prescription Drug Use."
25. Sargent, Marcucci, and Ellison, "Tiger Bones, Fire and Wine."
26. Harbison and Weishaar, "Samoan Migrant Fertility"; Ford, "Fertility of Immigrant Women"; Ford, "Diverse Fertility."
27. Nancie Gonzalez, "Giving Birth in America," in Simon and Brettell, *International Migration*, pp. 241–253; Wanda R. Trevathan, "Childbirth in a Bicultural Community: Attitudinal and Behavioral Variation," in Michaelson, *Childbirth in America,* pp. 216–227.
28. Janice M. Morse and Caroline Park, "Differences in Cultural Expectations of Perceived Painfulness of Childbirth," in Michaelson, *Childbirth in America*, pp. 121–129.
29. Carolyn Sargent and John Marcucci, "Khmer Prenatal Health Practices and the American Clinical Experience," in Michaelson, *Childbirth in America*, pp. 79–89.
30. Fishman, Evans, and Jenks, "Warm Bodies, Cool Milk."
31. Kendall, "Cold Wombs in Balmy Honolulu," p. 373.
32. Engle, Scrimshaw, and Smidt, "Sex Differences in Attitudes towards Newborn Infants," p. 142.
33. Cohen, *Culture, Disease and Stress.*
34. Westermeyer, Bouafuely, and Vang, "Hmong Refugees in Minnesota," p. 241.
35. Cohen, *Culture, Disease and Stress.*
36. Vega, Kolody, and Vallé, "Relationship of Marital Status, Confidant Support, and Depression."
37. Vega et al., "Depressive Symptoms," p. 650.
38. Vega et al., "Migration and Mental Health."
39. Lewin, "The Nobility of Suffering."
40. Chai, "Adaptive Strategies of Recent Korean Immigrant Women in Hawaii," and "Freed from the Elders but Locked into Labor."
41. Kirby, "Immigrants, Stress, and Prescription Drug Use."
42. Kay and Portillo, "Nervios and Dysphoria."
43. Kirby, "Immigrants Stress and Prescription Drug Use," p. 293.
44. Bell and Whiteford, "Tai Dam Health Care Practices."
45. Guendelman and Perez-Itriago, "Double Lives."
46. Lewin, "The Nobility of Suffering," p. 155.
47. Cohen, *Culture, Disease and Stress.*
48. Chavira, "Tienes Que Ser Valiente," p. 71.
49. Paule Marshall, "Black Immigrant Women in Brown Girls, Brownstones," in Mortimer and Bryce Laporte, *Female Immigrants,* pp. 1–13; Melville, "Mexican Women in the U.S. Wage Labor Force," in Melville, *Mexicans at Work,* pp. 1–11.
50. Helen I. Safa, "The Differential Incorporation of Hispanic Women Migrants in the United States Labor Force," in *Women on the Move*, pp. 159–173.
51. The informal economy is defined as the exchanges of transactions that occur among individuals or units of production that are totally outside the boundaries sanctioned by state or federal legislation. Fernandez-Kelly and Garcia, "The Making of an Underground Economy," p. 65. See the article for further clarification.
52. Margolis, "From Mistress to Servant." Not all immigrant women in the United States come from poor rural backgrounds and have minimal levels of education. Many have worked as professionals prior to their departure. Others have been recruited for their professional qualifications. This latter statement is perhaps most true for those women (Koreans, Filipinos, Caribbeans) who, in rather dramatic numbers, have come to North America to fill the shortages in the nursing profession.
53. Stafford, "Haitian Immigrant Women," p. 181.
54. Maria Garcia Castro, "Work Versus Life: Colombian Women in New York," pp. 231–259 in Nash and Safa, *Women and*

Change, mentions familial difficulties, particularly the repression of sexuality, as a major motive for the migration of younger single women.

55. Castro, "Work Versus Life," p. 243.
56. Boone, "The Uses of Traditional Concepts."
57. Kirby, "Immigrants, Stress, and Prescription Drug Use."
58. Prieto, "Cuban Women," p. 106.
59. As Safa, "Differential Incorporation of Hispanic Women," argues, the ideology of confinement to the home is a class ideology because it is only operative among elite women. See Gonzalez, "Multiple Migratory Experiences," for personal accounts of Dominican immigrant women of different class backgrounds.
60. Fernandez-Kelly and Garcia, "The Making of an Underground Economy."
61. Foner, "Sex Roles and Sensibilities."
62. Pessar, "The Dominicans," p. 123.
63. Melville, "Mexican Women Adapt to Migration"; Prieto, "Cuban Women and Work."
64. Monica Gordon, "Caribbean Migration: A Perspective on Women," in Mortimer and Bryce LaPorte, *Female Immigrants,* pp. 14–55.
65. Lamphere, "Bringing the Family to Work."
66. O'Connor, "Women's Networks"; Zavella, *Women's Work.*

Immigrant Women: Nowhere at Home?

✦ DONNA GABACCIA

Studies of immigrants, ethnics, and women in the United States share common roots in some ways. All developed as acceptable and even popular fields of inquiry during the same years, and in response to some of the same political movements and social forces. Often enough, too, students of women, immigrants, and ethnics seemed joined in a common research agenda which aimed at bringing previously excluded people to scholarly center stage.

Given the common purpose and the flowering of research on all these groups in the 1970s and 1980s, it is puzzling to survey today's historical accounts of immigrant and ethnic groups and of women in the United States (Archdeacon, 1983; Bodnar, 1985; Reimers, 1985; Clinton, 1984; Daniel, 1987; Evans, 1989). Female immigrants are exceedingly marginal figures in most of them.

The problem is not that immigrant women's lives have been either deliberately or accidentally ignored. To the contrary, two recent bibliographies document the existence of a considerable body of newer publications about immigrant women dating from the early 1970s (Cordasco 1985; Gabaccia, 1989). Interest in the topic continues strong[1] belying the possibility that ethnocentrism, political disagreement, or chauvinism explain its marginalization. What needs explanation is why interest rarely translates into integration: Why does research on immigrant women leave so few scholarly traces in the fields most concerned with them?

This question is not unprecedented; it resembles that of a group of African American women who titled their 1983 anthology *All the Women Are White; All the Blacks Are Men, But Some of Us Are Brave* (Hull et al. 1982). Just as women's studies and African American studies found it difficult to incorporate black women's experiences as central and important, immigrant women, too, have not found

Gabaccia, Donna. 1991. "Immigrant women: Nowhere at home?" *Journal of American Ethnic History*. Volume 10, Issue 4:61–75. Reprinted with permission of Transaction Publishers.

a comfortable scholarly home in ethnic or women's studies.[2]

This essay explores the reasons. Studies of immigrant women,[3] like those of men, are undertaken in several independent disciplines (sociology, history, literature) and the interdisciplinary field of ethnic studies. Unlike men, however, immigrant women can also be studied within women's studies. The result, however, is not greater visibility but greater marginality.

To understand why integration eludes scholarship on immigrant women requires a close look at the theoretical perspectives, methods, and categories used in the study of women and of immigrant or ethnic groups. Differences have developed both within particular disciplines (e.g., between immigration history and women's history) and between the interdisciplinary fields of ethnic studies and women's studies. When methods, theories, and categories diverge, those who study immigrant women must attempt to straddle several disciplinary boundaries; this can be a creative, but sometimes also an impossible challenge.

Four examples of this thesis are developed in separate sections following. A first section traces the contrasting questions and methods of immigration and women's history since the 1970s; a second addresses conflicting analytical categories used in studies of immigrant women. A third part examines the quite different treatment of the family in immigration scholarship and in women's studies in the 1980s. A final section discusses the development of apparently irreconcilable methodologies in women's studies and in sociology and the social sciences.

While the focus of this essay is on conflicts and divisions, these problems are analyzed mainly in the hope that they might be overcome. Each section offers some concrete suggestions to those who hope to bridge disciplinary boundaries and pursue integrative research. On the margins of many fields, those studying immigrant women are well placed to identify and expand the common ground shared by many disciplines.

Women and Immigration History: Different Drummers?

An excellent example of how conflicting questions and methods can relegate scholarship to obscurity comes from history. Even in the early 1970s, when immigration and women's history were newly popular fields, the two set differing methodological courses, posing troublesome choices for students of immigrants who were also women.

Of course, there were always some concerns common to historians of women and of immigration. One was the history of the family. In both areas too, interest in the working classes and a respect for human agency was evident. The many resulting studies of immigrant women as workers (Dickinson, 1980; Webster, 1978; Lintelman 1989; Hirata, 1979; Ichioka, 1977; Cheng, 1984; Glenn, 1981, 1984; Baum, 1973; Nea, 1976; Kessner and Caroli, 1978; Krause, 1977; Mormino and Pozzetta, 1982; Pleck, 1978; Vecchio, 1989; Ruiz, 1986; Taylor 1980) and as labor activists (Blumfeld, 1982; Schulman, 1986; Seller, 1986; Stjanstedt, 1981; Kessler-Harris, 1976; Hyman, 1980; Pratt, 1980; Turbin, 1979; Schrode, 1986; Hatzig, 1989) seem to have been widely read in both fields. So was Maxine Seller's excellent 1981 anthology which emphasized the diversity and the initiative of immigrant women, effectively countering earlier stereotypes of victimized foreign-born females (Seller, 1981).

Otherwise, immigration and women's history developed in opposing directions. A popular method for women's historians in the early 1970s was the documentation of notable women's lives and their contributions (Lerner, 1979). At precisely this time, by contrast, younger scholars in immigration history were abandoning "filiopietism"—the glorification of the contributions of great immigrants—as elitist, irrelevant, and defensive.[4] As a result, Cecyle Neidle's biographical studies (Neidle, 1975), and the lives of Emma Goldman (Shulman, 1970; Candace, 1984; Wexler, 1987, 1984), Mary "Mother" Jones (Fetherling, 1974; Long, 1976; Steel, 1985, 1988; Foner, 1983), Anzia Yezierska (Schoen and Yezierska, 1982; Dearborn, 1988; Henriksen and Yezierska, 1988), or the lesser-known foreign-born women of *Notable American Women*[5] and other works (McGovern, 1969; Feeley, 1972; Ritter, 1971; Wilson, 1970; Scharman, 1973; Dash, 1973) had some resonance in women's studies (Merriam, 1971; Nies, 1977), but little impact on immigration history.[6]

By the mid-1970s, immigration historians were involved in the task of writing histories of ethnic groups and communities—places where the lives of men and women intersected.[7] Women's historians instead focused on the uniqueness of women, a group they studied apart from men.[8] As immigration historians' understanding of community evolved, scholars interested primarily in immigrant women abandoned community studies for the methods of women's history.

Since both sexes make up the ethnic group or community, the community study initially seemed to offer good possibilities for an analysis of immigrant women. Case studies like Virginia Yans-McLaughlin's *Family and Community,* Judith Smith's study of Jews and Italians in Providence, or my own *From Sicily to Elizabeth Street* established women's contributions to ethnic-group formation (Yans-McLaughlin, 1977; Smith, 1985; Gabaccia, 1984; Slayton, 1986; Kleinberg, 1989). Community and ethnic loyalties were viewed as originating in the bonds of family solidarity, particularly in the kinship group where women's influence was most obvious.

Not all were satisfied with this model of community formation. Victor Greene has criticized early community studies for focusing so exclusively on family ties, and later works including his own sought the origin of ethnic solidarity elsewhere (Greene, 1987, p. 6). Unlike *Family and Community,* for example, John Zucchi's recent history of Toronto's early Italian community concentrates on ethnic business enterprises, voluntary associations, religious institutions, and the immigrant elite (Zucchi, 1988). Immigrant women scarcely appear in the account.

The dozens of community studies summarized in John Bodnar's recent synthesis, *The Transplanted,* do not ignore women but describe mainly those aspects of women's lives (wage-earning and labor activism) that most resemble men's. Distinctively female concerns—housework, marketing, pregnancy, or childrearing—receive little or no attention. Neither do private ones like sexuality or the dynamics of family life. The reason is obvious: Uniquely female or private familial events are assumed to have no direct impact on community life, which is the focus of these studies (Gabaccia, 1988).

Nowhere are immigration historians' difficulties in integrating women into accounts of community formation better demonstrated than in works based on oral history. Despite a preponderance of women in most elderly populations, women are typically one-third of the immigrants interviewed. Women's reminiscences appear almost exclusively in introductory chapters on family and early settlement (Pozzetta, 1987; Bodnar, 1982; Mormino, 1986; Tateishi, 1984; Lianes, 1982). Immigrant men became more important informants because they built institutions that immigration scholars now see as the center of the ethnic group.

Given the changing focus of immigration history, scholars influenced by women's history often abandoned the community study to concentrate separately on the lives of immigrant women of particular groups.[9] In the 1970s books and essay collections appeared on Jewish, Italian, and Mexican-American women (Baum et al., 1976; Glanz, 1976; Boyd et al., 1978; Cotera, 1976; Hembra, 1976; Mirand and Enriquez, 1979). General studies and essay collections on Jewish, Cuban, Japanese, Chinese, Korean, and Finnish women have appeared since 1980 (Doran et al., 1988; Marcus, 1981; Saiki, 1985; Ross and Brown, 1986; Yung, 1986; Yu and Phillips, 1987; Melville, 1980). The best of these was Hasia Diner's study of the Irish, *Erin's Daughters in America* (Diner, 1983). By studying a group in which women were particularly well-represented, Diner highlighted the biases of earlier works that ignored them. Also popular in the 1970s and 1980s were oral history projects focusing on the women of one or more groups (Kramer and Masur, 1976; Krause, 1981; Miller and Wedegartner, 1982; Weinberg, 1988), and shorter studies of female family roles (analyzed separately in the following paragraphs), women's educational patterns (Cohen, 1982; Birnbaum, 1986; Seller, 1978; Weinberg, 1983, 1987; Zinn, 1980) or female ethnic and religious organizations (Ewens, 1981; Golomb, 1980; Hyman, 1980; Balm, 1973; Peterson and Vaughn-Robertson, 1988; Radzialowski 1980; Szymczak, 1986).

The agendas of women's history and immigration history have not grown closer in recent years. In immigration history, studies of particular ethnic communities are giving way to important new efforts at synthesis (Bodnar, 1985), experiments with world-systems or "Atlantic" perspectives (Archdeacon, 1985; Hoerder, 1985), and interdisciplinary studies of the multiethnic American working class or of ethnic business and leadership (Greene, 1986; Hoerder, forthcoming). While immigration historians now seem involved in a search for commonalities, women's historians are moving in the opposite direction. Having abandoned earlier notions that women constitute a single group—comparable to a caste or class and defined by an essential femaleness or sisterhood—women's historians are now concerned with diversity and difference, particularly the impact of class and race on women's lines and feminist politics.[10]

Very few syntheses of immigrant women's lives have appeared; thus, studies of women remain "out of step" with developments in the field generally. This situation, however, may be appropriate and even necessary. A reading of Doris Weatherford's *Foreign and Female* (Weatherford, 1986), the most ambitious recent effort at synthesis, suggests why. Weatherford's examination of nineteenth-century white immigrant women is generally unsatisfying. It summarizes a number of important themes but offers no argument or interpretation. *Foreign and Female* seems premature and for simple reasons. Unlike John Bodnar, whose synthesis *The Transplanted* develops a number of general themes, Weatherford had only a handful of full-length interpretive studies of the women on which to draw.

Satisfactory synthesis of immigrant women's experiences will be possible only after completion of many more studies of immigrant women of one background. Historical surveys comparable to Diner's should be undertaken of Polish, French-Canadian, Chinese, Italian, Mexican, German, Scandinavian, and West Indian women. If informed by the questions of women's history, case studies like these can easily contribute to that field's analysis of the diversity of American women.

For scholars who wish to contribute to both immigration history and women's history, a comparative approach which simultaneously identifies commonalities *and* differences might satisfactorily address the currently conflicting agendas of the two areas. Two recent studies which deserve emulation are Louis Lamphere's *From Working Daughters to Working Mothers*—which traces changing work and family patterns among several generations of immigrant women from Europe and central and South America (Lamphere, 1986)—and Elizabeth Ewen's *Immigrant Women in the Land of Dollars,* with its focus on the changing identities of Italian and Jewish women in New York (Ewen, 1985).

Ewen and Lamphere were mainly familiar with the debates of women's history, but collaborative work by experts on several groups (and with appropriate language skills, which Ewen lacked) might easily address the questions of immigration and ethnic history.[11] While case studies are still useful, and synthesis almost certainly premature, comparative studies may have the greatest potential for bringing the diverging fields of women's history and immigration history closer, and for contributing to the integration of immigrant women in both.

Race, Nationality, Religion, and Ethnicity: Whose Categories?

The disciplines most interested in the study of immigrants do not share common analytical categories. Immigrants can be, and sometimes have been, studied as parts of groups defined by nationality, culture, or religion (each of which is sometimes called ethnicity), by race (also sometimes called ethnicity) or by class. To give an extreme example, an immigrant might be included in studies of Chicanos, Mexicans, Mexican-Americans, Latinos or Latin-Americans, Central Americans, Hispanics, Spanish-speakers, the Spanish-surnamed, or the working class (Hurtado and Arce, 1986).

Race, ethnicity, class, nationality, culture, and religion are all categories with important—and often overlapping—analytical uses.[12] However, it must be acknowledged that some categories focus better than others directly upon immigrants as immigrants.[13] Categories then inevitably shape research findings. To give just one example, if the recently arrived Haitian and the ancestor of an African brought to the British colonies in 1700 are both called African Americans, as they easily can be, we will see the impact of race on both, but we will not see those aspects of the Haitian's life which result from foreign birth, international migration, Haitian culture, or civil status in the United States.

For those interested in women, disciplinary training more than subject matter influences the choice of analytical category. Scholars in women's studies, like sociologists, and many ethnic studies' experts, prefer the analytical category of racial or ethnic minority (African American, Asian-American, Native-American, and Hispanic) and, like labor historians, that of class.[14] In women's studies and in sociology, the study of ethnicity often means the study of racial minorities.[15] With their more explicit focus on immigrants, by contrast, immigration historians study groups defined by nationality (e.g., Canadian; Jamaican), language or culture (e.g., prior to World War I, Polish), religion (e.g., Jewish), or combinations of these (e.g., German Jews; French-Canadians). The category Euro-American or European American,[16] which is increasingly used in ethnic studies and in women's studies to describe white immigrants, is almost never used by immigration historians.

The differing categories used in the disciplines that study immigrant women influence how research on foreign-born women is integrated in each field. Women's studies tends to treat the working-class of the nineteenth century and present-day racial minorities as homogeneous groups, with little attention to the foreign-born component of either. For example, most immigrant women today are nonwhite women from Asia, the Caribbean, and Central or South America, and research on them is still limited. Their experiences are often summarized together with the minority groups to which they can be assigned, and their lives are contrasted to the white or Euro-American majority.[17] As immigrants, these women are usually invisible. Considering immigrants as members of United States minority groups might be appropriate if women identified themselves in this manner, but the available evidence suggests that they do not; they remain acutely aware of their national or cultural origins, of their mother tongue and, in some cases, of their legal status.[18]

Foreign-born women of the past (when over 95% of immigrants were white Europeans) most often appear in women's history texts and women's history research as working-class wage-earners (Kessler-Harris, 1982; Tentler, 1979; Eisenstein, 1983; Stansell, 1983; Groneman and Norton, 1987) or as labor activists (Levine 1981, 1984; Milkman, 1985) in the years between 1880 and 1920. These, of course, were the years when the woman factory worker (typically an immigrant or her daughter) gripped the national imagination.[19] Histories of American women have summarized working-class women's distinctive reproductive work, leisure, and health more effectively than have immigration history's community studies (Borst, 1989; Dye, 1987; Kornblum and Frederickson, 1984; Boydston, 1986; May, 1984; Ogden, 1986). But because immigrants are viewed mainly as working class, women's history sometimes ignores ethnic differences, satisfied to compare working-class women to middle-class women whose lives are best documented and understood.[20] Both are considered Euro-Americans; only class is assumed to have divided them.

For similar reasons, immigration historians sometimes overlook studies of working-class women or racial minorities produced within women's studies, even when these studies contain significant information on the lives of foreign-born women. One example is Christine Stansell's *City of Women,* a broad and well-written study of nineteenth-century New York and its working-class women (many or most of whom were German and Irish). Stansell was uninterested in the nativity or ethnic identities of the women she studied; not surprisingly, *Journal of American Ethnic History,* an important source of information for immigration historians, did not review the book (Stansell, 1986).

While it is doubtful that scholars will ever settle upon one set of widely shared categories, a number of developments do point toward increasing rapprochement. Sizeable recent migrations of nonwhites have already brought assumptions about homogeneous minority groups into question. Both psychologists and sociologists, for example, specify nationality far more frequently in recent studies than they did in the early 1980s.[21] Women's studies will probably follow in this direction. Vicki Ruiz's excellent 1987 book on the Mexican immigrant women who make up the workforce of the food processing plants of the southwest, *Cannery Women* (Ruiz, 1987), has reached a broad women's studies audience. A number of studies of Jamaican, Haitian, and other Caribbean women are now available (Buchanan, 1979; Foner, 1986; Mortimer and Bryce-Laporte, 1981; Charkin et al., 1987; Cohen, 1977; Castro, 1986; Colen, 1986) and research on Hispanic women—like Ruiz's—also sometimes differentiate by cultural and national groups and by generation (Gurak, 1982). The use of cultural and national categories should open communication between immigration historians and scholars in both women's studies and the social sciences, to the benefit of all fields.

Whether agreement will be reached about the categories most appropriate for the study of white immigrant women in the past is harder to predict. If historians continue to pursue case studies, they will inevitably continue to emphasize ethnic and national differences, and also push women's studies towards a definition of ethnicity that covers a wider range of cultural differences. If they instead pursue comparison and synthesis, they may adopt the terminology of class (as John Bodnar did in *The Transplanted*) and find themselves at home in women's studies via this somewhat different route.

Comparison, too, seems an important antidote for the problem of mutually exclusive analytical categories. As long as class, race, religion, culture, and nationality are understood in isolation, we cannot discern how they intersect to create human identity or influence behavior.[22] Comparative studies of white and nonwhite immigrant women (e.g., Irish, Swedish, and Japanese domestic servants), or of nonwhite women of several backgrounds (e.g., Cuban, Dominican, Mexican, and Chinese garment workers), or of middle- and working-class immigrants should allow scholars to begin that important task.

Immigrant Families and Feminist Theory

While terminology is a troublesome matter, two obstacles loom even larger for those interested in improving interdisciplinary communication on immigrant women. This essay treats first one of concern to both social scientists and historians, and then, in a final section, a problem that affects sociologists most directly.

Neither historians nor social scientists who focus on immigrants and ethnics can at this time easily engage women's studies in a dialogue on women as members of families. The main reason is their conflicting, and in some ways opposite, understanding of family life. Here we have a case where students of immigrant women kept their feet firmly rooted in the assumptions of ethnic studies and immigration history; these assumptions have left them well outside the mainstream of women's studies.

Studies of women as family members made important early contributions to women's history and women's studies in the 1970s. Particularly influential for those analyzing rural, working-class, immigrant, and ethnic women was Louise Tilly and Joan Scott's *Women, Work and Family* (Tilly and Scott, 1978). Tilly and Scott argued that women's work lives were best understood as responses to the economies of the family units within which they lived and upon which they depended for their survival and well-being.

While immigration historians and ethnic studies scholars have continued to draw and build upon Tilly and Scott's work, many in women's studies criticized and ultimately rejected this approach to the study of women (Helmbold, 1987). In part, their rejection originated with the observation that attention to a family unit revealed too little about women's lives (Ross, 1979). Scholars following Heidi Hartmann also came to see the nuclear family as the key institution of patriarchy, and thus a place of conflict between the sexes and an arena of exploitation, not support, of women (Hartmann, 1981).

Within women's history, for example, study of women apart from nuclear families became an important way to document women's first efforts to free themselves (Meyerowitz, 1987, 1988). Books by Kathy Peiss and Christine Stansell both pointed to leisure activities and popular culture as important dimensions in this struggle.[23] At the same time, the immigrant nuclear family appeared in some women's studies scholarship as particularly patriarchal; several scholars emphasized the efforts—and failures—of immigrant women to use wage-earning as a means of breaking free of the self-sacrifice family life required of them (Bloom, 1985; Gonzalez, 1983; Gordon 1988).

Family solidarity, by contrast, continues to be a theme of considerable importance after twenty years of new research in immigration and ethnic studies. Many community studies of the 1970s reacted against Progressive Era portrayals of ethnic families as authoritarian, disorganized, or plagued by generational and pathological conflicts; had migration seriously undermined family life, these studies argued, then neither ethnic groups nor ethnic identities should have survived into the 1960s—as they so obviously had.[24] Thus family solidarity is interpreted positively, as benefiting the individuals who make up the family group. Indeed, it was his understanding of family solidarity that allowed John Bodnar to revise Oscar Handlin's view of immigrants as "the uprooted" (Bodnar, 1985). Viewed from the perspective of immigration history, women's studies' critique of immigrant patriarchy uncomfortably resembles old ethnocentric myths recently put to rest.

For those who have written specifically of immigrant women, the family also remains an important focus of attention, almost inseparable from the study of women themselves (Walkowitz, 1972; Bienstock, 1979; Weinberg, 1981; Rosa, 1982; Parto, 1982; Blackwelder, 1984; Weinberg, 1987; Anker, 1988). The concepts of family economies and family strategies are widely used and rarely criticized by historians, anthropologists, and sociologists alike.[25] Those who study immigrant women differ from their colleagues in women's studies in other ways, too: they rarely focus exclusively on nuclear families and they have shown little interest in sexuality, a topic of considerable concern to women's studies theorists in the 1970s and 1980s.[26]

Scholars of immigrant women usually portray women's family experiences positively. The kin network itself is often described as women-centered (Lamphere et al., 1980; Yanigisako, 1977; Keefe et al., 1979; Leonardo, 1984). Frequently, the kinship network and family are thus seen as arenas where women exercise considerable authority, an authority some scholars term matriarchal (Alcalay, 1984; Mancuso, 1978). Students of Mexican immigrants and Chicanos have been particularly adamant about rejecting the label of patriarchy (machismo) which was so often attached to these families. Many scholars now argue that Mexican women were resourceful participants in families where both husbands and wives enjoyed decision-making prerogatives. Early portrayals of dominating men and oppressed women, it is widely argued, were a myth invented by Anglos and perpetrated by social scientists to emphasize the otherness of the Mexican American (Hawkes and Taylor, 1975; Cromwell and Ruiz, 1978; Cromwell and Cromwell, 1978; Zinn, 1979).

Are those who study immigrant and ethnic women simply "nonfeminist" or "antifeminist," their methodologies and findings different from those in women's studies because of political differences? That possibility seems too simple, and most scholars would deny it. Those who study immigrant women continue to analyze them within a family context for many reasons, but the greatest probably is the overwhelming evidence of family identification and loyalty they find in immigrant women's written and oral sources. These sources suggest that immigrant women, past and often present, generally identified with their families; they did not think of themselves as individuals. (Some scholars have argued that the same was also true of immigrant men.[27]) By contrast, modern Americans, feminists among them, have difficulties accepting a concept of self or identity that is created primarily through relation to others within families.[28]

As women's studies struggles to come to terms with women's diversity, with racial minorities, working-class women, and the third world, the impasse between feminist theory and studies of ethnic and immigrant women may disappear. Worldwide feminist gatherings and research on poor and nonwhite women have both made scholars in the United States newly aware of their own class and cultural biases. In particular, one finds much recent discussion of just how "western" or "Anglo-American" are our assumptions that feminism originates in individuation and the pursuit of individualism.[29] Recognition that identity and even feminist politics in other cultures emerge through connection to others may encourage feminist theorists to reopen discussions of patriarchy and patriarchal families, concepts which are still too often treated as transcultural or transhistorical (Scott, 1988).

A second source for change may originate in women's studies' long-standing concern with documenting women's "voices," which usually means women's subjective understandings of their own experience.[30] Anthropologists Nancie Gonzalez and Nancy Foner, who study contemporary immigrant women from the Caribbean, have both recently emphasized the necessity of viewing the world through their eyes, and recognizing the sometimes intense difference—and validity—of their way of seeing (Gonzalez, 1986).

Unless feminist theorists are willing to dismiss massive evidence of immigrant women's identification and pleasure with their families as false consciousness, they will be forced to consider other possibilities. One of these will certainly be that immigrant women did indeed experience family life positively, in large part because the world beyond family and community as often meant economic exploitation and cultural alienation as autonomy and independence. Students of African American women have long pointed to conflicts between the ways middle-class feminists and minority women view families: The latter more often worry about threats to the family integrity, which underlies their survival-oriented cultures of resistance, than they do about male-domination within the family (Davis, 1971; Caulfield 1974; Glenn, 1987). Students of immigrant women could easily add their voices to this critique of feminist theory.

Structures and Subjectivity: Women's Studies and the Social Sciences

Precisely because the field of women's studies is concerned with female voices, experience, language, and ways of seeing (or interpreting), it cannot easily integrate quantitative and structural studies. Thus, a small scholarship on literature by and about immigrant women has found a home in women's studies' journals (Bannan, 1979; Rabine, 1987; Dearborn, 1986), while a much larger body of research on immigrant women by sociologists and demographers is published and read elsewhere.

While women's studies and the humanities have become ever more interested in culture and individual consciousness, sociologists and some other social scientists are less concerned with these matters. This development does not mean that sociologists have no interest in the culturally different, or the immigrants among them. In fact, study of immigrant women by sociologists and demographers has a long history in the United States. Moving away from Progressive Era concerns with assimilation (and the "backwardness" of immigrant mothers), social policy (including the protection of female immigrant workers), and social Darwinist theories of "race suicide," sociologists since the 1960s have undertaken considerable theoretical and empirical work on wage-earning, family roles, migration, race, minorities, and ethnicity (Hirschman, 1983).

Sociologists' research, however, is framed differently than in the humanities. Sociologists remain concerned with structure, theory and measurement, not with interpretation and experience.[31] Like other social scientists, they often undertake research in order to contribute to the formulation of public policy. That can make their research suspect in women's studies, a field that emphasizes the importance of non-exploitative and collaborative research (Westkott, 1979; Mies, 1983). The result is that only some sociological research—theories about minority women's "double," "triple," or "multiple" jeopardy; discussions of women in development; the creation of segmented labor markets—has been widely known or used in women's studies.[32]

In some respects, sociologists studying immigrant women share the concerns of immigration historians, especially their interest in immigrant women as wage-earners (Foner, 1987; Pessar, 1984; Cooney and Ortiz, 1978; Fernandez-Kelly and Garcia, 1985; Ortiz and

Cooney 1984; Prieto; Safa; Simon and DeLey, 1984; Tienda and Guhleman, 1985; Castro et al., 1987; Cardenas et al., 1982; Cooney, 1975; Kossoudji and Ranney, 1984; Carliner, 1981; Ong, 1987; Boyd, 1976; Tienda et al., 1984; Sullivan, 1984). Sociologists' theory of labor market segmentation (split labor markets) encouraged considerable study of the intersection of gender and ethnicity in shaping immigrant and minority women's rates of labor force participation, occupational preferences, and incomes (Woo, 1985; Wong and Hirschman, 1983; Segura, 1984; Haug, 1983; Harriet and Hartman, 1983; Cardenas et al., 1982). Of these, Evelyn Nakano Glenn's work on the segregation of Japanese women in domestic service (*Issei, Nisei, War Bride*)—based in part on oral histories—has found a women's study audience (Glenn, 1986). Studies of contemporary labor activism—or lack thereof—have also attracted some attention (Zavella, 1985; Lamphere, 1979, 1985, 1984; Loo and Ong, 1982; Mora, 1981; Shapiro-Perl, 1980). Growing interest in ethnic business enterprise is slowly generating a literature on self- or family-employed women, particularly Koreans (Bonacich and Park, 1987). The so-called new home economics raised questions about the relationship of women's wage-earning and familial power. Scholars interested in how and if wage-earning altered responsibility for household tasks or family decision-making often found immigrant women an appropriate group for empirical study, since many women had not earned wages prior to entering the United States (Bloch, 1976; Richmond, 1976; Hirayama, 1982; Chai, 1983; Kim and Hurh). Social scientists, unlike historians, have also given considerable attention to childrearing immigrant families (Zeskind, 1983; Strom et al., 1986; Lewin, 1980; Gray and Cosgrove, 1985; Luis and Escovar, 1985; de Cubas and Field, 1984; Chavez and Buriel, 1986; Bryan).

In other respects, the study of women and gender within sociology has scarcely kept pace with the more-rapidly changing humanities. Migration theory, always an important field within sociology, has only recently begun to consider gender a worthwhile variable. Recent statistical analysis documents a female majority among American immigrants at least since the 1930s (Houstoun et al., 1984). This empirical finding is gradually influencing migration theory, which for many years focused on the genderless pushes and pulls of national economies or on the equally genderless (but presumably male) labor migrants who chased capital flows about within a capitalist world system (Chaney, 1982; Morokvasic, 1984).

A number of important theoretical works on women's migration worldwide is also generating interest in the migration patterns of women who enter the United States.[33] Most studies, for example, point to United States immigration law, and its provisions for family unification, as a cause of changing sex ratios among immigrants over the past fifty years (De Jong et al., 1986; Donato and Tyree, 1986). But women immigrants, we learn, are also sometimes labor migrants, pioneering the way to the United States to find work and then sending for children, spouse, or kin from the homeland (Bryce-Laporte, 1977; Gonzalez, 1976).

Always an important field within sociology, demography reveals little about women's subjective experience, but it has long produced significant research about immigrant women. Studies abound of the fertility (Bachu and O'Connell, 1984; Card, 1979; Ford, 1985) and intermarriage of many immigrant and ethnic groups (Edno and Hirokawa, 1983; Gurak, 1987; Kim, 1978; Kitano and Chai, 1982; Kitano and Yeung, 1982; Kitano et al., 1984; Shin, 1987). Both birth rates and intermarriage are used as measures of women's social integration, cultural change, or assimilation (Gordon, 1964). Today, as in the past, popular racial fears seem to produce the fuel that fires much demographic research. Concern about the "browning" of the United States population has led to considerable attention to the fertility patterns, birth control, and abortion attitudes of Mexican-American women;[34] less is known about the behavior and attitudes of contemporary Asian immigrants (Swenson et al., 1987; Gordon, 1983; Kaku and Matsumoto, 1975; Leonetti, 1978; Leonetti and Newell-Morris, 1982; Hopkins and Clarke, 1983; Rumbaut and Weeks, 1986).

The lack of fit between sociologists' and women's studies' central questions threatens to undermine women's studies' ability to incorporate information on the lives of the large and growing population of immigrant women living in the United States today. Sociology is the discipline most likely to study contemporary migrations; this means we often must depend upon sociologists for what little information is currently available about the migration of women from Asia, the Caribbean and Central and South America since the 1960s.

Since most immigrants now originate in third world countries, however, anthropologists and folklorists who have specialized in studies of such lands are for the first time also beginning to examine immigrant life in the United States.[35] This development bodes well for women's studies' understanding of contemporary immigrant women, since anthropology's methods (participant observation), central concepts (culture, gender, subjectivity), and flexible use of theory can more easily be accommodated.

For many sociologists who study immigrant women, the possibility of finding a home in women's studies seems slim. Their dependence on survey data and their disinterest in culture are the main stumbling blocks. Both sometimes render sociologists blind to opportunities that would tempt other researchers. Unlike historians, sociologists could easily question and talk with the people they analyze. That they so rarely do so astonishes those who work with far less promising sources to limn the internal world of immigrant women.

Conclusion

This essay should put to rest an assumption, common in women's and ethnic studies, that the lives of immigrant women remain unexplored territory. To write this is not to deny that much remains to be done, only to emphasize that a great deal of research on immigrant women has been published in the last twenty years. Obviously, more than a few scholars have been brave enough to pursue the necessarily interdisciplinary study of immigrant women.

The results nevertheless have been disappointingly meager. The problem is not the paucity of research on immigrant women, but the unevenness of its reception. It is almost impossible to formulate research on immigrant women in a way that will be visible and exciting to all the disciplines logically interested in the topic. Often scholars must choose whether they will address an immigration history and ethnic studies audience *or* one of women's studies experts. Once research is completed, scholars find it difficult, if not impossible, to capture the attention of all of their colleagues. Ironically, the very proliferation of specialties that allowed ethnic and women's studies to develop as multidisciplinary fields has also helped institutionalize the conflicting categories, methods, and modes of analysis that contribute to the marginality of scholarship on immigrant women.

While common ground can always be found—and this essay has tried to point out the most hopeful areas for collaborative work—scholars in this field may long face difficult choices. Perhaps there will never be one disciplinary home for those researching immigrant women. Still, scholars in this field should recognize an opening: Current distress about the fragmentation of disciplines is strong and opens unique opportunities. Those who exist on the margins of many fields are in the best theoretical position to discover new analytical approaches that challenge existing paradigms and thus lead the way toward a more broadly inclusive scholarship. The comparative method seems to offer the possibility for resolving the first three conflicts explored in this essay. The fourth—the reconciliation of interpretive and theoretical approaches in the humanities and the social sciences—seems to allow for no such easy solution. This conflict is, however, not limited to those who study immigrant women. As scholars in many fields now recognize, the diverging goals of interpretation and explanation may well pose the most difficult intellectual challenges to humanists and social scientists for years to come.

NOTES

The author wishes to thank Sydney Weinberg, Christiane Harzig, Thomas Kozak, and participants in the Pittsburgh Social History Consortium for critical reading of earlier versions of this essay.

1. See special issues of *International Migration Review*, 18 (1984) and *Journal of American Ethnic History*, 8 (Spring 1989). For 1989-1990, sessions on *immigrant* women were scheduled for the Berkshire Conference as well as the meetings of the American Historical Association, the Organization of American Historians, and the Social Science History Association.
2. Some of the complex reasons are explored in Elizabeth V. Spelman, *Inessential Women, Problems of Exclusion in Feminist Thought* (Boston, 1989).
3. For the purposes of this essay, *immigrant* women are defined as those voluntarily crossing a national boundary to live or work in the United States, even if temporarily. The essay surveys works published since 1970, with some emphasis on the most recent years.
4. Thus the editors of The Harvard Encyclopedia of American Ethnic Groups (Cambridge, Mass., 1980) seemed disturbed by "authors. . . eager to recount the achievements of the groups about which they write," p. 436b.
5. Over one hundred *immigrant* and second generation women's lives are summarized in Edward and Janet James, eds., *Notable American Women*, 3 vols. (Cambridge, Mass., 1971); see also Barbara Sicherman et al., *Notable American Women, The Modern Period* (Cambridge, Mass. And London, 1980).
6. Archdeacon, *Becoming American* mentions only Neidle's book; Bodnar's *The Transplanted* does not consider works of biography.
7. Bodnar, *The Transplanted*, a synthesis of their studies, provides the best bibliographical introduction to them.
8. Or, in Lerner's words, "What would history be like if it were seen through the eyes of women and ordered by values they define?" *The Majority Finds Its Past*, p. 162.
9. Southern and eastern Europeans are by far the best-studied groups, see Cordasco, *Immigrant Women* or Gabaccia, *Immigrant Women*.
10. See the special issue "Rethinking Sisterhood: Unity in Diversity," *Women's Studies International Forum*, 8, 1 (1985); Johnnetta B. Cole, ed., All *American Women; Lines that Divide, Ties that Bind* (New York and London, 1986). For a more theoretical work, see Spelman, *Inessential Woman*.
11. A collaborative project by European scholars studying four groups of *immigrant* women in Chicago is currently underway with funding from the West German Volkswagen Foundation, directed by Christiane Hatzig at the University of Bremen.
12. Compare William Petersen, "Concepts of Ethnicity," *Harvard Encyclopedia*, pp. 235–237; Ronald Cohen, "Ethnicity: Problem and Focus in Anthropology," *Annual Review of Anthropology*, 7 (1978): 379–403; and Robin M. Williams, Jr., "Race and Ethnic Relations," *Annual Review of Sociology*, 1 (1975): 125–164.
13. The usefulness of studying cultural or ethnic groups and racial minorities together or apart remains controversial among scholars in ethnic studies. See Ronald Takaki, ed., From *Different Shores, Perspectives on Race and Ethnicity in America* (New York, 1987), pp 7–8, 1211. Milton Yinger, "Ethnicity," *Annual Review of Sociology*, 11 (1985): 151–180. Those who study Chicanos usually reject the *immigrant* analogy, emphasizing that native-American roots, not birth south or north of a border redefined by U.S. conquests, defines the group. See Alfredo Mirande, *The Chicano Experience, an Alternative perspective* (Notre Dame, Ind., 1985). For obvious reasons, distinctions be-

tween foreign born and native born are more commonly made in studies of Asian Americans. Studies of African Americans, however, rarely consider nationality.

14. See the special issue "Common Grounds and Crossroads: Race, Ethnicity, and Class in Women's Lives," *SIGNS*, 14 (Summer 1989); although the title appears to differentiate the two, the articles included conflate race and ethnicity, while distinguishing class as separate from either.
15. Besides the *SIGNS* special issue, see the April 1989 conference "Ethnic Women in the United States," Georgetown University, with its many fine sessions on minority women; Elizabeth Almquist, "Race and Ethnicity in the Lives of Minority Women," in *Women: A Feminist Perspective*, ed. Jo Freeman, 3rd ed. (Palo Alto, Calif., 1984), pp. 423–453.
16. Elizabeth Jameson, "Toward a Multicultural History of Women in the Western United States," *SIGNS*, 13 (Summer 1988): 763–773; Spelman, *Inessential Woman*, p. 157. The term "white ethnic" is also sometimes used; see James Stuart Olson, *The Ethnic Dimension in American History* (New York, 1979).
17. Daniel, *American Women*, ch. 6–7 provides just one example of this pattern.
18. See the interview material in "I Was Afraid but More I Was Hungry: Brooklyn's West Indians," in Thoman Kessner and Betty Boyd Caroli, *Today's Immigrants, Their Stories* (New York, 1982), pp. 186–1871 Hurtado and Arce, "Mexicanos," argue that those of Mexican descent identify with terms specifying Mexican origins in some way, but not with the commonly used category of Hispanic or Spanish-American.
19. Virginia Sapiro, *Women in American Society, An Introduction to Women's Studies* (Palo Alto, Calif., 1986). To be fair, these are also the best-studied of women *immigrants*, in large part because middle-class women reformers so effectively documented the lives of southern and eastern European arrivals during that time. Ironically, women were better represented among older *immigrant* groups travelling to rural destinations earlier in the century.
20. Probably the most careful to distinguish among women of various backgrounds is Kessler-Harris, *Out to Work*.
21. As a survey of the categories used in Psychological Abstracts and Sociological Abstracts over the last ten years will reveal. Psychological Abstracts, for example, dropped the category "Chicano" and substituted "Mexican-American." It still uses the category Hispanic, but now mainly for non-Mexicans.
22. For elaboration, see Spelman, *Inessential Woman*; for a concrete example of how teachers might approach this problem, see Alice Y Chai, "Toward a Holistic Paradigm for Asian-American Women's Studies: A Synthesis of Feminist Scholarship and Women of Color's Feminist Politics," *Women's Studies International Forum*, 8, 1 (1985): 59–66.
23. Stansell, *City of Women*; Kathy Peiss, *Cheap Amusements: Working Women and Leisure in Turn-of-the Century New York* (Philadelphia, 1986). Ewen, *Immigrant* Women handles some of the same themes as Peiss, but with better attention to ethnic origin.
24. For *immigrants*, this point is made most effectively by Yans-McLaughlin, *Family* and Community; see also Charles H. Mindel, *Ethnic Families in America, Patterns and Variations*. 3rd ed. (New York. 1988).
25. Generally, see Bodnar, *The Transplanted*, ch. 2; Tamara Hareven's *Family Time and Industrial Time: The Relationship between the Family and Work in a New England Industrial Community* (Cambridge, 1982); Kleinberg, *Shadow of the Mill*. Studies of *immigrant* women making explicit use of the concept include Louise Lamphere, "Working Mothers and *Family* Strategies: Portuguese and Colombian *Immigrant* Women in a New England Community," in *International Migration: The Female Experience*, ed. Rita J. -Simon and Caroline Brettell (Totowa, N.J., 1986), pp. 166–183; Gary Cross and Peter R. Shergold, "The *Family* Economy and the Market: Wages and Residence of Pennsylvania Women in the 1890s," *Journal of Family History*, 11, 3 (1986): 245–265; Evelyn N. Glenn, "Split Household, Small Producer and Dual Wage Earner: An Analysis of Chinese-American *Family* Strategies," *Journal of Marriage and the Family*, 45 (February 1983): 35–46.
26. Exceptions include Oliva Espin, "Cultural and Historical Influences on Sexuality in Hispanic/Latin Women," in *All American Women; Lines that Divide, Ties that Bind*, ed. Johnnetta B.

Cole (New York and London, 1986), pp. 272–284; Emma G. Pavich, "A Chicana Perspective on Mexican Culture and Sexuality," *Journal of Social Work and Human Sexuality*, 4 (Spring 1986): 47–65; Barbara Noda et al., "Coming Out. We Are Here in the Asian Community. A Dialogue with There Asian Women," *Bridge*, 7 (Spring 1979): 22–24; B. Ruby Rich and Lourdes Arguelles, "Homosexuality, Homophobia and Revolution: Notes toward an Understanding of the Cuban Lesbian and Gay Male Experience, Part II," *SIGNS*, 11 (Autumn 1985): 120–136.

27. Bodnar, *Workers' Lives*.
28. Weinberg, "The World of Our Mothers."
29. The discussion dates to the 1985 United Nations Decade for Women Conference in Nairobi.
30. Given their concerns with subjectivity, feminist theorists have become critical of objective methodologies; for the clearest statement see E.F. Keller, "Feminism and Science," *SIGNS*, 7 (1982): 589–602.
31. For a feminist's description of the structural approach of sociologists, see Myra M. Ferree and Beth B. Hess, "Introduction," *Analyzing Gender*, pp. 11–12.
32. Index of volumes 1–10, 1975-1985, *SIGNS*, 11, 4 (Summer 1986).
33. Andrea Tyree and Katharine M. Donato, "A Demographic Overview of the International Migration of Women," in *International Migration*, pp. 21–44; and "The Sex Composition of Legal *Immigrants* to the United States," *Sociology and Social Research*, 69 (July 1985): 577–84.
34. This sizeable literature is summarized in Katherine F. Darabi, comp., *Childbearing among Hispanics in the United States, An Annotated Bibliography* (New York, 1987).
35. Besides works cited by anthropologists Lamphere, Pessar, di Leonardo, Foner, and Gonzalez, see Rafaela Castro, "Mexican Women's Sexual Jokes," *Aztlan*, 13 (Spring and Fall 1982): 275–294; Rosan A. Jordan, "The Vaginal Serpent and Other Themes from Mexican-American Women's Lore," in *Women's Folklore, Women's Culture*, ed. Rosan A. Jordan and Susan J. Kalcik (Philadelphia, 1987), pp. 26–44; Kay F. Turner, "Mexican American Home Altars: Towards Their Interpretation," *Aztlan*, 13 (Spring/Fall 1982): 309–326.

Gender and Labor in Asian Immigrant Families

✦ Yen Le Espiritu, *University of California*

ABSTRACT

This article explores the effects of employment patterns on gender relations among contemporary Asian immigrants. The existing data on Asian immigrant salaried professionals, self-employed entrepreneurs, and wage laborers suggest that economic constraints and opportunities have reconfigured gender relations within contemporary Asian America society. The patriarchal authority of Asian immigrant men, particularly those of the working class, has been challenged due to the social and economic losses that they suffered in their transition to the status of men of color in the United States. On the other hand, the recent growth of female-intensive industries—and the racist and sexist "preference" for the labor of immigrant women—has enhanced women's employability over that of some men. In all three groups, however, Asian women's ability to transform patriarchal family relations is often constrained by their social positions as racially subordinate women in U.S. society.

Through the process of migration and settlement, patriarchal relations undergo continual negotiation as women and men rebuild their lives in the new country. An important task in the study of immigration has been to examine this reconfiguration of gender relations. Central to the reconfiguration of gender hierarchies is the change in immigrant women's and men's

AUTHOR'S NOTE: I thank Pierrette Hondagneu-Sotelo and two anonymous reviewers for their helpful comments and suggestions on an earlier draft.

Espiritu, Yen Le. 1999."Gender and labor in asian immigrant families." *American Behavioral Scientist*. Volume 42, Issue 4, 628–647. Reprinted by permission of Sage Publications, Inc.

relative positions of power and status in the country of settlement. Theoretically, migration may improve women's social position if it leads to increased participation in wage employment, more control over earnings, and greater participation in family decision-making (Pessar, 1984b). Alternatively, migration may leave gender asymmetries largely unchanged even though certain dimensions of gender inequalities are modified (Curtis, 1986). The existing literature on migration and changing gender relations suggests contradictory outcomes whereby the position of immigrant women is improved in some domains even as it is eroded in others (Hondagneu-Sotelo, 1994; Morokvasic, 1984; Tienda & Booth, 1991).

This article is a first attempt to survey the field of contemporary Asian immigrants and the effects of employment patterns on gender relations. My review indicates that the growth of female-intensive industries in the United States—and the corresponding preference for racialized and female labor—has enhanced the employability of some Asian immigrant women over that of their male counterparts and positioned them as coproviders, if not primary providers, for their families. The existing data also suggest that gender relations are experienced differently in different structural occupational locations. In contrast to the largely unskilled immigrant population of the pre-World War II period, today's Asian immigrants include not only low-wage service sector workers but also significant numbers of white-collar professionals. A large number of immigrants have also turned to self-employment (Ong and Hee, 1994). Given this occupational diversity, I divide the following discussion into three occupational categories and examine gender issues within each group: the salaried professionals, the self-employed entrepreneurs, and the wage laborers.[1] Although changes in gender relations have been slow and uneven in each of these three groups, the existing data indicate that men's dependence on the economic and social resources of women is most pronounced among the wage laborers. In all three groups, however, Asian women's ability to transform patriarchal family relations is often constrained by their social position as racially subordinated women in U.S. society.

As a review of existing works, this article reflects the gaps in the field. Overall, most studies of contemporary Asian immigrants have focused more on the issues of economic adaptation than on the effects of employment patterns on gender relations. Because there is still little information on the connections between work and home life—particularly among the salaried professionals—the following discussion on gender relations among contemporary Asian immigrants is at times necessarily exploratory.

Immigration Laws, Labor Needs, and Changing Gender Composition

Asian American's lives have been fundamentally shaped by the legal exclusions of 1882, 1917, 1924, and 1934, and by the liberalization laws of 1965.[2] Exclusion laws restricted Asian immigration to the United States, skewed the sex ratio of the early communities so that men were disproportionately represented, and truncated the development of conjugal families. The 1965 Immigration Act equalized immigration rights for all nationalities. No longer constrained by exclusion laws, Asian immigrants began coming in much larger numbers than ever before. In the period from 1971 to 1990, approximately 855,500 Filipinos, 610,800 Koreans, and 576,100 Chinese entered the United States (U.S. Bureau of the Census, 1992). Moreover, with the collapse of U.S.-backed governments in South Vietnam, Laos, and Cambodia in 1975, more than one million escapees from these countries have resettled in the United States. As a consequence, in the 1980s, Asia was the largest source of U.S. legal immigrants, accounting for 40% to 47% of the total influx (Min, 1995b, p. 12).[3] In 1990, 66% of Asians in the United States were foreign-born (U.S. Bureau of the Census, 1993).

Whereas pre–World War II immigration from Asia was composed mostly of men, the contemporary flow is dominated by women. Women make up the clear majority among U.S. immigrants from nations in Asia but also from those in Central and South America, the Caribbean, and Europe (Donato, 1992). Between 1975 and 1980, women (20 years and older) constituted more than 50% of the immigrants from China, Burma, Indonesia, Taiwan, Hong Kong, Malaysia, the Philippines, Korea, Japan, and Thailand (Donato, 1992). The dual goals of the 1965 Immigration Act—to facilitate family reunification and, secondarily, to admit workers with special job skills—have produced a female-dominated flow. Since 1965, most visas have been allocated to relatives of U.S. residents. Women who came as wives, daughters, or mothers of U.S. permanent residents and citizens are the primary component of change (p. 164). The dominance of women immigrants also reflects the growth of female-intensive industries in the United States, particularly in the service, health care, microelectronics, and apparel-manufacturing industries (Clement and Myles, 1994). Of all women in the United States, Asian immigrant women have recorded the highest rate of labor force participation (Gardner, Robey, and Smith, 1985). In 1980, among married immigrant women between 25 and 64 years of age, 61% of Korean women, 65% of Chinese women, and 83% of Filipino women were in the labor force (Duleep and Sanders, 1993). In 1990, Asian women had a slightly higher labor force participation rate than all women, 60% to 57%, respectively (U.S. Bureau of the Census, 1993).

Economic Diversity Among Contemporary Asian Immigrants

Relative to earlier historical periods, the employment pattern of today's Asian Americans is considerably more varied, a result of both immigration and a changing structure of opportunity. During the first half of the twentieth century, Asians were concentrated at the bottom of the economic ladder—restricted to retailing, food service, menial service, and agricultural occupations. After World War II, economic opportunities improved but not sufficiently for educated Asian Americans to achieve parity. In the post-1965 era, the economic status of Asian Americans has bifurcated, showing some great improvements but also persistent problems. The 1965 Immigration Act and a restructuring of the economy brought a large number of low-skilled and highly educated Asians to this country, creating a bimodalism (Ong and Hee, 1994). As indicated in Table 1, Asian Americans were over-represented in the well-paid, educated, white-collar sector of the workforce and in the lower paying service and manufacturing jobs. This bimodalism is most evident among Chinese men: Although 24% of Chinese men were professionals in 1990, another 19% were in service jobs.

Asian professional immigrants are over-represented as scientists, engineers, and health-care professionals in the United States. In 1990, Asians were 3% of the U.S. total population but accounted for close to 7% of the scientist and engineer workforce. Their greatest presence was among engineers with doctorate degrees, making up more than one fifth of this group in 1980 and in 1990 (Ong and Blumenberg, 1994). Although Asian immigrant men dominated the fields of engineering, mathematics, and computer science, Asian immigrant women were also over-represented in these traditionally male-dominated professions. In 1990, Asian women accounted for 5% of all

TABLE 1 Occupational distribution by gender and ethnicity—1990 (in percentages)

Occupation	All	Chinese	Japanese	Filipino	Korean	Vietnamese
Men						
Managerial	13	15	20	10	15	5
Professional	12	24	20	12	16	13
Technical, Sales	15	18	17	15	29	18
Administrative Support	7	8	9	16	6	8
Service	10	19	9	16	10	12
Fish, Forestry	4	<1	4	2	1	2
Production, Craft	19	8	12	12	12	19
Operators	20	9	8	15	12	22
Women						
Managerial	11	15	14	10	9	7
Professional	17	17	19	20	11	9
Technical, Sales	16	17	16	16	25	17
Administrative Support	28	21	28	25	14	18
Service	17	14	14	17	20	19
Fish, Forestry	1	<1	1	1	<1	<1
Production, Craft	2	3	3	3	6	10
Operators	8	13	5	7	14	20

Source: Mar and Kim (1994, p.25, Table 3). Reprinted with permission.

female college graduates in the U.S. labor force but 10% to 15% of engineers and architects, computer scientists, and researchers in the hard sciences (Rong and Preissle, 1997).

In the field of health care, two-thirds of foreign nurses and 60% of foreign doctors admitted to the United States during the fiscal years 1988 to 1990 were from Asia (Kanjanapan, 1995). Today, Asian immigrants represent nearly a quarter of the health-care providers in public hospitals in major U.S. metropolitan areas (Ong and Azores, 1994a). Of the 55,400 Asian American nurses registered in 1990, 90% were foreign-born (Rong and Preissle, 1997). The Philippines is the largest supplier of health professionals to the United States, sending nearly 25,000 nurses to this country between 1966 and 1985 and another 10,000 between 1989 and 1991 (Ong and Azores, 1994a). Due to the dominance of nurses, Filipinas are more likely than other women and than Filipino men to be in professional jobs. Table 1 indicates that in 1990, 20% of Filipino women but only 12% of Filipino men had professional occupations.

Responding to limited job opportunities, particularly for the highly educated, a large number of Asian Americans have also turned to self-employment. Asian immigrants are much more likely than their native-born counterparts to be entrepreneurs: In 1990, 85% of the Asian American self-employed population were immigrants (Ong and Hee, 1994). Korean immigrants have the highest self-employment rate of any minority and immigrant group (Light and Bonacich, 1986). A 1986 survey showed that 45% of Korean immigrants in Los Angeles and Orange counties were self-employed. A survey conducted in New York City revealed an even higher self-employment rate of more than 50% (Min, 1996). Because another 30% of Korean immigrants work in the Korean ethnic market, the vast majority of the Korean workforce—three out of four Korean workers—is segregated in the Korean ethnic economy either as business owners or as employees of coethnic businesses (Min, 1998). The problems of underemployment, misemployment, and discrimination in the U.S. labor market have turned many educated and professional Korean immigrants toward self-employment (Min, 1995a). Based on a 1988 survey, nearly half of the Korean male entrepreneurs had completed college (Fawcett and Gardner, 1994).

Although some Asian immigrants constitute "brain drain" workers and self-employed entrepreneurs, others labor in peripheral and labor-intensive industries. The typical pattern of a dual-worker family is a husband who works as a waiter, cook, janitor, or store helper and a wife who is employed in a garment shop or on an assembly line. In a study conducted by the Asian Immigrant Women Advocates (AIWA), 93% of the 166 seamstresses surveyed in the San Francisco-Oakland Bay Area listed their husbands' jobs as unskilled or semiskilled, including waiter, busboy, gardener, day laborer, and the like (Louie, 1992). Most disadvantaged male immigrants can get jobs only in ethnic businesses in which wages are low but in which only simple English is required (Chen, 1992). On the other hand, since the late 1960s, the United States has generated a significant number of informal sector service occupations—paid domestic work, child care, garment and electronic assembly—that rely primarily on female immigrant workers (Hondagneu-Sotelo, 1994). Due to the perceived vulnerability of their class, gender, ethnicity, and immigration status, Asian immigrant women—and other immigrant women of color—have been heavily recruited to toil in these low-wage industries. As indicated in Table 1, Asian women of all ethnic groups were much more likely than Asian men to be in administrative support and service jobs.

Gender Relations Among Salaried Professionals

Although the large presence of Asian professional workers is now well documented, we still have little information on the connections between work and home life—between the public and private spheres—of this population. The available case studies suggest greater male involvement in household labor in these families. In a study of Taiwan immigrants in New York, Hsiang-Shui Chen (1992) reports that the degree of husbands' participation in household labor varied considerably along class lines, with men in the professional class doing a greater share than men in the working and small-business classes. Although women still performed most of the household labor, men helped with vacuuming, disposing of garbage, laundry, dishwashing, and bathroom cleaning. In a survey of Korean immigrant families in New York, Pyong Gap Min (1998) found a similar pattern: younger, professional husbands undertook more housework than did men in other occupational categories, although their wives still did the lion's share. Professional couples of other racial-ethnic groups also seem to enjoy more gender equality. For example, Beatriz M. Pesquera (1993) reports that Chicano "professional men married to professional women did a greater share than most other men" (p. 194). This more equitable household division of labor can be attributed to the lack of a substantial earning gap between professional men and women, the demands of the women's careers, and the women's ability to pressure their husbands into doing their share of the household chores (Hondagneu-Sotelo, 1994; Hood, 1983; Kibria, 1993; Pesquera, 1993). On the other hand, Chen (1992), Min (1998), and Pesquera (1993) all conclude that women in professional families still perform more of the household labor than their husbands do. Moreover, Pesquera reports that, for the most part, the only way women have altered the distribution of household labor has been through conflict and confrontation, suggesting that, ideologically, most men continue to view housework as women's work. These three case studies remind us that professional women, like most other working women, have to juggle full-time work outside the home with the responsibilities of child care and housework. This burden is magnified for professional women because most tend to live in largely white, suburban neighborhoods where they have little or no access to the women's social networks that exist in highly connected ethnic communities (Glenn, 1983, p. 41; Kibria, 1993).

Given the shortage of medical personnel in the United States, particularly in the inner cities and in rural areas, Asian women health professionals may be in a relatively strong position to modify traditional patriarchy. First, as a much-sought-after group among U.S. immigrants, Asian women health professionals can enter the United States as the principal immigrants (Espiritu, 1995). This means that unmarried women can immigrate on their own accord, and married women can enter as the primary immigrants, with their husbands and children following as dependents. My field research of Filipino American families in San Diego suggests that a female-first migration stream, especially when the women are married, has enormous ramifications for both family relations and domestic roles. For example, when Joey Laguda's mother, a Filipina medical technologist, entered the country in 1965, she carried the primary immigrant status and sponsored Joey's father and two other sons as her dependents. Joey describes the downward occupational shift that his father experienced on immigrating to the United States: "My father had graduated in the Philippines with a bachelor's degree in criminology but couldn't get a job as a police officer here because he was not a U.S. citizen. So he only worked blue-collar jobs" (p. 181). The experience of Joey's father suggests that Asian men who immigrate as their wives' dependents often experience downward occupational mobility in the United States, while their wives maintain their professional status. The same pattern exists among Korean immigrant families in New York: while Korean nurses hold stable jobs, many of their educated husbands are unemployed or underemployed (Min, 1998).

Moreover, given the long hours and the graveyard shifts that typify a nurse's work schedule, many husbands have had to assume more child care and other household responsibilities in their wives' absences. A survey of Filipino nurses in Los Angeles County reveals that these women, to increase their incomes, tend to work double shifts or in the higher-paying evening and night shifts (Ong and Azores, 1994b). In her research on shift work and dual-earner spouses with children, Harriet Pressner (1988) finds that the husbands of nightshift workers do a significant part of child care; in all cases, it was the husbands who supervised the oft-rushed morning routines of getting their children up and off to school or to child care. Finally, unlike most other women professionals, Asian American nurses often work among their coethnics and thus benefit from these social support systems. According to Paul Ong and Tania Azores (1994b), there are "visible clusterings of Filipino nurses" in many hospitals in large metropolitan areas (p. 187). These women's social networks can provide the emotional and material support needed to challenge male dominance.

Despite their high levels of education,[4] racism in the workplace threatens the employment security and class status of Asian immigrant professional men and women. Even when these women and men have superior levels of education, they still receive economic returns lower than those of their white counterparts and are more likely to remain marginalized in their work organizations, to encounter a glass ceiling, and to be underemployed (Chai, 1987b; Ong and Hee, 1994; Yamanaka and McClelland, 1994). As racialized women, Asian professional women also suffer greater sexual harassment than do their Western counterparts due to racialized ascription that depicts them as politically passive and sexually exotic and submissive. In her research on racialized sexual harassment in institutions of higher education, Sumi Cho (1997) argues that Asian American women faculty are especially susceptible to hostile-environment forms of harassment. This hostile environment may partly explain why Asian American women faculty continue to have the lowest tenure and promotion rate of all groups (Hune and Chan, 1997).

Racism in the workplace can put undue stress on the family. Singh, a mechanical engineer who immigrated to the United States from India in 1972, became discouraged when he was not advancing at the same rate as his colleagues and attributed his difficulties to job discrimination based on national and racial origins. Singh's wife, Kaur, describes how racism affected her husband and her family: "It became harder and harder for my husband to put up with the discrimination at work. He was always stressed out. This affected the whole family" (Dhaliwal, 1995, p. 78). Among Korean immigrant families in New York, the husbands' losses in occupational status led to marital conflicts, violence, and ultimately divorce. Some Korean men turned to excessive drinking and gambling, which contributed to marital difficulties (Min, 1998). A Korean wife attributes their marital problems to her husband's frustration over his low economic status:

> Five years ago, he left home after a little argument with me and came back two weeks later. He wanted to get respect from me. But a real source of the problem was not me but his frustration over low status. (Min, 1998, p. 54)

Constrained by racial and gender discrimination, Asian professional women, on the other hand, may accept certain components of the traditional patriarchal system because they need their husbands' incomes and because they desire a strong and intact family—an important bastion of resistance to oppression.

Gender Relations Among Self-Employed Entrepreneurs

Ethnic entrepreneurship is often seen as proof of the benefits of the enterprise system: If people are ambitious and willing to work hard, they can succeed in the United States. In reality, few Asian immigrant business owners manage to achieve upward mobility through entrepreneurship. The majority of the businesses have very low gross earnings and run a high risk of failure. Because of limited capital and skills, Asian immigrant entrepreneurs congregate in highly competitive, marginally profitable, and labor-intensive businesses such as small markets, clothing subcontracting, and restaurants (Ong, 1984). In an analysis of the 1990 census data, Ong and Hee (1994) show that the median annual income of self-employed Asian Americans is $23,000, which is slightly higher than that of whites ($20,000). But there is a great deal of variation in earnings: a quarter earn $10,400 or less, another quarter earn at least $47,000, and 1% earn more than $200,000 (Ong and Hee, 1994). The chances for business failure appear particularly high for Southeast Asian immigrants; for every twenty businesses started by them each month, eighteen fail during the first year (May, 1987).

Given the labor-intensive and competitive nature of small businesses, women's participation makes possible the development and viability of family enterprises. Initially, women contribute to capital accumulation by engaging in wage work to provide the additional capital needed to launch a business (Kim and Hurh, 1985). In a study of professional and educated Korean couples in Hawaii, Alice Chai (1987) found that Korean immigrant women resisted both class and domestic oppression by struggling to develop small family businesses where they work in partnership with their husbands. Operating a family business removes them from the racist and sexist labor market and increases their interdependence with their husbands. Women also keep down labor costs by working without pay in the family enterprise (Kim and Hurh, 1988). Often, unpaid female labor enables the family store to stay open as many as fourteen hours a day, and on weekends, without having to hire additional workers (Bonacich, Hossain, and Park, 1987). According to Ong and Hee (1994), three quarters of Asian immigrant businesses do not have a single outside employee—the typical store is run by a single person or by a family.[5] Their profits come directly from their labor, the labor of their families, and from staying open long hours (Gold, 1994a). According to Ong and Hee (1994), approximately 42% of Asian American business owners work fifty hours or more per week, and 26% work sixty hours or more per week. Finally, the grandmothers who watch the children while the mothers labor at the family stores form an additional layer of unpaid family labor that also supports these stores (Bonacich et al., 1987).

Because of their crucial contributions to the family enterprise, wives are an economically valuable commodity. A 1996–1997 survey of Koreans in New York City indicates that 38% of the working women worked together with their husbands in the same businesses (Min, 1998). A study of Korean immigrants in Elmhurst, Illinois, indicates that "a man cannot even think of establishing his own business without a wife to support and work with" (Park, 1989, p. 144). Yoon (1997) reports a similar finding among Korean businesses in Chicago and Los Angeles: Wives are the most important source of family labor. Corresponding changes in conjugal relationships, however, have been slow and uneven. Unlike paid employment, work in a family business seldom gives women economic independence from their husbands. She is co-owner of the small business,working for herself and for her family, but she is also unpaid family labor, working as an unpaid employee of her husband. It is conceivable that, for many immigrant women in small businesses, the latter role predominates. Min (1998) reports that in almost all cases, when a Korean husband and wife run a business, the husband is the legal owner and controls the money and personnel management of the business. Even when the wife plays a dominant role and the husband a marginal role in operating and managing the family business, the husband is still considered the owner by the family and by the larger Korean immigrant community. In such instances, the husbands could be the women's "most immediate and harshest employers" (Bonacich et al., 1987, p.237).

Even though the family business, in some ways, is the antithesis of the separate gender spheres (men's public world of work and women's private world of domesticity), it can exacerbate dependency. Like housework, managing stores fosters alienation and isolation because it "affords little time and opportunity for women who run them to develop other skills or to establish close friendships" (Mazumdar, 1989, p. 17). Also, living and working in isolation, immigrant entrepreneurs may not be as influenced by the more flexible gender roles of U.S. middle-class couples and thus seem to be slower than other immigrant groups to discard rigid gender role divisions (Min, 1992). In most instances, women's labor in family businesses is defined as an extension of their domestic responsibilities. Kaur, a South Asian immigrant woman who manages the family grocery store, describes the blurred boundaries between home and work:

> I have a desk at home where I do my paperwork. This way I can be home when my daughters get home from school, and when my husband gets home from work I can serve him

> dinner right away. . . . I bought a stove for the store on which I cook meals for my husband and children during the hours when business is slow at the store. . . . I try to combine my housework with the store work such as grocery shopping. When I go shopping I buy stuff for home and the store. (Dhaliwal, 1995, p. 80)

The family's construction of Kaur's work as an extension of her domestic responsibilities stabilizes patriarchal ideology because it reconciles the new gender arrangement (Kaur's participation in the public sphere) with previous gender expectations and ideologies. Similarly, Min (1998) reports that in most Korean produce, grocery, and liquor stores that stay open long hours, wives are expected to perform domestic functions at work such as cooking for their husbands and, often, other employees.

When these small businesses employ coethnics, wages are low and working conditions dismal. Ong and Umemoto (1994) list some of the unfair labor practices endured by workers in ethnic businesses: unpaid wages and unpaid workers' compensation, violation of worker health and safety regulations, and violation of minimum wage laws. The exploitation of coethnic workers, specifically of women workers, is rampant in the clothing subcontracting business. Asian immigrant women comprise a significant proportion of garment workers. Asian immigrant men also toil in the garment industry but mostly as contractors—small-business owners who subcontract from manufacturers to do the cutting and sewing of garments from the manufacturers' designs and textiles. Because they directly employ labor, garment contractors are in a sense labor contractors who mobilize, employ, and control labor for the rest of the industry (Bonacich, 1994).

As middlemen between the manufacturers and the garment workers, these contractors struggle as marginally secure entrepreneurs on the very fringes of the garment industry (Wong, 1983). The precarious nature of the business is indicated by the high number of garment factories that close each year (Ong, 1984; Wong, 1983).[6] Given the stiff business competition, Asian male contractors have had to exploit the labor of immigrant women to survive. The steady influx of female limited-English-speaking immigrants puts the sweatshop owner in an extremely powerful position. Because these women have few alternative job opportunities, the owners can virtually dictate the terms of employment: They can pay low wages, ignore overtime work, provide poor working conditions, and fire anyone who is dissatisfied or considered to be a troublemaker (Wong, 1983). In retaliation, various unionization and employment organizations such as AIWA have worked for the empowerment of immigrant Asian women workers in the garment industry as well as in the hotel and electronics industries (Lowe, 1997, p. 275). It is important to stress that the problem of exploitation is not primarily gender- or ethnic-based but also inherent in the organization of the garment industry. Embedded in a larger, hierarchically organized structure, Asian immigrant contractors both victimized the workers they employ and are victimized by those higher up in the hierarchy. The contracting system insulates the industry's principal beneficiaries—the manufacturers, retailers, and bankers—from the grim realities of the sweatshops and the workers' hostility (Bonacich, 1994). Against these more dominant forces, Asian American men and women have, occasionally, formed a shared sense of ethnic and class solidarity that can, at times, blunt some of the antagonism in the contractor-worker relationship (Bonacich, 1994; Wong, 1983).

In sum,the burgeoning Asian immigrant small-business sector is being built, in part, on the racist, patriarchal, and class exploitation of Asian (and other) immigrant women. Barred from decent-paying jobs in the general labor market, Asian immigrant women labor long and hard for the benefit of men who are either their husbands or their employers or both—and in many cases, for the benefit of corporate America (Bonacich et al., 1987). The ethnic business confers quite different economic and social rewards on men and women (Zhou and Logan 1989). Whereas men benefit economically and socially from the unpaid or underpaid female labor, women bear the added burden of the double work day. Thus, it is critical to recognize that the ethnic economy is both a thriving center and a source of hardship and exploitation for Asian immigrant women.

Gender Relations Among the Wage Laborers

Of the three occupational groups reviewed in this article, gender role reversals—wives' increased economic role and husbands' reduced economic role—seem to be most pronounced among the wage laborers. In part, these changes reflect the growth of female-intensive industries in the United States, particularly in the garment and microelectronics industries, and the corresponding decline of male-dominated industries specializing in the production and distribution of goods (Clement and Myles, 1994). As a consequence, Asian immigrant women with limited education, skills, and English fluency have more employment options than do their male counterparts. Since the late 1960s, a significant number of U.S. informal sector occupations have recruited primarily female immigrant workers. The garment industry is a top employer of immigrant women from Asia and Latin America. The growth of U.S. apparel production, especially in the large cities, has been largely driven by the influx of low-wage labor from these two regions (Blumenberg and Ong, 1994). In Los Angeles, Latin American immigrants (mainly from Mexico) and Asian immigrants (from China, Vietnam, Korea, Thailand, and Cambodia) make up the majority of the garment workforce; in New York, Chinese and Dominican workers predominate; and in San Francisco, Chinese and other Asians prevail (Loucky, Soldatenko, Scott, and Bonacich, 1994). The microelectronics industry also draws heavily on immigrant women workers from Asia (mainly Vietnam, the Philippines, South Korea, and Taiwan) and from Latin American (mainly Mexico) for its low-paid manufacturing assembly work (Green, 1980; Katz and Kemnitzer, 1984; Snow, 1986). Of the more than 200,000 people employed in California's Silicon Valley microelectronics industry in 1980, approximately 50% (100,000 employees) were in production-related jobs; half of these production-related workers (50,000–70,000) worked in semiskilled operative jobs (Siegel and Borock, 1982). In a study of Silicon Valley's semiconductor manufacturing industry, Karen Hossfeld (1994) reports that the industry's division of labor is highly skewed by gender and race. At each of the fifteen subcontracting firms (which specialize in unskilled and semiskilled assembly work) that Hossfeld observed, between 80% and 100% of workers were third-world immigrants, the majority of whom were women. Based on interviews with employers and workers at these firms, Hossfeld concludes that "the lower with the skill and pay level of the job, the greater the proportion of third-world immigrant women tends to be" (p. 73).

In labor-intensive industries such as garment and microelectronics, employers prefer to hire immigrant women, as compared with immigrant men, because they believe that women can afford to work for less, do not mind dead-end jobs, and are more suited physiologically to certain kinds of detailed and routine work. The following comment from a male manager at a microelectronics subcontracting assembly plant typifies this "gender logic": "The relatively small size [of many Asian and Mexican women] makes it easier for them to sit quietly for long periods of time, doing small detail work that would drive a large person like [him] crazy" (Hossfeld, 1994, p. 74). As Linda Lim (1983)observes, it is the "*comparative disadvantage* of women in the wage-labor market that gives them a comparative advantage vis-à-vis men in the occupations and industries where they are concentrated—so-called female ghettoes of employment" (p. 78). A white male production manager and hiring supervisor in a Silicon Valley assembly shop discusses his formula for hiring:

> Just three things I look for in hiring [entry-level, high-tech manufacturing operatives]: small, foreign, and female. You find those three things and you're pretty much automatically guaranteed the right kind of work force. These little foreign gals are grateful to be hired—very, very grateful—no matter what. (Hossfeld, 1994, p. 65)

In Hawaii, Korean immigrant women likewise had an easier time securing employment than men did because of their domestic skills and because of the demand for service workers in restaurants, hotels, hospitals, and factories (Chai, 1987). These examples illustrate the interconnections of race, class, and gender. On one hand, patriarchal and racist ideologies consign women to a secondary and inferior position in the capitalist wage-labor market. On the other hand, their very disadvantage enhances women's employability over that of men in certain industries, thus affording them an opportunity to sharpen their claims against patriarchal authority in their homes.

The shifts in women's and men's access to economic and social resources is most acute among disadvantaged Southeast Asian refugees (Donnelly, 1994; Kibria, 1993). The lives of the Cambodian refugees in Stockton, California, provide an example (Ui, 1991). In Stockton, an agricultural town in which the agricultural jobs have already been taken by Mexican workers, the unemployment rate for Cambodian men is estimated to be between 80% and 90%. Unemployed for long periods of time, these men gather at the corners of the enclaves to drink and gamble. In contrast, Cambodian women have transformed their traditional roles and skills—as providers of food and clothing for family and community members and as small traders—into informal economic activities that contribute cash to family incomes. Women have also benefited more than men from government-funded language and job-training programs. Because traditionally male jobs are scarce in Stockton, these programs have focused on the education of the more employable refugee women (Ui, 1991). In particular, refugee women are trained to work in social service agencies serving their coethnics primarily in secretarial, clerical, and interpreter positions. In a refugee community with limited economic opportunities, social service programs—even though they are usually part-time, ethnic specific, and highly susceptible to budget cuts—provide one of the few new job opportunities for this population, and in this case, most of these jobs go to the women. Relying on gender stereotypes, social service agency executives have preferred women over men, claiming that women are ideal workers because they are more patient and easier to work with than men (Ui, 1991). Thus, in the Cambodian community of Stockton, it is often women, and not men, who have relatively greater economic opportunities and who become the primary breadwinners in their families. On the other hand, stripped of opportunities for employment, men often lose their "place to be" in the new society (Ui, 1991).

The shifts in the resources of immigrant men and women have challenged the patriarchal authority of Asian men. Men's loss of status and power—not only in the public but also in the domestic arena—places severe pressure on their sense of well-being, leading in some instances to spousal abuse and divorce (Luu, 1989, p. 68). A Korean immigrant man describes his frustrations over changing gender roles and expectations:

> In Korea [my wife] used to have breakfast ready for me.... She didn't do it anymore because she said she was too busy getting ready to go to work. If I complained she talked back

> at me, telling me to fix my own breakfast. . . . I was very frustrated about her, started fighting and hit her. (Yim, 1978, as cited in Mazumdar, 1989, p. 18)

According to a 1979 survey, martial conflict was one of the top four problems of Vietnamese refugees in the United States (Davidson, 1979, as cited in Luu, 1989, p. 69). A Vietnamese man, recently divorced after ten years of marriage, blamed his wife's new role and newfound freedom for their breakup:

> Back in the country, my role was only to bring home money from work, and my wife would take care of the household. Now everything has changed. My wife had to work as hard as I did to support the family. Soon after, she demanded more power at home. In other words, she wanted equal partnership. I am so disappointed! I realized that things are different now, but I could not help feeling the way I do. It is hard to get rid of or change my principles and beliefs which are deeply rooted in me. (Luu, 1989, p. 69)

Loss of status and power has similarly led to depression and anxieties in Hmong males. In particular, the women's ability—and the men's inability—to earn money for households "has undermined severely male omnipotence" (Irby and Pon, 1988, p. 112). Male unhappiness and helplessness can be detected in the following joke told at a family picnic: "When we get on the plane to go back to Laos, the first thing we will do is beat up the women!" The joke—which generated laughter by both men and women—drew upon a combination of "the men's unemployability, the sudden economic value placed on women's work, and men's fear of losing power in their families" (Donnelly, 1994, pp. 74–75).

The shifts in the resources of men and women have created an opportunity for women to contest the traditional hierarchies of family life (Chai, 1987; Kibria, 1993; Williams, 1989). Existing data indicate, however, that working-class Asian immigrant women have not used their new resources to radically restructure the old family system but only to redefine it in a more satisfying manner (Kibria, 1993). Some cultural conceptions, such as the belief that the male should be the head of the household, remain despite the economic contributions of women. Nancy Donnelly (1994) reports that although Hmong women contribute the profits of their needlework sales to the family economy, the traditional construction of Hmong women as "creators of beauty, skilled in devotion to their families, and embedded in a social order dominated by men" has not changed (p. 185). In the following quotation, a Cambodian wife describes her reluctance to upset her husband's authority:

> If we lived in Cambodia I would have behaved differently toward my husband. Over there we have to always try to be nice to the husband. Wives don't talk back, but sometimes I do that here a little bit, because I have more freedom to say what I think here. However, I am careful not to speak too disrespectfully to him, and in that way, I think I am different from the Americans. (Welaratna, 1993, p. 233)

The traditional division of household labor also remains relatively intact. In a study of Chinatown women, Loo and Ong (1982) found that despite their employment outside the home, three-fourths of the working mothers were solely responsible for all household chores. In her study of Vietnamese American families, Kibria (1993) argues that Vietnamese American women (and children) walk an "ideological tightrope"—struggling both to preserve the traditional Vietnamese family system and to enhance their power within the context of this system. According to Kibria, the traditional family system is valuable to Vietnamese American women because it offers them economic protection and gives them authority, as mothers, over the younger generation.

For the wage laborers then, the family—and the traditional patriarchy within it—becomes simultaneously a bastion of resistance to race and class oppression and an instrument for gender subordination (Glenn, 1986). Women also preserve the traditional family system—albeit in a tempered form—because they value the promise of male economic protection. Although migration may have equalized or reversed the economic resources of working-class men and women, women's earnings continue to be too meager to sustain their economic independence from men. Because the wage each earns is low, only by pooling incomes can a husband and wife earn enough to support a family. Finally, like many ethnic, immigrant, poor, and working-class women, working-class Asian women view work as an opportunity to raise the family's living standards and not only as a path to self-fulfillment or even upward mobility as idealized by the white feminist movement. As such, employment is defined as an extension of their family obligations—of their roles as mothers and wives (Kim and Hurh, 1988; Pedraza-Bailey, 1991; Romero, 1992).

Conclusion

My review of the existing literature on Asian immigrant salaried professionals, self-employed entrepreneurs, and wage laborers suggests that economic constraints (and opportunities) have reconfigured gender relations within contemporary Asian America society. The patriarchal authority of Asian immigrant men, particularly those of the working class, has been challenged due to the social and economic losses that they suffered in their transition to the status of men of color in the United States. On the other hand, the recent growth of female-intensive industries—and the racist and sexist "preference" for the labor of immigrant women—has enhanced women's employability over that of men and has changed their role to that of a coprovider, if not primary provider, for their families. These shifts in immigrant men's and women's access to economic and social resources have not occurred without friction. Men's loss of status in both public and private arenas has placed severe pressures on the traditional family, leading at times to resentment, spousal abuse, and divorce. For their part, Asian women's ability to restructure the traditional patriarchy system is often constrained by their social-structural location—as racially subordinated immigrant women—in the dominant society. In the best scenario, responding to the structural barriers in the larger society, both husbands and wives become more interdependent and equal as they are forced to rely on each other, and on the traditional family and immigrant community, for economic security and emotional support. On the other hand, to the extent that the traditional division of labor and male privilege persists, wage work adds to the women's overall workload. The existing research indicated that both of these tendencies exist, though the increased burdens for women are more obvious.

Notes

1. Certainly, these three categories are neither mutually exclusive nor exhaustive. They are also linked in the sense that there is mobility between them, particularly from professional to small-business employment (Chen, 1992). Nevertheless, they represent perhaps the most important sociological groupings within the contemporary Asian immigrant community (Ong and Hee, 1994).
2. The Chinese Exclusion Act of 1882 suspended immigration of laborers for ten years. The 1917 Immigration Act delineated a "barred zone" from whence no immigrants could come. The 1924 Immigration Act denied entry to virtually all Asians. The 1934 Tydings-McDuffie Act reduced Filipino immigration to fifty persons a year. The 1965 Immigration Law abolished "national origins" as a basis for allocating immigration quotas to various countries—Asian countries were finally placed on equal footing.
3. After Mexico, the Philippines and South Korea were the second-and third-largest source countries of immigrants, respectively. Three other

Asian countries—China, India, and Vietnam—were among the ten major source countries of U.S. immigrants in the 1980s (Min, 1995b).

4. According to the 1990 U.S. Census, 43% of Asian men and 32% of Asian women twenty-five years of age and older had at least a bachelor's degree, compared with 23% and 17%, respectively, of the total U.S. population (U.S. Bureau of the Census, 1993). Moreover, the proportion of Asians with graduate or professional degrees was higher than that of whites: 14% versus 8% (Ong and Hee, 1994). Immigrants account for about two-thirds to three-quarters of the highly educated population (Ong and Hee, 1994).
5. For example, in Southern California, many Cambodian-owned doughnut shops are open twenty-four hours a day, with the husbands typically baking all night, while wives and teenage children work the counter by day (Akast, 1993).
6. In New York City, more than a quarter of Chinatown garment shops went out of business between 1980 and 1981. Similarly, of the nearly 200 Chinatown garment shops that registered with California's Department of Employment in 1978, 23% were sold or closed by 1982 and another 8% were inactive (Ong, 1984).

26

Marital Relations

✦ Pyong Gap Min

The vast majority of post-1965 immigrants have come from third-world countries, especially Asia and Latin America. Many of these new immigrant groups show high female labor force participation rates (Foner 1986; Perez 1986; Pessar 1987), although married women in these third-world countries often do not work outside of the home. Korean immigrant women, following this pattern, usually did not work outside the home in Korea, but in the United States many play an active role in the family economy, particularly in the operation of family businesses. The increased economic role of Korean women has brought about significant changes in women's lives in general and marital relations in particular—the subject of this chapter.

Women's Increased Economic Role

According to the 1990 U.S. census, approximately 60% of married Korean American women participate in the labor force, in comparison to 58% of white married women (U.S. Bureau of the Census 1993b). Actually, the percentage is probably much larger. The census underestimates the labor force participation rate of Korean women because many Korean women who work for family businesses or other Korean businesses do not report their work to the census. In my 1988 survey of Korean married women in New York City, 71% of the respondents participated in the labor force and 54% worked full-time. With the exception of wives of successful business owners and successful professionals (lawyers, medical doctors, and accountants), almost all Korean immigrant wives participate in the labor force to increase their family earnings.

The situation is very different in Korea. There, only about a quarter of women thirty to fifty-nine years old in urban areas participated in the labor force, according to the 1990 Korean census (National Statistical Office, Republic of Korea 1993). The women in my New York City survey who had worked in

Gap Min, Pyong. 1998. "Marital relations," in *Changes and conflicts: Korean immigrant families in New York*, pp. 9–24. Allyn and Bacon: Boston.

Korea typically did so before they got married. A drastic change occurs when they come to the United States.

Most Korean immigrant women participate in the labor force out of practical needs rather than because of their career aspirations. The vast majority of the women in my New York City survey endorsed the statement that "in a normal family the wife should stay at home as a full-time housewife while the husband should be the main breadwinner." Jung Ja Kim, a forty-five-year-old woman, works as a manicurist at a Korean nail salon six days a week, nine hours each day, while her husband works as a manager for a Korean restaurant six days a week. Her son is a college freshman and her daughter is a high school sophomore. In responding to my question of whether she would like to work outside the home if her husband makes enough money, she commented:

> If my husband makes enough money for the family, why should I take this burden? Without me helping out economically, it is absolutely impossible to survive in New York City. I must work especially to send my children to college. You know about this better than I.

This suggests that many Korean women in this country are almost forced into undertaking the unfamiliar economic role, although they generally hold traditional gender role orientations.

Nearly half of the Korean working women work for their own or family businesses. Consider some figures from my New York City survey: 38% of the women in the labor force worked together with their husbands in the same businesses; another 12% ran their own businesses independently of their husbands; and 36% were employed in coethnic businesses. Working in a green grocery, a nail salon, or dry cleaning store—typical Korean businesses in New York—means that Korean working women put in exceptionally long hours. I found that Korean married working women in the survey spent fifty-one hours per week at their jobs, much longer than American working women (37 hours according to one survey conducted in the 1980s, see Shelton, 1992). Those engaged in their own businesses spent fifty-six hours a week in their businesses, five hours less than their self-employed husbands.

Korean immigrant working women make an important income contribution to the family finances, perhaps almost equal to their husbands, although this is difficult to accurately measure. When two partners run the same business, the wife is usually in charge of the cash register and the husband takes care of the total management of the store. The wife's control of the cash register is one of the central factors that make Korean retail businesses, such as produce, grocery, and liquor retail businesses, successful (Min, 1988). A grocery store owner in Bayside told me how important his wife's help was to the success of the business.

> I open the store at seven and work with an employee. My wife joins me at nine after sending our two children to school. During the daytime, I often have to go out to buy grocery items on sale from large chain stores. I can go out mainly because she takes care of the cash register. At six, my wife goes back home to prepare dinner and take care of our children while I work with our employee. I don't know how I can operate my grocery store without my wife.

Most Koreans, particularly new immigrants, start with small, family businesses where husbands and wives need to cooperate for economic survival. Large Korean business owners can manage without their wives: they run their businesses with employees and arrange for their wives to stay at home to take care of their children. In fact, Korean wives play a more important role than their husbands in many family-run businesses, particularly small dry cleaning shops and small restaurants. I was a regular client of a dry cleaning shop that was run by a Korean wife and her husband for several years (the shop has since closed). The husband played a marginal role in running the shop; he cleaned sidewalks and received laundry materials, while his wife ironed and altered dresses. The husband, an engineer in Korea, did not enjoy his job at all and was reluctant to talk with customers, probably because he felt the job was demeaning. In contrast, his high school graduate wife seemed to enjoy her job, most of the time smiling and talking with customers. The 1,500 Korean-owned nail salons in the New York area are usually owned and run by women. Some Korean men just drive their wives to and from the nail shop and help them open and close it while they either babysit or play golf during the daytime. They are often called "shuttermen" or "househusbands" in the Korean community. As will be shown later, in the Korean community where the husband's main role is considered to be financial support for the family this kind of role reversal puts pressure on husbands.

Korean immigrant wives can also find jobs in Korean-owned stores more easily than their husbands. Although various managerial jobs available in Korean-owned stores are filled by male immigrants, they are limited in number. There is more of a demand for blue-collar workers. But Korean male immigrants, mostly highly educated, are not attracted to blue-collar jobs in the ethnic economy. Korean business owners usually turn to inexpensive, hard-working, and compliant Latino male workers for these blue-collar jobs. The large number of sales-related white-collar jobs are usually filled by Korean women. Most Korean immigrant wives have received a high school education. As high school graduates, they are not satisfied with working as saleswomen or cashiers in coethnic businesses, but they do not consider it demeaning either. Thus, the structure of the Korean ethnic economy has helped Korean wives to play an active economic role. While it usually takes newly arrived Korean immigrant men a few months to find meaningful jobs, their wives often find jobs quickly and become the main breadwinners.

Women's Domestic Role

How has Korean women's increased economic role affected their domestic roles and their husbands' participation in housework? American working women still bear the main responsibility for housework and child care, although their increased economic role has reduced their share of these tasks (Hardesty and Bokermeier, 1989; Kamo, 1988; Ross, 1987). Korean immigrant working wives bear an even greater share of housework than American working wives. As a result, Korean immigrant wives suffer from overwork and work-related stress.

The results of my New York City survey show that Korean immigrant housewives bear almost all the responsibility for cooking, dishwashing, laundry, and housecleaning. Only in grocery shopping and garbage disposal did husbands take some responsibility. These findings come as no surprise, considering the fact that few husbands in South Korea take responsibility for a significant proportion of housework. When Korean working women get help around the house, it is most likely from their mothers, mothers-in-law, and daughters, not from their husbands. He Soon Lee is a Korean woman in her late forties who married her Korean husband in New York in 1975. They have their house in Bergen County, New Jersey, but own a dry cleaning store in Manhattan. Her husband works six days a week at the store in Manhattan while she works five days, taking Thursday off for housework. Each day, the shop is open seven to seven. They get up at six in the morning to open the shop and get home at eight. She told me that she could not sleep well without keeping her house clean every evening but that her husband did not help much. Mrs. Kim said:

> My husband is a good repairman. He takes care of electric, plumbing, and other maintenance problems. Other than that, he doesn't help me with housework at home. He never cooks or dishwashes. I don't think in his lifetime he can change his Korean habit of not working in the kitchen.

Younger, professional husbands undertake more housework than other Korean immigrants, although their wives still do the lion's share.

Choon Ran Park, a sociology major in a university in Korea, immigrated to this country several months after she got married to a Korean medical student in this country. She worked full-time to support her husband's graduate education at a medical school. She said:

> He does laundry and housecleaning, but he does not do kitchen work, that is, cooking and dishwashing. Further, he does not think he is obligated to take care of either laundry or housecleaning. He takes the attitude that he is simply kind enough to help me with either of the two. Thus, when he completes his laundry or housecleaning job, he expects me to thank him.

Two other professional husbands, one a college professor and the other an immigration broker, reported that they undertook dishwashing as well as laundry and housecleaning, but not cooking. One of them, Sung Jin Kang, said: "How can you expect me to cook Korean food, which is far more complicated than cooking American food?" Actually, he does not cook American food for his children either; his statement is simply a rationale for not cooking.

In Seoul and other large cities, middle-class wives often depend on housemaids for cooking and other traditional domestic tasks (Choe, 1985). In contrast, few Korean immigrant wives depend on maid service, although most spend long hours at paid work. Only 4.3% of the Korean families in my New York City survey had a housemaid working part-time or full-time. In sum, Korean immigrant wives spend many more hours doing housework and paid work than do wives in Korea, and most spend more hours in paid and unpaid labor than their husbands do.

My survey results make this very clear. Full-time housewives spent 46.3 hours per week on housework compared with 5.2 hours for their husbands. Among dual-earner couples, the wives' time on housework was reduced to an average of 24.8 hours per week while the husbands' time increased to only 6.7 hours. Working wives spent 75.5 hours weekly on their job and housework, 12 hours more than their husbands did. Since the vast majority of Korean immigrant wives assume the economic role, most work longer hours than their husbands. Although Korean immigrant men certainly work hard and experience a lot of work-related stress, their wives suffer even more stress and role strain due to the many, often conflicting demands of paid work, housework, and child care.

One can observe the patriarchal custom of women preparing food and serving men in group meetings as well as in individual families. When Korean immigrants have a party, several female guests usually help the hostess in the kitchen while their husbands drink in the living room. Work in the kitchen is never easy because Korean families usually cook elaborate dishes for a party. One can observe the gender division of labor easily in most Korean immigrant churches, too. Women are regularly involved in cooking and serving food for parties while men are responsible for organizational and financial affairs.

Korean men's double standard for boys and girls and their reliance on their wives for many services (without offering services to their wives) make an unfavorable impression on American-educated daughters. Korean women often respond to their husbands' unreasonable requests for various services to avoid family conflicts. Their daughters are critical not only of their fathers but also of their mothers who they think "accept a subservient position." Several years ago, Nina Shin, a second-generation Korean student at Stuyvesant High School (the best public high school in New York City), worked on her Westinghouse project under my supervision. One day when we were talking about second-generation Koreans' gender role changes, she said: "I plan not to marry anybody. Every day I have seen my mom providing all the services for my dad and not the other way. If that is a marriage, why should I marry a man." She said that several of her Korean friends at the high school felt the same way.

Of course, Nina's plan to remain single may not materialize. Yet many second-generation Korean women who are critical of their parents' unequal marital relations may well choose non-Korean, particularly white, partners. In fact, college-educated second-generation Korean women have a higher intermarriage rate than their male counterparts. American-born Korean men are ready to maintain more egalitarian marital relations than their parents, but they still cling to traditional gender-role notions.

Community Resistance to Women in Business

Resource theory (Blood and Wolfe, 1960; Centers et al., 1970) posits that a wife's employment increases her marital power because it provides her with economic and other resources to bring to her marriage. However, how much a wife's employment increases her marital power depends on the particular cultural context (Rodman, 1967). Earlier studies indicate that Asian and Latino immigrant women's economic role has not significantly improved their marital power and status mainly because of the traditional patriarchal system they brought from their native countries. In the Korean case, women's involvement in the family business is another factor that must be considered. Unlike paid employment, work in a family business does not give women economic independence from their husbands.

To be sure, Korean immigrant wives' increased economic role has given them more power and status relative to their husbands. Particularly those Korean women who run their own businesses independently of their husbands (12% of working wives in the New York Korean community) enjoy a level of independence and autonomy unimaginable in South Korea because they control personnel and money management. However, Korean women who assist their husbands in the family store do not enjoy the economic and psychological independence that most American working wives do. When a husband and a wife run a business, the husband is the legal owner in almost all cases. This has practical implications. For one thing, the social security tax for the self-employed family is deposited only for the husband, who is the legal owner. Also, the wife cannot sell the business even if she wants to discontinue the partnership because of marital conflicts. Jung Shin Suh, a woman in her fifties said: "When I was considering divorce after severe conflicts with my husband, I realized that I would have had nothing from the business, neither social security tax nor business ownership." After realizing these disadvantages, some of Mrs. Suh's Korean friends recently have registered themselves as co-owners. In the state of New York, even if the husband is the single legal owner of the family business, the wife is entitled to half of the proceeds when it is sold. However, the husband, as legal owner, is in control of how he sells it. One woman I interviewed said that one of her friends did not get a fair share of property settlement after divorce because her husband sold the store to her brother for an unreasonably small amount of money.

In addition, a husband practically controls the money and personnel management of the business, which gives him power in terms of making decisions concerning business operations. Although the wife takes care of the cash register in a retail business, the husband usually deposits money in the bank and orders merchandise. Moreover, it is usually he who hires and fires employees and decides whether the business should be extended. American employed women increase their bargaining power mainly because they bring home separate paychecks. Korean immigrant wives who work for the family business do not have this independent source of income, although they make a significant contribution to the family economy. The exclusion of many Korean women from money management in the family business has important implications for their marital power. A divorced interviewee said that her ex-husband used part of their business earnings for dating another woman, which ultimately led to their divorce. Since she was not involved in the money management of their business, she was not aware of her husband's spending money on another woman until it was too late.

The status of a Korean woman as a "helper" in the family business rather than as a co-owner also diminishes her social status and influence in the Korean immigrant community. Korean entrepreneurs establish associations based on business lines, and major business associations exercise a powerful influence on community politics in the Korean entrepreneurial community. Korean self-employed men, rather than self-employed women, represent their businesses and usually join a specialized business association and engage in organizational activities. Even if the wife plays the dominant role in managing the family business and the husband is the helper, Koreans usually consider the husband the owner. My wife operated a business for several years during my prolonged years of graduate education in Atlanta. Although I only helped my wife in the store irregularly I, rather than my wife, was the one invited to participate in meetings of a business association. Business associations in the Korean immigrant community consist almost exclusively of male members, although many Korean women are as active as or even more active than their husbands in business operation. My interviews with major Korean business associations in New York showed that only twenty-one Korean business women were affiliated with one or another of the five major Korean business associations, accounting for less than 1% of total affiliated members.

Successful Korean male entrepreneurs exercise a powerful influence on community politics through their leadership positions not only in trade associations, but also through other nonbusiness ethnic associations (Min, 1996). By virtue of their financial ability, many successful Korean businessmen are invited to be staff and board members of important nonbusiness ethnic associations. Those Korean businessmen with key positions in major business and nonbusiness ethnic associations spend a lot of time and money on their ethnic organizations. While they spend time and money on public activities, their wives are responsible for actual business operations. Although most self-employed Korean immigrants work long hours of work for moderate levels of income, many of them achieve a high level of economic success. When small family businesses turn into lucrative enterprises, both Korean husbands and wives enjoy economic benefits. However, business success often gives social status and positions only to Korean husbands.

Over the last twenty-five years, several successful Korean businessmen have served as president of the Korean Association of New York. Korean immigrants in New York choose the president of the Korean Association every two years through a direct election. In each election, two or three candidates for the president spend enormous sums of money, usually over $100,000, on election campaigns. Once elected, the president has to work almost full-time at the office and, instead of getting a salary, he spends a large amount of his own money for the operation of the organization. This is why only successful businessmen can volunteer for the position. In fact, twelve of the thirteen presidents between 1972 and 1997 were successful businessmen. They have been willing to donate so much money and time because of the high status associated with the position. And they can do so mainly because their wives continue to run their businesses to support their organizational activities financially. Many other successful Korean businessmen serve as presidents of various trade associations, and as leaders they expend smaller—but significant—amounts of their time and money.

Segregation and Patriarchal Ideology

The segregation of Korean immigrants at economic and religious levels also bolsters the patriarchal ideology they brought with them from Korea, and this is another reason Korean women's economic role does not significantly increase their power and status. Korean immigrants are socially segregated partly because of their group homogeneity. That is, they stick together because they share cultural characteristics and historical experiences. However, they are segregated also because of two other structural factors: the economy in which most work and their religious organization.

As I noted earlier, about 85% of the Korean immigrant work force is involved in the ethnic economy either as business owners or employees of co-ethnic businesses. This economic segregation gives Koreans advantages over other immigrant groups in maintaining their cultural traditions and social interactions with co-ethnics (Min, 1991). But it also hinders their interactions with American citizens. The vast majority of the employees in Korean-owned stores are either Korean or Latino immigrants (Min, 1989; 1996). Since Latino immigrants hired by Korean stores also have a severe language barrier, they often communicate with Korean owners and employees using a limited number of Korean words. It is also noteworthy that Latino workers hired by Korean stores usually hold a conservative gender role ideology similar to that of Korean immigrants. Although Korean-owned businesses usually serve native-born white and African American customers, their communications with customers for the most part are minimal. For these reasons, Korean immigrants concentrated in the Korean ethnic economy have little opportunity to learn U.S. customs, including a more egalitarian gender role orientation, accepted by the majority of Americans. In effect, Korean immigrants' language barriers and unfamiliarity with American customs have forced them into the ethnic economy, which, in turn, further hinders them from learning English and American customs.

Korean immigrants' economic segregation helps perpetuate the customs associated with the patriarchal ideology in the store as well as in the home. Most Korean produce, grocery, and liquor stores stay open long hours—usually fifteen hours—a day, and many stay open twenty-four hours. Most of these stores in New York have cooking facilities in the basement so the husband and wife can continue their work while eating. Wives usually cook in the basement and serve their husbands and often employees. Women are also expected to perform other domestic functions at work. In Korea, female employees usually make coffee to serve all employees in the office. The same custom has been transplanted to the Korean immigrant community. In Korean-owned travel agencies, real estate companies, and Korean community agencies, young women are usually responsible for making coffee, going on errands, and doing other miscellaneous chores not directly related to their work. Younger-generation Korean women in Korean-owned offices who are not familiar with the service-related role of women workers often have conflicts with male workers and managers.

The participation of most Korean immigrants in a Korean Christian church also perpetuates the patriarchal ideology and thus reduces the positive effects of Korean women's economic role on their power and status. Although neither Protestantism nor Catholicism is indigenous to Korea, both religions have incorporated much of Korean culture in their adaptation to Korean society. In their efforts to maintain Korean cultural traditions through their ethnic churches, Korean immigrants have Koreanized Christian religions even further (Min 1992b). The patriarchal ideology based on Confucianism is one of the central elements of Korean culture. As indicated by A. Kim (1996), the participation of most Korean immigrants in Korean churches bolsters the Confucian patriarchal ideology in two different ways. First, the hierarchical structure of Korean immigrant churches reinforces the patriarchal ideology. Like Christian churches in South Korea, Korean immigrant churches usually do not allow women to serve as head pastors or to hold important positions, although women compose the majority of church members both in South Korea and in the Korean immigrant community. The 1995–96 Korean Churches Directory of New York shows that only three out of about 500 Korean churches in the area have women as their main pastors. Women are usually involved in fundraising, prayer meetings, visiting the sick, and so forth, all related to women's traditional roles as nurturers and caretakers, while men hold important positions that involve decision making in organizational and financial affairs (A. Kim 1996; see also J. Kim 1996).

Second, Korean immigrant churches perpetuate the patriarchal ideology by teaching women their subordinate position in the family and society. Many Korean women—working women in particular—experience conflicts between the sexist and hierarchical Korean culture and the more egalitarian American culture. One way they try to resolve their inner conflicts is by appealing to "Christian" religious beliefs to legitimatize Korean culture and women's subordinate status (A. Kim 1996). Aira Kim, a Korean feminist scholar who also serves as the main pastor in an American church, interviewed many Korean Christian women to examine how they rationalized male supremacy by accepting sexist anthropomorphic views of God. One of her interviewees said:

> I believe men are superior to women. If men and women are equal, there is always collision. Therefore, God made women inferior to men so that He prevents collision. . . . Gee I had such a hard life after getting married. My husband and I fought so much during our twenty-five year marriage, but I could not win. Oh, I was miserable. Now, I've given up. I realized that to win against a husband is not possible because God made men superior to women. (p. 90)

Coping with Gender Role Reversals

Far from being a model of stability and consensus, many Korean immigrant families suffer from serious marital and generational conflicts. In fact, I was surprised by the high level of marital conflict that emerged in the in-depth interviews conducted for this book. My interviews with Korean immigrants and discussions with Korean family counselors suggest that divorce and separation occur far more frequently among Korean immigrants than in the population in Korea. Census data support this: Korean immigrant men have a divorce rate three times higher than men in Korea; Korean women's divorce rate is five times higher than women's in Korea (see Min 1997b).

Lillian Rubin's popular book, *Intimate Strangers* (1983), about American marriages in the 1970s, helps explain the marital conflicts and dissolutions in Korean immigrant families. Rubin wrote of how the discrepancy between changes in gender role behavior and persistence of traditional gender role attitudes caused serious marital conflicts. Many husbands Rubin interviewed felt threatened by their wives' increased economic role while many wives had difficulty accepting their husbands' reduced economic role. By now, wives' increased economic role has become the norm in contemporary America—but the problems Rubin described are still relevant for Korean immigrant families. Now that many Korean wives play a more important economic role than their husbands—some are even the main breadwinners for their families while their husbands are unemployed—traditional gender-role attitudes severely clash with reality.

Consider one example of the way in which gender role reversals have led to marital conflict. When Kyung Ja Choi married Mr. Lee in Korea, she did not know him well; her mother arranged the match because Mr. Lee was well educated, with a master's degree in linguistics. Upon immigration to the United States, Choi became the main breadwinner by taking several odd jobs, including taxi driving, while her husband was, for most part, unemployed. Mr. Lee's unemployment was prolonged because as a highly educated man he was unwilling to take the kind of blue-collar job that was available in a Korean business. He tried setting up a few semiprofessional businesses, such as real estate and insurance, but these failed. Choi had difficulty understanding her husband's "economic incompetence." When she argued with him, she often screamed, "Why won't you find a blue-collar job in a Korean produce store?" She also pressured him to take more responsibility for housework. This situation eroded the husband's patriarchal authority, which led him to react violently to his wife. When they argued, he often used physical force. When his punch caused a broken nose, she called the police and pushed him out of the house. She is now legally divorced.

I know of several similar cases where the husband's economic incompetence and role reversal led to marital conflicts, violence, and ultimately divorce. The men were highly educated and so unwilling to take blue-collar jobs, but they were not business-oriented and so were unsuccessful in running a business themselves. Meanwhile, their wives had stable jobs (many as nurses).

In most other Korean immigrant families, the wife plays an important, if not the dominant, role in the family economy. This increased economic role inevitably enhances their bargaining power in their marriages and this often causes tensions. Han Sik Chang, a forty-year-old Korean man, said: "My wife never talked back to me in Korea, but she began to talk back as soon as she assumed the economic role in this country. After seven years of paid work in this country, she now treats me, not as a household head, but as an equal. How can she change her attitudes so quickly?"

Some Korean men do not want their wives to work outside the home, and I found a few women who worked part-time without their husbands' knowledge. But most Korean men in New York expect their wives to participate in the labor force because it is almost impossible for their families to manage otherwise. The men are frustrated over their inability to support their families without the help of their wives. However, they do not accept the logic that because women now work they should reduce their patriarchal authority and increase their share of housework. When I said, "Don't you think you should assume more housework responsibility as your wife, too, works in the shop?" Dong Sik Lee, who runs a dry cleaning store in Manhattan with his wife, responded:

> Of course, in a normal situation my wife should not work outside the home. Now she is forced to work for family survival in a special

> situation. But how can we, men, change our custom of not working in the kitchen so quickly and maintain equal relations with them [wives]? Further, if marital relations are equal, we will have lots of conflicts. See, American families! They are more equal, women are more aggressive, but that's why they have lots of conflicts and divorces. There is no order in them.

Partly because of frequent marital conflicts in dual-worker families, Korean women as well as men often consider the wife's labor force participation undesirable. As one woman described:

> I deliberately decided not to work outside the home, although it is not easy to stay at home as a full-time housewife. I saw many Korean dual-worker couples having marital conflicts. When women make money they become aggressive and argue with their husbands. In order to maintain order in the family, we need to maintain the gender division of labor and the patriarchal system. This is why I decided not to work.

Korean men feel it is difficult to cope with the loss in occupational status they experience in this country. In the face of downward occupational mobility, they seek to assert their authority in the home, but increasingly they feel that their wives and children no longer accept it without question. Often their frustration over low status becomes serious when they reach middle age, leading to a mid-life crisis. Young Soo Lee, who worked as a manager for a major bank branch in Korea, immigrated to this country in the late 1970s to achieve his "American dream." In his early fifties now, he has been running his deli store for ten years. His wife said:

> He has often expressed his bitterness about his position as a small store owner. And his frustration over his low status greatly influences our relations. Five years ago, he left home after a little argument with me and came back two weeks later. He wanted to get respect from me. But a real source of the problem was not me, but his frustration over low status.

Some Korean women go through a mid-life crisis derived from status anxiety as well, complicating their marital relations. Women may feel that they have spent too much time caring for their families and not enough on their own careers. Husbands may resist their wives' new career goals and independence. I interviewed He Ran Park, a Korean woman in her late forties. She had four children under eighteen but had just begun a college degree program. He Ran taught for eight years in an elementary school in Korea, including two years after marriage, before she immigrated with her family to this country (at that time people were certified to teach in an elementary school in Korea with two years of college education). She spent all her years in this country helping her husband with his business and caring for her four children. She commented:

> I decided to start a college degree program at this stage of life to save myself, to save my career. For so many years I had been preoccupied with child care and family survival. But suddenly I realized that I had lost too much of myself. Of course, my study complicates my family life and marital relations. But I am now so determined that my husband cannot stop me.

She said that the Korean custom that stresses a mother's sacrifice for her children's education victimizes so many women. She emphasized that her career is as important as her children's education.

One way Korean men compensate for the low status associated with their occupations is to seek status in the Korean community by joining various ethnic organizations. There is strong competition and intense struggles for high-status positions (*gumtoo ssaoom*) as ethnic organizations can provide only a limited number of such positions. As previously noted, many successful businessmen spend large amounts of money ("face-saving money") to secure positions in large ethnic organizations, including churches (Min 1992b). Many Korean women resist their husbands' excessive donations and frequent social meetings to get *gumtoo* (a high position) in the Korean community. In one extreme case, a husband spent so much money and time on his election campaigns that he neglected his grocery business and children. To get his friends' strong support for his election campaign, he organized several golf trips and used credit cards to pay for the trips.

Status anxiety and frustration can lead Korean immigrant men to turn to excessive drinking, golfing, and gambling, which, needless to say, contributes to marital difficulties. Soon Hi Kwon, a woman in her mid-forties, commented on her husband's drinking problem:

> When our discount store did well, my husband began to drink in Korean clubs regularly. Each night, he paid over $300 for liquor and around $100 to the girls as tips. Sometimes, he drank until early morning and came back directly to the store. After sleeping in the store, he left for the club early evening with money from the cash register.

Another woman described her husband's "habitual drinking" as the most serious problem in their marital relations:

> Two or three times a month, he is involved in heavy drinking. Two weeks ago, the police called me from a Korean club. Because he did not want to leave the club when they were closing it, they called the police. At 3:00 in the morning, I tried to pick him up from the club, but he resisted. Two police officers helped me to put him into the car. He closed his business on the day.
>
> My sister-in-law, my mother-in-law, and even my mother in Korea do not consider heavy drinking as a serious problem. They often say, "If he doesn't beat you after drinking it is okay." But it is not acceptable to me. Why do I have to suffer so much because of his drinking problem. If he does not stop his excessive drinking soon, I will consider separation seriously.

Korean immigrants' excessive drinking is partly cultural. In New York as well as in Korea, many Korean men often go *eecha* (going to another place for drinking in the same night) and *samcha* (going to a third place for drinking in the same night) partly because it is an accepted custom. But Korean immigrants' boredom and status anxiety related to their monotonous lives in labor-intensive small businesses also contribute to heavy drinking. They are looking for an outlet for their stress and the monotony of their lives and want to get respect from women in Korean clubs. Hang Ja Kim, the former director of a Korean family counseling center, observed: "With $400 in a Korean club, each of them is treated like a king by young Korean girls. For at least two or three hours, they can release all their tensions and stress. With their blue-collar jobs, nowhere can they get that kind of treatment."

Still another important cause of Korean immigrants' frequent marital conflicts is their long hours of working together. Many Koreans who run family businesses spend twenty-four hours a day with their spouses, often in a very stressful environment. It is easy for them to argue over business matters. Since there is no clear demarcation between family and work life, tensions in one area can spill over and exacerbate tensions in the other area. Also a problem is that husbands can continue to exercise their patriarchal authority in the store. A few Korean women complained that their husbands try to restrict their freedom in the store as well as at home. He Soon Kim, a Korean woman in her late forties, has run a dry cleaning business with her husband for ten years. She commented:

> Staying together all day has increased our chance for arguments and conflicts. My husband, whether at home or in the store, always

> tries to exercise his patriarchal authority over me. Meeting him in the evening at home would give him enough chance to restrict my freedom. Staying together all day, he does not give me any breathing room. I wish he, like other professionals, could take business trips often. Korean women like professional husbands because they often stay away from home for a business trip.

It is ironic that many women in Korea complain that their husbands spend too little time with them, that they take too many business trips. In New York, it is precisely because husbands and wives spend too much time together that conflicts often arise.

There are two Korean family counseling centers in New York, one in Flushing and the other in Manhattan. They can help only a small fraction of the Korean immigrant families with marital difficulties in the New York metropolitan area. Moreover, Koreans usually do not want to talk about their marital problems with social workers. Korean church pastors play a more important role than social workers in helping couples with marital problems. My survey of Korean immigrant pastors indicate that over 80% of them provide counseling for their church members (1992b). Korean social workers are concerned that many of these pastors have not taken psychology and/or counseling courses and that therefore they cannot provide counseling effectively.

Benefits and Burdens: Immigrant Women and Work in New York City

✦ NANCY FONER

ABSTRACT

This article analyzes the complex and contradictory ways that migration changes women's status in New York City—both for better and for worse. The focus is on the impact of women's incorporation into the labor force. On the positive side, migrant women's regular access to wages—and to higher wages—frequently improves their position in the household, broadens their social horizons, and enhances their sense of independence. Less happily, many migrant women work in dead-end positions that pay less than men's jobs. Immigrant working wives also experience a heavy double burden since the household division of labor remains far from equal.

There is an underlying tension in much of the work on immigrant women. On the one hand, a growing number of studies show that women experience marked improvements in their status as women as a result of migration. These range from increased control over decision-making in the household to greater personal autonomy and access to resources in the community at large (e.g., Foner, 1986; Grasmuck and Pessar, 1991; Hondagneu-Sotelo, 1994; Lamphere, 1987; Pedraza-Bailey 1991; Pessar, 1998; Simon,

Nancy Foner is a professor of anthropology at the State University of New York, Purchase, and the author of several books on immigration, including *Jamaica Farewell: Jamaican Migrants in London* and *New Immigrants in New York*. Address for correspondence: Department of Anthropology, State University of New York, Purchase, NY 10077.

Foner, Nancy. 1998. "Benefits and burdens: Immigrant women and work in New York City." *Gender Issues*. Volume 16, Issue 4, 5–21. Reprinted by permission of Transaction Publishers.

1992; Brettell and Simon, 1986). On the other hand, the literature also emphasizes migrant women's continued oppression—what some call a triple burden or oppression, as gender inequalities are compounded by discrimination on the basis of class and race or ethnicity. Increasingly, recent research seeks to reconcile these two perspectives. As Patricia Pessar (1998) notes in a recent review of the literature, to ask whether migration is emancipating or subjugating for women is to couch their experiences in stark—and misleading—either/or terms. Feminist scholars now caution that migration often leads to losses as well as gains for women, and that, despite improvements, patriarchal codes and practices may continue to have an impact (see, for example, Espiritu, 1997; Morakvasic, 1984; Pessar, 1998).

In the spirit of the new feminist scholarship, this article offers an analysis of the complex and often contradictory ways that migration changes women's status—both for better and for worse. The focus is on the impact of women's incorporation into the labor force. This issue has been in the forefront of research on migrant women since it is wage work that so often empowers migrant women at the same time as it places severe burdens and constraints on them. The article is based on my larger comparative project on immigrants in New York City.[1] It draws on my own first-hand research on Jamaican women (see Foner, 1983, 1986, 1994)[2] as well as on available sociological and anthropological accounts for other immigrant populations. New York City continues to be a preeminent destination for the nation's immigrants: In 1996, about a third of its population was foreign-born (Moss, Townsend, and Tobier, 1997). The city's immigrants include a wide variety of Asian, Latin American, and Caribbean groups; in 1990, the top five were Dominicans, Chinese, Jamaicans, Russians, and Guyanese, in that order. While the analysis presented here is sensitive to different patterns of labor-market incorporation and cultural background among the various groups, the emphasis is on common themes, experiences, and processes that emerge.

Female Immigrants: The Background

To set the stage for the analysis of the impact of wage work on New York City's migrant women, some basic background information is necessary on their numbers, migration patterns, labor force, and occupational profile.

Women migrants now outnumber men in virtually all of the major groups coming to New York. In large part, this is because United States immigration law favors the admission of spouses and children as a way to reunite families and has made it possible for certain kinds of workers, like nurses, to get immigrant visas (Donato, 1992; Houston, Kramer, and Barrett, 1984). In the early 1990s, there were ninety-two male immigrants for every one hundred female immigrants entering New York City, up from ninety-eight males per one hundred females in the 1980s (Lobo, Salvo, and Virgin, 1996).

It is not just that women predominate. Many women come on their own rather than follow in men's footsteps. The structure of U.S. immigration law, changing gender roles, and economic opportunities for women are all responsible for this trend. Immigrant women's concentration in specific high-demand occupations—like private household work and nursing—has also enabled many to play a pivotal role as pioneer immigrants, establishing beachheads for further immigration (Salvo and Ortiz, 1992). This has been especially true for certain groups like Filipinos, with large numbers of nurses, and West Indians, with substantial numbers of private household workers.

Once in New York, the majority of immigrant women go out to work. At the time of the 1990 census, 60% of foreign-born female New Yorkers of working age were in the labor force. The percentages are much higher for certain groups. Filipino women, who often came specifically to work in health-care jobs, stand out as having the highest labor force participation rate at over 85%. West Indian women are not far behind, with labor force participation rates in the 70% to 80% range. Dominicans come out near the bottom, with 52% in the work force, and they have a relatively large proportion unemployed as well (Kasinitz and Vickerman, 1995). In trying to explain these different rates, Sherri Grasmuck and Ramon Grosfoguel (1997) argue that Dominican women's lower levels of education and limited English language skills have made it more difficult for them to find jobs, especially jobs that pay enough to cover the costs of child care. Because Jamaican women arrive with English and, on average, higher educational levels, they have better employment prospects. They are also more disposed to go out to work because they come from a society with a strong tradition of female employment: almost 70% of women in Jamaica were in the work force in 1990 compared to only 15% in the Dominican Republic.[3]

In New York, there is an enormous variety in the kinds of jobs occupied by female immigrants: a good many have professional and managerial positions while others end up in low-level service and factory work. Census data for 1990 on immigrant women in the labor force who arrived in the 1980s show this variation: 27% of Asian women, 13% from the Caribbean, and 10% from Central and South America were classified as professionals and manager; at the same time, 21% of Asian women, 14% from the Caribbean, and 23% from South and Central America were operators (Mollenkopf, Kasinitz, and Lindholm, 1995).

That many immigrant women are able to obtain professional and managerial jobs is not surprising given the human capital they bring with them. Immigration and Naturalization Service (INS) data, although limited, show that a fifth of the working-age women intending to live in New York City who reported an occupation to the INS when admitted for permanent residence between 1982 and 1989 were in professional/technical and administrative/managerial positions; in the early 1990s, the share in these categories went up to 36%. In both the 1980s and early 1990s, about one in every six immigrant women were in administrative support occupations such as secretaries, typists, and general office clerks (Lobo, Salvo, and Virgin, 1996).[4]

Of course, many immigrant women who had professional or white-collar jobs in their home society experience downward occupational mobility when they arrive in New York. Without American-recognized training, English proficiency, or greencards, highly qualified women are often consigned, at least temporarily, to relatively low-level positions when they arrive. Many Jamaican private household workers I interviewed in my research, for example, had been teachers and clerical workers back home, some experiencing what Maxine Margolis has called the transition from "mistress to servant" (Margolis, 1994; see also Colen, 1990). A number of Haitian and Hispanic aides in the New York nursing home I studied in the 1980s were full-fledged nurses before they emigrated, but their qualifications were not recognized here and language problems stood in the way of passing the requisite licensing exams to practice nursing in New York (see Foner, 1994).

In a time-worn pattern, women in each immigrant group gravitate in large numbers to particular occupations. As among men, English language ability and work skills help women in some groups gain a foothold in certain jobs; lack of English and specific job skills limit the employment possibilities of others. Once a beachhead is established, coethnics are likely to follow through a process of network hiring and referrals as well as employer preferences. Thus, for example, West Indian women are heavily concentrated in health care. Indeed, in 1990, close to a third of employed Jamaican women in New York were nurse's aides, orderlies, and attendants and registered or practical nurses (Kasinitz and Vickerman, 1995; see also Waldinger, 1996). Garment work has drawn in Dominican and Chinese women because it requires no English language ability, is quickly learned, and is often close at hand, in factories owned and managed by their compatriots. In the early days of the migration, Dominicans' entry into garment factories was also facilitated by the fact that the industry had already adjusted itself to Puerto Ricans, using bilingual supervisors and employee mediators (Grasmuck and Grosfoguel, 1997). Although the proportion of Dominican women in manufacturing has dramatically declined since 1980, substantial numbers still work in this sector. Chinese women remain the garment workers par excellence. Over half of all immigrant Chinese women workers in New York City are in the needle trades, virtually all as sewing machine operators. In recent years, new groups of immigrant women have also been drawn to the garment trades. The growing number of Korean-owned sewing shops—about 200 opened in midtown Manhattan in the late 1980s and early 1990s—are filled with Mexican and Ecuadoran workers, who are primarily women. Korean owners have had to look beyond the ethnic labor market for a source of cheap labor because Korean women are relatively well educated and have better opportunities elsewhere (Chin, 1997).

Wage Work: The Benefits

Wage work has, in many ways, improved the position of substantial numbers of migrant women in New York. This is not just the perception of the women themselves. From the outside looking in, it is clear that migrant women often gain greater independence, personal autonomy, and influence as a result of earning a regular wage for the first time, earning a higher wage than in the sending society, or making a larger contribution to the family economy than previously. How much improvement women experience depends to a large degree on their role in production and their social status in the home country as well as their economic role in New York. What is important is that, for the vast majority, the move to New York—and their involvement in work here—lead to gains in some domains of their lives, particularly in the household.

In cases where women did not earn an income, or earned only a small supplementary income, prior to migration, the gains in New York that come with a shift to regular wage work are especially striking. The much-cited case of Dominican immigrant women fits this pattern. Now that so many Dominicans work for wages—often for the first time—and contribute a larger share of the family income, they have more authority in the household and greater self-esteem. They use their wages, anthropologist Patricia Pessar observes, "to assert their rights to greater autonomy and equality within the household" (1995).[5]

In New York, Dominican women begin to expect to be co-partners in "heading" the household, a clear change from more patriarchal arrangements in the Dominican Republic. "We are both heads," said one woman, echoing the sentiments of many other Dominican women in New York. "If both the husband and wife are earning salaries then they should equally rule the household. In the Dominican Republic it is always the husband who gives the orders in the household. But here when the two are working, the woman feels herself the equal of the man in ruling the home" (Pessar, 1987, p.121). In a telling comment, a Dominican migrant visiting her home village told her cousin about New York: "Wait till you get there. You'll have your own paycheck, and I tell you, he [your husband] won't be pushing you around there the way he is here" (Grasmuck and Pessar, 1991, p. 147).

The organization of the household budget is in fact more equal in New York. In the Dominican Republic, men generally controlled the household budget even when wives and daughters put in income on a regular or semiregular basis. Commonly, men doled out an allowance to their wives, who were responsible for managing the funds to cover basic household expenses. The men had the last word when it came to decisions about long-term and costly outlays. When women contributed income, it was used for "luxuries" rather than staples, reinforcing the notion that the man was the breadwinner. In New York, Pessar found that husbands, wives, and working children usually pool their income; they each put a specific amount of their wages or profits into a common fund for shared household expenses. Often, they also pool the rest of what they earned for savings and special purchases. With this kind of arrangement, women's contributions are no longer seen as "supplementary" and men's as "essential." As men become more involved in developing strategies for stretching the food budget, they begin to more fully appreciate the skills women bring to these tasks. How critical women's wage work is to these new arrangements is brought out by what happens when women significantly reduce their contributions to the household budget, either in New York or when they return to the Dominican Republic. The man usually asserts his dominance once again by allocating a household allowance to his wife and reducing her authority over budgetary decisions.

No wonder that Dominican women are eager to postpone or avoid returning to the Dominican Republic where social pressures and an unfavorable job market would probably mean their retirement from work and a loss of new-found gains. One reason women spend large amounts of money on expensive durable goods like new appliances and home furnishings is to root their family securely in the United States and deplete the funds needed to return to the Dominican Republic.

Of course, many immigrant women, including some Dominicans, had regular salaries before emigration. Even these women often feel a new kind of independence in New York because jobs in this country pay more than most could ever earn at home and increase women's contribution to the family economy. For example, many Jamaican women I interviewed had white-collar jobs as secretaries, clerks, nurses, or teachers before they emigrated. Still, they said they had more financial control and more say in family affairs in New York where their incomes are so much larger. "We were brought up to think we have to depend on a man, do this for a man, listen to a man," said a New York secretary. "But here you can be on your own, more independent." Many told me that in Jamaica women usually have to depend on their husbands, whereas in New York they can "work their own money." Also, for those with training, there is a wider range of good jobs available. And there are better opportunities for additional training and education than in Jamaica, something that holds true for those from other Latin American and Caribbean countries as well (see Foner, 1986).

The sense of empowerment that comes from earning a regular wage—or a higher wage—and having greater control over what they earn comes out in studies of many different groups. Paid work for Chinese garment workers, according to one report, not only contributes to their families' economic well-being, but also has "created a sense of confidence and self-fulfillment which they may never have experienced in traditional Chinese society." "My husband dares not look down on me," one woman said. "He knows he can't provide for the family by himself." Or as another put it: "I do not have to ask my husband for money, I make my own" (Zhou and Nordquist, 1994, p. 201). For many Salvadoran women, the ability to earn wages and decide how they should be used is something new. As one woman explained: "Here [in the U.S.] women work just like the men. I like it a lot because managing my own money I feel independent. I don't have to ask my husband for money but in El Salvador, yes, I would have to. Over there women live dependent on their husbands. You have to walk behind him" (Mahler, 1996). Or listen to a Trinidadian woman of East Indian descent: "Now that I have a job I am independent. I stand up here as a man" (Burgess and Gray, 1981).

The female-first migration pattern involving adult married women that is common in some groups reinforces the effects of wage-earning on women's independence. Many women who initially lived and worked in New York without their husbands change, as one Dominican woman put it, "after so many years of being on my own, being my own boss" (Pessar, 1995, p. 60). One study suggests that Asian men who move to the United States as their wives' dependents often have to subordinate their careers, at least at first, to those of their wives since the women have already established themselves in this country (Espiritu, 1997).

Work outside the home in New York brings about another change that women appreciate. Many men now help out more *inside* the home than before they moved to New York. Of course, this is not inevitable. Cultural values in different groups as well as the availability of female relatives to lend a hand influence the kind of household help men provide. A study of the division of labor in Taiwanese immigrant households found that, as in Taiwan, men who held working-class jobs or owned small businesses did little around the house (Chen, 1992).[6] Korean men, staunch supporters of patriarchal family values and norms, generally still expect their wives to serve them and resist performing household chores like cooking, dishwashing, and doing the laundry. Such resistance is more effective when the wife's mother or mother-in-law lives in the household, a not infrequent occurrence in Korean immigrant families. Yet much to their consternation, Korean men in New York with working wives often find themselves helping out with household work more than they did in Korea—and that wives make more demands on them to increase their share (Min, 1998; Park, 1997; see also Lim, 1997, on Korean women in Texas).

Research on a number of Latin American and Caribbean groups shows that when wives are involved in productive work outside the home, there is a change in the organization of labor within it (cf. Lamphere, 1987). We are not talking about a drastic change in the household division of labor or the emergence of truly egalitarian arrangements. Indeed, Latin American and Caribbean women strongly identify as wives and mothers and they like being in charge of the domestic domain. What they want—and what they often get—is more help from men. Mainly, men oblige because they have little choice. Evidence also suggests that women's, and men's, conceptions of what men should do in the household begin to shift in the immigrant context.

West Indian men are definitely more helpful in the household than they were in the Caribbean. There, men hardly ever did housework, even when their wives had cash-earning activities. Work back home did not always take women out of the house for long periods of time. In the West Indies, neighbors and kin, especially mothers and sisters, frequently helped with child-minding. Those with salaried jobs employed domestics and nannies to cook, clean, and mind their children.

Although West Indian women in New York still do most of the cooking, cleaning, shopping, and washing, men often help out with this "women's work." However much they resent pitching in, men recognize that there is no alternative when their wives work and children (particularly daughters) are not old enough to lend a hand. "If she's working, we both chip in," is how one Trinidadian man put it (Burgess and Gray, 1981, p. 102). Working women simply cannot shoulder all of the domestic responsibilities expected of them, and they do not have relatives to help. Even if close kin live nearby, they are usually busy with work and their own household chores. Wives' wages are a necessary addition to the family income, and West Indians cannot afford to hire household help. "In order to have a family life here," said a middle-class Trinidadian woman, "[my husband] realizes he has to participate not only in the housework but in the childrearing too. It's no longer the type of thing where he comes home and the maid is there, having prepared the dinner. . . . Here if you're going to have a household, he has to participate. He has to pick up the children, or take them to the babysitter, or come home and begin the dinner" (p. 102). Several Jamaican men I met in New York—exceptions to be sure—even served as the main family cooks.

West Indian couples with young children often arrange their shifts so that the husband can look after the children while the wife works. I interviewed a number of Jamaican men in New York who worked night shifts and were at home during the day minding the children. "In Jamaica, oh, please," a Jamaican nurse told me."That was slavery. Bring the man his dinner and his slippers, do the laundry, you're kidding. Not anymore." In New York, her husband does the laundry, makes the children's breakfast and, in the past, got up at night to feed and change the babies.

More than behavior changes. As men become accustomed to doing more around the house, their notions of what tasks are appropriate—or expected—often also shift. Research shows that Dominican and Jamaican men and women believe that when both partners have jobs, and daughters are too young to help, husbands should pitch in with such tasks as shopping, washing dishes, and child care. Women tend to view their husband's help as a moral victory (Pessar, 1984); men accept their new duties, however reluctantly.

While the exigencies of immigrant life—women working outside the home, a lack of available relatives to assist, and an inability to hire help—are mainly responsible for men's greater participation in household tasks, American cultural beliefs and values play a role, too (see Foner, 1997). Many of the Dominicans whom Sherri Grasmuck and Patricia Pessar spoke to claimed that they self-consciously patterned their more egalitarian relations on what they believed to be the dominant American model. They saw this change as both modern and a sign of progress. One Dominican man and his wife said that soon after they were both working, they realized that "if both worked outside the house, both should work inside as well. Now that we are in the United States, we should adopt Americans' ways" (Grasmuck and Pessar, 1991, p. 152). Whatever men think, immigrant women may feel they can make more demands on their husbands in this country where the dominant norms and values back up their claims for men to help out.

In addition to the independence, power, and autonomy that wages bring, there are intrinsic satisfactions from work itself. Women in professional and managerial positions gain prestige from their positions and often have authority over others on the job. Certainly, this was true of the immigrant nurses in the nursing home I studied. The registered nurses were proud of their professional achievements, received deference from nursing aides below them, and exercised enormous authority in their units (Foner, 1994).

Many women in lower-level jobs also get a sense of satisfaction from doing their job well and from the new skills they have learned in New York. Dominican garment workers take pride in meeting the rigorous demands of the workplace (Pessar, 1995), and many immigrant women who do "caregiving work" in private homes or institutions get enormous pleasure from giving good care and from feeling needed and becoming close to their charges. "I like to help people," said a Jamaican woman who cared for a frail elderly couple on a live-in basis. "People don't realize how hard it is to work in the home and deal with sick people. Have to please them, make them comfortable, keep them happy. I like to work and I love my job. I may not be an R.N., but I help people" (Foner, 1986, p. 145). Deep attachments often develop between West Indian babysitters and the children they look after, and I found that many immigrant nursing home aides were close to elderly patients whose needs they saw to day after day (Foner, 1994).

An important aspect of work is the sociability involved. In factories, hospitals, and offices, women make friends and build up a storehouse of experiences that enriches their lives and conversations. Indeed, when women are out of work, they often complain of boredom and isolation. A Chinese garment worker said that when she was laid off "I had too much housework to do and I felt even busier than when I worked. Sometimes I get frustrated if I am confined at home and don't see my co-workers" (Zhou, 1992, p. 178). Dominican women say that when they are laid off they feel isolated at home; they not only miss the income, but also socializing with workmates and the bustle of the streets and subways (Pessar, 1995).

Typically, informal work cultures develop on the job that make work more interesting and liven up the day. Workers often chat and joke while they work, and they socialize at lunch and on breaks. Sometimes, they celebrate weddings or birthdays during free time or take up collections for sick co-workers. In the nursing home I studied, workers had formed a number of savings groups among themselves, with regular weekly contributions. Nursing aides also routinely lent each other a hand in difficult chores. In general, friendships formed on the job may extend outside the bounds of the workplace as women visit and phone each other or go to parties and on shopping jaunts with co-workers (see Foner, 1994).

Other Gains

Although the focus in this article is on the benefits that immigrant women reap from working outside the home, the move to New York has improved their status as women in other ways. In fact, women from some countries see the chance *not* to work as a gain. According to Fran Markowitz (1993), many Jewish emigre women from the former Soviet Union are freed from the triple role of worker, wife, and mother in New York because their husbands earn enough for them to stay at home or they are eligible, as refugees, for government assistance. While some Soviet emigre women feel depressed and useless because they no longer need to work full-time, others are glad to be able to take time off to care for young children. Couples who would never have dreamed of having more than one child in the old country may now have two or three.

For immigrants in some groups, welfare programs available in New York have provided new options for women on their own with young children to stay out of the paid labor force—or at least until the 1996 welfare reforms severely restricted noncitizens' access to welfare benefits. In the Dominican Republic, the lack of a system of public assistance increased the pressure on women without a man in the household to enter the labor force; in New York in the 1980s and early 1990s, Dominican women on their own, with young children and no spouse in residence, often preferred to seek public assistance than take the low-paying jobs available, since they could then care for their children (rather than spend a significant part of their wages on child care) and perhaps advance their own education and obtain future marketable skills (Gurak and Kritz, 1996).

Housework and other domestic chores are easier in New York for many immigrant women. In the case of Russian Jewish emigres, cooking, cleaning, and shopping, among other tasks, are less time-consuming than in the old country where keeping a family fed often meant standing on lines for hours each day just to purchase basic foodstuffs, bribing grocery store workers, and keeping abreast of news about special black market shipments (Markowitz, 1993; Orleck, 1987). In general, access to modern appliances like washing machines, vacuum cleaners, and microwave ovens makes life much easier for women who could never have afforded such luxuries in the countries they came from.

In New York, women may be able to engage in certain activities that were unacceptable or at least unusual for women in their home countries, which contributes to their sense that living abroad offers a new kind of freedom. Maxine Margolis describes a scene she observed in a Queens nightclub one Friday night, where a group of five Brazilian women in their forties and fifties sat at the bar drinking, smoking, and talking among themselves. Occasionally, the women were asked to dance by male patrons of the establishment. "What was so memorable about the scene is that it could not have occurred in these women's native land. In Brazil, it would be unthinkable for 'respectable' middle-aged women from the middle strata of society to go to a bar or a nightclub 'alone', meaning without appropriate escorts" (1994, p. 237). Several Jamaican women in my study spoke of the new opportunities to expand their cultural horizons in New York through the theater, concerts, and films—and of the opportunity to pursue their interests and lead their lives without the eyes, and censure, of the local community so closely upon them (Foner, 1986). Dominican women, too, say they feel liberated in their ability to travel widely on their way to and from work or to other activities without people gossiping that "they spend too much time away from their homes . . . [and] think the woman is up to no good" (Pessar, 1995, pp. 81–82).

Divorce is often easier and more acceptable in New York than it was back home. Despite the increasing prevalence of divorce in Taiwan, Chen (1992) explains, it is still very embarrassing for a divorced woman to face family and friends. In New York, Taiwanese divorced women can take care of themselves: "no one will question your past, and you can restart life here" (p. 254). Divorce, of course, is a risky business for immigrant women since, without the husband's financial contributions, their standard of living is in jeopardy and it is more of a struggle to make ends meet. Female-headed households typically have lower incomes and higher poverty rates than those with two working partners.

Still, better wage-earning opportunities in this country and, until recently, the widespread availability of welfare benefits to noncitizens, have meant that women can often manage on their own more easily in this country. Women may be more willing to make demands on their husbands than they would have done back home—and insist on more egalitarian relations—because they know these economic supports are on hand if the union breaks up. Also, they are spurred on by American norms that emphasize that husbands should be marriage partners who help out around the house and make decisions in concert with their wives—and by an American legal and social welfare system that supports them in cases of severe spouse abuse (cf. Kibria, 1993; Repak, 1995).

Wage Work: The Burdens

If wage work enables many immigrant women to expand their influence and independence, these gains often come at a price. Indeed, wage work in New York brings burdens as well as benefits to immigrant women and may create new sets of demands and pressures for them both on the job and at home. Moreover, despite changes in women's status in New York, premigration gender-role patterns and ideologies do not simply fade away; they continue to affect the lives of migrant women, often in ways that constrain and limit them.

Wage work, as immigrant women commonly explain, is not an option but a necessity for their family's welfare. As one Korean woman put it: "Without me helping out economically, it is absolutely impossible to survive in New York City" (Min, 1998, p. 38). Wage work typically brings a host of difficulties for women. On the job, women's wages are generally lower than men's. Moreover, women are limited in their choice of work due to gender divisions in the labor market—often confined to menial, low-prestige, and poorly paying jobs that can be described as industrialized homework. Working in the ethnic economy does not help most women either. Recent studies of Chinese, Dominican, and Colombian women in New York who work in businesses owned by their compatriots show that they earn low wages and have minimal benefits and few opportunities for advancement (Gilbertson, 1995; Zhou and Logan, 1989). Indeed, sociologist Greta Gilbertson argues that some of the success of immigrant small-business owners and workers in the ethnic enclave is due to the marginal position of immigrant women. The many Korean women who work in family businesses are, essentially, unpaid family workers without an independent source of income. Although many are working outside the home for the first time, they are typically thought of as "helpers" to their husbands; the husband not only legally owns the enterprise but also usually controls the money, hires and fires employees, and represents the business in Korean business associations (Min, 1998).[7]

For many immigrant women, working conditions are extremely difficult. Among the worst are those endured by garment workers who often have to keep up a furious pace in cramped conditions in noisy lofts. Despite federal and state laws, some sweatshops they work in are physically dangerous, located in windowless buildings with sealed fire exits and broken sprinkler systems. Often paid by the piece, many do not even make the minimum wage and are forced to work overtime at straight-time wages if they want to keep their jobs. Slow workers may make as little as $20 a day, fast workers more than $60 (Sung, n.d.). In the early 1990s, according to one account, Chinese women in unionized shops averaged $200 a week (Chin, 1997).

Domestic workers often have to deal with humiliating or demeaning treatment from employers as well as long hours, low pay, and lack of benefits (Colen, 1989). For those who clean houses, there are the dangers that come with using noxious and often toxic substances as well as the sheer physical strenuousness of the job. House cleaners, like many Salvadoran women, have to piece together a number of daily cleaning jobs so they can keep busy all week. Some immigrant women with full-time jobs have more than one position to make ends meet. I know many West Indian women, for example, who care for an elderly person on the weekend to supplement what they earn from a five-day child-care job. Others supplement their income through informal economic activities like selling homemade food or beauty products in various cosmetic lines.

Added to this, of course, are the demands of child care and burdens of household work. Only very affluent immigrants can afford to hire maids or housekeepers; female relatives, if present in New York, are often busy at work themselves. Occasionally, women can juggle shifts with their husbands so one parent is always around and sometimes an elderly mother or mother-in-law is on hand to help out.[8] Many working women pay to leave their children with babysitters or, less often, in day-care centers.[9] Child-care constraints are clearly a factor limiting women to low-paid jobs with flexible schedules; they may prevent women from working fulltime or, in some cases, at all. Sometimes, women leave their young children behind with relatives in the home country so they can manage work more easily, a common pattern among West Indian live-in household workers (Colen, 1989; Soto, 1987).

Immigrant women in all social classes have the major responsibilities for household chores as well as childrearing so that a grueling day at work is often followed or preceded by hours of cooking, cleaning, and washing. "I'm always working," is how Mrs. Darius, a Haitian nursing home aide with eight children put it. Although her husband, a mechanic, does not help much around the house ("some men are like that"), Mrs. Darius gets assistance from her mother, who lives with her. Still, there is a lot to do. "I have to work twenty-four hours. When I go home, I take a nap, then get up again; sometimes I get up at two in the morning, iron for the children, and go back to sleep" (Foner, 1994).

Korean working wives, according to sociologist Pyong Gap Min, suffer from overwork and stress due to the heavy demands on their time. After doing their work outside the home, they put in, on average, an additional twenty-five hours a week on housework, compared with seven hours done by their husbands. Altogether, working wives spend seventy-six hours a week on the job and housework—twelve more hours than men do. Although professional husbands help out more around the house than other Korean men, their wives still do the lion's share (Min, 1998) Kim Ai-Kyung, the wife of a physician, has run a boutique in New Jersey for more than thirteen years. She explained that she has not visited her family in Korea for many years because she cannot leave her husband and children alone:

> [T]he older boy is in medical school, and the younger one is working at a bank in New York City. But, when they come home, they still don't even open the refrigerator to get their own food or drink. I always serve them. And my husband—he does not know anything about the house. He doesn't even know how to make . . . instant noodle soup. If I went to Korea, he would starve to death. (Kim, 1996)

Or take the case of Antonia Duarte, a Dominican mother of three children, who put in a seventeen-hour day. At 5:00 A.M., she was up making breakfast and lunch for the family. She woke her three children at 6:00, got them dressed, fed, and ready for school, and then took them to the house of a friend, who cared for the four-year-old and oversaw the older children's departure to and return from school. By 7:15, Antonia was on the subway heading for the lamp factory where she worked from 8:00 A.M. to 4:30 P.M., five days a week. She collected her children a little after 5:00 and began preparing the evening meal when she got home. She didn't ask her two oldest children to help—the oldest is a twelve-year-old girl—because, "I'd rather they begin their homework right away, before they get too tired." Her husband demanded a traditional meal of rice, beans, plantains, and meat, which could take as long as two hours to prepare. She and the children ate together at 7:00, but her husband often did not get back from socializing with his friends until later. He expected Antonia to reheat the food and serve it upon his arrival. By the time she finished her child care and other domestic responsibilities, it was 11:30 or 12:00. Like other Dominican women, she explained that if she did not manage the children and household with a high level of competence, her husband would threaten to prohibit her from working (Pessar, 1982).

Women in groups where strong "traditional" patriarchal codes continue to exert an influence may experience other difficulties. In some better-off Dominican families, wives are pressured by husbands to stay out of the work force altogether as a way to symbolize their household's respectability and elevated economic status (Pessar, 1995). In many groups, working women who are now the family's main wage earners may feel a special need to tread carefully in relations with their husbands in order to preserve the appearance of male dominance. Indeed, one study shows professional Korean women making conscious attempts to keep their traditional lower status and to raise the position of their husbands by reducing their incomes. A nurse explained: "My basic salary exceeds his. If I do overtime, my income will be too much—compared to his—and so, when overtime work falls on me, I just try so hard to find other nurses to cover my overtime assignments. . . . By reducing my income, I think, my husband can keep his ego and male superiority" (Kim, 1996, p. 170).

Finally, there is the fact that women's increased financial authority and independence can also lead to greater discord with their spouses. Conflicts often develop when men resent, and try to resist, women's new demands on them; in some cases, the stresses ultimately lead to marital break-ups. There are special difficulties when men are unemployed or unsuccessful at work, and become dependent on women's wage-earning abilities, yet still insist on maintaining the perquisites of male privilege in the household (see Margolis, 1994; Min, 1998; Pessar, 1995). In extreme cases, the reversal of gender roles can lead to serious physical abuse for women at the hands of their spouses (Lessinger, 1995; Mahler, 1995). Indeed, in some instances, increased isolation from relatives in the immigrant situation creates conditions for greater abuse by husbands, who are freer of the informal controls that operated in their home communities.[10]

CONCLUSION

Wage labor, as one scholarly observer puts it, both oppresses and liberates immigrant women (Espiritu, 1997; see also Brettell and Simon, 1986; Morokvasic, 1984). On the positive side, women's regular access to wages—and to higher wages—in the United States frequently gives them greater say in household decision-making and more control over budgeting. Because immigrant working mothers are often absent from the home for forty to forty-five hours a week, or sometimes longer, someone must fill their place—or at least help out. Often, it is husbands. Women's labor force participation, in other words, frequently increases husband's participation in household work and leads to changes in the balance of power in many immigrant families. Working outside the home also broadens migrant women's social horizons and enhances their sense of independence. "A woman needs to work," said one Cuban sales worker. "She feels better and more in control of herself. She doesn't have to ask her husband for money. It seems to me that if a woman has a job, she is given more respect by her husband and her children" (Prieto, 1992). Many contemporary immigrant women would heartily agree. For a good number, the opportunities to work—and earn more money—represent a major gain that has come with the move to New York.

Yet, if migration has been liberating for women in some ways, it is clear that they are far from emancipated. Not only do they suffer from gender inequalities that are a feature of American society generally, but important vestiges of premigration gender ideologies and role patterns may place additional constraints on them. Like their native-born counterparts, immigrant women continue to experience special burdens and disabilities as members of the second sex. Many work in low-status, dead-end positions that pay less than men's jobs. Immigrant working wives in all social classes experience a heavy double burden since the household division of labor remains far from equal. If husbands help out with domestic burdens, they may do so only grudgingly, if at all, and it is women, more than men, who make work choices to accommodate and reflect family—and child-care—needs. Indeed, while many—perhaps most—immigrant women feel that the benefits of wage work outweigh the drawbacks, others would, if they could afford it, prefer to remain at home. As a Korean woman who worked as a manicurist in a nail salon fifty-four hours a week said, "If my husband makes enough money for the family, why should I take this burden?" (Min, 1998, p. 38).

If, as this article makes clear, studies of migrant women must consider the complex combination of gains and losses they experience in this country, additional research is needed to further specify the dynamics of these changes among different groups in a variety of domains, including the household, workplace, and community. Among the challenges ahead, as Patricia Pessar (1998) has recently pointed out, is to investigate how a host of interrelated factors—age, class, employment history, and legal status as well as family structures and gender ideologies (both prior to and after emigration)—affect the benefits as well as losses that migrant women experience. We have come a long way from the days when immigration scholars lamented that women were ignored in migration studies. Yet there is still much research to do to clarify and deepen our understanding of the complex and often contradictory ways that migration affects women.

NOTES

1. I am completing a book, *From Ellis Island to JFK,* that compares immigrants in New York today with immigrants at the turn of the century. In addition to analyzing the role of immigrant women then and now, it also examines such topics as education, transnationalism, race and ethnicity, and residence and work patterns.
2. My research among Jamaicans in New York in the early 1980s was based on in-depth interviews with forty immigrants (twenty men and twenty women) and participant observation. I also conducted research among health-care workers, largely Jamaican immigrant women, in a New York nursing home in the late 1980s (Foner, 1994).
3. These same factors, according to Grasmuck and Grosfoguel (1997), also account for the fact that Dominican female householders have a poverty rate almost twice that of Jamaican female heads.
4. Immigration and Naturalization Service data are the best we have for getting an idea of immigrants' occupational background, but they are not without problems. "Current" occupation asked on the immigrant visa can refer to last occupation held back home before immigrating but also, in some cases, to a job held in the United States or, for those entering under occupational preferences, to the occupation in the U.S. for which certification is being sought.
5. Pessar has developed her analysis of Dominican women in a number of publications. See Pessar, 1982, 1984, 1986, 1987, 1995, as well as Grasmuck and Pessar, 1991.
6. In his study of 100 Taiwanese households in Queens, Hsiang-Shui Chen (1992) found that men were most likely to help with garbage disposal and vacuuming, jobs seen as requiring physical strength. Taiwanese professional men helped out slightly more around the house than men in the working and business-owner classes. Chen links this to the work schedules of the different classes of men. He suggests that because professional men had shorter working hours, usually 9–5 work schedules, they could spend more time at home than business owners, who put in longer hours in their stores, or working-class men, who worked long hours at restaurant jobs. On the distribution of housework in Korean immigrant households in New York City see Min (1998) and Park (1997).
7. A 1988 survey, based on telephone interviews with a randomly selected sample of Korean married women in New York City, found that 38% of the women in the labor force worked together with their husbands in the same business; 12% ran their own businesses independently of their husbands; and 36% were employed in coethnic businesses (Min, 1998).

8. It is not infrequent for Korean immigrant couples to ask their mothers or mothers-in-law to come to New York to live with them to help out with child care (Min, 1998).
9. Day-care centres are in short supply, and they are often more expensive than babysitters in the immigrant community. Zhou notes that in 1988 there was only one subsidized day-care center for garment workers in Chinatown and a few home day-care services sponsored by the city government and some quasi-governmental organizations. The New York City Chinatown Daycare Center only had space for eighty children, chosen by lottery from among the families of the approximately 20,000 members of the International Ladies Garment Workers Union who worked in Chinatown's garment industry. The fee for subsidized day care in the late 1980s ranged from $8–$10 a week for each child from a low-income family (Zhou, 1992).
10. Hagan suggests a link between domestic violence among the Maya in Houston and the absence of the "watchful eyes of parents and other elderly kin" (1994, 58–59). Also see Ong's (1995) account of marital abuse experienced by two migrant Chinese women in San Francisco, one from an elite Beijing family, the other from a working-class Hong Kon background.

Selected Bibliography

ABAKER, REGINAL P., AND DAVIS S. NORTH. *The 1975 Refugees: Their First Five Years in America.* Washington, DC: New TransCentury Foundation, 1984.

ACUNA, RODOLFO. *Occupied American: A History of Chicanos.* New York: Harper and Row, 1981.

AGUEROS, JACK, et al. *The Immigrant Experience: The Anguish of Becoming American.* New York: Dial Press, 1971.

ALARCON, RAFAEL. "Norteñización: Self-Perpetuating Migration from a Mexican Town." In Jorge Bustamante, Clark Reynolds, and Raul Hinojosa, eds., *U. S.–Mexico Relations: Labor Market Interdependence* (pp. 302–318). Stanford: Stanford University Press, 1992.

ALBA, FRANCISCO. "Mexico's International Migration as a Manifestation of Its Development Pattern." *International Migration Review* 12 (Winter 1978): 502–551.

ALBA, RICHARD D. "The Twilight of Ethnicity Among American Catholics of European Ancestry." *Annals of the American Academy of Political and Social Science* 454 (1981): 86–97.

ALBA, RICHARD D. *Italian Americans: Into the Twilight of Ethnicity.* Upper Saddle River, NJ: Prentice-Hall, 1985.

ALBA, RICHARD D. *Ethnic Identity: The Transformation of White Identity.* New Haven: Yale University Press, 1990.

ALBA, RICHARD, AND VICTOR NEE. "Rethinking Assimilation Theory for a New Era of Immigration." *International Migration Review* 31 (1997): 826–874.

ALDRICH, HOWARD, AND JANE WEISS. "Differentiation Within the U.S. Capitalist Class."*American Sociological Review* 46 (1981): 279–290.

ALDRICH, HOWARD, AND ROGER WALDINGER. "Ethnicity and Entrepreneurship." *Annual Review of Sociology* 16 (1990): 111–135.

ALDRICH, HOWARD E., T. P. JONES, AND D. McEVOY. "Ethnic Advantage and Minority Business Development." In R. Ward and R. Jenkins, eds., *Ethnic Communities in Business* (pp. 189–210). Cambridge: Cambridge University Press, 1984.

ALLEN, JAMES P., AND EUGENE J. TURNER. *We the People: An Atlas of American's Ethnic Diversity.* New York: Macmillan, 1986.

ANDERSON, GRACE M. *Networks of Contact: The Portuguese and Toronto.* Ontario: Wilfrid Laurier University Press, 1974.

ANDERSON, NELS. *The Hobo, The Sociology of the Homeless Man.* Chicago: The University of Chicago Press, 1923.

ANSARI, ABDOULMABOUD. "A Community in Process: The First Generation of the Iranian Professional Middle-Class Immigrants in the United States." *International Review of Modern Sociology* 7 (1977): 85–101.

ANSARI, ABDOULMABOUD. *Iranian Immigrants in the United States: A Case of Dual Marginality.* New York: Associated Faculty Press, Inc., 1988.

ANSARI, ABDOULMABOUD. *The Making of the Iranian Community in America.* New York: Pardis Press, Inc., 1992.

ARDEBILI, MORTEZA H. "The Economic Adaptation of Iranian Immigrants in the Kansas City Metropolitan Area." Ph.D. Dissertation, University of Kansas, 1986.

AUSTER, ELLEN, AND HOWARD ALDRICH. "Small Business Vulnerability, Ethnic Enclaves and Ethnic Enterprise." In Robin Ward and Richard Jenkins, eds., *Ethnic Communities in Business: Strategies for Economic Survival* (pp. 39–56). Cambridge: Cambridge University Press, 1984.

AVERITT, ROBERT T. *The Dual Economy.* New York: Norton, 1968.

BACH, ROBERT L. "Mexican Immigration and the American State." *International Migration Review* 12 (Winter 1978): 536–558.

BACH, ROBERT L. "Immigration: Issues of Ethnicity, Class, and Public Policy in the United States." *Annals of the American Academy of Political and Social Science* 485 (May 1986): 139–152.

BACH, ROBERT L., LINDA W. GORDON, DAVID W. HAINES, AND DAVID R. HOWELL. "The Economic Adjustment of Southeast Asian Refugees in the United States." In *World Refugee Survey, 1983*, (pp. 51–55). Geneva: United Nations High Commission for Refugees, 1984.

BAILEY, THOMAS. *Immigrants and Native Workers: Contrasts and Competition.* Boulder: Westview, 1987.

BAILEY, THOMAS, AND ROGER WALDINGER. "Primary, Secondary, and Enclave Labor Markets: A Training System Approach." *American Sociological Review* 56 (1991): 432–45.

BARERA, MARIO. *Race and Class in the Southwest: A Theory of Racial Inequality.* Notre Dame, Indiana: University of Notre Dame Press, 1979.

BARKAN, ELLIOT. "Race, Religion, and Nationality in American Society: A Model of Ethnicity—From Contact to Assimilation." *Journal of American Ethnic History* 14 (1995): 38–101.

BARRINGER, H., R. W. GARDNER, AND M. J. LEVIN. *Asians and Pacific Islanders in the United States.* New York: Russell Sage Foundation, 1993.

BASCH, LINDA, N. GLICK SCHILLER, AND C. BLANC-SZANTON. *Nations Unbound: Transnational Projects, Post-Colonial Predicaments, and Deterritorialized Nation-States.* Langhorne, PA: Gordon and Breach, 1994.

BASKAUSKAS, LIUCIJA. "The Lithuanian Refugee Experience and Grief." *International Migration Review* 15 (1981): 276–291.

BAUBOCK, RAINER. *Transnational Citizenship: Membership and Rights in International Migration.* Aldershot, U.K: Edward Elgar, 1994.

BAUER, JANET. "A Long Way Home: Islam in the Adaptation of Iranian Women Refugees in Turkey and West Germany." In Asghar Fathi, ed., *Iranian Refugees and Exile Since Khomeini* (pp. 77–101). Costa Mesa, CA: Mazda, 1991.

BAXTER, SUE, AND GOEFF RAW. "Fast Food, Fetterd Work: Chinese Women in the Ethnic Catering Industry." In Sallie Westwood and Parminder Bhachu, eds., *Enterprising Women: Ethnicity, Economy, and Gender Relations* (pp. 58–75). New York: Routledge, 1988.

BEAN, FRANK D., AND MARTA TIENDA. *The Hispanic Population of the United States.* New York: Russell Sage, 1987.

BEAN, FRANK D., B. LINDSAY LOWELL, AND LOWELL J. TAYLOR. "Undocumented Migration to the United States: Perceptions and Evidence." *Population and Development Review* 13 (December 1987): 671–690.

BEAN, FRANK D., HARLEY L. BROWNING, AND W. PARKER FRISBIE. "The Socio-Demographic Characteristics of Mexican Immigrant Status Groups: Implications for Studying Undocumented Mexicans." *International Migration Review* 18 (Fall 1985): 672–691.

BEAN, FRANK D., HARLEY L. BROWNING, AND W. PARKER FRISBIE. "What the 1980 U.S. Census Tells Us About the Characteristics of Illegal and Legal Mexican Immigrants." Population Research Center, University of Texas at Austin, mimeographed, 1985.

BENEDICT, BURTON. "Family Firms and Firm Families: A Comparison of Indian, Chinese, and Creole Firms in Seychelles." In S. M. Greenfield, A. Strickon, and R. T. Aubey, eds., *Entrepreneurs in Cultural Context* (pp. 304–326). Albuquerque: University of Mexico Press, 1979.

BERGER, BRIGITTE. "The Culture of Modern Entrepreneurship." In Brigitte Berger, ed., *The Culture of Entrepreneurship* (pp. 13–22). San Francisco: ICS Press, 1991.

BERNARD, W. S. "Cultural Determinants of Naturalization." *American Sociological Review* 1 (December 1936): 943–953.

BERRY, JOHN W. "The Acculturation Process and Refugee Behavior." In Carolyn L. Williams and

Joseph Westermeyer, eds., *Refugee Mental Health in Resettlement Countries* (pp. 25–37). New York: Hemisphere, 1986.

BERRY, JOHN W., UICHOL KIM, THOMAS MINDE, AND DORIS MOK. "Comparative Studies of Acculturative Stress." *International Migration Review* 21 (Fall 1987): 491–511.

BIPARVA, EBRAHIM. "Ethnic Organizations: Integration and Assimilation vs. Segregation and Cultural Preservation with Specific Reference to the Iranians in the Washington, D. C. Metropolitan Area." *Journal of Third World Studies* 11, no.1 (1994): 369–404.

BLACKISTONE, KEVIN B. "Arab Entrepreneurs Take over Inner City Grocery Stores." *Chicago Reporter* 10 (1981): 1–5.

BLASCHKE, JOCHEN et al. "European Trends in Ethnic Business." In Roger Waldinger et al., ed., *Ethnic Entrepreneurs: Immigrants Business in Industrial Societies* (pp. 79–105). Newbury: Sage Publications, 1992.

BLAU, FRANCINE D. "The Use of Transfer Payments by Immigrants." *Industrial and Labor Relations Review* 37 (1984): 222–239.

BLAUNER, ROBERT. "Internal Colonialism and Ghetto Revolt." *Social Problems* 16 (1969): 393–408.

BODNAR, J. *The Transplanted: A History of Immigrants in Urban America*. Bloomington: Indiana University Press, 1985.

BÖHNING, W. R. *The Migration of Workers in the United Kingdom and the European Community.* London: Oxford University Press, 1972.

BOISSEVAIN, JERMY. "Small Entrepreneurs in Contemporary Europe." In Robin Ward and Richard Jenkins, eds., *Ethnic Communities in Business: Strategies for Economic Survival* (pp. 20–28). Cambridge: Cambridge University Press, 1984.

BONACICH, EDNA. "A Theory of Ethnic Antagonism: The Split Labor Market." *American Sociological Review* 37 (1972): 583–594.

BONACICH, EDNA. "A Theory of Middleman Minorities." *American Sociological Review* 38 (1973): 583–594.

BONACICH, EDNA. "Small Business and Japanese American Ethnic Solidarity." *Amerasia Journal* 3 (1975): 96–112.

BONACICH, EDNA. "Advanced Capitalism and Black/White Relations: A Split Labor Market Interpretation." *American Sociological Review* 41 (February 1976): 34–51.

BONACICH, EDNA. "Class Approaches to Ethnicity and Race." *Insurgent Sociologist* 10 (1980): 9–23.

BONACICH, EDNA. "Asian Labor in the Development of California and Hawaii." In Lucie Cheng and Edna Bonacich, eds., *Labor Immigration Under Capitalism* (pp. 130–185). Berkeley: University of California Press, 1984.

BONACICH, EDNA. "Korean Immigrant Small Business in Los Angeles." In Roy S. Bryce-Laporte, ed., *Sourcebook on the New Immigration* (pp. 167–184). New Brunswick, NJ: Transaction Books, 1987.

BONACICH, EDNA. "Asians in the Los Angeles Garment Industry." In P. Ong, E. Bonacich, and L. Cheng, eds., *The New Asian Immigration in Los Angeles and Global Restructuring* (pp. 137–163). Berkeley: University of California Press, 1994.

BONACICH, EDNA, AND TAE HWAN JUNG. "A Portrait of Korean Small Business in Los Angeles." In Eui-Young Yu, Earl H. Phillips, and Eun Sik Yang, eds., *Koreans in Los Angeles.* Koryo Research Institute and Center for Korean-American and Korean Studies, California State University, Los Angeles, 1982.

BONACICH, EDNA, AND J. MODELL. *The Economic Basis of Ethnic Solidarity: Small Business in the Japanese American Community*. Berkeley and Los Angeles: University of California Press, 1980.

BONACICH, EDNA, IVAN LIGHT, AND CHARLES WONG. "Koreans in Business." *Society* 14 (1977): 54–59.

BONACICH, EDNA, M. HOSSAIN, AND J. PARK. "Korean Immigrant Working Women in the Early 1980s." In E. Yu and E. H. Philipps, eds., *Korean Women in Transition: At Home and Abroad* (pp. 219–247). Los Angeles: California State University, Center for Korean-American and Korean Studies, 1987.

BONNETT, AUBREY W. "An Examination of Rotating Credit Associations Among Black West Indian Immigrants in Brooklyn." In Roy S. Bryce-Laporte, ed., *Sourcebook on the New Immigration* (pp. 271–283). New Brunswick, NJ: Transaction Books, 1980.

BORHEK, J. T. "Ethnic Group Cohesion." *American Journal of Sociology* 76 (1970): 33–46.

BORJAS, GEORGE J. "The Earnings of Male Hispanic Immigrants in the United States. *Industrial and Labor Relations Review* 35 (1982): 343–353.

BORJAS, GEORGE J. "The Economic Consequences of Immigration." *Science* 235 (1987): 645–651.

BORJAS, GEORGE J. *Friends or Strangers: The Impact of Immigrants on the U.S. Economy.* New York: Basic Books, 1990.

BORJAS, GEORGE J., AND M. TIENDA. "The Employment and Wages of Legalized Immigrants." *International Migration Review* 27, no. 4 (1993): 712–747.

BORJAS, GEORGE J., AND RICHARD B. FREEMAN, EDS. *Immigration and the Workforce: Economic Consequences for the United States and Source Areas.* Chicago: University of Chicago Press, 1992.

BOSWELL, TERRY E. "A Split Labor Market Analysis of Discrimination Against Chinese Immigrants, 1850–1882." *American Sociological Review* 51 (June 1986): 352–371.

BOSWELL, THOMAS D., AND JAMES R. CURTIS. *The Cuban-American Experience.* Totowa, NJ: Rowman and Allanheld, 1984.

BOUVIER, LEON L., AND ROBERT W. GARDNER. "Immigration to the U.S.: The Unfinished Story." *Population Bulletin* 14 (1986).

BOYD, MONICA. "Family and Personal Networks in International Migration: Recent Developments and New Agendas." *International Migration Review* 23 (1989): 638–669.

BOYD, ROBERT. "Ethnic Entrepreneurship in the New Economy: Business Enterprise Among Asian Americans and Blacks in a Changing Urban Economy." Ph.D. Dissertation, University of North Carolina, 1989.

BOZORGMEHR, MEHDI. *Internal Ethnicity: Armenian, Bahai, Jewish, and Muslim Iranians in Los Angeles.* University Microfilms International Dissertation Services. Ann Arbor: Michigan, 1992.

BOZORGMEHR, MEHDI, AND GEORGES SABAGH. "High Status Immigrants: A Statistical Profile of Iranians in the United States." *Iranian Studies* 21, no. 3–4 (1988): 5–36.

BRAY, DAVID. "Economic Development: The Middle Class and International Migration in the Dominican Republic." *International Migration Review* 18 (Summer 1984): 217–236.

BRETTELL, CAROLINE. *Men Who Migrate, Women Who Wait: The Demographic History of Portuguese Parish.* Princeton: Princeton University Press, 1987.

BRETTELL, CAROLINE, AND RITA SIMON. "Immigrant Women: An Introduction." In Rita Simon and Caroline Brettell, eds., *International Migration: The Female Experience.* Totowa, NJ: Rowman, 1986.

BRIGGS, VERNON M. "The Need for a More Restrictive Border Policy." *Social Science Quarterly* 56 (1975): 477–484.

BRIMELOW, PETER. *Alien Nation: Common Sense about America's Immigration Disaster.* New York: Random House, 1995.

BROWNING, HARLEY L., AND NESTOR RODRIGUEZ. "The Migration of Mexican Indocumentados as a Settlement Process: Implications for Work." In George J. Borjas and Marta Tienda, eds., *Hispanics in the U.S. Economy* (pp. 277–297). Orlando, FL: Academic Press, 1985.

BROWNING, HARLEY L., AND RODOLFO DE LA GARZA, EDS. *Mexican Immigrants and Mexican Americans: An Evolving Relation.* Austin: Center of Mexican American Studies, University of Texas, 1986.

BRUBAKER, ROGER S. *Citizenship and Nationhood in France and Germany:* Cambridge, MA: Harvard University Press, 1992.

BRUBAKER, ROGER, S., ED. *Immigration and the Politics of Citizenship in Europe and North America.* Lanham, MD: University Press of America, 1989.

BRUMBERG, STEPHEN F. *Going to America, Going to School: The Jewish Immigrant Public School Encounter in Turn-of-Century New York City.* New York: Praeger, 1986.

BUKOWCZYK, J. J. *And My Children Did Not Know Me: A History of the Polish-Americans.* Bloomington: Indiana University Press, 1987.

BULMER, M. *The Chicago School of Sociology: Institutionalization, Diversity, and the Rise of Sociological Research.* Chicago: University of Chicago Press, 1984.

BURAWOY, M. "The Functions and Reproduction of Migrant Labor: Comparative Material from Southern Africa and the United States."

American Journal of Sociology 81 (1976): 1050–1087.

BURGESS, JUDITH, AND MERYL GRAY. "Migration and Sex Roles: A Comparison of Black and Indian Trinidadians in New York City." In Delores Mortimer and Roy Bryce-Laporte, eds., *Female Immigrants to the United States: Caribbean, Latin America, and African Experiences*. Washington, DC: Research Institute on Immigration and Ethnic Studies, 1981.

BURMA, JOHN D. *Mexican-Americans in the United States: A Reader.* New York: Schenkman, 1970.

BUSTAMANTE, JORGE, AND GERONIMO MARTINEZ. "Undocumented Immigration from Mexico: Beyond Borders but Within Systems." *Journal of International Affairs* 33 (Fall/Winter 1979): 265–274.

CAIN, GLEN G. "The Challenge of Segmented Labor Market Theories to Orthodox Theory: A Survey." *Journal of Economic Literature* 14 (1976): 1215–1258.

CAMARILLO, ALBERT. *Chicanos in a Changing Society.* Cambridge, MA: Harvard University Press, 1979.

CARDOSO, LAWRENCE A. *Mexican Emigration to the United States, 1897–1931*. Tucson: University of Arizona Press, 1980.

CASTELLS, MANUEL. "Immigrant Workers and Class Struggles in Advanced Capitalism: The Western European Experience." *Politics and Society* 5 (1975): 33–66.

CASTELLS, MANUEL. *The Informational City: Information Technology, Economic Restructuring and the Urban–Regional Process*. Oxford: Basil Blackwell, 1989.

CASTLES, STEPHEN. "The Guest-Worker in Western Europe: An Obituary." *International Migration Review* 20 (Winter 1986): 761–778.

CASTLES, STEPHEN, AND MARK MILLER. *The Age of Migration: International Population Movements in the Modern World,* 2nd ed. New York: Guilford Press, 1998.

CASTLES, STEPHEN, HEATHER BOOTH, AND TINA WALLACE. *Here for Good: Western Europe's New Ethnic Minorities*. London: Pluto Press, 1984.

CHAI, ALICE YUN. "Freed from the Elders but Locked into Labor: Korean Immigrant Women in Hawaii." *Women's Studies* 13 (1987a): 223–234.

CHAI, ALICE YUN. "Adaptive Strategies of Recent Korean Immigrant Women in Hawaii." In Janet Sharistanian, ed., *Beyond the Public/Domestic Dichotomy: Contemporary Perspective on Women's Public Lives* (pp. 65–99). New York: Greenwood Press, 1987b.

CHAN, KWOK B., AND DAVID LOVERIDGE. "Refugees in Transit: Vietnamese in a Refugee Camp in Hong Kong." *International Migration Review* 21 (Fall 1987): 745–759.

CHAVEZ, LEO R. "Settlers and Sojourners: The Case of Mexicans in the United States." *Human Organization* 47 (Summer 1988): 95–108.

CHAVEZ, LEO R., AND ESTEVAN T. FLORES. "Undocumented Mexicans and Central Americans and the Immigration Reform and Control Act of 1986: A Reflection Based on Empirical Data." In *In Defense of the Alien*, Vol. 10 (pp. 137–156). New York: Center for Migration Studies, 1988.

CHEN, HSIANG-SHUI. *Taiwan Immigrants in Contemporary New York*. Ithaca, New York: Cornell University Press, 1992.

CHEN, JANET, AND YUET-WAH CHEUNG. "Ethnic Resources and Business Enterprise: A Study of Chinese Businesses in Toronto." *Human Organization* 44 (1985): 142–154.

CHILD, CLIFTON J. *The German-Americans in Politics, 1914–1917*. Madison: University of Wisconsin Press, 1939.

CHILD, IRVING L. *Italian or American? The Second Generation in Conflict*. New Haven, CT: Yale University Press, 1943.

CHISWICK, BARRY R. "The Effect of Americanization on the Earnings of Foreign-Born Men." *Journal of Political Economy* 86 (October 1978): 897–921.

CHISWICK, BARRY R. "The Economic Progress of Immigrants: Some Apparently Universal Patterns." In William Fellner, ed., *Contemporary Economic Problems* (355–399). Washington DC: American Enterprise Institute, 1979.

CHISWICK, BARRY R. "The Labor Market Status of American Jews: Patterns and Determinants." In W. A. Van Horne and T. V. Tonnesen, eds., *Ethnicity and the Work Force* (pp. 96–123). Milwaukee: University of Wisconsin System, American Ethnic Studies Coordinating Committee, 1985.

CHOCK, PHYLLIS P. "The Greek-American Small Businessman: A Cultural Analysis." *Journal of Anthropological Research* 37 (1981): 46–60.

CINEL, D. *From Italy to San Francisco.* Stanford: Stanford University Press, 1982.

CLEMENT, W., AND J. MYLES. *Relations of Ruling: Class and Gender in Postindustrial Societies.* Montreal, Canada: McGill-Queen's University Press, 1994.

COBAS, JOSE. "Paths to Self-Employment Among Immigrants." *Sociological Perspectives* 29 (1986): 101–120.

COBAS, JOSE. "Six Problems in the Sociology of the Ethnic Economy. *Sociological Perspectives* 32, no. 3 (1989): 201–214.

COBAS, JOSE, AND IONE DEOLLOS. "Family Ties, Co-Ethnic Bounds, and Ethnic Entrepreneurship. *Sociological Perspectives* 32 (1989): 403–411.

COCKCROFT, JAMES D. *Outlaws in the Promised Land: Mexican Immigrant Workers and America's Future.* New York: Grove Press, 1986.

COHON, J. DONALD, JR. "Psychological Adaptation and Dysfunction Among Refugees." *International Migration Review* 15 (Spring-Summer 1981): 255–275.

COLEMAN, JAMES. "Social Capital in the Creation of Human Capital." *American Journal of Sociology* 94 (1988): S94–S121.

COLEN, SHELLEE. "Housekeeping for the Green Card: West Indian Household Workers, the State, and Stratified Reproduction in New York." In Roger Sanjek and Shellee Colen, eds., *At Work in Homes: Household Workers in World Perspective.* Washington, DC: American Ethnological Society Monograph Series, no. 3. 1990.

CORCORAN, M. P. *Irish Illegal: Transients Between Two Societies.* Westport, CT: Greenwood, 1993.

CORNELIUS, WAYNE A. "Illegal Migration to the United States: Recent Research Findings, Policy Implications, and Research Priorities." Discussion Paper C/77-11. Center for International Studies, MIT, mimeographed, 1977.

CORNELLIUS, WAYNE A. "Mexican Migration to the United States: Causes, Consequences, and U.S. Responses." Working Paper. Center for International Studies, MIT, 1977.

CORNELIUS, WAYNE A., LEO R. CHAVEZ, AND JORGE G. CASTR. *Mexican Immigrants and Southern California: A Summary of Current Knowledge.* Research Report Series 36. Center for U.S. Mexican Studies. University of California Press, 1980.

CORTES, CARLOS E., ED. *Cuban Exiles in the United States.* New York: Oxford University Press, 1968.

CRESSEY, PAUL. *Taxi Dance Hall.* Chicago. The University of Chicago Press, 1932.

CUMMINGS, SCOTT A. "Collectivism: The Unique Legacy of Immigrant Economic Development." In Scott Cummings, ed., *Self-Help in Urban America* (pp. 5–32). Port Washington, NY: Kennikat Press, 1980.

CURRAN, JAMES, AND ROGER BURROWS. "The Social Analysis of Small Business: Some Emerging Themes." In Scott Cummings, ed., *Entrepreneurship in Europe: The Social Processes* (pp. 164–191). London: Croom Helm, 1987.

DALLALFAR, ARLENEE. "Iranian Immigrant Women in Los Angeles: The Reconstruction of Work, Ethnicity, and Community." University Microfilms International Dissertation services. Ann Arbor: Michigan, 1989.

DANZIGER S., P. GOTTSCHALK, EDS. *Uneven Tides: Rising Inequality in America.* New York: Russell Sage Foundation, 1993.

DAVID, HENRY P. "Involuntary International Migration: Adaptation of Refugees." In Eugene B. Brody, ed., *Behavior in New Environments* (pp. 73–95). Beverly Hills: Sage, 1970.

DE WIND, JOSH, TOM SEIDL, AND JANET SHENK. "Caribbean Migration: Contract Labor in U.S. Agriculture." *NACLA Report on the Americas* 11 (November–December 1977): 4–37.

DEFRIETAS, G. *Inequality at Work: Hispanics in the U.S. Labor Force.* New York: Oxford University Press, 1991.

DHALIWAL, A. K. "Gender at Work: The Renegotiation of Middle-Class Womanhood in a South Asian-Owned Business." In W. L. Ng, S.-Y. Chin, J. S. Moy, and G. Y. Okihiro, eds., *Reviewing Asian America: Locating Diversity* (pp. 75–85). Pullman: Washington State University Press, 1995.

DIAZ-BRIQUETS, SERGIO. "Cuban-Owned Business in the United States." *Cuban Studies* 14 (Summer 1985): 57–64.

DICKENS, WILLIAM T., AND KEVIN LANG. "A Test of Dual Labor Market Theory." *American Economic Review* 75 (1985): 792–805.

DINERMAN, INA R. "Patterns of Adaptation Among Households of U.S.-Bound Migrants from Michoacan, Mexico." *International Migration Review* 12 (Winter 1978): 485–501.

DINNERSTEIN, LEONARD. "The Last European Jewish Migration." In Leonard Dinnerstein and Frederic C. Jaher, eds., *Uncertain Americans: Readings in Ethnic History* (pp. 216–231). New York: Oxford University Press, 1977.

DIXON, H. "Black Cubans in the United States: A Case of Conflicts Between Race and Ethnicity." Paper Presented at the Annual Meeting of the American Studies Association, Miami, (October 27–30, 1988).

DIXON, HERIBERTO. "Emigration and Jamaican Employment." *Migration Today* 8 (1980): 24–27.

DONATO, KATHARINE. "Understanding U.S. Immigration: Why Some Countries Send Women and Others Send Men." In Donna Gabaccia, ed., *Seeking Common Ground: Multidisciplinary Studies of Immigrant Women in the United States*. Westport, CT: Praeger, 1992.

DONATO, KATHARINE M., JORGE DURAND, AND DOUGLAS S. MASSEY. "Stemming the Tide? Assessing the Deterrent Effects of the Immigration Reform and Control Act." *Demography* 29 (1992): 139–157.

DONNELLY, N. D. *Changing Lives of Refugee Hmong Women*. Seattle: Washington University Press, 1994.

DULEEP, H., AND S. SANDERS. "Discrimination at the Top: American-Born Asian and White Men. *Industrial Relations* 31 (1993): 416–432.

EDMONSTON, BARRY, AND JEFFREY PASSEL. "The Future Immigrant Population of the United States." Paper presented at the Conference on Immigration and Ethnicity. The Urban Institute, Washington, D. C. (June 1991): 17–18.

EDWARDS, ROBERT, ROBERT REICH, AND DAVID GORDON. *Labor Market Segmentation*. Lexington, MA: D. C. Heath, 1975.

ENTZINGER, HAN B. "Race, Class and the Shaping of a Policy for Immigrants: The Case of the Netherlands." *International Migration Review* 25 (March 1987): 5–20.

ESCHBACH, K. "The Enduring and Vanishing American Indian: American Indian Population Growth and Intermarriage in 1990." *Ethnic Racial Studies* 18 (1995): 89–108.

ESPENSHADE, THOMAS J., AND CHARLES A. CALHOUN. "An Analysis of Public Opinion Toward Undocumented Immigration." *Population Research and Policy Review* 12 (1993): 189–224.

ESPENSHADE, THOMAS. J., AND W. YE. "Differential Fertility Within an Ethnic Minority: The Effect of Trying Harder Among Chinese American Women." *Social Problems* 41, no.1 (1994): 97–113.

ESPIRITU, YEN LE. *Filipino American Lives*. Philadelphia: Temple University Press, 1995.

ESPIRITU, YEN LE. *Asian American Women and Men*. Thousand Oaks, CA: Sage, 1997.

FAIST, THOMAS. *Social Citizenship for Whom? Young Turks in Germany and Mexican Americans in the United States*. Aldershot, U.K: Avebury, 1995.

FAIST, THOMAS. "Transnational Social Spaces Out of International Migration: Evolution, Significance and Future Prospects." *Archive Europeenne Sociologique* 39 (1998): 213–247.

FARLEY R. "The Common Destiny of Blacks and Whites." In H. Hill and J. E. Jones, eds., *Race in America: The Struggle for Equality* (pp. 197–233). Madison: University of Wisconsin, 1993.

FARLEY, R., AND W. R. ALLEN. *The Color Line and the Quality of Life in America*. New York: Russell Sage Foundation, 1987.

FATHI, ASGHAR. "Theories of Involuntary Migration and the Iranian Experience." In Asghar Fathi, ed., *Iranian Refugees and Exiles Since Khomeini* (pp. 8–18). Costa Mesa, CA: Mazda, 1991.

FAWCETT, JAMES T. "Network, Linkages, and Migration System." *International Migration Review* 23 (1989): 671–680.

FAWCETT, JAMES. T., AND R. W. GARDNER. "Asian Immigrant Entrepreneurs and Non-entrepreneurs: A Comparative Study of Recent Korean and Filipino Immigrants." *Population and Environment* 15 (1994): 211–238.

FEAGIN, J. R. *Living with Racism: The Black Middle-Class Experience*. Boston, Beacon Press, 1994.

FEBREGA, HORACIO, JR. "Social Psychiatric Aspects of Acculturation and Migration: A General Statement." *Comprehensive Psychiatry* 10 (July 1969): 314–329.

FERNÁNDEZ-KELLY, M. PATRICIA, AND ANNA M. GARCIA. "Informalization at the Core: Hispanic Women, Homework, and the Advanced Capitalist State." In Alejandro Portes, Manual Castells, and Lauren A. Benton, eds., *The Informal Economy* (pp. 247–264). Baltimore: Johns Hopkins University Press, 1989.

FERREE, M. M. "Employment Without Liberation: Cuban Women in the United States." *Social Science Quarterly* 60 (1979): 35–50.

FILER, R. K. "The Impact of Immigrant Arrivals in Migratory Patterns of Native Workers." In G. Borjas, and R. Freeman, eds., *Immigration and the Work Force: Economic Consequences for the United States and Source Areas* (pp. 245–269). Chicago: University of Chicago Press, 1990.

FITZPATRICK, JOSEPH. *Puerto Rican Americans: The Meaning of Migration to the Mainland,* 2nd ed. Englewood Cliffs, NJ: Prentice-Hall, 1987.

FOERSTER, ROBERT. *The Italian Emigration of Our Times.* Cambridge, MA: Harvard University Press, 1919.

FONER, NANCY. *Jamaica Farewell: Jamaican Migrants in London.* Berkeley and Los Angeles: University of California Press, 1978.

FONER NANCY. *Jamaican Migrants: A Comparative Analysis of the New York and London Experience.* Center for Latin American and Caribbean Studies, New York University, Occasional Paper 36, 1983.

FONER, NANCY. "Sex Roles and Sensibilities: Jamaican Women in New York and London." In Rita Simon and Caroline Brettell, eds., *International Migration: The Female Experience.* Totowa, NJ: Rowman and Allenheld, 1986.

FONER, NANCY. "The Immigrant Family: Cultural Legacies and Cultural Changes." *International Migration Review* 31 (1997): 961–974.

FONG, NG. BICKLEEN. *The Chinese in New Zealand.* Hong Kong: Hong Kong University Press, 1959.

FORBES, SUSAN S. "Residency Patterns and Secondary Migration of Refugees." *Migration News* 34 (January-March 1985): 3–18.

FOST, DAN. "Iranians in California." *American Demographics* (May 1990): 45–47.

FRAZIER, E. FRANKLIN. *The Negro in the United States.* New York: Macmillan, 1949.

FRAZIER, E. FRANKLIN. *Race and Culture Contacts in the Modern World* . New York: Knopf, 1957.

FREEMAN, GARY. "Modes of Immigration Politics in Liberal Democratic States." *International Migration Review* 29 (1995): 881–902.

FURNIVALL, J. S. *Colonial Policy and Practice.* New York: New York University Press, 1956.

GABACCIA, D. R. *From Italy to Elizabeth Street.* Albany: State University of New York Press, 1983.

GAERTNER, MIRIAM L. "A Comparison of Refugee and Non-Refugee Immigrants to New York City." In H. B. Murphy, ed., *Flight and Resettlement* (pp. 99–112). Lucerne: UNESCO, 1955.

GAFFARIAN, SHIREEN. "The Acculturation of Iranians in the United States." *The Journal of Social Psychology* 127, no. 6 (1987): 565–571.

GAMIO, MANUEL. *Mexican Immigration to the United States.* Chicago: University of Chicago Press, 1930.

GANN, L. H., AND PETER J. DUIGNAN. *The Hispanics in the United States: A History.* Boulder, CO: Westview Press, 1986.

GANS, HERBERT J. *The Urban Villagers: Group and Class in the Life of Italian Americans.* New York: Free Press, 1962.

GANS, HERBERT J. "Foreword." In Neil Sandberg, ed., *Ethnic Identity and Assimilation: The Polish Community* (pp. vii–xiii). New York: Praeger, 1973.

GANS, HERBERT J. "Symbolic Ethnicity: The Future of Ethnic Groups and Cultures in America." *Ethnic and Racial Studies* 2 (1979): 1–20.

GANS, HERBERT J. "The Second Generation Decline: Scenarios for the Economic and Ethnic Futures of Post-1965 American Immigrants." *Ethnic and Racial Studies* 15 (1992): 173–192.

GANS, HERBERT J. "Toward a Reconciliation of Assimilation and Pluralism: The Interplay of Acculturation and Ethnic Retention." *International Migration Review* 31 (1997): 875–892.

GARCÍA, MARIO. *Desert Immigrants: The Mexicans of El Paso, 1880–1920*. New Haven, CT: Yale University Press, 1981.

GARDNER, R., B. ROBEY, AND E. C. SMITH., EDS. "Asian-Americans: Growth, Change, and Diversity." (Special Issue). *Population Bulletin* 40 (1985).

GARIS, ROY L. *Immigration Restriction*. New York: Macmillan, 1927.

GEERTZ, CLIFFORD. *Peddlers and Princes*. Chicago: Chicago University Press, 1963.

GILBERTSON, GRETA. "Women's Labor and Enclave Employment: The Case of Dominican and Colombian Women in New York City." *International Migration Review* 19 (1995): 657–671.

GLASER, WILLIAM A., AND CHRISTOPHER HABERS. "The Migration and Return of Professionals." *International Migration Review* 8 (Summer 1974): 227–244.

GLASGOW, DOUGLAS G. *The Black Underclass*. San Francisco: Jossey-Bass, 1980.

GLAZER, NATHAN. "Ethnic Groups in America." In Morroe Berger, Theodore Abel, and Charles Page, eds., *Freedom and Control in Modern Society* (pp. 158–173). New York: Van Nostrand, 1954.

GLAZER, NATHAN. *Clamor at the Gates: The New American Immigration*. San Francisco: Institute for Contemporary Studies Press, 1985.

GLAZER, NATHAN. "Is Assimilation Dead?" *Annals of the American Academy of Political and Social Sciences* 530 (1993): 122–136.

GLAZER, NATHAN, AND DANIEL P. MOYNIHAN. *Beyond the Melting Pot*. Cambridge: MIT Press, 1963.

GLAZER, NATHAN, AND DANIEL P. MOYNIHAN. *Beyond the Melting Pot: The Negroes, Puerto Ricans, Jews, Italians, and Irish of New York City*. Cambridge: MIT Press, 1970.

GLENN, E. N. "Split Household, Small Producer, and Dual Wage Earner: An Analysis of Chinese-American Family Strategies." *Journal of Marriage and the Family* 45 (1983): 35–46.

GLENN, E. N. *Issei, Nisei, War Bride: Three Generations of Japanese American Women at Domestic Service*. Philadelphia: Temple University Press, 1986.

GOLD, STEVEN J. "Refugees and Small Business: The Case of Soviet Jews and Vietnamese." *Ethnic and Racial Studies* 11 (November 1988): 411–438.

GOLD, STEVEN J. *Refugee Communities*. Newbury Park, California: Sage, 1992.

GOLD, STEVEN J. "Chinese-Vietnamese Entrepreneurs in California." In P. Ong, E. Bonacich, and L. Cheng, eds., *The New Asian Immigration in Los Angeles and Global Restructuring* (pp. 196–226). Philadelphia: Temple University Press, 1994a.

GOLD, STEVEN J. "Patterns of Economic Cooperation Among Israeli Immigrants in Los Angeles." *International Migration Review* 28, no. 1 (1994b): 114–135.

GOLDRING, LUIN. *Diversity and Community in Transnational Migration: A Comparative Study of Two Mexico-US Migrant Communities*. Unpublished Ph.D. Dissertation, Department of Rural Sociology, Cornell University, 1992.

GOLDSCHEIDER, CALVIN, AND FRANCES KOBRIN. "Ethnic Continuity and the Process of Self-Employment." *Ethnicity* 7 (1980): 256–278.

GORDON, DAVID M. *Theories of Poverty and Unemployment: Orthodox, Radical, and Dual Labor Market Perspectives*. Lexington, MA: Lexington Books, 1972.

GORDON, MILTON M. *Assimilation in American Life*. New York: Oxford University Press, 1964.

GRANOVETTER, MARK. "Economic Action and Social Structure: The Problem of Embeddedness." *American Journal of Sociology* 91 (1985): 481–510.

GRASMUCK, SHERRI. "Immigration, Ethnic Stratification, and Native Working-Class Discipline: Comparison of Documented and Undocumented Dominicans." *International Migration Review* 18 (Fall 1984): 692–713.

GRASMUCK, SHERRI, AND PATRICIA PESSAR. *Between Two Islands*. Berkeley: University of California Press, 1991.

GRASMUCK, SHERRI, AND RAMON GROSFOGUEL. "Geopolitics, Economic Niches, and Gendered Social Capital Among Recent Caribbean Immigrants in New York City." *Sociological Perspectives* 40 (1997): 339–364.

GREELEY, ANDREW M. *Why Can't They Be Like Us?* New York: Dutton, 1971.

GREELEY, ANDREW M. *The American Catholic: A Social Portrait*. New York: Harper and Row, 1977.

GREELEY, ANDREW M. "Immigration and Religio-Ethnic Groups: A Sociological Reappraisal." In B. R. Chiswick, ed., *The Gateway: U.S. Immigration Issues and Policies* (pp. 159–192). Washington: American Enterprise Institute for Public Policy Research, 1982.

GREEN, S. *Silicon Valley's Women Workers: A Theoretical Analysis of Sex-Segregation in the Electronics Industry Labor Market*. Honolulu, HI: Impact of Transnational Interactions Project, Cultural Learning Institute, East-West Center, 1980.

GREENWOOD, MICHAEL J. *Migration and Economic Growth in the United States*. New York: Academic Press, 1981.

GREENWOOD, MICHAEL J. "Human Migration: Theory, Models, and Empirical Evidence." *Journal of Regional Science* 25 (1985): 521–544.

GREENWOOD, MICHAEL J., GARY L. HUNT, AND JOHN M. McDOWELL. "Migration and Employment Change: Empirical Evidence on the Spatial and Temporal Dimensions of the Linkage." *Journal of Regional Science* 26 (1987): 223–234.

GUARNIZO, LUIS, AND MICHAEL P. SMITH. "The Locations of Transnationalism." In Michael P. Smith and Louis Guarnizo, eds., *Transnationlism from Below*, Vol. 6 (pp. 3–34). *Comparative Urban and Community Research*. New Brunswick, NJ: Transactions Publishers, 1998.

GURAK, DOUGLAS, AND MARY KRITZ. "Social Context, Household Composition, and Employment Among Migrant and Nonmigrant Dominican Women." *International Migration Review* 30 (1996): 399–422.

GURAK, DOUGLAS T., AND FE CACES. "Migration Network and the Shaping of Migration Systems." In Mary Kritz, Lin Lean Lim, and Hania Zlotnik, eds., *International Migration System: A Global Approach* (pp. 150–176). Oxford: Clarendon Press, 1992.

HAGAN, JACQUELINE. *Deciding to Be Legal: A Maya Community in Houston*. Philadelphia: Temple University Press, 1994.

HAINES, DAVID W. *Refugees in the United States: A Reference Handbook*. Westport, CT: Greenwood Press, 1985.

HAINES, DAVID W., ED. *Refugees as Immigrants: Cambodians, Laotians, and Vietnamese in America*. Totowa, NJ: Rowman & Littlefield, 1989.

HAMMER, THOMAS. *Democracy and the Nation State: Aliens, Denizens and Citizens in a World of International Migration*. Aldershot, U.K: Avebury, 1990.

HAMMER, THOMAS, ED. *European Immigration Policy*. New York: Cambridge University Press, 1985.

HANDLIN, OSCAR. *Boston's Immigrants: A Study of Acculturation*. Cambridge, MA: Harvard University Press, 1941.

HANDLIN, OSCAR. *The Uprooted: The Epic Story of the Great Migration That Made the American People*. Boston: Little, Brown, 1973. Originally published 1951.

HANDLIN, OSCAR. *The Newcomers: Negroes and Puerto Ricans in a Changing Metropolis*. Cambridge: Harvard University Press, 1959.

HANNERZ, ULF. *Exploring the City: Inquiries Toward an Urban Anthropology*. New York: Columbia University Press, 1980.

HANSEN, M. L. *The Atlantic Migration, 1607–1860: A History of the Continuing Settlement of the United States*. Cambridge: Harvard University Press, 1940a.

HANSEN, M. L. *The Immigrant in American History*. Cambridge: Harvard University Press, 1940b.

HANSEN, NILES, AND GILBERTO CARDENAS. "Immigrant and Native Ethnic Enterprises in Mexican American Neighborhoods: Differing Perceptions of Mexican Immigrant Workers." *International Migration Review* 22, no. 2 (1988): 226–242.

HANSSAB, SHIDEH. "Acculturation and Young Iranian Women: Attitudes Toward Sex Roles and Intimate Relationships." *Journal of Multicultural Counseling and Development* 19 (1991): 11–21.

HARRIS, J. R., AND MICHAEL P. TODARO. "Migration, Unemployment, and Development: A Two-Sector Analysis." *American Economic Review* 60 (1970): 126–142.

HATTON, TIMOTHY J., AND JEFFREY G. WILLIAMSON. " International Migration and World Development: A Historical Perspective." *Historical paper no.41*. National Bureau of Economic Research, Cambridge, MA. 1992.

HEALEY JOSEPH. *Race, Ethnicity, Gender, and Class: The Sociology of Group Conflict and Change*. London: Pine Forge Press, 1995.

HEIN, J. "Refugees, Immigrants, and the State." *Annual Review of Sociology* 19 (1993): 43–59.

HEISLER, MARTIN. "Citizenship—Old, New and Changing: Inclusion, Exclusion, and Limbo for Ethnic Groups and Migrants in the Modern Democratic State." In Jurgen Fijalkowski, Hans Merkens, and Folker Schmidt, eds., *Dominant National Cultures and Ethnic Identities,* Vol. 1 (pp. 91–128). Berlin: Free University, 1991.

HEISLER, MARTIN, AND BARBARA SCHMITTER HEISLER, EDS. *From Foreign Workers to Settlers? Transnational Migration and the Emergence of New Minorities.* The Annals of the American Academy for Political and Social Science. Beverly Hills: Sage, 1986.

HERMAN, HARRY VJEKOSLAV. "Dishwashers and Proprietors: Macedonians in Toronto's Restaurant Trade." In Sandra Wallman, ed., *Ethnicity at Work* (pp. 71–90). London: Macmillan, 1979.

HIGHAM, JOHN. *Strangers in the Land: Patterns of American Nativism, 1860–1925.* New Brunswick, NJ: Rutgers University Press, 1955.

HIRSCHMAN, C., AND M. G. WONG. "Socioeconomic Gains of Asian Americans, Blacks, and Hispanics: 1960–1976." *American Journal of Sociology* 90 (1984): 584–607.

HODSON, RANDY, AND ROBERT L. KAUFMAN. "Circularity in the Dual Economy: A Comment on Tolbert, Horan, and Beck, 1980." *American Journal of Sociology* 86 (1981): 881–887.

HOERDER, DIRK, ED. "Acculturation Twice: Return Migration," In *Labor Migration in the Atlantic Economies: The European and North American Working Classes During the Period of Industrialization*, Part II, (pp. 353–434). Westport, CN: Greenwood Press, 1985.

HOFFMAN, DIANE M. "Language and Culture Acquisition Among Iranians in the United States." *Anthropology and Educational Quarterly* 20 (1989): 118–132.

HOLLIFIELD, JAMES. "Migration, Trade, and the Nation-State: The Myth of Globalization." *UCLA Journal of International Law and Foreign Affairs* 3 (1998/99): 595–636.

HOLLINGSWORTH, L. W. *The Asians of East Africa.* London: Macmillan, 1960.

HONDAGNEU-SOTELO, PIERRETTE. *Gendered Transition: Mexican Experiences in Immigration.* Berkeley: University of California Press, 1983.

HONDAGNEU-SOTELO, PIERRETTE. *Gendered Transitions.* Berkeley: University of California Press, 1994.

HOOD, J. G. *Becoming a Two Job Family.* New York: Praeger, 1983.

HOUSTOUN, MARION, ROGER KRAMER, AND JOAN MACKING BARRETT. " Female Predominance of Immigration to the United States Since 1930: A First Look." *International Migration Review* 18 (1984).

HURH, W. M., AND K. C. KIM. "The Success Image of Asian Americans: Its Validity, and Its Practical and Theoretical Implications." *Ethnic Racial Studies* 12, no.4 (1989): 512–537.

HUTCHINSON, EDWARD P. *Legislative History of American Immigration Policy, 1798–1965.* Philadelphia: University of Pennsylvania Press, 1981.

ICHIHASHI, YAMATO. *Japanese in the United States.* Stanford: Stanford University Press, 1932.

JACOBSON, DAVID. *Rights Across Borders: Immigration and the Decline of Citizenship.* Baltimore, MD: Johns Hopkins University Press, 1996.

JACOBSON, MATTHEW. *Special Sorrows: The Diasporic Imagination of Irish, Polish, and Jewish Immigrants in the United States.* Cambridge, MA: Harvard University Press, 1995.

JALALI, BEHNAZ. "Iranian Families." In M. McGoldrick, J. Pearce, and J. Giordano, eds., *Ethnicity and Family Therapy* (pp. 289–309). New York: Gulford, 1982.

JASSO G., AND M. R. ROSENZWEIG. "Self-selection and the Earnings of Immigrants: Comment." *American Economic Review* 80, no.1 (1990): 298–304.

JASSO, GUILLERMINA, AND MARK R. ROSENZWEIG. *The New Chosen People: Immigrants in the United States.* New York: Russell Sage, 1990.

JEFF, A. J., RUTH M. CULLEN, AND THOMAS D. BOSWELL. *The Changing Demography of Spanish Americans.* New York: Academic Press, 1980.

JENCKS, C. "Is the American Underclass Growing?" In C. Jencks, and P. E. Peterson, eds., *The Urban Underclass* (pp. 28–100). Washington DC: Brookings Institute, 1991.

JENKINS, RICHARD. "Ethnicity and the Rise of Capitalism." In Robin Ward, ed., *Ethnic*

Business in Britain (Chapter 4). New York: Cambridge University Press, 1984.

JEROME, HARRY. *Migration and Business Cycle.* New York: National Bureau of Economic Research, 1926.

JIOBU, ROBERT M. "Ethnic Hegemony and the Japanese of California." *American Sociological Review* 53 (1988): 353–367.

JONES, M. A. *American Immigration.* Chicago: University of Chicago Press, 1960.

JOPPKE, CHRISTIAN. "Immigration Challenges the Nation State." In Christian Joppke, ed., *Challenge to the Nation-State: Immigration in Western Europe and the United States* (pp. 5–44). Oxford: Oxford University Press, 1998.

KAMPHOEFNER, W. D. *The Westfalians: From Germany to Missouri.* Princeton: Princeton University Press, 1987.

KASINITZ, PHILIP, AND MILTON VICKERMAN. "Ethnic Niches and Racial Traps: Jamaicans in the New York Regional Economy." Paper presented to the Social Science History Association, Chicago, Illinois, 1995.

KATZ, E., AND ODED STARK. "Labor Migration and Risk Aversion in Less Developed Countries." *Journal of Labor Economics* 4 (1986): 131–149.

KAZAL, RUSSELL. "Revisiting Assimilation: The Rise, Fall, and Reappraisal of a Concept in American Ethnic History." *American Historical Review* 100 (1995): 437–472.

KELLER, S. L. *Uprooting and Social Change: The Role of Refugees in Development.* Delhi: Manohar Book Service, 1975.

KELLY, R., JONATHAN FRIEDLANDER, AND ANITA COLBY. *Irangeles: Iranians in Los Angeles.* Los Angeles: University of California Press, 1993.

KENNEDY, RUBY JO REEVES. "Single or Triple Melting Pot? Intermarriage Trends in New Haven, 1870–1940." *American Journal of Sociology* 49 (1944): 331–339.

KENNEDY, RUBY JO REEVES. "Single or Triple Melting Pot? Intermarriage in New Haven, 1870–1915." *American Journal of Sociology* 58 (1952): 56–59.

KESSNER, T. *The Golden Door: Italian and Jewish Immigrant Mobility in New York City, 1880–1915.* New York: Oxford University Press, 1977.

KIBRIA, NAZLI. *Family Tightrope: The Changing Lives of Vietnamese Americans.* Princeton, NJ: Princeton University Press, 1993.

KIBRIA, NAZLI. "Household Structure and Family Ideologies: The Dynamics of Immigrant Economic Adaptation Among Vietnamese Refugees." *Social Problems* 41, no. 1 (1994): 301–315.

KIM, AI RA. *Women Struggling for a New Life: The Role of Religion in the Cultural Passage from Korea to America.* Albany: State University of New York Press, 1996.

KIM, HYUNG-CHAN. "Ethnic Enterprises Among Korean Immigrants in America." In Hyung-Chan, Kim, ed., *The Korean Diaspora.* Santa Barbara: ABC-CLIO, 1977.

KIM, ILLSOO. *New Urban Immigrants: The Korean Community in New York.* Princeton University Press, 1981.

KIM, ILLSOO. "The Korean: Small Business in an Urban Frontier." In Nancy Foner, ed., *New Immigrants in New York* (pp. 219–243). New York: Columbia University Press, 1987.

KIM, KWANG CHUNG. "Ethnic Resource Utilization of Korean Immigrant Entrepreneurs in the Chicago Minority Area." *International Migration Review* 19, no. 1 (1985): 82–111.

KIM, KWANG CHUNG, AND WON MOO HURH. "Two Dimensions of Korean Immigrants' Sociocultural Adaptation: Americanization and Ethnic Attachment." Paper presented at the annual meeting of the American Sociological Association, Atlanta, August 1988.

KINDLEBERGER, CHARLES P. *Europe's Postwar Growth: The Role of Labor Supply.* New York: Oxford University Press, 1967.

KIRKPATRICK, CLIFFORD. *Intelligence and Immigration.* Baltimore: Williams and Wilkins, 1926.

KITANO, H. *Japanese Americans: The Evolution of a Subculture.* Upper Saddle River, NJ: Prentice Hall, 1976.

KIVISTO, PETER. *Immigrant Socialists in the United States: The Case of Finns and the Left.* Rutherford, NJ: Farleigh Dickinson University Press, 1984.

KOENIG, SAMUEL. "The Socioeconomic Structure of an American Jewish Community." In Isaque Graeber and S. H. Britt, eds., *Jews in a Gentile World* (pp. 200–242). New York: Macmillan, 1942.

KRAUT, ALAN M. *The Huddled Masses: The Immigrant in American Society, 1180–1921.*

Arlington Heights, IL: Harlan Davidson, 1982.

KRITZ, M. M. *U.S. Immigration and Refugee Policy: Global and Domestic Issues.* Lexington, MA: Lexington, 1983.

KUNZ, EGON F. "Exile and Resettlement: Refugee Theory." *International Migration Review* 15 (Spring-Summer 1981): 42–51.

KUO, WEN H., AND YUNG-MEI TSAI. "Social Networking, Hardiness, and Immigrants' Mental Health." *Journal of Health and Social Behavior* 27 (June 1986): 133–149.

LADBURY, SARAH. "Choice, Chance, or No Alternative? Turkish Cypriots in Business in London." In Robin Ward and Richard Jenkins, eds., *Ethnic Communities in Business: Strategies for Economic Survival* (pp. 105–124). Cambridge: Cambridge University Press, 1984.

LAMM, RICHARD D., AND GARY IMHOFF. *The Immigration Time Bomb: The Fragmenting of America.* New York: Dutton, 1985.

LAMPHERE, LOUISE. *From Working Daughters to Working Mothers: Immigrant Women in a New England Industrial Community.* Ithaca, NY: Cornell University Press, 1987.

LAMPHERE, LOUISE. "The Shaping of Diversity." In Louise Lamphere, ed., *Structuring Diversity: Ethnographic Perspectives on the New Immigration* (pp. 1–34). Chicago: The University of Chicago Press, 1992.

LAUBY, JENNIFER, AND ODED STARK. "Individual Migration as a Family Strategy: Young Women in the Philippines. "*Population Studies* 42 (1988): 473–486.

LEE, EVERETT S. "A Theory of Migration." *Demography* 3 (1966): 47–57.

LEE, S. M. "Asian Immigration and American Race Relations: From Exclusion to Acceptance?" *Ethnic Racial Studies* 12, no.3 (1989): 368–391.

LESSINGER, JOHANNA. *From the Ganges to the Hudson: Asia Indians in New York City.* Boston: Allyn and Bacon, 1995.

LIEBERSON, STANLEY. *A Piece of the Pie: Black and White Immigrants Since 1980.* Berkeley and Los Angeles: University of California Press, 1980.

LIEBERSON, STANLEY, AND MARY C. WATERS. "The Location of Ethnic and Racial Groups in the United States." *Sociological Forum* 2 (Fall 1987): 780–810.

LIEBERSON, STANLEY, AND MARY C. WATERS. *From Many Strands: Ethnic and Racial Groups in Contemporary America.* New York: Russell Sage, 1988.

LIGHT, IVAN H. Ethnic Enterprise in America: Business and Welfare Among Chinese, Japanese and Blacks. Berkeley and Los Angeles: University of California Press, 1972.

LIGHT, IVAN H. "The Ethnic Vice District, 1880–1944." *American Sociological Review* 42 (1977a): 464–479.

LIGHT, IVAN H. "Disadvantaged Minorities in Self-Employment." *International Journal of Comparative Sociology* 20 (1979): 31–45.

LIGHT, IVAN H. "Asian Enterprise in America." In Scott Cummings, ed., *Self-Help in Urban America* (pp. 33–57). Port Washington, New York: Kennikat Press, 1980.

LIGHT, IVAN H. "Immigrant and Ethnic Enterprise in North America." *Ethnic and Racial Studies* 7 (1984): 195–216.

LIGHT, IVAN H., AND ANGEL SANCHEZ. "Immigrant Entrepreneurs in 272 SMSAs." *Sociological Perspectives* 30, no. 4 (1987): 373–399.

LIGHT, IVAN H., AND CHARLES WONG. "Protest or Work: Dilemmas of the Tourist Industry in American Chinatowns." *American Journal of Sociology* 80 (1975): 1342–1368.

LIGHT, IVAN H., AND EDNA BONACICH. *Immigrant Entrepreneurs: Koreans in Los Angeles 1965–1982.* Berkeley: University of California Press, 1988.

LIGHT, IVAN H., AND STAVROS KARAGEORGIS. "The Ethnic Economy." In Neil Smelser and Richard Swedberg, eds., *Handbook of Economic Sociology* (pp. 1–78). New York: Russell Sage Foundation. 1993.

LIGHT, IVAN H, AND STEVEN GOLD. *Ethnic Economies.* New York: Academic Press, 2000.

LIGHT, IVAN H., GEORGES SABAGH, MEHDI BOZORGMEHR, AND CLAUDIA DER-MARTIROSIAN. "Internal Ethnicity in the Ethnic Economy." *Ethnic and Racial Studies* 16, no. 4 (1993): 581–597.

LIGHT, IVAN H., GEORGES SABAGH, MEHDI BOZORGMEHR, AND CLAUDIA DER-MARTIROSIAN. "Beyond the Ethnic Enclave Economy." *Social Problems* 41, no. 1 (1994): 65–80.

LIGHT, IVAN H., IM JUNG KWUON, AND DENG ZHONG. "Korean Rotating Credit Associations in Los Angeles." *Amerasia* 16, no. 1 (1990): 35–54.

LIM, IN-SOOK. "Korean Immigrant Women's Challenge to Gender Inequality at Home." *Gender and Society* 11 (1997): 31– 51.

LIN, KEH-MING, LAURIE TAZUMA, AND MINORU MASUDA. "Adaptational Problems of Vietnamese Refugees: I. Health and Mental Health Status." *Archives of General Psychiatry* 36 (August 1979): 955–961.

LIPSON, JULIENE G. "The Health and Adjustment of Iranian Immigrants." *Western Journal of Nursing Research* 14, no. 1 (1992): 10–29.

LIU, WILLIAM T., MARYANNE LAMANNA, AND ALICIA MURATA. *Transition to Nowhere: Vietnamese Refugees in America.* Nashville: Charter House, 1979.

LOBO, ARUN PETER, JOSEPH SALVO, AND VICKI VIRGIN. *The Newest New Yorkers, 1990–1994.* New York: Department of City Planning, 1996.

LOEWEN, JAMES. *The Mississippi Chinese: Between Black and White.* Cambridge: Harvard University Press, 1971.

LOGAN, JOHN R., RICHARD D. ALBA, AND THOMAS L. McNULTY. "Ethnic Economies in Metropolitan Regions: Miami and Beyond." *Social Forces* 72 (1994): 691–724.

LORENTZ, JOHN, AND JOHN T. WERTIME. "Iranians." In Stephen Thernstrom, ed., *Harvard Encyclopedia of American Ethnic Groups* (pp. 521–524). Cambridge, MA: Harvard University Press, 1980.

LOVELL-TROY, LAWRENCE A. "Clan Structure and Economic Activity: The Case of Greeks in Small Business Enterprise." In Scott Cummings, ed., *Self-Help in America* (58–85). Port Washington, NY: Kennikat Press, 1980.

LOVELL-TROY, LAWRENCE A. "Ethnic Occupational Structures: Greeks in the Pizza Business." *Ethnicity* 8, no. 1 (March 1981): 82–95.

MADHAVAN, M. C. "Indian Emigrants: Numbers, Characteristics, and Economic Impact." *Population and Development Review* 11 (September 1985): 457–481.

MADHAVAN, M. C. "Migration of Skilled People from Developing to Developed Countries: Characteristics, Consequences, and Policies." Paper presented at the United Nations Development Program Conference on Transfer of Knowledge Through Expatriate Nationals, New Delhi, India, February 1988.

MAHAJANI, USHA. *The Role of Indian Minorities in Burma and Malaya.* Bombay: Vora, 1960.

MAHLER, SARAH J. *American Dreaming: Immigrant Life on the Margins.* Princeton, NJ: Princeton University Press, 1995.

MALDONADO, EDWIN. "Contract Labor and the Origin of Puerto Rican Communities in the United States." *International Migration Review* 13 (Spring 1979): 103–121.

MALZBERG, BENJAMIN, AND EVERETT S LEE. *Migration and Mental Disease: A Study of First Admissions to Hospitals for Mental Disease, New York, 1939–1941.* New York: Social Science Research Council, 1956.

MAR, DON. "Another Look at the Enclave Economy Thesis: Chinese Immigrants in the Ethnic Labor Market." *Amerasia* 17 (1991): 5–21.

MARGER, MARTIN, AND CONSTANCE HOFFMAN. "Ethnic Enterprise in Ontario: Immigrant Participation in the Small Business Sector." *International Migration Review* 26, no. 3 (1992): 968–981.

MARKOWITZ, FRAN. *A Community in Spite of Itself: Soviet Jewish Émigrés in New York.* Washington DC: Smithsonian Institution Press, 1993.

MASSEY, DOUGLAS S. "Dimensions of the New Immigration to the United States and the Prospects for Assimilation." *Annual Review of Sociology* 7 (1981): 57–85.

MASSEY, DOUGLAS S. "The Settlement Process Among Mexican Immigrants to the United States." *American Sociological Review* 51 (October 1986): 670–684.

MASSEY, DOUGLAS S. "Understanding Mexican Migration to the United States." *American Journal of Sociology* 92 (May 1987): 1372–1403.

MASSEY, DOUGLAS S. "Do Undocumented Immigrants Earn Lower Wages than Legal Immigrants? New Evidence from Mexico." *International Migration Review* 21 (Summer 1987): 236–274.

MASSEY, DOUGLAS S. "International Migration and Economic Development in Comparative Perspective." *Population and Development Review* 14 (1989): 383–414.

MASSEY, DOUGLAS S. "Social Structure, Household Strategies, and the Cumulative Causation of Migration." *Population Index* 56 (1990a): 3–26.

MASSEY, DOUGLAS S. "The Social and Economic Origins of Immigration." *Annals of the American Academy of Political and Social Science* 510 (1990b): 60–72.

MASSEY, DOUGLAS S. "The New Immigration and Ethnicity in the United States." *Population and Development Review* 21, no. 3 (1995) : 631–652.

MASSEY, DOUGLAS S. *World in Motion: Understanding International Migration at the End of the Millennium.* Oxford: Clarendon Press, 1998.

MASSEY, DOUGLAS S., AND AUDREY SINGER. "New Estimates of Undocumented Mexican Migration and the Probability of Apprehension." *Demography* 32 (1995): 203–213.

MASSEY, DOUGLAS S., AND ZAI LIANG. "The Long-Term Consequences of a Temporary Worker Program: The U.S. Bracero Experience." *Population Research and Policy Review* 8 (1989): 199–226.

MASSEY, DOUGLAS S., AND FELIPE GARCÍA ESPAÑA. "The Social Process of International Migration." *Science* 237 (1987): 733–738.

MASSEY, DOUGLAS S., RAFAEL ALARCON, JORGE DURAND, AND HUMBERTO GONZALEZ. *Return to Aztlan: The Social Process of International Migration from Western Mexico.* Berkeley: University of California Press, 1987.

MASSEY, DOUGLAS S. et al. "Theories of International Migration: A Review and Appraisal." *Population and Development Review* 19 (1993): 431–466.

MASSEY, DOUGLAS S. et al. "An Evaluation of International Migration Theory: The North American Case. "*Population and Development Review* 20 (1994): 699–751.

MASUDA, MINORU, KEH-MING LIN, AND LAURIE TAZUMA. "Adaptational Problems of Vietnamese Refugees: II. Life Changes and Perceptions of Life Events." *Archives of General Psychiatry* 37 (April 1980): 447–450.

MCCOY, TERRY L. "The Political Economy of Caribbean Workers in the Florida Sugar Industry." Paper presented at the fifth annual meeting of the Caribbean Studies Association, Willemstad, Curacao, mimeographed, May 1980.

MEZEY, A. G. "Psychiatric Illness in Hungarian Refugees." *Journal of Mental Science* 106 (April 1960): 628–637.

MILLER, JAKE C. *The Plight of Haitian Refugees.* New York: Praeger, 1984.

MILLER, KERBY A. *Emigrants and Exiles: Ireland and the Irish Exodus to North America.* New York: Oxford University Press, 1985.

MILLIS, H. A. *The Japanese Problem in the United States.* New York: Macmillan, 1915.

MIN, PYONG GAP. "From White-Collar Occupations to Small Business: Korean Immigrants' Occupational Adjustment." *The Sociological Quarterly* 25 (1984a): 333–352.

MIN, PYONG GAP. "A Structural Analysis of Korean Business in the United States." *Ethnic Groups* 6 (1984b): 1–25.

MIN, PYONG GAP. "Factors Contributing to Ethnic Business: A Comparative Synthesis." *International Journal of Comparative Sociology* 28, no. 3–4 (1987): 171–193.

MIN, PYONG GAP. "Problems of Korean Immigrant Entrepreneurs." *International Migration Review* 24, no. 3 (1990): 436–455.

MIN, PYONG GAP. *Caught in the Middle: Korean Communities in New York and Los Angeles.* Berkeley: University of California Press, 1996.

MIN, PYONG GAP. *Traditions and Changes: Korean Immigrant Families in New York.* Needham Heights, MA: Allyn and Bacon, 1998.

MIN, PYONG GAP AND CHARLES JARET. "Ethnic Business Success: The Case of Korean Small Business in Atlanta." *Sociology and Social Research* 69 (1985): 412–435.

MINES, RICHARD. "Network Migration and Mexican Rural Development: A Case Study." In Richard C. Jones, ed., *Patterns of Undocumented Migration: Mexico and the United States* (pp. 136–158). Totowa, NJ: Rowman and Allanheld, 1984.

MINK, GWENDOLYN. *Old Labor and New Immigrants in American Political Development.* Ithaca, New York: Cornell University Press, 1986.

MIYAMOTO, SHOTARO F. *Social Solidarity Among the Japanese in Seattle.* Seattle: University of Washington Publication in the *Social Science* 11 (December 1939): 57–130.

MOALLEM, MINOO. "Ethnic Entrepreneurship and Gender Relations Among Iranians in Montreal, Quebec, Canada." In Asghar Fathi, ed., *Iranian Refugees and Exiles Since Khomeini* (pp. 180–199). Costa Mesa, CA: Mazda, 1991.

MOBASHER, MOHSEN M. "Class, Ethnicity, Gender, and the Ethnic Economy: The Case of Iranian Immigrants in Dallas." Ph.D. Dissertation, Southern Methodist University, 1996.

MODARRES, ALI. "Ethnic Community Development: A Spatial Examination." *Journal of Urban Affairs* 14, no. 2 (1992): 97–107.

MODEL, SUZANNE. "A Comparative Perspective on the Ethnic Enclave: Blacks, Italians, and Jews in New York City." *International Migration Review* 19 (1985): 64–81.

MODELL, JOHN. "Class or Ethnic Solidarity: The Japanese American Company Union." *Pacific Historical Review* 38 (May 1939): 193–206.

MODELL, JOHN. *The Economics and Politics of Racial Accommodation: The Japanese of Los Angeles, (1900–1942)*. Urbana: University of Illinois Press, 1977.

MOGHADDAM, FATHALI, DONALD TAYLOR, AND RICHARD N. LALONDE. "Individualistic and Collective Integration Strategies Among Iranians in Canada." *International Journal of Psychology* 22 (1987): 301–313.

MOMENI, JAMSHID. "Size and Distribution of Iranian Ethnic Group in the United States: 1980." *Iran Nameh* 2 (1984): 17–21.

MONTERO, DARREL. "The Japanese Americans: Changing Patterns of Assimilation over Three Generations." *American Sociological Review* 46 (1981): 829–839.

MORALES, R., AND F. BONILLA, EDS. *Latinos in a Changing U.S. Economy.* Newbury Park, CA: Sage Publication, 1993.

MORAWSKA, EWA. T. *For Bread with Butter: The Life-Worlds of East Central Europeans in Johnstown Pennsylvania, 1890–1940.* New York: Cambridge University Press, 1985.

MORAWSKA, EWA. "The Sociology and Historiography of Immigration." In Virginia Yans McLaughlin, ed., *Immigration Reconsidered: History, Sociology, and Politics* (pp. 187–240). New York: Oxford University Press, 1990.

MORAWSKA, EWA. "In Defense of the Assimilation Model." *Journal of American Ethnic History* 13 (1994): 76–87.

MORGOLIS, MAXINE. *Little Brazil: Ethnography of Brazilian Immigrants in New York City.* Princeton, NJ: Princeton University Press, 1994.

MOROKVASIC, MIRJANA. "Birds of Passage Are Also Women." *International Migration Review* 18 (1984): 886–907.

MOSLEHI, SHAHNAZ. *A Look at the Psychology of Iranians and Iranian Immigrants.* Palo Alto: Peninsula Printing, 1988.

MOSS, MITCHELL, ANTHONY TOWNSEND, AND EMANUAL TOBIER. "Immigration Is Transforming New York City." Taub Urban Research Center, Robert F. Wagner School of Public Service, New York University (1997).

MULLER, T., AND T. J. ESPENSHADE. *The Fourth Wave: California's Newest Immigrants.* Washington: Urban Institute, 1985.

NAGEL, JOANE. "The Political Construction of Ethnicity." In Joane Nagel and Susan Olzak, eds., *Competitive Ethnic Relations* (pp. 93–112). Orlando, FL: Academic Press, 1986.

NASH, JUNE. "The Impact of the Changing International Division of Labor on Different Sectors of the Labor Force." In June Nash and Patricia Fernandez-Kelly, eds., *Women, Men, and the International Division of Labor* (pp. 3–38). Albany: State University of New York Press, 1983.

NEE, VICTOR, AND JIMY SANDERS. "The Road to Parity: Determinants of the Socioeconomic Achievement of Asian Americans." *Ethnic and Racial Studies* 8 (January 1985): 75–93.

NEE, VICTOR, AND JIMY M. SANDERS. "On Testing the Enclave-Economy Hypothesis." *American Sociological Review* 52 (1987): 771–773.

NELSON, CANDACE, AND MARTA TIENDA. "The Structuring of Hispanic Ethnicity: Historical and Contemporary Perspectives." *Ethnic and Racial Studies* 8 (1985): 49–74.

NOEL, D. "A Theory of the Origin of Ethnic Stratification." *Social Problems* 16 (1968): 157–172.

NOVAK, MICHAEL. *The Rise of the Unmeltable Ethnics.* New York: Macmillan, 1971.

NOWIKOWSKI, SUSAN. "Snakes and Ladders: Asian Business in Britain." In Robin Ward and Richard Jenkins, eds., *Ethnic Communities in Business: Strategies for Economic Survival* (pp. 149–165). Cambridge: Cambridge University Press, 1984.

NUGENT, WALTER. *Crossings: The Great Transatlantic Migrations, 1870–1914.* Bloomington: Indiana University Press, 1992.

ONG, AIHWA. "Women Out of China: Traveling Tales and Traveling Theories in Postcolonial Feminism." In Ruth Behar and Deborah Gordon, eds., *Women Writing Culture.* Berkeley: University of California Press, 1995.

ONG, P. "Chinatown Unemployment and the Ethnic Labor Market." *American Journal* 11 (1984): 35–54.

ONG, P., AND T. AZORES. "The Migration and Incorporation of Filipino Nurses." In P. Ong, E. Bonacich, and L. Cheng, eds., *The New Asian Immigration in Los Angeles and Global Restructuring* (pp. 164–195). Philadelphia: Temple University Press, 1994b.

ORITZ, VILMA. "Changes in the Characteristics of Puerto Rican Migrants from 1955 to 1980." *International Migration Review* 20 (Fall 1986): 612–628.

ORLECK, ANNELISE. "The Soviet Jews: Life in Brighton Beach, Brooklyn." In Nancy Foner, ed., *New Immigrants in New York.* New York: Columbia University Press, 1987.

OSTERGREN, R. C. *A Community Transplanted: The Trans-Atlantic Experience of Swedish Immigrant Settlement in the Upper Middle West, 1835–1915.* Madison: University of Wisconsin Press, 1988.

PARK, KYEYONG. "Impact of New Productive Activities on the Organization of Domestic Life: A Case Study of the Korean American Community." In G. Nomura, R. Endo, S. Sumida, and R. Leong, eds., *Frontiers of Asian American Studies* (pp. 140–150). Pullman: Washington State University Press, 1991.

PARK, KYEYONG. *Korean American Dream.* Ithaca, NY: Cornell University Press, 1997.

PARK, ROBERT. *The City: Suggestions for Investigation of Human Behavior in the Urban Environment.* Chicago: The University of Chicago Press, 1925.

PARK, ROBERT E. *The Immigrant Press and Its Control.* New York: Harper, 1922.

PARK, ROBERT E. "Human Migration and the Marginal Man." *American Journal of Sociology* 33 (1928): 881–893.

PARK, ROBERT E. "The Nature of Race Relations." In Edgar T. Thompson, ed., *Race Relations and the Race Problem* (pp. 3–45). North Carolina: Duke University Press, 1939.

PARK, ROBERT E. *Race and Culture: Essays in the Sociology of Contemporary Man.* New York: Free Press, 1950a.

PARK, ROBERT E. "Our Racial Frontier on the Pacific." In R. Park, *Race and Culture* (pp. 138–151). Glencoe, IL: Free Press, 1950b (1926).

PARK, ROBERT E. *Race and Culture.* Glencoe, IL: Free Press, 1950c.

PARK, ROBERT E. "Racial Assimilation in Secondary Groups." In R. Park, *Race and Culture* (pp. 204–220). Glencoe, IL: Free Press, 1950d (1913).

PARK, ROBERT E., AND E. W. BURGESS. *Introduction to the Science of Sociology.* Chicago: University of Chicago Press, 1921.

PARK, ROBERT E., AND H. A. MILLER. *Old World Traits Transplanted.* New York: Harper, 1921.

PASSEL, JEFFREY S., AND KAREN A. WOODROW. "Geographic Distribution of Undocumented Immigrants: Estimates of Undocumented Aliens Counted in the 1980 Census by State." *International Migration Review* 18 (Fall 1984): 642–671.

PASTOR, ROBERT. *Migration and Development in the Caribbean.* Boulder, CO: Westview Press, 1985.

PEDRAZA-BAILEY, SILVIA. "Cubans and Mexicans in the United States: The Functions of Political and Economic Migration." *Cuban Studies* 11 (July 1979): 79–97.

PEDRAZA-BAILEY, SILVIA. "Cuba's Exiles: Portrait of a Refugee Migration." *International Migration Review* 19 (Spring 1985): 4–34.

PEDRAZA-BAILEY, SILVIA. *Political and Economic Migrants in America: Cubans and Mexicans.* Austin: University of Texas Press, 1985.

PEDRAZA-BAILEY, SILVIA. "Women and Migration: The Social Consequences of Gender." *Annual Review of Sociology* 17 (1991): 303–325.

PEPAK, TERRY. *Waiting on Washington: Central American Workers in the Nation's Capital.* Philadelphia, PA: Temple University Press, 1995.

PERSONS, S. *Ethnic Studies at Chicago, 1905–1945.* Urbana: University of Illinois Press, 1987.

PESSAR, PATRICIA. "Kinship Relations of Production in the Migration Process: The Case of Dominican Emigration to the United States." *Occasional Paper,* no. 32. New York: Center for Latin American and Caribbean Studies, New York University, 1982.

PESSAR, PATRICIA. *The Filipinos in America: Macro/Micro Dimensions of Immigration and Integration.* Staten Island, NY: Center for Migration Studies, 1984a.

PESSAR, PATRICIA. "The Linkage Between the Household and Workplace of Dominican Women in the United States." *International Migration Review* 18 (1984b): 1188–1211.

PESSAR, PATRICIA. "The Role of Gender in Dominican Settlement in the United States." In June Nash and Helen Sara, eds., *Women and Change in Latin America.* South Hadley, MA: Bergin and Garvey, 1986.

PESSAR, PATRICIA. "The Dominicans: Women in the Household and the Garment Industry." In Nancy Foner, ed., *New Immigrant in New York.* New York: Columbia University Press, 1987.

PESSAR, PATRICIA. "On the Homefront and in the Workplace: Integrating Immigrant Women into Feminist Discourse." *Anthropological Quarterly* 68 (1995): 37–47.

PESSAR, PATRICIA. *A Visa for a Dream: Dominicans in the United States.* Needham Heights, MA: Allyn and Bacon, 1996.

PESSAR, PATRICIA. "The Role of Gender, Households, and Social Networks in the Migration Process: A Review and Appraisal." In Josh Dewind, Charles Hirschman, and Philip Kasinitz, eds., *Immigrants and the Transformation of America.* New York: Russell Sage Foundation, 1998.

PETERSEN, WILLIAM. *Japanese Americans: Oppression and Success.* New York: Random House, 1971.

PETRAS, ELIZABETH. "The Global Market in the Modern World Economy." In Mary Kritz et al., eds., *Global Trend in Migration: Theory and Research on International Population Movements* (pp. 44–63). New York: Center for Migration Studies, 1981.

PHIZACKLEA, ANNIE. "Entrepreneurship, Ethnicity, and Gender." In Sallie Westwood and Parminder Bhachu, eds., *Enterprising Women: Ethnicity, Economy, and Gender Relations* (pp. 20–33). New York: Routledge, 1988.

PHOENIX, ANN. "Narrow Definitions of Culture: The Case of Early Motherhood." In Sallie Westwood and Parminder Bhachu, eds., *Enterprising Women: Ethnicity, Economy, and Gender Relations* (pp. 153–176). New York: Routledge, 1988.

PIORE, MICHAEL J. *Birds of Passage: Migrant Labor in Industrial Societies.* Cambridge: Cambridge University Press, 1979.

POLANYI, KARL, C. ARENSBERG, AND H. PEARSON. *Trade and Markets in the Early Empires.* New York: Free Press, 1957.

PORTES, ALEJANDRO. "Dilemmas of a Golden Exile: Integration of Cuban Refugee Families in Milwaukee." *American Sociological Review* 34 (August 1969): 505–518.

PORTES, ALEJANDRO. "Determinants of Brain Drain." *International Migration Review* 10 (Winter 1976): 489–508.

PORTES, ALEJANDRO. "Immigrant Aspirations." *Sociology of Education* 51 (1978a): 241–260.

PORTES, ALEJANDRO. "Migration and Underdevelopment." *Politics and Society* 8 (1978b): 1–48.

PORTES, ALEJANDRO. "Illegal Immigration and the International System: Lessons from Recent Legal Mexican Immigrants to the United States." *Social Problems* 26 (April 1979): 425–438.

PORTES, ALEJANDRO. "Modes of Structural Incorporation and Present Theories of Labor Immigration." In M. Kritz, C. B. Keely, and S. M. Tomasi, eds., *Global Trends in Migration: Theory and Research on International Population Movements* (pp. 279–297). New York: Center for Migration Studies, 1981.

PORTES, ALEJANDRO. "The Rise of Ethnicity." *American Sociological Review* 49 (June 1984): 383–397.

PORTES, ALEJANDRO. "The Social Origins of the Cuban Enclave Economy of Miami." *Sociological Perspectives* 30 (October 1987): 340–372.

PORTES, ALEJANDRO. "Immigration Reform: The Theory and the Realities." *Baltimore Sun* (January 2, 1987): 15A.

PORTES, ALEJANDRO. "Children of Immigrants: Segmented Assimilation and Its Determinants." In Alejandro Portes, ed., *The Economic Sociology of Immigration* (pp. 248–279). New York: Russell Sage, 1995a.

PORTES, ALEJANDRO. "Economic Sociology and the Sociology of Immigration: A Conceptual

Overview." In Alejandro Portes, ed., *The Economic Sociology of Immigration* (pp. 1–41). New York: Russell Sage, 1995b.

PORTES, ALEJANDRO. "Immigration Theory for a New Century: Some Problems and Opportunities." *International Migration Review* 31 (1997): 799–825.

PORTES, ALEJANDRO. "Divergent Destinies: Immigration, the Second Generation, and the Rise of Transnational Communities." In Peter Schuck and Rainer Munz, eds., *Paths to Inclusion: The Integration of Migrants in the United States and Germany* (pp. 33–57). New York: Berghahn Books, 1998.

PORTES, ALEJANDRO, AND A. ROSS. "Modernization for Emigration: The Medical Brain Drain from Argentina." *Journal of Inter-American Studies and World Affairs* 18 (1976): 395–422.

PORTES, ALEJANDRO, AND ALEX STEPICK. "Unwelcome Immigrants: The Labor Market Experiences of 1980 (Mariel) Cuban and Haitian Refugees in South Florida." *American Sociological Review* 50 (August 1985): 493–514.

PORTES, ALEJANDRO, AND CYNTHIA TRUELOVE. "Making Sense of Diversity: Recent Research on Hispanic Minorities in the United States." *Annual Review of Sociology* 13 (1987): 359–385.

PORTES, ALEJANDRO, AND JOHN WALTON. *Labor, Class, and the International System*. New York: Academic Press, 1981.

PORTES, ALEJANDRO, AND JOZSEF BOROCZ. "Contemporary Immigration: Theoretical Perspectives on Its Determinants and Modes of Incorporation." *International Migration Review* 23 (Fall 1989): 606–630.

PORTES, ALEJANDRO, AND JUAN CLARK. "Mariel Refugees: Six Years After." *Migration World* 15 (1987): 14–18.

PORTES, ALEJANDRO, AND JULIA SENSENBRENNER. "Embeddedness and Immigration: Notes on the Social Determinants of Economic Action." *American Journal of Sociology* 98 (1993): 1320–1350.

PORTES, ALEJANDRO, AND LEIF JENSEN. "What's an Ethnic Enclave? The Case for Conceptual Clarity." *American Sociological Review* 52 (1989): 768–771.

PORTES, ALEJANDRO, AND MIN ZHOU. "The Second Generation: Segmented Assimilation and Its Variants Among Post-1965 Immigrant Youth." *Annals of the American Academy of Political and Social Sciences* 535 (1993): 74–96.

PORTES, ALEJANDRO, AND R. L. BACH. *Latin Journey: Cuban and Mexican Immigrants in the United States*. Berkeley and Los Angeles: University of California Press, 1985.

PORTES, ALEJANDRO, AND RAFAEL MOZO. "The Political Adaptation Process of Cubans and Other Ethnic Minorities in the United States." *International Migration Review* 19 (Spring 1985): 35–63.

PORTES, ALEJANDRO, AND ROBERT MANNING. "The Immigrant Enclave: Theory and Empirical Examples." In Susan Olzak and Joane Nagel, eds., *Competitive Ethnic Relations* (pp. 47–66). New York: Academic Press, 1986.

PORTES, ALEJANDRO, AND RUBEN RUMBAUT. *Immigrant America: A Portrait*. Berkeley and Los Angeles: University of California Press, 1990.

PORTES, ALEJANDRO, JUAN M. CLARK, AND MANUEL M. LOPEZ. "Six Years Later, The Process of Incorporation of Cuban Exiles in the United States: 1973–1979." *Cuban Studies* 11–12 (1981–1982): 1–24.

PORTES, ALEJANDRO, ROBERT N. PARKER, AND JOSE A. COBAS. "Assimilation or Consciousness?" *Social Forces* 59 (September 1980): 200–224.

POSTON, D. L. "Patterns of Economic Attainment of Foreign Born Male Workers in the U.S." *International Migration Review* 28, no. 3 (1994): 478–500.

PRIETO, YOLANDA. "Cuban Women in New Jersey: Gender Relations and Change." In Donna Gabaccia, ed., *Seeking Common Ground*, Westport, CT: Praeger, 1992.

RAMIREZ, ANTHONY. "Cubans and Blacks in Miami." *Wall Street Journal* (May 29, 1980).

REICHERT, JOSHUA S. "The Migrant Syndrome: Seasonal U.S. Wage Labor and Rural Development in Central Mexico." *Human Organization* 40 (Spring 1981): 59–66.

REICHERT, JOSHUA S. "Social Stratification in a Mexican Sending Community: The Effect of Migration to the United States." *Social Problem* 29 (1982): 422–433.

REIMERS, CORDELIA W. "A Comparative Analysis of the Wages of Hispanics, Blacks, and

Non-Hispanic Whites." In George J. Borjas and Marta Tienda, eds., *Hispanics in the U.S. Economy* (pp. 27–75). Orlando, FL: Academic Press, 1985.

REIMERS, D. M. "An Unintended Reform: The 1965 Immigration Act and Third World Immigration to the United States." *Journal of American Ethnic History* 3 (1983): 9–28.

REIMERS, D. M. *Still the Golden Door: The Third World Comes to America.* New York: Columbia University Press, 1985.

REITZ, JEFFREY G. *The Survival of Ethnic Groups.* Toronto: McGraw-Hill, 1980.

RESNICK, MELVYN C. "Beyond the Ethnic Community: Spanish Language Roles and Maintenance in Miami." *International Journal of the Sociology of Language* 69 (1988): 89–104.

RHOADES, ROBERT E. "Intra–European Migration and Rural Development: Lessons from the Spanish Case." *Human Organization* 37 (1978): 136–147.

RISCHIN, MOSES. *The Promised City: New York Jews 1870–1914.* Cambridge, MA: Harvard University Press, 1962.

RIST, RAY. "Guestworkers in Germany: Public Policies as the Legitimation of Marginality." *Ethnic and Racial Studies* 2 (October 1979): 401–415.

ROGG, ELEANOR. "The Influence of a Strong Refugee Community on the Economic Adjustment of Its Members." *International Migration Review* 5 (1971): 474–481.

ROMERO, M. *Made in the U.S.A.* New York: Routledge, 1992.

RONG, X. L., AND J. PREISSLE. "The Continuing Decline in Asian American Teachers." *American Educational Research Journal* 34 (1997): 267–293.

ROSE, PETER I. "Some Thoughts About Refugees and the Descendants of Theseus." *International Migration Review* 15 (Spring-Summer 1981): 8–15.

ROSENBLUM, GERALD. *Immigrant Workers: Their Impact on American Radicalism.* New York: Basic Books, 1973.

ROTHBART, RON. "The Ethnic Saloon as a Form of Immigrant Enterprise." *International Migration Review* 27, no. 2 (1993): 332–357.

ROTHMAN, DAVID J. *The Discovery of the Asylum.* Boston: Little, Brown, 1971.

ROUSE, R. "Mexican Migration and the Social Space of Post-Modernism." Unpublished Manuscript.

RUBENSTEIN, HYZINE. "Remittances and Rural Underdevelopment in the English-Speaking Caribbean." *Human Organization* 42 (Winter 1983): 295–306.

RUMBAUT, RUBEN D., AND RUBEN G. RUMBAUT. "The Family in Exile: Cuban Expatriates in the United States." *American Journal of Psychiatry* 133 (April 1976): 395–399.

RUMBAUT, RUBEN G. "Portraits, Patterns, and Predictors of the Refugee Adaptation Process." In David W. Haines, ed., *Refugees as Immigrants: Cambodians, Laotians, and Vietnamese in America* (pp. 138–182). Totowa, NJ: Rowman & Littlefield, 1989.

RUMBAUT, RUBEN G. "The Structure of Refuge: Southeast Asian Refugees in the United States, 1975–85."*International Review of Comparative Public Policy* 1 (1989): 97–129.

RUMBAUT, RUBEN G. "Immigration Research in the United States: Social Origins and Future Orientation." *American Behavioral Scientist* 42 (1999): 1285–1301.

RUMBAUT, RUBEN G., AND JOHN R. WEEKS. "Fertility and Adaptation: Indochinese Refugees in the United States." *International Migration Review* 20 (Summer 1986): 428–466.

RUMBAUT, RUBEN G., AND KENJI IMA. "Determinants of Educational Attainment Among Indochinese Refugees and Other Immigrant Students." Paper presented at the annual meeting of the American Sociological Association, Atlanta, August 1988.

RUMBAUT, RUBEN G., AND KENJI IMA. *The Adaptation of Southeast Asian Refugee Youth: A Comparative Study.* Washington, DC: U.S. Office of Refugee Resettlement, 1988.

RUMBAUT, RUBEN G., LEO R. CHAVEZ, ROBERT J. MOSER, SHEILA PICKWELL, AND SAMUEL WISHIK. "The Politics of Migrant Health Care: A Comparative Study of Mexican Immigrants and Indochinese Refugees." In Dorothy C. Wertz, ed., *Research in the Sociology of Health Care* 7 (pp. 143–202). Greenwich, CT: JAI Press, 1988.

SABAGH, GEORGES, AND MEHDI BOZORGMER. "Are the Characteristics of Exiles Different from Immigrants? The Case of Iranians in Los Angeles." *Sociology and Social Research* 71, no. 2 (1987): 77–83.

SALMON, T. W. "The Relation of Immigration to the Prevalence of Insanity." *American Journal of Insanity* 64 (July 1907): 53–71.

SALVO, JOSEPH, AND RONALD ORTIZ. *The Newest New Yorkers: An Analysis of Immigration into New York City During the 1980s*. New York: Department of City Planning, 1992.

SAMORA, JULIAN. *Los Mojados: The Wetback Story.* Notre Dame, IN: Notre Dame University Press, 1971.

SANCHEZ-KORROL, V. E. *From Colonia to Community: The History of Puerto Ricans in New York City, 1917–1948.* Westport, CT: Greenwood, 1983.

SANDEFUR, G. D., AND W. J. SCOTT. "Minority Group Status and the Wages of Indian and Black Males." *Social Science Research* 15 (1983): 347–371.

SANDERS, JIMY M., AND VICTOR NEE. "Limits of Ethnic Solidarity in the Enclave Economy." *American Sociological Review* 52 (1987): 745–773.

SANDERS, JIMY M., AND VICTOR NEE. "Problems in Resolving the Enclave Economy." *American Sociological Review* 57 (1992): 415–418.

SANDHU, KERNIAL SINGH. *Indians in Malaya.* Cambridge: Cambridge University Press, 1969.

SANJIAN, AVEDIS K. *The American Communities in Syria Under Ottoman Dominion.* Cambridge: Harvard University Press, 1965.

SASSEN-KOOB, SASKIA. "Formal and Informal Association: Dominicans and Colombians in New York." *International Migration Review* 13 (Summer 1979): 314–332.

SASSEN-KOOB, SASKIA. "Immigrant and Minority Workers in the Organization of the Labor Process." *Journal of Ethnic Studies* 8 (Spring 1981): 1–34.

SASSEN-KOOB, SASKIA. "Changing Composition and Labor Market Location of Hispanic Immigrants in New York City, 1960–1980." In George J. Borjas and Marta Tienda, eds., *Hispanics in the U.S. Economy* (pp. 299–322). New York, Academic Press, 1985.

SASSEN-KOOB, SASKIA. *The Global City: New York, London, and Tokyo.* Princeton, NJ: Princeton University Press, 1988.

SASSEN-KOOB, SASKIA. *The Mobility of Capital and Labor.* Cambridge, MA: Cambridge University Press, 1988.

SASSEN-KOOB, SASKIA. "Exporting Capital and Importing Labor: The Role of Caribbean Migration to New York City." Center for Latin American and Caribbean Studies, New York University, *Occasional Papers*, no. 28, 1981.

SASSEN-KOOB, SASKIA. *Losing Control? Sovereignty in an Age of Globalization.* New York: Columbia University Press, 1996.

SCHERMERHORN, R. A. *Comparative Ethnic Relations.* New York: Random House, 1970.

SCHERMERHORN, R. A. *Comparative Ethnic Relations: A Framework for Theory and Research.* Chicago: University of Chicago Press, 1978.

SCHMITTER HEISLER, BARBARA. *Immigration and Citizenship in West Germany and Switzerland.* Unpublished Ph.D. Dissertation, Department of Sociology, University of Chicago, 1979.

SCHMITTER HEISLER, BARBARA. "Sending States and Immigrant Minorities: The Case of Italy." *Comparative Studies in Society and History* 26 (1984): 325–334.

SCHMITTER HEISLER, BARBARA. "Sending Countries and the Politics of Emigration and Destination." *International Migration Review* 19 (1985): 469–484.

SCHMITTER HEISLER, BARBARA. "Contexts of Immigrant Incorporation: Locating Dimension of Opportunities and Constraints in the United States and Germany." In Hermann Kurthen, Jurgen Fijalkowski, and Gert Wagner, eds., *Immigration, Citizenship, and the Welfare State in Germany and the United States* (pp. 91–106). Stamford, CT: JAI Press, 1998.

SENGSTOCK, MARY C. "Iraqi Christians in Detroit: An Analysis of an Ethnic Occupation." In B. C. Asward, ed., *Arabic Speaking Communities in American Cities* (pp. 21–38). New York: Center for Migration Studies, 1974.

SHARMA, MIRIAM. "The Philippines: A Case of Migration to Hawaii, 1906–1946." In Lucie Cheng and Edna Bonacich, eds., *Labor Immigration Under Capitalism* (pp. 337–358). Berkeley: University of California Press, 1984.

SIMON, RITA J. *The Economic Consequences of Immigration.* Oxford: Basil Blackwell, 1989.

SIMON, RITA J. "Refugee Families' Adjustment and Aspirations: A Comparison of Soviet Jewish and Vietnamese Immigrants." *Ethnic and Racial Studies* 6 (October 1983): 492–504.

SIMON, RITA J. "Sociology and Immigrant Women." In Donna Gabaccia, ed., *Seeking Common Ground.* Westport, CT: Praeger, 1992.

SIU, PAUL C. P. "The Sojourner." *American Journal of Sociology* 58 (July 1952): 34–44.

SJAASTAD, LARRY A. "The Costs and Returns of Human Migration." *Journal of Political Economy* 70 (1962): 80–93.

SMITH, ROBERT. " Transnational Localities: Community, Technology and the Politics of Membership Within the Context of Mexico-US Migration." In Michael Peter Smith and Luis G. Guarnizo, eds., *Transnationalism from Below,* Vol. 6 (pp. 196–238), *Comparative Urban and Community Research.* New Brunswick, NJ: Transaction Publishers, 1998.

SNOW, R. "The New International Division of Labor and the U. S. Workforce: The Case of the Electronics Industry." In J. Nash and M. P. Fernandez-Kelly, eds., *Women, Men, and the International Division of Labor.* Albany: State University of New York Press, 1986.

SOTO, ISA MARIA. "West Indian Child Fostering: Its Role in Migrant Exchanges." In Constance Sutton and Elsa Chaney, eds., *Caribbean Life in New York City.* New York: Center for Migration Studies, 1987.

SOWELL, THMAS. *Ethnic America: A History.* New York: Basic Books, 1981.

SOYSAL, YASEMIN. *Limits to Citizenship: Migrants and Postnational Membership in Europe.* Chicago: University of Chicago Press, 1994.

SRIDHAR, KAMAL K. "Language Maintenance and Language Shift Among Asian-Indians: Kannadigas in the New York Area." *International Journal of Sociology of Language* 69 (1988): 73–78.

STARK, ODED J. "Migration Decision Making: A Review Article." *Journal of Development Economics* 14 (1984): 251–259.

STARK, ODED J. *The Migration of Labor.* Cambridge: Basil Blackwell, 1991.

STARK, ODED J., AND DAVID E. BLOOM. "The New Economics of Labor Migration." *American Economic Review* 75 (1985): 173–178.

STARK, ODED J., AND J. EDWARD TAYLOR. "Relative Deprivation and International Migration." *Demography* 26 (1989): 1–14.

STARK, ODED J., AND J. EDWARD TAYLOR. "Migration Incentives, Migration Types: The Role of Relative Deprivation." The *Economic Journal* 101 (1991): 1163–1178.

STARK, ODED J., AND SHLOMO YITZHAKI. "Labor Migration as a Response to Relative Deprivation." *Journal of Population Economics* 1 (1988): 57–70.

STARK, ODED J., EDWARD TAYLOR, AND SHLOMO YITZHAKI. "Remittances and Inequality." *The Economic Journal* 96 (1986): 722–740.

STARK, ODED J., EDWARD TAYLOR, AND SHLOMO YITZHAKI. "Migration, Remittances, and Inequality: A Sensitive Analysis Using the Extended Gini Index." *Journal of Development Economics* 26 (1988): 309–322.

STARR, PAUL D., AND ALDEN E. ROBERTS. "Attitudes Toward New Americans: Perceptions of Indo-Chinese in Nine Cities." *Research in Race and Ethnic Relations* 3 (1982): 165–186.

STEIN, BARRY N. "The Experience of Being a Refugee: Insights from the Research Literature." In Carolyn L. Williams and Joseph Westermeyer, eds., *Refugee Mental Health in Resettlement Countries* (pp. 5–23). New York: Hemisphere, 1986.

STEINBERG, STEPHEN. *The Ethnic Myth.* New York: Atheneum, 1981.

STEPICK, ALEX. "Haitian Refugees in the U.S." Minority Rights Group Report, no. 52. London: MRG, 1992.

STEPICK, ALEX, AND ALEJANDRO PORTES. "Flight into Despair: A Profile of Recent Haitian Refugees in South Florida." *International Migration Review* 20 (Summer 1986): 329–350.

STEVENS, ROSEMARY, LOUIS W. GOODMAN, AND STEPHEN MICK. *The Alien Doctors: Foreign Medical Graduates in American Hospitals.* New York: Wiley, 1978.

STONEQUIST, EVERETT V. *The Marginal Man: A Study in Personality and Culture Conflict.* New York: Russell & Russell, 1961.

STRAND, PAUL J., AND WOODROW JONES, JR. *Indochinese Refugees in America: Problems of Adaptation and Assimilation.* Durham, NC: Duke University Press, 1985.

STRYKER, SHELDON. "Social Structure and Prejudice." *Social Problems* 6 (Spring 1959): 30–54.

SWAY, MARLENE. "Gypsies as a Middleman Minority." Ph.D. Dissertation, University of California, Los Angeles, 1983.

SZAPOCZNIK, JOSE, RAQUEL COHEN, AND ROBERTO E. HERNANDEZ, EDS. *Coping with Adolescent Refugees: The Mariel Boatlift.* New York: Praeger, 1985.

TABORI, PAUL. *The Anatomy of Exile: A Semantic and Historical Study.* London: George Harrap, 1972.

TAYLOR, J. EDWARD. "Undocumented Mexico—U.S. Migration and the Returns to Households in Rural Mexico." *American Journal of Agricultural Economics* 69 (1978): 616–638.

TEITELBAUM, MICHAEL S. "Right Versus Right: Immigration and Refugee Policy in the United States." *Foreign Affairs* 59 (1980): 21–59.

THOMAS, BRINLEY. *Migration and Economic Growth: A Study of Great Britain and the Atlantic Economy.* Cambridge: Cambridge University Press, 1973.

THOMAS, W. I., AND FLORIAN ZNANIECKI. *The Polish Peasant in Europe and America.* Chicago: The University of Chicago Press, 1918–1920, 1984.

THOMAS, W. I., AND F. ZNANIECKI. *The Polish Peasant in Europe and America.* New York: Knopf, 1927.

THOMPSON, RICHARD H. "Ethnicity vs. Class: Analysis of Conflict in a North American Chinese Community." *Ethnicity* 6 (1979): 306–326.

THOMPSON, RICHARD H. "From Kinship to Class: A New Model of Urban Overseas Chinese Social Organization." *Urban Anthropology* 9, no. 3 (1980): 265–293.

THOMPSON, VIRGINIA, AND RICHARD ADLOFF. *Minority Problems in Southeast Asia.* Boston: Beacon Press, 1955.

TIENDA, M., AND F. D. WILSON. "Migration and the Earnings of Hispanic Men." *American Sociological Review* 57 (1992): 661–678.

TIENDA, MARTA, AND K. BOOTH. "Gender, Migration and Social Change." *International Sociology* 6 (1991): 51–72.

TILLY, CHARLES. "Migration in Modern European History." In William S. McNeil and Ruth Adams, eds., *Human Migration, Patterns and Policies* (pp. 48–72). Bloomington: Indiana University Press, 1978.

TILLY, CHARLES, AND C. H. BROWN. "On Uprooting, Kinship, and the Auspices of Migration." *International Journal of Sociology* 8 (1967): 139–164.

TODARO, MICHAEL P. "A Model of Labor Migration and Urban Unemployment in Less Developed Countries." *The American Economic Review* 59 (1969): 138–148.

TODARO, MICHAEL P. *Internal Migration in Developing Countries.* Geneva: International Labor Office, 1976.

TODARO, MICHAEL P., AND LYDIA MARUSZKO. "Illegal Migration and U.S. Immigration Reform: A Conceptual Framework." *Population and Development Review* 13 (1987): 101–114.

TSENG, YEN-FEN. "Chinese Ethnic Economy: San Gabriel Valley, Los Angeles County." *Journal of Urban Affairs* 16, no. 2 (1994): 169–189.

TURNER, F. J. "The Significance of the Frontier in American History." In *The Frontier in American History* (pp. 1–38). New York: Holt, 1920(1893).

TURNER, JONATHAN H., AND EDNA BONACICH. "Toward a Composite Theory of Middleman Minorities." *Ethnicity* 7 (1980): 144–158.

TYHURST, LIBUSE. "Displacement and Migration: A Study in Social Psychiatry." *American Journal of Psychiatry* 101 (February 1951): 561–568.

TYHURST, LIBUSE. "Psychosocial First Aid for Refugees: An Essay in Social Psychiatry." *Mental Health and Society* 4 (1977): 319–343.

UI, S. "Unlikely Heroes: The Evolution of Female Leadership in a Cambodian Ethnic Enclave." In M. Burawoy, ed., *Ethnography Unbound* (pp. 161–177). Berkeley: University of California Press, 1991.

U.S. DEPARTMENT OF JUSTICE. *Statistical Yearbook of the Immigration and Naturalization Service.* Washington D.C: U.S. Printing Office, 1989.

U.S. DEPARTMENT OF JUSTICE. *Statistical Yearbook of the Immigration and Naturalization Service*. Washington D.C: U.S. Printing Office, 1993.

U.S. DEPARTMENT OF JUSTICE. *Statistical Yearbook of the Immigration and Naturalization Service*. Washington D.C: U.S. Printing Office, 1998.

VAN DER KROEF, JUSTUS M. "The Eurasian Minority in Indonesia." *American Sociological Review* 18 (October 1953): 484–493.

VENABLE, ABRAHAM S. *Building Black Business: An Analysis and a Plan*. New York: Earl G. Graves, 1972.

VIDICH, ARTHUR, AND STANFORD LYMAN. *American Sociology*. New Haven: Yale University Press, 1985.

WALDINGER, ROGER. "Immigration and Industrial Change in the New York City Apparel Industry." In George J. Borjas and Marta Tienda, eds., *Hispanics in the U.S. Economy* (pp. 323–349). New York: Academic Press, 1985.

WALDINGER, ROGER. *Still the Promised City?* Cambridge, MA: Harvard University Press, 1996.

WALDINGER, ROGER D. *Through the Eye of the Needle: Immigrants and Enterprise in New York's Garment Trades*. New York: New York University Press, 1986.

WALDINGER, ROGER D. "Structural Opportunity or Ethnic Advantage? Immigrant Business Development in New York." *International Migration Review* 23 (1989): 48–72.

WALDINGER, ROGER D. "The Ethnic Enclave Debate Revisited." *International Journal of Urban and Regional Research* 17 (1993): 444–452.

WALDINGER, ROGER D. "The Making of an Immigrant Niche." *International Migration Review* 28 (1994): 3–30.

WALDINGER, ROGER D., R. WARD, AND H. ALDRICH. "Ethnic Business and Occupational Mobility in Advanced Societies." *Sociology* 19 (1985): 586–597.

WALDINGER, ROGER D., AND J. PERLMAN. "Second Generations: Past, Present, and Future." *Journal of Ethnic and Migration Studies* 24 (1988): 5–24.

WALDINGER, ROGER D., AND MEHDI BOZORGMEHR, EDS. *Ethnic Los Angeles*. New York: Russell Sage, 1996.

WALDINGER, ROGER D., HAWARD ALDRICH, ROBIN WARD, AND ASSOCIATES. *Ethnic Entrepreneurs: Immigrant Business in Industrial Societies*. Newbury Park: Sage Publications, 1990.

WALKER, S. LYNNE. "The Invisible Work Force: San Diego's Migrant Farm Laborers from Oaxaca." *San Diego Union* (December 18–22, 1988): A–1.

WARD, ROBIN. "Ethnic Entrepreneurs in Britain and Europe." In Robert Goffee and Richard Scase, eds., *Entrepreneurship in Europe: The Social Processes* (pp. 83–104). London: Croom Helm, 1987.

WARNER, W. L., AND L. SROLE. *The Social Systems of American Ethnic Groups*. New Haven, CT: Yale University Press, 1945.

WARRUERM, SHRIKALA. "Migration, Maternity, and Female Economic Activity: Gujarati Mothers in Britain. In Sallie Westwood and Parminder Bhachu, eds., *Enterprising Women: Ethnicity, Economy, and Gender Relations*. New York: Routledge, 1988.

WATSON, J. L. *Emigration and the Chinese Lineage: The Mans in Hong Kong and London*, Berkeley and Los Angeles: University of California Press, 1975.

WEBER, MAX. *The Protestant Ethnic and the Spirit of Capitalism*. New York: Scribner, 1958.

WEBER, MAX. "The Distribution of Power Within the Political Community: Class, Status, Party." In G. Roth and C. Wittich, eds., *Economy and Society*, Vol. 2 (pp. 926–939). Berkeley and Los Angeles: University of California Press, 1978.

WEIL, PATRICK. "The State Matters: Immigration Control in Developed Countries." New York: United Nations, Department of Social and Economic Affairs, Population Division, 1998.

WERBNER, PNINA. "Enclave Economies and Family Firms: Pakistani Traders in a British City." In Jermy Eades, ed., *Migrants, Workers, and the Social Order* (pp. 213–233). London: Tavistock Publication, 1987.

WERBNER, PNINA. "Taking and Giving: Working Women and Female Bonds in a Pakistani Immigrant Neighborhood." In Sallie Westwood and Parminder Bhachu, eds., *Enterprising Women: Ethnicity, Economy, and Gender Relations* (pp. 177–202). New York: Routledge, 1988.

WIEST, RAYMOND E. "External Dependency and the Perpetuation of Temporary Migration to the United States." In Richard C. Jones, ed., *Patterns of Undocumented Migration: Mexico and the United States* (pp. 110–135). Totowa, NJ: Rowman and Allanheld, 1984.

WILEY, NORBERT. "The Ethnic Enclave Mobility Trap and Stratification Theory." *Social Problems* 155 (1967): 147–159.

WILLIAMS, CAROLYN L., AND JOSEPH WESTERMEYER, EDS. *Refugee Mental Health in Resettlement Countries.* New York: Hemisphere, 1986.

WILLMOTT, W. E. "The Chinese in Southeast Asia." *Australian Outlook* 20 (December 1966): 252–262.

WILSON, KENNETH L., AND ALEJANDRO PORTES. "Immigrant Enclaves: An Analysis of the Labor Market Experience of Cubans in Miami." *American Journal of Sociology* 86 (1980): 295–319.

WILSON, KENNETH L., AND ALLEN W. MARTIN. "Ethnic Enclaves: A Comparison of the Cuban And Black Economies in Miami." *American Journal of Sociology* 88 (1982): 135–160.

WILSON, W. J. *The Truly Disadvantaged: The Inner City, the Underclass, and Public Policy.* Chicago: University of Chicago Press, 1987.

WIRTH, LOUIS. *The Ghetto.* Chicago: The University of Chicago Press, 1928.

WONG, BERNARD. "The Role of Ethnicity in Enclave Enterprises: A Study of the Chinese Garment Factories in New York City." *Human Organization* 46, no. 2 (1987): 120–130.

WONG, CHARLES CHOY. "Black and Chinese Grocery Stores in Los Angeles' Black Ghetto." *Urban Life* 5 (1977): 439–64.

WONG, M. G. "Post-1965 Asian Immigrants: Where Do They Come From, Where Are They Now, and Where Are They Going?" *Annals of the American Academy of Political and Social Science* 487 (1986): 150–168.

WONG, MORRISON G., AND CHARLES HIRSCHMAN. "The New Asian Immigrants." In William C. McReady, ed., *Culture, Ethnicity, and Identity* (pp. 381-403). New York: Academic Press, 1983.

YANCEY, WILLIAM, EUGENE ERIKSON, AND RICHARD JULIANI. "Emergent Ethnicity: A Review and Reformulation." *American Sociological Review* 41 (1976): 391–402.

YOON, IN-JIN. "The Changing Significance of Ethnic and Class Resources in Immigrant Businesses: The Case of Korean Immigrant Businesses in Chicago." *International Migration Review* 25, no. 2 (1991): 303–332.

YU, EUI-YOUNG. "Occupation and Work Patterns of Korean Immigrants." In Eui-Young Yu, Earl H. Phillips, and Eun-Sik Yang, eds., *Koreans in Los Angeles.* Koryo Research Institute and Center for Korean-American and Korean Studies, California State University, Los Angeles, 1982.

ZENNER, WALTER P. "Arabic-Speaking Immigrants in North America as Middlemen Minorities." *Ethnic and Racial Studies* 5 (1982): 457–477.

ZENNER, WALTER. *Minorities in the Middle.* Albany, NY: State University of New York Press, 1991.

ZENTGRAF, KRISTINE M. "Gender, Immigration, and Economic Restructuring in Los Angeles." *California Sociologist* 12 (1989): 111–136.

ZHOU, MIN. *Chinatown: The Socioeconomic Potential of an Urban Enclave.* Philadelphia: Temple University Press, 1992.

ZHOU, MIN, AND JOHN LOGAN. "Return on Human Capital in Ethnic Enclaves: New York City's Chinatown." *American Journal of Sociology* 86 (1989): 295–319.

ZHOU, MIN, AND REGINA NORDQUIST. "Work and Its Place in the Lives of Immigrant Women: Garment Workers in New York City's Chinatown." *Applied Behavioral Science Review* 2 (1994): 187–211.

ZIMMER, CATHRINE, AND HOWARD ALDRICH. "Resource Mobilization Through Ethnic Networks: Kinship and Friendship Ties of Shopkeepers in England." *Sociological Perspectives* 30, no. 4 (1987): 422–445.

ZLOTNIK, HANIA. "Empirical Identification of International Migration System." In Mary Kritz, Lin Lean Lim, and Hania Zlotnik, eds., *International Migration System: A Global Approach* (pp. 19–40). Oxford: Clarendon Press, 1992.

ZOLBERG, A. R., A. SUHRE, AND S. AGUAYO. *Escape from Violence: Conflict and the Refugee Crisis in the Developing World.* New York: Oxford University Press, 1989.

ZORBAUGH, HARVEY. *The Gold Coast and the Slum.* Chicago: The University of Chicago Press, 1929.